Praise for *First Person Accounts of Mental Illness and Recovery*

"*This book is a stellar r̶e̶s̶o̶u̶r̶ ̶.̶.̶.̶ ̶e̶d̶u̶c̶a̶t̶o̶r̶s̶ ̶.̶.̶.̶s̶o̶c̶i̶a̶l̶ ̶.̶.̶.̶ ̶t̶h̶o̶s̶e̶ ̶o̶t̶h̶e̶r̶ ̶h̶e̶l̶p̶i̶n̶g̶ ̶f̶i̶e̶l̶d̶s̶.̶ ̶W̶h̶.̶.̶.̶ ̶.̶.̶.̶ in the past assigned single b̶o̶o̶k̶-̶l̶e̶n̶g̶t̶h̶ ̶f̶i̶r̶s̶t̶ ̶p̶e̶r̶s̶o̶n̶ ̶a̶c̶c̶o̶u̶n̶.̶.̶.̶,̶ ̶I̶ ̶w̶i̶l̶l̶ ̶u̶s̶e̶ ̶t̶h̶i̶s̶ ̶c̶o̶l̶l̶e̶c̶t̶i̶o̶n̶ ̶t̶o̶ ̶g̶i̶v̶e̶ ̶m̶y̶ ̶s̶t̶u̶d̶e̶n̶t̶s̶ a broader understanding of the tremendous heterogeneity in the ways that different people experience and cope with mental illness.*"

Beth Angell, PhD
Associate Professor, School of Social Work and Institute for Health, Health Care Policy, and Aging Research
Rutgers University

"*The authors have compiled an important collection of first person narratives of mental illness and recovery. Every course in mental, emotional, and behavioral disorders should seek to give voice to the diverse lived experiences of consumers who want so much that we listen, understand their struggles and triumphs, and truly appreciate their humanity. This book will help us do that.*"

Kia J. Bentley, PhD
Professor and Director
Virginia Commonwealth University
School of Social Work

"*In their book* First Person Accounts of Mental Illness and Recovery, *LeCroy and Holschuh offer the student, researcher, or lay person the intimate voice of mental illness from the inside.* First Person Accounts of Mental Illness and Recovery *is a wonderful book, and it is an ideal, even indispensable, companion to traditional mental health texts. I am grateful that they have given the majority of this book to the voices that are too often unheard.*"

John S. Brekke, PhD
Frances Larson Professor of Social Work Research
Fellow, American Academy of Social Work and Social Welfare
School of Social Work
University of Southern California

"*This book provides a major new resource for education in the mental health professions and contains an extraordinary range of personal accounts of mental illness in one volume. These are given context and meaning through the introductions and study questions that precede each chapter.*"

Linda Chafetz, RN, DNSc
Professor, Department of Community Health Systems
University of California, San Francisco

"*This is one of the most compelling, comprehensive, and powerful compilations of first person accounts of resiliency and recovery that I've read. It will be an excellent teaching resource for instructors and professionals. The firsthand accounts will engage students in discussions that promote a more humane understanding and less stigmatizing image of mental illness. The book should be required reading in all schools of social work with a strengths-based mental health curriculum. It is a marvelous book and a gift to the reader.*"

Jan S. Greenberg, PhD
Professor, School of Social Work
University of Wisconsin-Madison

FIRST PERSON ACCOUNTS OF MENTAL ILLNESS AND RECOVERY

FIRST PERSON ACCOUNTS OF MENTAL ILLNESS AND RECOVERY

Edited by
Craig Winston LeCroy
Jane Holschuh

WILEY

John Wiley & Sons, Inc.

Library of Congress Cataloging-in-Publication Data:

LeCroy, Craig W.
  First person accounts of mental illness and recovery / Craig Winston LeCroy, Jane Holschuh.
    p. cm.
  Includes bibliographical references and index.
  ISBN 978-0-470-44452-8 (pbk.)
  ISBN 978-1-118-25859-0 (ebk)
  ISBN 978-1-118-23393-1 (ebk)
  ISBN 978-1-118-22024-5 (ebk)
  1. Mentally ill—Personal narratives.   2. Mental illness—Case studies. I. Holschuh, Jane. II. Title.
  RC464.A1L43 2012
  616.89—dc23   2011043308

Printed in the United States of America

10 9 8 7 6 5 4 3 2 1

To people with mental illness everywhere who struggle, prevail, and recover.

Contents

Acknowledgments   *xv*
Introduction   *xvii*
About the Editors   *xxxi*

1   **Schizophrenia and Other Psychotic Disorders**   **1**

Schizophrenia   6

* *The Best Medicine*   6
    SUSAN A. SALSMAN

* *Recovery as Discovery*   9
    PAOLO SCOTTI

* *Understanding Health as a Continuum*   *14*
    LESLIE GREENBLAT

* *Psychiatry and Oppression: A Personal
    Account of Compulsory Admission and Medical Treatment*   *19*
    BENJAMIN GRAY

* *Powerful Choices: Peer Support and Individualized
    Medication Self-Determination*   *25*
    CORINNA WEST

Schizoaffective Disorders   38

* *Snapshots: The First Symptoms of Psychosis*   *38*
    KRISTEN B. FOWLER

* *Why Having a Mental Illness Is Not Like Having Diabetes*   *43*
    ANONYMOUS

2	**Mood Disorders**	**49**
	Depressive Disorders	*53*
	• *Depression: Disease, Loneliness, Social Isolation, Suicide, Negative Thoughts . . .*	
	BEC MORRISON	*53*
	• *My Confession: My Life Had Come to a Stop*	*57*
	LEO TOLSTOI	
	• *Willow Weep for Me: A Black Woman's Journey Through Depression*	*61*
	MERI NANA-AMA DANQUAH	
	• *I Wish I Had Gotten Help Sooner: My Struggle With Postpartum Depression*	*66*
	MARCIE RAMIREZ	
	• *My Journey Through Postpartum Depression*	*72*
	JESSICA RODRIGO-DUNICAN	
	Bipolar Disorders	*76*
	• *Living with the Dragon: The Long Road to Self-Management of Bipolar II*	*76*
	PETER AMSEL	
	• *On Madness: A Personal Account of Rapid Cycling Bipolar Disorder*	*91*
	ANONYMOUS	
	• *Random Scribblings on Bipolar Disorder*	*97*
	MICHAEL NAPIORKOWSKI	
	• *Being Bipolar: Living on Both Sides of the Coin*	*101*
	SUSAN MICHELE VALE	
3	**Anxiety Disorders**	**105**
	Panic Disorder	108
	• You *Have Anxiety?*	*108*
	KELLY ORBISON	
	• *Susan's Story*	*115*
	SUSAN LUDEMAN	
	Phobias	122
	• *On the Outside Looking In*	*122*
	DANIELA GRAZIA	
	• *Mysophobia*	*133*
	CATHERINE TAYLOR	

Obsessive-Compulsive Disorder (OCD)   142
- *Flux*   *142*
  FRANK R. DeFULGENTIS
- *Rituals, Routines, and Recovery: Living With OCD*   *153*
  JARED DOUGLAS KANT WITH MARTIN FRANKLIN AND
  LINDA WASMER ANDREWS
- *"It'll Be Okay." How I Kept Obsessive-Compulsive*
  Disorder (OCD) From Ruining My Life   *160*
  SHANNON SHY

Posttraumatic Stress Disorder (PTSD)   175
- *Emotional Triangle*   *175*
  BLAZIE HOLLING
- *Panic, Anxiety, PTSD, and My Experiences of*
  Healing Through Multiple Avenues of Psychotherapy   *181*
  CATHERINE McCALL
- *The Demons of War Are Persistent: A Personal*
  Story of Prolonged PTSD   *189*
  ART W. SCHADE

4   Personality Disorders   **197**
- *My Path to Recovery*   *199*
  MELANIE GREEN
- *A "Classic" Case of Borderline Personality Disorder*   *203*
  LYNN WILLIAMS
- *Loud in the House of Myself*   *207*
  STACY PERSHALL

5   Substance-Related Disorders   **215**
- *Goodbye, Johnnie Walker*   *217*
  NEIL DAVIDSON
- *Untitled*   *228*
  AARON J. FRENCH
- *A Nurse's Journey Through Loss, Addiction, and Recovery*   *232*
  MICHELLE WALTER

6   Eating Disorders   **237**
- *Dying by Inches*   *239*
  EMILY TROSCIANKO
- *Big Little*   *263*
  PRISCILLA BECKER

- *Binging and Purging to Stay Alive*   *276*
  ANONYMOUS
- *Life With an Eating Disorder*   *281*
  LAURA BETTE

7   Impulse Control Disorders   285
- *The Numbers of My Obsession*   *286*
  MIA ZAMORA
- *Memoirs of a Compulsive Firesetter*   *294*
  SARAH WHEATON
- *Dan's Story*   *298*
  ANONYMOUS

8   Delirium, Dementia, and Amnestic and Other Cognitive Disorders   303
- *Before It's Too Late*   *306*
  JANE MCALLISTER
- *Poor Memory: A Case Report*   *310*
  MALCOLM L. MELTZER
- *Parkinson's: A Patient's View*   *317*
  SIDNEY DORROS

9   Somatoform Disorders   323
- *A Psychosomatic Study of Myself*   *325*
  F. WERTHAM
- *Bigorexia: Bodybuilding and Muscle Dysmorphia*   *339*
  ANONYMOUS
- *Hypochondria*   *341*
  HEATHER MENZIES JONES

10   Dissociative Disorders   345
- *Coping Strategies*   *348*
  RUTH DEE
- *Family Talk*   *358*
  BARBARA HOPE
- *Fractured Mind, One Heart?*   *361*
  ROBERT B. OXNAM

11   Sexual and Gender Identity Disorders   365
Sexual Pain Disorders   *369*
- *Vaginismus: The Blessing of Botox*   *369*
  RACHEL

Paraphilias   374
- *The Armed Robbery Orgasm: A Lovemap Autobiography of Masochism*   374
  RONALD KEYS AND JOHN MONEY

Gender Identity Disorders   377
- *A Rose in Bloom*   377
  APRIL ROSE SCHNEIDER
- *Time for a Good Transgender Story*   388
  KAM WAI KUI

12 Sleep Disorders   **401**
- *An Insomniac's Slant on Sleep*   404
  GAYLE GREENE
- *My Story of Narcolepsy*   414
  PATRICIA HIGGINS

13 Disorders Usually First Diagnosed in Infancy, Childhood, or Adolescence   **421**
Pervasive Developmental Disorders   426
- *Communication Impairment*   426
  JOHN ELDER ROBISON
- *Alien: A Story of Asperger's Syndrome*   431
  STEPHANIE MAYBERRY
- *The Experience of Infantile Autism*   440
  TONY W.

Attention-Deficit/Hyperactivity Disorder (ADHD)   444
- *The Only Me That We Have Ever Known*   444
  KATY ROLLINS

Tic Disorders   450
- *A Tourette Story*   450
  RICK FOWLER
- *Searching for Answers*   455
  CRYSTAL THOMAS

Index   **467**

Acknowledgments

This book would not have seen completion were it not for the tremendous support we received from many students. As we further understood the task in front of us, it became clear that we were going to need considerable support and assistance to put this manuscript together. Our strategy was to build a team of students who could assist in all details—finding first person accounts, selecting parts of books to use as accounts, tracking down individuals who we could ask to write accounts, typing up accounts, requesting permission from publishers, reviewing and critiquing the accounts, and so forth.

Our team in various phases consisted of Kim Bingham, Michelle Urban, Andrea Riendl, Aindrea McCammon, Erin McClain, Chris James, Janet Reed-Verdusco, Rich Hinton, Clinton Sandoval, and Mandy Bergstrom. Mandy, in particular, worked on this project while in school and continued with us after graduating. She was essential to the final product we created.

We also would like to acknowledge the Wiley team. Rachel Livsey provided needed support as we worked to find these accounts and meet deadlines.

Introduction
More Than a Diagnosis: First Person Accounts of Mental Illness and Recovery

There is a long history of personal narratives written by individuals who have suffered from a mental illness or mental disorder (we use these terms interchangeably in this book). That history has been traced to the 15th century (Barlow & Durand, 2004), and there are many well-known accounts from the 1800s. For example, Leo Tolstoi wrote his account of suffering from depression in 1887. As such, narrative descriptions of the subjective experiences of mental illness have a lengthy and established presence in the mental health field. Indeed, a major impetus for the current book was the rediscovery of Bert Kaplan's *The Inner World of Mental Illness,* published in 1964. This marvelous book gathered first person accounts that described varied experiences of mental illness. As Kaplan (1964) notes, "there is no better starting point for those seeking to understand ... than accounts of this experience ... we can come into intimate contact with the reality of mental illness itself" (p. vii). This classic book included four sections: the psychotic experience, a variety of psychopathologies, drug-induced states, and historic statements. In the past half-century, the interest in and list of first person narratives has continued to grow.

These many accounts have contributed to an ongoing interest in memoirs. The public is familiar with such first person accounts (FPAs) as *An Unquiet Mind, Girl Interrupted* (a major motion picture), *Wasted, A Beautiful Mind* (also a major motion picture), *Prozac Nation, Drinking: A Love Story, Darkness Invisible, Down with the Rain, Quitting the Nairobi Trio,* and numerous other stories. And although these particular accounts have achieved commercial success, there are many others written by people who simply want to tell their stories. Gail Hornstein (2008) has created a comprehensive "bibliography of first person accounts of madness in English" current to 2008, which includes 642 separate written accounts (See www.mtholyoke.edu/acad/assets/Academics/Hornstein_Bibliography.pdf). Sommer and colleagues (Sommer, Clifford, & Norcross, 1998; Sommer & Osmond, 1960, 1961, 1983) have created lists of accounts starting in 1960 and published them in highly regarded peer-review psychiatric journals. They list over 150 titles. In 1982, Peterson published *A Mad People's History of Madness* and listed 305 titles.

There are compendiums of accounts that focus on more specific themes such as depression (*Unholy Ghost*), eating disorders (*Going Hungry*), or mental health professionals telling their own stories (*Breaking the Silence: Mental Health Professionals Disclose Their Personal and Family Experiences of Mental Illness* and *Wounded Healers: Mental Health Workers' Experiences of Depression*). *Different People, Different Voices* (Fleteren & Fleteren, 2008) is a book of first person accounts written, published, and marketed entirely by Canadians with mental disabilities. Similarly, *Voices of Experience* (Basset & Stickley, 2010) acknowledges the recipients of mental health services as "experts in their own right," and provides readers with the personal narratives of psychiatric "survivors" in the United Kingdom. People with a story to tell are publishing e-books, and one publisher, Chipmunka, specializes in stories of mental illness and recovery. Beyond this is the World Wide Web, which hosts Internet sites such as the Experience Project, where you can post almost any experience you want to write about. In England, there is Health Talk, which is a database of personal and patients' experiences where individuals share their stories. The advent of online organizations such as Intervoice, Asylum, MindFreedom, and the Hearing Voices Network represents the development of democratic psychiatry and the hearing voices movement (Gray, 2009; see Gray's first person account, p. 18, for URLs). In the United Kingdom, Dr. Benjamin Gray is working with Intervoice to publish a book of first person accounts of hearing voices that invites "all sorts of voices and voice hearers and all sorts of points of view, experiences, and personal journeys" and will include "journeys to recovery" (Gray, 2009, p. 663).

MOTIVES AND PURPOSES OF FIRST PERSON ACCOUNTS

Storytelling has become a large enterprise as authors have increasingly recognized its value. There is something fundamental about telling one's story (LeCroy, 2012). In discussing the sociology of illness, Arthur Frank (1997) describes the "wounded storyteller" and notes that the storytelling of people with an illness is guided by a sense of responsibility and represents one way of living for the other. As Frank (1997) notes, "People tell stories not just to work out their own changing identities but also to guide others who will follow them" (p. 17). He puts his finger on a critical aspect of storytelling by recognizing that it has an element of testimony and that such testimony is inherently valuable—even therapeutic. People who suffer need to tell their stories in order to heal.

Frank (1997) began his work looking at illness and the role narrative stories might play in helping people cope and manage their conditions. He classifies three types of narratives that emerge from people who are ill. The *restitution story* is told frequently, but this type of story makes illness appear only transitory. *Chaos stories* are embedded in the crisis of the illness and cannot get beyond that stage. *Quest stories* address suffering directly and are motivated by the person's belief that something is to be gained by the experience. *Restitution* and *quest* stories are found most often in published accounts. Frank (1997) provides an eloquent description of this process: "Realizing who they always have been, truly been, each becomes or prepares to become the re-created, moral version of that self" (p. 131). In this display of character, memory is revised, interruption assimilated, and purpose grasped. "Whatever has happened to me or will happen," the *storyteller as hero* implicitly claims, "the purpose remains mine to determine" (p. 131).

The use of first person accounts has been supported further by evidence from a study (Banyard, 2000). Reading or listening to the experiences and perspective of someone with a mental disorder can deepen our understanding and empathy. Furthermore, an increased understanding helps the audience grasp the extent of the challenges faced. This can inspire efforts to help the person and his/her family. The study administered a survey to students in a required abnormal psychology class. Students answered questions that compared the traditional textbook with the readings of first person accounts. Students assessed what they had learned from the textbook and from the first person accounts by answering questions on a five-point scale and through open-ended questions. Results found significant differences on six of eight of the ratings that compared the two learning modes. For example, students rated first person accounts as significantly more useful than textbooks in being able to understand how someone with the disorder feels and in their ability to feel empathy for the person with the disorder. All open-ended responses about the use of first person accounts were coded as positive. Comments included, "it made it easier to understand the disorder," "helps bring to life what was learned in the textbook," "makes the information more real," and "really brought into focus what living with a mental disorder is like." The author notes that enhancing students' understanding and empathy may reduce the "stigmatizing of those with mental disorders" (Banyard, 2000, p. 43). Research consistently has found that stigmatizing attitudes were reduced for those who were introduced to or knew individuals with mental disorders or understood their experiences (Corrigan & Gelb, 2006; Link, Yang, Phelan, & Collins, 2004; Penn et al., 1994; Thornton & Wahl, 1996).

Our hope is that this book will inform readers about mental illness/ mental disorder and help instructors, students, and the general public talk about their experiences with it whether a client's, their own, a family member's, or a close friend's. Our small city, Tucson, Arizona, experienced the tragedy of multiple shootings targeted at our congresswoman, Gabrielle Giffords, in January 2011. The young man arrested for the killing spree has been assessed to have mental illness that went unrecognized and untreated. As we write this introduction, one of us (Craig) just days ago was deeply impacted by another tragedy indicative of mental illness. His 17-year-old son's chemistry lab partner committed suicide—by shooting himself in the head. All of us are in disbelief. This young man suffered from bouts of depression. The private high school where this happened has never witnessed such an event. Yet, as we know from putting this book together, often we cannot escape the impact that mental illness will have on any of us. In the wake of these recent tragedies, we and our community are left with many nagging questions.

Like other common illnesses such as diabetes and heart disease, mental disorders are part of society. Nunes and Simmie (2002) describe it this way:

> There are really only eight kinds of people affected by mental disorder. It's a very small list, but we all know someone on it: someone's mother, daughter, sister, or wife; someone's father, brother, husband, or son. In other words, people just like us. Just like you. (p. 3)

Our hope is that this book will, in some small way, reduce the stigma and discrimination that so many people with mental illness experience in their daily lives.

EMERGING THEMES

An important aspect of first person accounts is that they have brought recognition to and validation of the recovery process that many individuals engage in and achieve. This is consistent with the landmark Surgeon General's Report (1999) on mental health and the report of the U.S. President's New Freedom Commission on Mental Health (2003), which assert that mental health systems should adopt a recovery orientation. Ridgway (2001) notes that "first person recovery narratives are important source materials that can help us refocus our thinking beyond the myopic and outdated deficit perspective" (p. 336).

In studying first person accounts, Ridgway (2001) identified eight core themes:

1. Recovery is the reawakening of hope after despair.
2. Recovery is breaking through denial and achieving understanding and acceptance.
3. Recovery is moving from withdrawal to engagement and active participation in life.
4. Recovery is active coping rather than passive adjustment.
5. Recovery means no longer viewing oneself primarily as a person with a psychiatric disorder and reclaiming a positive sense of self.
6. Recovery is moving from alienation to a sense of meaning and purpose.
7. Recovery is a complex and nonlinear journey.

8. Recovery is not accomplished alone—the journey involves support and partnership.

Her work is significant in that it represents ongoing efforts to shift the field from the language of "chronicity" to one of recovery. Ridgway (2001) claims that first person accounts often challenge the field to critically examine service delivery systems, which can either support resilience and recovery or act as a barrier to restrain recovery. When systems focus on deficits and pathology, strength-based interventions are de-emphasized, and recovery is not promoted (Rapp & Goscha, 2006; Saleebey, 2005, 2008).

Indeed, this cultural shift toward "transformative" narrative story telling is a welcome addition to the mental health field. The field is experiencing a critical movement toward recovery-oriented approaches and toward systems that promote and support the recovery process (see Rapp & Goscha, 2006). Professionals in the mental health field have worked with consumers to develop a broader understanding of the dimensions of recovery (Whitley & Drake, 2010). Our book contributes to this movement by promoting first person accounts to enhance understanding of the recovery process as well as the challenges faced by those with mental disorders. Ridgway (2001) sums up the potential of such accounts, stating that "narratives can engender a 'contagion of hope' (Deegan, 1994, p. 159) and reorient both staff members and people with psychiatric disabilities toward alternative and more rewarding life paths, by restorying the possibility for positive growth after destabilizing life events" (p. 342).

Steven Hinshaw's book *Breaking the Silence* is a collection of first person accounts by mental health professionals who openly describe their personal experiences with mental illness in some fashion. Hinshaw (2008) concludes that, while some progress has been and is being made to increase understanding and counteract stigma, there is a long road ahead. Indeed, mental health professionals themselves can contribute to stigma. He identified a set of core themes that emerged from the first person accounts in his book, and these same themes have emerged from the accounts in our book. They are summarized here:

Confusion: When an individual experiences mental illness, the symptoms can be confusing—for everyone. This is discussed directly in many of the first person accounts in our book. Individuals struggle to understand themselves: Why did I say that? Why am I hearing voices or seeing things? Often, individuals experience an exaggeration of an aspect of themselves or may begin to act in ways that are inappropriate. This confusion can be the tipping point at which the person either recognizes the need to seek help or family members/ others do. Eventually, the person or a family member realizes there is truly something wrong that is not getting better.

Pain: One of the difficult aspects of reading first person accounts is the high level of pain that may be expressed. It can hurt just to read the detailed description of what the person is feeling. The darkness of despair, the hopelessness about the future, the anguish that one cannot escape—these can be painful aspects of having a disorder. Many times they are felt in a direct and even physiological manner. The stories of depression come to mind since often they are filled with the pain of hopelessness. For others, the pain of seeing a loved one afflicted or not being able to help is also present. For many, the loneliness and social stigma that can accompany the disorder are painful.

Aloneness and Isolation: Many individuals who have a mental disorder experience loneliness and isolation from others. Certainly, unusual behaviors push people away, scare people, and are misunderstood. Symptomatic individuals often are preoccupied with and overwhelmed by their "inner world" and lose touch with the surrounding social world. Sometimes people with a mental disorder lack the social skills needed to maintain consistent social connections. As symptoms worsen, individuals can be stigmatized in a manner that leads to blame, decreased social interaction, and isolation. Yet, it is also important to know that people with schizophrenia might engage in withdrawal as a strategy to manage their exposure to stimuli. Social stigma and self-stigma remain serious issues that have not been addressed adequately in the mental health field (Corrigan & Watson, 2002).

Vulnerability: Individuals with serious mental disorders sometimes may have limited decision-making ability, and their capacity to be fully informed about therapeutic choices can be compromised. At times, they are vulnerable because of inadequate social and coping skills as well as difficulties in communication. As people with mental disorders process their experiences, they sense and are aware of their vulnerability. This has been reflected in the way institutions have treated people with mental disorders in the past and can be true today in how they are treated by mental health professionals and systems.

Everyday Lives and Experiences: Many of the accounts you will read here depict not only the big events of the disorder but what everyday life is like living with it. What happens when you get up in the morning? What are the challenges you face today? Living with mental illness is about the everyday effort to cope, work, and live your life—just like it is for all of us. The more we understand what this is like in the everyday sense, the more likely we are to develop a deeper level of understanding and empathy. This increases our ability to identify with others and can reduce stigma by shortening the distance between us and those with mental health problems (Angermeyer, Beck, & Matschinger, 2003).

Strength and Courage: Too often, our understanding of mental disorders is based on the tragedies and failures of individuals. Increasingly, the mental health field is focusing on the strengths and courage of people with these disorders. Indeed, the recovery movement is about helping people identify their strengths, assets, and talents. Most individuals who experience the worst symptoms have times when symptoms abate and functioning improves. The most popular memoirs are testimonies to strength and courage, and they inspire hope and remind us of the resilience that is possible.

Shaping Identity and Career: Frequently, these accounts describe the all encompassing and overwhelming nature of mental illness. Yet many of our authors have written "transformative" narratives in which they have accepted their illness and understood its value in shaping their identity and career. Often, people "give back" as they recover, and this has encouraged the field to recognize the strengths, not just the vulnerabilities, of those with such experiences.

Stigma and Treatment: Too many of the first person accounts in this collection recount the devastating impact of stigma and the inadequate services that our authors have received. Indeed, one of the most frustrating aspects of reading these accounts has been coming face to face with the disrespect and inappropriate treatment that our authors divulge. Fear of discrimination and stigma often prevent people from seeking critical mental health care. We hope one clear message from reading these accounts is that people with a mental disorder, like all of us, deserve to be listened to, understood, helped, and provided access to quality care. Today, there is no excuse for those needing treatment not to get it.

DEFINITIONS AND DIAGNOSIS

Putting together a book of first person accounts of "mental illness" immediately calls into question what constitutes a mental illness. Although our book educates about and conforms to the *Diagnostic and Statistical Manual of Mental Disorders,* 4th edition, Text Revision (*DSM-IV-TR*) categories, it should not be perceived as an endorsement of the *DSM*. A common understanding of psychiatric disorders is that a person is undergoing extreme distress, is experiencing something that is rare, is engaging in behaviors that might violate social norms, and/or is suffering from a disability or has an impairment in functioning. Yet the *DSM-IV-TR* (American Psychiatric Association, 2000) itself acknowledges: "although this manual provides a classification of mental disorders, it must be admitted that no definition adequately specifies precise boundaries for the concept of 'mental disorder,'" which "lacks a consistent operational definition that covers all situations" (p. xxx). Wakefield (1992) discusses the idea of "harmful dysfunction analysis" in understanding mental disorders. He defines a disorder as existing when "the failure of a person's internal mechanisms to perform their functions as designed by nature impinges harmfully on the person's well-being as defined by social values and meanings" (Wakefield, 1992, p. 373). Wakefield's harmful dysfunction analysis combines scientific fact with socially constructed values. More specifically, the scientific facts describe the biological process that is not functioning normally, while the social values define the harm that results from that dysfunction.

How mental illness is defined has been the target of controversy since psychiatry emerged as a medical specialty. It continues today and is the subject of Richard McNally's (2011) new book, *What Is Mental Illness?* As with many others (Corrigan, 2007; Hagen, 2000; Kendell, 2002; Kirk & Kutchins, 1992; Wakefield & Spitzer, 2002; Wylie, 1995), McNally is not content with the traditional *DSM* definitions and understanding of mental disorders. His book begins: "Nearly 50 percent of Americans have been mentally ill at some point in their lives, and more than a quarter have suffered from mental illness in the past twelve months. Madness, it seems, is rampant in America" (McNally, 2011, p. 1). As a critique of the *DSM*, his book is an attempt to bring a greater degree of the scientific perspective to our understanding of mental disorders. Many have wondered how the *DSM* can include what would seem to be very nonpsychiatric difficulties such as mathematics disorder and caffeine intoxication. While our book often will be used side by side with the *DSM* in the classroom, our intent is to provide a broader understanding, that people with a mental disorder and their first person accounts are *more than a diagnosis*.

In identifying the first person accounts for this book, we used a multipronged approach. First, we searched the Internet, read blog entries, and googled specialized Web sites to see who might be writing narrative accounts of their experiences with mental illness. This yielded some excellent contributions. However, in spite of the great number of written memoirs, assembling a comprehensive collection was challenging. In the end, our efforts resulted in a varied and interesting set of accounts. Some were written on request, some were reprinted from well-known sources, some were derived from self-published books, and a few historic accounts that demonstrate consistency over time were included. We hope the reader appreciates the diversity represented in the collection.

LIMITATIONS AND A NOTE TO STUDENTS

As you will learn from reading these accounts, mental disorders affect all types of people everywhere—urban and rural, rich and poor, young and old, male and female, educated and uneducated, happy people and sad people. In these pages, you will find the stories of individuals who have much to share about their diverse experiences, ranging from extreme frustration at the mental health services delivery system to incredible gratitude for the help they received. Some authors describe family members who were essential to their recovery, and some describe family members who seemed essential to their demise. Each first person account can teach you something different.

Your challenge is to discover what each story offers to further your understanding.

The chapters in this book are organized by *DSM-IV-TR* categories so that students (and other readers) can relate the first person accounts to what they are learning about diagnosis and mental disorders in the classroom and internship settings. We have taken a teaching approach in the introductions to the chapters for each category of disorders. We intentionally included well-written memoirs that have inspired an entire field of writing and more common accounts that have not made the *New York Times* bestseller list. Sometimes, the well-written memoir is strikingly effective at describing the disorder and does so in an especially engaging manner. Other times, a simple account is basic but establishes a clear and meaningful everyday story. Our goal was to obtain a good mix of personal narratives for the reader.

This book includes subjective firsthand accounts, and as such it is biased, not objective; it does not attempt to represent the true or complete range of experiences that individuals may have. The account is not tantamount to the experience of mental illness itself. It reflects the limits of communication, memory, and potential distortion. Yet it is this subjective experience—the inside view—that we want to present and honor. One challenge for students is to look across these accounts for lessons that can be learned and then applied to their general understanding of the various disorders.

Some of these accounts may, indeed, be accurate representations of a particular disorder. However, in many cases the disorder is not clearly identified and symptoms may overlap with other disorders. We believe this contributes to a greater understanding of the complexity of symptoms and disorders—psychiatric classification is far from perfect, and these accounts should provide indirect evidence of this fact. We have taken our contributors' stories as they were written, and as such they stand. Our goal has been to provide the reader with the subjective viewpoints of people who have experienced living with a "mental disorder." Promoting a broader, more humane perspective is central to an enhanced understanding of mental illness in our society. We hope that reading this collection of first person accounts promotes greater compassion and empathy; an increased commitment to quality services and treatment; reduced stigma, pain, and suffering; and an expansion of hope and recovery.

REFERENCES

American Psychiatric Association. (2000). *Diagnostic and statistical manual of mental disorders* (4th ed., Text Revision). Washington, DC: Author.

Angermeyer, M. C., Beck, M., & Matschinger, H. (2003). Determinants of the public's preference for social distance from people with schizophrenia. *Canadian Journal of Psychiatry, 48*(10), 663–668.

Banyard, V. L. (2000). Using first-person accounts to teach students about psychological disorders. *Teaching Psychology, 27,* 40–43.

Barlow, D. H., & Durand, V. M. (2004). *Abnormal psychology: An integrative approach.* Pacific Grove, CA: Thompson.

Basset, T., & Stickley, T. (2010). *Voices of experience: Narratives of mental health survivors.* Sussex, England: Wiley.

Corrigan, P. (2007). How clinical diagnosis might exacerbate the stigma of mental illness. *Social Work, 52*(1), 31–39.

Corrigan, P., & Gelb, B. (2006). Three programs that use mass approaches to challenge the stigma of mental illness. *Psychiatric Services, 57*(3), 393–398.

Corrigan, P. W., & Watson, A. C. (2002). The paradox of self-stigma and mental illness. *Clinical Psychology: Science and Practice, 9*(1), 35–53.

Deegan, P. W. (1994). Recovery: The lived experience of rehabilitation. In W. A. Anthony & L. Spaniol (Eds.), *Readings in psychiatric rehabilitation* (pp. 149–162). Boston, MA: Boston University, Center for Psychiatric Rehabilitation.

Fleteren, M., & Fleteren, M. V. (2008). *Different people, different voices.* Rockford, MI: Outsider Press.

Frank, A. W. (1997). *The wounded storyteller: Body, illness, and ethics.* Chicago, IL: University of Chicago Press.

Gray, B. (2009). Psychiatry and oppression: A personal account of compulsory admission and medical treatment. *Schizophrenia Bulletin, 35*(4), 661–663.

Halgin, R. P. (Ed.) (2000). Part I: Classification and diagnosis. *Taking sides: Clashing views on controversial issues in abnormal psychology: Issue 1.* Is the DSM-IV a useful classification system? (pp. 3–38). Guilford, CN: Dushkin/McGraw-Hill.

Hinshaw, S. P. (2008). *Breaking the silence: Mental health professionals disclose their personal and family experiences of mental illness.* New York, NY: Oxford University Press.

Hornstein, G. (2008). *Bibliography of first-person narratives of madness in English* (4th ed.). Retrieved from: www.mtholyoke.edu/acad/assets/Academics/Hornstein_Bibliography.pdf

Kaplan B. (1964). *The inner world of mental illness.* New York, NY: Harper & Row.

Kendell, R. E. (2002). Five criteria for an improved taxonomy of mental disorders. In J. E. Helzer & J. J. Hudziak (Eds.), *Defining psychopathology in the 21st century: DSM-V and beyond* (pp. 3–17). Washington, DC: American Psychiatric Publications.

Kirk, S. A., & Kutchins, H. (1992). *The selling of DSM: The rhetoric of science in psychiatry.* New York, NY: Aldine De Gruyter.

LeCroy, C. W. (2012). *The call to social work* (2nd ed.). Thousand Oaks, CA: Sage.

Link, B. G., Yang, L. H., Phelan, J. C., & Collins, P. Y. (2004). Measuring mental illness stigma. *Schizophrenia Bulletin, 30*(3), 511–541.

McNally, R. J. (2011). *What is mental illness?* Cambridge, MA: Harvard University Press.

Nunes, J., & Simmie, S. (2002). *Beyond crazy: Journeys through mental illness.* Toronto, Ontario, Canada: McClelland & Stewart.

Penn, D. L., Guynan, K., Daily, T., Spaulding, W. D., Garbin, C. P., & Sullivan, M. (1994). Dispelling the stigma of schizophrenia: What sort of information is best? *Schizophrenia Bulletin, 20,* 567–578.

Peterson, D. (1982). *A mad people's history of madness.* Pittsburgh, PA: University of Pittsburgh Press.

President's New Freedom Commission on Mental Health. (2003). *Achieving the promise: Transforming mental health care in America. Final Report.* Retrieved from: www.mentalhealthcommission.gov/reports/FinalReport/FullReport.htm

Rapp, C. A., & Goscha, R. J. (2006). Strengths assessment: Amplifying the well part of the individual. In C. A. Rapp & R. J. Goscha (Eds.), *The strengths model: Case management with people with psychiatric disabilities* (2nd ed., pp. 91–120). New York, NY: Oxford University Press.

Ridgway, P. (2001). Restorying psychiatric disability: Learning from first person recovery narratives. *Psychiatric Rehabilitation Journal, 24,* 335–343.

Saleebey, D. (2005). Balancing act: Assessing strengths in mental health practice. In S. A. Kirk (Ed.), *Mental disorders in the social environment: Critical perspectives* (pp. 23–44). New York, NY: Columbia University Press.

Saleebey, D. (2008). *The strengths perspective in social work practice* (5th ed.). New York, NY: Longman.

Sommer, R., Clifford, J. S., & Norcross, J. (1998). A bibliography of mental patients' autobiographies: An update and classification system. *American Journal of Psychiatry, 155,* 1261–1264.

Sommer, R., & Osmond, H. (1960). Autobiographies of former mental patients. *Journal of Mental Science, 106,* 1030–1032.

Sommer, R., & Osmond, H. (1961). Autobiographies of former mental patients: Addendum. *Journal of Mental Science, 107,* 1030–1054.

Sommer, R., & Osmond, H. (1983). A bibliography of mental patients' autobiographies, 1960–1982. *American Journal of Psychiatry, 140,* 1051–1054.

Thornton, J. A., & Wahl, O. F. (1996). Impact of a newspaper article on attitudes toward mental illness. *Journal of Community Psychology, 24,* 17–25.

Tolstoi, L. (1887). *My confession.* New York, NY: Crowell.

U.S. Department of Health and Human Services. (1999). Mental health: A report of the Surgeon General. Washington, DC: Author.

Wakefield, J. C. (1992). The concept of mental disorder: On the boundary between biological facts and social values. *American Psychologist, 47*(3), 373–388.

Wakefield, J. C., & Spitzer, R. L. (2002). Why requiring clinical significance does not solve epidemiology's and DSM's validity problem. In J. E. Helzer & J. J. Hudziak (Eds.), *Defining psychopathology in the 21st century: DSM-V and beyond.* Washington, DC: American Psychiatric Publications.

Whitley, R., & Drake, R. E. (2010). Recovery: A dimensional approach. *Psychiatric Services, 61*(12), 1248–1251.

Wylie, M. S. (1995, May–June). The power of DSM-IV: Diagnosing for dollars? *Family Therapy Networker,* 23–33, 65–68.

About the Editors

CRAIG WINSTON LECROY is a professor in the School of Social Work at Arizona State University. He also holds an appointment at the University of Arizona in the John & Doris Norton School of Family and Consumer Sciences, Family Studies and Human Development division. He has been a visiting professor at the University of Canterbury, New Zealand; the Zellerbach Visiting Professor at the University of California at Berkeley; and a senior Fulbright specialist. Professor LeCroy has published 10 books previously, including *Parenting Mentally Ill Children: Faith, Hope, Support, and Surviving the System; Handbook of Evidence-Based Treatment Manuals for Children and Adolescents; Handbook of Prevention and Intervention Programs for Adolescent Girls; The Call to Social Work: Life Stories; Case Studies in Child, Adolescent, and Family Treatment; Case Studies in Social Work Practice; Empowering Adolescent Girls: Examining the Present and Building Skills for the Future with the "Go Grrrls" Program; Go Grrrls Workbook;* and *Social Skills Training for Children and Adolescents.* Professor LeCroy has published over 100 articles and book chapters on a wide range of topics, including mental health, the social work profession, home visitation, and research methodology. He is the recipient of numerous grants, including (as principal investigator or co-principal investigator) interventions for risk reduction and avoidance in youth (NIH), Go Grrrls Teen Pregnancy Prevention Program, evaluation of Healthy Families (a child abuse prevention program), a mental health training grant for improving service delivery to severely emotionally disturbed children and adolescents (NIMH), and Youth Plus: Positive Socialization for Youth (CSAP).

JANE HOLSCHUH is Professor Emerita in the Department of Social Work at Humboldt State University. She was a predoctoral and postdoctoral National Institute of Mental Health Fellow during her training at the University of California at Berkeley and the University of Wisconsin–Madison. She has taught a range of courses in mental health while on the faculty at UW-Madison, Humboldt State University, and Arizona State University, including assessment of mental disorders, mental health problems and community services, and social work practice and severe mental illness. Professor Holschuh currently teaches assessment of mental disorders, mental health issues and policy, and advanced mental health practice in the MSW program at Arizona State University. She chaired the Mental Health Concentration at UW-Madison and helped develop coursework for the mental health specialization at ASU. Her interests and research in serious mental illness focus on consumers' perspectives, stigma, social networks, and homelessness. Professor Holschuh received an NIMH grant to study the social networks of adults with schizophrenia. She was the principal investigator on two major survey research projects that interviewed homeless adults in Humboldt County, California, and Pima County, Arizona.

1

Schizophrenia and Other Psychotic Disorders

INTRODUCTION

We begin this book with the first person accounts (FPAs) written by people who have been diagnosed with or have experienced the symptoms of a psychotic disorder. The *Diagnostic and Statistical Manual of Mental Disorders,* 4th edition, text revision (*DSM-IV-TR*) groups together under this category disorders that involve a variety of serious symptoms that have considerable impact on people's daily lives. Of these disorders, schizophrenia is the prototype. Earlier versions of the *DSM* took a unitary approach that conceptualized psychopathology on a continuum; neurosis reflected a higher level of functioning and psychosis signified the greatest impairment in functioning. Arieti's (1974) concept of a "break with reality" defined psychosis more narrowly and is why the first signs/symptoms or episode of schizophrenia has been termed a *first break.* Psychosis represented an inability to distinguish between internal and external stimuli. The break with reality referred to this loss of ability to reality test, or to tell whether, for example, the voices a person hears are real and are being heard by others or not. This way of thinking about psychosis has endured. In neurotic disorders as defined by the first two *DSMs*, this capacity remained intact. Beginning with *DSM-III,* the manual abandoned the unitary approach and, instead, defined psychopathology as discrete or distinct categories of disorders and developed a core set of criteria for each disorder.

People who have been diagnosed with any of the psychotic disorders may experience problems in perception (hallucinations in any of the five sensory areas, but most often auditory or visual hallucinations), delusions or false beliefs, disorganized speech (and thought), and/or disorganized or catatonic behavior. While these psychotic symptoms are common across the disorders in this category, such symptoms are not thought of as the core parts of every disorder in this section, and there is variation in the symptoms that are considered psychotic for different disorders in this category. In *schizophrenia, schizophreniform disorder, schizoaffective disorder,* and *brief psychotic disorder,* the following are psychotic symptoms: delusions, any hallucinations (with or without accompanying insight) that are prominent, disorganized speech, and disorganized or catatonic behavior. In substance-induced psychotic disorder and psychotic disorder due to a general medical condition, only delusions and hallucinations with no insight are considered to be psychotic. In *delusional disorder* and *shared psychotic disorder,* the term psychotic is interchangeable with the term delusional.

It is important to note that some cognitive disorders, mood disorders, dissociative disorders, and substance withdrawal disorders may also involve more transient psychotic symptomatology. And, increasingly, there is no assumption of common etiology in the psychotic disorders. For example, current research posits that schizophrenia is thought to be etiologically more similar to schizotypal personality disorder than to the other psychotic disorders (Tsuang, 2002).

While certain symptoms were thought of as pathognomonic of schizophrenia in the past (e.g., Kurt Schneider's first-rank symptoms of schizophrenia/1939), we now know that there is no one sign or symptom that defines or predicts the disorder. People with schizophrenia can experience a variety of cognitive and emotional difficulties that must, by definition, be related to social and/or occupational dysfunction. These include problems in perception, in communication and language, in the content and process of thought and speech, in attention, in volition and drive, in the ability to experience pleasure, in affect and mood, behavior, and inferential thinking. Symptoms of schizophrenia are classified as either positive or negative. Positive symptoms represent an exaggeration or distortion of normal functions (e.g., delusions and hallucinations). Negative symptoms involve a reduction in or loss of normal functions (e.g., affective flattening and avolition).

The subjective experience of signs and symptoms has been viewed as especially critical to an understanding of schizophrenia (Estroff, 1989; Strauss, 1989). *Schizophrenia Bulletin* dedicated an entire issue to this topic (Strauss & Estroff, 1989). Viewing the illness through the eyes of those who have been diagnosed with it has contributed to a renewed focus on designing psychosocial treatment and services that will be more responsive to consumers' needs, reduce stigma, and enhance their quality of life. Honoring the subjective experiences of those with schizophrenia (or any mental disorder) requires us to shift perspectives from thinking of ourselves as the experts to viewing those who experience symptoms of mental illness as experts in their own right. We can learn a great deal about the challenging aspects of their experiences from listening to their stories. Perhaps more important, we also learn about courage, persistence, and the strength to endure and even triumph.

The FPAs in this chapter describe individuals' experiences with schizophrenia and with schizoaffective disorder in which there is an added mood component. People who meet criteria for schizoaffective disorder must first meet the symptoms criterion for schizophrenia (Criterion A), and then also meet criteria for a major mood episode (depressive, manic, or mixed) during a significant period of the course of the illness. For individuals who meet criteria for any of the psychotic disorders, the personal experience of signs/symptoms can and does vary greatly. These can be frightening and disabling, especially initially. Probably no two people with a diagnosis of schizophrenia have identical symptoms or the exact same course or trajectory of the illness. The onset of schizophrenia most often occurs in late adolescence to mid-twenties (18–25) for men and from 25 to mid-30s for women. There is a bimodal distribution for women, with an additional peak of onset after 40. But the timing and process of onset varies across individuals, too. The onset for schizoaffective disorder occurs typically in early adulthood, although it can range from adolescence to much later in life. Women have a higher incidence of schizoaffective disorder than men and more often experience the depressive than the bipolar type.

As you read the FPAs in this chapter, we think you will be struck by the contrast between the *DSM*'s portrayal of these disorders and the subjective, personal experience of living with schizophrenia or schizoaffective disorder that our authors provide. In focusing solely on the symptoms and the *DSM* diagnostic criteria as we have done as background in this introduction, we risk coming away with a limited understanding of these problems. We have found that by "listening" to what the personal narratives in this chapter tell us about the lived experience of psychotic disorders, our understanding is broadened and greatly enriched.

Susan Salsman wrote the FPA that begins this chapter. Her life with schizophrenia changed greatly when someone else with mental illness identified with her and said, "Yeah, that happened to me too." In the next selection, Paolo Scotti describes his experience of having schizophrenia and talks about his recovery as a process of "discovery." Leslie Greenblat's account of hearing voices reveals not only the challenges she has faced but also the resourcefulness she has shown in developing a strategy to cope with them and move on with her life. Benjamin Gray draws on what he experienced during a 12-month involuntary hospitalization for schizophrenia to critique services based on a medical model. He advocates for patients' rights, discusses the rise of democratic psychiatry, and tells the reader about several alternative approaches such as the hearing voices movement. In an account of how she uses her own experience of schizophrenia and her recovery to work with others, Corinna West discusses her role as a peer specialist in helping those who are struggling with the illness.

Kristen Fowler's moving story of her "first symptoms of psychosis" portrays how her illness changed from serious depression to include symptoms of psychosis that eventually were diagnosed as schizoaffective disorder. She describes this process as a descent into suicidality and psychosis. The final FPA in this chapter, written by an anonymous author, highlights the differences in having and receiving treatment for a mental illness versus a physical illness. The author makes her point by comparing her experiences of having schizoaffective disorder to the experiences that someone with diabetes might have.

QUESTIONS FOR REFLECTION

What are some common strategies that these authors have used to cope with having a psychotic disorder? What strengths have they revealed in dealing with the symptoms and other challenges they experienced? Do these accounts fit your stereotype of people with schizophrenia or schizoaffective disorder? Why or why not?

REFERENCES

Arieti, S. (1974). *Interpretation of schizophrenia* (2nd ed.). New York, NY: Basic Books.

Estroff, S. E. (1989). Self, identity, and subjective experiences of schizophrenia: In search of the subject. *Schizophrenia Bulletin, 15*(2), 189–196.

Strauss, J. (1989). Subjective experiences of schizophrenia: Toward a new dynamic psychiatry—II. *Schizophrenia Bulletin, 15*(2), 179–187.

Strauss, J., & Estroff, S. E. (1989). Subjective experiences of schizophrenia and related disorders: Implications for understanding and treatment. *Schizophrenia Bulletin, 15*(2), 177–178.

Tsuang, M. T. (2002). Schizotaxia and the prevention of schizophrenia. In J. E. Helzer & J. J. Hudzial (Eds.), *Defining psychopathology in the 21st century: DSM-V and beyond* (pp. 249–260). Washington, DC: American Psychiatric Publishing.

SCHIZOPHRENIA

The Best Medicine

SUSAN A. SALSMAN[1]

Wouldn't it be great if all mental health professionals were required to have a mental illness? I'm just talking about those who want to deal with people who have been diagnosed with a mental illness. If a professional wanted to work with neurotics then, no requirements necessary, because all people have neuroses! I think that's an inborn trait. But to help the mentally ill, you must be mentally ill.

I have lived with schizophrenia since about age 15. I knew there was something wrong, so I sought help. I saw school counselors and even went to see a psychologist a few times. Had I kept going to him, I might have learned early on that I had a mental illness. I found out many years later, after my hospitalization and diagnosis, after many years of seeking counsel from this doctor or that, or this counselor or that, that that early psychologist had suspected psychosis.

I wonder sometimes if I would have been better off if I had caught it early. But I'm okay with the fact that I didn't, because life is good. I am who I want to be today. I probably couldn't get any closer to being normal than I am right now. I'm not 100 percent and it's not perfect. But will it ever be for anyone? Everyone has something to deal with at some time. Mine just happens to be schizophrenia.

I can't count the number of mental health professionals I have seen in my search for answers. I just know that there have been many. All of them were unique individuals, all of them were well educated, and all of them, I hoped, had the best reason for choosing the profession they did: to help people. I understand that that may not always have been the case, but the majority of them surely meant well, and I appreciate that.

I hopped from one mental health professional to the next, getting fixed up a little only to fall back into madness and return once again to a little office with a big desk and a new face. I would sit in desperation, longing to find the answers, longing for something to hold onto that would take away

---

[1]From "The Best Medicine," by Susan A. Salsman, 2003, *Schizophrenia Bulletin, 29*(3), 615–616. Copyright 2003 by Oxford University Press. Reprinted with permission.

all of my pain. I was hoping to learn how to live, how to cope. I always wanted to be told what to do and how to do it.

After I realized that this would never happen, the mental health professionals just became sounding boards. If I babbled on enough, if I cried enough and complained enough, it would release some of the tension—at least for a while. And that's all I could do because I knew then that nothing they said or did would ever help me beyond the little hour we shared—that little hour filled with hopelessness and good intentions.

Finally I was hospitalized in 1989 at the age of 24 and came to some important realizations. First, something was seriously wrong in my head. Second, medication could help to take away some of that craziness. And third, I was not alone.

Realizing that I was not alone was a revelation. To this day I hear that one sentence in my head spoken from a beautiful person sitting next to me who came from some other place, whose life I knew nothing about—a complete stranger whose face I caught only intermittent glimpses of as I faded in and out of reality the first few days. Seeing her clearly now, this perfect, beautiful stranger said to me, "Yeah, that happened to me too."

The medicine helped, I became friends with a staff member, and I started to enjoy a little sanity for the first time in months. But nothing in that hospital experience mattered more than what happened in that one little fragment of time. And I still find it humorous how it was said so nonchalantly and almost matter-of-factly, in a manner that one could have as easily said, "Your hair is red."

I don't know this girl's name. I wouldn't recognize her if I saw her on the street. I don't know who she is or where she came from or where she is now. But a part of her lives in me just as strongly today as it did in the moment we first spoke.

I have shelled out a lot of money over the years. All the time and effort I put into my career as a patient, all the hard work and sweat these people poured out to me from behind their tidy desks, all the little hopes and twists of starlight fading into dawn, left me disillusioned by the realization that in order for healing to begin, we need only to hold in our hearts the love, understanding, and compassion of a fellow sufferer.

I can tell a mental health professional what I am experiencing: how it feels, my perception of it. I can describe hallucinations, pouring out expressions like water. I can be as eloquent as possible, laying open my soul. I can take the time to try to explain, to find the right words, knowing there are none, and then leave feeling more frustrated than before. I can do this. I can bang my head against a wall for hours too. The results are pretty much the same.

Unless I have a doctor who also lives with mental illness, the plain fact is, the doctor will never understand. The doctor cannot learn it from a book. No matter how strong the desire to learn, to feel, to know and understand—it will never happen.

Healing may begin with a simple sentence that may forever leave an impression on your soul. But it is a journey from that point on. I have learned a few things over the years that only experience can teach. And what I found to be true, at least in my life, is that there must be a desire to get well.

Intrinsically the answers are already there inside of us. Whether they exist in the head or heart or soul, they are there, and we are all aware of that. It's this part of us that keeps us alive in times of total despair. It kept us sane long enough for us to begin our relationship with it, even if it was only sporadic in the beginning. It's the source we tap into that gives us hope and insight. And it is the very part of us that allows us to lead normal, happy lives.

I'm so adamant about directing my own recovery not just because of my disillusionment and frustration with the mental health field. My desire is also based on the fact that we are all unique. My experiences are never exactly the same as someone else's. It is this uniqueness that makes treatment so difficult. But this very thing has brought joy into my life and a deep appreciation of tiny little moments that take place between two people at a single point in time—moments that can lead to epiphanies. It's this uniqueness that allows us to learn from one another and always leaves a little mystery lingering so we can appreciate that some things will always be sacred.

Hospitals are necessary. Meds are necessary. In the beginning, I needed them more than anything. Meds have become an extension of my mind. If I don't take them, I will not survive.

In the beginning, denial became my defense. I was angry and resentful. I hated life and felt singled out because of all the people this thing could have chosen, it picked me. At the time my diagnosis was equal to the death sentence. Nothing could have been more devastating. Not even death itself. No matter how hard I fought—kicking and screaming—it would not go away. It was like a pit bull growling at me that would stop only if I fed it. After it gobbled down its food, it would corner me again, continuing to growl and threaten. I decided to keep feeding it. And after awhile, the dog took on the role of man's best friend. I learned to live with it the best I knew how.

This is what I know. I made an effort to open my eyes, to become very aware of myself. I made a decision to quit wallowing in self-pity and to become responsible for the course my life would take. I came to see the important truth that only I know what is best for me in my journey of re-covery—that I have the answers in me and have learned to draw on them. Through trial and error, I have learned what works and what doesn't.

Experience teaches us how to live well. In time, the mental illness di-minishes in importance. And some days it's not any more significant than a little bug bite. Some days, it seems to have disappeared. I have learned that reaching out to family and friends with mental illness and taking meds—striving to be the very best I can be—are essentials. If my eyes are open and my mind is clear, I can see what I need to do. If I can reach out and share what I know, it may be that everything I say means nothing at all. Or it could be too that I might say one thing that seems to be of little importance to me, yet opens a new door for someone I don't even know.

So, in our fellowship with one another, friends in the struggle, always keep in mind that there is no better medicine in the world than for one person who has a mental illness to say to another, "Yeah, that happened to me too."

Peace and good cheer.

Recovery as Discovery

PAOLO SCOTTI[2]

The story of my recovery-related journey begins in the fall of 1992, when I was doing my Masters in Organic Chemistry at the University of Toronto. Slowly, slowly, something terribly wrong began to occur in my life. I began missing important meetings. I began thinking that fellow graduate students were out to get me and sabotaging my research work. I became ambivalent and could not decide what research to conduct and which professor to work under.

---

[2]From "Recovery as Discovery," by Paolo Scotti, 2009, *Schizophrenia Bulletin, 35*(5), 844–846. Copyright 2009 by Oxford University Press. Reprinted with permission.

Now, I was not a born chemist, and I had to work very hard at it to do well; but the stress of graduate school, along with other factors, triggered the beginning of my illness. I began fearing for my life because I thought that people wanted to harm or kill me. I became afraid to take the subway, believing that I was being followed, and withdrew from everyone thinking that they were plotting against me. I believed that my house was bugged, that people could read my mind, and that people were trying to insert evil/ destructive thoughts in my mind. The television and radio began to send me secret messages and were referring directly to me in their broadcasts. I sometimes heard voices saying negative statements about my religious faith, and I felt that I was being persecuted religiously.

Eventually, things got to the point where I became so disabled by delusions and other psychotic symptoms (although no one in my family, including myself, knew it was this) that I was admitted into a psychiatric ward at a general hospital. And thus began my experience with the mental health system. I was in an inpatient unit twice within a period of 3 months, after which I spent over a year in day hospital.

The hospital experience was not particularly positive. No one ever explained mental illness except for depression to me or to my family while I was there, and I was made to feel responsible for my misfortune (or at least I felt that way). The staff was not always helpful. I will never forget one of my meetings with my hospital psychiatrist. In one of my weekly visits that lasted no more than 15 minutes, my psychiatrist was becoming annoyed and impatient with me as usual because I could not finish my sentence, and I would start to repeat the same thing over again (this was due to thought disorder caused by my illness, although I did not know it at the time). Rather than trying to help me, he told me quite coldly: "You are always saying the same thing over again, it's so boring." I could have died at that moment. Just because someone is ill does not mean that they are any less human without feelings. Reflecting back, I now think of Psychiatric/ Psychosocial Rehabilitation (PSR) Core Principle 7: All people are to be treated with respect and dignity and PSR Core Principle 8: PSR practitioners make conscious and consistent efforts to eliminate labeling and discrimination, particularly discrimination based on a disabling condition. I wish the mental health workers back then would have known and practiced such principles.

I thought that everything that was happening to me was my fault and that I was to blame because I had some "character flaw." I thought that I had lost everything, my life was over, and I was a failure. I became depressed, and although I did not actively think of suicide, my will to live had never been less.

I started seeing another psychiatrist outside the hospital who fortunately was very caring. He listened to me patiently, got me on the right dose of medication, and after 6 months diagnosed me with schizophrenia. He described to me what the illness was and gave me literature references to read to help me understand the illness. I remember sitting in the family room with my mom and spending hours reading everything I could get my hands on.

I never felt labeled or stigmatized by my diagnosis. In the beginning, it was a relief to know of it because now I had an understanding of what caused my precarious circumstances, and I realized that it was not my fault or anyone else's fault. The guilt that haunted me disappeared, and I no longer felt so helpless because now there was a name to my enemy.

With understanding, however, came the overwhelming realization of the powerful force that was against me, and I felt devastated. The negative symptoms of the illness kicked in, and I felt incapacitated and depressed. I could do nothing, and I lost all hope in myself and in life. For several years, I lived in darkness and despair.

Fortunately, I had people in my life, like my mom, who genuinely loved me and who believed in me and never lost hope in me. With her steadfast support, along with that of my psychiatrist and the rest of my family and along with my faith that guided me through the darkest hours of my life, I very, very slowly began to recover.

Recovery was not some magic wave that swept over me. I had to learn to live life all over again, and it occurred in painstakingly small, tiny steps over long periods of time. In and of its own, each step may have seemed insignificant, but with a steady reinforcement of incremental growth, progress was miraculously achieved. It was incredible how disabled I had become. At first, I was unable to do anything. Something as basic as grocery shopping was both frightening and overwhelming for me. I remember my mom taking me along to do grocery shopping as a form of rehabilitation. Initially, I would just cling to the shopping cart too terrified to move while my mom began busily loading the shopping cart. I did this for the longest time until 1 day, after many observations, I actually decided to venture away from the cart and gather some apples. This was how small my steps were, and it may sound silly, but then I was faced with the daunting task of deciding which apples to choose from the bunch. Everything seemed so difficult.

Eventually, I was well enough that I felt like working again. I thought I could try and return to the field of science, so I tried returning to graduate school; however, because 5 years had passed, they no longer would accept me. I enrolled in a program called Work on Track that helps people with mental illness prepare to reenter the work force, and at the end of the program I began to look for work. Although Work on Track had helped me to prepare a good resume, again I had a 5-year gap in my resume, which, I was to find out the hard way, worked sorely against me. Even when I did get an interview, the question of the gap would arise. I was told to say that it was due to a medical condition but that it was now under control and that it would not be a factor in my job. It was unbelievable how, after saying this, I immediately sensed that any hope of getting the job disappeared and that we then went only through the motions of a superficial interview with no chance to succeed. I never got a second interview. In one way, I felt discriminated against; however, I would never have been able to prove it even if I wanted to. This was my first "failure." I became convinced that I would only be accepted to work as a janitor and spend the rest of my life cleaning other people's toilets. Not that there is anything wrong with that. It is a noble and honest job, but I felt that I wanted to do something different.

After some time reflecting and regrouping, I was determined to find a meaningful job and to contribute positively and constructively to society. So I went back to college and got accepted into George Brown College's Dental Technology Program in Toronto. I thought that if I worked with my hands and did something practical, I would be happy. I told no one about my illness, and I was terrified that someone would discover my "secret." Returning to school full-time (and with no accommodations) was incredibly difficult; however, after 3 years, I graduated with my diploma in dental technology. Schooling was not, however, my most difficult step. After graduation, I found work in a dental laboratory and soon realized that this was an even more stressful, fiercely competitive, and productivity-oriented business. The law of the day seemed to be that if you were not better and faster than the next person, your days were numbered. After a very difficult year of working in the field, it was clear that I would not be able to work effectively in this field. Both my employer and I agreed that the situation was not working out, and I resigned. I told no one about my illness. Maybe, I erred;

however, I did not think that this was a field open to accommodations. This was my second failure.

It was now 2004, and I was in my early 40s. I was afraid that my life would amount to nothing and that I had little purpose in this life. Then, my psychiatrist suggested one day that I consider shadowing a peer support worker on an Assertive Community Treatment (ACT) Team. Up until now, I wanted nothing to do with the mental health system or its users, and I was still unwilling to disclose my illness. I found the experience, however, to be very interesting and positive. It was encouraging to see the dedication and the care that the ACT Team demonstrated in improving the quality of life for people who suffer from mental illness, and I wanted to contribute to this dedication and caring. After some thought, I enrolled in the PSR Certificate Program at Humber College in Toronto. I found the PSR courses to be totally amazing. They were also a double blessing in that they taught me how to work with and care about people with a mental illness, but I could also apply the teachings to my own life. Recovery took on a totally new meaning for me. I joined the PSR/Réadaption Psychosociale Canada Ontario Chapter Board of Directors (of which I am still a board member), and I began volunteering at a drop-in for a case management organization. My life seemed to take on new meaning and purpose. Things came to me naturally, and I really enjoyed what I was doing.

Then I lucked out. While I was doing my PSR Field Experience Course in Toronto East General Hospital's ACT Team, an opening for a peer support worker arose on Canadian Mental Health Association's West Metro ACT Team in Toronto. I applied, and in February 2006, I was hired as their peer support worker. I still work there, and I love my job. I am even happier now than I was before my illness started.

They say that recovery is knowing oneself under new circumstances, redefining one's role, and reevaluating oneself to develop a new sense of respect for oneself. After living in darkness for many years and having died to my old self, thinking that my life was over and futile, a new birth emerged from within me that has made my life more meaningful and purposeful than before. Whereas before I was a "thing" person, I now discovered a part of me that is a "people" person. I treasure relationships, everything from my relationship with our Creator, family, service users, coworkers, fellow peers, and friends.

They also say that the goal of recovery is to be more human. All the pain and suffering of the past was not a waste because it has helped me to be more human in that now I feel I am a more compassionate and empathic person, and I can use that new enlightenment to help others. Thus, my recovery has been a precious discovery for me and hopefully for others, which I happily share here.

Acknowledgments

This article is edited by Abraham Rudnick, BMedSc, MD, MPsych, PhD, FRCPC, Associate Professor, Departments of Psychiatry and Philosophy, University of Western Ontario (UWO); Chair, Division of Social and Rural Psychiatry, Department of Psychiatry, UWO; Physician-Leader, Psychosis Program, Regional Mental Health Care, 850 Highbury Avenue, London, Ontario N6A 4H1, Canada, tel: 519-4555110, ext. 47417/47333, fax: 519-4552677.

Understanding Health as a Continuum

Leslie Greenblat[3]

"That's enough cherries."

That sounds like Pat. But Pat, sitting across from me, said I could have as many cherries as I like. It's a hot July night, they're tart and smooth, and I like them.

"You'll feel it in the morning. That's enough cherries."

These are good cherries. Just one more. I promise this will be the last one.

"You're making a pig of yourself."

Yes, the seeds and stems are piling up. But Pat said I could have as many cherries as I like, and I'm the one who's going to feel it in the morning. Besides, she told me she won't eat them. She doesn't like sour cherries.

This is what my summer evening was like. Chatting with a friend, eating cherries, and trying to filter out a constant commentary from the vocalized thoughts in my mind. My ability to screen out the "free advice" is hard won. For many years I responded to the constant commentary as if it were coming from someone powerful—sometimes smarter, healthier, and more active

---

[3]From "Understanding Health as a Continuum," by Leslie Greenblat, 2000, *Schizophrenia Bulletin, 26*(1), 243–245. Copyright 2000 by Oxford University Press. Reprinted with permission.

than I was, or sometimes dark and cruel. Even when I was told that I was contaminating everything I touched, I still listened. Family and friends told me to ignore the thought-voices. I couldn't.

Ten years ago I was diagnosed with schizophrenia, and for the first three years I lived the revolving door syndrome: I was hospitalized 13 times. On May 24, 1999, I graduated magna cum laude with a degree in women's studies from the University of Maryland. I'm now enrolled in a master's program in the Johns Hopkins School of Public Health.

Before, I'd take the meds, I'd start to feel better, and then I'd think I didn't need them anymore. Other times I'd convince myself that I could rise up out of the psychosis faster by not being on meds. Regardless of my reasons, I'd still end up hospitalized. Somewhere along the line—I still can't say when or exactly how—I came to realize that I had to stay on the meds and that I needed to trust someone else's perceptions. As I write this, it's hard for me to think about walking on the Verrazano Bridge, believing that because I wanted to go south for the winter, going over the bridge was the quickest way to get to Florida. Three women stopped and gently restrained me from walking off the sidewalk. I regret to this day that I don't know their names to thank them. They saved my life. I wish I could tell them who and what I am today.

Surrounded by boxes of books and household items to be moved, I am struck by how far I've come.

Hearing voices is a lot like having a child pulling at your skirt, asking questions 24 hours a day. Yelling and screaming at the child doesn't stop the barage of questioning and does little to calm yourself. On the other hand, patience and respect works with children and thought-voices. I've tried both—screaming and calm intervention—and calm works better. Even learning that much, though, took time and energy. While driving, I may hear that child ask, *"What are you doing?"* and I think, "I'm driving." If that doesn't satisfy her, I'll visualize the engine. I don't know much about combustion engines, you understand, but I know enough to soothe a child.

I had to learn to manage what I constantly heard if I was ever going to be healthy and independent. One of the hardest things is privacy. Am I as transparent to others as they sometimes seem to me? I miss the feeling of solitude. While I intellectually know that I am alone, it doesn't diminish the fact that I still feel as if my head is full of other people.

My thought-voices come up with some very intense perspectives. When I think of my voices as external or separate entities, I find myself feeling demoralized, asking, "Why didn't I think of that?" Sometimes I have a very hard time thinking of these thoughts as mine. When I find myself in this situation, I can be very critical of myself, constantly pushing to be creative and clever. I am, however, coming to understand that what sounds to me like an outside commentary is from my own thinking. So even if I "hear" someone saying, *"Look, she's at the computer writing,"* I can rephrase it to myself, "I am at the computer writing." I shift from third person to first person.

Sometimes it's hard to accept that I generated these seemingly external observations. I avoid the use of "voice" to describe what occurs in my thinking. Instead, I prefer to conceptualize these occurrences by saying it is *as if* I hear "voices." As I move along in my recovery, I am better able to own what I think as belonging to me.

Ironically, I am learning to talk to myself. But this time I know to whom I am directing my ideas—myself. I used to think that I could project telepathically—that someone else could hear me. I remind myself that everyone processes and deliberates before sharing with others.

One of the most effective tools I have for coping is sharing. I have an excellent working relationship with my psychiatrist. All of my close friends know I was very ill, and as I continue to make new friends, they, too, learn of my struggle. My illness is not a dirty little secret. This given, I have to be careful about what I share and with whom. The concept of "voices" can be frightening and difficult to understand. My friends and family are enormously supportive, but I had to be willing to recognize that a trained professional is better equipped to untangle my distorted thinking.

Asking for help in appropriate ways and not letting a situation get out of control are critical processes. Being willing to let go of your ego and ask for and accept feedback are part of the healing process. Even so, I believe that "the patient is the expert." The idea that a doctor knows all the answers doesn't click with me. This isn't to say that professionals don't have valuable input, but I know my illness better than anyone.

I attribute much of my recovery to my hard work. I have been on many medications, including clozapine, but I have had the same doctor now for nearly 10 years. Dr. Ann Alaoglu is the person I feel had the greatest impact on my return to health. Before I met her, I didn't trust doctors. Doctors doped me up, locked me in, and were generally distant.

Dr. Alaoglu, unlike so many of my past therapists, was willing to put herself on the line, sharing with me her sense of my progress and lapses. One of her greatest strengths is her ability to paraphrase. When I was stressed or unhappy, she may have said, "You seem really down today. What's going on?" I remember psyching myself up for a flight home but telling Dr. Alaoglu that the trees were warning me not to go. Dr. Alaoglu responded by saying, "You seem a bit nervous about your trip." If I had said that to a former therapist of mine she would have suspended my visit and told me (yes, told me!) I was crazy. I think paraphrasing is critical: Hearing how others interpreted what I said gave me a sense of how I was communicating. Later in my treatment, Dr. Alaoglu gave me more rein in my recovery, listening to my input about the level of medication I was on and taking me seriously when I asked for a decrease or even an increase in my medications. I felt empowered in my recovery.

I can remember one doctor who never said a word to me during therapy except to say, "Please sit down, Ms. Greenblat. Tell me about your day." He would take notes, nodding occasionally, and then at the end of a session say, "Thank you, Ms. Greenblat. I will see you later this week." He completely lacked warmth or affection.

There is one more person I must mention: my mother, Dr. Cathy S. Greenblat. She is among the most energetic, positive, determined persons I know. That drive was evident throughout the course of my illness. She searched out the best hospitals and investigated alternative therapies like megavitamins (which, by the way, are very helpful) and visual therapy. As psychotic as I was, within 2 weeks of my discharge she had me pounding the pavement, looking for a job. She supported my decision to go back to school. It was her perpetual optimism that kept me afloat, swimming with me until I was able to swim on my own.

I am fortunate to live in a community with a strong commitment to vocational rehabilitation. The community college I attended before the University of Maryland—Montgomery Community College—had tuition breaks for disabled students. Scholarships to the University of Maryland that would have been unavailable to me because of the credit minimum (a minimum of 12 credits was considered full-time and determined eligibility for the scholarship) were negotiated through the Department of Disability Services.

Being treated as a human and not an illness is critical to recovery. I am increasingly accepting that I may think this way for the rest of my life—*that*

I think differently. Sometimes my thoughts-voices (I still haven't found a good way to describe them) are a real pain in the ass. I have found numerous ways to cope, but still they can/I can be very draining.

What I can say about my recovery is that I had to accept that I played a role in my wellness. It no longer was satisfying to defy or protest treatment—I knew I had to have a working relationship with a therapist and accept my part of the job. I carry with me today the question I was asked several years ago: "Are you ready to be well?" I wasn't then. I am now.

I think the quality of the thought-voices evolved as my health evolved. I no longer hear suggestions to run into traffic; if I did, I would refuse. I'm able to judge the appropriateness of the advice. More often than not, the thought-voices are reasonable—if nagging. Now they tell me not to eat too many cherries, for example. I hear advice to get enough sleep, eat sensibly, get my exercise. They really bug me about exercise, but I believe it's *me* telling me to get my exercise. I'm a thinking, intelligent woman. I know I need to get exercise. But for some reason, I tend to hear it as coming from someone or somewhere else. It's difficult to really concretely define "voices" for someone else. Sometimes it seems they serve as reminders of things I should or shouldn't do—doubts vocalized.

What's the magic cure? How did I go from being an angry, distrusting, "treatment-resistant schizophrenic" to a woman entering graduate school, who lives with schizophrenia? There's no magic cure. All I offer to my fellow travelers is this: Be patient with yourself. Take time to have fun. Work hard. Be passionate. Be willing to trust yourself and others. Take your meds. If you have issues about your meds, negotiate with your doctor. Have courage. If you are in a difficult or stressful situation, plan your response. Have someone to call. Know your limits, and most important, be willing to grow beyond them, but know where to go for support. I am open to alternative health therapies, too. I've tried visual therapy and vitamin therapy and still practice meditation, controlled breathing, and visualization. I'm involved in a study on the effects of fish oil, and think it's working for me. I am sharper and clearer and was able to reduce my neuroleptic medications.

Therapists will say that a move to another city to go to graduate school is about a 10 on the stressor scale. I know it all too well. I also know that I have tools to manage this life event. I know if I start being unable to sleep, I need to call my support network (my therapist, mom, sister, stepfather, and friends) and get feedback on what is happening. "Leslie, take a warm bath, get in bed, shut your eyes, don't open them. Or even take a PRN..." If my thought-voices become too overwhelming or frequent, I know I need to call for support. True, my phone bill is enormous, but think what hospitalization would cost. Final exam? Breathe slowly, hold it, push it all out of my mouth slowly, follow the breath.

A diploma is not a certification of mental health for anybody. I believe health is not an end point; health is an ongoing process of self-reflection and action. I now understand, too, that my illness exists as a continuum. I can find lots of ways to make myself totally crazy. I can now find as many ways to keep myself sane.

Emerson said, "There are voices which we hear in solitude, but they grow faint and inaudible as we enter into the world." I wonder sometimes, as I grow even healthier, if the voices will fade away completely. Will I miss them? Having lived with them for so many years, I wonder if it will feel empty or lonely without them. Thought-voices are part of who I am, and what makes me unique. With what will I replace them? I believe I will find other ways to be unique.

Can I do it? I believe so. I am willing to try.

Psychiatry and Oppression: A Personal Account of Compulsory Admission and Medical Treatment

BENJAMIN GRAY[4]

Hearing Voices: A Personal Story

Certainly, my negative conception of traditional psychiatry and compulsory treatment is colored by the 12 months that I spent in a psychiatric acute unit. Kept under Section 3 of the Mental Health Act of the United Kingdom, I was both obliged to stay in hospital and forced to take antipsychotic medication against my wishes, though physical force was never used against me.

My strange religious beliefs were perhaps quite rightly classified as delusions and discounted by my psychiatrist, nurses, and also my family, but

---

[4]From "Psychiatry and Oppression: A Personal Account of Compulsory Admission and Medical Treatment," by Benjamin Gray, 2009, *Schizophrenia Bulletin, 35*(4), 661–663. Copyright 2009 by Oxford University Press. Reprinted with permission.

this left me with the impression that my experiences, however negative and painful, were also being discounted and that I was not being listened to in order to be more deeply and humanely understood. The famous line of Szasz (1973, p. 113) often came to my mind: "If you talk to God, you are praying; If God talks to you, you have schizophrenia."

Among the people I met during my time in hospital was Rosemary. She was an unassuming, quietly spoken woman, unremarkable apart from an air of sadness. Rosemary had told me and many of the nurses that she would be better off dead than hearing any more of the terrible voices that kept her from sleeping. Better up there with her mother in heaven, she told me, than down in the hell of the psychiatric ward with her voices. Within a few days of being discharged, Rosemary was with her mother again. The nurses called a meeting in the communal lounge. There had been an accident. Rosemary had thrown herself in front of a train. The girl next to me at the meeting broke into tears.

Night after sleepless night and through the long, seemingly endless days in the ward, where smoking and television stood in place of any attempt of therapy, I and my fellow patients experienced similar feelings to those of Rosemary: feelings of loss, isolation, pain, sorrow, self-pity, confusion, and helplessness.

"You're alone," an insidious voice whispered to me. "You're going to get what's coming to you." "You're going down there!" it shouted. "You wait until you see what I'm going to do to you!"

When I heard my voices, which would often shout at me, no one around me moved or looked startled. It was just me hearing the voices. I tried not to answer them. Better to ignore the voices, repress them, and soldier on, I thought. I had seen others screaming back at their voices, and it had left me with mixed feelings of consternation, pity, and fear. I did not want to look mad, like them. Any symptoms of hearing voices would go on medical case notes, be raised as proof of insanity at my case reviews, and keep me locked up in the hell of the ward away from family, friends, and what seemed like a long-distant normal life.

I learned several important lessons too: never admit that you hear voices; certainly never answer them; do exactly as you are told by staff or concerned family or you will be seen as ill; never question your diagnosis or disagree with your psychiatrist; and be compliant and admit your mental illness or you will never be discharged.

All the time, the voices got worse. "Hot fire in your eyes!" shouted a voice to me in the hell of the ward. "That's where you're going. In the fire of the sun!"

Many of the people, and there have been hundreds, with mental illness who I have talked with both as a patient and as a researcher and academic, tell me that they have had to suppress and hide their voices in order to be considered well, stable, and healthy. Not only is this a suppression of symptoms, but it is also a suppression of people's personhood. Traditional psychiatry, in this gloomy and pessimistic view, could be argued to be little more than an instrument of social control and of oppression and a system of scientific belief that perhaps unintentionally crushes people's subjectivity, choices, human rights, and free will.

The majority of individuals with schizophrenia and mental illness that I have spoken with, and from my own personal experience in a psychiatric acute unit I have to agree, find meeting with their consultant psychiatrist threatening because any unusual thoughts or behavior can be taken out of context and construed as psychotic. Many people with mental health problems are genuinely afraid of meeting with their psychiatrist or other members of the mental health team. I remember a teenage boy in the ward literally shaking and wringing his hands with fear before his weekly case review with his psychiatrist, much to the concern of nurses, the boy's mother, myself, and the boy's mental health advocate.

Many people with mental health problems hide their symptoms, their aberrant beliefs, and their voices to stay out of hospital, but this means that they are ostracized and that there is a lack of dialogue between mental health professionals and people with mental health problems. This also means that there may be a lack of disclosure and of what is really going on in people's lives and what voices they may be hearing. Because people with mental health problems fear the psychiatric encounter and are afraid of punitive intervention or compulsory treatment, psychiatrists and mental health professionals are not getting the full picture so as to agree a consensus on care plans and treatment. This is also true of family carers, who are increasingly being called upon to provide around the clock support for people with mental health problems in the community. Family carers are often little more than the unpaid workhorses of community care, who lack the skill and information necessary to provide adequate support to their family members with schizophrenia and mental health problems who may hear voices.

More worryingly, when in hospital, violence is sometimes used as a tool for getting noncompliant patients to take their medication, usually via depot injection. This violence is often conceived of as right, as just, and in the patient's best interest. Certainly, many nurses I have spoken to have not only said that they do not like administering forcible injections but also say that they have a duty of care. Violence as care is an oxymoron and hides the institutionalized abuse of people with schizophrenia and mental health problems. I myself have witnessed 8 occasions where patients have had to be very violently restrained by staff and only 2 assaults by mental health patients on nurses. This is in line with evidence that people with mental health problems are more likely to experience violence on their person rather than attacking other people.

Psychiatry has taken a biomedical approach, with the prescription of powerful antipsychotic medication, including drugs such as olanzapine, risperidone, and clozaril, all of which I have been prescribed. These powerful antipsychotics have serious and debilitating side effects, are toxic, and have also been suggested to be harmful to those taking them in the long term. These antipsychotic medications have often been described as a "chemical cosh," leaving people who take them passive, debilitated, and zombie like. This could be suggested to lead to the tranquilization of people's personal beliefs, however irrational, and their thoughts, subjectivity, and feelings. Such an approach could certainly be argued to crush diversity and discount the diversity of people's experience of life and the world, in the name of normalization and keeping a stable social and medical order.

Put very crudely, popping a pill is far less of a burden on a health service that has limited resources, a lack of money, severe pressures on beds, and a lack of inpatient provision, which often depends on family carers who lack the knowledge and expertise of dealing with people with mental health problems who may be in distress and where care in the community is limited in scope and often means no care in the community, leaving people with mental health problems with the feeling that they are alone, invisible, and ostracized.

All this means that there is little study of what schizophrenics' voices say to them, which would make people's experiences more valid and meaningful and also lend itself to a more human account of mental illness. People's experiences of hearing voices are silenced, which can only augment ignorance and fear, both in society and in the mental health-care system. Little attention has been given to what people with mental health problems think and feel and what treatments they would prefer. Psychiatry overrelies on powerful antipsychotic medications, and there are long waiting lists for less invasive treatments such as counseling and cognitive behavioral therapy.

To complicate and make matters worse, it is almost impossible to talk with other people and relate the pain that voices inflict when they are raging inside you and shouting you down. It is even harder to face the voices and achieve what psychiatrists and mental health professionals call "insight." My voices, in particular, often sounded telepathic, as though people were speaking to me through their minds. My voices would often be racist or abusive about mental health staff and other patients. It is perhaps not surprising that voices like these, if dismissed as bizarre delusions and not discussed as at least phenomenologically or subjectively "real," may sometimes lead to violent behavior toward staff and other patients or—as I have witnessed—the smashing of hospital furniture, equipment, and the television from which the voices emanated.

The main point to reiterate is that these voices are silenced and dismissed as delusions and that they are managed mostly by medical treatment and thus not addressed in human and sympathetic terms that might begin to tackle the root cause of the problem, which in turn might help people cope more profoundly and insightfully with their voices.

Certainly, the overreliance on medication is perhaps not surprising, given that people who hear voices can be perceived as aggressive, irrational, and violent. My voices often took on a demonic or hellish quality: "You think you've been exploited and abused?" a demonic voice often shouted at me. "You wait until you see what I'm going to do to you! You wait until you see what I look like!"

But this is partly the point: other people cannot hear the schizophrenic's voice. There needs to be a dialogue so as to treat the voice hearer's experience as valid and meaningful (Foucault, 1992; Laing, 1967). A more democratic psychiatrist listens to people with mental health problems and is open to their experiences and voices, so not stigmatizing the voice hearer, which in turn may lead to more holistic, democratic, and sensitive packages of mental health care.

Discussion: The Rise of Democratic Psychiatry and the Hearing Voices Movement

What I have learnt as an academic and researcher, as well as a mental health patient labeled with schizophrenia, is that what people with mental health problems want is to be treated as equal citizens with equal human and medical rights. People with mental health problems who hear voices or hallucinate want to be valued, as we all do, not feared and ostracized. They want their views and opinions taken into account, especially as regards what sorts of treatment they have and in their care plans. They want a right to accept or refuse medication and not have it forced upon them supposedly for their own good. At the very least, people with mental health problems want their stories, narratives, and voices to be valued and taken into consideration. Such an approach would take people's diversity, and their diverse experiences and beliefs, into consideration and not label people as mad or bad but value them as human beings, with all the faults and strengths that being a human being entails. Such an approach would give rise to a more democratic and person-centered psychiatry, which would also view mental health patients' experiences as a form of expertise to be shared with professionals rather than discounted as delusions.

What is required is a balance of perspectives between traditional psychiatry and the diverse experiences of people with mental health problems, with the aim of achieving a consensus on pathways of treatment and new, innovative, and alternative methods of mental health practice (Stastny & Lehmann, 2007). Hearing voices groups and voice hearers' Internet discussion forums are just 2 contemporary examples as is the use of advance agreements and directives.

Central to this process is the rise of democratic psychiatry and the hearing voices movement, headed by the eminent psychiatrist Marius Romme and organizations such as Intervoice (http://www.intervoiceonline.org/), Asylum (http://www.asylumonline.net/ and http://studymore.org.uk/mpuzasy.htm), MindFreedom (http://www.mindfreedom.org/), and the Hearing Voices Network (http://www.hearing-voices.org/andhttp://www.hvn-usa.org/).

Democratic psychiatry and the hearing voices movement do not ostracize and silence people who hear voices but create space for their voices, narratives, stories, personal thoughts, and experiences, which will lead to more humane and holistic approaches of understanding and treating schizophrenia and mental illness in the future. This means that psychiatry rather than doing things "to" or "for" people must begin to work "with" them. According to Romme and Morris (2007):

> The term 'schizophrenia' is not just stigmatising, but also fundamentally flawed. It is a label without scientific validity. Diagnosis ignores connections between life experiences and core illness experiences. We urge mental health professionals to listen to what their patients are telling them and help them understand their experiences. (p. 7)

References

Foucault, M. (1992). *Madness and civilisation*. London, England: Routledge.

Laing, R. D. (1967). *The politics of experience and the bird of paradise*. Harmondsworth, England: Penguin.

Romme, M., & Morris, M. (2007). The harmful concept of schizophrenia. *Mental Health Nursing, 27*, 7–11.

Stastny, P., & Lehmann, P. (2007). *Alternatives beyond psychiatry*. Shrewsbury, England: Peter Lehmann.

Szasz, T. (1973). *The second sin*. Garden City, NY: Anchor/Doubleday.

Powerful Choices: Peer Support and Individualized Medication Self-Determination

CORINNA WEST[5]

Introduction

I am a certified peer specialist. I have helped homeless people and people with mental illnesses reclaim their lives by sharing my story of recovery from both homelessness and mental illness. I use many tools and creative talents each day at work: poetry, PowerPoint presentations, personal conversations,

[5]From "Powerful Choices: Peer Support and Individualized Medication Self-Determination," by Corinna West, 2011, *Schizophrenia Bulletin, 37*(3), 445–450. Copyright 2011 by Oxford University Press. Reprinted with permission.

recovery research, and extensive social networking. I believe that the mental health system can change to provide recovery for every single person with mental illness. I think that 2 of the important science-to-service gaps in real-world schizophrenia treatment are the ability to inspire people to make changes in their own lives and to help people decide to take responsibility for important choices that will affect their recovery. As a peer specialist, I tackle both issues. I think that we need both more peer support and more medication self-determination and individualization of treatment.

My message is a story of hope that all people with mental illness can take control of their lives on the other side of a diagnosis. We can regain a productive and fulfilling membership in the community. By combining my life passions, my recovery story, my dreams, and my joys, I am able to create novel presentations and workshops. I perform these for day programs, support groups, consumer-run organizations, and staff trainings at community mental health centers. These are active and participatory learning experiences that incorporate performance or spoken word poetry, PowerPoint slides, and cutting-edge research that challenge how the current mental health system is being funded and operated. I am a storyteller, and I tell a tale of change: taking the power back to help oneself, taking risks, and finding new dreams. I create short or long workshops where people can become inspired by both giving and receiving peer support in order to learn the importance that mutual relationships can have. I believe that peer support is the future of the mental health system, and we will be some of the most powerful forces in transforming the mental health system to a "recovery-oriented community of hope" (Missouri Department of Mental Health, 2009).

My recovery involved finding a way to maximize my strengths and move beyond my weaknesses, and active transportation, including walking, running, and bicycling, is an important element in my daily routine. Patricia Deegan, PhD, a psychologist who has also recovered from schizophrenia, has come up with a term called "personal medicine," which is what we do for ourselves. Pill medicine is what we take, and personal medicine is what we do, both how we stay well and the reasons we find for wanting to stay well (Deegan, 2005). I have incorporated my art, my work, and my life, in a way where many of the things I do will enhance my recovery. I ride a bicycle everywhere I go and advocate for the 8.3% of Missouri households that have no access to an automobile (Missouri Bicycle Federation, 2009). I use exercise as a positive coping tool for stress, I am out and involved in the community, and I have made a great group of friends and supporters who enjoy my personality with or without mental illness. My plan, my power, and my way is to do what I can to be a positive, inspirational person who has immense potential to make the world a better place.

Reclaiming Dreams

A few years ago, when I was more ill, I read somewhere that when an initial diagnosis of mental illness is made, what should happen is that the doctor should give the diagnosis and give some basic information about the illness and the treatment. Then the doctor should walk out of the room, and a person with that diagnosis should walk in and say, "I have this illness, and I have a life. I have some really good things going for me on the other side of this diagnosis."

When I first read that, I thought, "I'd like to be that person." Now I am. I am a certified peer specialist working for Mental Health America of the Heartland, an information and advocacy organization in Kansas City. My last peer support assignment was at a local homeless shelter, where I gave my peers information on recovery, helped them look for jobs, helped advocate for their residential needs, taught people how to prepare an agenda for their medication appointments, assisted with transportation planning, and served as an example that recovery is possible. I also co-coordinate a warmline, a consumer-operated alternative to a crisis line where people with mental illnesses can call and just talk to someone else who is experiencing the process of recovery. Our warmline is all volunteer staffed with about 28 consumers who answer about 350 calls a month while learning employment skills, recovery information, assertiveness, and how to build their own personal peer support networks. My job is to help people rebuild their lives. What I try to communicate as a peer specialist is that it is worth digging a mile through stone. I try to give people the tiny hope of a baby dream that they can recover; however, they need to hear it. I try to help people connect and to learn to help themselves. My story, along with my joys and passions, is part of the peer support movement that is transforming the mental health system (Peebles et al., 2007). I advocate for clients' larger possibilities in staff meetings, I challenge stigmatizing statements made in the back rooms, I share updated information about recovery, and I bring in creative client-centered solutions to my coworkers. Most important, I provide an example of productivity and recovery for every staff member with whom I interact.

This ability to change attitudes and perceptions for both clients and other staff is unique to the peer support role.

Spoken word poetry is one of the most powerful tools in my arsenal. This is a dense art form that can communicate emotion, ideas, and my ambitious personality in a brief amount of time using intonation, gestures, and choreography. I have a 7½-minute poem about being a member of the 1996 Olympic Judo team that contains the same important images, skills, character, and a lot more emotion than the original 60-minute PowerPoint presentation. After hearing this poem, people have said, "That is the most inspirational thing I have heard in a long time," and "I was so hopeful that it brought tears to my eyes." One of my poems was selected for publication in *Mind Matters Monthly,* a newsletter for people inside Oswatomie State Hospital, the biggest inpatient institution in the state of Kansas. A peer specialist who works in the hospital said, "When people read the poem, and saw all that you had accomplished, the light bulb went off for them. They just realized, 'Yeah, I can do this.' It was really powerful and amazing to watch."

Peer Support as an Evidence-Based Practice

Peer support is qualitatively different than other mental health staff interactions. A client at the homeless shelter where I worked told the other peer support worker and me, "I really like working with you two because it seems like you understand where I am coming from. You two are the best part of this facility." Paulson et al. (1999) compared practice patterns of consumer and nonconsumer providers of mental health services and found a much greater qualitative than quantitative difference. "While the activity log analyses showed that both teams had similar patterns in *what* they did, that is the type and distribution of time spent doing case manager activities, there were observable differences in *how* the teams carried out these same activities. In other words, there were differences in the practice 'cultures' operating in the two teams [italics and quote original]." The kind of differences included boundary issues such as a greater willingness to self-disclose, less expressions of fear of the clients, and less rigid issues of personal space like a friendly "goodbye" hug. The consumer team had less emphasis on adherence to rules and seemed to work more cooperatively rather than imposing sanctions. Perhaps, the most important difference observed was a more relaxed pace "where the case manager seemed to 'be there' for the client, where it was not the task but rather the relationship and being fully present with the consumer which was considered paramount in the recovery process" (Paulson et al., 1999).

Sells, Black, Davidson, and Rowe (2008) found that " clients with peer providers perceive that their providers' communications are more validating compared with clients with traditional providers. Moreover, peer providers' invalidating communication appeared to be linked to clients' subsequent improvements in social relationships and health, whereas no corresponding associations were found for clients of traditional providers." Often when I have had to disagree with a client, I have been able to bring in first hand experience. I remember one particular conversation discussing the merits of hospitalization with a person who was not really suicidal or a danger to others. I was able to bring in my own experience of multiple hospitalizations that not only kept me safe but also somewhat delayed me in the process of finding solutions to my primary problems of a job, friends, and housing.

Peer support was designated as an evidence-based practice by the Centers for Medicare and Medicaid Services (CMS) in August 15, 2007, letter to State Medicaid Directors that said, "CMS recognizes that the experiences of peer support providers, as consumers of mental health and substance use services, can be an important component in a State's delivery of effective treatment." The letter emphasized that plans and goals must be individualized and person centered (SMDL, 2007).

[*sic*] Report of Eiken and Campbell (2008) on Medicaid coverage concluded that "1) when provided in addition to other mental health services, a majority of studies suggest peer support helps participants improve psychological outcomes and reduce hospitalization; and 2) a majority of studies suggest peer providers perform as well as non-peers when peer-delivered services are an alternative to traditional mental health services." Gates and Akabas (2007) found that barriers to integrating peer staff include attitudes toward recovery among nonpeer staff, role conflict and confusion, lack of clarity around confidentiality, poorly defined peer jobs, and lack of opportunity for networking and support. The authors suggest workplace strategies to respond to each of these issues. The agency I work for, Mental Health America of the Heartland, employs 9 peer specialists who work in collaborating nonprofit agencies throughout our bistate metro Kansas City area. Although we are one of the largest groups of peer specialists in our region, we have

barely scratched the surface of the demand. Many other states have yet to make the effort to create a certification process so that they can bill Medicaid for providing peer support. Increasing the amount of peer support would remedy an important science-to-service gap in the real-world treatment of schizophrenia.

The Importance of Choices

I think that the science-to-service gap can be summed up in one word: choices. In an ideal world, all people with schizophrenia would have access to available evidence-based treatments. The power of choices is summarized in Patricia Deegan's article "Recovery as a Journey of the Heart" that explains how those of us with psychiatric disabilities can choose to become helpless rather than hopeless when our efforts feel futile. Deegan explains that choices are essential to help someone come out of this place and says " ... the staff must not fall into despair, feel like their efforts are futile, grow hard of heart, and stop caring themselves. If they do this, they are doing exactly what the person with the psychiatric disability is doing" (Deegan, 1996).

Role modeling of hope is one of my most important jobs as a peer specialist. By sharing my recovery story, I can help staff avoid the trap of feeling that their efforts are wasted by pointing out that people do indeed recover. At the homeless shelter, I started a process of collecting success stories of clients so that they could be used to inspire other clients for grant writing, to reassure staff, and to reward the clients who were so recognized. One of the clients I approached said, "Well, I didn't really consider myself a success, but I guess I have made a lot of progress." I help both the clients and the other staff recognize small milestones. I learned in a support group that I helped to facilitate that recovery is best understood in hindsight—just as it is possible to travel most of the way from Miami to California without seeing a single sign for over 1500 miles that you are on your way to California (Crowley, 2000). I help both clients and staff to see the signs and keep hope alive. Fisher and Ahern (2002) have described how the role modeling of hope works by providing hope, social connection, and a belief that people can regain control of their life.

When I was going through the certification training to become a peer specialist, Beth Filson, also a certified peer specialist and one of the trainers, told us, "In no other field could I take those ten years of my life that were so much misery and pure hell, and turn all that negativity into something positive. All those experiences that were so terrible when I lived through them have now become valuable and have the potential to help someone else, and it's like, 'Wow, those years weren't wasted'." Hearing people respond to my recovery story with a new sense of encouragement is incredibly powerful for both me and the person with whom I am working.

The Choice of Medication

Nowhere does the importance of choices have such a social and emotional impact as in the area of medication. [sic] Article of Roe and Swarbick [sic] (2007) on "A Recovery Oriented Approach to Psychiatric Medication" mentions that efforts to develop and integrate concepts such as shared decision making, self-determination, and informed consent are transforming the mental health system. The authors suggest that supporters can help by empowering consumers to ask questions, to help consumers prepare ahead of time for a meeting or to be present as an advocate, by role-playing aspects of the medication meeting, and by teaching consumers to ask for the drug prescribing information. As a peer support specialist, I have never once advocated medication discontinuance. Instead, I try to ask effective questions like, "How is that working for you?" or "What is your biggest barrier to reaching that goal?" or "Is there a way you can tell your doctor what you really need next time?"

Because I was first diagnosed with a psychotic illness relatively recently (2001), I was able to participate in a mental health system that allowed me some degree of choice. My initial symptoms of visual hallucinations were met with a prescription of an atypical antipsychotic, which worked for me. Later, a different doctor diagnosed me with a nonpsychotic mood disorder and abruptly took me off the antipsychotic with my consent. After about 2 months, I became floridly psychotic, with visual, tactile, and olfactory hallucinations. I remember vividly one time when I was trying to drive home and the hallucinations were so frequent that I was afraid to drive off the road or run into something that may or may not have been there. I finally pulled over and called a friend who is a mental health consumer. "Do you have any Thorazine?" I asked her. "I don't care if it's a bad drug, I'll take anything at this point." I was well aware at that time that atypicals were supposedly superior, although that assertion has come into dispute more recently (Geddes, Freemantle, Harrison, & Bebbington, 2000). My friend did not have any meds for me but did talk to me about how to calm down and try to separate the real from the unreal enough to get myself home that evening. I got back on atypicals, and after a rough 2 or 3 more months including one more hospitalization, the psychotic symptoms were abated enough that I could live independently and work again. In fact, the job and the house I found to share were also very important steps as I learned to take responsibility for my own life and to build a new life instead of trying to get back to the life I had before I was ill.

As a peer support specialist, I can use my personal experience with medication to reinforce both the benefits and the disadvantages to medications, and I can help the clients weigh their goals in order to make a more informed decisions. This helps to create the individualized plan of care necessary for each person. I often have more time available than do my nonpeer clinicians, and I can try to work out the important values for the choice. I never tell people to discontinue medication, and in fact, when I do presentations, when people ask me about my medications, I tell them about Lance Armstrong, the cyclist. He is often asked about medications by people with the same kind of testicular cancer, and he tells them that medications and their effects are incredibly individual and have to be handled on a case-by-case basis, so what meds work for one person is irrelevant to another person's treatment.

Medication Issues, Peer Support, and Self-Determination

There are people in the consumer movement who say, "I couldn't have recovered without my medications," and when I was more ill I was definitely in that category, although not so much anymore. Some people even advocate for a greater role of medication decisions made on behalf of consumers who may not see the need for medications (Frese, Stanley, Kress, & Vogel-Scibilia, 2001). However, there are also people who say, "If I had stayed on my medication, I don't think there's any way my life would be as together as it is now" (Carey, 2006). All these positions need to be recognized and validated. Bola and Mosher (2002) suggest that "An outright dismissal of antipsychotic medication use as well as an uncritical and universal prescription of these medications for all psychoses might be equally regarded as ideological positions."

Ignoring the fact that some people do well off medications might be another large science-to-service gap in the real-world treatment of schizophrenia (Harding & Zahniser, 1994; Harrow & Jobe, 2007). I am aware that many of the studies showing greater rates of relapse for people on placebo (Beasley et al., 2006) are abrupt withdrawal studies, whereas gradual withdrawal, following sound pharmacological principles, has a much lower rate of relapse (Viguera, Baldessarini, Hegarty, van Kammen, & Tohen, 1997). I have found out that antipsychotics cause a discontinuation syndrome that can be confounded with relapse (Moncrieff, 2006). This may be based on the fact that antipsychotics increase the density of dopamine receptors and convert dopamine D2 receptors from the low-affinity state to the high-affinity state that is implicated in psychosis (Seeman et al., 2005). These increased numbers of high-affinity dopamine D2 receptors are invariably associated with behavioral supersensitivity to the brain's dopamine, the release of which is increased by stress, street drugs, and other factors. In addition, combinations of different genes in different people can be associated with such dopamine supersensitivity. No single gene is sufficient to account for behavioral supersensitivity and psychotic symptoms. For example, the removal or knockout of a particular gene will cause changes in the activity of other genes, which can converge to trigger dopamine supersensitivity and psychosis, so the race to find a single gene for schizophrenia is essentially futile (Seeman et al., 2006). This supersensitivity has been proposed to cause treatment failure over time (Samaha, Seeman, Stewart, Rajabi, & Kapur, 2007) and has been suggested, along with side effects, as an important reason for the high rate of discontinuation during the Clinical Antipsychotic Trials Of Intervention Effectiveness (CATIE) trial (Chouinard & Chouinard, 2008). It is possible that by medicating everyone, we are missing out on a group of people who are overrepresented in the best outcomes category (Kurihara, Kato, Reverger, & Yagi, 2002). More extreme detractors of medication have hypothesized that medications cause more harm than good and that lower use of medications explain the better outcomes found by the World Health Organization studies in the developing world (Whitaker, 2004).

Even though I understand these issues with medications, I still know from personal experience, from work observations, and from research data that medications do indeed have value. As a peer support worker, I have to try to avoid any dogmatic or judgmental characterization that would be unhelpful to my clients. I am very aware that although I am a trained professional, I am not a doctor. Instead of giving any specific medication advice, I teach clients self-advocacy skills, negotiation strategies, and problem-solving techniques to address their concerns with their doctor. I teach self-determination so that people can optimize their medication regimes for themselves. My job is to model hope, as Patricia Deegan said, to keep offering options and choices, and to help the staff I work with to keep from falling into despair. I know recovery is possible, and I help people to see how they still do have the ability to impact the world and make changes. I teach them to ask themselves questions like, "What is stopping me from working?" or "Was it really true when that doctor told me that taking the bus would be too stressful for me?" or "Who else can I find to talk to about this problem?"

I have helped other mental health consumers to apply for the peer specialist training after not working for long periods of their life. One of them said, "I still believe I have a lot to contribute to the world and I would like to make a difference for someone else the way other people have done for me." The choice of seeking employment is a powerful assist to recovery, yet a study on conformant care found that 52% of people had not been assessed for work potential. The same study found that 24% of people were undergoing polypharmacy with multiple antipsychotics, which the author defined as nonconformant to the Schizophrenia Patient Outcomes Research Team guidelines (Bollini et al., 2008). Because atypical antipsychotics cost $300–$600 a month, that could have bought quite a lot of peer support. In the wake of the CATIE trial results questioning the superiority of atypicals, Luchins (2006) says, "The decision to reduce resources for other interventions while enormously expanding the medication budget was not necessarily one that would have been supported by consumers, but it was a decision we made. In hindsight it was a mistake."

As a peer supporter, my job is to challenge all the assumptions. The first assumptions I had to challenge were my own fears of never being able to work again at the same level and fears of not having friends or a family or a life worth living. I was very ill for a long time, and now I am not. I have a remarkable life with friends, passions, hobbies, and interesting and ever expanding opportunities. I have a practical and durable bicycle that gets me all over town while meeting amazing people and having interesting adventures along the way. Connecting with resources in the consumer movement helped me decide to keep trying after I had given up numerous times. Now it is my turn to keep asking questions, to help people to find what works the best for them, and to keep pushing their limits. My role is unique with [*sic*] the mental health system because I affect both clients and the other staff as they provide services. I help both groups see that there are many powerful choices available.

Acknowledgments

To my compassionate ear co-coordinator, Lois Hohn, who is as dedicated as I am to consumer-provided services. To Randy Johnson, my boss, and the entire staff at Mental Health America of the Heartland, where I have been [*sic*] learned to harness my unique talents. To the countless leaders of the consumer movement who came before me and paved the way—we are the evidence.

References

Beasley, C. M., Sutton, V. K., Taylor, C. C., Sethuraman, G., Dossenbach, M., & Naber, D. (2006). Is quality of life among minimally symptomatic patients with schizophrenia better following withdrawal or continuation of antipsychotic treatment? *Journal of Clinical Psychopharmacology, 26,* 40–44.

Bola, J. R., & Mosher, L. R. (2002). Clashing ideologies or scientific discourse? *Schizophrenia Bulletin, 28,* 583–588.

Bollini, P., Pampallona, S., Neiddu, S., Bianco, M., Tibaldi, G., & Munizza, C. (2008). Indicators of conformance with guidelines of schizophrenia treatment in mental health services. *Psychiatric Services, 59,* 782–791.

Carey, B. (2006, March 21). Revisiting schizophrenia: Are drugs always needed? *New York Times.* Quoting Will Hall. http:// www.nytimes. com/2006/03/21/health/psychology/21schiz.html?_ r=1#.

Chouinard, G., & Chouinard, V. A. (2008). Atypical antipsychotics: CATIE study, drug induced movement disorder and resulting iatrogenic psychiatric-like symptoms, supersensitivity rebound psychosis and withdrawal discontinuation syndromes. *Psychotherapy and Psychosomatics, 77,* 69–77.

Crowley, K. (2000). *The Power of Procovery.* Los Angeles, CA: Kennedy Carlisle Publishing.

Deegan, P. (1996). Recovery as a journey of the heart. *Psychiatric Rehabilitation Journal, 19,* 91–97.

Deegan, P. E. (2005). The importance of personal medicine: A qualitative study of resilience in people with psychiatric disabilities. *Scandinavian Journal of Public Health Suppl.*, *66*, 29–35.

Eiken, S., & Campbell, J. (2008). Medicaid coverage of peer support for people with mental illness: Available research and state examples. *Thompson Reuters Healthcare Report*. Washington, DC: Centers for Medicare & Medicaid Services (CMS).

Fisher, D. B., & Ahern, L. (2002). Evidence-based practices and recovery. *Psychiatric Services*, *53*, 632–633.

Frese, F. J., Stanley, J., Kress, K., & Vogel-Scibilia, S. (2001). Integrating evidence based practices and the recovery model. *Psychiatric Services*, *52*, 1462–1468.

Gates, L. B., & Akabas, S. H. (2007). Developing strategies to integrate peer providers into the staff of mental health agencies. *Administration and Policy in Mental Health and Mental Health Services Research*, *34*, 293–306.

Geddes, J., Freemantle, N., Harrison, P., & Bebbington, P. (2000). Atypical antipsychotics in the treatment of schizophrenia: Systematic overview and meta-regression analysis. *BMJ*, *321*, 1371–1376.

Harding, C. M., & Zahniser, J. H. (1994). Empirical correction of seven myths about schizophrenia with implications for treatment. *Acta Psychiatrica Scandinavica Suppl.*, *384*, 140–146.

Harrow, M., & Jobe, T. H. (2007). Factors involved in outcome and recovery in schizophrenia patients not on antipsychotic medications. *The Journal of Nervous and Mental Disease,195*, 406–414.

Kurihara, T., Kato, M., Reverger, R., & Yagi, G. (2002). Clinical outcome of patients with schizophrenia without maintenance treatment in a nonindustrialized society. *Schizophrenia Bulletin, 28*, 515–524.

Luchins, D. J. (2006). Letter. *Psychiatric Services*, *57*,139–140.

Missouri Bicycle Federation. (2009). http://mobikefed.org/2005/09/ how-many-missourians-are-non-drivers.php.

Missouri Department of Mental Health, Office of Transformation. (2009). http://www.dmh.missouri.gov/transformation/transformation.htm.

Moncrieff, J. (2006). Does antipsychotic withdrawal provoke psychosis? Review of the literature on rapid onset psychosis (supersensitivity psychosis) and withdrawal-related relapse. *Acta Psychiatrica Scandinavica*, *114*, 3–13.

Paulson, R., Herinckx, H., Demmler, J., Clarke, G., Cutler, D., & Birecree,

E. (1999). Comparing practice patterns of consumer and non-consumer mental health service providers. *Community Mental Health Journal, 35,* 251–269.

Peebles, S. A., Mabe, P. A., Davidson, L., Fricks, L., Buckley, P.F., & Fenley, G. (2007). Recovery and systems transformation for schizophrenia. *The Psychiatric Clinics of North America, 30,* 567–583.

Roe, D., & Swarbrick, M. A. (2007). A recovery-oriented approach to psychiatric medication. *Journal of Psychosocial Nursing and Mental Health Services, 5,* 35–40.

Samaha, A. N., Seeman, P., Stewart, J., Rajabi, H., & Kapur, S. (2007). "Breakthrough" dopamine supersensitivity during ongoing antipsychotic treatment leads to treatment failure over time. *The Journal of Neuroscience, 27,* 2979–2986.

Seeman, P., Schwarz, J., Chen, J. F., Szechtman, H., Perrault, M., McKnight, G. S., . . . Sumiyoshi, T. (2006). Psychosis pathways converge via D2high dopamine receptors. *Synapse, 60,* 319–346.

Seeman, P., Weinshenker, D., Quirion, R., Srivastava, L. K., Bhardwaj, S. K., Grandy, D. K., . . . Tallerico, T. (2005). Dopamine supersensitivity correlates with D2high states, implying many paths to psychosis. *Proceedings of the National Academy of Sciences of the United States of America, 102,* 3513–3518.

Sells, D., Black, R., Davidson, L., & Rowe, M. (2008). Beyond generic support: Incidence and impact of invalidation in peer services for clients with severe mental illness. *Psychiatric Services, 59,* 1322–1327.

SMDL #07-011, U.S. Centers of Medicare and Medicaid Services, August 15, 2007. http://www.cms.hhs.gov.

Viguera, A. C., Baldessarini, R. J., Hegarty, J. D., van Kammen, D. P., & Tohen, M. (1997). Clinical risk following abrupt and gradual withdrawal of maintenance neuroleptic treatment. *Archives of General Psychiatry, 54,* 49–55.

Whitaker, R. (2004). The case against antipsychotic drugs: A 50-year record of doing more harm than good. *Medical Hypotheses, 62,* 5–13.

SCHIZOAFFECTIVE DISORDER

Snapshots: The First Symptoms of Psychosis

KRISTEN B. FOWLER[6]

Episodes of significant depression have been a part of my life for as long as I can recall, but psychosis was unknown to me until I was in my mid-thirties, months after the birth of my second child. At first, all I recognized were the emerging symptoms of postpartum depression in the weeks after the birth: a familiar scenario, since it had also occurred with my first child. My OB/GYN immediately prescribed 50mg of Prozac daily. I took the medication, felt much better, and continued to breastfeed my second daughter with no apparent problems.

In fact, for about four months I felt better than I had in years. My therapist, an LCSW, was thrilled with my progress. She had been treating me with a technique called Eye Movement Desensitization and Reprocessing (EMDR) for about a year in order to abate the symptoms of depression, anxiety, and panic attacks I had suffered nearly all of my adult life. The therapy worked; I successfully overcame the anxiety and panic attacks, and the Prozac ameliorated the depression. I felt like I had been healed, cured, was a new person, for the first time truly enjoying the many blessings in my life: two beautiful daughters, a doting husband, a good income, and a teaching career I loved. But in the fifth postpartum month, and for no apparent reason, something went very, very wrong. The depressive mood returned—despite the Prozac—in a form it had never taken before, with a frighteningly self-destructive severity and a subtle but definite descent into psychosis. No one recognized it at first, although eventually it would be diagnosed by most professionals as schizo-affective disorder. The following essays are my recollections of some of these new, and very foreign, moments in the beginning of that process, as my mind gradually turned from sane to psychotic.

June 2002

Tim is away, traveling on business this week. I don't like it when he's gone. It's not the lack of conversation or sleeping in an empty bed that's the problem. The hard part is that time in the evening when the girls are in bed and the house is silent and dark. I know this sounds very strange, but I am sensing something awful in the shadows at night. In darkened spaces, I feel a presence is lurking; I fear that it is watching me. I don't like to think about what it might be, but I think it's something dead, something that is alive and yet shouldn't be alive. Something silent, stealthy, evil, made of bones, or bloody, decaying body parts. I am terrified to look in the closets, or behind doors, or in the garage. I am constantly turning my head to look behind me. Even a familiar sound such as the cat jumping off the counter startles me. My heart pounds while the water sprays over me in the shower, for fear that my eyes might be closed or my back turned and my body vulnerable as something advances toward me. I wish Tim would come home. The evil things keep hidden when he is around in the evening. They want me alone.

I told my therapist, Diane, about the evil things in the dark shadows. "I'm really embarrassed to tell you about this," I said. "You're going to think I'm schizophrenic or something." I looked away, rubbing my finger over a small spot on my khaki pants. Even the closet in her office, dark behind folding doors, looked suspicious to me at the moment.

"No, no, it's not that," she said. "I'm not an expert on schizophrenia, but I would recognize it if I saw it. Besides, if you were schizophrenic, it would have developed in your teens and twenties."

I breathed a sigh of relief.

"These might be some memories of childhood nightmares," she continued. "We've been digging into your past while doing the EMDR, and all kinds of subconscious thoughts can resurface during the therapy."

"I can't tell you how glad I am to hear you say that," I said.

"These creepy things have really been scaring me." "More than likely, you'll find that it will go away now that you've recognized the fear and discussed it with me," Diane said. She smiled, and her clear green eyes looked relaxed.

She's not worried, I thought.

I left her office feeling better, but the evil things in the shadows remained.

August 2002

It was late, past 10:00 p.m., when I went into the kitchen for a glass of water and realized the dishes hadn't been done. Tim was hunched over his laptop in the family room, chuckling occasionally at the television. Frowning, I reached under the counter for the dishpan, squirted in some lemon-scented dish soap, and filled it with hot water.

The baby bottles got washed first, while the water was clean. All the pastel-colored plastic caps and bottles of various sizes clunked around in the dishpan as I inserted a bottle brush inside each one and twisted it. Gradually I became aware of a tapping sound on the screen sliding door. *What is that?* I peered over the counter to see if the dog was scratching to go out. She wasn't there.

Tap. Tap-tap. Tap. I stacked the clean bottles to dry and moved on to the glasses and utensils, saving the messy pans for last. My gaze flicked back and forth between the dishpan and the screen door and the tapping sound. Suddenly I understood. Large moths were throwing themselves against the screen in an effort to get in. I could see them now. *Tap, buzz. Tap. Tap.*

But I was not entirely reassured. The tapping sound was creepy, and not just because I didn't want the big brown moths to come in. I rinsed some cooking spoons and placed them in the dish drainer, not wanting to look at the screen anymore. *What if those are fingers tapping on the screen? Long, crusty, brown fingers, not human. Alien. Trying to get in.* Carefully I picked up a crystal wine glass and dunked it in the warm water. The dried purple residue of merlot colored a dimple at the bottom of the glass, just farther than the reach of my fingers.

Tap, tap. Buzz, tap. I had to look. *It's just moths, okay? It's not fingers. It's moths. Look, you can see them.* They were ugly, fuzzy-looking things, some of them walking around on the gray screen that separated the yellow incandescent light inside from the charcoal darkness. I shuddered and felt that anxious tightening in my chest.

Crack. A stab of pain jerked my attention back to my hands. The wine glass had broken in my hands while I was washing it. A half-inch gash on my right hand started to bleed as I held it up, as though it had only just been cut with a scalpel. I stood there and watched the blood well up and run over my water-wrinkled hand; I turned it slightly so that it would drip into the dishwater and not run down my arm onto my clothes.

It was a very curious sensation, and one I had never felt before. I felt glad. *Look at that. Fascinating, the blood dripping into the water and winding around, like drops of food coloring. This is a good thing, and you deserve such things. Very good. Well done.* The sight of the blood swirling into the water captivated my attention and froze my body for many minutes. *Yes.*

In another moment, or perhaps many, I walked around the counter and closed the sliding door, locking out the moths and whatever else was out there. I forgot about the alien fingers, because I was busy looking at my own hand, which I had just cut wide open but seemed to have healed itself again. It took a few minutes of studying it before I realized, to my disappointment, that I had merely imagined the incident. I hadn't really cut myself. *But now I wanted to.*

September 2002

For as literate as I am, I am having a terrible time coming up with the words to explain what this is like. At first I just thought that it was different moods, but now it's more than that. I feel like my personality is somehow unraveling, and each mood takes on its own personality. There are no names for them, only descriptions: the fearful adult, the cold adult, the caring adult, the teenager, the child, the Others—those are the ones who are not me. They speak inside my head; I don't hear them out loud, and I don't "become" them—they are just there. The milder ones just talk about the way they see my world. The harsher ones, particularly the cold adult and the Other voices, shout and hiss a lot and order me to do things like cut myself. I can't tell anymore if these are my own thoughts, or if they are something else. (But what?) Oh, boy—I told you this was confusing. If you understand this, you are way ahead of me.

Diane looked up after she finished reading the page. "Well, I admit that this seems unusual, and I can understand why you're confused. Maybe we've uncovered some unconscious issues, and when you've worked through them, these 'moods' will disappear."

"I certainly hope so," I said. "They're making me feel awfully strange. I'm still taking Prozac, so it couldn't be depression, could it?"

"No, probably not." She smoothed her dyed-blonde hair while she thought for a minute. "Let's not get too discouraged about it, okay? You're working very hard to get through these things, and I have no doubt in my mind that you'll succeed. Just think what you accomplished while you were pregnant! You thought you would never get over those panic attacks, and then one day you did." She paused for a moment to take a drink of water. "I'll bet, by the time I come back from my vacation, you and Liz will have all this figured out, and you'll be just perfect."

October 2002

The craft store had the exact paint set I wanted; it was a portfolio of water-colors in a box, instead of tubes. I opened the box and stared at the colors for what must have been ten or fifteen minutes, captivated by the luxurious sensory impact of each one. My confused, splitting mind was somehow drawn to, connected with colors, lines, and shapes in a very visceral way. Women wheeled their shopping carts past me, laden with eucalyptus-scented dried flowers, decorative pots, and wide cloth ribbons; they looked at me standing there studying the sixteen semi-moist paint squares, and no doubt wondered what I was doing.

After a while my attention broke away from the paint box and I walked down the next aisle, where the paintbrushes and colored pencils were stocked. Adjacent to the display of paintbrushes, there was a display of carving tools. I selected a detail brush and a mop brush for my water-colors, and across the aisle, several new Prismacolor pencils. That was all I really needed, but my mind turned back to the carving tools. *Just look. You've got time.*

Hanging there on the white pegboard racks were dozens of cutting and wood-carving tools, packaged separately and labeled with sizes and suggested uses. I was as fascinated by all these sharp little tools as I had been by the colors, but for a different purpose; I wanted these to cut *myself.* Instead of resorting to sharp scissors or broken glass shards (Tim had already locked up the kitchen knives), I could have my very own secret sharp tool.

There were all kinds of little knife tools; I only had to decide which one. Some had small blades, and some looked like chisels. One had a two-pronged point. *I could stab myself in the stomach with that one.* Another very tempting choice was a C-curved blade. *I could dig into my wrists and pull out the tendons with that one.* Finally, I decided on a more ordinary Exacto knife, which had a small, fine-pointed blade and a plastic cap that went over the top, so that I could carry it in my purse without cutting my fingers while I was rooting around for stuff. *Sharp, practical, easy to hide, easy to make an excuse for. Oh, that? I need that for the building projects the kids are working on at school. The one I had got lost.*

The knife and its sharp, triangular blade called to me from my purse like a chocolate bar. *I'm here, don't forget me. I'm so easy, so convenient.* The voice in my head, in its low, almost whispering tone so like my own voice, concurred. *Yes, yes, it's a lovely little knife, so simple for you to use. Get it out, why don't you? Cut that place on your hand where you burned yourself a couple years ago. You already have a scar there. It'll be quick; it won't even hurt much. There, see? Good girl. Just stick a Band-Aid on it and no one will know except us. Later you can do it again.*

I had never before allowed my personal problems to creep into the school day; in fact, I really didn't have time for them. I hardly had time to use the restroom. A fifteen-minute recess in the morning, forty minutes for lunch, and once a week an hour of prep time while the kids went to music or art; that was all I got. Five minutes, even three, or two, was enough time to get out supplies, set up a science project, or grade a few math tests. My prep time was golden, and there I was, using it to cut up my hands and arms. This was not a good sign, and I knew it. The voices were influencing me while I was at school, their commands taking precedence over my attention to the job that I loved and had been deeply involved with for years.

Not good. Not good at all. The knife reminded me constantly of its presence, like the One Ring to Frodo Baggins. The voices spoke softly, giving encouraging reminders. *Let's get out the knife. This is what we want you to do. Don't worry, we are on your side. Think how it will feel. Think of the warm, red blood inside you, and how much we like to see that. Look at your wrists, the inside, where the larger veins are. Think about how much you want to cut yourself there. Think. Think.* I could hear them out loud now, whispering in a chorus of voices. *We will be with you, whenever you are ready.*

Why Having a Mental Illness Is Not Like Having Diabetes

Anonymous[7]

A number of times during the course of my illness I have been told by health professionals that it is useful to think of having a mental illness (in my case

[7]From "Why Having a Mental Illness Is Not Like Having Diabetes," Anonymous, 2007, *Schizophrenia Bulletin, 33*(4), 846–847. Copyright 2007 by Oxford University Press. Reprinted with permission.

schizoaffective disorder) as having a lifelong disease that requires lifelong management and drug treatment—in fact, just like diabetes, a well-known disease affecting a large proportion of the population. Diabetics, so the story goes, need to accept that they have an illness that will require treatment for the rest of their lives; and if they continue the treatment, they will maintain their health insofar as this is possible, while if they discontinue treatment, they will suffer dire consequences, including blindness, loss of limbs, diabetic coma, and so on. Looked at in this light, treatment of a mental illness is just the same; if medication and other treatments are continued, the prospects are relatively good, and if not, the prospects are dire.

This story is common among health professionals who treat those with mental illness, but it also occurs in some medical research in which schizoaffective patients have been explicitly compared with diabetes patients. In a series of studies a team based in Lund, Sweden, took schizoaffective patients and compared their social networks and background factors (Nettelbladt, Svensson, & Serin, 1996; Nettelbladt, Svensson, Serin, & Öjehagen, 1995). The rationale for making a comparison between schizoaffectives and diabetics is as follows:

"From a medical and psychological point of view there are similarities between diabetes and schizoaffective disorder. In both diseases you may prevent a relapse by taking medication (insulin or lithium) and the risks of pregnancy and delivery are greater than for healthy women. Further, the chances that a child to a parent with diabetes or schizoaffective disorder will subsequently develop a diabetes or a schizoaffective disorder are considerable. Thus, the medical and mental strain caused by diabetes and schizoaffective disorder to some extent may be the same (Nettelbladt et al., 1995, p. 906).

I would like to spend the rest of this article showing why this parallel, so frequently made, is ill conceived and unhelpful.

Hospital Experience

A diabetes patient in hospital can expect a clean, hygienic ward peopled by staff who treat the patient with respect, as an equal, who explain the illness and the treatment regime, and who co-opt the patient as an important agent in his or her own recovery. A psychiatric patient, however, might well find a ward that is rundown and peopled by staff who do not seem to have the same expectations of respect for patients and of a generally good professional working relationship between staff and patients. A psychiatric patient might instead, as I did in one of my hospitalizations, find staff who avoided talking to the patients as far as possible and whose only interaction with patients was to give commands.

As a diabetes patient, one would certainly not expect violence or abuse from fellow patients; and if this did occur, one could expect a swift reaction from the staff. However, as a psychiatric patient, violence from other patients is at times a real risk, and one that staff might seem to regard as inevitable.

A diabetes patient would certainly not expect to come out of the hospital experience feeling belittled and demeaned, whereas this is something that has been reported by psychiatric patients; and certainly it was my own experience in one hospital.

Finally, in a diabetes ward there is no sense of being in a prison, even though diabetic patients, just as much as schizoaffective patients, are necessarily confined to the ward for their health and safety. Mental patients in hospital, by contrast, frequently report feeling as though they were in prison; certainly during one of my hospitalizations I spent most of my time trying to devise ways to escape.

Attitude of Family and Friends

Schizoaffective disorder rips straight into the heart of the family, causing shame, anger, guilt, and self-blame from parents and siblings, as well as casting blame on the patient. Parents ask, where did I go wrong, and patients ask, if I had had a different upbringing could I have avoided this disease? With diabetes, however, there is no sense of blame, guilt, or shame; rather, people hear the diagnosis, learn (perhaps over time) about the condition, and come to accept the limitations of the condition.

After receiving a diagnosis of diabetes, a person could expect that their friends, on inviting them over for dinner, might inquire how they could best fit in with the patient's new diet, if that were necessary. However, after receiving a diagnosis of schizoaffective disorder, a patient would be waiting a long time for someone to ask how he or she could fit in with the sickness. This is a pity because there are many very simple ways to make life easier for those who suffer from psychosis and other mental illness problems. In my own case, for purely psychotic reasons, I would love to be assured that there would be no electronic beeps in any house I was going to visit. However, I find it difficult to imagine asking even close friends to turn off any electronic beeping machines when I am coming over; the request would be embarrassing and weird. It is not confronting to conform to a diabetic diet, but it is confronting to adapt to a psychotic patient's needs.

With diabetes, there is no stigma. People are not afraid of a diabetes patient. A diabetes patient would probably feel free to tell anyone that he or she has diabetes, without expecting possible rejection or shunning. I have frequently been warned by health professionals never to tell anyone, apart from close family, the name of my sickness. Diabetes patients can even tell an employer about their disease, whereas schizoaffective patients would be most unwise to.

Even if the general public does not know the causes or exact effects of diabetes, knowing only perhaps that it is something to do with sugar in the blood, which means that someone with diabetes has to be careful what they eat, their ignorance does not lead to fear and ridicule. Diabetes is in fact quite easy to explain to a layperson. Schizoaffective disorder is very hard to explain to a layperson. My own child is getting to be old enough where she will soon need an explanation from me of what exactly my sickness is and why I need to go to [sic] hospital now and then. Such an explanation for a diabetes patient would be easy. For schizoaffective patients it is very hard.

In the media diabetes generally receives an impartial, unemotive treatment. I have never seen schizoaffective disorder referred to in the media (another problem contributing to ignorance in the general public), but its close relative schizophrenia is almost universally dealt with in simplistic, lurid, and often violent terms—in any case generally with more hysteria than information.

The Disease Course

The course, and consequences, of the 2 diseases are very different. Diabetes does not get out of control and make a person do things for which they could be civilly or criminally liable. Diabetes does not gradually erode a person's ability to think and reason or leave one unable to decide what is true and what is not true in the world, crippling his or her ability to act as an independent adult. Diabetes does not affect the very way people think, who they are, and how they operate socially, professionally, and within their family. Schizoaffective disorder does.

Treatment

Diabetes medicine does not change who a person is; it does not turn one into a zombie, negating the highs as it flattens out the lows; it does not change the way one operates or, in fact, change what it is to be that person. Medicine for schizoaffective disorder does.

Diabetes treatment does not require the same sacrifice of personal privacy that nonmedical treatment for schizoaffective disorder does.

These facts, each one perhaps small in itself, combine together in schizoaffective disorder to contribute toward an insidious erosion of the sense of self that is compounded by the action of the disease itself and the side effects of the medication. I therefore reject the analogy of schizoaffective disorder as being like diabetes. If I could choose a replacement analogy, I would say schizoaffective disorder is like a whirlwind: it comes out of nowhere, strips you naked and sucks you dry, and swiftly vanishes, leaving you empty and shaken but alive, wondering if it really did happen and whether, and how soon, it will come back again.

References

Nettelbladt, P., Svensson, C., & Serin, U. (1996). Background factors in patients with schizoaffective disorder as compared with patients with diabetes and healthy individuals. *European Archives of Psychiatry and Clinical Neuroscience, 246,* 213–218.

Nettelbladt, P., Svensson, C., Serin, U, & Öjehagen, A. (1995). The social network of patients with schizoaffective disorder as compared to patients with diabetes and to healthy individuals. *Social Science & Medicine, 41*(6), 901–907.

2

Mood Disorders

INTRODUCTION

The mental health problems listed under this category in the *Diagnostic and Statistical Manual of Mental Disorders* (*DSM-IV-TR*) have a disturbance in mood as their central or key feature. The mood has to be more than "feeling blue" or "down in the dumps" or feeling really happy, elated, or energized. These are familiar feelings that most of us have had at one time or another in response to stress or loss or to having good fortune or a really good day. *DSM*-defined mood disorders involve sets of criteria that go beyond the feelings we experience as part of the normal ups and downs of everyday life. And, perhaps most critical, the mood disturbance must cause significant distress or impairment in social and/or occupational functioning.

A number of large, epidemiological studies in the past several decades have attempted to better understand the distribution of mental disorders in the general population in this country. Results from the National Epidemiological Survey on Alcoholism and Related Conditions show that the lifetime prevalence rate of major depressive disorder was 13.23% (Hasin, Goodwin, Stinson, & Grant, 2005). For women and for men, the lifetime prevalence rates were 21.3% and 12.7%, respectively (Kessler, Abelson, & Zhao, 1998). So, while mood disorders are not common experiences for most of us, they also are not entirely uncommon in our society. According to the National Comorbidity Survey Replication (NCS-R), the lifetime prevalence rate for any *DSM* mood disorder was 21%, the second highest of any group of the mental disorders (the highest was anxiety disorders at 29%) (Kessler et al., 2003). The personal, social, and economic toll of these disorders is devastating.

From a *DSM* diagnostic perspective, an individual must be experiencing relevant signs and symptoms, then meet criteria for one or more of the four types of mood episodes, and finally must meet the core criteria for one of the actual disorders. The signs/symptoms and mood episodes (major depressive, manic, mixed, hypomanic) act as building blocks for the diagnoses. The two general types of disorders are *depressive* and *bipolar*, with a third type that allows for mood disorders due to medical conditions or due to the use of or exposure to substances. Further description is possible through the application of specifiers for clinical status (mild, moderate, severe with or without psychotic features), specifiers that describe features of the current or most recent episode (e.g., postpartum onset), and specifiers noting the course/pattern of recurrent episodes (e.g., rapid cycling).

The signs and symptoms of depressive episodes include depressed mood, decreased interest or pleasure in activities, marked weight loss or weight gain, insomnia or hypersomnia, psychomotor agitation or retardation, fatigue/loss of energy, feelings of worthlessness or guilt, problems in concentration, and recurrent suicidal ideation or thoughts of death. Manic or hypomanic episodes involve elevated, expansive, or irritable moods during which some or all of the following are present: grandiosity or inflated self-esteem, decreased need for sleep, excessively talkative or pressured speech, racings thought or flight of ideas, distractibility, psychomotor agitation or increase in goal-directed activity, and/or overinvolvement in pleasurable activities with a high potential for negative consequences (e.g., buying sprees or sexual indiscretions). These symptoms can be intense, prolonged, and incapacitating.

Many people experience some of the symptoms listed above and yet do not meet the full criteria for a *DSM-IV-TR* mood disorder. This should in no way invalidate their experiences. The *DSM*'s categorical approach defines disorders as discrete entities; either you meet the criteria and have the disorder, or you do not. This approach inherently is problematic because those who experience a subclinical level of symptoms that do not qualify them to meet the full criteria do suffer, and their experiences are real. The first person accounts (FPAs) in Chapter 2 describe a variety of personal experiences that involve many of the symptoms listed above.

In the first account, Bec Morrison talks about the many aspects of depression that she has experienced and its impact on her life. In his account of suicidal ideation, Leo Tolstoi provides a powerful description of the desperation he felt. As an African American woman who emigrated from Ghana at age 6, Meri Nana-Ama Danquah grew up straddling two distinct cultures, and it was difficult for her to accept her depression. Both Marcie Ramirez and Jessica Rodrigo-Dunican have written personal narratives of their experiences with postpartum depression—a problem that is being increasingly recognized. Peter Amsel provides a detailed portrayal of "living with the dragon" in his account of bipolar II. In her account of living with rapid-cycling bipolar disorder, an anonymous author describes its pervasive effect on her life. Michael Napiorkowski offers a glimpse into his life with bipolar disorder in a series of "random scribblings" about it. And, last, but certainly not least, Susan Michele Vale tells her story about living with bipolar disorder and, after struggling through 15 hospitalizations, how she survived and began recovery to become a mental health care professional who lives to serve her community.

QUESTIONS FOR REFLECTION

What are the essential differences between depression and the bipolar disorders? How do these impact the personal experiences of the problems discussed by the authors of these accounts? How did their experiences of depression and/or mania influence their perspective on living? Do the coping strategies that the various authors develop differ?

REFERENCES

Hasin, D., Goodwin, R., Stinson, F., & Grant, B. (2005). Epidemiology of major depressive disorder: Results from the National Epidemiological Survey on Alcoholism and Related Conditions. *Archives of General Psychiatry, 62,* 1097–1106.

Kessler, R. C., Abelson, J. M., & Zhao, S. (1998). The epidemiology of mental disorders. In J. W. Williams & K. Ell (Eds.), *Advances in mental health research: Implications for practice* (pp. 3–24). Washington, DC: NASW Press.

Kessler, R. C., Berglund, P., Demler, O., Jin, R., Koretz, D., Merikangas, K. R., ... Wang, P. S. (2003). The epidemiology of major depressive disorder: Results from the National Comorbidity Survey Replication (NCS-R). *Journal of the American Medical Association, 289*(23), 3095–3105.

DEPRESSIVE DISORDERS

Depression: Disease, Loneliness, Social Isolation, Suicide, Negative Thoughts ...

Bec Morrison[1]

These are only some of the words that I think of when I remember DE-PRESSION.

It is a harsh and nasty illness that unfortunately affects more people than you and I would know. How do I know? Because unfortunately or fortunately, hard to say, I suffer from the disease. I am in remission after four and a half very long years. I write this on the day, the big day, that I was discharged from the outpatient program, which I attended at a private psychiatric hospital in Tasmania for two and a half years. It is the day I take the big step and venture into the big wide world and walk this earth, a survivor of this illness.

My path has not been easy. I was a young 23-year-old girl who had the world ahead of me. One day, without even realizing it, everything changed. I moved from Victoria, my home for six years, to escape an abusive relationship, to Tasmania, the place I was born and bred. My mum started to notice changes in me; I was no longer the happy girl that I was in Victoria. My energy dropped, I was spending longer in bed and my mood was low. Mum strongly suggested that I see our general practitioner (GP) for advice. After explaining the symptoms to my GP, he decided that I was experiencing a form of depression due to my past relationship, leaving a good job in Victoria and returning to Tasmania unemployed. It was here that I started my first, and I thought, my only course of antidepressants.

Questions wandered through my head: how could I have depression? I didn't want to believe it. I took the antidepressant Zoloft and started to see a psychologist to help with the unwanted thoughts. Later I applied for a position with the Health Department as a school dental therapist and was successful with the position. I started work and going to the gym, which I loved, and thought I was on the road to recovery.

[1]From "Depression: Disease, Loneliness, Social Isolation, Suicide, Negative Thoughts ...," by Bec Morrison, 2008, *Social Alternatives Journal, 27*(4), 51–53. Copyright 2008 by Social Alternatives. Reprinted with permission.

How could I be so wrong? Zoloft didn't help my mood and I found my symptoms getting worse. I returned to the GP, was weaned off Zoloft and put on Effexor. This was the answer to my prayers, or so I thought. I started off on a small dose of the drug, but then it had to be increased to help battle off my symptoms. I cried a lot of the time and even little issues seemed huge. I had little energy, felt run down, didn't want to get out of bed, was in my negative thoughts all the time, couldn't manage my life, and I couldn't get the energy to go to work. I withdrew from friends and family and withdrew into my self more and more. Mild suicidal thoughts even entered my head. This drug held me stay strong and healthy for ten months, but then the long, hard, unforgettable journey of a major depressive disorder began.

I sit here, as I am writing this, with tears in my eyes as I re-encounter the road I have travelled. If I thought things couldn't get worse, I was mistaken; there is no word to describe the pain, torture and heartache I experienced over the last four years. It got to the point where my GP could no longer help me medically. I was referred to a psychiatrist. I never in my wildest dreams could imagine what came next. After seeing my psychiatrist, I was admitted to a private psychiatric hospital, which was thought to be the best way to treat my depression at this stage. I still remember the day. I was put in a private room with a bed, TV, and chair and I was all alone, frightened, and scared. What was going to happen to me?

My stay was long but eventually re-medicated and feeling slightly better and I was discharged. This wasn't for long and for the first time in my history of depression I began to experience strong suicidal thoughts. After many discussions I was re-admitted to the hospital and so began the road to electroconvulsive therapy (ECT). Eleven bilateral doses, so can you imagine what this did to my memory? I don't think anyone could. I suffered short and long term memory loss. This was very scary, simple things I could not remember and people. I saw faces, but knew no names. ECT was stopped and it was deemed to be unsuccessful.

Throughout the time after ECT I tried numerous medications but nothing could lift me. I wanted to die; I no longer wanted to be in this pain I was feeling. I felt like I was a burden on my family and society. I was in the hospital for twenty months out of twenty-four. How sad, a young girl and many other men and women of varying ages were all in a hospital battling some form of mental illness. My psychiatrist tried everything,

Trans Magnetic Stimulation (TMS) and many medications, so many I can't remember all of them. I put on a lot of weight, due to medication, bad diet, and little exercise.

One week two years on, still battling, my psychiatrist went on holiday. I was admitted by another psychiatrist in another psychiatric hospital in Hobart. I was on the waiting list to see a professor at the Melbourne Clinic and was biding my time at the Hobart Clinic. A bed came up at the Melbourne Clinic. It all happened so quickly, I was discharged from the Hobart Clinic, flew to Melbourne and was admitted to the Melbourne Clinic. I saw the professor. I began another medication change, saw another psychologist and then was advised, along with medical treatment, that I should undergo a depression course that ran at the clinic every day for four weeks. I did what I was encouraged to do and it looked like the medications were slowly agreeing with me. Nine weeks later I was discharged and returned home. Happy, but still with issues, I tried so hard to be happy, but sometimes the pain in my body, the thoughts and tears in my eyes were all too much.

When home, I saw another psychologist who was based two hours away. I was again readmitted to a hospital but kept up my weekly visits while undergoing medical treatment, thanks to my mum, dad, and grandparents. I hate to say that things got to be too much, but something snapped in my head. I told my nurse I was going for a walk, which was not a lie, but my destination was a lie. I went to the local pharmacy, bought some tablets, stuffed them in my pockets, walked around the block back to my room, and headed straight to the bathroom. I did it, I never thought I would but I did I took all the tablets I had. I was so scared I was dying that I called a nurse and told him what I had done. I was transferred to the public emergency hospital and stayed in emergency for eighteen hours.

I survived, but did I want to? I was seen by the head psychiatrist—they told me they could see the pain in my eyes and believed if discharged I would try even harder to harm myself—they were right. I was admitted to the Psychiatric Intensive Care Unit (PICU), a ward for very sick people who suffer severe forms of mental illness. It involved cameras in your room, no jewelry, and all visits in a small room with three cameras. I wasn't allowed to make coffee or meals; this was all done for me. The worst thing was the plastic utensils. I remember the first time I saw mum and dad after the overdose, I could see sadness, tears and pain in my parents' eyes—what had I done?

My parents are the most supportive people that I know. My parents, as well as my brother and sisters, have been through every day of this journey with me. I changed psychiatrists after this incident and have been lucky enough to meet a kind and helpful doctor. Someone who had a lot of work ahead of them to try and give me a life back, the GP too tried many medications, again, nothing worked. I decided, with my doctor, to have a course of unilateral ECT when suicidal thoughts entered my head. They were unwanted thoughts—why did I have them and why couldn't I control them?

After many admissions at the Hobart Clinic during 2007/2008 my doctor tried Nardil, an old style antidepressant. It has worked and I have been stable now for seven months—not long, but I have made many changes. Not only was it the help from my professional support, but I also made a decision in my own mind that I no longer wanted to be in and out of the hospital, I had enough, and I needed to start living. I had let four years pass me, years I cannot replace.

I hadn't worked for two and a half years and had been told by one doctor that I would never work again. I returned to my profession, dental therapy, for three hours two days a week. It was hard, stressful, and a struggle. My employer hired a Rehabilitation Consultant who negotiated with management and me. They agreed to let me return to work on a part time basis, not in dental therapy, but in administration. This too was difficult, but with self-determination and the help of many people, I returned to work two half days, two full days, three full days and now full time. My department doesn't have a position for me, but is supporting me by employing me until I find another position. I am a full time employee and who would have guessed it?

Throughout the last two years I have attended an outpatient program. I have gone from attending the clinic three days a week to finally being discharged. Do you know I am happy? I am proud of my achievements thus far. Many a time I would and have given up. I have learnt to dream, to look forward to the next day, and to have positive thoughts. I have been in a relationship for six months and love my boyfriend and best friend dearly. He is supportive, there for me, and always encourages me to be the person I want to be. I now challenge my thoughts and feel positive about the future and my life. I am on this earth for a reason and I want to fill every day with as much as I can. I have a lot of catching up to do.

I would like to thank my mum and dad for their support, which is always there. Without them I would be lost. I love them so much. I couldn't achieve this without the constant love of my brother, sisters, grandparents, and extended family. Also, thank you to my psychiatrist, psychologist, rehabilitation consultant, employer, and all who have been there over the last four years. I am learning to fly and I have met many special people throughout my many visits to the hospital.

I want to help others who suffer from DEPRESSION. I want to give them hope that with medication and the right mental attitude, you too can live. I have my days, but that is the nature of the illness and I see my psychiatrist as an outpatient. Please know that the bad days will pass, life will get better, and I am living proof. Keep going, it is worth it!

"Shoot for the moon, even if you miss you'll land among the stars." Les Brown.

My Confession: My Life Had Come to a Stop

LEO TOLSTOI[2]

My life had come to a sudden stop. I was able to breathe, to eat, to drink, to sleep. I could not, indeed, help doing so; but there was no real life in me. I had not a single wish to strive for the fulfillment of what I could feel to be reasonable. If I wished for anything, I knew beforehand that, were I to satisfy the wish, nothing would come of it, I should still be dissatisfied. Had a fairy appeared and offered me all I desired, I would not have known what to say. If I seemed to have, at a given moment of excitement, not a wish, but a mood resulting from the tendencies of former wishes, at a calmer moment I knew that it was a delusion, that I really wished for nothing. I could not even wish to know the truth, because I guessed what the truth was.

The truth lay in this, that life had no meaning for me. Every day of life, every step in it, brought me nearer the edge of a precipice, whence I saw clearly the final ruin before me. To stop, to go back, were alike impossible; nor could I shut my eyes so as not to see the suffering that alone awaited me, the death of all in me, even to annihilation. Thus, I, a healthy and a happy man, was brought to feel that I could live no longer, that an irresistible force was dragging me down into the grave. I do not mean that I had an intention

---

[2]From *My Confession: My Life Had Come to a Sudden Stop* (pp. 407–411), by Leo Tolstoi, 1887, New York, NY: Crowell.

of committing suicide. The force that drew me away from life was stronger, fuller, and concerned with far wider consequences than any mere wish; it was a force like that of my previous attachment to life, only in a contrary direction.

The idea of suicide came as naturally to me as formerly that of bettering my life. It had so much attraction for me that I was compelled to practice a species of self-deception, in order to avoid carrying it out too hastily. I was unwilling to act hastily, only because I had determined first to clear away the confusion of my thoughts, and, that once done, I could always kill myself. I was happy, yet I hid away a cord, to avoid being tempted to hang myself by it to one of the pegs between the cupboards of my study, where I undressed alone every evening, and ceased carrying a gun because it offered too easy a way of getting rid of life. I knew not what I wanted; I was afraid of life; I shrank from it, and yet there *was* something I hoped for from it.

Such was the condition I had come to, at the time when all the circumstances of my life were pre eminently happy ones, and when I had not reached my fiftieth year. I had a good, a loving, and a well-beloved wife, good children, a fine estate, which, without much trouble on my part, continually increased my income. I was more than ever respected by my friends and acquaintances; I was praised by strangers, and could lay claim to having made my name famous without much self-deception. Moreover, my mind was neither deranged nor weakened; on the contrary, I enjoyed a mental and physical strength which I have seldom found in men of my class and pursuits. I could keep up with a peasant in mowing and could continue mental labor for ten hours at a stretch, without any evil consequences.

The mental state in which I then was seemed to me summed up in the following: my life was a foolish and wicked joke played upon me by I knew not whom. Notwithstanding my rejection of the idea of a Creator, that of a being who thus wickedly and foolishly made a joke of me seemed to me the most natural of all conclusions, and the one that threw the most light upon my darkness. I instinctively reasoned that this being, wherever he might be, was one who was even then diverting himself at my expense, as he watched me, after from thirty to forty years of a life of study and development, of mental and bodily growth, with all my powers matured and having reached a point at which life as a whole should be best understood, standing like a fool with but one thing clear to me, that there was nothing in life, that there never was anything, and never will be. "To him I must seem ridiculous. . . .

But was there, or was there not, such a being?" Neither way could I feel it helped me.

I could not attribute reasonable motive to any single act, much less to my whole life. I was only astonished that this had not occurred to me before, from premises which had so long been known. Illness and death would come (indeed they had come), if not today, then tomorrow, to those whom I loved, to myself, and nothing would remain but stench and worms. All my acts, whatever I did, would sooner or later be forgotten, and I myself be nowhere. Why, then, busy one's self with anything? How could men see this, and live? It is possible to live only as long as life intoxicates us; as soon as we are sober again we see that it is all a delusion, and a stupid one! In this, indeed, there is nothing either ludicrous or amusing; it is only cruel and absurd.

There is an old Eastern fable about a traveler in the steppes who is attacked by a furious wild beast. To save himself the traveler gets into a dried-up well, but at the bottom of it, he sees a dragon with its jaw wide-open to devour him. The unhappy man dares not get out for fear of the wild beast, and dares not descend for fear of the dragon, so he catches hold of the branch of a wild plant growing in a crevice of the well. His arms grow tired, and he feels that he must soon perish, death awaiting him on either side, but he still holds on; and then he sees two mice, one black and one white, gnawing through the trunk of the wild plant, as they gradually and evenly make their way round it. The plant must soon give way, break off, and he will fall into the jaws of the dragon. The traveler sees this, and knows that he must inevitably perish, but, while still hanging, he looks around him and, finding some drops of honey on the leaves of the wild plant, he stretches out his tongue and licks them.

Thus do I cling to the branch of life, knowing that the dragon of death awaits me, ready to tear me to pieces, and I cannot understand why such tortures have fallen to my lot. I also strive to suck the honey which once comforted me, but it palls on my palate, while the white mouse and black, day and night, gnaw through the branch to which I cling. I see the dragon too plainly, and the honey is no longer sweet. I see the dragon, from whom there is no escape, and the mice, and I cannot turn my eyes away from them. It is no fable, but a living, undeniable truth, to be understood of all men. The former delusion of happiness in life which hid from me the horror of the dragon, no longer deceives me.

However I may reason with myself that I cannot understand the meaning of life, that I must live without thinking, I cannot again begin to do so, because I have done so too long already. I cannot now help seeing that each day and each night, as it passes, brings me nearer to death. I can see but this, because this alone is true—all the rest is a lie. The two drops of honey, which more than anything else drew me away from the cruel truth, my love for my family and for my writings, to which latter I gave the name of art, no longer taste sweet to me. "My family," thought I; "but a family, a wife and children, are also human beings, and subject to the same conditions as myself; they must either be living in a lie, or they must see the terrible truth. Why should they live? Why should I love, care for, bring up, and watch over them? To bring them to the despair which fills myself, or to make dolts of them? As I love them, I cannot conceal from them the truth—every step they take in knowledge leads them to it, and that truth is death."

But art then; but poetry? Under the influence of success and flattered by praise, I had long persuaded myself that these were things worth working for, notwithstanding the approach of death, the great destroyer, to annihilate my writings, and the memory of them; but now I soon saw that this was only another delusion, I saw clearly that art is only the ornament and charm of life. Life having lost its charm for me, how could I make others see a charm in it? While I was not living my own life, but one that was external to me, as long as I believed that life had a meaning, though I could not say what it was, life was reflected for me in the poetry and art that I loved. It was pleasant to me to look into the mirror of art, but when I tried to discover the meaning of life, when I felt the necessity of living myself, the mirror became either unnecessary or painful. I could no longer take comfort from what I saw in the mirror, that my position was a stupid and desperate one.

It warmed my heart when I believed that life had a meaning, when the play of the light on the glass showed me all that was comic, tragic, touching, beautiful, and terrible in life, and comforted me. But when I knew that life had no meaning at all, and was only terrible, the play of the light no longer amused me. No honey could be sweet upon my tongue when I saw the dragon and the mice eating away the stay which supported me. Nor was that all. Had I simply come to know that life has no meaning, I might have quietly accepted it as my allotted portion. I could not, however, remain thus unmoved. Had I been like a man in a wood, out of which he knows that there is no issue, I could have lived on; but I was like a man lost in a wood, and who, terrified by the thought, rushes about trying to find a way out, and, though he knows each step can only lead him farther astray, cannot help running backward and forward.

It was this that was terrible, this which to get free from I was ready to kill myself. I felt a horror of what awaited me. I knew that this horror was more terrible than the position itself, but I could not patiently await the end. However persuasive the argument might be that all the same something in the heart of elsewhere would burst and all be over, still I could not patiently await the end. The horror of the darkness was too great to bear, and I longed to free myself from it by a rope or a pistol ball. This was the feeling that, above all, drew me to think of suicide.

Willow Weep for Me—A Black Woman's Journey Through Depression

Meri Nana-Ama Danquah[3]

My relationship with depression began long before I noticed it. The first conscious thought that all was not well with me came in 1989, when I was twenty-two. I had been living in Los Angeles for two years, working various temp jobs while trying to establish myself as a writer and performance artist. Out of nowhere and for no apparent reason—or so it seemed—I started feeling strong sensations of grief. I don't remember the step-by-step progression of the illness. What I can recall is that my life disintegrated; first, into a strange and terrifying space of sadness and then, into a cobweb of fatigue. I gradually lost my ability to function. It would take me hours to get up out of bed, get bathed, put clothes on. By the time I was fully dressed, it was well into the afternoon.

When I went out into the city, I would always become disoriented, often spacing out behind the wheel of my car or in the middle of a sentence. My thoughts would just disappear. I'd forget where I was driving to, the point I was about to make in conversation. It was as if my synapses were misfiring, my brain off kilter. A simple stroll to the coffee shop down the

[3]From *Willow Weep for Me—A Black Woman's Journey Through Depression* (pp. 27–35), by Meri Nana-Ama Danquah, 1988, New York, NY: W.W. Norton, 1998. Reprinted with permission of Ann Edelstein Literary Agency.

block overloaded my senses: sounds of feet shuffling on sidewalks, honks from cars, blinking of traffic lights, loud colors of clothing. It was all bewildering. I started to have panic attacks every time I went outside.

After a while I stopped showing up at my temp job, stopped going out altogether, and locked myself in my home. It was over three weeks before I felt well enough to leave. During that time, I cut myself off from everything and everyone. Days would go by before I bathed. I did not have enough energy to clean up myself or my home. There was a trail of undergarments and other articles of clothing that ran from the living room to the bedroom to the bathroom of my tiny apartment. Dishes with decaying food covered every counter and tabletop in the place. Even watching TV or talking on the phone required too much concentration. All I could do was take to my pallet of blankets and coats positioned on the living room floor and wait for whatever I was going through to pass.

And it did. Slowly. That's the thing about depression, it will generally vanish on its own. The problem is that there is no telling when it will go away or for how long it will stay gone. When I felt better I bathed, took the garbage out, did laundry, plugged my telephone back in, and made plans to venture forth into the weird outside.

The first person to call me was an actress friend who wanted to brag about her trip to Berlin. She proudly told me that she had recently returned with a piece of the Wall. "The Berlin Wall?" I asked in disbelief. The last time I had heard mention of the Berlin Wall was in a high-school history class. My friend had to start from square one and explain to me that the Berlin Wall had come down.

"Wait, wait, wait. Like, you don't know? You're joking, right? My gosh, Meri, where've you been, Mars?"

It was humiliating. I felt like Rip Van Winkle. During the time I was laid up in my apartment making huge efforts to do simple things like brush my teeth and pull open the curtains, people had traveled, landscapes had changed; the world as I had known it before I surrendered and crawled into bed was no more. There was no escaping that episode without acknowledging that something extraordinary had happened to me. Ordinary folks just don't hole themselves up for weeks on end without bathing, working, reading the newspaper, talking to friends, or watching TV. Deep down, I knew that something had gone wrong with me, in me. But what could I do?

Stunned and defenseless, the only thing I felt I could do was move on. I assured myself that my mind and the behaviors it provoked were well within my control. In the future I would just have to be extremely aware. I would make sure that what happened did not happen again. But it did. Again and again, no matter how aware, responsible, or in control I tried to be. Each time, I buried the fear. I chastised myself for not paying attention to my emotions, for allowing myself to sink to such disgusting depths.

Each wave of the depression cost me something dear. I lost my job because the temp agencies where I was registered could no longer tolerate my lengthy absences. Unable to pay rent, I lost my apartment and ended up having to rent a small room in a boarding house. I lost my friends. Most of them found it too troublesome to deal with my sudden moodiness and passivity so they stopped calling and coming around. There were some that tried to hang in there and be supportive, but before long the depression took its toll on those relationships as well. Whenever I resurfaced from my episodes of depression, it was too hard to pick up where we had left off. "You've changed," my friends told me. "You're not the same person." How could I be? How could anyone be the same after their entire world has come to a screeching halt?

Thankfully, there were a few major reprieves, weeks, sometimes months, when it seemed as if the nails of despair weren't digging as deeply into my skin. During one of these times, I entered a new relationship.

In early 1990, I met Justin Armah, a tall, bespectacled thirty-eight-year-old accountant from Ghana, my native country. He was, on the surface, everything I believed I wanted a mate to be: charming, ambitious, and employed. We met at "Positive Vibrations Through Spoken Word," a twice-monthly poetry series, which I founded and organized at Rosalind's, a small Ethiopian restaurant in Los Angeles. He learned about the readings through *LA Weekly*, an alternative newspaper, which had recently featured me in its "Local Heroes" segment. As an active participant in the literary community, I was just beginning to gain a bit of recognition for my work as a writer and events organizer.

Justin and I quickly became romantically involved. We suffocated each other with our constant togetherness. After a few weeks, I moved into his home, a two-bedroom duplex on the west side of town. It was the perfect solution come right on time. What I felt I needed in my life was an anchor in case I began to drift away again. I hoped my relationship with Justin would be that grounding force. Depression is a very *"me"* disease. There is an enormous amount of self-criticism, self-loathing, and low self-esteem. Everything revolves around the perception of self. Most depressives find themselves—as much to their own disgust as to everybody else's—annoyingly and negatively self-obsessed.

I was not so much in love with Justin as I was with the prospect of having someone other than myself be the focal point of my life. We were not at all a compatible pair. There was a sixteen-year age difference between us. He was a stable, well-established professional. I was the opposite—a college drop-out who spent the bulk of her time writing poetry, something he eventually began to ridicule as a futile, unproductive hobby. Whatever forces of passion, lust, or need that brought us together disappeared as quickly as they appeared. By that time, I was already pregnant.

The pregnancy was an added point of contention between us. Justin wanted me to abort. Motherhood was not something to which I had ever aspired but for some reason I could not bring myself to end the pregnancy. There was another life inside of me, growing, changing my physical form, and I loved it. But morning sickness and the stress of a failing relationship turned what should have been a joyous time into a thick, lengthy period of depression. I grew increasingly unhappy and agitated. Very little brought me pleasure. Everything seemed complicated and burdensome, including "Positive Vibrations Through Spoken Word," my reading series. Eventually I stopped organizing it. I even stopped writing. It seemed as if the world was closing in on me, squeezing me dry.

There was no one close by that I felt I could rely on or confide in. My parents, though divorced, both lived in Washington, D.C. Ordinarily, we were not very close, but throughout the course of my pregnancy I spoke with them pretty frequently. At the time, my relationship with them could be described, at best, as turbulent. However, being able to talk to them, no matter how short or shallow the conversations, made me feel like I was not alone, like someone cared.

In my seventh month of pregnancy, my mother and father flew to L.A. to attend my baby shower and to meet Justin. It was a tremendous display of love for them, to take leave from their lives, at my request, to share the occasion with me. Still, I found their visit to be particularly traumatizing. When they arrived, all the underlying issues that had inspired me to move and place the distance of an entire country between us came with them. Suddenly, I felt like a child, not a woman carrying a child.

Like my parents, Justin had immigrated to the States as an adult, so the three of them carried on for hours about schools they had attended and friends they had in common. I had nothing to offer the discussion. I was either too young or too estranged from Ghanaian culture. They even talked to each other in *Twi*, a language I can't speak and have trouble understanding. I felt shut out. The remarks that were meant for me to hear were made in English. These remarks were generally jokes made by my mother about my inability to cook or clean house properly and my flare for melodrama—all faults I had supposedly acquired because I was too Americanized.

It was a pretty devastating experience to have my parents come and belittle me in front of a man who belittled me on a daily basis. To say the least, it wreaked havoc on my self-esteem. At one point during the visit, Justin took us out to dinner at an elegant Chinese restaurant in Beverly Hills. During our meal, my mother made a remark that upset me. I don't remember what it was. So many things that my parents said and did during that trip were upsetting but, for the most part, I never let them know that. To do so in Justin's presence would have caused them embarrassment.

From the age of six, I was raised in the United States. Like many other immigrant children, I grew up trying to find my own personal balance between two distinct cultures. I have always felt torn between the rigid mores of Ghanaian culture and the overly permissive attitudes of Americans. If a choice had to be made that evening, I felt obligated to err on the side of heritage. By remaining stoic and nonresponsive, I hoped to disprove my parents' accusations that I had become too Americanized. Before I could stop myself though, I started sobbing hysterically over my meal. Mum, Dad, and Justin were dumbfounded. They looked at each other curiously. I excused myself from the table, rushed through the dimly lit restaurant and headed for the bathroom, knowing that I had only proved them right. I was melodramatic, thin-skinned, and whiny, just like their image of the average American.

When I returned, Mum and Justin made jest of my outburst. My father seemed genuinely concerned.

"Are you sure you're alright?" he asked, gently placing his hand on my back. His concern came a little too late.

"Yeah, Daddy. I'll be fine," I said coolly, pulling my chair closer to the table. For the rest of the evening, and the rest of their visit, I wore an armor of indifference.

In hindsight, I must admit that I was being oversensitive. My emotions were delicate enough that any comment, however innocent, could have easily been perceived as negative and prompted tears. Nevertheless, that evening was as accurate a representation as any of the way my parents and I related to each other. They criticized, I cried. We were complete strangers to one another. Like many children of divorce, I felt abandoned by them at a time in my childhood when I needed them most, and the disappointment of that stayed with me in my young adulthood.

Becoming a parent has enabled me to see my own parents as fragile and fallible people. Understanding how difficult it is to raise a child in the face of life's unpredictable circumstances, I no longer find myself standing in such harsh judgment of them or the choices that they made so long ago. I believe that my individual therapy was instrumental in bringing me to this point.

When I first started therapy, I found myself unable to talk about my parents or admit that I felt a tremendous amount of rage toward them. I imagine that it was because in African as well as African-American cultures, talking about one's parents is frowned upon; only an ingrate would do such a thing. Even talking about other people's parents is a no-no. When I was a kid, the worst thing you could say to somebody was "Yo' Mama." That was like an invitation to a fight.

I have often heard it said that depression is anger turned inward. I don't know how true this is, but there is no denying that the events of my child-hood played a major role in fostering my vulnerability to depression. In fact, it is believed that an individual's susceptibility to depressive disorders is usu-ally formed early in childhood, especially with people who have experienced traumatic loss. This theory notwithstanding, I doubt that the unspoken anger that has fueled my depressions was caused solely by my parents. Suffice it to say, the pain that has already passed between us could claim a lifetime of tears.

I Wish I Had Gotten Help Sooner: My Struggle With Postpartum Depression

Marcie Ramirez

Postpartum depression screening saved my life. Period. There can be no argument or debate. If I hadn't been screened by my OB, I would be dead.

There is a good chance my son would be dead, too. I am living proof that screening saves lives. When Jacob was born I felt nothing. No happiness, no sadness, just emptiness.

I put on a good show, though, and no one was wiser. No one knew that I wasn't happy. No one knew that the reason I asked my husband to give Jacob his baths was because every time I passed by the bathroom images popped in my head of drowning him. No one knew and no one was ever going to know. What kind of mother would think about harming her child? I didn't want to hurt him and I certainly didn't want to kill him, but I didn't know how to talk about it. How does a woman, a strong, successful woman tell her husband that she wants to hurt her baby? How does she tell him that she is afraid of a 5-pound precious little being? I couldn't.

I wanted to tell my OB, after all postpartum depression had been talked about at every prenatal visit and in the hospital before discharge. It was obviously something they saw needed to be discussed. What if they took my baby? I couldn't let that happen. Or could I? Maybe my life could go back to normal if I didn't have this thing robbing me of my sanity anymore.

My chance came at my six-week postnatal OB exam. As with every single visit from my first prenatal until now, I filled out the Edinburgh PPD screening. I marked the highest number on everything except having thoughts of hurting myself or the baby. I was still too nervous to be honest about that. I had my exam and the OB talked to me, asking how I was feeling and adjusting. I told him I was tired and stressed but left it at that. He asked if I felt safe at home and I told him I did. He left and I got dressed.

Before I could leave he knocked on the door and sat himself down. He had just seen the results of my screening. He had this look in his eyes like he wanted to make everything better. I had never seen so much compassion as I had seen in his face at that moment. He took time and talked to me, really talked to me. He told me that there was a therapist on staff who could see me in just over an hour and asked me if I would please stay and talk to her. The head nurse came in, too. She told me how important it was for me to get help and made me promise I would get some lunch and come back. I did.

I talked to the therapist and was very careful as to what to say and not to say. My guard was very much up. I started seeing her weekly and she would always ask if I had thoughts of hurting my child. She would tell me that it was common and very treatable. After several weeks, I finally opened up and told her about the images I was having. I did not tell anyone else. I continued to see her weekly but the images were getting more intense and even though in my head I did not want to act on what I was seeing it got to a point where physiologically I could feel the muscles in my arms start to react. I was afraid that I would throw him against the wall or drown him or put him in the dishwasher.

I put Jacob in his crib, closed the door, and sat in my living room. I was unable to cry. I just sat there terrified and feeling like a complete failure as a mother. I finally got up the courage to call my therapist. We talked on the phone several times and the psychiatrist she worked with called me, too. She asked if I felt safe until our next appointment, which was the day after next, and I told her I thought so, but I really wasn't so sure.

My husband came home. OH CRAP! He didn't know about any of this. He knew I'd been seeing someone about the fact that I wasn't sleeping but that's it! What would happen when they called back and my husband was there? I couldn't let him find out. He would divorce me for sure and I would never see my kids again! I turned off my phone. Jacob was asleep so I lay down in my bed and pretended to be asleep, too. I imagined myself not being there or having to deal with this. My family deserved better than I could give them. They would be better off without me.

A little while later I heard a loud knock on the front door. I knew deep down who it was. My heart sank and I just wanted to run. Instead, I pretended to be asleep and imagined I was dead. I heard my husband answer the door. Then I heard what I had feared most. I heard the sound of walkie-talkies and a loud voice that said "we just got a call that a woman was about to throw her baby out the window." My husband insisted they had the wrong house until they mentioned Jacob and me by name. I heard them talk for a few minutes before the police officer insisted on Jacob and I coming out of the bedroom. My husband came in to get me and I just lay there. I wanted to be dead. I did not want to go out there and face my demon. The police would take Jacob, I would go to jail for the rest of my life, and my husband would leave me and never let me see my family again.

My husband practically had to carry me out to the living room. I stood there, barely able to keep my balance and barely able to keep my eyes open. The police evaluated me. They asked if I had taken anything or if I was just out of it. I told them I was out of it. I waited for them to take me to jail. Instead, they sat and talked with us. They told my husband what to watch for. They made him promise not to leave me alone with the baby and made me promise to be more open about how I was feeling to my husband. They were wonderful, supportive, and understanding. There was absolutely no judgment at all, not by the police and not by my husband. I found out later that the police in San Diego had a PERT (psychological emergency response team) that was specially trained to deal with situations that involved mental illness. I turned on my phone again after the police left and had several messages from my therapist and the psychiatrist. A few minutes later my phone rang and it was my therapist. My husband talked to her and we all decided it would be best if he went to my next appointment with me.

My husband and I went to my appointment, and after talking for a few minutes it was suggested I go to the hospital. I had never been so afraid in my life, not even when the police were at my door. My therapist told me that the goal was to keep both Jacob and me safe. After a lot of tears I finally agreed. The hospital was right across the street so my husband and therapist walked me over. Both of them stayed with me all afternoon until I was finally taken back to my room. The hospital was a scary place and no one knew a thing about PPD. I had to go to classes on how to control my schizophrenia, which I didn't have, but since many others had it I had to tag along. I was definitely in the wrong place. Everyone knew it. I wanted to leave. My therapist tried to get me out, but since I had admitted to being suicidal and hadn't eaten since I had arrived two days prior, they told her that if I tried to leave they would put me on a 5150 psychiatric hold. I was stuck there.

My mission was to get out, so I put on a show. Everyone knew I was lying but since I was saying I was better and I was eating, they eventually had to let me go. Two weeks went by. My husband could no longer work. I would not go near the baby except to nurse and I would no longer leave my bedroom. I had to have all the blinds closed and the lights off. I wouldn't eat. I wouldn't get out of bed. I barely slept. I probably slept a total of 10 hours and ate maybe 1,000 calories total over the next two weeks. My intention was to disappear. I don't know how many times I held pills in my hand. Sometimes I even put them in my mouth. I tried to get my husband to buy razors, telling him I needed them for something but he conveniently "forgot" them every time he went to the store. I visualized shooting myself in the head. I didn't want anyone to be able to save me. I wanted to save my baby and the only way that would happen was if I killed myself. There must have been some part of me that wanted to live, though, because I still made it to my appointments with my therapist.

I ended up in the hospital a second time. This time it was a hospital that was supposedly more suited for PPD patients, but now my therapist didn't have privileges so I wasn't able to see her like I had been able to at the other hospital. When I met with the doctor there he said that I would have to start in the locked unit, given my situation. I was in a private room. I did everything I could to make myself comfortable. I'd always been somewhat of a germophobe, but now I was in a full-blown OCD cleaning spree. I scrubbed every nook and cranny of the room with my toothbrush, including the ceiling, underside of the desk, chair, and bed.

After about six hours of sanitizing my space, the nurse came in and told me I was being moved to share a room with another woman. The fear threw me into what I heard them say was a semicatatonic state. I stayed at the sink in the dining hall scrubbing my hands in the hottest water available until the nurses literally pulled me off about 30 minutes later. I stood at the door of my new room all night unable to bring myself to step inside. When the nurse asked me why I wouldn't go in, I told her it was not sanitary. Another nurse promptly came up behind her and whispered that nothing would be clean enough for me.

Bright and early the next morning the doctor showed up and moved me to the open unit after asking me all kinds of questions about my fear of germs. I think he knew that there was no chance of healing for me in that area of the hospital so even though I was moved to the open unit, I still noticed "Close Watch" written in bold red letters on my chart and "CW" posted at every nurses station next to my name. I spent several weeks there trying like crazy to get better. I went to every class, every therapy session, and ate every meal. My goal was simple. I wanted to be safe around my family. I didn't care if I was happy. I just wanted to be safe. I would look at my four-year-old when he would visit me and feel so guilty that the only way he could see his mommy was to visit her in a mental hospital. Thankfully, he was none the wiser. The hospital looked more like a recreation room.

I was finally released and went home only to start going downhill again. The images came back and the fear of leaving my bed was just as bad as before. Why couldn't I give my family a normal mom? A normal wife? Once again I wanted to die. I started going to a support group. There were other moms who were also dealing with PPD. It was so comforting to hear other moms say that they weren't happy either. Not that I would wish PPD on anyone, but at least I was not alone. I still wouldn't be alone with Jacob, though, so I was the only mom there without a baby. I actually looked forward to going every week. Even with the support group, therapy, alternative treatments (light therapy, walking, nutrition, etc.) and medication, I was still not getting better. I was sinking again and I was sinking fast.

I ended up in the hospital for the third and final time. There was an option that had been discussed before that my husband and I had always decided was not what we wanted. It was ECT (better known as shock therapy). I hadn't gone into the hospital for that purpose but after seeing the drastic change in other patients (I literally saw it bring a young woman out of a catatonic state) and doing a lot of research, we decided to try it. At this point we were willing to try anything. I had several rounds of ECT, each time getting better. I was not perfect by any means but something about the ECT "reset" my brain and allowed me to go for longer and longer periods of time without the images and without wanting to kill myself. After several more weeks in the hospital and the ECT treatments, I was finally able to go home.

My therapist had arranged for my family and me to have a postpartum doula when I was released. She cooked us dinner, checked in to see how I was doing, and made a point to see how my husband was, too! But most importantly, she helped me bond with my baby and helped me not to be so afraid of him. She was such a blessing. My postpartum OCD had been so consuming for my family that it was necessary to have someone from the outside come into our craziness and help bring us back to normal. I was finally getting better.

I eventually had my first outing with Jacob. I took him to my support group. It was a 15-minute car ride and then we'd be with people again. I know it made everyone's day to see him. Jacob was a pint-sized celebrity. He reminded us all that with help we could recover from PPD. It was a huge step for me to take him that day, but I did. I slowly started taking him other places such as to my therapy appointments and my friend's house. I remember when I took Jacob to see my friend she burst into tears and said, "I've got my friend back! I never thought I would get my friend back!" That was the moment when I knew without a doubt that I was on the road to recovery.

I owe my life to so many people: my therapists, doctors, my amazingly wonderful and supportive husband, my doula, my support group, the day care that took Jacob in pro bono so my husband could somewhat keep his sanity, my family, my friends, my church, the PERT team, and more than anyone, my boys, who reminded me every day why I was fighting to stay alive. I love all of them and could never repay them for everything I put them through.

If it hadn't been for the screening my OB had done, I would never have gotten the treatment I so desperately needed. I most likely would have committed suicide and I very possibly would have taken Jacob with me. I had educated professionals who worked with me to provide the best treatment for my individual situation. I had an entire community that wrapped its arms around me and held me during the darkest part of my life so that I could be the wife and mother I am today. Did I enjoy going through it? Absolutely not. Am I thankful for it? I am thankful with every ounce of my being.

I am a much stronger person than I ever dreamed possible. My family has a bond that only going through tragedy together can bring. I have a new sense of compassion for families dealing with postpartum issues and mental illness in general. I realized that each and every one of us is only one chemical, one trauma, one injury away from losing our sanity. I grew as a wife, mother, and person. I hate to think of what would have happened if I had lived in a community where I was told PPD was a myth or the Baby Blues. PPD is real and it is common. Most of all, it is treatable.

We must stop turning a blind eye to postpartum depression. As a society we must realize that it is the number one complication of pregnancy, and act accordingly. We need education and we need to figure out what we can do about it. No woman should have to go through this alone, and no woman should be called a crybaby when she tries to talk to her doctor. Moms deserve better than that. Babies deserve better than that. Families deserve better than that.

My Journey Through Postpartum Depression

JESSICA RODRIGO-DUNICAN

I became pregnant for the first time at the age of 18, less than a year out of high school. We were young but excited at the prospect of becoming parents and starting our life together. My husband (boyfriend at the time) and I moved into our first apartment and began to prepare for the arrival of our first blessing. On December 30,1994, at 9:55 p.m., I gave birth to a beautiful dark-haired baby girl weighing in at 6 lbs 7 oz. We named her Rain Carey. We were discharged the following day and went home to our tiny apartment with our new addition in tow.

The first three or four days postpartum were uneventful save for getting the hang of nursing and lack of sleep. Around the first week mark I began to notice something wasn't "right." I could not sleep, I felt "revved up," and my mind was racing and it would not be shut down. I had insomnia for days at a time. At the time I blamed it on the "birth high." Actually, I was pretty pleased with myself because I was taking care of my baby, my house, and I even started to exercise again at about three weeks postpartum. I had never been more energetic in my life.

At the same time, I could not eat. I had no appetite for food and no desire to sit for as long as it took to eat a meal. I spent my days cleaning and exercising and, even though it was winter, bundling the baby and walking for hours at a time trying to dispel all this pent-up energy. This mania lasted some weeks and I dropped well below my pre-pregnancy weight; I was living on little more than water and air. Eventually, I began to run out of steam. My thoughts began to slow down and I wasn't thinking rationally. Actually, I spent much of my time living in a fantasy world and just going through the motions of my day-to-day life. Within 18 months I was feeling more like myself, and although I knew something was strange about my postpartum experience, I didn't have a name for it nor had I ever heard of postpartum mood disorder.

Within three years I was pregnant for the second time, but sadly, I lost that baby at 14 weeks' gestation. I was pregnant for the third time less than five months later. After an uneventful pregnancy I gave birth to my second daughter on March 18, 1999. We named her Celeste and she was a joyful, happy baby. Within days the revving of my mind began again. I didn't sleep, I didn't eat, I couldn't shut down. At about five or six weeks postpartum, new and terrifying symptoms began for me. I began to have days-long panic attacks and I wasn't thinking rationally. At one point I even was convinced we were all going to die of rabies because I saw a raccoon in our yard.

I was frozen with the fear of dying and it consumed my every thought. I was also afraid to tell anyone how off I felt. I wasn't even sure I could verbalize what I was feeling, and if I told anyone I was positive they would take my children from me. Along with the panic I began to "see" demons. I couldn't close my eyes without horrific images flashing through my mind. I knew that my brain was broken. I thought that I had gone insane, that I had schizophrenia.

I had never heard of anything besides the baby blues. The most terrifying symptom to me was the incessant thoughts of hurting my children. I would imagine throwing them, biting them, or hitting their heads on walls. I didn't want to do these things but I believed my mind was so far gone that I may not be able to control my actions any longer. I also thought about driving off the highway, jumping out of windows, or driving into trees. I didn't want to die. These thoughts were so horrifying and I couldn't seem to control them. During this whole period I was still living and putting on a normal face, trying to fight what was happening. I still had no idea what it was and I tried in vain to find a physical cause for this. I went to the cardiologist for my heart palpitations, I visited an endocrinologist to have my thyroid tested, and a naturopathic doctor to have my hormones tested, and nothing panned out.

At about the 1-year mark, I started to slowly feel better when I discovered I was pregnant for the fourth time. I was so petrified with fear. During this pregnancy I experienced my first depressive episode. I cried through most of the nine months. I felt sorry for myself. I just wanted to have a normal pregnancy and be a normal mother after my children were born. I knew this wasn't going to happen. I tried to confide in every health care professional I came into contact with during the whole nine months. I would tell them I was scared that I had experienced some postpartum issues. Usually, I got a pat on the leg and a condescending smile.

In February of 2001 I gave birth to my third daughter, a round-faced baby we named Riley. I cried right after birth and I told her I was sorry but there was something wrong with me. Like clockwork the revving began at three days postpartum and the full-blown OCD/Panic/Anxiety right around the four-week mark. I was also majorly depressed at this time. I had three small children and I knew I was losing my grip on reality. I felt all alone. I felt like no one understood or wanted to help. I tried to tell people how I was feeling, but I usually got responses such as "You need to get out of the house," "Get a hold of yourself," or "You have three healthy children! Why are you depressed?" I gained weight, rarely got dressed, and cut myself off of any outside life. I stopped watching TV or reading the news because my mind was so open to any violent or disturbing imagery and I just couldn't handle any more stimulus. I was effectively cut off from the world.

Interestingly, one of my major fears was going on medication. I had some really terrifying experiences with illegal drugs in high school and I was sure that SSRIs would produce the same symptoms in my already fragile mind. I was desperately trying to hold onto the small strand of sanity I had left. I tried again through counseling and different doctors to get help, but nothing worked. I really wanted someone to say to me "this is what you are going to do" and make me do it. I don't think, looking back, that I was mentally capable of making the decisions I was making about my own health. I don't think most of the health care people I came in contact with were even familiar with what I was experiencing. I know that some thought I was exaggerating or being overly sensitive.

Slowly, very slowly, my brain began to heal. I was sad thinking I had missed out on all this time with my children while I was trying to fight my own mind. I was also sad because I knew I would never be able to give birth to another child. I knew if I did I would never come back mentally. We made the decision to take permanent action against further pregnancies. We have since adopted another baby girl, a tiny fairy of a baby we named Brooke.

Postpartum mood disorders are very real and very terrifying. No one should have to go through it alone. It is my hope that the more people tell their stories, the more people reach out, the more educated people will become about this topic. No one should have to be ashamed or scared to have a mental illness, and it is my sincere wish that my story helps even one person. Talk until somebody listens. Talk until someone takes you seriously.

BIPOLAR DISORDERS

Living With the Dragon: The Long Road to Self-Management of Bipolar II

PETER AMSEL[4]

After living with an affective disorder for over 25 years one might assume that I would be living a symptom-free, healthy and 'fully functioning' life. Given the fact that I am a reasonably successful composer of contemporary classical music and that I am presently writing a book about living with mental illness, the story is not all that it appears. While I am able to project a veneer of normalcy to many, people do not see the full story of what I am experiencing: they do not know how much pain I am in all the time, nor do they have any idea about the anxiety that grips me when I am away from home; they are unaware of the savagely swirling emotions that threaten to rise to the surface without warning. Most of all, people do not understand that I am living with a dragon: a beast that seeks to devour me at every opportunity, seeking to destroy my spirit by taking away the things that are important to me through the manifestations of this pernicious affective disorder. Those things are my ability to be creative, the ability to create a sculpture with sound or paint a picture with words; these are my passions, my reasons for living. While I am still currently in treatment for the management of bipolar disorder, it has not been possible to eradicate all of the symptoms that I experience at any given time, nor has it been possible to fully control those symptoms. If it were possible, I could well find myself in a situation where I was rendered unable to compose or write at all due to the close link between creativity and this often malicious disease. This situation has been explored in much greater detail by many writers exploring the relationship between the disease and creativity, including a chapter in the seminal work on the illness, *Manic Depression* [sic] by Goodwin and Jamison (2007), and a chapter written for the book *Learning About Mental*

---

[4]From "Living with the Dragon: The Long Road to Self-Management of Bipolar II," by Peter Amsel, 2010. In T. Basset & T. Stickley (Eds.), *Voices of Experience: Narratives of Mental Health Survivors* (pp. 58–60, 62–71, 74). Copyright 2010 by John Wiley & Sons. Reprinted with permission.

Health Practice (Amsel, 2008), which also explored the challenges of treating creative individuals.

When it was first suggested by my family doctor that I might benefit from taking an antidepressant, my reaction was to stare at her in disbelief: I sat in her office feeling stunned and scared, completely unsure of what my future held. An antidepressant spelled out only one possible thing: *mental illness*. Surely my doctor had not suggested that I had a mental illness, I thought to myself, how can this be happening to me? At the same time I was struck by the thought that if I denied my doctor's suggestion of treatment, I might never find a solution to the problems that had been plaguing me for so long. It was this inner voice that drove me to look at the evidence confronting me with the blackness that had descended on my life like a dark storm that would not dissipate. Yes, it was true, I thought to myself, as my doctor read the conflicted emotions on my face and tried to comfort me. My life had been led down a path of darkness by something that I did not understand beyond the periphery; beyond the engulfing darkness of its seething hunger, my own life was being consumed and robbed of the few things that had not only given me joy but had provided me with my identity. If I only knew one thing about depression at that moment it was that it could kill: if not physically, then spiritually. The truth was, it was in the process of killing me and if something was not done to stop that from happening it was only going to be a matter of time before the disease won the day and the job was completed.

My reasons for going to see my doctor had not been trivial in any respect: I was truly in desperate shape. Aside from being unable to sleep for more than a few fitful hours at a time, I was experiencing extreme, debilitating migraines, and I was in the midst of a creative block the likes of which I had never known before: I had not been able to write a thing or compose a note for several months. In truth, it was this block in my creativity that I found to be more disturbing than anything else, even more than how I was physically feeling. When everything finally became too much for me to bear, when I could not stand another day without being the creative individual that I had been born to be, I was ultimately led to seek the help of my doctor. It must be understood that being unable to express myself creatively in the ways that had become so important to me had begun to make the thought of living unbearable. For as long as I could remember there had been music playing in my mind, not what you would think of in a bad sense or songs that I had heard on the radio, but rather the music that I was composing and would eventually work on, the music that would ultimately become the foundation for each of the pieces that I had worked on over the past 20 years. This 'soundtrack' was now gone and with it my desire even to *listen* to music; the prospect of living without my music was something that I had difficulty even imagining, it was a life that I simply did not want to live. How could I continue to call myself a composer if I could not *compose* or even *listen* to music? How could I be a writer that *could not write?* These were questions that pained and tortured me as I tried, for naught, to rekindle the creative flames that I was certain were still buried somewhere inside, just waiting for the right time for it to once again be revealed.

Patience is often a difficult virtue for someone to maintain when dealing with healthcare practitioners who give the impression that your care is not the most important thing in the world, an impression that can be gained when the process of diagnosis seems to take longer than it should; an impression that often arises out of legitimate frustrations, but can also be based on a purely subjective assessment. It is difficult to imagine how much I can appreciate the complexity involved in the process of untying the knot of pathologies involved in what I was experiencing considering the symptoms that I presented: a doctor, after all, can only work with what they are given. While an initial diagnosis of major depressive disorder, otherwise known as 'clinical depression,' began my path towards a correct diagnosis, it also began a period of intense inner battles as my moods vacillated even more rapidly than before and the migraines that I was experiencing became almost paralysing in their intensity.

What I could not have known at the time was that my doctor had only diagnosed half of my problem. After taking the antidepressants that had been prescribed for about a year it was decided that my progress on the medication was not what it should be, and my headaches were posing issues that needed another medical perspective, so I was referred to both a neurologist and a psychiatrist. When I saw the psychiatrist—a psychopharmacologist—I was told that my problem was not depression. 'You do not have clinical depression,' he told me, which I could not believe, especially since I was still struggling with some very difficult, very dark episodes. 'If I am not depressed,' I countered, 'how come I want to jump off of my balcony?' This was delivered with a laugh and a smile in order to make sure that my 'threat' of self-harm would not be taken too seriously. It was not, but it managed to elicit an answer that I had not expected: 'No, no', he said quickly, 'you *have* depression, just not *clinical* depression. You have *bipolar affective disorder*', he paused and then quickly added, *'type II'*.

Bipolar disorder, type II, whatever that meant; I knew that it was also known as 'manic depression', something that I had seen in all its 'glory' while in university when a flute player experienced a full-blown manic episode and ended up hospitalised for several months. I knew what this meant: I really *was* crazy. Having spent a year reading about depression and its related conditions, I had thought that I actually knew something about what I had been experiencing, but I was wrong. After we had spoken for a while the psychiatrist put it perfectly when he said, 'You possess a great deal of knowledge but not very much insight about the illness'. Nothing could have inspired me more, nothing could have driven me to become better informed, more insightful regarding the nature of what I was experiencing, than the words of that psychiatrist. After all, who could become a better expert about my own mind and body than me? Understanding the nature of an illness was one thing, understanding its manifestation in *my* body and mind, on the other hand, was something that I could relate to better than any textbook. It was then that I decided that I might in fact be crazy, but I most certainly was *not* insane. Doctors may know about the mental illnesses, but precious few of them know what it *feels* like to experience the various aspects of those illnesses.

Ultimately, it was faith that saved me: not merely spiritual faith, but the belief that my creativity would return and with it, my ability to do the things that made my life worth living. I knew that faith meant that you sometimes believed in things that could not necessarily be seen or proved to be true, but if I did not believe, how could I stand another day without my creativity? The choice was simple—I could either believe that I would be able to compose and write again, and that I would produce things that were beyond anything that I had done in the past, or I could give up and surrender to the illness. The choice was made: I have never surrendered. There were many pieces remaining to be composed, stories, poems and books to be written, and so much more I could not begin to make a list. Once I began to think of the music that remained to be written, when I stopped thinking of all that I had lost and began to focus on all that remained to be done, the inner soundtrack that had been gone for over a year returned, softly at first, but it was back: music was once again flowing from my pen.

My Journey Had Truly Begun

Describing what it was like to live with bipolar disorder seemed to be difficult considering that the more I found out about the disease the more I realised that I had actually been living with it for many more years than I had initially believed. Unlike what I had seen as a university student, when I witnessed some of the classic symptoms of mania, bipolar disorder, type II can manifest itself in many subtle ways that often makes diagnosis very difficult. Episodes of depression, for example, are common elements to both types of bipolar disorder (American Psychiatric Association, 2000) which often leads to individuals being diagnosed with depression first, before receiving a more accurate diagnosis when other symptoms are brought to the attention of the doctor. One of the main difficulties in diagnosing bipolar disorder is that it is not always easy for the person experiencing the illness to recognize that something is wrong when they are not feeling depressed. Very few people are likely to go to their doctor with the complaint that they are 'too happy' or that they have 'too much energy', which are often characteristics of hypo-mania, or simply not being depressed.

While there are many clinical distinctions between the two types of bipolar disorder, with subtypes within the main types, the essence of the illnesses are quite straightforward: it is important to point out that the main difference between the two is that the condition of full-blown mania only manifests itself in bipolar, type I while people with bipolar, type II may experience what is known as hypo-mania. It should also be noted that individuals with bipolar, type I may also experience episodes of hypo-mania (American Psychiatric Association, 2000). In essence, hypo-mania is an episode that does not reach the heights or breadth of a manic episode, making it 'small' or 'less than' full-blown mania while it can also be similar in many ways, without being as dangerous, self-destructive or lengthy in duration.

If asked to describe the difference between mania and hypo-mania I often offer the following scenario: a person experiencing a manic episode may decide to run down the middle of the street naked, singing some Beatles songs at the top of his lungs. Someone experiencing an episode of hypo-mania, on the other hand, might look at the person experiencing mania and think to themselves, 'That looks like a *really good idea*'. The person experiencing hypo-mania might write about it, draw pictures of it, obsess about it and tell friends about how it looked like a really brilliant thing to do, but the likelihood of their going through with it would be extremely low. By the time a person experiencing hypo-mania gets around to doing something about it the episode may already have ended. While hypo-mania may sound similar to mania on the surface, there is a distinctly qualitative difference to the 'energy' that one experiences and what that energy is able to drive the afflicted individual into doing, as well as a quantitative difference. Manic episodes can last for over a week, and often longer, while true hypo-manic episodes last a minimum of four days (American Psychiatric Association, 2000). Mania is generally associated with behaviour that severely impairs one's ability to function in both a social and a professional environment. Another characteristic of manic episodes may be the presence of psychotic features and the need for hospitalisation. It must be remembered that this is an illness which has, when left untreated, led to the death of individuals as a result of exhaustion.

The energy that I have occasionally experienced through an episode of hypo-mania, unlike the debilitating nature of a manic episode, was actually something that could be enjoyed on many occasions. Unfortunately, there are often other symptoms involved with my hypo-manic episodes that make it difficult to harness the potentiality of the creativity that is regularly associated with the energy of hypo-mania. Symptoms such as free-floating anxiety and feelings of angst seemed to be particularly fond of expressing themselves at the same time as the various hypo-manic episodes, as well as a general irritation that was either manifested as a short temper or simply extreme irritability. It turns out that it is extremely rare for me to experience an episode of 'pure' hypo-mania, far rarer than the episodes that began to make up what I began to call the *rollercoaster ride from hell*. The worst part about this ride is not so much the ride, but what awaits me at the end: each twist and turn ultimately leads me inevitably closer to the dark tunnel that signals the end of the ride and the open mouth of the most terrible giant dragon, waiting to devour me once the ride comes to a halt.

When living with bipolar affective disorder, especially the type II variant which has brought a whole new meaning to the term 'rapid cycling', you get a great appreciation of the proverb *what goes up must come down*. Life often seems to be defined by the ups and downs of an unseen, mad conductor, who is wildly beating out an oddly syncopated piece of music for an invisible orchestra that nobody can hear … except those few who have been granted the 'backstage pass' that comes with having this illness. Having these diverse mood swings takes on an entirely different meaning when you find yourself cycling through various mental and emotional states in rapid succession. When cycling becomes what is euphemistically called 'rapid cycling'—a term which hardly encompasses the turmoil that exists—where moods alternate between everything from depression, agitation, hypo-mania, anxiousness, and several combinations thereof—things take on an entirely different complexion. I have found this to be especially true when tracking my own mood swings or 'shifts' and discovered that there were often 17 or more episodes in a day, something that is not only psychologically exhausting, but physically exhausting as well, leaving me drained of both energy and a desire to do anything constructive. It often feels as though I am racing through the tunnel at the end of the rollercoaster ride towards a solid brick wall.

Hitting that wall translates into a frighteningly rapid plunge into a dark depressive episode, barely escaping the jaws of the dragon as it tries to snap off my head. These depressive episodes can sometimes last longer than others, often for days or even weeks at a time; but soon enough the cycling resumes and the rollercoaster ride begins all over again. Perhaps the oddest times for this illness takes place when I am in a depressed state and still experience rapid cycling; with moods ranging from deeply depressed to varying states of agitation it is impossible to predict how I am going to feel from one hour to the next, let alone one day to another. These cycles merely avoid the 'higher', or elevated affects associated with the illness.

This may be where you can find the one silver lining about having bipolar disorder, particularly the rapid-cycling variant: you can always be certain that an episode of depression will end at some point, usually of its own accord and without the need for any emergency interventions. Unfortunately, on the other side of the coin, there is the likelihood that there will be many more episodes of darkness than would be experienced by someone living with clinical depression and no other underlying affective disorder. However, this should not be seen to imply that there are measurable or somehow qualitative differences between the intensity and potential seriousness of the depressive episodes experienced by people suffering from either bipolar disorder or clinical depression. It is not practical, possible or ethical to compare the seriousness of one's personal suffering with an illness such as depression based solely on something as transient as the duration of the illness or the number of episodes an individual has experienced during their life. Ultimately, the relative comparison of suffering that one may experience to that of another is both entirely impossible and meaningless on the grounds of the experiential subjective relationship between each individual and the manifestation of their illness.

While one person may find that certain symptoms are virtually impossible to live with, these same symptoms may not be as bothersome for someone else living with the same medical condition; the experiences are purely personal, with one caveat: while these comparisons become purely subjective and, as such, meaningless, they do provide the opportunity for individuals living with similar illnesses to be able to relate to each other under the umbrella of common suffering. People find it easier to relate to someone who has experienced a similar ordeal even if the path to where they presently are is not the same one as that taken by the other person; it is somewhat like comparing scars and boasting about how many stitches it took to sew up one's flesh. If a scar is covering a laparoscopic procedure it could be hiding something much more serious than the scar across a knee that came about from falling down a hill. Both are scars, but they have entirely different stories and, subsequently, totally different meanings. The result, however, is still a scar, and that will allow for common ground to exist, a point from which sharing can begin and where healing can begin. People who realise they are not alone are less apt to feel the desolation that can come with the diagnosis of a mental illness; feeling as though you are the only person in the world going through what you are experiencing. Being alone against the world is not a place you ever want to be, believe me, I have been there and it is a very scary place.

Having spent nearly a year studying depression I was now totally unprepared to start again on the journey towards understanding what I was now facing, or at least, I thought I was; once I began studying bipolar disorder I began to realise that it really was—in essence—depression *plus* the extra components of the illness. Of course, it was those 'extra' parts that had been making my life so interesting for the past few decades, and even more so over the past year since I had been taking the antidepressant prescribed by my doctor. As someone who experiences rapid cycling, the antidepressant that I had been prescribed before the final diagnosis was made could well have worked against my condition. The medication came from the SSRI (selective serotonin reuptake inhibitor) class of medications and seemed to cause me to cycle even more rapidly than I had been before seeking help.

After seeing the psychiatrist a different SSRI was recommended, along with some mood stabilisers.

Before Things Get Better They Sometimes Get Worse

Very few things can make you feel as helpless, or as desperate for help, than when you are embarking on a new treatment protocol for an affective disorder and you happen to be alone. My doctor had referred me to a psychiatrist at the Royal Ottawa Hospital with whom I was able to make an immediate connection, and he decided to change my medications for the simple reason that I was not having the desired effects (or affects) on them, and I was experiencing extreme insomnia. We discussed the proposition of my becoming an inpatient but, in the end, decided that it would be better for me to remain an outpatient. Part of this decision was based on the idea that I am, ostensibly, a 'high-functioning' individual for whom being an inpatient would be extremely difficult. Unfortunately, this also meant that at those times when I ended up needing support the most, in the middle of the night when I could not sleep and was alone, trying to outrun the snapping jaws of the dragon, I had nobody to talk to, nobody to get advice from or anything supportive ... so, I read, I read almost anything and everything that I could find relating to bipolar affective disorder and what I was experiencing, including new studies that I was finding through medical journals on the internet.

Aside from seeing my new psychiatrist regularly in the hope that we would find a pharmaceutical cocktail that would help me the most, accompanied by the fewest side-effects, I became involved in the Psychiatric Rehabilitation programme available at the hospital at that time. This consisted of offering different groups which were designed to provide both psychiatric rehabilitation and education to those living with mental illnesses. The different groups focused on providing the necessary tools needed to prevent the relapse of serious episodes of illness and to recognise the most disturbing stressors in our environment that influenced our wellbeing, and which may exacerbate our illnesses. They also assisted in the planning and completion of goals, allowing us to achieve as much as we are willing to believe that we are capable of achieving. These groups proved to be extremely helpful for my recovery process, not to mention the many others who participated in them over the many years that they ran, long before I came into the programme. The groups offered by the Psych Rehab programme that I took included Goal-Setting, Symptom Self-management, Thoughts and Feelings, and Stress Management. Each group contributed its own set of tools which allowed members to become better prepared at dealing with our illnesses. While the programme was heralded by visiting members of the medical community for its effectiveness and it became a model for the treatment of mental illness, it was cancelled due to the hospital taking a 'new direction' in 'client care'. For those fortunate enough to have taken both the Goal-setting and Symptom Self-management groups, the tools acquired and the support received will be impossible to replicate, but they will still be able to use those tools for the rest of their lives. These were ongoing groups that allowed people to continue to work on their 'wellness', or 'recovery' goals, discussing their concerns with both the group members and the group facilitator.

Since my lack of sleep was an ongoing and important symptom for me I began to monitor how much sleep I had, leading me to discover that there were many nights where I slept as few as one or two hours, or less, if you include the occasional night where I did not sleep at all. The several weeks that I monitored at one point averaged between 11 and 15 hours' sleep over a seven-day period. When this was reported in the group the response was unanimous: 'How can you live like that?' This was a question that I had asked myself on more than one occasion, but I could not allow myself to listen to such questions for the simple reason that they drew on the sense of hope that I was clinging to for recovery. Losing hope can be very easy, especially when you experience a cyclical condition such as bipolar disorder, and that can become crippling. Hope can be lost over virtually anything, no matter how seemingly insignificant; had I allowed myself to enter that stream of hopelessness I may well have lost my battle with this illness altogether, especially with the negative feelings associated with not being able to sleep. This could very well have become an overwhelming burden, creating an avalanche of self-pity from which I may not have been able to recover.

If you do not think for an instant that learning about your enemy is one of the most important things you can do if you have any hopes of victory, believe me, it truly is, for knowledge is power. If you believe that living with a mental illness is anything less than a war for your mind, you need to reconsider the power of these diseases. These are illnesses that can drive the strongest individuals towards the unthinkable; people who would ordinarily never consider hurting themselves or anyone else can be driven by these diseases to commit acts of self-destruction that you would never have thought possible, including that one, final act of desperation that cannot be undone; an act that speaks of such anguish it can only be the result of the darkest side having claimed victory over yet another desperate soul. Many people find it difficult even to discuss suicide, thinking it a shameful thing, a dark secret, something that must be concealed from the prying eyes of the public, but it is a part of this illness, whether you like to admit it or not. Thinking about suicide, often referred to as 'suicidal ideation', is a very common symptom of bipolar disorder and is something I have frequently experienced. Thinking about something, however, does not necessitate acting on those thoughts. It is only when we give power to those thoughts that they gain control over our lives. Suicidal ideation does not have to lead to suicide.

The truth of the matter is that suicide will only lose the power that it holds over us when it is exposed to the light; it thrives on the darkness that is secrecy and shame, allowing people who have treatable illnesses to take their lives for the simple reason that they did not have someone they could talk to in their deepest moments of need. In many ways it can be said that society induces individuals to commit suicide, encouraging the pursuit of that which is unattainable by most through the idealised version of 'perfection' that is marketed to the world through what is generally identified as 'American' culture, and which is clearly seen through the representations in the popular media and the constant depiction of the 'good life', as reflected in the possession of money, fame and the power to influence others. Some people get so caught up in the very idea of this 'rat race' that they are unable to extricate themselves from it, even when that is something that they desperately desire. While we may think that this is a too simplistic dismissal of the myriad contributory factors to suicide today, it is difficult to deny that one of the main stressors on contemporary youth, and of those identified as being members of generations 'x' and 'y', are bombarded with cleverly crafted media marketing campaigns that deliver specific socioeconomic messages regarding what success is, and that anything else is, by inference, a failure.

The starkness of this truth, and its importance to my life, was something that was made more real to me than I ever wanted to know when there came a knock on my door three years ago. At the time I was living near a pizza shop and had become friendly with one of the cooks. It turned out that his girlfriend was the sister of a very dear friend of mine from high school whom I had not been in touch with for several years. On this cold December night the delivery boy from the pizza shop gave me a message from his boss: his girlfriend's sister was dead. After I called the restaurant her sister called me and told me the entire story; it made me want to curl up in a corner and die. She was one of the sweetest women you could ever hope to know, the type of person that could make you smile even if you were in a lousy mood; and through all of that she was living a life that left her feeling miserable. Unfortunately, it turned out that she and I had far more in common than I could have ever imagined when we first met in high school. Through the intervening years time had made us closer through pathologies if not distance. Like me she also had fibromyalgia and suffered from severe migraines; instead of bipolar disorder she lived with repeated bouts of major depressive disorder, or just plain old depression. She did not want to go back into the hospital, according to her sister, and had been in a great deal of physical and emotional pain. All she wanted was the pain to end, a sentiment that I can certainly relate to given the chronic pain that I find myself in from fibromyalgia. Without the type of medical support that I have received—including a family doctor who has been willing to help me control my pain—my friend decided that she had experienced enough and it was time for the pain, and everything else, to end.

I had never understood why some people called suicide a 'selfish' act until I was told that she was dead; it hurt so much to hear those words, it felt as though a part of me died that night—part of me wanted to die that night—but I knew that I had too much to do, too much to live for. Death was not—is not—an option.

While I say that death is not an option for me, for my friend—well, I cannot pretend to understand what she was experiencing; part of me was angry that she did not call, part of me was angry because I thought that she *should have known* that I would understand her problems, that I would be willing to listen. I then realised that I was being just as judgmental about her as those who condemn that act of suicide without looking at the people who are behind the word; the only difference was that I was couching my judgement in the things she 'should have done' rather than focusing on the obvious state of despair that she must have been in to have allowed herself to be overcome by something that she had been seemingly able to defeat in the past. Of course, people do not call if they do not want to be talked out of something, which leads me to believe that she *really* wanted to end her life. I could not help but imagine her small form being engulfed in the jaws of that sinister dragon, its mouth seemingly curled into a smile as it raised its head to allow the small but precious parcel of food to slide down its gullet.

As My Eyes Meet Those of the Dragon It Realises That I Am Going to Kill It and, for the First Time in My Life, It Is Scared

With increased understanding of the nature of my illness came a new level of liberation that had previously not been possible. While it was important to take the information provided by the groups and put those tools into practice, it was equally important to combine what I learned there with what I had already learned from other sources, from books, articles, and resources found online, and use them to become more than an ordinary 'patient'. In many ways I was fortunate in that the philosophy at the hospital promotes the idea of a 'partnership in care', as well as 'clients' working with their 'healthcare team', so it never even occurred to me that there was anything wrong with taking up the position of patient advocate for myself and others. Perhaps my background in teaching and my facility with communication opened the door for my decision to become so involved in my care, but it all seemed perfectly natural; the fact that I was encouraged by my psychiatrist certainly did not hurt.

While I had become an advocate for mental healthcare I was also becoming more involved in my own care. Rather than being a passive recipient of medical care, as I had been for many years, I was now able to take a more active role; much to my surprise I discovered that the members of my healthcare team were not only not opposed to my proactive approach to my health, they were enthusiastically supportive. Apparently, or so it would seem from the responses I received, doctors would rather have patients that take an active interest in their own care than those that rely on them to make all of the decisions. In the end, the final decision regarding medical care is going to be made by the doctor, but it is the right of the patient to be involved in that decision. The burden of making those decisions is not as difficult when the doctor is not struggling with a patient who is not being open with them. Developing this type of doctor–patient relationship is not something that can be created after only one or two sessions; it must be cultivated through open communication with the doctor, demonstrating that there is a genuine desire on your part to be an active participant in your care. The best way to accomplish this is through asking topical, relevant questions relating to your treatment and about what you could do to learn more about your illness. Doctors are usually more than willing to recommend something to read, and many are gifted teachers who welcome the opportunity to share their knowledge. It is important to understand that there is a distinct difference between being active in your care and merely asking your doctor for different or more drugs. More than anything, it is essential to demonstrate that you are interested in recovery: that may sound odd, but some patients are not ready to recover at the beginning of their illness; they are more interested in being sick than working at what is entailed in the recovery process.

There is a distinctly different healthcare paradigm involved in a true partnership rather than with the conventional healthcare model with which most individuals find themselves entrenched. Most partnership-based models have the benefit of featuring recovery as a central component of the treatment plans. Without approaching recovery as something more than a vague concept, the idea that one day the symptoms of illness may go away is not enforced through the interactions between the healthcare professionals and the client. In order to foster the idea of recovery we must first be ready to *work* on recovery. In the case of other illnesses, such as measles or pneumonia, the process of recovery is quite straightforward: once the illness has been diagnosed, medication is prescribed and, after a certain period of time, there is the expected recovery. Things do not work that way in the case of mental illnesses such as bipolar disorder. You must be an active component of your own recovery process, otherwise there is no chance that it will work.

On the surface it sounds as though I am saying, 'You've broken your leg, now hop on over to Urgent Care and get yourself a cast'. But that is not the case at all; it is simply that the recovery process for an affective disorder requires a personal investment from the individual that is seemingly not as essential a component when dealing with the other realms of medicine. Of course, we have all seen, or heard, of how someone who has a positive attitude will tend to recover faster than someone with a negative attitude. Is this a function of genetics at play or merely a response to the power of 'positive' energy? Perhaps it is more a response to the fact that when we make a connection between our minds and our desire to recover we con- nect with a greater power than is necessarily understandable at this point in contemporary science. It is certainly a concept that made itself known to Dr. Frankl when he was imprisoned in a concentration camp during the Holocaust and saw people who had said they would die do so right before his eyes. Others said they would survive, and they did; testament to the power of the human spirit to survive when there is a *why* to continue (Frankl, 1959).

Therein lies the crux of the recovery process: why do you *want* to recover? If you can answer that question, you are on the *road* to recovery. It is simplicity itself, if you can understand the idea that your recovery is predicated on the idea that you must be actively involved in every aspect of your recovery, as though you were fighting the battle of your life; you will then have a better chance of succeeding than were you merely passively receiving treatment for the same condition. Remember, when battling affective disorders we are talking about the *mind*, not treating a back injury or a broken leg, but an illness that is influencing the way we *think* and *feel*. In order to be able to overcome these wretched illnesses we must first believe that it is possible to achieve some level of recovery, otherwise, why bother? If you do not believe the pills you are taking are going to help, why take them? If you think they are poison, why swallow them? If you want them to work, believe that they are working, even as they slide down your throat and begin to dissolve in your stomach.

When I look at what could be called my 'recovery process' I sometimes laugh; I still cycle, still get depressed, still get irritated . . . and sometimes I still feel downright awful. However, I am able to compose and write, and I am not thinking about killing myself, most of the time. If I do have a moment where those thoughts creep in I simply start thinking of all the work that remains and well, quite frankly, I have far too much to do to die; perhaps in 50 years or so.

There is a photograph of an extreme close-up of a retaining wall near the Rideau Locks behind the Chateu Laurier in Ottawa, Canada. I find it reflects the idea of strength in imperfection, for even with the crack in the wall, the wall remains intact, capable of completing its job. It is something like the struggle that people with a mental illness face every day of their lives: people do not understand that we can make substantive contributions to society—that we can be bricks in the wall—even with our cracks and imperfections, and it will not cause the structure to crumble. There is great beauty in diversity.

References

American Psychiatric Association (2000). *Diagnostic and statistical manual of mental disorders* (4th ed., Text Revision). Washington, DC: Author.

Amsel, P. (2008). Treating creatively: The challenge of treating the creative mind. In T. Stickley & C. T. Basset (Eds.), *Learning about mental health practice* (pp. 495–510). Chichester, England: Wiley.

Frankl, V. E. (1959). *Man's search for meaning.* New York, NY: Washington Square Press.

Goodwin, F. K., & Jamison K. R., (2007). *Manic depressive illness* (2nd ed.). New York: Oxford University Press.

On Madness: A Personal Account of Rapid Cycling Bipolar Disorder

ANONYMOUS[5]

I became unwell suddenly, unexpectedly, and severely five years ago. I was working as a full-time GP at the time with a growing list and four small children. Initially, I had days when I was intensely irritable with my family and suffered from episodes of anxiety and tension headaches. I put these down to the long hours I was working and a full social life at the time. Then driving down the motorway one day I decided it would be appropriate for me to crash the car and end my life. This was the start of very strong suicidal thoughts and impulses that would pop into my head unbidden and needed real mental energy to resist acting them out.

In the meantime I was also having difficulty working, at times literally dragging a deeply fatigued body and an equally befuddled brain into the consultation, managing by treating one person at a time, rather than look at a whole fully booked surgery. On other days I found work a useful distracter from the milder symptoms of my depression. Then again, at other times I was full of energy, enjoyed patient contact and was continually looking around for extra things for myself and the family to do.

Gradually, I noticed that working long nights and weekends became intolerable, which I initially put down to having young children rather than

---

[5]"On Madness: A Personal Account of Rapid Cycling Bipolar Disorder," Anonymous, 2006, *British Journal of General Practitioners, 56*(530), 726–728. Reprinted with permission.

believing that I might be ill. As my mood fluctuated so widely and on a day-to-day basis, it was difficult for me to see that I needed help. In the end, my husband encouraged me to make an appointment with my GP.

My GP wisely referred me straight on to a psychiatrist. Unwisely, she started me on an antidepressant not having asked about symptoms of elevated mood, as I was clinically so depressed at the time. My psychiatrist signed me off work initially with depression, but eventually with bipolar disorder, and thus began several years of treatment. Antidepressants, mood stabilizers, ECT, antipsychotics, thyroid hormones, lithium, psychotherapy, and hospital admissions made no difference to the unstable pattern of abrupt mood swings, rapid cycling, bipolar depressions, and mixed mood states with psychotic features woven throughout.

What Is It Like to Live With This Condition on a Day-by-Day Basis?

This illness is about being trapped by your own mind and body. It's about loss of control over your life. Bipolar disorder is multipolar, affecting not just energy levels but behavior and physiology. To onlookers it seems that your whole personality has changed; the person they know is no longer in evidence. At times they can be sucked into believing that the changes are permanent.

My mood may swing from one part of the day to another. I may wake up low at 10 a.m., but be high and excitable by 3 p.m. I may not sleep for more than two hours one night, being full of creative energy, but by midday be so fatigued it is an effort to breathe.

If my elevated states last more than a few days, my spending can become uncontrollable and I have to hand over my credit cards to my husband, which takes a great effort of willpower; otherwise I make purchases I will later regret. I remember being entranced by 18-meter lengths of coiled yellow extension wire. In my heightened state of awareness, the coils of yellow looked exquisitely beautiful and irresistible. I wanted to buy several at once.

I will sometimes drive faster than usual, need less sleep, and can concentrate well, making quick and accurate decisions. At these times I can also be sociable, talkative, and fun, focused at times, distracted at others. If this state of elevation continues, I often find that feelings of violence and irritability towards those I love will start to creep in. Concentration and memory start to wane and I can become hypersensitive to noise. The children making their usual noise and my husband singing can drive me to distraction.

My thoughts speed up and I can lie in bed for hours at a time watching pictures on the inner-sides of my eyelids. Sometimes words are present and I read them as if engrossed in a good novel. If I were asked to read them out loud, they would not make sense. They are a fascinating blur of words and pictures, snatches of poetry and music. I become impatient with myself and those around me who seem to be moving and talking so slowly.

I frequently want to be able to achieve several tasks at the same moment. I may want to read two novels, listen to music, and write poetry all simultaneously, becoming rapidly frustrated that I cannot do this. Physically my energy levels can seem limitless. The body moves smoothly; there is little or no fatigue. I can go mountain biking all day when I feel like this and if my mood stays elevated not a muscle is sore or stiff the next day. But it doesn't last. My elevated phases are short, mild, and generally manageable, but the shift into severe depression or a mixed mood state occurs sometimes within minutes or hours, often within days, and will last weeks without a period of normality. Indeed I often lose track of what normality is.

Initially my thoughts become disjointed and start slithering all over the place. I feel that I am physically trying to pin them down in my brain, trying to run ideas together in a coherent way. They will sometimes remain rapid and are accompanied by paranoid delusions, causing an inner tension that can only be relieved to some extent by physical activity, such as pacing a corridor. I start to believe that others are commenting adversely on my appearance or behavior. I can become very frightened and antisocial.

The children will detect the mood shift early on and play by themselves as I become more isolative and angry. My sleep will be poor and interrupted by bad dreams. I will change from being the person who has the ideas—is the decision maker—to not being interested in anything at all. The world appears bleak and a pointless round of social niceties. I will wear my most comfortable, often black clothes; everything else grazes and chafes at my skin.

I become repelled by the proximity of people, acutely aware of interpersonal spaces that have somehow grown closer around me. I will be overwhelmed by the slightest tasks, even imagined tasks. I will see dirt on every surface, weeds all over the garden, and grubby children, and feel solely responsible for improving these things.

Physically there is immense fatigue. My muscles scream with pain and an old nephrostomy scar plays up. I ache down to my bone marrow and my joints feel swollen. I become breathless weeding a small patch of garden and have to stop after two minutes. I become clumsy and drop things. The exhaustion becomes so complete that eventually I drop into bed fully clothed. Sometimes I will vomit, my digestive processes halted. I will often sleep without being refreshed for up to 18 hours. At times every muscle in my body will tense up and be totally resistant to relaxation. Sweat will pour off me or I will be caught in an attack of shivering unrelated to the ambient temperature. I will shout over and over again in my mind for help, but never get the words past my lips.

Food becomes totally uninteresting or takes on a repulsive flavor, so I will lose weight rapidly during a long depressive phase. Sometimes, I will crave only sweet foods in small quantities. It will often be difficult to bother to drink adequately, which can affect my drug levels and my bowels do not function. I become unable to concentrate to read a novel for pleasure, for escape. Even a newspaper or magazine becomes impossible to follow.

I start to feel trapped, that the only escape is death. At this point or earlier it becomes a rational decision. My brain slows right down. I become stuck, unable to answer a simple question, unable to establish eye contact and unable to comprehend what is being asked of me. I avoid answering the phone or the door. My voice deepens and slows sometimes to the point of slurring. My skin becomes pale and grey in hue. I feel the cold more readily. I will look in the mirror and fail to recognize the person there.

As I begin to slip into a more psychotic state of mind I become unable to recognize something as familiar as the palm of my hand or my children's faces. My sense of space alters and rooms that are familiar appear to have changed dimensions. Simple objects in a room can take on sinister meanings for me. At this point the world begins to take on a malevolent aspect, which is difficult to describe. Those I love around me become part of a conspiracy to harm me. Their faces will alter and their voices develop a mocking ring. I will hate my husband and other loved ones.

Images just out of my field of vision will be waiting to pounce, leaving me in a constant state of vigilance. I have been under the impression that I was rotting under my skin, that my bone marrow is being gnawed away by evil spirits. Soon the voices and images in my head start telling me what to do. Stop taking my medications, injure or kill those I love. Destruction. No other way out. Ultimately they tell me that everything would be better if I killed myself. I am evil, a burden; I deserve only punishment. Twisted tales and delusions.

I become passionate about one subject only at these times of deep and intense fear, despair, and rage: suicide. The suicidal impulses and images can come at any stage of the illness, even in mania, but are at their most intense and irresistible during psychotic phases. For months at a time I have carried ropes, blades, and enough tricyclic antidepressants to kill myself twice over, in the boot of my car. In the past I have had access to a fatal pharmacopeia of emergency drugs through my general practice work. I know where to buy a gun. I know the fatal dosages of the drugs I take. I have considered railway crossings, bridges over rivers, driving off roads into valleys, and electrocution. I have made close attempts on my life by hanging and drowning over the last few years. Sadly, the impact of suicide on my children does not avail me when I am ill. I consider myself to be such a huge burden on them at these times that I believe suicide to be a relief, a final gift to them from a mother who can do no more. A person who has reached the limit of endurance.

At times I will experience images of extreme violence toward others, often family members and those close to me, but on occasions even complete strangers. Sometimes I feel completely detached and dispassionate and compelled to act on these images: more often they are extremely distressing to me. When in a normal state of mind, I find these images abhorrent in the extreme. Fortunately, those who care for me have been able to recognize these unsafe states and admit me to hospital. Then inexplicably, my mood will shift again.

The fatigue drops from my limbs like shedding a dead weight, my thinking returns to normal, the light takes on an intense clarity, flowers smell sweet, my mouth curves to smile at my children, and my husband and I are laughing again. Sometimes it's for only a day, but I am myself again, and the person that I was is a frightening memory. I have survived another bout of this dreaded disorder. It's a continuous round fought on a daily basis. If I'm lucky I will get a few days every few months when I am completely normal and don't have to make continual allowances for my mood state.

So why am I still here? I don't know. Possibly luck. Possibly the tiny scrap of humanity that remains even in my most psychotic and suicidal states, which allows me to express the desperation and loss of control that I am experiencing so that caregivers and treating clinicians can respond appropriately and keep me safe. A little hope. Some denial.

I have lost my job, intellectual stimulation, and my social life. Sometimes I wonder how my marriage holds together. I am continually anxious about the effects of my illness on my children and whether I will end up like too many other people with severe bipolar disorder, separated from them permanently.

There have been relationships broken and distorted, and relationships that have held fast and true through the worst of its manifestations. Making new friends has often been too difficult. Those who know of my illness have sometimes become accommodating and flexible, but others have not. I have had to tolerate opinions from all sorts of people who think that if I only did something differently I would be restored to full health. People offer varied advice like multivitamins, regular massage, a holiday, a return to my country of origin, meditation, regular prayer, church attendance, or avoidance of atmospheric pollutants and negative thinking.

It's taught me that even with the best psychiatric care some people do not respond to medication and do not get better. However, I am grateful that I have had the best care available to me throughout and that I had completed my family before the onset of this illness. I am also grateful that I was able to take out income protection insurance several years prior to becoming ill; otherwise, like many other mentally ill people, we would be impoverished.

This illness is about having to live life at its extremes of physical and mental endurance and having to go to places that most people never experience and would never want to experience. It has been about having unthought-of limitations placed on your life, your career, and your family. For my family it's been about adjusting to totally altered dynamics and having a mother who is often unable to be there for them, for them to have to live with the flux of my moods and the disturbance that comes with recurrent hospitalizations. It's about having to rely on others for help when you are feeling at your most vulnerable and exposed. It's about being stigmatized. It has become about trying to stay alive and live life fully in the brief periods of normality or mild elevation that occur from time to time. Otherwise, rapid cycling bipolar disorder is an unrelenting scourge.

Random Scribblings on Bipolar Disorder

Michael Napiorkowski

20:20 Hindsight—Monday, November 19, 2007

Since I was about 17 years old I've known that there was something a little different with me, but I never thought for a second that it was bipolar disorder. Bipolar people are crazy, aren't they? It's amazing how our perception and understanding is shaped by stigmas and ignorance. What did I actually know about bipolar disorder until I was diagnosed? Nothing. I knew it was an illness that affected the mind, but I had no idea about what it looked like or, more importantly, how it felt.

I went through my highs and lows year after year without a clue. I knew that when my mood was low that I was depressed, but I thought that when my mood was high that this was me, my normal state. I felt great when I was high. People loved being around me. I was full of energy and I had a never-ending desire to experience life. I was wild and didn't care about anything. I wanted to be everywhere at all times. I didn't want to miss anything. This was the person I wanted to be all the time and I was convinced that it was me, until the low mood would eventually kick in. This is where my excited, energetic self would fizzle away and I would be left feeling empty and detached from the world. I would disappear for four to six months of the year. No contact with friends, no going out, no laughter, and no energy. The only thing I desired was being alone.

This cyclical pattern of highs and lows would continue year after year, and each year the intensity of my highs and lows appeared to increase. My highs would bring on dangerous erratic, impulsive behavior, and my lows would leave me feeling helplessly empty and detached. I thought this was just me. This was my personality. It wasn't until I lost all my friends and began seriously damaging my marriage and family life that I realized that there was something wrong with me. I was out of control.

Becoming the Ups and Downs—Monday, November 19, 2007

Looking back on my up phases usually leaves me feeling confused, regretful, and ashamed. It honestly feels like I'm looking back on a person who isn't me, the me that is now. I was reckless, irresponsible, and dangerous.

I remember the situations, the intense excitement, my inexhaustible hunger for constant never-ending experiences. The drive behind my impulsive decisions and actions. The endless nights of random confrontations with the unknown. I could never get enough to fulfill the thrill-seeking energy that was bursting out of every pore in my body. All those stupid choices I made. The ones I now regret, the ones that haunt me.

It leaves me asking myself, who am I really? The personality that exists with each phase of mood is so different that these personalities appear to belong to completely separate people. When I'm up I can't personally relate to my down, and when I'm down I can't personally relate to my up. I become my mood, and my mood transforms everything in my life to reflect its current state. From bright wonderful days to dark lonely emptiness, my sense of self shifts and my personality becomes a temporary notch in a cycle of ups and downs.

Dark Winter Days—February 2009

You never see these [dark] periods coming when they come. Overwhelming sensations flood your mind from every direction as you try your hardest to stand firm and continue functioning as usual and try not to drown in the onslaught of normal responsibilities that now have transformed into giant weights that are holding your head under water and preventing you from breathing. You try your hardest, but what was once an easy task has become an impossibility.

The naturalness of your character and associated behaviors have become dislodged, distorted, and broken, and you are vividly aware of how lost you feel as you desperately try to find something that you recognize in yourself that will bring you back. There is a hopelessness that envelops your existence. Thoughts flood your mind about how you are incapable of continuing like you have for so long. You ask yourself what you are going to do, but this question just piles more pressure on you as you slowly retract into yourself.

Indecisiveness takes over and even small decisions feel like they are impossible to make. The mental paralysis toward decision making is excruciating and quickly becomes a form of physical paralysis as you give up on decision making and instead sit and watch time pass moment by moment, until it is once again time to sleep. All I can do now is sit and wait for that morning when everything suddenly lifts and my mind returns to its nondepressed state and my relationship to the contents of my mind changes once again.

Stress: Our Worst Enemy—February 2008

It's so scary to trace your mind backward from a mental breakdown and to see how it so easily got the best of you. How your now-slumped-over, hopeless, aching body and tear-filled eyes stemmed from a simple negative thought that got out of control. You're left with a chicken and egg question about what came first, the thought or the feeling. How did I end up here? Why did I act that way? Why did I say those things? Why did I have those thoughts? Was that really me? You see how easy it is to lose yourself in a runaway mood. How easy it is for your mind to get stuck in an infinite loop of negativity, agitation, frustration, anger, and hopelessness. A downward spiral into hell.

Finding Sense in It All—May 2008

It's sometimes so difficult to see what is real and what is not when your mind is possessed by your mood. Mood is like the light that illuminates objects and thoughts, and when it becomes distorted, so do the objects and thoughts that it illuminates. You change and so does your world. The difficulty in all of this is how real your mood-driven behavior and thoughts become. You don't see them as mood-driven behavior or thoughts because you become them and you can't see through their influence because you become the influence. It's not until your mood shifts along the spectrum and pauses somewhere where a different perspective can take place that you realize that you've been deluded once again. The scary thing, though, is that most of the behavior that happens during these mood-driven phases is far from passive and usually has far-reaching impacts on your life and the people close to you. This inevitably increases your stress and anxiety once you've realized that you lost control once again and have to deal with the consequences, which usually sets you off once again.

My behavior and thoughts don't make sense all the time in a logical linear fashion. They don't always neatly add up in a rational way. My behavior and thoughts are filled with contradictions and opposing viewpoints. One month the world will reveal itself one way and I will attempt to derive conclusions and insights from it. The next month it will appear in another way that opposes the conclusions and insights formed from the month before. I never really know which viewpoint best represents the world around me because the feelings behind the viewpoints keep changing so dramatically. I can only imagine how confusing it must be for the people in my life to comprehend and predict who I am.

The Mind's Sense of Freedom—June 2008

The influence of inconsistent moods and the opposing realities they attempt to create and then perpetuate within a single mind are daunting. Identity becomes a confusing mess of contradictions played back in memory, and your vision of the future continually shifts as your inconsistent mood continues to influence the atmosphere of your mind. Freedom begins to haunt you as you begin to realize your only choice in life is to continue choosing while not fully trusting your judgment, even though in every moment that judgment feels right.

Identity becomes split into three modes of functioning: manic, normal, and depressed. You identify differently with each identity, and although your overall identity remains the same, each different mood transforms you into something far different than the other. Parts of your life can't function properly together and things start to become a mess and fall apart. You do things in one mood that you would never do in the other and you have to somehow find a way to reconcile this conflict during one of your fleeting moments of stability.

Left alone to your sense of freedom, you see the world around you happening and you try to understand how you fit into it. You find things to surround yourself with to tell you who you are, to reassure your insecurities that inevitably present themselves in every choice you make so that you think you understand the reasoning behind your choices. But as time goes by, the things you surrounded yourself with lose their effect and influence and you're lost once again to your sense of freedom and the unpredictability of who you will be in the months to come.

Consistency is Key—February 2008

It sometimes seems like the world isn't made for us. Like we don't fit the mold of what a human being should be. Employers don't want workers who will suffer uncontrollable bouts of depression or mania and exhibit associated behaviors. Friends don't want the unpredictability of friends who one moment are filled with energy and excitement and the next moment won't leave their house or talk to anyone because they are so depressed. They want consistency. They want reliability. They want to know that who you are now is who you will be tomorrow and six months from now.

The fact is that we would love to have this consistency as much as everyone else wants it from us, but evolution and chance have given us a set of cards that are a little more difficult to play. Like any minority that doesn't fit the bill of the majority, we face our challenges, but for us these challenges are more than just fitting into a social/cultural structure. For us it means dealing with our social/cultural structure as well as dealing with our internal struggles for self-survival. Our simple existence is a challenge for us at times and especially during an episode of mania or depression. We feel the normal struggles of daily life along with you, but we also feel the struggle of convincing ourselves that this life is actually worth living and losing so much control of our ability to properly judge and reason that we end up risking it all—both outcomes, unfortunately, having a bad conclusion. In our extremes, things can seem to be unbearable for all involved, but much of our time is spent in milder forms of the disorder's expressions, and at other times we appear to be like everyone else. We live, play, and work among you, and although you may not easily see us, we are there.

Being Bipolar: Living on Both Sides of the Coin

Susan Michele Vale

It was the spring of 1993. Hours before, I had joined the ranks of the unemployed. I had gone from clinician to civilian in the blink of an eye. Devastated, I was shaking; I felt that I had nothing left and that there was no one I could ever trust again. I was fifty thousand dollars in debt without counting my student loans. At the age of 31, I had rheumatoid arthritis; I was in pain every day. The only way my family handled problems was to ignore them; to them, I was just another problem. I couldn't go to them. I had no friends. I could feel my mind racing.

Alone in my bathroom, I looked around. There were bottles of prescription medications that my psychiatrist had prescribed for me. I had pain medications and muscle relaxants; it did not occur to me that there was definitely enough there to "do the job." I just simply made the decision that I was ready to die, and in doing so, it was the first time ever that I was overcome with an indescribable sense of peace. I can't tell you how many pills I took. I just know I took every bottle—probably at least 10—that I had of prescription medication (many of them full) plus all the over-the-counter stuff that I could possibly add to the mix for the purpose of lethality. So, I contacted my psychiatrist and asked him if I could go into the hospital, stating I was in crisis but did not tell him I had begun to overdose with a plan to commit suicide. My plan was to be found dead the next morning in a place where people would know what to do with my body after I was gone. The doctor arranged for my admission. I drove over to the facility (completely under the influence), presented to the technicians, and calmly went in my room for what I hoped would be my final sleep. What I didn't count on was that I would fail.

Hours later, alone in a room at Tucson Psychiatric Institute, I woke up only to realize that I was alive and that the attempt I had made at death was not to be. I needed to come clean and tell the staff what I had done. So, I went to a trusted staff member with whom I had a rapport and confessed that I had swallowed an ungodly amount of medication. Soon after, we were on our way across the street to St. Joseph's Hospital, and I was having my stomach pumped.

My first symptoms began around the age of 16. I had moods, but a lot of it was thought to be related to my periods. The doctor put me on Valium. After going away to college, my depression worsened. I hit rock bottom one time in Buffalo. I stopped going to classes and would not leave the house. I saw a psychiatrist at Campus Health, but he didn't give me a formal diagnosis. The worst was yet to come.

I was hospitalized for the first time at University Medical Center in 1984. I was an undergrad at the University of Arizona; the doctors treated me for depression with tricyclic antidepressants and released me. I went home to New York for the rest of the semester. Three years later, in 1987, I was driving all over town at all hours of the night. I couldn't relax. My mind would race. I would sit on the edge of my bed in the morning and stare into my closet, crying because I couldn't decide what clothes to wear in the morning. I was depressed one minute and in manic oblivion the next. I tried talking to my boss. His response was that I needed to lay out my clothes the night before; it was silly. But it only got worse. Eventually, I went to Palo Verde Hospital for help. At Palo Verde, they admitted me to the unit, and a doctor there started me on Lithium. Within 24 hours, I was a completely new person. It was magical. My diagnosis was bipolar disorder, and they finally knew what was wrong with me.

The problem with being on a drug like Lithium is that it can cause toxicity, particularly in my case since I had thyroid issues. So, finding the right "cocktail," so to speak, proved to be pretty daunting for my doctors. You name it, they tried it. Ultimately, the drug (along with some others, as I also had PTSD and other issues) that began to turn things around for me was Depakote. I was doing well enough that by 1994, I had my last and final hospitalization at Charter Hospital in Tucson. I knew then that I was doing better because the staff at the hospital was not doing their 10-minute checks on me; not only did I write all of them up, but I filed a formal complaint with the medical director. The real Susan was back. I have not seen the inside of a psychiatric unit as a patient since that day.

Eighteen years later, I can proudly say that I am a survivor of bipolar disorder. I had four other overdoses after the first one and a total of more than 15 voluntary hospitalizations. I think that my recovery has had a lot to do with the fact that I have had really special people in my life who were my cheerleaders. It is because of them that I learned what boundaries are and how to use coping mechanisms in a proactive manner. They also helped me to learn how to trust people again, although I must say that even now, I am still a work in progress. Today, I am blessed to still have some of those same cheerleaders in my life and new ones in place of those who have gone off on their own journeys.

For me, I think the hardest thing has been living in a world where you need to "keep your secret." As a professional in the psychiatric field, there are a lot of people out there who still want to keep the stigma of mental illness alive—many of them are psychiatrists and other clinicians—so being open about my mental illness is not something I am always able to do. I like to let people get to know me first and respect me for the woman I am. After a while, I might disclose, but it depends on the relationship that I have with a person. If I could stand in front of an audience and teach them one thing, it is that people with mental illnesses have a lot to teach them. I am a living lesson in what can go *right*.

I am proudest of the fact that I have earned a master's degree in rehabilitation counseling and that I am about to earn a second one in social work, both with specialties in the behavioral health field. I am also proud of the fact that I proved the doctor wrong; when I had my first psychotic break, the doctor said I might never work again. I did. I will again, too.

Since 1994, I have dedicated my life to being able to give back to my community, and I think I have been successful in doing that. The local Mental Health Art Show sponsored by our region's behavioral health organization was something that I helped to launch, and it recently celebrated its 12th year. I love nothing more than to help a person who wants help by giving them the wisdom that others gave me, only to watch them grow and change for the better. I will continue to do that until I take my last breath … due to natural causes, of course.

3

Anxiety Disorders

INTRODUCTION

All of us have experienced anxiety to one degree or another; it is an ordinary human feeling or response. A certain degree of anxiety can motivate us to try new things or to deal with challenging situations. Anxiety becomes problematic when it occurs frequently or with great intensity, when the response is out of proportion to the stimulus or event, when it interferes with psychosocial functioning, and/or when it involves a high or prolonged level of discomfort. The disorders in this *DSM-IV-TR* category represent a range of conditions in which people experience a level of anxiety that is beyond the normal response to a situation that is unfamiliar or poses a threat. Symptoms may differ across the types of anxiety disorders, but core symptoms that are common to all types are exaggerated or irrational fear and heightened apprehension.

Data from the National Comorbidity Survey Replication found the 12-month prevalence rate for any *DSM*-diagnosed anxiety disorder for U.S. adults was about 18% (Kessler, Chiu, Demler, & Walters, 2005). The lifetime prevalence rate for any anxiety disorder was 29%, with the anxiety disorders having the highest rate of any group of *DSM* mental disorders (Kessler, Berglund, et al., 2005). Anxiety disorders were more prevalent among women than men, and low income and education were risk factors for developing an anxiety disorder (Kessler, Chiu, et al., 2005). These were the most common type of disorder among older adults, more frequently experienced than depression or severe cognitive impairment (Kessler, Chiu, et al., 2005). For all adults, the four most prevalent anxiety disorders were *generalized anxiety disorder, panic disorder, social anxiety disorder* (social phobia), and *posttraumatic stress disorder*. By definition, the anxiety disorders greatly impact individuals' functioning and can be extremely debilitating.

The personal narratives in this chapter reveal the authors' struggles with a variety of anxiety symptoms and conditions. In each account, the stark reality of dealing with these challenges on a daily basis appears overwhelming. Yet, the most impressive aspects of their stories are the strengths these individuals possess and the resilience they ultimately demonstrate. The first two first person accounts (FPAs) by Kelly Orbison and Susan Ludeman draw us into their worlds of living with the anxiety and panic attacks that are part of having a panic disorder. Next, Daniela Grazia and Catherine Taylor vividly describe the nature of phobic anxiety in their accounts of social anxiety disorder and mysophobia, or the obsession with germs, which is an example of a *specific phobia*. The authors of two FPAs about *obsessive-compulsive disorder* (OCD) portray how the symptoms of this condition limit their lives. Frank DeFulgentis relates his experience of living with a hand-washing obsession/compulsion, and Jared Kant recounts his experience of living with OCD and the process of recovery.

Posttraumatic stress disorder (PTSD) is one of the few *DSM-IV-TR* disorders that requires a clear and known precipitant—exposure to an extreme traumatic event. Blazie Holling describes the panic attacks that she experienced as part of her PTSD and her understanding of the role of stressful events in it. Catherine McCall's story of "healing through multiple avenues of psychotherapy" shows the persistence with which she sought help and the power of the therapeutic relationship. In his narrative about combat-related PTSD, Art Schade provides a heart-wrenching account of his combat experiences in Vietnam and the long-term impact these had on his life across four decades until he sought help at the VA during the media coverage of the Gulf War.

QUESTIONS FOR REFLECTION

How does the nature of anxiety present itself in the various stories and disorders our authors write about? What are the common symptoms these individuals have dealt with? What symptoms are unique to their particular disorders? Have you ever experienced excessive anxiety? If so, how was this similar or different to the accounts presented in this chapter?

REFERENCES

Kessler, R. C., Berglund, P., Demler, O., Jin, R., Merikangas, K., & Walters, E. (2005). Lifetime prevalence and age of onset distributions of *DSM-IV* disorders in the National Comorbidity Survey Replication. *Archives of General Psychiatry, 62*(6), 593–602.

Kessler, R. C., Chiu, W., Demler, O., & Walters, E. (2005). Prevalence, severity, and comorbidity of twelve month *DSM-IV* disorders in the National Comorbidity Survey Replication (NCS-R). *Archives of General Psychiatry, 62*(6), 617–627.

PANIC DISORDER

You *Have Anxiety?*

KELLY ORBISON[1]

"*You* have anxiety?" People often ask with surprise. "But you're so calm and peaceful! I would have *never* guessed it!" It's true. I'm not high strung or a classic type-A personality. I feel calm a lot of the time. I have many friends who confide in me because I'm a calming presence for them and a good listener. But, internally, I've struggled with anxiety and panic since I was 26 years old.

My first panic attack happened when I was traveling for spring break with my mom. I was about to graduate with my master's in social work and wondered what adventures might be open to me in Colorado. My mom was recovering from divorce after 22 years of marriage and was up for some fun herself. After a few days in Colorado Springs, we hopped in the car and made our way up toward Estes Park. Nearing Denver during rush hour, my mind wandered as I drove with gorgeous green mountains surrounding us under skies promising snow.

My dad also struggled with anxiety and panic, his beginning in childhood. When I was growing up, he often drove alone because he didn't want anyone to see him panic. I know now that he had a lot of feelings of embarrassment around his anxiety, even though he faced it with courage driving to work every day. But, as a child, I don't remember picking up on it at all. My younger brother will say to me, "Don't you remember when...?" but the only memory for me is the imprinted feeling of shame when my own anxiety arises.

So, for some reason, while I was driving with all the beauty and serenity the Rockies had to offer, a random thought entered my head, "I wonder what it was like for dad when he couldn't drive?" and BOOM—it was like my body, genetically predisposed for this stuff, had been waiting for an invitation and jumped me right in to a full-blown panic attack. I felt huge waves of warm adrenaline surging across my chest and back, my hands were shaking, and I felt scared that I was losing control—whatever that meant.

---

[1]Kristin, theanxietygirl.com. Reprinted with permission.

"I've got to pull over," I said, feeling like I could barely drive the car. Looking back at that pivotal moment, I know that even though I felt out of control, I still very carefully put on my turn signal, changed lanes, and exited the highway before asking my mom to take over at the wheel. Catching my breath, a part of me knew I had experienced a panic attack, but was still utterly bewildered at why it happened and how quickly it came on, taking over body and mind.

If I go back further, I can remember having existential angst as a grade school child. Lying in bed at night, my mind would wander to "I wonder what happens when I die? Is there a heaven? What does forever mean or feel like?" Adrenaline would begin racing alongside my brain when these thoughts popped up, and the impulse to get away from the feelings was overwhelming. Before I knew it, I was running down the stairs as fast as my feet would carry me, landing in my mother's arms, crying, "I don't want to die!"

If you've never had a panic attack before, it feels as scary as if someone jumped out from a dark alley and put a gun to your head, leaving you pleading for your life. You would do whatever it took to get away and fast. In the case of panic, though, you look around, body shaking, heart racing, adrenaline coursing, and see that you're simply driving a car, presenting to colleagues at work, or shopping for groceries. It's so intense that in the height of panic, the survival instinct kicks in and it seems like a toss-up whether you'll make it out alive or with your mental faculties in place.

I've learned over the years that if I had been able to simply experience the symptoms without creating a story about them, it would have been no big deal and the sensations would have melted away. David Barlow, PhD, founder, and director emeritus, Center for Anxiety and Related Disorders at Boston University, cites that up to 10% of the population regularly experiences panic, but these people don't label it as such. This is fascinating to me. How we attribute meaning to our experience and symptoms has much to do with how much we suffer. In the case of my first panic attack, I quickly moved to catastrophic thoughts like:

What if this happens all the time?
I can't function when I'm panicking!
What if I'm the woman who stopped driving at 26 years old!
Something's very wrong with me!
I'd better not tell anyone or they'll think I'm crazy!

Although the stories we tell ourselves are not rational, they feel true because we're trying to make sense of what just happened and stay safe. Who would believe that those crazy intense sensations were not dangerous? I believed the story created in my head, and it didn't take long before I feared I would always panic while driving on the highway. In no time, I greatly limited my interstate driving in hopes I could keep panic at bay. When I did venture out, I felt better if a "safe person" came along just in case I needed to pull over. Before long, though, I worried about getting anxious on "regular" roads that were unfamiliar, and the avoidance that was meant to reduce my anxiety simply built more fear.

As a perpetual student, I bought a workbook and started doing my homework. I wanted to be over this problem *yesterday* and kept asking the rhetorical question, *"Why is this happening to me?"* Reading stories of others' experiences was not as comforting as I had expected. Instead, I realized that panic could strike anywhere, not just on the highway.

What? People can panic during a haircut? Oh, no! That would be so weird and embarrassing! Panic attacks can pop up at work? Everyone thinks I'm calm and competent—what if that's not true and I'm just a fraud? I used to like flying, but now I see that people with panic often feel trapped on the plane. What if I freak out on an airplane and can't get off? Why am I getting scared by these stories? These people are not me. Uh-oh, what if my panic gets so bad that I never really recover and they have to lock me up?

I was being hijacked by irrational worries that would never happen. But patterns of fear and avoidance quickly began wearing deep grooves in my brain and I began to feel like a spider caught in a web.

Back at school, I sought out help through student counseling. In graduate school, our program encouraged all budding social workers to try therapy; knowing how it felt to be on the other side of the couch was an important piece of our education. With this connection in place already, I went for advice on how to cure my anxiety in the last few weeks of school. Looking back, I feel I could have been saved years of struggle if I had been given proper direction and wise counsel at this crucial point. What I needed was information, coping skills, and someone to help get me back on the road as soon as possible; I needed to know with absolute certainty that anxiety did not have the power I imagined; and I needed to be surrounded by people taking on similar challenges and having success.

Instead, I was encouraged to take Xanax before driving and my case was closed at the end of the school year with the message "you'll be fine." I spent the next four years trying to find a pathway out of anxiety. I met with a few recommended therapists who told me to relax, lighten up, do yoga, and try EMDR; this was a stage and I would eventually outgrow it. Although these were lovely people with good intentions and excellent stress management skills, none of them really knew what it took to effectively work with anxiety disorders. I was surprised at how often medication was suggested as the first course of action. Eventually, I sampled a few SSRI antidepressant medications, but always stopped short because of the side effects. From reading everything I could get my hands on, I knew that anxiety was treatable without medication and, honestly, I worried that when I decided to come off of the meds, anxiety would just be hanging outside my door, saying, "Hey, welcome back! I've been waiting for you!"

Isolation is such a big part of anxiety for me. For a long time, I knew there were other people out there struggling like I was in silence, but I couldn't seem to find them. One day, my neighbor, a dynamic young lawyer, gave me the gift of disclosing his panic disorder. That exchange gave me the courage to slowly open up to others about my anxiety, and I found that many people had the same or similar issues—doctors, teachers, social workers, lawyers—educated, successful people who were living with anxiety and still doing amazing things with their lives. Many were on SSRI medication, in counseling, and, often, were frustrated with not making enough progress. I came to realize that there are a lot of people quietly struggling with chronic anxiety and panic, wondering, "Is this as good as it gets?" Years later, as a way to reach out to others and build a community, I would start a blog called "The Adventures of Anxiety Girl."

My turning point came when I became a mother and realized that I needed a better game plan to tackle my fears, not only for myself, but to set a positive example and have resources in place should my children need them. My dad did the best he could with his anxiety and the little information available at the time, but it wasn't something we talked about until I was a young adult. I wanted to be open with my kids, teach them how to work with fear and not have it be such a secret.

Over the next few years I found books by Jerilyn Ross, Claire Weekes, R. Reid Wilson, and Dave Carbonell that were hopeful, discussing the benefits of exposure practice; that is, purposefully putting yourself into feared situations, learning to work with the thoughts and feelings, and not running away. I enlisted the help of a new therapist, and we spent an hour each week driving the local highways and bridges together, often employing her clever distraction techniques. During the week, I also practiced on my own and kept a log tracking routes, thoughts, and emotions.

I would love to say that this was the end of the story and I was cured, but my anxiety was still not going away. Some routes got better, but during others I still had big waves of adrenaline and wondered what I was doing wrong. My therapist was enthusiastic and helpful, but we both grew frustrated when her distraction techniques were not making the anxiety go away.

"I don't know why you're still feeling anxious during your practice drives," she pondered. "I think it goes back to your wiring and we should consider Celexa. It won't be forever, but if you go on for about two years it's going to help reset your brain. When you come off of it, you'll be happily surprised that your anxiety is completely manageable. I'm just not sure what else to do."

Research tells us now that using distraction to cope with anxiety can actually make it worse, but neither of us knew that then. I wasn't sure what to do next, but knew that medication was not what I wanted. With another roadblock up, I stopped counseling and kept working on my own. All the while, motherhood was teaching me that I had innate strength and power and that coping with anxiety was within my reach. After my second child was born, a friend recommended a great therapist who used to direct the anxiety clinic at our local medical school. I enjoyed her straightforward, spunky nature and her depth of knowledge. She often spoke of not looking for a cure but for finding acceptance. Each week I heard that I could handle whatever anxiety threw at me. Again, I came in with my practice charts, taking back most of the driving routes and bridges I had avoided.

By this time, anxiety was also starting to bother me in some social situations and public speaking. Anxiety's insidious nature is that what we fear is what fear can do to us. So, even though I was getting desensitized to anxiety on all of my regular driving routes, at my core I still feared that having a panic attack could drag me down into a constant state of fear. You start to feel like just when you've climbed to the top of one mountain, there are three or four still waiting on the other side.

I still held on to the hope that if I could only work harder, I could be cured. I desperately wanted to go back to the person I was before that first panic attack in the mountains of Colorado. I grew tired of hearing that I just needed to accept my anxiety. How was this acceptable? I had always been a person that could achieve what I wanted to if I was willing to really work. My counselor would look at me and say with kindness, "Kristin, there's no one in my practice that works harder than you. You just need to accept that this is how it is. Maybe it's time to think about medication? With your genes and wiring, this might be what you need, and there's no shame in taking meds."

I trusted and liked this woman a lot, so I decided to give Lexapro a try this time. It didn't take away all the anxiety, but it did help a little until I became pregnant with our third child and needed to get off of the medication. During my third trimester, though, panic started popping up again, and, during those moments, I felt very afraid that I was getting swept away by panic. "What if I panic during labor?" "What if I have to have a cesarean?" "I can't live like this." Now a childbirth educator and doula, I felt (my own) pressure to do a "good job" in birth and knew enough about hospitals to be afraid of having to enter them. I felt stuck in anticipatory anxiety with no way out.

As with all irrational anxiety, none of these worries came to pass. I had the most amazing, powerful home birth with our third child. Sitting with my counselor a few months later and telling her my birth story, she said, "Wasted energy. All that worry and wasted energy." I agreed. By the time I hit three months postpartum, my anxiety had come back with a vengeance. What if I go crazy? What if I can't parent my children? I'm losing my mind for certain this time. Again, the intangible hold of anxiety that I couldn't just go out and drive the same loop over and over again and make go away. On the outside I looked calm and cool, but inside I felt the constant threat of storms and took solace in another round of low-dose Lexapro. An unintended consequence of the medication, I believe, is that you start thinking you can't do the work on your own. I stayed on the medication for six months and slowly came off of it because I knew there was no freedom in having to take a pill every day.

As I kept working with my body and mind, the research also caught up, bringing about new ideas and results in best practices. I began to realize that success was being willing to show up and feel any sensations that came out to play. In my willingness to feel everything, there was a way out. I dog-eared the pages about attitude and the use of paradox in *Don't Panic* by Dr. R. Reid Wilson. I learned that it's not only okay to be anxious; it's what I need to seek out on a daily basis. The more I sincerely want to feel the symptoms of anxiety and panic, the stronger my skills will grow. This is not easy work, but it felt freeing because it was no longer my job to make anxiety go away. Yes, this was a mental trick, but when I had enough courage to ask my anxiety to show up and to "bring it on," it actually grew bored and went away.

Mulling over the ideas of struggle, acceptance, and paradox, I wrote a blog post early on called "When King Kong Sits on Your House, Invite Him In."

So, I have this comic strip image in my head where a woman is inside of her house. The sun is shining through the open windows and as she gazes out, she sees anxiety (personified as a little chimpanzee) lurking outside by the back fence, climbing in the trees. She's gripped by fear and begins locking the windows, sweat beads forming on her brow. Over and over again, she peers out the window from behind the now closed curtains, while the chimp (anxiety) opens the front door and taps her on the shoulder.

The woman, already hypervigilant and on guard for any sight of the beast, tackles the chimp to the ground, puts it in a head lock and kicks it back outside. She throws all the locks, as she trembles and shakes, and puts a chair beneath the doorknob to keep it from coming back in. The more frightened she gets, the bigger the chimp becomes until it's as big as King Kong and sitting on her house, it's eye filling up the entire window as it peers inside.

Finally, after trying everything she can think of to force him to leave (think of something else, call a safe person to help ground her, turn the music up loud, thumb through her anxiety workbook, get down on her knees and pray), she gives up and opens up the door. "Come on in," she gestures with exhaustion. As soon as the door is open, King Kong shrinks back down to the size of a baby chimp, and jumps into her lap. The woman strokes his soft fur, but offers nothing for him to sink his teeth into. Realizing that tonight he won't be getting fed, he slips out the back door, swings over the fence and moves onto the next guarded house.

With a head full of knowledge and years of practice, I still find it hard to muster up the courage to ask anxiety to "bring it on!" every day. I go through periods of time where I feel pretty good and others when my anxiety flares back up again. From experience, I know that choosing avoidance is scarier than feeling anxiety in the moment, so the hint of avoidance can serve as a motivator.

What still bothers me is the daily undercurrent of anxiety; the "what if" questions and images that rise to the surface with such ease. There's always a part of my brain that's on guard, waiting for anxiety to show up. I want to be prepared. I still feel like I've done my time and would like to be done with anxiety, thank you very much. I suppose this guru, anxiety, has valuable lessons I have not fully grasped yet.

Most days I work through anxious thoughts, if not feelings, and they seem to still focus on driving new routes, large bridges, anxious thoughts, and being anxious in front of other people. When anxiety feels overwhelming, I try to get out in the world and take it on through regular exposure practice or cognitive exposure. I'm also sensitive to making sure I'm exercising and practicing self-care. I work toward a welcoming, even anxiety-provoking, attitude. Ever so slowly, my ability to accept how I'm feeling grows stronger, and I'm thankful because the hand given to me could have been a lot worse.

My husband once suggested that I write a post about all the things that don't create anxiety for me (or that are important enough to do anyway), so here are a few: I've given birth naturally three times—twice at home; I like to rock climb; I've run a marathon and completed a handful of triathlons (two in open water); riding on the back of a motorcycle is big fun to me; I like to get past small talk and really connect with people; I teach childbirth classes; I spent a year living on top of a mountain taking kids through caves, behind waterfalls, and on long hikes; I can ask the hard questions and sit with other people's pain; I have attended about 20 births as a doula and flown to Italy, California (once by myself while I was pregnant), and the Virgin Islands.

It's important to remember that anxiety is just one small piece of what makes me who I am. Or, as a fellow anxiety superhero once said, "Anxiety is just the Side B to being a highly passionate, creative, and empathic person. I wouldn't give one side up for the other."

Susan's Story

SUSAN LUDEMAN

The day of the space shuttle *Challenger* disaster—January 28, 1986—was the day that my life changed forever.

While trying to focus on the news, I became increasingly preoccupied with physical symptoms that intensified over the day. My heart was pounding, my chest was tight, I felt lightheaded, and I seemed to be having difficulty breathing. After several hours of struggling with these symptoms, I decided to go to my doctor's office. But after getting in my car, I felt that I could not drive. I asked a coworker to take me. We had not gotten far before I instructed him to skip the doctor's office and head straight for the emergency room at the nearest hospital.

I felt as though I could not breathe, my blood was pounding in my ears, my heart was racing, my knees were weak, my vision seemed "dark," and I felt as though I was going to pass out. I thought I *must* be having a heart attack.

In the ER, a nurse asked if the events of the day had upset me. I knew instantly what she meant: that somehow my physical symptoms were connected to "upset"—something psychological. This was *inconceivable* to me. I was *certain* I was having a heart attack. But if it had really been a heart attack, I would now be in the Guinness Book of Records for the longest heart attack on record!!

I answered the nurse: "No." The space shuttle disaster had not upset me. Of course, my answer was not even remotely true. But I needed to make it clear that what was going on in my mind had nothing to do with what was happening to my body. My symptoms were so strong that they *couldn't* be psychological!

After six hours and various tests in the ER, a doctor told me I had probably had a panic attack, *but* I might have a heart problem and I should see a cardiologist. In the meantime, I should go home, take Valium, and stay in bed.

The doctor's advice to stay in bed was possibly the worst I could have received. It triggered a reaction of fear and reinforced my idea that something dreadful could happen to me at any moment. I only had a vague notion of what a panic attack might be and, thus, I focused on the heart attack scenario. This episode of January 28, 1986, was so powerful, that to this day, when I mean to say "panic attack," I often say "heart attack" by mistake!

What followed was a nightmare that lasted five years.

I had the "million dollar workup." I saw cardiologists, neurologists, respiratory specialists, and gynecologists, each ordering their own medical tests. At the end of each workup, all I ever came away with was a prescription for Valium or Xanax.

For the first nine months, the Xanax was actually very helpful. But then my symptoms began to reappear. At this point, I felt very trapped. The Xanax wasn't working like it once had, but I was afraid to stop it. If I stopped it, my symptoms might get even worse. I felt I was in a worse "fix" than when I had started.

I kept trying to get help from doctors. On two occasions, doctors gave me a new medication with instructions to simply stop the Xanax and start the new drug. On both occasions, I experienced a huge increase in the symptoms that I was trying to get rid of. I assumed the new medications were not working and quickly went back to Xanax. I now know that what I experienced was actually withdrawal from the Xanax. For many people—including myself—changes in anxiety medications are best accomplished gradually.

With all the medical examinations, tests, and drugs, I received no help in treating the cause of my symptoms. The most common explanation I was given was that "it was *just nerves.*"

Once, after describing my ordeal in detail to a new doctor, he had a simple reply: "It doesn't sound so horrible to me." I felt stunned, shamed, and humiliated. Perhaps, he *meant* to say that my condition was not life threatening. But he failed to understand that it *was horrible to me.*

I did my best to adjust to my condition. I became a catalog shopper and a 7-Eleven shopper, because I could be "in and out" in the shortest possible time. I avoided "unnecessary" trips out of the house, and I avoided as many social activities as possible.

My life revolved around two things: avoidance and planning for escape. I invented excuses I could use to "get out of" any situation where I would feel anxiety. While the successful avoidance would initially bring relief, I soon realized how small my world was becoming. I became increasingly isolated, lonely, and demoralized. I was not *physically* housebound—but *mentally* I certainly was.

During this time, there was one thing I could not avoid: my work. I was teaching college chemistry—a position that had once been a tremendous joy in my life but had turned into a nightmare. I walked into every lecture believing that I would pass out before the hour was complete. I dreaded seeing students at my office door knowing that this could mean I would be "trapped" in a conversation.

One doctor had recommended a "change of scene" as a cure for my problems. So, when an opportunity arose for me to move from Washington, D.C., to Baltimore, I decided to give it a try. The move meant giving up something that I had once loved—teaching. But I felt that I could no longer live up to my responsibilities to my students. I thought that if I could get away from the anxiety of the teaching commitments for a little while, perhaps I would "get better" and could then return to teaching.

In Baltimore, I found myself in a new environment with new challenges and expectations—and an *escalation* of my symptoms. So much for "change of scene" as a cure!

I found a new gynecologist. At the end of our first meeting, he was clear and firm in his message to me: *He* could not help me, but I *had* to see a mental health professional. He gave me the name and phone number of a psychiatrist he recommended.

Other doctors had vaguely suggested that maybe I should "see someone." But this was the first time I had been given a referral to a mental health professional. Also, I was ready. I had really "hit bottom." I felt that I had nowhere else to turn.

I made an appointment with the psychiatrist. At the end of our first meeting, he said I could continue to see him or I could see an expert. Thank goodness I still had the presence of mind to make a rational decision. I said I wanted the expert.

And that is how my five-year nightmare came to an end.

My first meeting with Dr. Sally Winston was the turning point in my life. Within a few minutes, she was describing the symptoms I had been experiencing for five years! She was the first to explain the physiological basis of my symptoms—the effects of hyperventilation and adrenaline surges. She was the first to acknowledge that my symptoms were *real*, and there was a *cause*. She explained that my symptoms were horrible but not dangerous. And Dr. Winston was the first to give me a *plan*—a plan for *recovery*—and a reason to hope. (Note: Dr. Winston is the co-director of the Anxiety and Stress Disorders Institute of Maryland. She has an outstanding Web site at www.anxietyandstress.com.)

The foundation of Dr. Winston's plan was education. The first book she suggested was Claire Weekes's *Hope and Help for Your Nerves*. It was amazing to see my fears, thoughts, and actions described in print—it made me feel less alone.

Learning coping skills—life skills, really—was also part of the education process. Dr. Winston taught me specific skills that addressed both the mental and physical aspects of anxiety disorder. Here are some of the skills that were *key* in my recovery process. (I've included links to some helpful pages on paniccure.com.)

1. Learning to use an "anxiety scale" of "0" to "10." All levels of anxiety are not the same. For example, being in a restaurant might be a "10," but being in a grocery store might be a "6." Discovering this means you can start your recovery work by going to grocery stores before you go to restaurants. Using the anxiety scale is a lot more helpful than saying "I can't do anything—everything is hard!".

2. Learning to do slow, abdominal breathing. See this page for a similar breathing technique: www.paniccure.com/Approaches/Meditation/Belly_Breathing.htm

3. Learning to stay "in the now": focusing on the present instead of worrying about the future.

4. Learning to *accept* feelings of anxiety. This attitude of acceptance actually lowers anxiety. See this page for a good explanation of this idea: www.paniccure.com/Short_Essays/Allowing.htm

5. Learning to correctly identify emotions (for example, "I am angry, not anxious").

6. Learning to correctly estimate the risk that a scary event might happen. (See this page: www.paniccure.com/Approaches/CBT/Mastering_Panic/Pizza-7.htm)

As I became more confident and knowledgeable, I began to take on more aspects of Dr. Winston's plan for recovery. I participated in "in vivo" or "exposure" therapy, which means going to places and putting yourself in situations that actually provoke anxiety. This is all about facing your fears, and it is not easy! You really have to be willing to experience the discomfort—to be willing to suffer!

Initially, my in vivo experiences were guided by a therapist. She planned the sessions and the degree of difficulty and helped me through each outing. In a grocery store, for example, she would have me go down every aisle, read labels, and select the longest checkout line. Many of these sessions were about learning how to slow down, how to focus on the moment, and how to wait—whether it be in a checkout line, in a traffic jam, or in a conversation.

Doing these outings on a regular basis is called "practicing." As I continued to do my outings, it was essential for me to learn to accept my feelings and go on. I could see my progress, and I learned that the key to recovery is practice, practice, practice! (See this page: www.paniccure.com/Overcoming_Agoraphobia/Practice_key.htm)

Dr. Winston suggested that I have both individual and group therapy sessions. The group therapy was difficult for me, as it was hard for me to express my personal thoughts and feelings in a group setting. But I learned to do better—and this was extremely important in breaking the isolation I had felt.

My favorite therapy experiences were my individual sessions with Dr. Winston. Here, I had the opportunity to explore the underlying causes of my anxiety, as well as strengthen my new skills.

So, Dr. Winston's plan for recovery included both "behavioral" and "cognitive" therapy—practicing specific tasks as well as changing my attitudes. Through this approach, the tasks are transformed into a meaningful exploration of self.

For me, the concept of "recovery" involves an ongoing process of understanding, coping, and succeeding. I still can experience uncomfortable levels of anxiety, and sometimes this anxiety leads to a panic attack. But today, compared with my pretreatment days, there is a *big* difference in how I feel and how I respond. I know what is happening and I know how to deal with it. I have already had my worst panic attacks—the ones that occurred when I had no concept of what was happening to me. That level of extended fear and incapacitation can never happen again. I know too much now.

When I first met Dr. Winston, I told her I wanted my old life back. But what happened, through learning to deal with my anxiety, was something different. I found a *new* life—a *better* life—one with greater self-confidence and self-awareness.

There are two stories that I like to tell. I always liked dangling earrings, but I never thought I was mature enough or "cool" enough to wear them. Now, as a result of learning how to deal with my anxiety, I wear them. And every time I put them on, I get a charge out of it! It is a powerful symbol to me of how much I have grown.

The second story is from my experience at an Anxiety Disorders Association of America conference I attended in 2001. One night, there was to be a dance. My first thought was "I will *never* go." But I *did* go—and I danced! It was the first time in 30 years that I danced while sober!! And I so enjoyed it that, when I went home, I took dancing lessons—because I intended to dance again!

Panic—and learning to deal with it and its causes—has opened new and wonderful facets of my life that I never imagined possible.

I started with the grocery store, but it has become *so* much more. I could not have done this alone—I had support from my family, from others with anxiety disorders, and, most important, from Dr. Sally Winston. In Dr. Winston, I had a therapist who made me believe I could get better and have a better life. I trusted her, and it has made all the difference.

I hope that you, too, can find that belief, that support, that hope. And I hope that you will go out and buy the dangling earrings and, in the words of a popular song, "when you have the choice to sit it out or dance, I hope you dance!"

PHOBIAS

On the Outside Looking In

Daniela Grazia[2]

Many people know what it's like to have an allergy to something. They do what they have to in order to avoid whatever it is they have a bad reaction to. Imagine if that catalyst were people. Then what would you do?

At the age of 12, I boarded the school bus for the first time on my way to begin junior high school. It was then that I was overcome by panic and an overwhelming sense of alienation and detachment from those around me. I wanted to flee, but I couldn't. I sat immobilized in my seat, unable to speak. This is when my real issues began, although I believe I'd already been showing earlier signs of social anxiety disorder (SAD).

It's been a daily struggle ever since. I lived with this torture for over 30 years, mostly in silence, too ashamed to expose this humiliating part of myself. I've made considerable progress the past several years, but I continue to battle the effects of this disorder on a daily basis. Today, at the age of 44, I've finally managed to achieve a fairly "normal" existence through perseverance, the love of family and a few close friends, a sense of longing to "fit" in the world, and the knowledge that I couldn't end my own life. The journey to get to this point was nothing short of painful and pure torture.

As a child, I thoroughly enjoyed myself by easily engaging other kids and being involved with whatever games or mischief the neighborhood kids were getting into. I was more than eager to try new things. Each new endeavor was so exciting. I was good at sports and wanted to be part of whatever was going on at the time, be it softball, tennis, roller skating, skateboarding, etc. I loved to laugh and make others laugh. I wanted to be chosen first for the team, lead of the play, or winner of the spelling bee. I wanted to be noticed for my efforts. I gave whatever it was at the time my focus and energy and wanted to do it well. Life for me then was full of possibilities, excitement,

---

and happiness. Friends, family, and teachers commented on my energy and the fact I was always laughing and enjoying myself.

Looking back, I realize this need for excelling also brought with it an excessive sensitivity to criticism or not being acknowledged for my efforts. Perfection is what I sought, and this expectation for myself brought on undue stress and anxiety. I couldn't help it, though; it was who I was. I'd take the smallest criticism much harder than it was meant to be and it would stay with me for days. At the age of eight, I was hospitalized after complaining of chronic stomach pain and not wanting to attend school. The problem stemmed from a teacher who was more critical than I was used to. She was harsh when she spoke, and the good grades I was used to were harder to achieve. Of course, nothing was discovered by the tests that were performed on me.

I'm sure this need for "perfection," the extreme sensitivity to being perceived in a negative light, and the stress it brought with it were the initial symptoms of SAD. After that day on the bus, things gradually began to change for me. The transition from grade school to junior high was overwhelming. I was being separated from the kids and the routine I'd grown accustomed to. It was a much bigger world, with many more kids, and I was a very small part of it.

I was still able to engage other kids and make some new friends in school, but getting on that bus was excruciating. The other kids noticed I was backward and quiet, and I was targeted as one of the kids they could pick on. I was so self-conscious and full of anxiety, my brain wouldn't work to put together a sentence let alone be able to stand up for myself. My entire body tensed, my facial muscles tightened, my mouth went dry, and my gut knotted. It was extremely uncomfortable to even ask for a seat. I sat rigid and quiet, anticipating the moment I could flee. I would ride the bus when it was cold out, but when the first warm weather came, I walked the three miles home to avoid it.

I kept this part of me all to myself and hidden. I didn't understand what was wrong with me. I was sure it was just me and who I was. I couldn't even tell my own mother. She was very loving but her expectations were also very high. I knew the expectation she and I both had for me was that I would make something great of myself. I'd come home angry and exhausted from the stress and humiliation of the day and would take it out on my family. I was so irritated with myself for being this pathetic person.

In grade school, my gym teacher was also the coach of the junior high girls' softball team. She saw how well I'd played and asked me to join the team. I was thrilled and accepted, but once I was in that team environment, the same feelings as on the bus took over. I felt detached and out of place—like a stranger in a foreign land. My body tensed and I was paralyzed with anxiety. I did not feel like a part of the team. I sat off to the side by myself, unable to engage or enjoy myself. It was too uncomfortable, so I quit and cried on the way home trying to understand what was happening to me.

As time went on, this became the norm for me in social situations. I managed to make a few friends in school, but eventually, I became uncomfortable even around them. There were only a few situations I was comfortable in—the most comfortable being when I was alone. It became very difficult to attend school every day. I craved for the end of the day to come when I could walk home alone and be free from the anxiety for a while. I could feel my entire body loosen up, and it was incredibly freeing. At the same time, I felt extremely lonely. It was so difficult to be around people, and yet I hated to be alone. It was a ruthless contradiction.

I began a life of pretending just to fit in and be part of my surroundings. I pretended to fit in and enjoy myself when really, inside, I was a quivering mess. I wanted so badly just to be like everyone else but I couldn't relax enough to let things happen naturally. My actions and conversations became forced. I laughed when I thought I should laugh. I went out of my way to please people, thinking it was the only way I could get them to like me.

As with many other people who suffer with SAD, I discovered at a young age how alcohol could help me feel less inhibited, enough to be part of my surroundings. It was the start of a vicious cycle. Over the years, it would become my crutch. Many times the decision of whether I would attend a social function was based on the whether there would be alcohol available. I became very choosy as to where I would go.

Holding a conversation became an impossible task. I couldn't maintain eye contact or focus on the words coming from the other person's mouth. I could only focus on how my body was reacting—the way my facial muscles tightened, my face grew red, and I was acutely aware of my awkwardness. I stumbled and stammered over my words and I just knew the other person could see all this and was thinking what a strange person I was. I'd say I'd have somewhere to be and hurry off while all the way bombarding myself with destructive self-talk, "You're such an idiot!" "You're pathetic!" "You're nothing!"

The look on my face became that of a permanent frown compared to when I was younger and always smiling. I started walking with my head down. I became very depressed and started having thoughts of suicide, but I knew no matter how badly I felt, I wouldn't have the courage to see it through. I was stuck in a living hell—my own head.

Many times I sat around tables and watched other people talking and laughing so easily—as if it took no effort at all—while I sat so uneasily wanting to flee and yet wanting so badly to fit in. I so envied them. They lived a life outside themselves while I was living a life inside my own head. One that started telling me what a pathetic excuse for a human being I was. I wanted so desperately to feel a part of their world, but I didn't. As hard as I tried, I just couldn't. I was not a part of their world any longer. I could only watch from the outside, and it was an extremely agonizing and lonely place.

Over the years, I watched the friends I did have grow as people and make their way in the world. They made new friends, developed new interests, and took part-time jobs after school. They moved easily from one phase of their lives to the next while my world stood still. I knew I couldn't take my own life, so all I could do was push myself to get through each day and then the next. I didn't want to live this way, but I also didn't want to die. I cried all the time when no one could see me. No one knew this secret I was keeping. My parents both worked evenings, so many nights were spent alone. I didn't want the people closest to me to know the person I was out in the world.

I wanted desperately to be doing the things my friends were doing. I would've liked to have earned my own money, but both attempts at working during my teens ended horribly. I tried to work in a pizza shop, but when a customer approached the counter my body tensed. I became incredibly awkward and stumbled and stammered over my words. I could barely look at them. It was too uncomfortable, and I knew I wasn't doing a good job. I felt I was only embarrassing myself and quit after a short time.

As a senior in high school, I made one more attempt to work at a new local grocery store that was opening. We were given good training before the store opening as cashiers using scanners. It was difficult just going through the training, but when the first customer approached me to check out, I froze. I became very awkward and clumsy, nearly dropping the items as I scanned them. I felt the customer was watching my every movement so closely and thinking what a klutzy and inept employee I was. I barely lasted a week.

I was always so concerned about what others thought of me to the point that if a car was following behind me, I was sure the driver was criticizing how I drove and I'd try to drive at the "perfect" speed—not too fast or too slow. As I walked through the mall, I believed all eyes were on me and people were saying what a strange person I was. Walking through the grocery store, I'd be sure to check the aisle for someone I knew or someone who I thought knew someone I knew. I would quickly move to the next aisle in an effort to avoid conversation. I was sure they saw me doing this and were thinking how strange and unfriendly I was. If I wanted to go out for a walk and saw someone approaching on the street, I would wait till they passed before going out. I'd also take the path I thought would be least traveled by others. It was nearly impossible for me to sign my name in front of the teller at the bank. If I had an item I wanted to return to the store, I'd much rather keep whatever it was than have to deal with customer service. It would take me days to make a phone call. I would practice for days what I wanted to say and even then the words came out jumbled.

Attending family functions was the absolute worst for me. Our extended family is quite large, with many aunts, uncles, and cousins. These people were family but it didn't matter. It also didn't matter how long I'd known someone. SAD doesn't discriminate that way. At family functions, I did not fit. I didn't have a thing to say. The others talked and laughed, enjoying each other's company while I stood off to the side feeling completely awkward and out of place. I didn't know what to do with myself. I was so self-conscious—acutely aware of my ineptness and movements. If it wasn't obvious to someone watching me how uncomfortable I was, I'd be completely amazed. I'd find a place to hide—the bathroom or outdoors—to cry and beat myself into the ground.

I realized as a teenager my behavior was mirroring that of my dad's. It was obvious how uneasy he was in social situations. I watched him go back inside and wait till someone passed on the street before exiting the house. He fought my mother to go to family functions or basically anywhere. Others talked and laughed around him while he sat quietly and apprehensively. He came home from his long hours at work with tension and sadness written all over his face. He'd sit alone on the back porch for hours—I'm sure thinking of the humiliation he had experienced that day and wondering how he was going to get through the next. He could barely sign his own signature because his hands had started to shake so badly. I, better than anyone, understood how exhausting and excruciating it could be to be forced to be around people for any extended period of time. It was so difficult to watch him. You expect your parents to be strong. It made me ache inside to know he was struggling the same way. I knew I had inherited my traits from him, but as of yet, I didn't know there was a name for it. I assumed it was just our personalities. I thought to myself that I could never have children and subject them to this kind of life. It would be unbearable to know they hurt this way.

As the end of our senior year in high school approached, my friends talked about college and their future plans. Some attended college close by, while others went away. I simply said I wanted to take some time off first, but in reality, I had no idea where I was headed. I didn't know in what environment I could function. I was so afraid and worried of what my future would be. I really didn't see one for myself.

After a few months of sitting at home with my parents, I decided I had to do something. I couldn't just sit around doing nothing but thinking how depressing my life was. I had to push myself to move on. Since I'd done well in school because it was something I could do on my own, I decided I could handle sitting in a classroom again. I didn't have to participate. I didn't have to talk to anyone if I didn't want to. So that's what I did. But just walking into the building brought on a very strong and uneasy feeling of alienation. I didn't belong there. I didn't fit in there. It was another new world filled with people I didn't know. I went to my classes, didn't speak to anyone, and went home. If I had a break between classes, I would go to a drive-thru, then go to a park to sit by myself. While my friends were having the best time of their lives, I was headed into the worst time of mine.

Things began to decline further for me. I began to experience a "darkness" and "heaviness" that was truly crushing. I felt myself becoming "numb." A sense of impending doom hovered over me from the time I woke. My mind raced with dark, negative thoughts. I was struggling to get through each day, and truly, every hour of every day was a struggle. I didn't want to go out in the world, but I didn't want to not be in it either. What an excruciating place to be. I remember thinking, "I wish the earth would just open up and swallow me in."

I decided I had to talk to someone. It was getting too difficult to live. I went to a school counselor because I really didn't know where to turn. I thought it would be a good starting point. When facing and talking to people is the issue, it's very difficult to get across what it is you need to get across. I tried the best I could to explain how sad and lonely I felt and that the only time I could relax and feel calm was when I was by myself. He said I was making myself feel sad and lonely by being alone. I hadn't heard there was something called social anxiety yet, and apparently not even the counselors had. I left feeling even more defeated and alone. No one could understand and no one could help me. I was truly on my own in the world, in this hell which was in my own head.

I experienced my first panic attack during this time. While sitting in the classroom, I could see the professor's lips moving but was unable to comprehend the words coming from her mouth. A sense of panic overtook me and I was unable to breathe. I fled the classroom to my car. My life spiraled out of control and I couldn't continue in school. I couldn't even drive. After years of inner turmoil, anxiety, and worry, I was breaking down. My mind and body had just had too much.

Still unaware there was a name for what I was dealing with, I was too ashamed to explain to my mother or friends. I believed it was me and who I was. I was this pathetic excuse for a human being. Only able to tell them I was depressed, I was treated for it with medication but received no counseling or hospitalization. The medicine only made me gain weight and feel extremely tired. The extreme anxiety had spiraled into a deep depression. I fought every day. I didn't want to end up in a mental facility, nor did I want to waste my life. In time, I made myself get out for walks, and eventually, I forced myself to go back to school. I was determined to finish, even though I didn't know in what capacity I'd be able to use my education out in the world.

In my entire life, I've only had a few people I felt comfortable being around. I can count them on one hand. I call these people my "comfort" people because while in their company I was able to relax and enjoy myself. The time I spent with them was incredibly freeing, and I craved it. In their company, I realized there was another person still there deep down inside trying desperately to escape. If I could just be this other person all the time, I could be productive, content, and feel I had some purpose for being in this world.

They have no idea how much I relied on them for some relief from the outside world. I clung to them as if they were my lifeline. They didn't need me to be happy or to make their way in the world, but I was truly lost without them. They were the reason why I got through each day—a reason to live and be in this world. Each time one of them moved forward in their life, it was a huge adjustment and loss to me. I felt a part of me leave with them. The loss felt as great as the death of a loved one.

I managed to graduate college with an associate degree, but I didn't give myself any credit for it. I wasn't able to give myself any recognition for the good things I did, but I sure knew how to put myself down when I didn't do something the way I thought I should. It was never my doing if something was accomplished; it was only by the efforts of others.

From my past limited experience in the work environment, I knew I had to find work that required minimal interaction. So for 16 years of my life, I worked in manufacturing environments. For the most part, I could work on my own, but there were instances I had to work in closer proximity to others. I would go an entire eight-hour shift without uttering more than a few words to the person next to me.

I felt bad for my coworker. Eight hours is long enough, without even having some conversation to help the time pass. I watched the others around me talking and laughing and wished so badly I was like them. The harder I tried to engage, the less I could think of to say. I became paralyzed with anxiety. My brain would not work to put together a sentence. At one point someone asked if I was mute because I spoke so infrequently. I wished I could work alone. I knew I was a hard worker, but social anxiety was such a hindrance.

At lunchtime, I was too uncomfortable to join the others in the cafeteria. I would go out to my car even when it was cold out. The others thought I was strange for doing that because I didn't smoke. I prayed for the shift to end so I could seek the solitude of my car and the drive home. All the way I cried and begged God to help me. I didn't want to go back the next day, but I knew I had to. I had to earn a living. Each day was as excruciating as the one before. There was no escape from this living hell.

It wasn't until my early 20s that I discovered there was a name for what I was experiencing. By chance one day, I came across an article in *Dear Ann Landers* and read a submission by a woman who worked as a nurse and loved her job but had great difficulty interacting with the patients. The response given to her was there was something then called social phobia and she might seek the advice of a doctor. As I read the symptoms listed for the disorder, I realized it was a description of me. I was ecstatic! Not that I was happy someone else was hurting this way, but it meant it wasn't just me and who I was. There was a name for it. I can't describe the relief I felt at that moment.

I spent countless hours on the Internet and in the library researching the disorder. I read articles online and bought books to learn how to get better. After I gained the courage to seek help, I made an appointment with a local therapist. I was elated to think someone would finally understand what I'd been dealing with and would help me get better. It turned out that I would be highly disappointed. My experiences with therapists over the years consisted of me talking and/or crying while they sat staring at the floor, the clock, or looking at me in disbelief. It was difficult even looking the therapist in the eye as I spoke, but I did the best I could. I was desperate for help. I'd learned from the books that what was necessary was to change my thought patterns and the way I perceived things to be in my head. I thought they would give me exercises to do to learn how to do this. Instead, I was given medications from which I got no relief.

With each new therapist, I had renewed hope, but each time was the same. I knew what I needed was to be treated at an intensive inpatient clinic but there were few around the country and they were very costly. My insurance would not cover the treatment. I'd basically given up on getting the help I needed. On my own, I practiced the exercises I learned from books I'd purchased. In the meantime, I continued to push myself to get through each day. I lay on my floor crying each day before leaving for work thinking of the humiliation I would experience that day. The best I would ever be was a factory worker, even though I knew I had the intelligence to have a more lucrative career. I was left with only a sense of degradation and self-loathing. I prayed desperately to God to keep me strong and dreamed of a day free of anxiety, hopelessness, and sadness—all the while keeping the horror of this secret to myself.

I tried discussing my issues with my comfort people but they couldn't understand it, not having gone through it themselves. They saw how quiet and "backward" I was around other people, but they didn't understand the depth of my inner turmoil. What they perceived was someone with a "subdued" personality who was able to engage in certain situations and somewhat enjoy herself when she was under the influence of alcohol or in the presence of people she was comfortable with. I'm sure what they thought was it couldn't be so much worse for me in other social situations. After all,

I was "okay" in their company. I was left to deal with this nightmare on my own.

The strain and humiliation of my "human inadequacies" not only consumed my hours at work, but invaded my every waking moment. This is what works to destroy the relationships you do have. SAD, like other afflictions, is extremely selfish. I was so consumed by how I was struggling inside and worrying how I was going to get through the next day that I was unable to live in the moment and experience the joy of being with my comfort people. At times, I felt I was sucking the life out of my vibrant friends. I felt I brought nothing to their lives compared to what they provided me.

When the company I worked for closed its doors and relocated after 12 years, I was scared, but also relieved that I wouldn't have to go to work every day. It would turn out to be a turning point in my life. When we were given the opportunity to return to school with our tuition paid, I found it a much better option than having to go out and look for work. I didn't have to speak to anyone if I didn't want to and the students' attention would be on the professor, not me. At least, that's how I remembered it.

The reality was that things had changed considerably since my previous college days. The focus now was teamwork. A lot of the projects assigned were to be completed as a team, and presentations were a big part of the curriculum. How was I ever going to do it? At one point, a professor inquired as to why I hadn't signed up for the extra credit presentation he offered at the end of the year to boost our average. He expressed it in a way that implied I wasn't interested in working for such an easy means of earning extra credit and it touched a nerve in me. I became angry at the implication and thought, "Sure, I've given up on so much in my life because I'm lazy and not interested in improving myself! What an ass!"

It just so happened the course was Organizational Behavior—a business psychology course. I was sure he'd heard of social anxiety, so I decided at that moment it was time for me to get better by speaking up about what I was dealing with. I also thought what better place to get help but in an educational environment? When I explained my issues to him, he apologized and said I was brave for returning to school.

With all the stress of the anticipatory anxiety that came with the team projects and presentations, a deep depression soon set in. I cried walking to class thinking I'd be unable to continue. Between classes, I found a secluded area in the library to contemplate the continued emptiness and hopelessness that was my life. I had to seek help again if for only to have someone to talk to. I didn't expect much more than that from my previous experiences with therapy.

The man I saw could not believe the lack of care I'd received. He explained a course of treatment for me and promised to help me feel better. I didn't know what it was exactly about him, but I believed him. In time, with his direction and support, I was able to learn the steps I needed in order to "deprogram" the automatic thoughts that had plagued me nearly every minute of every day. I had to recognize them, stop them, and replace them with more positive thoughts. I had to understand that these thoughts were not really how things were, but how I perceived them to be. This negative "self-talk" that had played over and over in my head for many years would not go away quickly or without much effort. I knew that. It would take time to "unlearn" it. I had become accustomed to only perceiving myself in a negative light to the point I was unable to look at myself in a mirror, afraid of the ugliness that would be looking back at me.

I managed to get through the presentations and the whole college experience, not with much dignity, mind you. I mostly memorized what it was I wanted to say or basically read from my notes without looking up, but I did get through it. It was a first huge step in the right direction. In December 2006, I graduated earning a bachelor of science degree in business administration with a 3.73 average (magna cum laude).

Right out of college, and after some very uncomfortable interviewing experiences, I was fortunate enough to be hired by a very patient and kind employer whose wife helped run his business. I was given good training and the job provided me very beneficial work experience in a subdued work environment. I couldn't have asked for a better first job out of college. Granted, it wasn't easy. I was extremely uneasy when either sat beside me during my training. I still stumbled over my words and my mind would go blank. Sometimes my fingers got knotted on the keyboard. Performance anxiety went hand-in-hand with the social anxiety. We were the same age, but I found it very difficult to maintain a conversation with either of them. This is what can make a grown woman feel completely inadequate and inept. I had to fight the negative self-talk. I had to give myself credit for even being there and attempting to hold this job. I went to work every day, and some days I would still go home crying, but I made myself go back the next day.

What choice did I have? Life went on and I wanted to be part of it. My world had stood still for too long. I had to earn a living. I had to be here, and I wanted my time on earth to not be so horrendous. I wanted to actually enjoy living again. I wanted a family, stability, and a home. This had been my pursuit for over 30 years. Unfortunately, after only two years with the company, the economy experienced a severe recession and my employer was forced to let me go. His acknowledgment and gratitude of my hard work went a long way to lifting my self-esteem. I could not be more appreciative of the experience he'd given me.

It was times like these I realized God was with me and had been with me all along. He didn't actually give me what I'd asked for (a life free of anxiety and sadness), but he put it within my reach. Looking back now, I see he had done this all along but he required me to work for it so I could be a better and stronger person.

Today, I work as a staff accountant for a medium-sized company. I went through the inner turmoil of the interviewing process all over again, and it took some time for me to integrate, but now I have more days than not of feeling I "fit in." Certain occasions still bring on heightened levels of anxiety—meetings, luncheons, and other social events still bring on the familiar feelings of uneasiness, but for the most part, on a daily basis, the subdued and quiet environment is a perfect working environment for someone with SAD. My social interaction is just enough to not make me feel overly anxious, and just enough to know I have a place in the world and am making a small contribution. I'm doing much better than I used to. I could not have held this job even 10 years ago.

There are still times I avoid social gatherings. There are still times SAD rears its ugly head and makes me cry, but I know I've made considerable progress. I attribute it to the love of my family and close friends, perseverance, and the understanding that others are dealing with much worse circumstances than I am. I thank God for being by my side and giving me the strength to continue on. This is what it's like to live with social anxiety disorder.

Mysophobia

CATHERINE TAYLOR

One thing a lot of people don't realize is that I haven't always been so scared of germs. Growing up, I had no problems sharing a Mountain Dew with my best friend or swiping food off my sister's plate. Of course, today, the thought of doing either of those is enough to make me nauseous.

The change came after I married. My first husband and his mother were very unclean people. He stopped brushing his teeth and only showered once or twice a week. His mother had a nasty rash that was spreading everywhere, but she wouldn't see a doctor. She used to sit at the dinner table and scratch it nonstop. I can remember watching little patches of her skin fall everywhere. The dog had a cut on his tail, so every time he wagged, blood would fly everywhere. I cleaned and cleaned, but the house could never get clean enough. There was dog hair, dog blood, and tiny patches of skin everywhere. I believe living like this is what caused me to be mysophobic.

The change in my thoughts and behavior was slow, so slow I didn't realize what was happening. At first I would just move away when someone coughed or sneezed. Then I started turning my head when my husband tried to kiss me. After a while, I started getting physical reactions such as my throat closing and getting physically sick. Then one day I was driving with a friend's 6-year-old son and he sneezed. My throat closed and I couldn't breathe. I almost wrecked my van trying to pull over so I could stop and get out. That's when I knew it was something serious, but I had no idea what it was.

That was about 10 years ago. Since then, my life has changed in many ways. I have a new husband. I live 2,000 miles away. I have a new career. I have a completely new life. But with everything that's changed, one thing has stayed the same. I still have that same intense fear of germs, although it's a little easier to deal with today. Living with it for the past 10 years has helped me to understand my triggers, so I'm able to predict what will set me off. Plus, I have a very understanding husband who helps me get through the daily attacks without making me feel guilty. Today, my life is structured around my fear of germs. Many of the things I do are to prevent the many anxiety attacks.

First of all, let me explain that I'm not scared of all germs. I can dig in the dirt and kiss my dogs on the mouth without even thinking about germs. The only germs I worry about are germs from people and germs from dairy products. I believe people, me included, are just covered with germs, both inside and out. Some people get offended by this. They think I think they're "dirty," but that's not it at all. It doesn't matter how often you shower, how often you brush your teeth, or how often you wash your hands. The germs are still there. And I include myself in this. I have the exact same physical reaction when I sneeze or cough. I know this might sound ridiculous, but I don't even want my own germs.

Food Anxiety

I deal with a lot of my food anxiety by using separation. Because I can't eat food that others may have touched or breathed on, I have my own separate fridge, freezer, and food cupboard. To ensure no one gets in them, they are right outside my bedroom door. I have to have my own milk, peanut butter, jelly, bread, lunch meat, and anything else that is meant to be opened and resealed. If my family runs out of milk or needs some of my food for some reason, I have to be the one to get it from my fridge and pour it. Plus, I have to rewash the cup before I pour the milk in it. For some reason, if I think the cup is contaminated, the act of pouring the milk into it will contaminate my milk. I know it doesn't make sense, but that's how it is.

When I cook, I stay in the kitchen the whole time so that I can make sure no one coughs or sneezes in the kitchen. If they do, I'll throw all the food away and start over. If I make too much and I know there will be leftovers, I have to save a little before anyone else even knows the food is done because it's the only way I can be sure that the food hasn't been contaminated. I always have to get my food first, which means a lot of people think I'm rude when I have a dinner party. Most of the time, I eat by myself. If I eat around family, I usually end up throwing my meal away because someone will sneeze or cough. In fact, if the person sitting next to me even breathes or talks in my direction, I can't eat my food. Sometimes, I will eat my meal before everyone else just so I can sit at the table with them while they're eating.

I can't eat food that someone else has cooked. I just can't be sure that they washed their hands. I can't be sure that they didn't sneeze or cough. I can't be sure that they didn't do a couple of taste tests using the same spoon. There's just too many what ifs. So if someone else decides to cook, I just make a small meal for myself. If we're going to a family dinner, I bring my own food and tell everyone it's because I'm on a diet. When we do eat at someone else's house, I keep my food covered with a napkin and only uncover it to take a bite. I tell them it's because of flies. My close family understands about my mysophobia and they aren't offended by my refusing to eat their food, but I'm too worried about offending those relatives we rarely see to tell them the truth.

Drinking is another problem for me. I can only drink out of containers that have lids. I can't drink tap water, so I buy water bottles by the case. I have special coffee cups with lids to drink my hot drinks. Those mugs and lids are washed and kept separate from anyone else's. Plus, I have plastic toppers to attach to my soda cans. If I leave the room and forget to take my drink, I throw it away because I can't be sure that someone didn't drink out of it. You wouldn't believe how many sodas and waters I waste.

My biggest problem with food is dairy. For some reason my mind associates dairy food with germs, like germs are more liable to grow in dairy products. My mind imagines all the little germs just swimming around the dairy products and I know they're waiting to infect me. If I want a glass of milk or if I want milk in my cereal, I have to drink it within 3 minutes of pouring it. Plus, there can't be anyone else around. If I'm eating a milk product and my husband enters the room, I yell "milk product!" and he knows to just turn around without saying a word. Oddly enough, my favorite food is cheese. I have to eat it within one week of buying it, and I only eat it if I'm alone in the house or if I'm alone in my room.

Other Germs

When someone sneezes or coughs while I'm in the same room as them, I have an actual physical reaction that lasts until I'm out of the room. My throat closes and won't open again until I'm safe. When this first started happening, I would freak out because I couldn't breathe. It was very embarrassing and sometimes scary because I came close to passing out a few times. But now I know if I just stand up and walk outside, everything will be okay. However, if someone sneezes or coughs on me, like on my arm or face, I get physically sick. And after vomiting, I have to seriously scrub in the shower, and then rub alcohol on whatever parts of me got sneezed on, but even then I can still feel the germs. Sometimes I swear I can feel the wetness from a sneeze for hours afterwards. But it's not just sneezing or coughing. I also get affected by someone breathing too close to me, or talking in my direction (although this is mostly when I'm eating). This makes many daily actions that most people take for granted completely impossible for me. I can't eat a piece of birthday cake because I know blowing the candles out means you're basically covering the cake with millions of germs. I can't sit next to someone and have a face-to-face conversation with them. If I deem someone as generally dirty, I can't be near them. For instance, today there is one person in my house who only showers once a week. If he accidentally brushes against me, I get nauseous. If he comes in the room, even for a second, while I'm eating or while I have the lid off my bottle to take a drink, everything gets thrown away.

Perhaps one of the hardest things about mysophobia is my inability to kiss. Most of the time, my husband can't kiss me on the lips. If he does, it can't be after he's eaten or drunk anything. He has to brush his teeth and make sure his lips are completely dry. If he does this and my symptoms aren't going haywire, I'll let him give me a small peck on the lips, after which I have to brush my teeth and wash my face. Oddly enough, mysophobia doesn't affect having sexual relations with my husband at all.

Sweating is a big deal for me. It's disgusting and I don't want any part of it. If I sweat, I shower. Sometimes that means I'll shower 6 or 7 times a day. If someone else is sweating, they can't come anywhere near me because if their sweat touches me, I get physically sick. In fact, I'm getting nauseous just writing about it.

I can't shake hands with anyone. God only knows if they washed their hands after using the bathroom. Who knows what they might have touched? Or if they used their hands to catch a sneeze or cough? I just can't risk it, so I politely refuse by telling another fib, usually something about just putting lotion on my hands. I know I could just shake hands and then wash mine, but something might happen to prevent me from getting to a sink. I figure I'm better safe than sorry.

Cleaning

I disinfect the house one to two times a day with antibacterial spray. I make sure to get all the doorknobs, light switches, remote controls, and staircase bannisters. Once or twice a week, I'll spray all the furniture. I have to clean the shower before I can use it, but only if someone else has showered since my last shower. I also clean the toilet before I use it. Because of this, I keep a small bottle of disinfectant and some wipes in my purse in case I have to use a public restroom. I have to clean the sink handles before I can touch them and after I wash my hands, I dry them on my own personal towel (which I hide so no one else accidentally uses it). I can't use bar soap because there might be germs from the last person that used it.

When I cook, I wash every pot, pan, and utensil before using it, even if they're already clean. I also rewash my plate and bowl before eating. I wash the table and my chair minutes before sitting down to eat so that I know it hasn't been contaminated since the last wipe-down.

I wash my sheets twice a week. I have my pillow and pillowcase marked so they don't get mixed up with my husbands. I also mark the sheets and blankets so that they are put on the bed the exact same way every time. That way, any germs that survived the wash will stay on their side of the bed. We each have our own side of the couch, and we each have our own chairs.

When I fold the laundry, I can only touch certain items. I can't touch any socks or underwear that belongs to someone else. And if the clothes belong to someone I see as particularly dirty, I can't touch their shirts or the towels they used either. Although I know better, for some reason I'm scared that the germs may have survived the wash.

I've tried to wear gloves in my daily life, but my hands always end up sweating.

Family and Friends

Society thinks mysophobia is funny. I think it's mostly because on TV, it's always portrayed as something to laugh at. Unfortunately, this just causes problems for those of us who are actually suffering from it.

When I tell people I'm terrified of germs, I usually get one of three reactions:

I get laughed at and not taken seriously.
They get offended, like I pick and choose who has germs and who doesn't.
Or they just don't care, meaning they're going to keep coughing and sneezing on me.

Very few people understand the two very basic facts that I try to impress on them. First, that it's very real. And second, that it has nothing to do with them.

My husband is one of the few that understand. He helps me tremendously by not making it a big deal. If I won't let him kiss me, he'll laugh and say, "That's fine, but I get extra later." Sometimes he even jokes about sneezing on my food if I don't do what he wants. He's even gone so far as to lick the last cookie because he knows that will keep me from eating it.

He lets me do what I need to (like separating our food) and gives me space. He knows there are certain rules, and he sticks to them without question. And he never makes me feel bad about ruining a special day or a special moment with one of my anxiety attacks. Although he's always aware of my fear, he never focuses on it. If he has a question, he asks it straight out. He's never skated around the issue because he knows that would make me feel like there was something wrong with me. To him it's just a fact of life, something he has to live with.

Feelings

Obviously, the base emotions of mysophobia are fear and panic, but that's not all it involves. There's also intense guilt, disgust, confusion, and frustration.

For me, the worst feeling (after fear and panic) is guilt. I feel guilty all the time. I know it's my fault that my husband and I don't have a normal relationship. I feel guilty because we can't do the things normal couples do. We rarely kiss at all, and although he won't show it, I know that upsets my husband. I feel guilty when we go out to eat because we can't sample each other's food and we can't share a romantic dessert. I feel guilty when he asks if he can make me breakfast in bed and I have to say no. I feel guilty when he comes home from work because I won't let him touch me until after he showers. I know that most of this may not seem important, but the small things mean more when you can't do them. I also feel guilty when someone misunderstands when I tell them I don't want their germs. Many of my friends have ended up with hurt feelings because they take my fear personally and think it has something to do with them.

My biggest source of guilt is with my kids. Even as babies, I could never kiss them on the mouth. I had to wash my hands after holding them. I could never give them a bite of my food or a sip of my drink. They grew up watching me get worse and worse. Then last year, my son kept bugging me to try his soda that he made. I kept refusing because he had already drunk out of it. When I realized he was truly upset at my refusal, I took a sip. Of course, then my plan backfired because he felt even worse when I got sick afterward. I know my fear affects them more than anybody, and most of the time I hate myself for it. I mean, these are my kids and I'm scared to touch them! What kind of mother does that make me? One of my biggest fears is that by growing up watching me act like this, they will somehow grow to fear germs, too. I don't know if I could handle that.

Disgust is a daily part of mysophobia. When I watch a person eat off of someone else's plate, share their drink with someone, double dip, or continue to eat their food after someone has coughed nearby, I get completely disgusted. The disgust is so intense I can liken it to the same feeling of disgust I feel when I hear about a woman doing drugs when she's pregnant. Sometimes it's all I can do to stop myself from getting physically sick. I see it and all I can think is, "Don't they know how disgusting that is? How can they do that?" Seeing how careless some people are about germs has actually affected my entire opinion of them. A few times, it's even been the reason for me ending a friendship. I just can't be around someone if I view them as disgusting.

I really don't understand why everyone isn't like me. I don't understand how people can be so thoughtless about the germs they get from others. I mean, there are so many illnesses and viruses going around, I just don't understand how people can go through life not thinking about germs and how to avoid them. I understand that my fear is a little extreme and I don't expect everyone to be like this, but I just don't think it's healthy to have *no* fear of germs!

How Others Can Help

The first thing I ask for is understanding. When I'm explaining mysophobia to someone, I ask that they sit and talk with me until they really understand what I'm saying. Those that won't take the time to understand usually end up cutting off our friendship because they either think I'm a freak or they get offended because "I think they're dirty."

Those that actually try to understand usually end up changing their behavior around me. For instance, my mother-in-law and sister-in-law used to be unconcerned about germs in general. But now when they sneeze, they usually lift their shirt above their nose and sneeze in it. In my mind, this stops the germs in their tracks, so I don't have any negative response at all. They no longer get offended when I rewash the dishes before I use them. They used to get upset that I won't eat with them, but then they realized it's because my father-in-law coughs without covering his mouth multiple times during every meal. I thank them for their understanding by attempting to eat with them when my father-in-law is gone. Their understanding and their seemingly small actions make a huge difference. Plus the fact that my friends and family care enough to actually change their behavior makes me feel like I'm doing the right thing with being honest about it.

Like I mentioned before, one of the biggest things that has helped me has been my husband acting like it's no big deal. I can't even imagine how much more intense my guilt would be if he made a big deal about certain things. But it's not just that. A huge chunk of my life is focused on mysophobia. There are so many things I have to watch out for, so many things I can't do, so many rules I have to follow. I really don't need anyone else bringing attention to it and focusing on it, too. Aware, yes. Focused, no.

When I ask my father-in-law to cover his mouth when he coughs, he always makes a big deal out of it. He'll complain and talk about it until I leave the room from embarrassment. He makes my fear the center of attention and makes me feel guilty for it. He won't even try to understand, and that makes our relationship extremely rocky.

The one thing I insist on is that people follow my "rules" if they're around me. If you can't cover your mouth when you sneeze or cough, you don't need to be around me. If you insist on eating with me, you don't need to be around me. If you feel the need to touch me, you don't need to be around me. I try my hardest to make others feel comfortable with their own quirks and dislikes, so I don't think it's unreasonable to expect the same in return.

One thing I really appreciate is people being direct when they talk about my fear of germs. I don't hide it. I'm not ashamed of it. Although I don't like it too much, mysophobia is a part of who I am. When someone is embarrassed to talk about it or too shy to ask a question about it, it makes me wonder if they think I'm weird or crazy. I end up feeling like a freak. I end up feeling like maybe I should be ashamed of it, like maybe I should hide it and not tell anyone. To prevent this, I try to be as open and direct as I can. I try to show people that it's nothing to be ashamed of. I know it's a curious condition, so I encourage them to ask questions and I answer as honestly as I can. In the end, I think education and information are the keys to ending the stigma of mysophobia.

OBSESSIVE-COMPULSIVE DISORDER (OCD)

Flux

FRANK R. DeFULGENTIS[3]

Example of the Hand-Washing Dilemma

Let's look at a situation in which a concern is resolved with a mental compulsion. Back when I attended Universal Technical Institute, it was imperative that I arrive to class on time. If I missed a part of the lecture, I could fail the written test (or not be able to perform the hands-on task in the shop). My grade as a whole could suffer and I could cause the grades of others to suffer as well.

Let's say that one morning, before my "street legal" class is about to begin, I use the bathroom. Afterwards, I wash and dry my hands, hold the door open for the students walking in, and take my seat for the lecture on superchargers that is about to begin. To my dismay, I realize that as I had held the door open with my left hand it had come into contact with a yucky kind of wet substance. "What was it that I had touched? What if someone had gone to the bathroom and not washed their hands afterwards. What if that was urine on the door. What if it was someone's nasty sweat. Ugh, I can't go back and wash my hands right now, class is starting. I guess I will just have to wait until the first fifteen-minute break."

Interestingly enough, these open-ended, self-directed types of questions do not in themselves constitute an obsession. . . . After all, is it wrong to feel a little grossed out if you touch a wet bathroom door? Not necessarily. And this kind of situation could happen to anyone. It doesn't mean we are obsessing.

Clearly, it has only just now strolled through my mind for the first time. Therefore, here in stage 1 it is merely a concern. So, I turn my attention to the instructor who is now beginning the first slide of his PowerPoint presentation. Only, the concern once again reappears. But as I begin to wonder once again what that wet, yucky substance might have been, I feel

---

[3]This story is part of the larger book *Flux—A Strategy Guide for OCD* by Frank DeFulgentis. Copyright 2009. Reprinted with permission.

uneasy, and start to shift around in my seat (stage 2). It is intrusive because I do not want to explore this concern any further. There is nothing I can do about it right now. I want to pay attention to the lecture. This concern has become an anxiety-provoking thought. And to make matters worse, it is now recurrent.

This is not a passing concern, and so here in stage 2 this has now become an obsession. However, we still do not know if it will result in rumination or a compulsion. It is still open-ended, at the moment anyway. To be sure, let's once again look at the *DSM-IV-TR* criteria of an obsession and see how this situation matches up. Obsessions: recurrent, intrusive, and anxiety-provoking thoughts, impulses, or images. Yes, it is definitely an obsession.

I have not decided how I want to respond to it yet. It may be seen as an interruption to "Mr. Jones" if I get up in the beginning of his lecture. I know from various remarks that he has made in the past to others that he feels it is inappropriate for students to leave within the first fifteen minutes. As a result, I fear that I might anger Mr. Jones and maybe even my peers as well. Therefore, I decide to stay seated and just pay attention to the lecture until it is appropriate to use the restroom. "Whatever. Dirty hands are no big deal, time to move on with life. The lecture is more important!"

Stage 2 has now ended since no steps were taken toward a resolution. Until I decide on a resolution, every repetition of this is rumination. I once again turn my attention to the instructor and begin to focus in on what he is saying. But the obsession is waiting there for me, like a forgotten aunt that I am supposed to pick up at the airport. "I want to wash my dirty hands. Hmmm ... yeah my hands may have something disgusting on them—this thought again. Yeah, there is nothing I can do about it, so I must ignore it." And so once again, I press on as if I am behind the wheel of a car and have to manually shift my transmission (brain) out of first gear and press on down the road. "So, back to what the instructor is saying ..."

A few minutes later, I feel the hand-washing issue tugging at my attention again! Once again my heart rate increases. Only now, I am overtaken with a feeling of dread. "This hand-washing issue is really bothering me. I can't seem to put it out of my mind.... It's OK ... it's no big deal.... Why am I reacting to it like this? I can't do anything about it right now." It is as if my obsession is a car crash—that I notice in my rearview mirror as I pass it—and there is a person standing in the middle of the road waving his hands shouting, "Come back, help!" Only I can't stop and go back.

Meanwhile, in class, the instructor has just flipped to the third page of the power point presentation. "Ugh, I am missing this!" To make matters worse, there is a discussion taking place between the students on the material that was just presented on the previous slide. In fact, the person next to me asks a question on what engine component it is that increases intake air flow? "Oops, I missed that slide also. What did he say? I was thinking about the stupid hand-washing. I better keep up with this discussion."

But even now, it's too late, and I have missed the answer he gave to the student next to me—that could have helped me to catch up to the current slide—because of this internal dialogue. "If only I wouldn't have touched the door. I would be able to pay attention. What if I hadn't touched the door? I would be taking in all of this information now. Did it feel like water? Or was it a more gooey kind of substance?"

Stage 3 has now begun, and it signifies the beginning of a covert compulsion. This is because I have chosen a course of action. Essentially, I have chosen to revisualize the event in hopes of convincing myself that I hadn't touched anything disgusting. Because I feel that if I can do this, the impulse to wash my hands will go away, and the problem will be solved. Therefore, I have chosen a mental-compulsion to resolve it. Of course, there is no way that I am going to be able to produce this kind of clarity from revisualizing it.

Does this happen in cases of OCD? You bet it does! What a mess we have on our hands. So where do we even begin? Welcome to the study of psychology. Because as a sufferer of OCD you have now become your own part-time psychologist, whether you like it or not. If you don't take personal responsibility for your anxiety (yet learn to not inflate this responsibility), there is not a thing anyone can do to help you.

Even though there is still a general consensus among clinicians that compulsions are physical acts, we know that they are not necessarily as overt as some may think. Often, we are driven to perform compulsions, covertly. Covert compulsions (mental compulsions) are repetitive thoughts designed to organize events through visualizing images or rehearsing silent strings of words. In a sense, it is a mental replacement for the physical act, or the condensing of many mental interpretations within a small time frame. The "bathroom door dilemma" provides an example of a covert compulsion.

In the movie *Two for the Money*, there is a scene where Al Pacino begins to verbalize the suspicious feelings he has about his wife and a new employee (played by Matthew McConaughey). As he thinks out loud, this introspection takes a turn for the worse, and before long his words sound increasingly jealous and paranoid. Finally, his wife, played by Rene Russo, interjects, "You are in your own head again. What'd I tell you about that? Stay out of there, it's a bad neighborhood!"

I love that quote because it illustrates an important point. Namely, that a mental compulsion is a bad neighborhood. Yet we go there, again and again, like gluttons for punishment. We are like junkies driving downtown to cop a fix, without any regard for our safety or whether we will get caught and arrested. What could we possibly need so badly? What is it that takes hold of our brains and forces us to navigate through endless cycles of disturbing obsessive-compulsive behavior? What are we really after? The answer, of course, is the feeling of certainty. What makes the green grass green? What makes a light switch, switched off? What makes a locked door locked?

Practicing Imperfection

Tolman's idea of the cognitive map is an insightful one. Clearly, we do form cognitive maps and use them as the basis for much of our reality. Indeed, this is a part of human living that we couldn't shake even if we wanted to. Whether we are attempting to navigate ourselves through an actual territory or we are making decisions about our personal relationships, we owe it to ourselves to have a brutally honest—consistently revised—map at our disposal. But what we do not want to do is kid ourselves into thinking that we can obsess our way into a perfect accuracy.

We will never be absolutely certain about whether or not our maps are accurate, and that, of course, is the whole point! There is always something we can do to improve our maps (and as Peck says, it is important to realize this), but as those of us with OCD know, the timing must be appropriate. The immediacy of life may require us to suspend the need for certainty. It is indeed a paradox. On the one hand, we desperately want to make—on the spot—revisions of our maps because this correction may be vital to understanding not only the present situation but a situation that may immediately follow. But if our outward focus suffers because we are trying to make on-the-spot revisions, many new problems may develop as a consequence.

One of the things that I have had to do in order to spend five hours less a day in compulsive activity was give up the need for perfection (certainty, about whether or not the door is locked, or the oven is off, am I making the right decision, interacting with people correctly, etc.). I had to give up what had become a radical and deep desire to be completely certain about everything I ever did or wanted to do. Certainty is not always possible—as Korzybski's proposal that "the map is not the territory" so eloquently illustrates.

Certainty has been my security blanket for a long time. Using a mental compulsion to resolve whatever doubt I am feeling about something at the moment may or may not relieve my anxiety, but the point is there is a much bigger picture to consider. If I am talking to my boss and he is explaining how he wants me to carry out a specific task, but I am caught up in my head reflecting on something, I am going to fail miserably at what I am attempting to do (even if he doesn't notice that I was faking the funk). This may cause me to feel demoralized and embarrassed because I know that, once again, I let my urge to become mentally compulsive take over. Eventually, what I realized is I am damned if I do and damned if I don't.

If I am able to refrain from carrying the mental compulsion I can then regain peace of mind as I continue to engage in what I am doing. The truth is that something else is likely to rear its ugly head, only a minute later anyway. In my efforts to be more in tune with the world around me I have discovered that the whole is greater than the sum of the little uncertain parts. I remember many times in the past when I was not as successful at shifting out of my modes of uncertainty. My compulsions were stifling because of my inability to focus on what I was doing. Interestingly, I rarely remember what triggered my confusion in the first place. What I remember is how poorly I had dealt with it.

In his book, *Science and Sanity* (1933) Korzybski describes his concept of "time binding." Grammatical meanings change throughout the years, and the truth about ourselves, and the world, changes along with them. Time changes the meanings and contexts of words. What is true now might not be true—even five minutes from now. As Korzybski points out, after a while, it's not even about the territory anymore. Map making can become a map-making compulsion—maps of maps of maps, etc. There is no end to this.

We are all imperfect, we will always be imperfect, and there is not a thing that we can ever do about it. At some point, we have to practice imperfection, if we want to function at all. I once had a doctor tell me that I was crazy for wanting to write this book. "You are not a doctor and you are not a writer," he said. For years, I had told myself this also, but not anymore. And that is because, whether I have a PhD or not, I will still never be perfect.

I am not claiming to be a scientist, a doctor, or even Ernest Hemingway. I have put together a strategy guide of ideas, things that have worked for me. This book may not contain as "perfect" an analysis as the good doctor claims he has—that he wants to charge me weekly for—but it is a starting point, nonetheless. I may never (in some people's eyes) have a complete enough map of reality to write this book. And, indeed, I could have vowed to not publish this book until I became a doctor, and as a result I would have spent my life stewing and feeling sorry for myself. The truth is that any attempt to hold on to the ideal of absolute perfection (PhD or not) is nothing but a detour in oblivion because we all suffer from uncertainty.

The Cognitive Maze

Werner Heisenberg, the German theoretical physicist, introduced the idea of the uncertainty principle, and the resulting, observer effect. According to Heisenberg, the accuracy of your observations is inversely proportional to the position that you are making them from in that particular moment in time. In other words, not only am I limited to the information that I presently have available to me, but that information changes as I observe it! This is similar to Korzybski's observation, and just as Korzybski points to the potential for "obsessional map-making," so Heisenberg can help us to understand this as well. Sometimes, we inadvertently create sub-obsessions while observing ourselves, and as a result we sidetrack ourselves.

The German physicist Werner Karl Heisenberg found that the very act of observing an electron influences its activity and casts doubt on the validity of the observation. Heisenberg concluded that nothing can ever be known with certainty in science. Translated into psychology, this principle says that, although human behavior is indeed determined, we can never learn at least some causes of behavior because in attempting to observe them we change them.... Such a position is called indeterminism (B. R. Hergenhahn).

Once I begin to measure what my position is, I have changed it. "If I am not really worried about this, then why do I keep thinking about it?" And so, not only has my concern become an obsession but I now have a second obsession running parallel with the first.

The danger often lies in trying to find the quick fix, the instant certainty that we are right, and that everything is okay, so that our anxiety will be relieved. As Rollo May has said many times throughout his career, anxiety comes from the space between where we are now and where we want to be. If right now I work at Wendy's, but within the span of the next six months I want to write a book, sell millions of copies, and buy a boat to sail around the Caribbean, I am going to have a lot of anxiety. But it takes more than just realizing this to change it.

It is always tempting to take the gamble that I can resolve an internal conflict by splitting my consciousness, plugging in a quick rationalization—through a mental compulsion—and stepping right back into the shoes of my present awareness. Not only is this not a good idea for reasons that I gave above, but I am taking a huge gamble by doing this. At the point that I split my consciousness, I roll the dice. I am, in a sense, betting on the odds that I can resolve my compulsive urge quickly enough to not miss any of the potentially important things that are presently taking place around me. I may miss information that later may be essential to my survival. It is like putting a piece of chewing gum in the hole of a racing tire before you head out to the track.

Engaging in mental compulsive rituals while undertaking responsibilities that I need to be focused on is always a risk. Unwittingly, I am entering a metaphorical-like maze. But let's take this metaphor one step further and imagine ourselves as rats, searching for cheese in this maze. The cheese for us represents the feeling of certainty. We want it, we want it now, and we are determined to get it. With each probing thought of our covert compulsion we race further in and around to one adjacent corridor after another, deeper and deeper. We either arrive at this reassurance that we are after, or we get so lost in the split between reflection and our "I" awareness that our anxiety and fear is now creating compulsions as fast as we are resolving them. This can have a treadmill-like effect where we are constantly trying to retrace our steps quickly to get back into the present flow of what's going on.

I call this trap of quick-fix certainty "the cognitive maze." We can, in a sense, become just like Tolman's rats, creating little pseudo-landmarks, while we race around our minds with red flags, leaving behind a trail of peanuts. Some of the pressure we put on ourselves, and the deep probing issues we feel we must we resolve—within the span of a minute—are at times ludicrous. To illustrate just how irrational taking the certainty plunge is in some circumstances, let me give one more example.

In the beginning of my book I mentioned the pre-Socratic philosopher Heroclitus and how he proclaimed that the world is in a constant state of flux and so it is impossible to achieve true knowledge of it. He is known for saying, "You cannot step in the same river twice." He said this because he believed that since both we and the world are constantly changing, what is true one moment is not necessarily true the next. Parmenides of Elea came along and said, "Wait a minute, there are some things that are unchanging." And he proceeded to present *his* argument.

Moreover, Socrates went to great lengths to endlessly question the nature of people and the world, and so did the philosophers that followed him. Plato used the allegory of the cave and talked about the "forms" of reality. Rene Descartes famously declared, "I think, therefore I am," and used this as the main premise for reflecting on his world. Much later, David Hume shed light on the causal connections we often take for granted and got us to consider whether these conjoined cause-and-effect assumptions we made daily were even true at all. Immanuel Kant's approach to human affairs states that thoughts organize and modify the outer world; thus, people can change both (perhaps where most OCD people get stuck). At one point, the American philosopher William James, in response to the endless philosophizing over what we can and cannot know, suggested that we focus on the more pragmatic and useful concerns of humanity. Later, Wittgenstein claimed that ultimately, it is our diverse, individual interpretations of grammar that get in the way of our ever knowing the true nature of reality, and that these discursive turns must be taken into account.

The argument about what we can and cannot know has gone on for centuries. The argument has not gone away, it has simply changed hands (Ludwig Wittgenstein).

This is only the tip of the iceberg. Imagine having all of the people that have ever philosophized about this sort of thing, in one room, at one time. This would be a big room, with many people in it, and the conversation would be concentrative and intense, to say the least. Can you imagine trying to resolve all of the arguments on the true nature of reality, and how you fit within this spectrum, within the span of a minute? It is crazy, of course!

We cannot even be sure that philosophers have adequately explained it—even now—after a thousand years. Socrates once proclaimed that the only thing he knew was that he knew nothing. The point is: The more certain we wish to become about anything, the more likely it is that we will thwart these efforts. At some point, you have to be satisfied enough for the moment—with yourself, with your life, with your decisions.

Suspension of Disbelief

Stop trying to ignore your obsessions and compulsions. What happens when you try to ignore anything? You force yourself to notice it more. Rather, suspend your immediate concerns, put them off until a more appropriate time (like you would put a virus in quarantine until you have a cure). This way you are not trying to convince yourself that you are being irrational by rearranging words in your head while on the freeway in heavy traffic! Maybe you have some valid issues that you need to look at about yourself. But know when it is appropriate. If, later, you want to read large volumes of philosophical arguments on the nature of reality and what we can be sure we know, then go ahead! Right now, pay attention to your life.

Find your derivative desires. You can't always get what you want, but if you strive for something else that you want just as much or almost as much, sometimes you can even wind up getting both in the end. Let's say you have tripped on yourself while walking into class on the first day of school and al- most fell on someone's desk. No doubt, you look stupid. Maybe your desire to make a friend to have lunch with just went out the window. Maybe you feel you ruined your chance to make a good first impression. Don't let it get you down and don't obsess. Instead, just become engaged in the lecture and class discussions. After all, you desire to do well in your class. Let this more important desire take precedence; it will carry its own momentum. In the process you may inadvertently make a friend by attentiveness to the subject matter. Perhaps somebody will agree with a comment you made in class and will want to tell you at lunch. Now two desires have been gratified! Don't waste your time in obsessive thought convincing yourself you are okay. You are okay!

Suspend your disbelief, remind yourself that even though you will sometimes mess up in life, whenever you miss gratifying one desire there is always something else that you can shoot for five minutes later. If you can suspend disbelief long enough, plug in your derivative desire (the one you have of not being caught up in your head during conversations), and let the emotional weight generated by your contact with others take hold through conversational turn taking and pacing, then you have just pulled the truck out of the ditch. At least until the next obsession, which may be just around the corner. But don't get discouraged. As you become adept at feeling the pain of uncertainty, and using that unresolved tension, you will begin to experience the natural rhythms and the pleasant, spontaneous, flowing conversations they produce.

Example of the Rabbit

The fear of germs is a central feature of OCD. I have heard many stories about the cleaning frenzies of others, scrubbing kitchen floors and bathroom tiles with ammonia, bleach, etc. Indeed, a fear of contamination is the driving force behind many of our compulsive activities. And with the use of cleaning products, many people can compulsively subdue this fear, at least temporarily. However, compulsive cleaning does not help me at all (my wife wishes it did). Interestingly, I once heard a nurse at Walter Reed comment, "For someone with OCD, you are one of messiest people I have ever met!"

The fact is: cleaning in itself makes me nervous. I don't mean showering, straightening up my room, putting things away, folding clothes, etc. I mean cleaning agents. Although I shower at least once a day and will at times scrub my hands furiously with soap in order to remove germs, that is as far as I am willing to take it. This is because of a special that I saw on TV a long time ago. It was a documentary about spray agents such as deodorant, perfume, cologne, hair spray, bathroom scents, cleaning solutions, etc. The makers of this documentary were animal rights activists who wanted to expose the cruelty that goes into the testing of these kinds of spray-bottle chemicals.

In order to illustrate this, they showed several pictures of animals that were used during the testing process. Of course, some of the manufacturers had to test the chemicals several times on several animals before they were considered to be safe enough for humans. Consequently, these animal test subjects had suffered horribly during this development process. They showed some extremely graphic pictures of a rabbit's eyes rotting out and the sickly, purplish skin tone of his fur. It really had an effect on me at a deep level. To this day, I sometimes hold my breath either when I spray deodorant or have to walk through a room where someone else has sprayed chemicals. When my wife cleans the house, often I will open all of the windows and turn on the ceiling fans because just the scent of cleaning chemicals can set off a fear of contamination within me. And even though they freak me out, I can deal with them, for the most part.

Another fear of contamination that I have stems from my life here in Orlando, Florida. Florida does not require emissions testing (for automobiles).

There are some old nasty cars being driven that have sickly emissions coming out of them. I often find myself being stuck behind one of these cars for long periods of time (while in heavy traffic). I may turn off my air conditioning or close my air vents to avoid breathing in the chemicals. But one of the things I have begun to understand is that these small (minor threat) kind of germs are probably healthier than anything else in life. And that is because they prepare me for the bigger (major threat) germs.

I attribute part of my success of dealing with this to the biologist Bruce Lipton and his work with cloning. In his book, *The Biology of Belief* (2005), Lipton writes about the work he has done with cells, and what he found is that genes aren't the actual determinants of inheritable disease. Basically, to paraphrase Lipton: the nucleus is not the brain of the cell. Rather, there is a much bigger picture. He talks about cell communities, the antennas of cells and how they use our windows of perceptions as their means of interpreting the environment.

Lipton did some crazy stuff with cells; like exposing them to toxic agents in a Petri dish. To his amazement, these cells thrived! It was the internal environment (complete with the person's belief system) that did these cells in. In these cases, the internal environments of these people were more poisonous than the supposed toxic agents that could destroy them. Cells follow the collective voice of the community. Cancer may be the result of cells trying to escape from the "status quo" of their community in order to start their own.

Our beliefs are the determining factors in what triggers disease; genes are only a blueprint. Our cells will realign themselves with the danger that we ourselves are determined to predict. In a sense, worrying about getting a disease may ultimately cause the onset of a disease. Lack of forgiveness, fear, or hypervigilance may all be conduits of this.

The diseases that are today's scourges—diabetes, heart disease, and cancer—short-circuit a happy and healthy life. These diseases, however, are not the result of a single gene, but of complex interactions among multiple genes and environmental factors. What activates genes? The answer was elegantly spelled out in 1990 in a paper entitled "Metaphor and the Role of Genes and Development" by H. F. Nijhout (1990). When a gene product is needed, a signal from its environment, not an emergent property of the gene itself, activates expression of that gene. In other words, when it comes to genetic control, "It's the environment, stupid" (Bruce Lipton).

I recommend this book to anyone who has a severe fear of contamination or disease. Let it challenge your thinking and open up some new neural pathways in your brain!

I once heard a clever anecdote on germs, given by George Carlin on his CD *Napalm and Silly Putty.* Carlin talks about how the fear of germs has become a sickness in society and that it is this sickness in itself that keeps people from strengthening their immune systems and living healthy lives. He talks about growing up in New York City and how he used to swim in the Hudson River. The Hudson River is historically known for being dirty, filthy, unswimmable water. Yet on extremely hot summer days, he and his friends would succumb to the urge to dive in and swim for hours at a time.

Furthermore, he goes on to say that while everyone was lecturing him and his friends about their swimming in the Hudson River, they had gotten polio and everything else that was prominent back then. He gives a rather sarcastic chuckle and says that his immune system was as strong as iron, because of all of the times he swam in it. When hearing Carlin's anecdote I had to chuckle myself because there is a simple yet eluding truth in it. There comes a point when we have to just let our immune system do its job! It's there for a reason and it will not get stronger if we live in a sealed-off, germ-free world. Sometimes, I consciously have to remind myself of this.

Rituals, Routines, and Recovery: Living With OCD

Jared Douglas Kant with Martin Franklin and Linda Wasmer Andrews[4]

My Story

It was during my junior year of high school that I experienced the most horrific and terrifying obsessions. These intrusive thoughts included images that superimposed themselves upon the world around me like an acetate overlay. For instance, in the middle of a conversation with my best friend, Corrine, I would suddenly see myself burying a hatchet into her chest. It was the most

---

[4]From *The Thought That Counts: A Firsthand Account of One Teenager's Experience With Obsessive-Compulsive Disorder,* by Jared Douglas Kant with Martin Franklin and Linda Wasmer Andrews (2008, pp. 99–108). Copyright 2008 by Oxford University Press. Reprinted with permission.

terrifying thing I could think of, since I loved Corrine (and still do to this day). Yet this sort of image kept coming back at random times, and when it did, it left me shaking.

I also developed a fear that if I didn't tell my therapist every single thing I had done the entire day, it would turn out that I had omitted the part where I killed someone and left the body in the woods. To my knowledge, I've never actually killed anyone, and I've certainly never left a dead body in the woods. But the thought kept returning. This was my OCD telling me that I had done something I found morally reprehensible.

Sometimes in the middle of a therapy session, I would tell my therapist that I was afraid I was going to hit him or do him bodily harm in some other way. I expected him to be horrified and offended, but he explained that this is a very common belief among people being treated for OCD. If the violent thoughts truly are due to OCD, there's very little chance that they'll turn into real acts of violence. On the other hand, they could easily give rise to compulsive rituals. In my case, I would exhaustively confess every tiny wrongdoing, often while sitting on my hands to make sure I didn't do something even more terrible.

There were also occasions when I mentally saw myself rape or molest someone, and the images scared the hell out of me. When I told my therapist about these intrusive thoughts, I started to shake. Over and over, I said that I didn't think I had done it, but what if I had? What if I were a super-villainous serial rapist who had figured out how to elude the police and the FBI where others had failed? I was terrified that I was leading a double life—sweet on the outside but with a personality on the inside that made Jack the Ripper look like a Boy Scout.

Staring Down OCD
Dr. C., my cognitive-behavioral therapist, has degrees in several fields, one of which is divinity. This made me wonder if perhaps I might be confessing my sins rather than explaining my obsessions to him. And though I feared that I possibly could be sort of a serial killer, over time, I came to accept Dr. C.'s assurances that I was not. At first, I was a little skeptical, but I trusted the man. Here was someone who not only was a doctor who healed people mentally and emotionally, but also had a connection to God. I believed this connection would require him to drive a stake through my

heart if he deemed me to be anywhere near as evil as I had previously assumed myself to be.

Dr. C. asked whether I enjoyed the thoughts about acting violently—a very straightforward question I probably should have asked myself long before. My immediate reaction was that *of course* I didn't. The thoughts were sometimes so terrible that I lost sleep and had to be sedated for panic-induced shortness of breath and palpitations. Then Dr. C. asked another really good question that should have been obvious: Was it likely that I would be an evil murderer if the mere thought of violence was so distressing to me? Finally, Dr. C. asked whether I had been visited by the police. I told him I hadn't. I realized right then that he was showing me how completely illogical it was to believe that the horrible images were true.

The next thing we did was extremely unnerving. Dr. C. asked me to free associate words related to all manner of violent acts, particularly the ones I found most abhorrent and unforgivable, such as molestation, rape, and murder. I went through a thesaurus' worth of words, then continued into words that had been causing me to think of these violent thoughts. Dr. C. wrote it all down on his scratchpad. When he was finished, he asked if it was okay for him to show me what he had written. I was surprised that the request scared me so deeply.

On the page were words so vile and disturbing that they went against everything I held sacred and important. The acts named there were far removed from what I believed to be morally correct and not even in the vicinity of anything I would ever do. As I stared at the words, images flashed through my mind like a rapid-fire slide show of the most horrible scenes I could imagine. I was terrified. This, Dr. C. told me, was the first step toward facing down my OCD.

I just wanted to puke on the rug. I felt compelled to call everyone who was an authority figure in my life and ask if they could check in their area to make sure I hadn't done anything bad or hurt anyone. I also had a strong urge to call the police myself to make sure there weren't any missing person reports or crime scenes that matched the images in my head. But I didn't do these things. Instead, I just sat there and sweated it out, drenching my shirt with salty tears and sweat. In short, I went through the basic steps of EX/RP—exposure plus response prevention.

I felt very empowered knowing that the things I most feared about myself were extremely unlikely and, in some cases, utterly impossible. Yet the words didn't lose their anxiety-provoking ability overnight. When the therapy session ended, I took the list with me and tucked it away, feeling almost as if I needed a biohazard bag to contain it. Over repeated exposures, though, I came to know the words intimately. I also exposed myself to violent media and challenged myself by asking if I could even remotely be the sort of person who did such terrible things.

On the plus side, I got the privilege of viewing some really nasty horror movies that the other kids weren't allowed to watch at school. Some of the kids were even jealous of my therapy.

Life Beyond High School

Before I found EX/RP, I was struggling—not only with the symptoms of OCD itself, but also with related problems. As I later discovered, having other psychological and behavioral problems in addition to OCD is quite common. In my case, I found myself using drugs to make the pain go away, and I smoked cigarettes, too, in a sarcastic approach to casual and gradual suicide. At various times, I also had to contend with panic attacks, depression, and recurring tics.

After I began getting my symptoms under control with effective treatment, I made a lot of progress. I quit smoking, graduated from high school with honors, and became more comfortable with who I was. It wasn't an overnight miracle cure, however, and the comfort had its limits. Although the symptoms became milder and more manageable, they didn't disappear.

In college, I started allowing obsessions and rituals back into my life like unwanted houseguests who wouldn't go away. My schedule of college activities dictated that I have a routine every day, and I followed it precisely, even compulsively. I spent most of my college career using several alarm clocks at once, setting them to go off at different times in a sequence that wasn't predictable. I also made sure each clock was at least five feet away from my bed so that I wouldn't be able to just hit the snooze button and go back to sleep. Yet I still lost a lot of sleep to perpetual anxiety over the possibility of missing a single minute of class.

The stress of not getting enough sleep combined with the transition to college life was tough on me. Almost all teenagers yearn for greater freedom. But suddenly being plopped into a situation with very few restrictions after the structure of a therapeutic boarding school was harder than I had expected. Of course, I wasn't alone in that feeling. Many college freshmen are shocked to discover that there is such a thing as having too much freedom. When OCD symptoms are added to the mix, however, the pressure can feel overwhelming.

Hoarding 101

College students aren't known for their tidiness, so when you live in the basement of a dorm the way I did, dirt is unavoidable. I resigned myself to the knowledge that I was constantly surrounded by germs and there was nothing I could do about it. In that environment, I made great strides toward overcoming my contamination fears, but new problems with hoarding cropped up.

In college, it's easy to become a packrat. I got into the habit of throwing things onto my desk in between classes and social activities. Later I would stuff everything into a drawer or shove it out of sight. For most students, this might lead to nothing worse than a messy room. But for me, it triggered a tendency toward compulsive hoarding.

During my first year of college, like many people, I went through a sort of reinvention of self that included refining how I dressed. I bought a new wardrobe, but still I kept all the clothing I no longer wore. I would estimate that I used up to 75% of my closet space to store clothes that didn't fit me or that I didn't like. The fear was that, if I did throw them away, I would be losing something of myself. Although many people feel that way about a certain blanket or favorite old sweater, I felt that way about everything I owned. I could not, to the point of absurdity, part with anything. More to the point, I had to keep it all on hand.

In addition to clothes, I also kept all kinds of old computer equipment in case I ever needed it—which meant I planned to save it for eternity. As a technician building computers out of old junk parts, my job was to extract what I needed from machines that still ran well and scrap the rest. Instead, my office in the engineering building began to overflow with old intake fans, floppy discs, and cables. Whenever forced to justify keeping these things, I became quite defensive, creating elaborate scenarios in which I might need a five-inch floppy drive in the future despite the fact that they had been obsolete for nearly two decades. I sometimes felt the overwhelming sense that, if I didn't have the parts on hand, I would one day be unprepared for a catastrophe.

Then there were the mounds of paper. I remember looking around my dorm room one day and thinking that it was gradually and inexplicably shrinking. When I sifted through my drawers later that night, a pile of receipts from the bookstore, drugstore, and several dozen other stores fell onto the floor. Pulling out a big trunk from underneath my bed, I found more receipts inside.

On my bookshelf, there was a binder with several pocket folders designed to store receipts and record transactions. Its intended purpose was to help me organize my finances. But as noble as that goal was, it really wasn't the underlying motive. The true driving force was an unexplained fear that one of these days I would find myself in dire need of proof that I had paid for some random item. I also worried that my personal information might leak out if I didn't keep a tight lid on it, and that meant not casually tossing out receipts. The problem was that I was keeping the receipts indefinitely for every single item I paid for.

I had such limited space to begin with that I wasn't able to rationalize the hoarding for long. I couldn't afford to keep collecting extraneous trash if I didn't want to be evicted for health reasons. Besides, I was starting to lose my current homework in the piles of homework from long ago.

Yet I reasoned that I could never be absolutely sure that a piece of paper or scrap of information was no longer useful. I kept all my old assignment sheets, telling myself that one day the professors could somehow lose all of my work and I would have to reproduce it. Many of the papers were either expired assignments turned in long ago or drafts of essays that had been long since revised, so part of me realized that they were unlikely to be of use, but the very idea of parting with them was still terrifying.

Cleaning Up My Act

I realized it was time to do a serious intervention with myself to clean out the drawers, clear off the shelves, and sort through my trunk and closet. By a stroke of good fortune, Radio Shack was having a sale on paper shredders—the heavy-duty, crosscut kind. I bought one of those bad boys and made a pile of papers to get rid of. Then I promptly panicked and had to run outside for a deep breath.

By coaxing a friend to come back inside with me, I finally was able to start the destruction of many pounds of unwanted paper under the guise of showing off a new toy. Never underestimate the young male's desire to demonstrate his masculinity by destroying stuff. The allure of grinding gears wasn't lost on my friends, and I eventually had what I called a shredding party. Seven shopping bags later, you could see dust clouding in the room from the gears tearing away at all that paper. I haven't lived without a shredder since then.

Next I decided to take on the old, unworn clothes. First I took some big brown paper bags and started to stuff them with old jackets. Then I began filling garbage bags with designer skater clothing. When I donated the bags to Goodwill afterward, I realized that I had just managed to not only do an exposure for myself, but also help others who were less fortunate in the process—a really worthwhile return on my investment of time, energy, and effort.

Finally, I tackled the old computer equipment I had been saving for the proverbial rainy day that never came. I was (and still am) heavily into computers and technology, so there was a lot of it. I took out the old components and stripped them down to their base level. Then I dusted them, repainted a couple, installed upgraded parts, and made whole computers out of the garbage that had been invading my personal space. I donated the computers to a local nonprofit organization that provides services and support to survivors of domestic abuse. So in another exposure, I not only sharpened my computer repair skills, but also made new computers for people who really needed them. Now that's something to feel doubly good about.

The Big Picture

OCD can be simultaneously your worst enemy and your best friend. Every time I overcame obsessive-compulsive thoughts and behavior, I learned more about myself and took greater charge of my life. As a result, I'm of the sincerely peculiar opinion that some good has come from my illness. I can't honestly say that I'm grateful for OCD, but I do think it has made me a stronger, better person.

Comorbidity—in other words, the coexistence of two or more disorders in the same person—just adds to the challenge. Mental health professionals use strict criteria to define different disorders for purposes of diagnosis, treatment, and research. This creates the illusion of neat, orderly categories. But real life is much messier than that, and many teens have symptoms of more than one condition.

As I've mentioned, I faced several challenges—including depression, substance abuse, and a tic disorder—in addition to OCD. I learned that it was important to address *all* of them. Otherwise, the symptoms tended to feed each other and keep the problems going. It's hard to concentrate on OCD in therapy, for instance, when your motivation is sapped by depression or your ability to think clearly is undermined by drugs. That's one reason treatment needs to be individualized. You're one of a kind, and your exact mix of symptoms and conditions is unique, too.

"It'll Be Okay." How I Kept Obsessive-Compulsive Disorder (OCD) From Ruining My Life

SHANNON SHY[5]

"OCD? So, What, Did You Wash Your Hands a Lot?"

When I tell people today that I struggled with OCD, I usually get asked about my symptoms. More times than not, folks specifically mention a very common OCD symptom and ask, "OCD? So, what, did you wash your hands a lot?" This [article] describes my OCD symptoms…and the OCD episode that finally caused me to decide to seek help.…[I] explicitly describe how OCD tortured me. I discuss these symptoms in detail because in order to understand how significant my turnaround was, one must understand how deeply and darkly I was affected by OCD. If you are trying to help someone you believe may have OCD, the detailed descriptions will give you an idea about how OCD works. Having OCD was exhausting. The intrusive, irrational thoughts were haunting and caused embarrassment, anguish, and physical pain. Physically, my heart rate increased, my heart pounded as if my chest was going to burst open, my body temperature rose, I perspired, and my stomach tied itself into knots. (For those of you with OCD, remember, as I discuss my symptoms, it's okay if the power of suggestion puts some or all of these thoughts in your head. It doesn't mean you agree with those thoughts. They are not your thoughts.)

1. ***Objects on the Side of the Road.*** *Every* time I would drive, I would see something on the side of the road, which I would immediately

---

identify as the object it was (a log, for example) and then a thought would come to me that it might be a person laying there dying or dead. I would turn the car around again and again and again (twenty to thirty times would not be a stretch) to go back and look at it, to confirm that it was not a dead or dying person.

2. ***Hitting Bumps in the Road While Driving My Car.*** *Every* time I ran over a noticeable bump while driving my car, I would think immediately that I might have hit a person. My first reaction would be to look in the rearview mirror to ensure I didn't hit anyone. That, of course, would be followed by a line of reasoning that would convince me that I had a bad view in the mirror and therefore would have to turn around to go check—again and again and again. When I would arrive at my destination, the first thing I would do is get out of the car and check to ensure there wasn't a body part, blood, or a piece of clothing on the bumper. I then waited for hours, sometimes days, sure that the police would arrive at my door and arrest me for hit and run.

3. ***Bodies of Water.*** Pools, ponds, lakes, rivers, and oceans caused me great grief. *Every* time I would drive by or be near a body of water, I would see something that caused me to think that a person was in distress. Again, if I was in my car, I would turn around to go back for another look, repeatedly, until I was able to convince myself on a prayer that a person was not drowning. Sometimes I would drive by a body of water and deliberately not look into the water (thinking that if I didn't look, I couldn't see anything that might be a problem). That didn't work. I would merely think that my failure to look was a deliberate act that prevented me from seeing the person in distress, so therefore, I was more culpable in the distressed person's death.

4. ***Accountability of People Swimming.*** Related to issue number three, I could not go to a pool, a lake, or an ocean without keeping careful watch of who went into the water and who came out of the water. I remember being at the beach along the Atlantic Ocean at Camp Lejeune and losing track of two women who I had seen go in the water. I approached the lifeguard, and said, "It's probably nothing, but I saw two women go in the water about a half hour ago. I never saw them come out." He gave me a long blank stare. "Are you telling me that you think two women drowned out there?" he asked. "No,"

I replied. "I just wanted you to know what I saw." "Thanks," he said, with a hint of sarcasm in his voice. "We'll keep an eye out." He looked at the other lifeguard as if to say, "What a nut." I walked away embarrassed, but at least I was relieved to know that I let someone know about the two women. I told myself that their lives were no longer *my responsibility.*

5. ***Risk of Fire.*** The risk of fire commanded my attention in all venues— at work, at home, in businesses, at gas stations, and while traveling down the road (particularly in wildfire-crazy California, where I was stationed from 1992 to 1994 and visited quite often on business afterward). If I saw anything that had the potential of sparking or catching fire, no matter how remote that possibility might have been—coffeepots, irons, stoves and ovens, discarded cigarettes and matches, candles, electrical cords, and overused outlets—I focused on it. If I saw it, I wouldn't rest until I brought it to someone's attention.

I remember once leaving a business, going home, and then finally succumbing to the thoughts, the anguish, and the pain, driving about ten miles back to the business to let them know that they might want to check the plugs in a particular outlet that wasn't in plain view. In classic OCD form, there were days I could not even get to my car in the driveway without going back inside the house numerous times to make sure the coffeepot, the stove, and the iron were off. There were even times when I would get halfway to my office, only to have my OCD tell me that the coffeepot or stove might be on, and as a consequence, my house would burn down and my family would be in grave danger. In response to this, I would either call my wife or turn around myself to go home to check it.

Gas stations were always an OCD-rich experience for me. If I dripped any gasoline (even a drop) while returning the gas nozzle to the pump, I would report it to the attendant. After returning the nozzle to the pump and putting the gas cap back on my tank, I would check and recheck several times to make sure both were in place before I would get into my car. Also, I would avoid driving over the covers to the underground gasoline storage tanks out of fear that I would dislodge the cover, causing either gas vapors to leak out or someone to step on the cover and fall in. If I did by chance happen to drive over a cover, I would go into the gas station and tell the attendant what I had just done. To make matters worse, gas presented a dual threat for me. Gas either meant there was a risk of fire or explosion or it meant there was an environmental/safety hazard, which leads me to my next group of symptoms.

6. ***Environmental/Safety Hazards.*** Anything that looked like it could cause an environmental or safety concern became, for all intents and purposes, my sole focus. For example, a discarded container of any chemical, such as antifreeze, on the side of the road, broken glass, spills of any liquid on a floor or walkway, missing gas caps, gas spilled on the ground (even just a few drops and even at a gas station), and the smell of gasoline (even at a gas station) received my undivided attention. Basically, I was in physical pain, sweating, and in great distress until I brought the issue to the attention of someone who had responsibility for the area. Here are a few anecdotes to give you a clearer image of my condition.

- In 1995, I was getting ready to mow the lawn of the house I was renting. I filled the lawnmower's gas tank, started the engine, and proceeded to mow, only to discover quickly that I forgot to put the gas cap back on the tank. A small amount of gas (less than an ounce) splashed on the ground. Within seconds, I concluded that the gas would seep through the ground into the ground water and poison the entire community. I had moved the mower about two feet, so it wasn't as if I could point to one particular small spot on the ground to identify where the gas was. I knelt down with my nose nearly touching the earth and proceeded to smell the ground to see where the gas had spilled. I then dug a hole with a perimeter about one foot outside where I figured the gas had spilled and about one foot deep. I put the partially contaminated dirt in a trash bag (lined by another trash bag) and took it to the dump to turn it in as hazardous waste. After I got back home, and for the next week, I conducted my sniff tests to make sure I had removed all of the gas. Seven months later, I conducted the sniff test on this spot once again prior to moving out of the house.
- I was an environmental lawyer for the Marine Corps at Camp Lejeune. As Marines do, we would go out for a three- to five-mile

run around noon every day. I dreaded going. First, we usually ran near the water (we've already discussed this problem). Second, I could not go for a run without inspecting every piece of trash that was lying on the ground, to make sure it wasn't something that could cause an environmental spill. One of the majors in my office used to rib me (in a good-natured way), saying, "Shannon is the Camp Lejeune trash man" and "Shannon never saw a piece of trash he didn't like."

• On one occasion, I noticed some broken glass laying sporadically over a half-mile stretch of a dirt path used by joggers and cyclists at Camp Lejeune. The thought that a Marine or civilian family member or base employee might fall and cut themselves or blow out a bicycle tire plagued me all day until late in the evening. From my home, I telephoned the Base Officer of the Day and reported it. "Okaaaayyy," he said, not knowing what to make of my report. "I'll let Base Safety know about it and I'm sure they'll send someone there to clean up the glass on Monday." I was embarrassed, *but at least the blood of the soon-to-be injured was off of my hands.*

• In 1996, my younger sister and her family visited us in Jacksonville, North Carolina. I was giving them a windshield tour of the base when I saw what looked like a bag of lawn fertilizer lying on the side of the road, across from one of the ammunition supply points. I turned the car around, stopped, got out, and sure enough, it was a half-empty bag of fertilizer. I immediately thought about the fact that fertilizer was one of the ingredients to make the explosives used in the 1994 Oklahoma City bombings. Over the course of an hour, as we continued to sightsee and then drove toward my house, I struggled, openly and verbally, in the presence of my sister and her husband as to whether I should report this to the military police. It was all they could do to keep me from calling. My sister, noticing this peculiar behavior that she had not witnessed before in me, asked, "Is everything okay with you?" I did not call and for the next several *weeks,* I simply awaited the report that the ammunition supply point had been hit by a terrorist and then about how much I would be shamed because I could have prevented it.

• I helped coach my five-year-old son's soccer team. While the head coach warmed up the team prior to each game, I would walk every square inch of the soccer field to ensure that there were no rocks or other objects that could hurt the kids. If I ran out of time and was unable to check a particular part of the field, I would tell the head coach and referee that I had found some rocks on one part of the field but was unable to check the other part. I hated the looks they would give me, but at least *it would not be my fault if one of the kids fell and got hurt.*

7. **Safety Issues with Other Vehicles.** I constantly kept a watchful eye out for problems with other vehicles. Missing gas caps, objects hanging low or dragging beneath or behind the vehicle, and tire abnormalities were just a few of the problems that garnered my attention. I remember getting behind a newer pickup truck on the way home from work in Jacksonville one evening. It appeared as if the left back tire on the truck was wobbling. I tried to wave at the driver but to no avail. I followed him off the route that I would normally take, down a few country roads, and finally into a not-so-well-lit industrial park. He jumped out of the truck and ran back to my car. "What the f** do you want?" he demanded, ready to fight. "You've been following me for thirty minutes." Rather embarrassed, I simply said, "I was trying to get your attention. Your left rear tire looks like it was wobbling." He glanced at his tire, which had some dirt on it (thus causing the optical illusion of a wobble as the tire rolled) and said, "My tire is fine. Mind your own f***in' business! You're going to get yourself killed following people like this." My wife agreed with this assessment after I told her this story when *I finally* got home that night.

8. **Checking Cars Parked on the Roadside.** Cars parked on the side of the road presented huge dilemmas for me. Some roadside cars have occupants; some do not. Some are broken down; some are simply sitting there while the driver waits for someone. For me, *every* car on the side of the road was a potential site of a person who might be dead or dying. If there was a car stopped on the side of the road, it received a quick glance from me to see if anyone was inside (possibly in need of help). More times than I care to remember, I would rightly conclude that the car was empty, but then be convinced that I either didn't get a good look or maybe that I did see a person. This, of course, led to countless checks and rechecks, only to discover the car was empty, or more often than not, that the "person" I saw was just

a headrest on the seat. The distant sight of a car on the roadside used to make my stomach turn because I knew what awaited me.

I remember once seeing a car on the side of the road in Jacksonville. A man (yes, I actually did know this was a person) was lying back in the driver's seat with his head tilted back. I drove on. Quickly convinced that the man was probably dead, I decided to go back and check. I turned around, drove back, stopped my car, approached the driver's side window, and tapped on the door. The guy sprang up and nearly came through the open window at me. "What are you doing?" he screamed. Stuttering through it, I said, "I thought you were hurt." "Well, I'm not. I'm sleeping. Leave me be," he replied. This story also prompted my wife to tell me that "Someday, someone is going to shoot you."

9. ***Kids and Animals Left in Cars.*** I dreaded driving or walking through parking lots because of my focus on the possibility that there might be kids or animals left in cars. I would avoid going to grocery stores, malls, and other businesses because of this reason alone. I could not walk through a parking lot, particularly during the summer, without *going out of my way* to look in car windows or listen carefully for sounds of distress, to ensure there were no kids or animals left in cars. If I wasn't convinced that I did a good enough job of looking or listening after going into the store or getting back into my car to leave, I would return to the parking lot to try to satisfy my doubt.

10. ***How Parents Treat Their Kids.*** This will sound odd coming from a father who at the time had two small children, but I dreaded going to places where there were children. I knew that I would become focused (to the exclusion of my own family and even to the exclusion of why I was there in the first place) on the actions or words of other parents in dealing with their kids. I would actively watch and listen to how parents were interacting with their children. I *always* found a reason to be concerned. It got to the point where I would try not to focus on what others were saying around me so I wouldn't hear anything objectionable, which resulted in me *only* focusing on what others were saying. One incident stands out in my mind. I still regret the way I handled it, because my behavior affected one of my sons.

When my oldest son was four, he got really sick. I took him to the emergency room at the naval hospital on Camp Lejeune. While we were in the waiting room, a woman across the room behind me was trying to deal with her rambunctious small children. I listened to her repeatedly tell the kids to settle down, and then at one point I thought I heard her say (or my OCD convinced me that she said) something about slapping her child in the face. *Did she really say that?* I glanced in the direction of where the comment was made. I was alarmed by what I thought I had heard, but I didn't do or say anything about it initially.

Over the next ten to fifteen minutes (at which point my son's name was called to be seen) I struggled over whether to do anything about the mother. I became convinced that my inaction would result in those children being beaten and tortured by their mother. I told my son's nurse what I thought I may have heard, although I did not know where the mother had gone. She agreed that the woman should not have said what she said (if she even said it), but indicated if I didn't have a name or couldn't point the woman out, there was nothing they could do. I immediately panicked, thinking that my failure to act back in the waiting room meant that those children were in danger of being beaten for the rest of their childhood. (And it would be my fault and when people found out that I could have done something to stop it, I would be shamed out of the Marine Corps.) I told the nurse that I would be right back. I left my son on the gurney in the ER with her so that I could go find the woman and then point her out to the hospital staff. After searching for a while, I found her on another floor of the hospital. I confronted her and her husband. She denied ever saying it and her husband told me that such accusations were pretty serious and he did not understand why I would make something like that up. Embarrassed, I left them and returned to my son. I had been gone about fifteen minutes. He was crying because I had left him for such a long time, and the nurse was fuming. I felt two inches tall.

11. **Locked Doors.** Whether it was leaving home or leaving work, I checked, rechecked, and checked some more to make sure doors were locked. I would almost instantaneously play out the potential consequences (e.g., murderer entering the house and mutilating my family) of leaving a door unlocked. Again it would not be a stretch to say that I rechecked door locks up to twenty to thirty times before I would finally move on, still unsure whether the door was locked. I

often would twist the knob and violently push and pull on the knob while saying aloud to myself, "I'm holding the knob and pushing the door. It is locked. It is locked." I would get into my car, begin to drive off, and I would think, *You were concentrating so hard on the words you were saying, you didn't pay attention to whether the door was actually locked.* I would turn around and go check it again. This became life-altering in 1993 and 1994 in California after my first son started walking and we lived just off of a well-traveled road. It once took me about forty-five minutes to actually get further than a quarter mile away from my house, because I turned around so many times to check the door.

12. ***Perceived Defects in the Wings of Airplanes.*** I traveled frequently for the Marine Corps. *Every* time I got on a plane, I would visually inspect the wing while sitting in my seat to ensure there were no defects such as cracks. I remember at least two occasions where, after OCD convinced me that the plane crash was going to be my fault if I didn't disclose what I had discovered, I called the flight attendant (once pre-flight and once in-flight) to point out what appeared to be a crack in the wing. On both occasions, the flight attendants explained that the plane underwent a thorough pre-flight safety inspection and it would be "okay."

13. ***Proofreading Documents.*** As an attorney, I wrote many legal opinions, some rather lengthy. That wasn't problematic because conscientious attorneys write thorough legal opinions. What was problematic was when I would make one or two changes in a document. Instead of simply printing the page with the change, I would print the entire document and then read every word of the document each time it was printed. I was convinced there was a potential that making the change(s) might cause the document to change in some other way and that this would result in providing incorrect legal advice (which, in turn, might result in the client taking a course of action that either got the client in trouble or would result in environmental harm). I was convinced that if I didn't print and read the entire document word for word (again), I would not know with certainty whether there had been any other deletions or changes. It would take me hours upon hours to get a document finalized.

14. ***Contamination/Poison.*** I can't count how many times a day I washed my hands, out of fear that I would contaminate or poison

other people, especially my children. If I came into contact with anything remotely related to waste, dirt, bacteria, or a chemical substance (including animals, fish, reptiles, and even containers holding the waste, dirt, bacteria, or chemical), I would go to great lengths to remove all traces of the source. I washed my hands when most folks do (when they are actually dirty, such as after using the restroom) and when most folks don't. It became ritualistic. I would wash my hands and then wipe down any surface that I might have contacted, such as doorknobs, countertops, spray bottles that held the chemical, the sink, the faucet handles, and the soap dispenser. I would then wash my hands again to complete the cycle.

The concern over contamination and poison wasn't just limited to my hands. It extended to my clothes and shoes. If my clothes or shoes came into contact with anything "dirty," I would change them as soon as possible (and clean anything with which they came into contact). When walking on or across a parking lot, driveway, or road, I was extremely careful not to step in or let my children step in any type of fluid leakage or spill on the ground or even a slight stain from a previous leak or spill. If I did, I would immediately take my shoes off, and as soon as I got home, either clean them with soap and water (which, in turn, triggered issues about releasing contaminants into the sewage system, or if I used a hose in the yard, about contaminating the earth and ground water). If I didn't feel like worrying about the issues related to washing my shoes, I would simply throw the shoes away. (Yet another reason to avoid my garage, gas stations, and parking lots.)

15. ***Checking Out of Hotels or Rented Houses.*** As I already stated, I traveled quite often with the Marine Corps. Consequently, I stayed in countless hotel rooms. As an additional by-product of serving in the military, my family moved a lot. We lived in six different rented houses between 1989 and 1997. Interestingly, notwithstanding issue number fourteen above, I was never concerned about whether the rooms or houses had any existing contamination when I got there. What sent me into the "endless loop" was trying to check out of the room or the house, recognizing that I would never return. The finality of leaving the place and the thought that I might have left the room or house in unsafe (e.g., forgetting to turn off an iron, coffeepot, lamp,

or the stove, or forgetting to lock the doors and windows), unsanitary (e.g., forgetting to flush the toilet or spilling something and the carpet getting moldy), or damaged (even just a nick) condition caused me to revisit and reinspect the room or the house over and over and over.

In 1995, when my wife and I moved from Charlottesville, Virginia, to Jacksonville, North Carolina (after living in a rented house for only nine months), it took four days to get the house in "perfect" condition and nearly a half a day to stop going back into the house to reinspect everything. I made the same circuit through the house each time, checking every light in every room, checking the stove, checking the water, checking the windows, and checking the locks. Oh, and yes, as I mentioned before, I even conducted another "sniff" test on the lawn because it was here where I had spilled a small amount of gasoline seven months before.

16. *Standing "Duty" as the Command Officer-of-the-Day.* Standing "duty" is a regular part of life in the military. It requires one to report to the command headquarters building once a month or so to serve as the Commanding Officer's after-hours representative from the close of business until the morning of the following day. A normal tour of duty generally encompasses presiding over evening/morning Colors, windshield inspections of the geographic area of responsibility for the command, answering phones, handling Red Cross notifications and emergency travel, etc. The officer of the day records significant events in a duty logbook, which is turned in to the command Chief of Staff or Executive Officer at the end of the duty period. For most officers, an average logbook for a tour of duty would run one to two pages.

Enter my OCD. I dreaded standing duty. The average length of my logbook entries ran somewhere around seven pages. For me, practically every phone call, observation, and occurrence was at least potentially significant and worth verifying, reverifying, or otherwise worth reporting. It got to the point—so I was told by a Gunnery Sergeant who stood duty with me a few times at Camp Pendleton in 1993 and 1994—where staff noncommissioned officers would check the duty roster to see if they had duty with me. If they did, they would do everything within their power to switch dates.

I remember a particular incident in 1995 while standing duty in the Army's Judge Advocate General School in Charlottesville, Virginia

(I was attending the school working on a Master of Laws degree in 1994–95). On one of my rounds inside the building in the middle of the night, I looked out a window into the parking lot and saw someone placing a large brown paper grocery bag into a dumpster. Initially, I thought it was probably a resident student throwing away some trash. My OCD tried to convince me that someone may have been placing a bomb in the dumpster. After an hour of fretting that I had witnessed the next Oklahoma City bombing in progress and failed to do anything about it, I finally went out and climbed into the dirty dumpster only to find out that the "bomb" was really just a bag of trash.

The Episode That Triggered My Decision to Seek Help— Someone's Bleeding to Death

October 23, 1997, Jacksonville, North Carolina. (Told in the first person present so you can stand in my shoes and experience this as I did.)

I am a Major in the U.S. Marine Corps. I've been on active duty for almost nine years and a Major for a little more than a year. My oldest son is five years old and my youngest son recently turned one. It's 5:45 a.m., still dark, on a cool October morning in Jacksonville, North Carolina. I want to get to my office on Camp Lejeune by 6:00 a.m. to put the final touches on a memo due to one of my senior clients by 8:00 a.m.

I dread going out of the house because I know *something* is going to happen. It is an eleven-mile drive to my office. I get into my car and begin the painful trek. *What's it going to be today? A dead body on the side of the road? Someone drowning in the New River? A wheel about to fall off a car? A strong smell of gasoline fumes in the air? Just get to work.* My stomach is already in knots.

About halfway to the base, I stop at a red light at a major intersection. An industrial park sits dark and lifeless across the intersection on the right side. My windows are down to take advantage of the cool air. There's no traffic anywhere. *CRACK!*—a noise shatters the pre-dawn morning. *What was that? It came from the direction of the industrial park.* I immediately identify the sound as a piece of lumber falling on concrete. I look over in the direction of the industrial park but don't see anything. *Just a piece of lumber.* Light turns green. I start to drive. *Piece of lumber ... or was it a gunshot? A gunshot?! No, it wasn't a gunshot; it was a piece of lumber. Just drive. No, it was a gunshot. Someone's probably hurt.*

I give a half-glance into the industrial park as I drive by, hoping not to see anything so I can confirm in my mind the "falling lumber" theory. I don't want to look too carefully, however, because I'm afraid I'll actually see something that will cause me to investigate further. I don't see anything, so I continue to drive. I get about a half mile down the road and my heart starts to beat faster and my hands get clammy. *You idiot, you didn't look. Someone is bleeding to death back there and you're just going to drive on to work? That poor soul's blood is on your hands. . . . It was a piece of lumber! It wasn't a gunshot. . . . Just check and make sure.* "Damn it," I say out loud. I turn the car around and drive back past the industrial park, staring intently, but I don't see anything. *See, it was nothing.*

I turn the car back around and head toward Camp Lejeune. I pass the industrial park, this time not looking because I've "confirmed" that it was nothing. About a quarter mile past the industrial park, I see a person walking along the side of the road in a direction away from the industrial park. He's wearing a hooded sweatshirt with the hood pulled up over his head. I think I see something in his hand. *What's that in his hand? Is that a gun? No it's not a gun. It's something else.* My heart is racing. My chest is getting tighter. I get hot flashes. I start to perspire. *God, that might have been a gun! A person is bleeding to death in the industrial park, the guy who pulled the trigger is walking down the street with a gun in his hand, and YOU'RE just going to drive to work?!* "F***!" I scream, pounding my fist on the steering wheel. "What is wrong with me?!" I yell. "It was just a piece of lumber!" I turn back around and drive very slowly past the industrial park. I see nothing. I turn the car around to head toward Camp Lejeune. It's now 6:00 a.m.

I drive past the industrial park toward the base and past the point where I saw the guy walking. *Oh Jesus, where did he go!? Shit, you should've followed him. There's a potential killer on the loose. You were in a position to do something about it and you were too afraid to do anything. You f***ing coward. And had you driven into the industrial park, you would have found the person bleeding to death. But that person has got to be dead by now. You at least have to call the police and let them check it out. People are already going to be ashamed of you for not taking action quicker. You're no Marine, you're nothing but a f***ing coward. You don't deserve to live. Just kill yourself to spare yourself the shame.* I get about three miles from the industrial park toward the direction of Camp Lejeune and see a pay phone at a gas station parking lot. *Police? 9-1-1? They're going to laugh at me. The only thing I have to report is a noise that sounded like* *lumber. I can't call 9-1-1.* I look in the phone book for the non-emergency number for the police department and dial the phone. It rings and rings and rings. No answer. I'm relieved because I at least attempted to call the police and now I don't have to be embarrassed about reporting the "mystery of the falling lumber." I get back in my car and continue toward work. It's 6:15 a.m. *Damn it! I'm late.*

As I drive toward the base, my heart is pounding so hard it feels like it is going to burst out of my chest. Like every other time I discover a problem and fail to do something about it, I get hot flashes, my chest tightens, I start to sweat, and I have a knot in my stomach. *There is still someone dying back there and the murderer is loose—probably breaking into someone's house getting ready to kill again. In fact, he's probably killing someone else right now. You have to go back and help the person dying in the industrial park or at least report it.* "F***, f***, f***!" I scream, pounding my fist on the dashboard. "What's wrong with me?!" I turn the car around and head back to the industrial park. In a strip mall parking lot near the industrial park I see two patrol cars with their parking lights on. I take a deep breath, pull into the lot, and prepare to embarrass myself. *I can hear the officers now, "You heard a gunshot and saw a suspect almost an hour ago, and now you're reporting it?" "What's wrong with you? And you're a Marine? You better hope that person is not dead."*

It is now past 6:30 a.m. I approach the officers and attempt to determine how best to convey the information in a way that will prompt them to check it out, but not alarm them and not emphasize my own dereliction. "May I help you?" one officer asks. I begin the way I've begun when alerting someone in authority about a self-imposed "problem" so many times before.... "It's probably nothing, but I just wanted to let you know what I heard and what I saw about forty-five minutes ago...." I explain about the noise that sounded like a piece of lumber but that could have been a gunshot, and about the guy I saw walking. The officers look at each other and the driver turns to me and says, "I'm sure it's okay. We would have heard something about it if it was a gunshot." I thank them, walking away embarrassed but relieved. *I let them know about it; if they don't want to do anything about it that's on them.*

The hot flashes and the pounding heart go away. *Until the next thing happens, that is.* I feel as though I have a tortured soul. For the first time in thirteen years, since my mother's early death, tears begin to well up in my eyes. As I completed my drive to my office on that morning in October

1997, I finally concluded that I needed professional help. *Your career is over. You are such a failure as a father and husband. What a disappointment.* But I concluded I had no other reasonable choices. I had boiled it down to either being seen by a doctor, living forever in my own prison of anguish and pain, or simply ending it all. Later that morning, from my office, I called the psychiatric unit at the Camp Lejeune Naval Hospital. It was the smartest decision I ever made.

POSTTRAUMATIC STRESS DISORDER (PTSD)

Emotional Triangle

BLAZIE HOLLING

August 3, 1993, is a day I will remember forever. I woke up full of anxiety and began rushing around preparing to leave for a family gathering that afternoon. We were having a baby shower at my sister Pat's house just a mile away. I'd been irritated with everyone and everything I came into contact with that morning. I kept telling myself that all I had to do was just get to the party and relax, but I felt like a ticking time bomb about to explode at any moment. My emotions were consuming me. I cried at the slightest upset. I was perspiring profusely and felt like I had a ton of bricks on my chest crushing the breath out of me.

I hadn't been making good judgment calls for months and at the time I thought this was just due to all the stress I felt from my job. On my way to the party I decided to stop at the neighborhood bar for a cold beer hoping this would take the edge off my anxiety. I had two beers, but I can't say they made me feel any better. The party had already started and I knew my family would be really upset if I got there much later. I left the calm darkness of the bar behind, stepped out into the glaring light of day, and drove to my sister Pat's baby shower.

I walked into the back yard of my sister's house and heard the familiar voices laughing, Mexican music turned up a little too loud, and the children chasing each other around in delight. I didn't hear these sounds the same way as everyone else. They were all smiling and they seemed happy to be together, but to me everything was amplified ten times the normal and this was quickly becoming unbearable.

As I looked around at their faces, something began to happen that I didn't understand. It seemed like I didn't know anybody there, they all looked different, their faces had become distorted and I began to feel extremely nervous. Everything seemed to start spinning around and suddenly I didn't feel safe. I thought I might feel better if I could just block it all out, but I couldn't find a quiet corner anywhere. Then I knew one thing for sure—I was going to get physically ill at any moment.

Somehow I managed to move through the crowd of people and duck into the house without anyone stopping me.

As I quickly pushed the bathroom door closed behind me, my stomach lurched and I vomited so violently that my body shook and tears came to my eyes. I continued to vomit and vomit until nothing was left in my stomach, but my body didn't seem to know this and so I crouched over the toilet and continued to heave and gag until I couldn't catch my breath. I feared that I was going to faint onto the floor. How long could I endure this? I then became horrified by the realization that I was not gaining back any control of my own body, my chest began to ache and pain shot through me.

I knew I needed to get help, but I couldn't even call out or move toward the door. My sisters were in the back yard, just a few yards from the bathroom window, but there was no way for me to get their attention. The words could not come out, and the thoughts kept speeding through my mind, "This is it. I'm either dying or having a nervous breakdown." It seemed like I was in that bathroom for hours, but it couldn't have been hours because someone would have looked for me if I had been missing that long.

Finally, I got a break in the attack and I was able to run out of the house and get to the safety of my car. The moment I turned the key in the ignition, my emotions took over again and I began crying like I'd never cried before in my entire life. I just sobbed. There were so many tears pouring from my soul. My heart was breaking and I didn't even know why. Somehow I drove home, but I must have been in a complete blackout, because I don't remember what streets I turned on or when I came across a signal light. I just remember pulling into the driveway and running for the safety of the house.

My partner, Ruby, held me as I cried for the next two hours. I was so nervous I couldn't even speak; I was having a complete emotional breakdown. In my mind I was telling myself, "This is not the way I am supposed to go. I'm going to end up curled up in some corner in some mental hospital because I had a nervous breakdown."

After a few hours, I started to calm down. I was listening to some soft music and then I put on the TV. I was very quiet and moving very slowly around the house. A few hours later, I thought, "Okay, I'm going to be okay." But I was scared because at this point in my life my mind, my body, and my spirituality had been on empty for a very long time. I felt like I was being held together with little pieces of string.

I went to bed that evening feeling very scared. Holding a rosary in my hand, I went into our guest room, surrounded myself with pillows, and piled on tons of blankets. I left the window wide open and slept with a nightlight on. That was the only time I've ever slept with a nightlight on. I was very, very scared.

Then it happened. Just when I thought I was going to be okay, I started choking and getting chest pains. It was one o'clock in the morning and I could not breathe. I just knew that this was going to be a stroke that could paralyze me or that I was about to die from choking on something I ate the day before. My roommate heard me and ran into the room. She could see I was in great distress and called paramedics. When the paramedics got there they tried to clear an airway so that I could breathe. They strapped on an oxygen mask and with siren wailing rushed me to the emergency room. On the way, I thought I saw something out of the corner of my eye. I lifted my head off the stretcher for a moment to look and I thought I saw my mother's face outside the window. All I could think was, "Oh my God, she's going to lose another child.... I'm going to die."

We arrived at the hospital and they ran hour after hour of tests. When the doctor finally came to talk to me he told me there was nothing blocking my breathing, nothing in my throat. He told me I was suffering from something called a "panic attack."

I didn't believe this doctor. My mother, who had come to the hospital to be with me, didn't believe him either. After a few hours we left the hospital. That morning on the drive home I had my third panic attack and it was even worse than the first two. My mother and Ruby rushed me to another emergency room. We were sure the first hospital must have made an incorrect diagnosis. My mind was racing. I felt sure I was going to die at any moment and I told myself I was okay with it. I was okay with God and I was ready for it to just happen now.

When we arrived at the second hospital they repeated all the tests. By this time I was completely hysterical. A doctor came in and after asking my family to leave he sat down next to me. I remember him saying a few magic words. He said, "You are going to be okay. Tell me what's on your mind."

I thought they just couldn't get a priest there fast enough for my last rites and this doctor was there to hold my hand for a few moments until I died. I wanted to get everything off my chest and out of my mind before I made my transition. I didn't want to die with the secret untold, and so for the very first time I told someone about the violent murder I had witnessed as a child. I told him about my night terrors and described to him all the ugly images that I couldn't keep out of my mind. After about an hour and a half I think I had told him about every single person I had known who had died and how.

Out of all the experiences I've had in life I will never forget this night. It was the scariest physical feeling I have ever experienced. The doctor wanted to send me to someone who specialized in grief and posttraumatic stress disorder. At the time I was thinking, "What the hell for! How could that possibly help me with the choking?" He sent me home with a prescription for sedatives and a few phone numbers for therapists.

My first counseling appointment was in two weeks. During that waiting period I barely said one or two words a day. I know this sounds very dramatic, but I was actually supervised by various family members 24 hours a day. I was never left alone even for a moment. I ended up being off from work for four months. I started a seemingly endless series of appointments—stress management classes, counselors, and doctors.

During that four-month period I didn't even put the key in the car ignition. I was driven to every single appointment by my nephew Michael or by my friends. After about four months of therapy I started to feel a little patched together and I felt up to driving again. Even though I was ready to return to work, I was worried about how I was going to manage going back to supervising my department. But it turned out there was even a special course for people returning to work after having been away for a while, just to show them how to get through that first week back at the job.

I wrote this book to show that anyone, regardless of how emotionally strong and how physically healthy they are, no matter how strong their spiritual foundation—*anyone* with such traumatic events in their life occurring one after the other can crumble like a house of cards.

I now realize if I had gotten counseling after the first or second trauma or even read a few books explaining posttraumatic stress and the grieving process, things would not have gotten so bad. I would have had some idea of what I was going through and maybe found some comfort in this understanding. But I didn't know about these things. All I knew was that I didn't want to burden my family or my friends with the terrible feelings I was having or the horrible images that bombarded my mind constantly. I thought I could take care of things myself—and I was wrong.

I remember every minute detail of the day my carefree childhood was stolen from me, the day my life forever changed. It was just before lunch and my mother needed a quart of milk to make macaroni and cheese—my favorite. I was seven years old and would be a second grader when school started in a few weeks. I was so proud of myself to be old enough to go on an errand by myself, and I bounded out the door with a dollar tucked safely in my pocket.

It was one of those perfect California days, sunny and breezy with a slight autumn crispness, and I whistled happily as I walked to the little store around the corner. I remember looking back and seeing my mother sitting worry-free on the front porch. She waved to me and I waved back as I made my way up the sidewalk of our block where everyone knew each other, the kids played ball safely in the street and no one even locked their front door during the day.

I loved the corner store. My big sister, Karen, worked there summers and on weekends after school started in September. It had just about everything you could need in the way of groceries, all jammed together in one small room. I took my time walking around the store looking at cans of fruit and boxes of cereal, making my way slowly to the dairy section. I carefully chose just the right bottle of milk. The bottle was heavy and the glass felt so cold as I carried it carefully, holding it tight against my chest with two hands. I brought it to the front counter and handed my sister the money.

She smiled at me and played along with my pretend game of being a grownup shopper, until I got to the door where she couldn't resist admonishing me to be careful and not drop the bottle or lose the change on the way home. I smiled back, too happy to be offended, and let the screen door swing shut behind me with a satisfying "Bang!"

As I walked back home, whistling a little tune, I had no sense of foreboding, no premonition that my innocence was about to be lost forever, my sense of trust destroyed, and that I would *never* feel safe again. I walked up the block, rounded the corner, and stopped. There, on the ground in broad daylight, lay a man, prone, exposed, and surrounded by three menacing men, one of whom I recognized.

Quickly, my eyes darted away, hoping I hadn't been noticed staring at the group. I dared another glance and realized that someone had placed a funnel into the man's mouth. One of the surrounding men held a little bottle and he was pouring a liquid through the funnel into the struggling man's mouth.

I'll never forget that funnel. It was extra wide at the top and narrow at the base; the steel glistened in the sun. The liquid started foaming in the man's mouth and on his face where it splashed while he thrashed about, wild eyed, trying to escape. I was horrified, terrified, and fascinated all at the same time.

I tried to pretend not to see, but I couldn't seem to tear my eyes away from what was happening. Fear seized my muscles and I dropped the bottle. It shattered loudly and I peed my pants as suddenly all eyes were on me. One of the men looked directly into my eyes. He knew me. His name was Victor (name changed), and he was one of my uncles.

Victor motioned at me, waving me past the group of men while the man they were holding down continued his desperate struggle. I was frozen in horror and paralyzed by fear. Nervous anxiety swept over me and I began to softly whistle a little made-up tune. From that moment to this, whenever fright overtakes me I unconsciously whistle the same tune, note for note, the little melody forever imprinted in my mind.

Petrified, I tried to will my body to move. My mind raced in confusion, trying to understand the violence I was witnessing. I was mesmerized by its viciousness and terrified by its reality. Suddenly, my body shifted into survival mode and began propelling me toward home. My mind attempted to protect and distract me by repeating a series of nonsensical numbers—one-two, one-two-three, one-two, one-two-three—through the whistling. The numbers made no sense, but I couldn't stop myself from repeating them over and over again until I reached the safety of home.

I burst through the front door of our house and began searching for my mother, *needing* to tell her what I had witnessed, silently praying I would find her quickly so she could comfort me and restore my sense of security. I raced through the house searching each room. Unable to find her I headed for the back yard.

There she was! She was hanging laundry without a care in the world. She was positioning a bedsheet on the line as I reached for the handle to the sliding door leading to the backyard. It was a tricky door and difficult to open. As my little fingers grasped the door handle and I frantically attempted to open it, I felt a heavy weight on my shoulder. Panic filled me as I was forcibly pulled away from the door. Death had followed me home.

Panic, Anxiety, PTSD, and My Experiences of Healing Through Multiple Avenues of Psychotherapy

CATHERINE MCCALL

I've been a marriage and family therapist for almost 30 years. I'm a 62-year-old mother of four, grandmother of six, and I've been married to my husband, Peter, for over 40 years. Ours is a deeply connected, stable, affectionate marriage. Not that it's always been that way; it hasn't. There were years—just as our daughters were beginning college—when our marriage required open heart surgery and extensive rehab: marital therapy, sex therapy, individual therapy, family therapy, group therapy, and hypnotherapy, in varying sequence depending upon what was going on.

The Beginning

I initially sought therapy when I was in my late 20s, and at that time I had no idea that I would eventually become a therapist myself. I was suffering with panic attacks and agoraphobia, though I'd never heard of either. Errands as simple as running to the grocery store for milk and bread became terrifying. My heart would race, I'd break into a sweat, and then hyperventilate. My internist told me that if I'd stick my finger down my throat and gag, my heart would resume normal pacing, so I did that. My husband taught me that I could stop hyperventilating by breathing into a paper bag, so I carried one in my purse, and lived in fear that despite following their suggestions something was horribly wrong with me. The panic attacks would only happen again and again … which they did.

I had four young children who needed a responsible, loving mommy and were involved with various activities around town, so I forced myself to do things. But when I took our youngest to her pediatrician for a routine vaccination and the sight of the needle nearly catapulted me out of the room, I decided it was time to get professional help. I was afraid that I was going crazy or worse … dying of a brain tumor.

We were living in Auburn, Alabama, at the time, and I made an appointment with a professor on the graduate school faculty of the Marriage and Family Therapy Program at the university. Looking back, it's remarkable that I had the courage to seek therapy. Though my father was a physician who had been taught by Carl Jung and Alfred Adler during psychiatry rounds in medical school, he was vehemently opposed to psychotherapy. I can still remember him leaning toward me at the dining room table, pointing his finger only inches from my face: "Let me tell you something, young lady," he said, "you'll be a lot better off in this life if you leave some things unexplored. And don't *ever* go near a psychiatrist or anyone connected with psychology in any way, if you know what's good for you." But now it was time to taste the forbidden fruit; there was too much at stake.

I was relieved when I first met my therapist, Mary Anne Armour. She was tall, had thick healthy-looking gray hair, and a strong yet gentle voice. There was a reverence about her tone and an almost holy quality to the way she carried herself and listened to me. At the end of my first session she told me that she couldn't promise any guarantees about the outcome of therapy, but she could promise that she would do everything in her professional ability to help me. When I asked how long it would take, she said that when the time came, we'd know. The time came 16 years later, and I'll be forever grateful for every hour of every year I spent in her care, though if anyone had told me at that time that I'd be in therapy for 16 years, I'd have said they were nuts.

Background

My family of origin was nuts, a treasure-trove of psychopathology. My father was an esteemed ophthalmologist, gifted pianist, an untreated manic-depressive, and an alcoholic. My mother was artistic, had a college degree in French, a beautiful, first soprano operatic voice, hosted bridge parties, and was an advanced alcoholic by the time I became a teenager. I'd been a serious child, conscientious, parentified, lonely, though I had friends, a brother three years older than myself, a sister three years younger, and a brother six years younger.

We grew up in a large, elegant brownstone in Brooklyn, New York, and went to parochial schools through high school. I also went to a Catholic women's college: Georgian Court, in Lakewood, New Jersey, where I majored in elementary education. Though many have experienced horrific abuse at the hands of Catholic clergy, that was not my experience. In fact, the Catholic influences in my life were, for the most part, positive for me— nurturing, strengthening, inspiring.

I began going to daily Mass when I was 10 and continued to do so through elementary school, high school, and college. Despite what might have gone on at home—Mother's drunken stupors; Dad's despotic bursts of rage, deep depressions, or manic spending sprees—participation in the ritual of the Mass soothed me and taught me about the power of love, through the teachings of Holy Scripture. Also, because I was aware that the same Mass was being celebrated in churches throughout the world, I felt supported and encouraged by a large spiritual family. As Kathleen Norris puts it in *The Cloister Walk*: "… I could dare to conceive of the Church as a refuge, a place to find the divided self made whole, the voice of the mocker overcome by the voice of the advocate … and I could dare to imagine it as home…."

Looking back, I can see that the mornings I prayed in front of the Blessed Sacrament as a young person prepared me to recognize and be attracted to the reverence I heard in Mary Anne's voice. And if you'll please excuse the cliché, I can tell you that I took to therapy like a duck to water.

My Experience as a Psychotherapy Patient

Seeing Mary Anne helped me to work through the issues that had created my symptoms. Her comments, interpretations, and questions revealed a depth of understanding about my family of origin and the family Peter and I had created. For the first time in my life I felt like I had found someone who heard me accurately, and cared. My anxiety symptoms abated.

Early in treatment she had Peter come in for a few marital sessions and she had the girls come in for a family therapy session. Our girls were ages three, seven, eight, and nine at the time. One of my sweetest therapy memories occurred toward the end of that session when our youngest got up from her chair, walked over to Mary Anne, and asked if she could sit on her lap. Once there, she looked Mary Anne in the eye, smiled and said, "I like you." I've always believed that three-year-olds are the best judges of character, so in my estimation she had bestowed upon our therapist her seal of approval. Mary Anne could be trusted.

Insurance didn't cover Mary Anne's fee, so I got a part-time job with Servpro, washing clothes and linens from houses with smoke damage and hanging them outside on the line to dry. I shudder to think this given the dangers of today's society, but I also sold *World Book* encyclopedias door-to-door, in town and out in the country. Meanwhile, seeing Mary Anne weekly, my therapy developed a momentum and I developed an attachment to her. Though I knew nothing about Object Relations Theory at the time, Mary Anne Armour became all-important, my psychological mother, the internal object who would reorganize my whole history of internal objects.

Through our evolving relationship, which was almost exclusively individual therapy at this phase, I began to feel as if I were being reparented, as if she were picking up where my own mother had left off when I was about 10. She helped me to unravel unconscious conflicts, coached me into a systemic understanding of the function of my anxiety in my marriage, and influenced my mothering style with my children. She helped me to parent them differently, better than I had been parented, and helped me to become a better person. Therapy was a constant quest for truth, a constant dose of reality, which I needed, after growing up in a psychotic, alcoholic family.

I had entertained thoughts of becoming a midwife from the time our youngest daughter was born, but because of my experience as a patient in therapy, psychological processes had become as awe-inspiring to me as childbirth. I began to entertain thoughts of becoming a therapist myself. I also hoped that through doing so I might continue to learn things that would help Peter and I rear our own family.

The Marriage and Family Therapy Program at Auburn emphasized a Psychodynamic orientation at the time when I applied and was accepted, and students were required to be in therapy themselves. However, that soon changed as one professor resigned and another came on board, shifting the program to an experiential perspective. At this point students were encouraged but not required to be in their own therapy, but even this was short-lived. Yet another professor left and two more came on board—a purist strategic therapist and a not-so-purist Ericksonian—both of whom discouraged students from being in therapy. Though I continued seeing Mary Anne and felt that it enhanced my work as a therapist, most of my classmates had never been patients themselves, which in my opinion, was unfortunate for both them and their clients.

I worked my way through graduate school with a teaching assistantship and developed a ravenous appetite for learning, devouring the writings of Klein, Mahler, Winnicott, Whitaker, Napier, Boszormenyi-Nagy, Bowen, Framo, Minuchin, Stierlin, and others. Their concepts awakened insights about my clients' families as well as my own, while the drum roll of the feminist movement lured me into the march for women's rights. As mother of four future women, I was ripe for the writings of Betty Friedan, Gloria Steinem, Letty Cottin Pogrebin, and Adrienne Rich. Meanwhile, my work with Mary Anne helped me to integrate all that I was learning, to renegotiate my relationships with Peter, my parents and siblings, to continue to be attuned to the developmental needs of each of my daughters, and it gave me a deepened appreciation for the sacredness of life and the power of relationship, particularly the therapeutic relationship.

PTSD: The Siege of Symptoms That Bombarded My Life

Ten years into my therapy, there was a major crisis. Mary Anne was diagnosed with breast cancer and went into the hospital for a mastectomy. When she returned from medical leave I had a flashback, while making love with Peter, of being raped by my father when I was 10 years old and Mother was in the hospital.

I had studied about flashbacks, had worked with clients who'd accessed long-repressed memories through the trigger of a sight, a sound, a feeling, or a constellation of factors. I had been intrigued and respectful of the psyche's power. But now, in the wake of my own flashback, I was deeply grieved, and flooded with insights and questions. Devastated, I was soon plagued with intrusive thoughts, images, feelings, flashbacks of more sexual abuse, and nightmares. By this time Mary Anne had moved to Macon, Georgia, and Peter and I had moved to a suburb of Atlanta, where I'd developed a full-time private practice. I needed to reorganize my personal and professional life to accommodate the demanding process of recovery from my new diagnosis: posttraumatic stress disorder (PTSD).

I reduced my client load to less than half, referring out people for whom I felt I might be psychologically compromised. I consulted with a psychiatrist well versed in the nuances of trauma recovery for supervision of my clinical work. I developed a peer supervision group, modeled after Carl Whitaker's cuddle groups, with three colleagues who, like myself, were committed to examining how their personal lives affected their clinical work and vice versa.

My need for therapy intensified. I got into a therapy group in Atlanta for incest survivors and continued seeing Mary Anne for individual therapy weekly. Because she was on the faculty of Mercer University School of Medicine and practiced there in Macon, for me, this meant a two-and-a-half-hour drive south of my suburban Atlanta home. I'd rise at 5:00 and depart ahead of the Atlanta rush hour traffic to make my 8:00 appointment, then return home in time to rest and reorient myself to the needs of my family before school let out. When I was having flashbacks, horrible nightmares, was plagued with vivid memories and suffering from the emotional fallout of these ordeals, my relationship with Mary Anne provided a holding place, and helped me to extricate the poison of shame and repressed rage that tipped me into the depressed side of my emotional landscape.

Expanding the Therapeutic Terrain

Mary Anne and I consulted with a hypnotherapist sporadically, for the purpose of helping me manage flashbacks and nightmares. I benefited also from two intensive weekends of Psychodrama with a therapist trained by Moreno, intermittent sex therapy with another therapist, and marital and family therapy with Mary Anne and a co-therapist. It was a tough time for me, for my husband, and for our daughters, and it was expensive. These were the hell years. They were also years of tremendous personal growth.

Clinical literature on trauma recovery emphasizes the importance of assigning language to experience. As my need for self-expression grew, I wrote journals, letters, prayers, songs. I also needed more therapeutic help and practical support than my husband, treatment team, friends, and family could provide. By this time my siblings had left the burden of care for my parents, who had become destitute and ill, on Peter's and my shoulders, our daughters were working at their own separation–individuation processes, which presented us with challenges characteristic of adolescence. Though earlier in my life the Church had been a source of strength, I could no longer tolerate active participation in Catholicism once I understood how patriarchal systems breed sexual abuse.

Once again, I turned to authors—Mary Anne called it bibliotherapy. I devoured memoirs by Maya Angelou, Louise Wisechild, Nancy Venable Raine, Patricia Weaver Francisco, Carolyn Knapp, Kay Redfield Jamison, Jacki Lyden, Alice Walker, Jill Kerr Conway, Kaethe Weingarten, and Sue William Silverman. The writings of Matthew Fox, Elizabeth Johnson, Rita Nakashima Brock, Joan Chittister, Rosemary Reuther, Judith Crist, and

Megan McKenna nourished my spiritual life. To borrow author Kennedy Fraser's (1997) words:

> I needed all this murmured chorus, this continuum of true-life stories, to pull me through. They were like mothers and sisters to me, these literary women ... more than my own family, they seemed to stretch out a hand ... I was looking for directions, gathering clues. (pp. 3–4)

Soon, out of gratitude and a sense of solidarity with other abuse survivors, I felt compelled to write my own memoir. Through the story of what my father did to me, I hoped to show the world what horrors are inflicted on children, and through the story of my experience as a patient in therapy, I hoped to show how healing happens. I also wanted to illustrate how the wounds of incest can reveal themselves in a long-term monogamous marriage, and how a couple grapples to heal those wounds through the hard work of love. I wanted the intimacy of my story to inspire hope in readers, along with resolve to do their part in making the world a safer place for children.

The writing and publishing of my memoir took 10 years. People often asked me during that time if writing it was cathartic, but it wasn't. I began writing the memoir after terminating therapy, and for me, catharsis came during the therapy. What came as a result of the writing was deeper integration. Southern author Rosemary Daniell, in a writing group of hers that I was in, often said that "revision revises the writer." Now I understand the powerful truth of that statement, and something more: the gift of publication, a profound sense of liberation gained by giving my testimony to the world.

When the Piano Stops: A Memoir of Healing From Sexual Abuse was released by Seal Press in 2009 and the European print, *Never Tell: The True Story of Overcoming a Traumatic Childhood,* was released in the United Kingdom and all the countries of the British Commonwealth by a division of Random House in 2010. It was on the London Sunday Times Paperback Nonfiction Bestseller List for four weeks in the spring of 2010. This has been a source of great joy for my husband and me. In fact, I experience a burst of joy even as I sit here at my computer recounting the events to you.

I've received many e-mails and Facebook fan page messages from readers all over the world, which is deeply touching, gratifying, inspiring, and humbling. In truth, the writing and publication of my memoir has itself been a therapeutic process for me—an unexpected continuation of therapy and healing.

Concluding Comments

These days I rarely suffer from symptoms of PTSD. When symptoms do get activated they're usually circumscribed around a particular event, like the day I was scheduled to fly to New York to visit one of my daughters and became so panicked by a heightened terrorist alert that I couldn't get on the plane. I've learned to reach out to Peter or a close friend since that episode, or to get into therapy with another trusted therapist for a brief period of time, who's trained in EMDR (Eye Movement Desensitization Reprocessing), a therapy modality that has been particularly helpful to me in recent years.

When I first entered Mary Anne's office so many years ago, I hoped that she could help me, but I had no idea about how that might happen, or how long it might take. I had not the faintest glimpse into how our therapeutic relationship would enrich my life, my marriage, my family, nor did I have even a hint about what it would require from either of us. Long-term, in-depth work requires, from both the patient and the therapist, a dedicated commitment to healing, and the ability to endure. Kaethe Weingarten (2010) articulates it well when she notes that "trauma is a circumstance in which the invitation to withdraw from the partnership—on either side—can be great, and the willingness to remain in partnership is ultimately rewarding for both."

I am now a seasoned therapist myself with many years of clinical experience. Mary Anne is retired, in her 80s, and though experiencing the painful realities of her physical decline, she still exudes compassion. We visit several times a year, and enjoy a deep affection and mutual admiration for each other. She keeps a copy of my memoir on her nightstand; I keep a prayer for her in my heart, and a sense of gratitude for this therapist's journey of healing through multiple avenues of psychotherapy.

References

Fraser, K. (1997). *Ornament and silence: Essays on women's lives* (pp. 3–4). New York, NY: Knopf.

Norris, K. (1996). *The cloister walk* (pp. 46, 144–145). New York, NY: Riverhead Books.

Weingarten, K. (2010). Intersecting losses: Working with the inevitable vicissitudes in therapist and client lives. *Psychotherapy Theory, Research, Practice, Training, 47*(3), 374.

The Demons of War Are Persistent: A Personal Story of Prolonged PTSD

ART W. SCHADE

Forty years have passed since my deployment as a combat Marine to Vietnam. Nevertheless, only several years since I acknowledged I was unable to continue to suppress the demons alone. Like many veterans, the "demons" have haunted me through nightmares, altered personas, and hidden fears. Even as many veterans manage the demons' onslaught successfully, millions survive in destitution, finding solitude through social disconnection. Countless live in denial and loneliness, protecting a warrior's pride. As the most vulnerable—too often—choose to "end" their lives: tormented by guilt and feeling forever alone. Whereas, like me, scores consider themselves cowards, should they concede to the demons' hold?

Even today, as friends and family gather to celebrate another joyful holiday, I am melancholy. Saddened by vivid memories of lost friendships and battlefield carnage that erratically seeps from a vulnerable partition of my mind. A cerebral hiding place I concocted decades before, to survive in society. Consequently, I unwittingly clutch a profound loneliness as I avoid searching for memories of my youthful years. For if I dare to gaze to my past, I must transcend through the cloak of darkness I weaved to restrain the demons so many years before.

My pledge to God, Country, and Marine Corps was 40 years ago, or more. As a young, unproven warrior, I consented to the ancient rules of war. At 18, like many others, I was immersed in the ageless stench of death and carnage, in the mountains and jungles of Vietnam.

However, my journey began much earlier, on a 60-mile bus ride with other nervous teenagers, to New York City's legendary Induction Center at 39 White Hall Street. We went through lines of examinations and stood around for hours. We recognized one another's bare asses before we had the chance to learn each other's names. Nor did we realize so many of us would remain together in squads and fire teams, building deep-seated bonds of friendships along our journey. Our initial "shock" indoctrination began immediately at Parris Island, by intimidating drill instructors, who scrambled our disoriented butts off the bus. Then they organized us into a semblance of a formation, and herded us to barracks for a night of hell! Anxiety, second-guessing our decision to join, and apprehension was our welcoming. Followed by what we thought would be sleep, was merely a nap. We were woken in awe by explosive clamor, as they banged on tin garbage can lids next to our bunks, yelling "get up, you maggots." Even the largest recruits trembled in accord with the smaller guys.

We remained maggots for the next few weeks as we began the intense physical and mental training of boot camp. Slowly recognizing the ultimate importance of the team, not the individual, had been entrenched in our minds. In less than sixteen weeks we were proud United States Marines! It was a short celebration as we loaded our gear and headed to Camp Lejeune, North Carolina; Camp Pendleton in California; Okinawa; and the Philippines, where we continued to enhance our stealth killing skills, until the time came to execute our new talents on the blood-soaked fields of Vietnam.

We argued and fought among ourselves as brothers often do. But never lost sight of the bonds we shared: We were United States Marines with an indisputable commitment to "always cover each other's back." Crammed into the bowels of Navy carrier ships, we slept in hammocks, with no more than 3 inches from your brother's butt sleeping above you. The sailors laughed as these self-proclaimed "bad-ass Marines" transformed into the wimpy "Helmet Brigade," vomiting for days on our way to Okinawa for counter guerrilla warfare training. Nevertheless, aware we were going to Vietnam, we partied hard in every port. The first of our battles began as slugfests in distant barroom brawls.

Conversely, our minds were opened to the poverty and living conditions on these famous islands in the Pacific, brought to life through stories we heard about in the war with Japan, or movies starring everyone's hero, John Wayne. Instead, we found overpopulated, dirty cities and were barraged constantly by poor children seeking any morsel of food. In the fields, families lived in thatched huts with no electricity and unsanitary conditions. As well as the horror, while training, of being chased by a 2-ton water buffalo, with only blanks in my rifle, who moments before was led around by a ring in its nose by a 5-year-old boy. Worse, hearing the laughter of brother

Marines watching me run at full speed trying to find something to climb. I was feeling as though I was losing the "macho" in Marine, and we were still thousands of miles from Vietnam.

In confidence, we spoke as brothers about our fears, hardships growing up, family, girlfriends, times of humiliation, prejudice, and what we planned to do in our lifetime once our tour of duty in Vietnam was over. We knew how and what many of us were thinking about, and spoke as though we would all be returning home alive, never considering the thought of death or defeat: We had not learned that lesson yet. Moreover, we dreamed of going home as respected American warriors who defended democracy in a remote foreign land. Standing proud, feeling a sense of accomplishment, and experiencing life, as none of our friends at home would understand. Our country had called, and we answered.

We transferred to a converted World War II aircraft carrier that carried helicopters and Marines instead of jet planes. To traverse the coast of Vietnam and deploy by helicopter into combat zones from the Demilitarized Zone, the imaginary line separating North and South Vietnam, to the provinces and cities of Chu Lai and Da Nang. Then further south, to the outer fringes of Vietnam's largest city, at that time named Saigon.

Within sight of land, we heard the roar of artillery, mortars, and the familiar crackling of small-arms fire. Sounds we were accustomed to, through months of preparing ourselves for battle. However, for the first time we understood the sounds were not from playing war games. Someone would be dead. Anxiety, adrenaline highs, and fear of the unknown swirled within my mind. Was I prepared? Could I kill another man? Would another man kill me? From that point forward, death was part of my life. We would eventually load into helicopters, descending into confrontations ambivalent, yet assured we were young invincible warriors. We were convinced the South Vietnamese people needed us, as many of them did. Thus, our mission in enemy encounters was simple: Save the innocent and banish the enemy to Hell!

The first time we touched down on Vietnamese soil, we mechanically spread out in combat formation. Immediately, everything I was taught to watch out for rushed through my mind: Was the enemy around us, was I standing near an enemy grenade trap, or stepping toward a punji pit filled with sharpened bamboo spikes? Seeing our company walking through the low brush gave me comfort, until an unexpected explosion deafened our senses. We immediately hit the ground and went into combat mode, each understanding our zone of fire. There was nothing to think about except engaging the enemy. We were ready for battle. We waited, but heard no gunfire or rockets exploding, only a few Marines speaking several hundred feet away. One was yelling, "I can't f***ing" believe it!" We learned our first meeting with death was due to one of our brothers' grenade pins not being secured, and we assumed it was pulled out by the underbrush. Regardless, he was dead. I felt the loss of youthful innocence gush away.

Throughout a number of engagements we plunged by helicopters from their soaring formation to hovering a few feet off the ground. We anxiously leapt—some fell to the ground—into the midst of an already heated battle. The enemy sprung a deadly assault upon us; I became engrossed in the shock, fear, and adrenaline rush of battle. It was surreal! It was also not the time to ponder the killing of another human being, recall the rationale behind the ethics of war, or become absorbed in the horror of men slaughtering one another. Thoughts of war's demons certainly were not on my mind.

When the killing ceased and the enemy withdrew, I remained motionless, exhausted from the fighting. With only a moment to think about what had just occurred, shock, hate, and anger were buried under the gratitude of being alive. I had to find out which brothers did or did not survive, and as I turned to view the combat zone, I witnessed the reality of war: dreams, friendships, and future plans vanished. We knelt beside our brothers, some dead, many wounded and screaming in pain. A few lay there dying silently.

As I moved about the carnage, I noticed a lifeless body, face down, twisted abnormally in jungle debris. I pulled him gently from the tangled lair, unaware of the warrior I had found. Masked in blood and shattered bones, I was overwhelmed with disgust and primal obsession for revenge, as I realized the warrior was my mentor, hero, and friend. I shouted at him as if he were alive: "Gunny, you can't be dead! You fought in World War II and Korea. Wake up! Wake up, Marine! I need you to fight beside me!" Tears flowed down my face as I held him close and whispered that he would not be forgotten. I placed him gently in a body bag, slowly pulling the zipper closed over his face, engulfing him in darkness.

Navy corpsmen—our extraordinary brothers—worked frantically to salvage traumatized bodies. We did our best to ease the pain of the wounded as they prayed to God Almighty. "With all my heart I love you, man," I told each friend I encountered. However, some never heard the words I said, unless they were listening from heaven. I was unaware of the survivor's guilt brewing deep inside me. In 2 or 3 weeks our mission was completed, and we flew by helicopter from the jungle to the safety of the ship. None of us rested, instead remembering faces and staring at the empty bunks of the friends who were not there. I prayed for the sun to rise slowly, in order to delay the forthcoming ceremony for the dead.

Early the next morning, we stood in a military formation on the aircraft carrier's deck. I temporarily suppressed my emotions as I stared upon the dead. Rows of military caskets, identical in design, with an American flag meticulously draped over the top, made it impossible to distinguish which crates encased my closest friends. As *Taps* played, tears descended. For the first time I understood that in war, you never have a chance to say goodbye. I pledged speechlessly to each of my friends that they would never be forgotten: A solemn promise I regretfully only kept, through years of nightmares or hallucinations.

Combat is vicious; rest is brief; destroying the enemy was our mission. We fought our skillful foes in many battles, until they or we were dead, wounded, or overwhelmed. Engaging enemy troops was horrific. Memories of guerrilla warfare in jungles and villages were equally, if not more, agonizing. We had to either accept or build psychological boundaries around the terror. Nonexistent were the lines of demarcation; we constantly struggled to identify which Vietnamese was a friend and which was a foe. The tormenting acknowledgment that a woman or child might be an enemy combatant that had to be confronted was often overwhelming.

I was not aware of the change in my demeanor. In time, I realized that I had adjusted emotionally to contend with the atrocities and finality of war. I acquired stamina, could endure the stench of death, eliminate enemy combatants with little or no remorse, suppress memories of fallen companions, avoid forming new deep-rooted friendships, and struggled to accept the feasibility of a loving Lord. I never detected the nameless demons embedding themselves inside of me.

At the end of my tour, I packed minimal gear and left the jungle battlefields of Vietnam for America, never turning to bid farewell or ever again wanting to smell the pungent stench of death and fear. Within 72 hours, I was on the street I left 14 months prior, a street untouched by war, poverty, genocide, hunger, or fear. I was home. I was alone. Aged well beyond my chronological age of 19, I was psychologically and emotionally confused. I had to transform from a slayer back into a (so-called) civilized man.

Except for family members and several high school friends, returning home from Vietnam was demeaning for most of us. There were no bands or cheers of appreciation or feelings of accomplishment. Instead, we were shunned and ridiculed for fighting in a war that our government assured us was crucial and for an honorable cause. I soon found that family, friends, and coworkers could never truly understand the events that transformed me, in 14 months, from a teenage boy to a battle-hardened man.

I was not able to engage in trivial conversations or take part in the adolescent games many of my friends still played. For them, life did not change, and "struggle" was a job or the "unbearable" pressure of college they had to endure. It did not take me long to realize that they would never understand; there is no comparison between homework and carrying a dead man.

The media played their biased games by criticizing the military, and never illuminating the thousands of Vietnamese saved from mass execution, rape, torture, or other atrocities of a brutal Northern regime. They never showed the stories of American "heroes" who gave their lives, bodies, and minds to save innocent people caught in the clutches of a controversial war. For years, my transition back to society was uncertain. I struggled against unknown demons and perplexing social fears. I abandoned searching for surviving comrades or ever engaging in conversations of Vietnam.

Moreover, I fought alone to manage recurring nightmares. I locked it all away in a chamber labeled, "Do not open: horrors, chaos, and lost friends from Vietnam." However, suppressing dark memories is almost impossible. Random sounds, smells, or even words unleash nightmares, depression, anxiety, and the seepages of bitterness I alluded to before. I still fight to keep these emotions locked away inside me.

Today, my youth has long since passed and middle age is drifting progressively behind me. Still, unwelcome metaphors and echoes of lost souls seep through the decomposing barriers fabricated in my mind. Vivid memories of old friends, death, guilt, and anger sporadically persevere. There may be no end, resolution, or limitations to the demon voices that began as whispers and have since intensified over decades in my mind. "Help me, buddy!" I still hear them scream. As nightmares jolt me from my slumber, I wake and shout, "I'm here! I'm here, my friend," and envision their ghostly, blood-soaked bodies. Even today, I wonder if more Marines would be alive if I had fought more fiercely. "I had to kill!" I tell myself. Visions of lost friends and foes hauntingly reappear at inappropriate times. Guilt consumes my consciousness as I wonder why I did the things I did as well as the question: Why did they not survive? More dreadful, however, is the conflicting torment I feel when I acknowledge that I am thankful it was others instead of me.

Regardless of the war one fought, I am sure many memories are similar to mine, and mine to yours. I never recognized the persistency of the demons to mature, each time I thought I beat them; they were simply hiding deep within my soul. Disguised and deep-rooted, I assumed anxiety, loneliness, depression, alcohol abuse, nightmares, and suicidal thoughts were traits that haunted every man. For 35 years, I would not admit to these demons in my mind, and believed asking for medical assistance was a weakness as a man.

It was not until the first Gulf War began that I sensed the demons bursting from within. No matter how hard I tried to avoid them, I saw vivid images and news coverage of every aspect of the war. The bodies and faces in the media were not strangers anymore. Instead, they were my brothers from a much older and forgotten war. I sought refuge with VA doctors to help me try and understand, that PTSD is real and asking for help did not make this warrior a lesser man.

Semper Fi!

4

Personality Disorders

INTRODUCTION

The term *personality* seems familiar enough. Most of us would agree that it signifies something like the essence of a person or the expression of the core part of each of us. In Jung's psychology, *persona* is the personality adopted by an individual in relation to the outside world, the actor's mask or the character being acted. Webster's (2008) definition of personality is "the total of the psychological, intellectual, emotional, and physical characteristics that make up an individual, especially as others see her/him." Personality traits, then, are the intrinsic and enduring patterns of perceiving, relating to, and thinking about ourselves and the world around us that are expressed across a variety of contexts and are characteristic of who a person is. So, we might ask, how can a personality be *disordered*? It seems odd to think that something so fundamental to each of us as our personality or character could be disordered. Yet, this is exactly how the *Diagnostic and Statistical Manual of Mental Disorders* (*DSM-IV-TR*) defines personality disorders.

According to *DSM-IV-TR,* a personality disorder is a stable, long-term pattern of internal experience and outward behavior that differs notably from the expectations of one's sociocultural or reference group. The pattern is exhibited in at least two of the following areas: cognition, affectivity,

interpersonal functioning, impulse control. This pattern is rigid and enduring. It is pervasive across multiple situations and contexts, and it causes distress or negatively impacts functioning in one or more life domains. When
personality traits that originate in adolescence or early adulthood become
inflexible and maladaptive in adulthood, the individual is considered to have
a personality disorder. While a number of dimensional models of personality dysfunction have been proposed and are being researched, the current
DSM-IV-TR diagnostic approach remains a categorical one; the various
personality disorders are viewed as distinct entities.

Often, individuals who meet the criteria for one of the personality disorders do not acknowledge the dysfunctional patterns as described by the
DSM and, thus, do not seek treatment or services for them. Alternative ways
of thinking about these patterns might cast them as problems in living or
difficulties in interpersonal relationships rather than as mental disorders.

The names of the personality disorders are indicative of the personality traits inherent to them: for example, *paranoid, antisocial, narcissistic,
avoidant, dependent, obsessive-compulsive.* The type most frequently seen in
treatment settings is *borderline personality disorder* (BPD). Individuals who
meet the criteria for BPD often engage in disruptive behaviors, including
self-mutilation, suicidal gestures, or attempts that bring them to the attention of service providers. From the late 1930s into the 1970s, the term
borderline was used to describe people with symptoms on the borderline
between neurosis and psychosis. Individuals with "borderline disorders"
were thought to be experiencing a kind of latent schizophrenia. This way of
thinking about these problems shifted with the introduction of *DSM-III*,
in which divisions were no longer clearly drawn between neurosis and psychosis. While people with BPD can experience psychotic-like symptoms,
these are transient and more often of a dissociative than psychotic nature.
Current theory on BPD holds that a central part of the disorder is emotional dysregulation, an inability to regulate intense emotions that become
overwhelming.

The three first person accounts (FPAs) in this chapter are written by
people with a diagnosis of BPD. Melanie Green writes about finally becoming ready to understand her out-of-control emotions and that this was a
crucial stage in the process of recovery. As she learned skills to deal with
emotional dysregulation, she found the "power to regulate" her emotions
and "began to develop an identity." As someone with a "classic case of BPD,"

Lynn Williams offers a perspective on it that she feels will be helpful to service providers and family members. Her symptoms caused her to feel desperate, and she thinks it is critical that people understand that the distress is real, not behavior enacted to get attention from others. Her account focuses on the misconceptions about BPD, how the disorder feels, and how mental health professionals can help. In the final narrative in this chapter, Stacey Pershall talks about being diagnosed with multiple *DSM* disorders, but that only bulimia and BPD were valid. Her story of recovery began when she finally learned coping skills that helped her manage her feelings through dialectical behavioral therapy (DBT).

QUESTIONS FOR REFLECTION

Can a personality be disordered? Should the personality disorders in *DSM-IV-TR* be considered mental disorders? What are the common themes identified by the three authors in this chapter in terms of their experiences of having BPD, and what has made a difference in their recoveries? Does BPD fit the *DSM-IV-TR*'s definition of personality disorder?

REFERENCE

Webster's new college dictionary (3rd ed.). (2008). Boston, MA: Houghton Mifflin Harcourt Publishing Company.

My Path to Recovery

Melanie Green[1]

When my alarm goes off on a typical weekday, I reluctantly roll out of bed and jump into the shower. I hurry through breakfast and race off to school. After class, I grab some coffee or a sandwich and then hurry to work. I return phone calls and e-mails and juggle through the tasks at hand. I stress over prioritizing my responsibilities and figuring out how I will get it all

---

[1]From "My Path to Recovery," by Melanie Green, 2005, *Focal Point: Research, Policy and Practice in Children's Mental Health, 19*(1), June 2005, Research and Training Center on Pathways to Positive Futures, Portland State University. Reprinted with permission.

done. When the day is done, I return home to face my homework, put in some time on the treadmill, and eventually collapse into bed.

Sometimes things are pretty overwhelming. I convince myself there is no way to manage everything that's going on and that I simply can't handle it. But then I stop and think. I think of what I've gone through and what I've achieved. I laugh at myself for stressing so much over work and school. I think of how thankful I am to be working and pursuing my education. And I think about the days when I was simply fighting for my life.

A mere three years ago I lived in a completely different world. I was depressed, anxious, obsessive-compulsive, and mildly psychotic. My emotions were so torturously intense at times that it took all of my strength just to live in my own skin. I had no goals and no plans for the future. I wasn't entirely convinced there would even be a future. Self-injury became my primary coping mechanism—as well as my identity.

For several years I was intensely involved with the mental health system. I was hospitalized once per month on average, both in local and state hospitals. I was once described by a psychiatrist as "the number one utilizer of crisis services in the county." With a diagnosis of borderline personality disorder, I was often misjudged by professionals with a lack of understanding of my disorder and of self-injury. I was accused of "just doing it for attention" and told that I was "taking up time and resources that could be used to treat real patients." It was difficult and confusing to be repeatedly put down when I needed help the most.

Fortunately, there were people who did understand what I was going through. After a meeting with several therapists for various amounts of time, I met one at a local mental health center that I truly connected with. She was trained and experienced in the area of borderline personality disorder and was able to look past my illness and truly appreciate who I was as a person. I slowly gained support and learned new ways to cope with things that were difficult. After long periods of being "drugged-up" on medications like Thorazine, I began to work with an excellent nurse practitioner. Together we found a medication regimen that helped manage my symptoms and, at the same time, permitted me to function. However, even though I was receiving excellent care and support, I continued to struggle. Life was still tumultuous, and I didn't think I could tame it.

It wasn't until an early morning in the emergency room that things started to change. I was in a seclusion room waiting for a psychiatric consultation, having been transferred from a medical bed after overdosing the night before. My stomach ached with regret and I started to cry. "I don't want to do this anymore," I thought. I didn't want to continue living from one cut to the next. I didn't want to spend half my life in hospitals and emergency rooms. I didn't want to be my illness anymore.

It took years for my mental illness to develop to such substantial proportions, and it would take a significant amount of time for me to regain control of my life. But I was finally ready. I was determined to make it happen. Appointments with my therapist changed from being a way to kill some time to being a way to learn new skills. We talked a lot about why I felt the way I did and about the difference between how things sometimes feel emotionally and how they are in reality. I began to understand my emotions and I gained the power to regulate them rather than be controlled by them. I was fortunate to be working with a therapist who understood and supported me. For every bad feeling I had about myself, she could point out something good. She helped me understand that my life wasn't over. All the skills and attributes I had before my bout with mental illness were still there, there was just other stuff in the way.

I was fortunate to have a mentor as well. By chance, I met a woman who had gone through many of the things I was experiencing. Although her story was different from mine, she recognized enough of what I was going through to convince her to make a commitment to me. She told me she would be there for me and that we'd "get through this together." We spent a lot of time together, sometimes just hanging out, sometimes in serious crisis. The point is, she was there. She still is.

My family also played a significant role in my recovery. My mother relentlessly researched everything connected with my mental illness. Her wealth of acquired knowledge included the details of each diagnosis I received and every medication I took. The rest of my family did everything they could to stand by me and encourage me to grow strong again. I never understood the value of family until I saw what they all went through for me.

Things didn't get better immediately. It took a lot of time and a lot of hard work. Sometimes I'd give up, but just for a day or two. Every time things got intense I was able to poke my head out of the chaos just long enough to get a look at the big picture. I started thinking about what I wanted to do with my life and began working on accomplishing it. I started slowly, adding one thing at a time. I went back to school and took one class per quarter. I gradually increased my schedule to two classes, then three. I began volunteering at Consumer Voices Are Born, a local consumer-run agency and "warm line" to adults dealing with mental illness.

As my responsibilities increased, so did my confidence. I began to develop an identity. Rather than a mental illness with a person inside, I was becoming a person with a little mental illness inside. My efforts were initially slight but quickly gained momentum. Once things started rolling, they never stopped.

In the spring of 2003, I was given the opportunity to help conduct some focus groups in preparation for a new mental health grant that had been awarded to Clark County, Washington. I was flattered by the offer and eager to participate. It never occurred to me that offer would mark the start of a new beginning. The focus group project led to an invitation to join the steering committee for Clark County's Partnerships for Youth Transition. Later that year I was asked to travel to Washington, DC, with the program for a cross-site meeting. Within a few months of the trip, I was offered a job as the youth coordinator for the program.

Now, with a little over a year of employment with Clark County, I have to take a moment from time to time to reflect on what I've accomplished. Sometimes I still feel like I'm stuck in my old world and that I'll never get out. I remember the way things used to be and wish that I could just erase it all from my life. There are times when I give myself a pat on the back. I think about the youth I work with and the fact that I'm on the other side now. I think about the people I sit in meetings with, people from the same agencies that used to provide me with services. I think about the numerous presentations I've given at national conferences and the people who come up to me afterwards with compliments and ask for more information. They're asking me—professionals in the mental health field are coming up and asking me for advice. It's amazing. I've been able to take the worst part of my life and turn it into something positive for other people.

I think about the things people tell me and the compliments I receive. They're the same kinds of compliments I received when I was younger, when I knew I was worth something. I went so long without feeling value. It is amazing to listen to people and to truly believe that I mean something again. People value me and the contributions I make. I've come back to life.

Recovery is a remarkable thing. For me it has meant gaining my life back. For others it may look different, but it is a possibility for everyone. There is no person alive who can't have things at least just a little bit better, and to me, that's recovery. Recovery is a process. It doesn't necessarily mean that everything will be better and problems will cease to exist. It may mean being able to cook dinner, manage medication, or simply control emotions. It is still important, though. Individuals brought down by the weight of mental illness need to be reminded that there is more to their life. They deserve the opportunity to discover who they really are.

A "Classic" Case of Borderline Personality Disorder

LYNN WILLIAMS[2]

As someone who once suffered world-class symptoms of borderline personality disorder that resulted in multiple admissions to hospitals, but who has since gone on to rejoin society, I can offer some perspectives on this disorder.

Misconceptions About Borderline Personality Disorder

The first misconception most people have about borderline personality disorder is that its dramatic manifestations such as reckless or suicidal behavior are merely deliberate, manipulative attempts to get attention. That is not true. The distress is real.

For me, when I was acutely ill, no other options besides my suicidal behavior existed. I often fervently hoped each overdose would be the last or that finally someone would "see" how much help I needed. I had complete tunnel vision and couldn't envision yesterday or tomorrow. While having my stomach pumped in an emergency room or while running away from a psychiatric hospital, I would careen from high to low in euphoric bursts; I felt as if I was watching someone else. Even if the experience was unpleasant, which it usually was, I was unable to learn from it. Brief moments bordering on lucidity were too painful. It was as if part of me was asleep and I couldn't wake myself up, or I was too afraid or felt too hopeless to wake myself up.

[2]From "Personal Accounts: A 'Classic' Case of Borderline Personality Disorder," by Lynn Williams, 1998, *Psychiatric Services, 49,* 173–174. Copyright 1998 by American Psychiatric Association. Reprinted with permission.

I was accused of intentionally reacting in certain ways and was once asked sarcastically by a doctor, "Is this enough attention for you?" But inside I was more like a frightened two-year-old than the cunning individual he thought I was. I couldn't see what I was doing. Mostly I felt desperate, with a longing to be permanently looked after, and I felt addicted to looking for help. I can explain these feelings only on reflection.

Some people believe people with borderline personality disorder "enjoy" it and don't want to get well. Wrong. I was out of control and couldn't have changed my behavior if I wanted to because I was looking for rescue. But each time the response from health care providers would be different. I felt, in a warped way, that their concern did clarify my existence, but my panic, fear, and anger took over when my racing thoughts and attempts to flee were stopped.

When I would overdose and when medical intervention, usually by force, was deemed necessary, I would feel temporarily hopeful, and then threatened, judged, and thwarted in meeting some sort of need. Oh, how I see the futility of it now. I was incapable of seeing it then, and I secretly wanted to be respected, liked, and approved of, but I didn't know how to attain these privileges or whether I was worthy of them in the first place.

How the Disorder Feels

The best way I have heard borderline personality disorder described is having been born without an emotional skin—with no barrier to ward off real or perceived emotional assaults. What might have been a trivial slight to others was for me an emotional catastrophe, and what would be a headache in emotional terms for someone else was a brain tumor for me. This reaction was spontaneous and not something I chose.

In the same way, the rage that is often one of the hallmarks of borderline personality disorder, and that seems way out of proportion to what is going on, is not just a "temper tantrum" or a "demand for attention." For me, it was a reaction to being overwhelmed by present pain that reminded me of the past. To put it simply, think of something that would really hurt you and multiply it by a hundred.

If several stressors occurred in sequence, I sometimes started to generalize, negatively. The past and the present became one. Feelings swept over me like one of those nets used to trap animals in the jungle—black, dark, persistent, and at times suicidal feelings. Those feelings, accompanied by flawed logic, fantasies of rescue, and a kind of self-preservation system gone awry, created chaos in my mind. I would feel hopeless, my world would compartmentalize, and I'd enter an unremitting state of shock. The pain would seem interminable.

Thus the pain experienced by people with borderline personality disorder is not just a result of simple immaturity, a brilliant imagination, or the longings of a so-called spoiled child. We don't end up certified, in police lockups waiting to see a psychiatrist, or even dead because we're morally deficient. Our pain is real, but the equation creating that pain is faulty. Something is shut down in our brains, which means we can't listen at first because we're in survival mode.

My longing for rescue made me, especially after I entered the treatment system, run, flee, turn to authorities for help, be chased. In fact, I fled from security (that is, I left the psychiatric unit), running away but still wanting to be caught, to be contained but not suffocated—primal feelings that I couldn't verbalize then. To say it was an altered state of consciousness is putting it mildly. All I can say now is that there was something I wanted to be gone but at the same time didn't wish to lose.

How Mental Health Professionals Can Help

The most important thing is, do not hospitalize a person with borderline personality disorder for any more than 48 hours. My self-destructive episodes—one leading right into another—came out only after my first and subsequent hospital admissions, after I learned the system was usually obligated to respond. Nothing that had happened to me before being admitted to a psychiatric unit for the first time could even approach the severity of the episodes that followed.

What I did after I entered the system was to survive using maladaptive tools as a result of knowledge I acquired in the hospital. The least amount of ill-placed reinforcement kept me going. It prevented me from having to make a choice to get well or even finding out that I wasn't as helpless as I believed myself to be.

In the community, a person with borderline personality disorder can discover how to live. Hospitalization activates needy feelings and perpetuates the patient's sick self-image in her own eyes and those of staff. I believe if you live with the lame, you learn to limp. I know I did. Hospitalization is too easy an "out," but episodes of self-harm may very well reduce or disappear if the patient knows the response will be minimal.

A person with borderline personality disorder is often just looking for reassurance rather than admission when she hints at or threatens suicide—she doesn't yet know how to directly and safely express her feelings. If she is admitted, however, she will probably regret it five minutes after she gets in. Without hospitalization, she can see that what seems beyond endurance usually is not. This realization has allowed me, albeit slowly, to grow and learn to cope. Tolerating pain and uncertainty is the only way this can happen.

The person with borderline personality disorder doesn't know how to wait and a system that immediately responds doesn't give her a chance to soothe herself. Therefore, she continues to believe she is helpless. A man in an emergency room once said I would have to grow up and take care of myself. Reflecting the helplessness that I felt, I screamed at him, "I can't! Don't you know that alone I'm going to die?" It was flawed, but to me believable logic, with emotions literally blocking the intellect.

When you as a service provider do not give the expected response to these threats, you'll be accused of not caring, but what you are really doing is being cruel to be kind. When my doctor wouldn't hospitalize me, I accused him of not caring if I lived or died. He replied, referring to a cycle of repeated hospitalizations, "That's not life." And he was 100 percent right!

I would never have the life I have today if I had continued to get the intermittent reinforcement of hospitalization. The longer I stayed out of the hospital, the less I wanted to be in. The devastation I would have felt at supposedly losing my foundation of recovery would have been far worse than what I was feeling at the time. When I started to struggle to put my life together, sometimes all I had was that ever-growing time out of the hospital—which, with the exception of a short stay during the summer of 1997, has spanned five years—as something positive I could point to.

A word of advice to mental health professionals that cannot be stressed too strongly: don't define people with borderline personality disorder too strictly by any textbook limitations you have read. I have exceeded my doctor's expectations for improvement, and he doesn't know how far I can progress. For the most part I've stayed out of the hospital, maintained long-term full-time employment, live independently, have a motor vehicle, and plan to pursue further educational opportunities. If I, as one of the most chronic, regular, well-known, persistent visitors to emergency rooms in my community between the late 1980s and early 1990s, as one of the most chronic hospital escapees, as someone who was written off and told so—could triumph over borderline personality disorder to this extent, I'm sure other people with the disorder can at least improve the quality of their lives.

Someone answering to my name was once a terrified, angry person who was showing up in emergency rooms nearly every night and throwing up into a basin, or being looked for regularly by the police when threatening suicide. Someone answering to my name also once fought nasogastric tubes and ran from nurses, doctors, police, and hospital security. But that wasn't the real me. That's not who I want to be. Nor are the other people who are seen through the pathology of borderline personality disorder showing their real selves. As frustrating as these acutely ill people may be, please don't write them off. Maybe, just maybe, you'll be able to help one of them. I'm living proof that—over time—we can be helped.

Loud in the House of Myself

STACY PERSHALL[3]

While working at a shop in Brooklyn, my tattoo artist Denise had an apprentice named Tasha. One day we were all hanging out in the shop looking at a book of tattoo designs by the legendary artist Sailor Jerry. The drawings were crude but beautiful, and we laughed at three little pieces that had obviously been some sailors' nicknames years ago. The first one was an eight ball, and beneath it, in plain block letters, it said, "8-ball." The next was a beer keg, and underneath it said, "Guzzler." But the best by far was the third, a crossed fork and knife, with the words "Chow Hound." It didn't take long before Tasha and I decided that, once she had Denise's approval, she'd tattoo "Chow Hound" on my butt. And indeed, one night several months later, Tasha got out her machine and half an hour later I had Chow Hound on my ass. While lying there with the two of them cackling over my flesh, I thought, what in

[3]From *Loud in the House of Myself: Memoir of a Strange Girl,* by Stacy Pershall. Copyright 2011 by Stacy Pershall. Used by permission of W.W. Norton & Company.

God's name am I doing? Here I am, a former anorexic, getting a tattoo pro-
claiming that not only do I like to eat, I like to eat a lot.

I am trying on identities again.

It's 1978, and I'm with my mother in the Kmart in Fayetteville, Arkansas, which, at age seven, seems like the big city to me. I sit at a dressing
table, wearing a Farrah Fawcett-style wig (because in those days, Kmart sold
wigs) and a large floppy beige hat that is supposed to look like straw but is
actually made of cheap nylon. Perched precariously on my nose is a pair of
pink-tinted sunglasses several sizes too big. I am eating puffy peppermint
meringue candies, for which my mother has not yet paid, and writing in a
small blue notebook with yellow pages and a cutesy drawing of a flapper on
the cover, for which she also has not yet paid. This is important work. I am
taking notes.

Two women pass me and giggle. I glance at their reflections in the
dressing table mirror and proceed to record every detail of their appearance
and conversation, congratulating myself on how inconspicuous I am. I am
Harriet the Spy, and I am training myself to be as surreptitious as possible.

Kmart doesn't have everything my mother wants, so we make a stop at
Wal-Mart, which, besides the various Baptist churches in the area, is the hub
of northwest Arkansas social life. My mother stops to chat with someone she
knows and I am free. Wigless now, myself again, I run for my next disguise.

The crafts section is in the far right corner of the store, a distant wonder-
land of rickrack, fake flowers, and cheap fabric.

In Wal-Mart, I am a dancer. I have the power to defy gravity. I fold
myself into the bolts of multicolored mesh, trying to wrap myself so that it
completely obscures my vision. I want to see nothing but my future, nothing but the costume I will wear when I am a decade older and famous and
thousands of miles away from my thousand-person hometown of Prairie
Grove, twenty miles south of Fayetteville. With age will come grace and
sophistication. I will be magically teleported to New York City on waves of
talent. I will be carried on a magic carpet of tulle. This is what I live for. It is
what I have to believe to survive.

I learned about New York City from an episode of *The Love Boat* featuring Andy Warhol. He prowled around the ship with a Polaroid camera,
a silver wig, and a pair of big red plastic glasses. From that point on, I
relentlessly compared Prairie Grove to New York and knew it was where I
belonged.

Prairie Grove is one of those small towns that seem removed from time. Fayetteville is, like the rest of America, being subsumed by subdivisions and strip malls, but Prairie Grove has hardly changed at all. There is still no McDonald's, no Starbucks. There are still only two traffic lights. They still hang the same battered light-up Santas and snowmen they've used for at least thirty years on the light poles of Main Street at Christmas.

You can still stroll past Lou Anna Bellman's flower shop, and if the door is open you'll smell carnations. You can fill prescriptions at Rexall Drug, where the same cracked orange plastic sign still announces the place, and the same three bottles of Lemon-Up shampoo sit on a half-empty shelf, a layer of dust cascading like snow down their plastic lemon caps. There are still cowboy boots and stiff indigo Wrangler's to be bought at Crescent's, where the dressing room still has pine paneling.

At the other end of the street is the Farmers & Merchants Bank and the Beehive Diner, where the air is saturated with countless years of cigarette smoke, cooking grease, and stale coffee, and the same faded photos of chimps in human clothing, dumping plates of spaghetti over their heads, still hang on the wall. The old Laundromat is still there, but the front of it is now a beauty shop.

Once you've ridden your bike through the ditch outside the Dersams' house enough times, and made multiple barefoot treks to the One-Stop Mart to get the same slightly overfrozen Rocky Road ice cream cones, and worn a path through the overgrown field that is a shortcut between Marna Lynn Street and home, you've basically seen it all. If you're a strange and sensitive kid, you're ready to blow the joint by the time you're seven.

And I was that kid, the weird kid, the strange girl, the crazy one. In a town of a thousand people, reputations are hard to live down. There was a forced intimacy there I am deeply grateful not to have today, in New York City, where even though I'm a tattooed lady with flaming red dreadlocks, I can exist in relative anonymity on a day-to-day basis. In Prairie Grove, people thought nothing of going to the gas station barefoot or with perm rods in their hair; they knew their neighbors well enough they might as well have been in their own living room. When you went to town, you saw the same characters, like the old lady who rode around with her poodle in the basket of her bike, or Mary Frances the square-dance teacher, or the unsmiling Hendersons, with their five kids lined up in the driveway half an hour before all the garage sales opened. And, most spectacularly and terrifyingly, there was Susannah, the March of Dimes poster child.

Susannah was the younger sister of Sheridan, one of the most popular girls in school, and she had a disease called Apert syndrome, which meant her face was all messed up, the middle part sunken in and her eyes bulging. They hung her posters in the window of Dillon's grocery store, and although they terrified me, I had an intense urge to steal one. I wanted to do with it what Ramona Quimby did with her Halloween mask, hiding it under the couch cushions so she could sneak peeks at it and scare herself when she chose. I wanted to have Susannah's picture all to myself, knowing that just beneath my butt on the sofa was her crumpled weird eye. I wanted to stare at her face until I could almost see her reaching out to nub my own with her fused-together fingers, their one large nail growing straight across, then safely turn away at the last possible second. Most of all, I wanted to use her image as a tool, a barometer, that would help me test how off things were inside my head. I would know by how long it took before her picture started to look like it was going to come to life—I often thought photographs or inanimate objects might just do so. As a child, my grasp on reality was tenuous, and it only became more so as I got older. (I spent a lot of time staring at my stuffed animals and looking away just before they turned into demons, as I felt certain they would if I stared too long. I felt compelled to do this most nights before falling asleep, perhaps as a way of assuring myself I had some degree of control over my terror.)

When I saw Susannah's mother pushing her around town in her tiny wheelchair, goose bumps swam to the surface of my skin. Anytime I left the house, I took the chance of seeing her, which meant I sometimes wanted to leave the house and sometimes didn't. It depended on how out-of-control my thoughts already were that day. *Make me crippled,* I prayed at night, *make me like Susannah: make it able to be seen. Give me bright shiny crutches with gray plastic cuffs and free me from living in this brain. Make me pretty or hideous but nothing in between. Pose me on matted beige carpet, save me on film, hang me in the window so my birth defects can be seen. Make it bad enough that parents will tell their kids teasing me isn't funny*

This is the story of how a strange girl from Prairie Grove discovered she had a multitude of disorders and how she survived. The names of my disorders came later, and start with *b:* borderline, bipolar, bulimic. The only *a* was anorexia. These disorders have a chicken-and-egg quality. Was I bulimic because I was borderline, anorexic before bulimic, is the bipolar even real? Some physicians and researchers suggest that borderline personality disorder should be reclassified as a mood, rather than personality, disorder, and that in fact it may live on the bipolar spectrum. The symptoms overlap. If your mood swings last a week, you're bipolar; if they last a few hours, you're borderline. This is of course a drastic oversimplification, and when you're in the midst of colossal emotional overwhelm, you don't care what your disorder is called, you just want it to stop—or, in the case of early mania, go on forever.

It's only slightly better as an adult. You give your feelings melodramatic names, grandiose status, because melodramatic and grandiose are how you're feeling. You're the most depressed person EVER, or, on the rare good days, the happiest—no, not happy, ECSTATIC. There is no gray, there is only the blackest black and shimmering white. The white, for which you live, is like being illuminated by a god in whom you have long since stopped believing. The black is what you more often get.

If you are this child, or this hypersensitive, emotionally skinless adult who might as well be a child, there will be therapists, long lines of them, each offering drugs and, if you have no health insurance, as much counseling as they can offer before their internships expire. Then it's on to the next one, who may or may not have a different diagnosis and/or different drugs. The drugs usually make you gain weight and sleep a lot—or not at all—but if you're lucky they lift the blackness for a while. If you're bipolar, you tend to only show up in therapists' offices when depressed, which means you will likely be diagnosed with unipolar depression and fed a steady stream of antidepressants, which will send you into glorious hypomania for a while before bottoming out and leaving you desolate again. It will generally take quite some time before someone works with you long enough to see that you have more than just depression, that there is a cycle to your moods.

I was diagnosed in this order: bulimia, major depression, attention deficit disorder (briefly, in 1993, when it first became trendy; it was later discounted), bipolar disorder, anorexia, borderline personality disorder. The first and last diagnoses were most accurate. In the spring of 2005, I entered a three-day-a-week Dialectical Behavioral Therapy (DBT) program for borderlines at New York-Presbyterian Hospital. The skills learned in the four modules of DBT—Mindfulness, Distress Tolerance, Emotion Regulation, and Interpersonal Effectiveness—are things most people learn as children. Borderlines, however, due to having been raised in what DBT creator

Marsha Linehan calls an "invalidating environment," need help figuring out how not to drown in the undertow of our own feelings.

It is embarrassing to admit I didn't begin to acquire these skills until the age of thirty-four, when after a breakdown I began to get my life together through medication, therapy, and tatooing. *Borderline* means you're one of those girls who walk around wearing long sleeves in the summer because you've carved up your forearms over your boyfriend. You make pathetic suicidal gestures and write bad poetry about them, listen to Ani DiFranco albums on endless repeat, end up in the emergency room for overdoses, scare off boyfriends by insisting they tell you they love you five hundred times a day and hacking into their e-mail to make sure they're not lying, have a police record for shoplifting, and your tooth enamel is eroded from purging. You've had five addresses and eight jobs in three years, your friends are avoiding your phone calls, you're questioning your sexuality, and the credit card companies are after you. It took a lot of years to admit that I was exactly that girl, and that the diagnostic criteria for the disorder were essentially an outline of my life:

[Borderline Personality Disorder is characterized by] a pervasive pattern of instability in interpersonal relationships, self image, and affect, and marked impulsivity beginning by early adulthood and present in a variety if contexts, as indicated by five (or more) of the following:

1. *Frantic efforts to avoid real or imagined abandonment.*
   Note: Do not include suicidal or self-mutilating behavior covered in criterion 5
2. *A pattern of unstable and intense interpersonal relationships characterized by alternating between extremes of idealization and devaluation*
3. *Identity disturbance: markedly and persistently unstable self-image or sense of self.*
4. *Impulsivity in at least two areas that are potentially self-damaging (e.g., spending, sex, substance abuse, reckless driving, binge eating). Note: Do not include suicidal or self-mutilating behavior covered in criterion 5.*
5. *Recurrent suicidal behavior, gestures, or threats, or self-mutilating behavior.*
6. *Affective instability due to a marked reactivity of mood (e.g., intense episodic dysphoria, irritability, or anxiety usually lasting a few hours and only rarely more than a few days)*

7. *Chronic feelings of emptiness.*
8. *Inappropriate, intense anger or difficulty controlling anger (e.g., frequent displays of temper, constant anger, recurrent physical fights)*
9. *Transient, stress-related paranoid ideation or severe dissociative symptoms.*

The first time I read these criteria, I felt like someone had been following me around taking notes. DBT and tattoos taught me how to accept and survive pain, a lesson I needed to learn physically as well as emotionally. Tattooing, like therapy, has allowed me to control the occasions on and degree to which I experience discomfort. I would not go back to my life before age thirty-five for anything in the world, but life after is shaping up to be pretty good.

Throughout my life I've felt the constant pull between a powerful force that wants to make art and save the world and one that wants to destroy me and everyone in my path. I have been driven by a frantic need for overachievement, which becomes even more frantic when I'm hypomanic. My mood goes up, I commit myself to grandiose plans, I feel certain I can take on the universe. In my case, for every seventy-two hours of unadulterated manic bliss, there are weeks of unremitting depression and obsessive rumination. These are the psychiatric cards I was dealt. I have lost years to depression so crippling I lay in bed for days at a time, my head sunken into my pillow because I couldn't bear its weight.

But this body in which I am trapped is made, now, of color and life. My skin is made of lightning bolts, robots, rockets, cats, the Bride of Frankenstein, Laurie Anderson quotes. My tattoos remind me who I am and what I'm made of, and the unfilled lines of a work in progress remind me where I want to go. Learning who I am and creating a skin in which I can bear to live has taken this long and required this much effort.

5

Substance-Related Disorders

INTRODUCTION

The use and abuse of substances is as old as humankind. Various mood-altering and/or mind-changing substances have been used by individuals and groups as part of cultural and religious ceremonies for thousands of years. Pictures carved in rock caves that depict beer being made from barley date as far back as the fourth millennium B.C. People in China made and drank an intoxicating beverage from rice around 2200 B.C. American Indians have used plants and other organic substances such as peyote routinely as an integral part of their spiritual practices. Societies and cultures have engaged in activities involving the use of psychoactive beverages and substances across the seasons and across the continents. While there is a long and colorful history of these customs, it probably always has been difficult to determine the true extent of substance use in any culture or population. Reliable estimates of the prevalence of substance use and abuse in this country are hard to obtain because definitions of misuse and abuse vary widely, campaigns to bring about temperance often have moral overtones that skew the extent of problematic use, and users themselves frequently are reluctant to say how much they drink and/or to admit to the overuse of prescription drugs or the use of illegal drugs.

Nevertheless, troublesome use of substances appears to be a common occurrence, and people with alcohol and/or drug problems are found in every walk of life. To compound these problems, results from the National Epidemiological Survey on Alcohol and Related Conditions (2001–2002) revealed considerable comorbidity between mood and anxiety disorders and substance use disorders. Of adults with drug and alcohol problems, 78% meet the criteria for an independent mental disorder at some point in their lives. Those who abuse alcohol and/or other substances have been found to have higher rates of mood and anxiety disorders than the general population. And people with mental disorders abuse substances at greater rates than those with no psychiatric diagnosis (Comsay, Compton, Stinson, & Grant, 2006).

The *DSM-IV-TR* includes the following substances in its list of substance-related disorders: alcohol, amphetamines, caffeine, cannabis, cocaine, hallucinogens, inhalants, nicotine, opioids, phencyclidine, sedatives, polysubstance, other (MDMA, steroids, anticholinergics). The manual distinguishes between *substance dependence* and *substance abuse* based on the nature of the consequences experienced by users. *Substance dependence* involves the harmful use of any of these substances that results in psychological and/or physiological dependence and can include signs and symptoms of tolerance and/or withdrawal. It is what is commonly thought of as addiction. *Substance abuse* is the harmful use of any of these substances that leads to marked distress or impairment but falls short of dependence. The two substance-induced disorders in this section of the *DSM* are *substance intoxication* and *substance withdrawal.*

This chapter includes three first person accounts (FPAs) written by people with substance abuse problems. While it is not clear that these authors meet criteria for *DSM* disorders, they describe in vivid detail the impact that substance misuse has had upon their lives. Only one of the narratives is able to convey a real sense of the recovery process. In *Goodbye Johnnie Walker*, Neil Davidson tells the story of his "love affair with the bottle." After years of being a functioning alcoholic, his around-the-clock drinking finally got out of control. He got to the point of feeling a sadness that he "just couldn't drown anymore" and flew across the country to enter treatment at the Betty Ford Center. The title of his narrative comes from the letter he wrote in treatment to say farewell to the booze. Aaron French writes about his polysubstance addiction and says that he never was addicted to any particular drug. From an early age, he used drugs to escape fears of the world around him. As a direct result of his drug use, he experienced paranoia, panic attacks, and psychosis. From methamphetamine to alcohol to prescription painkillers, his addiction endured. Now drug free, he struggles with the "whispering voices of addiction" and tries to live life one day at a time. Michelle Walters first used prescription narcotics to relieve the physical pain resulting from two surgeries. As a nurse, she had access to these drugs and began to use them to deal with emotional pain and stress. Through losing her job and being arrested, her recovery finally began when she was introduced to another nurse who was in recovery.

QUESTIONS FOR REFLECTION

What do the authors of the narratives in this chapter have in common in terms of their experiences with alcohol and/or drugs? Does acceptance of one's addiction inevitably lead to recovery for every user? What else might be a critical component of recovery? Why is substance abuse such a common problem?

REFERENCE

Comsay, K. P., Compton, W., Stinson, F. S., & Grant, B. F. (2006). Lifetime co-morbidity of DSM-IV mood and anxiety disorders: Results from the National Epidemiological Survey on Alcohol and Related Conditions. *Journal of Clinical Psychiatry, 67*(2), 247–257.

Goodbye, Johnnie Walker

NEIL DAVIDSON[1]

Until recently, I hadn't gone to bed sober in twenty-five years. I was a drunk when I first met my wife of twenty-three years, and I have been one ever since. I have been a pretty good drunk, as drunks go, without the usual DWIs, abusive behavior, or too dear a price paid for being too honest after

---

[1]Neil Davidson, 2010, modified from "Goodbye, Johnnie Walker," 1998, Beacon Press and *The Sun.*

my seventh or tenth drink. I am a flirt when drunk but have never been unfaithful. I worked hard while I drank, and once wrote three novels and hundreds of nonfiction articles in four years. I believe my work was more lyrical with the help of alcohol. The problem was that my love affair with the bottle finally began to threaten my continued existence on this shaky earth.

In the past year, I started drinking in the shower each morning. I was drunk by nine, drunk at noon, drunk at three, drunk at seven, and drunk at ten o'clock. I had pretty much stopped eating, although I still made dinner for my wife, our dogs, and myself, and pretended to enjoy a fine meal in a fine little house on a pretty street in a nice little town. Eventually, my body started eating itself to stay alive. Ketosis is the medical term.

Why my drinking got so out of control after so many years of my being a functioning and productive alcoholic remains a mystery to me. I just know that I had become (and still am) one sick son of a bitch just a step away from the grave because I suffer from the disease of alcoholism. I drink too much. It is as simple, and as difficult, as that.

I love drinking, and am having a hard time accepting that being sober is somehow a superior state of being. It's also hard to accept that I have to expend even more energy to stay clean then I did when the first thing I thought about in the morning was whether I had enough scotch for the following night. Never having had hangovers, I don't feel any better when I wake up now than I did when I drank and literally have to remind myself that I didn't drink yesterday.

I do not, however, miss all those questions for which I seldom found answers: Did I black out last night? Are apologies due? Is my wife pissed? How did I get home, and where the hell is the car? Who did I call, and did I insult them? What happened to all the money in my wallet? How much did I put on the card? Think now, Davidson. These are questions most drunks have to ask themselves at one time or another. Usually every night. After a while, I just stopped asking them.

I want to run away and drink. If I die, I die. No excuses or regrets. I want to run away and drink, but I won't. I will try to make it in this new world I don't know. I will try those silly meetings that many drunks believe are chaired by God. I am scared now. I am afraid of success and failure in equal measure. But I will try.

If I didn't begin drinking early and keep drinking, I got the sweats so bad that my entire head became soaked with perspiration. My heart hurt so much, I was afraid a heart attack was imminent. My hands shook so much; I couldn't drink a glass of water, not that I was so inclined. But of course there was an antidote to my pain—a panacea so profoundly satisfying that virtually everything else became unimportant or nonexistent. One drink of good scotch, and everything stopped. Well, almost everything. I still had quiet cries and a sadness that I just couldn't drown anymore.

During my pre-admission interview with a counselor from Betty Ford, I asked what I should do about needing a jolt in the morning. She said, "Take a drink and don't try to detox yourself or you might not make it here." So I took a drink. It was now officially my medicine. My psychiatrist had once said that I was one of the most self-medicated persons he had ever met. At last, I understood precisely what he meant: I was a doctor with a fool for a patient.

I find most books that deal with drinking and rehab somewhat smug and self-congratulatory. I am neither confident enough nor sufficiently proud of getting through a day sober to take that attitude. Truth be told, I am confident only that I will have another drink at some point in my life. Maybe today.

I was surprised and more than a little delighted to find that at least some of the bars in the Philadelphia International Airport were open at six thirty in the morning. Of course, I was prepared if they weren't. I had purchased twelve miniature bottles of Johnnie Walker Red for the trip. I was on the way to the Betty Ford Center: sun and palm trees and drunken, pill-popping celebrities. Jesus, maybe I could get a free golf lesson. I was ready.

I remember having a few doubles in the bar in Philly before I took off, perhaps another five or so aboard the plane, five or six more in Denver, a few more after we took off again, and then upon my arrival at Palm Springs at about twelve-thirty in the afternoon (California time), another seven or eight. These last several drinks I downed after telling a very nice gentleman from the center who was there to pick me up and deliver me to my new life—in my most apologetic tone—that I needed to have a couple of more belts before leaving. This very nice alcoholic stood with me at the bar in the Palm Springs airport, a tender hand on my shoulder, while I put away one after the other.

After that, I don't remember much. They told me later that I had my last five or six mini-bottles in the nurses' office. Once word got out that some guy was drinking over in "meds," my soon-to-be fellow patients came over as a group and carried me back to the dorm, singing, "Show him the way to the next whiskey bar. No, don't ask why." Several of them inquired as to whether I had any more booze and tried to impress upon me that sharing was a noble and selfless act. I didn't have anything left, I am happy to report. The damage I could have caused!

I am also told that, before going to bed that night, I asked the women in charge of searching my bags for anything that might contain alcohol (including shaving cream), if she would tuck me in, and would it be possible to get a good night kiss? She smiled and said no, then left with my razor. I was on suicide watch.

The next couple of days are fuzzy. I know that they were giving me some sort of drugs, but not enough, and that I was falling down a lot and hurting myself in the process, then crying when they told me I needed a wheelchair and round-the-clock nursing. A short time later, the maggots and leeches showed up. I kept telling the pretty nurse to find me some Raid. Then told her to forget it, because my sweet black Lab puppy was somehow between my legs (even though I was damn sure Betty Ford had said no pets and that my dog was really three thousand miles away with my wife), and Raid would be toxic to her. I kept opening her mouth and pulling out maggots, but more kept coming from inside of her. They were in my eyes and mouth, too, but I didn't care. I needed to help my innocent baby first.

In the beginning I was cranky and critical of what I perceived to be rather stupid and pointless rules at the center, such as no saying hello to anyone, especially women from the other dorms; no newspapers, except from Saturday at five until Sunday night; no caffeine, no unauthorized books; no telephones, faxes, or televisions; no hats or sunglasses indoors; no walking alone after dark; no smoking in the boys' room or on our private verandas; and no removing the rubber mattress covering from your bed, no matter how much you suffered from the hot, then cold sweats.

The fact that most of these rules came to make some kind of twisted sense as I progressed through the program was a revelation to me. The counselors talked about the need to surrender, and although the word *surrender* is not in my vocabulary—I have always been suspicious of anything even remotely smacking of authority due to a run-in with a dirty pervert who was a YMCA camp counselor when I was about ten and he was a thousand—I did experience some sort of giving-in to many requirements I either hadn't agreed with or hadn't understood at the beginning.

The Betty Ford Center is located in Rancho Mirage, California (a small town with more than a hundred golf courses) on a beautiful campus covering some ten acres. It consists of four dormitories—two for men and two for women—housing twenty patients each, an overpriced bookstore that sells only approved drug-and alcohol-related books, a cafeteria, a swimming pool, a nurses station, an auditorium, and assorted office spaces. Although legally it is a hospital, it feels, at best, like a hotel; at worst like a minimum-security prison.

In spite of its reputation as an expensive retreat (twelve thousand bucks up front, probably a lot more by the time you read this and our insurance company refused to help) for rich elites and pretty people who just need to get straight for a while (there is an element of that), Betty Ford offers a program of tough love, a caring and talented staff with the patience of Job, and a rigid schedule designed to educate patients about substance abuse and keep people busy.

Former first lady Betty Ford is on the board of the center and is a frequent visitor who dines often in our cafeteria with an affluent coterie of Republican-looking geezers and geezettes (she lives nearby), but away from the riff-raff. Though not inclined to make small talk with the patients, she will, with studied ease, stand up in front of a bunch of drunks and addicts and say, "Hi, I'm Betty Ford, and I'm an alcoholic and drug addict." And she will go on to tell her story of too much Valium and booze, usually mixed.

A normal day at Betty Ford begins with a 6 a.m. wake-up call with one of the patients going from room to room to awaken each person. Mickey Mantle, who once lived in our dorm, went from door to door on all fours barking and growling like a manic dog to get people going. Not an easy task in most cases. I would get out of bed for the Mick. You shower, make your bed, visit meds, then do your daily chores.

Each person is given weekly job assignments that get easier as you make your way through the program. I started out cleaning the laundry room and ended up as clothing monitor, which consisted of telling people not to wear their hats or shades indoors. After breakfast, there's a short meditation reading from two books of dated platitudes and wishes for drunks. The rest of the morning is taken up by a "meditation talk," a thirty-minute lecture on anything from anger management to the medical consequences of alcohol abuse (no lecture lasts longer than thirty minutes, since it is a contention at Betty Ford that the brains of alcoholics and addicts can absorb information for only that long), a peer review of the lecture, and then an hour of group therapy.

After lunch there is a "first step" session, in which a patient admits to his addiction and says how sorry he is for messing up. A first step can be boring, dramatic, touching, informative, or funny. For example: "I forgot my wife was with me and left the bar with another woman. I remembered my wife in the morning, though she wasn't there when I went back to pick her up. I guess she left when the place closed." After first step comes a mandatory recreation period, I never did get to it, then perhaps grief counseling or a smoking-cessation program which I never got to either.

Before dinner you're expected to work on your assignment, such as writing in your diary (which goes to your counselor every day where it sits on his desk several hours and is then returned to you), or some other expressive activity. Then there's another visit to meds, and dinner.

After dinner (the food is quite good but rumored to be spiked with drugs which will kill your libido) you attend another lecture, another peer review of said lecture, and then an Alcoholics Anonymous meeting or a Narcotics Anonymous meeting for an hour. From 9 p.m. until bed, you're expected to read alcohol-related materials or AA's "Big Book," but more often than not it's a chance for a snack, a smoke, or surreptitious stroll over to the women's dorms.

They dispense a minimum of drugs at the Betty Ford and don't seem at all concerned when new arrivals show up at the dorm office complaining of thousands of insects in their beds. One young man, not yet familiar with just how tough the Betty Ford program can be, boasted that by putting half an Alka Seltzer tablet in his mouth and shaking uncontrollably, he could get the staff to give him morphine. He said he had done it successfully at other hospitals. Hearing of this, a counselor said, "You know what we would do? We'd throw the little shit out on the lawn and tell him he had an NA meeting in ten minutes and not to be late." I know from my own experience that the counselor was not exaggerating. The philosophy seems to be that a little suffering goes a long way toward helping you remember what it was that brought you there in the first place.

As I sobered up, I became very concerned about whether I would be able to write without my source of inspiration and comfort. The fact that I had become moderately successful in my chosen craft only while drunk did not escape me. The glib pronouncements of many people, both in and out of the program, that I would be a better writer sober ("just imagine how many new emotions you'll have!"), was less than reassuring since most of them couldn't write a simple declarative sentence if their lives depended on it.

I did worry, after reading over the few letters I wrote to people while at Betty Ford, that I was losing the ability to express myself on paper, not to mention finding it exceedingly difficult to write legibly due to my uncontrollable shakes. Which I continue to have in spades while a couple of weeks later, sans the tremors and with a more clear mind, I wrote the following for our last assignment before being released, a goodbye letter to whatever put us there, read aloud to the group:

Goodbye, Johnnie Walker.

Unlike so many of my peers, I have not based my goodbye to you on the assumption that you are male or female, best friend or hated lover. In all the years of your dubious friendship, never once, even in my most drunken state, did you ever manage to pour yourself into my twelve-ounce glass, containing five half-moon ice cubes, and jump into my waiting hands. You are a fine bottle of whiskey—not a bad thing to be, by any means—but nothing more and nothing less.

It is late Friday night, and here I am having an illicit smoke in the bathroom at the Betty Ford Center and thinking about you. I am wondering if I will be able to find the words to tell you that, as much as I have enjoyed our reckless but enduring friendship, it's time for us to say goodbye. Alas, I will miss you terribly, but there comes a time when it is not only necessary, but best, to go our separate ways.

You have been a good and loyal friend. When my soul hurt, you were there to numb me. When my heart was broken, you helped me forget. When my dear old man died on Easter Sunday, I said, Goodbye, Daddy, with you in hand. But in the end, I was just another barfly, last guy down on the left. The last guy still there after my drinking friends had babies, changed jobs, bought new homes, or found other places that had five-buck all-you-can-eat lunches. I was left in a place I didn't like anymore, but stayed anyway.

Then I saw your power: your ability to put me in the hospital, legs shot, liver wounded, cold sweats, a wheelchair. I saw maggots and leeches on my body, in my mouth. Even before, you made me sneaky, which, by nature I am not. You made me think of Hemingway and putting a gun in my mouth, too. But then my dog barked and I took her for a walk. Maybe tomorrow. Maybe next week. But maybe, always maybe, when you are there.

I live in a small house at the end of a quiet cul-de-sac in the pretty town of Ardmore, Pennsylvania. It is a prosperous and safe place. I happily share my life with my wife of more than twenty years. She is beautiful and caring, but, best of all, she loves me. We have a fine dog—a black lab named Samantha—who was born on the fourth of July in 1995. I rake leaves in the fall, shovel snow in the winter, plant flowers in the spring, and take care of my little garden in the summer; last year—due to noisy storms and assorted quiet animals—it yielded exactly one fat green pepper, after an expenditure of $487.

I am an author—a profoundly satisfying calling—and work in a complete and attractive office on the second floor of our home. I am indeed a lucky man. And yet, with your help, I am killing myself, and I don't know why. So we are over, you and I. I take this action with a deep and abiding respect for both your power and your charm. I will miss you.

Since I began writing this, I have slipped three times. "Slipped" is the term AA uses to describe a relapse. The Betty Ford people say you "fucked up." I am neither proud nor ashamed that I did indeed fuck up. Nothing will give me back my yesterdays or allow me to relive them, so I won't try. I will just go on and hope that someday, somehow, I will finally win (if staying sober really is winning).

The first time I slipped, it was out of some strange curiosity about what a drink would do to me now and how it would taste. I decided to have a vodka and tonic. The biggest mistake I made (besides just having the drink) was to pour myself a drink of the same proportions—in the same fourteen-ounce glass, no lemon (it takes space away from the booze), just three small ice cubes—I'd used when I was a certifiable drunk. My preferred ratio was about 80 percent vodka to 20 percent tonic.

So here I was, enjoying what I thought would be one little drink, and all of a sudden I was toasted, baked, fried. Of course, once a drunk gets toasted, baked, and fried, all thoughts of moderation go out the window, and the only thought left is whether I *really* need three ice cubes in the second drink. I did, after a time, call the Betty Ford people to say that I had fucked up. I was crying and disappointed in myself and needed to hear some encouraging words. They were very nice and understanding and said that most of their lambs stray at some point, and that drinking is part of the recovery process, so I shouldn't be too hard on myself—but a little bit hard was OK.

They also suggested that I go to an AA meeting as soon as possible. Drunk but not disorderly, I went to a meeting that night and ended up being asked to leave and not come back if I'd had anything to drink. I was embarrassed and humiliated. The incident was a new one to everyone I told about it, especially to the Betty Ford people, who pointed out that membership to AA is open to all who have a desire to stop drinking. That's it. There are no other requirements to be a member of that organization. Basically, I'd been tossed out of a club that will accept anybody. Haven't been back to one since.

Since then I've given up on AA and decided to make do with my trusty expensive psychiatrist, my supportive and caring wife, our dog (who seems to have a great deal to say about everything that happens around here), my counselors from Betty Ford, and my fellow drunks and addicts and co-conspirators from the program. I came to truly love and depend on the assorted wackos I lived with in the dorm at Betty Ford. There was a usually profane, even vulgar sense of shared pain, caring, and camaraderie among us. We banded together against the ignorance and antagonism many people showed toward our disease.

One night on *Sixty Minutes,* the resident curmudgeon and commentator, Andy Rooney, was discussing the Baltimore Ravens' chosen name. He pointed out that Edgar Allan Poe, whose poem "The Raven" had inspired the name, ended up dying in Baltimore on a barroom floor, penniless (certainly a crime in Rooney's neat white world of the Hamptons) and nothing more than a common drunk. He spit out the word *drunk* with a venom all too familiar to us alcoholics. So when we, the sick, have the chance to be together in a place where our flaws are not only accepted, but embraced, it's a meaningful and transforming experience.

The first day or two that I was in the wheelchair, I decided, quite admirably I thought, that I could do everything without help. But the damn doors were just too heavy, the chair kept tipping, and I kept falling and was always late for meals because I wouldn't accept a helping hand. Finally, after a particularly nasty fall, I got up the courage to ask someone to help me back into the chair. It was then that I finally understood why Betty Ford urges people to ask for help: we all need it and can't make it without it.

After I left Betty Ford, my psychiatrist said that I'd been "engaged" there, and now needed sustained and continuing engagement if I was going to make it as a former drinker in a drinking world. So I have tried several private counselors who are supposedly experts in dealing with people like me—that is, drunks. The one I've settled on is a gray-haired woman, an M.D., smart and hard—and expensive. She told me the insurance companies "fucked her over" too much in the past, so she doesn't deal with them anymore. Another 120 bucks a week that we don't have, and for what? To try to keep me alive, I guess. She tells me I'm worth it, but for that much money she'll probably tell anybody anything. Nonetheless, I will probably see her again. My shrink said engagement, engagement, engagement. That's what I need.

So I will try engagement. I want to try heroin. I want to try prescription drugs. I want to get high again on my favorite scotch. I want to lose myself. But right this minute, this second really, I am sober and I like it.

Addendum

It is some years later and for every song I sang, every tango I danced, cigarette I smoked, and jigger of good whiskey that rolled down my thirsty gullet, the bills have come due. The costs are high and all sales are final. I am ill and have been for about the last six or seven years. I suffer like hell. All due to my bad habits.

Several years ago my doctor wrote a letter for me for some reason I can't remember now: "1. Laenec's cirrhosis with portal hypertension and progressive liver failure. 2. Chronic obstructive pulmonary disease with advanced emphysema. 3. Spinal stenosis with painful bilateral radiculopathy. 4. Stage III testicular carcinoma, disseminate, S/P radiation and aggressive chemotherapy." He basically went on to say that I was severely limited in my capacity to ambulate and to care for myself. This was not news to me; I cannot make it up a short flight of stairs without having to gasp for breath. My prognosis is poor.

It has been hard these last ten years or so. I am lucky to be alive. I am still happily married but guilty as hell that I've become so damn helpless to my wife. My sweet lab Sam is dead and I'm afraid to get another because I couldn't walk her and will probably not outlive her. I have tried to adopt an attitude of complaining or talking about my illnesses as little as possible. Thinking about them and trying to work are another matter entirely. It's tough to write when you are in pain and loaded up with morphine, Trazodone, Prozac, Wellbutrin, and at last count, 19 other drugs.

There are so many other things I could tell you about but who the hell wants to hear about someone else's bad times. I tried to give you the information that was needed without being too maudlin, and that's it. Except for smoking—a constant battle—and not being Catholic and too old, I could be a fucking choirboy the way I live now. No booze—scotch smells horrible to me now—like medicine. (We have a bottle of beer in the fridge, which has been there several months; we keep for a friend who likes to split one with me.) So, I have the occasional beer—purely social—and never want more than one or two unless really pushed. I can go six months without even thinking about drinking. I have no desire to drink at all. Zero. Nada. Zip. None. Kind of a hollow victory, I guess.

So, this formerly handsome young man who used to get the pretty girls, was a fairly decent athlete, and who felt infallible, has been mugged by reality. I can't really win here since the portal hypertension makes surgery out of the question in terms of the liver, emphysema is not curable and just gradually steals your breath away, and now they are saying that my kidneys are involved.

Please don't feel sorry for me. I don't. I am surrounded by people every day who would never let me be if I were so inclined, which I am not anyway. So when a test comes back from the hospital and the results are an arrow in the heart, completely unexpected, don't mope and cry why me, why me. Boo, hoo, hoo. Go visit the kids on the oncology floor of the hospital. Or, when faced with nasty results, do what I now do, rip it up, toss it away, and don't look back.

Untitled

Aaron J. French

Imagine wandering around your front yard at 6 a.m., armed with a baseball bat, convinced people are hiding in the bushes. Imagine pacing before a television with the lights turned down, the blue glow of the screen filling the room. Imagine sitting in a bathroom, chin cradled in palms, with a loaded rifle close at hand, listening to the voices in your head.

To tell you how I ended up this way, I'd have to go back through the fear, the underlying terror that fuels the destruction, and the disintegration of the healthy mind. It was always about fear with me: fear of myself, fear of other people, and fear of the outside world. My fear during childhood was a different kind of fear; the kind that washed away with the passing days, that was felt in the moment then let go of, that dissolved like sugar into water with each successive playground visit.

So unlike my fear during adolescence, that fear entered into my being and penetrated my mind. It lingered in my body, growing like a cancerous tumor. The fear was so terrible that I would do anything in order to escape. I thought the problem was in *me*, in my personality. I thought it was keeping me from assimilating, from joining the rest of the world, who, at the time, seemed to be getting along just fine. I hated this about myself. I wanted to assimilate. I didn't want to be different. I decided to kill the kind, innocent, peaceful, blissfully ignorant being that resided inside of me. The world wanted anger, violence, sex, materialism, and cynicism. The world wanted to glorify its darker half, its brutish ways.

To escape the fear of the world, which was really just my own fear reflected back at me, I looked to my parents for guidance. My mother has been a closet drug addict for as long as I can remember. During my adolescence, I discovered this fact about her and I had a realization. I can even recall when this conception took root in my brain. *So this is how you do it,* was my thinking. *This is how you tolerate the fear of the world, how you blend in, how you cope.*

Once I began to assimilate alongside everybody else, they liked me and wanted to be my friends. Girls started talking to me. They started seeing me as a man, instead of a gentle, pacifist child. I could damage things now, be it myself or others, just like the rest of the world damaged things. I remember thinking, *I'm doing it now, I'm finally doing it … I'm finally growing up.*

There was no way I could give up the drugs. To do so was to return to my previous state: that of a gentle, compassionate child. A state that, in my mind, the entire world despised. I was never addicted to any particular drug. It was the drugs themselves I needed, whether smoking or snorting or huffing or drinking, because without them I became a different person. I reverted to my former child ego, an ego I eventually became so detached from that to be in it was bewildering and confusing. I felt like two separate people, and one of them wanted to murder—literally, *murder*—the other. This murderous ego I supported, for the world around me seemed to support it, and I soon tricked myself into thinking I *was* it.

As years progressed, I leapfrogged through drugs. During my teens it was cigarettes and marijuana. I eventually started selling marijuana. I met other dealers, gradually worked my way up the drug chain. But I was constantly aware that on some level I was two people. The one on the exterior: a hardcore, drug-dealing tough guy; and the one on the interior, a terrified and embarrassed child.

At 17 or 18, I switched from marijuana to alcohol. When my friends asked why, I told them it was because I wanted a larger profit. But truthfully, the child presence—the former "me"—had begun to break free whenever I smoked marijuana. Instead of deadening my fear and shame, it intensified it. In other words, it had the opposite effect. I suffered panic attacks whenever I got high, and not the usual type of paranoia associated with the drug—"our parents may catch us, the teachers may catch us, the police may catch us," and so on.

When this paranoia hit me (and usually around other people, the same people I was supposed to act tough and emotionless around), I was immobilized with fear. I imagined that everyone was looking at me, at least thinking about me, criticizing me, and I became terrified I was worthless, an empty void in the room sucking the "normalness" out of everyone. My terrified child ego rose to the forefront and I had no control over it. Suddenly I was reminded of the fears I had about my mother's drug addiction, my fears about girls and sex, and every other fear in my soul. It took tremendous willpower, but during such attacks I eventually managed to say, "Well I got to get going now, guys" through clenched teeth, and depart silently. I always hated myself afterward. I remember wanting to be dead.

So I quit marijuana, though I continued selling it in large amounts. But I soon discovered alcohol one night when I got drunk at a party. I'd flirted with alcohol plenty of times, but never had I embraced it with the same passion as I had the marijuana. I discovered the extensive deadening effects of alcohol, its bolstering of self-confidence, its capability to incite raucousness. I continued the alcohol for about a week, with soaring relief, as I realized the child ego could not break through when I was drunk, no matter how hard it tried.

Somewhere around my late teens, I was introduced to cocaine. This was done in two ways. First, my mother did cocaine every day and so I periodically dipped into her stash. I hadn't taken to the coke, not really, because it was hard to get and expensive, and I didn't quite understand the effects. The second way I was introduced to cocaine was through my mother's dealer. He came to the house frequently during my adolescence. When I started selling pot he somehow caught wind and asked if I would like to sell pot for him. I said yes and so we exchanged beeper numbers and started a relationship that was, for the most part, kept private from my mother.

My behavior eventually became too much even for her, so she booted me out. Homeless, I went to stay with various drug-dealing "buddies." I even lived in a house full of strippers for a while. During this period I discovered meth. Almost instantly, I was massively addicted. Using this drug impaired me so badly that my drug dealing enterprise went down the tubes and I soon found myself living on the streets. I was only 18.

Eventually I went crawling back to my parents. My father let me work at his business, and he even set me up in a studio apartment owned by some lawyer friend of his. I'd stopped selling drugs completely. I was only using now. That apartment became a psychotic's playpen. I was using heavy, heavy amounts of meth, staying up for days at a time. I managed to hold down my job, but I was a total wreck, and people could tell. I entered a dream state, a nonreality. To a degree, I'd been in this nonreality since I was 12 years old, but here I lost my grip on what was real. There were voices and hallucinations. Terrible voices, telling me how worthless I was. Telling me to go out and purchase more meth.

I got my supply from a house inhabited by a notorious biker gang. I have this memory of standing in the living room after getting my fix when suddenly a violent brawl erupted between three members. I swear as they pummeled each other, smashing glass and furniture, I stood right in the middle of it, and yet their lunging bodies passed right through me. I wasn't locatable. You couldn't touch me or speak to me, could barely even *see* me, like I was an image fading from an old photograph.

The voices hounded me. Total psychosis occurred each night as I paced the apartment. I experienced fits of violent eruption. On the few occasions when I had people over, it was not uncommon for me to explode. Once I grabbed a baseball bat and smashed the coffee table in front of three friends. I screamed at the top of my lungs and ended up outside, swinging the bat to and fro, shouting at them to come outside and fight me. Who knows how long I had been without sleep.

One of my friends moved in. In a month I had him hooked on meth. He was absorbed into my "dream" world. My nonexistence acted as a vacuum, sucking whatever awareness he had of reality into the void. It got to be too much. He eventually moved out and stopped smoking meth. I was utterly alone. People stopped coming by the apartment. I drifted further into my head.

This is the moment at which the nightmare became real. Now the voices were broadcast on a loudspeaker. I never slept, never ate. The mornings would find me sitting in the bathroom, holding the glass meth pipe, head cocked toward the window, straining to hear voices. I had little awareness that the voices were in my head. I actually believed they were a part of the external world. I often paced the yard and peered into bushes with the baseball bat propped over my shoulder. I can't really explain what happened the night I decided to stop using. But I can recount my experience.

My mother and her family were on vacation. I somehow wound up at their house. Alone. I had been up for five days. I remember lying in my old bedroom, staring at the walls, which were covered over with black scorpions and Egyptian scarabs. My ex-girlfriend had called and we'd had a fight. She claimed she was sending her new boyfriend and a bunch of his friends over to attack me. In a panic, I started gathering weapons in the house, formulated a plan, even tried to devise booby traps. I then hid in the shadows, waiting.

But no one showed up. There was a moment when I looked out the window, and instead of seeing the dark street beyond, I saw myself reflected in the glass. A single thought ran through my head: *What the hell are you doing?* At once, almost on top of the thought, I made a decision. Not halfheartedly, but with the inmost power of my will. *I'm not going to do this anymore.* That was the last time I ever used meth. My life started over, but my addiction remained. Again I funneled it into alcohol and soon became a functioning alcoholic. Years of heavy drinking ensued.

Following a similar experience in which I broke down into tears and cried like a child, I quit drinking. My life started over once more, but still the addiction remained. This time it was funneled into painkillers, pharmaceuticals. But that only lasted a year or two and eventually I was able to stop taking them. Presently I am drug-free, though even now the whispering voice of addiction endures.

I've managed to throw a leash around this monster of mine, tether it to a hitching post, so to speak. But it has not gone away. The best I can hope for is control. I have funneled my addictive personality into coffee, which is far less severe, as well as legal, but sometimes I experience a similar craving for it. Someday I'll funnel it into an addiction that is nondamaging—sunshine and fresh air, perhaps—but until then, I take things a day at a time, and I have a cup of coffee.

A Nurse's Journey Through Loss, Addiction, and Recovery

MICHELLE WALTER

At some point in their lives, many people see an image that haunts them, an image that changes their lives, an image they will never forget. For me, that image was a brain tumor. That image was the beginning of a downward spiral that almost killed me.

My mom was not only a mother to me, but also my best friend. She was a healthy 52-year-old teacher when the unthinkable happened. We noticed her smile had looked funny and she was very tired. She had attributed it to the fact that it was the end of the school year and she was finishing up her master's degree. I convinced her to go to the doctor anyway.

At first, they thought she might have had a small stroke, so they sent her to get a CAT scan. The scan was being done at the hospital I worked at, so I went in with her. That moment, that very moment is when I saw the haunting image on the screen. A brain tumor. A deadly brain tumor, a glioblastoma. My heart sank, my knees went weak. I knew that life as I knew it was never going to be the same. What I didn't know was just how bad it was going to get. I knew deep down that my mom was going to be taken away from us very soon. What I didn't know was that I was also going to become addicted to narcotics.

As far back as I can remember, I knew I wanted to be a nurse. I was that girl who was never grossed out. So, when it was time for college, I studied nursing. After college, I went to work at a wonderful hospital. I loved working ICU/CCU, and most of my 15 years there was in that area. I worked as a nurse in acute care all those years and never had an issue with addiction. I was happily married, had two healthy kids, and a great job. Life was going just as I had planned it. Then, life threw me a curveball—mom was diagnosed with brain cancer. Then, another curveball—I had to have a major surgery. Finally, curveball number three—I had to have another unplanned major surgery related to the first one.

I was full of grief, despair, and emotional pain, as well as physical pain. Bad combination. Once my physical pain was gone, I continued to use the narcotics to dull the emotional pain. Since my mom's illness, I hadn't been sleeping well. My mind just wouldn't turn off. I noticed that when I would take the narcotics, I could sleep. My mind would turn off for a little while and I could actually rest.

It didn't take long before I was hooked. Not only was I hooked, but I was also taking more and more pills to have that "numbing" effect. I had also been prescribed a benzo (Xanax) to calm my anxiety about my mom's illness. So, now I was combining narcotics and benzos. This next part may sound crazy, but being a nurse, I started to worry about my liver due to all the Tylenol I was ingesting in the pain pills. So, I got the bright idea to switch to pain meds without Tylenol. Those meds are stronger meds—Demerol, morphine, Dilaudid. Like the others, those started as pill form, but eventually I turned to the injectables. What is crazy is the fact that I hate needles. Yes, I am a nurse and I don't mind giving injections, but I hate getting them. My addiction had its claws in me and I was spiraling down.

Even at this point, I was still convinced I was in control and I could stop when I wanted to. But that's what an addiction does. It changes your whole life. What you knew as right and wrong, black and white, gets distorted and becomes gray. I had been confronted at work and my husband knew I had a problem, but they didn't know how bad it was. I had told them the truth, but not the whole truth. Another aspect is they attributed my behavior to the fact my mom was dying. My addiction had consumed me and all I thought about was how I was going to get the meds.

234 FIRST PERSON ACCOUNTS OF MENTAL ILLNESS AND RECOVERY

By this time, I was injecting anything I could get my hands on. I was in trouble and I had no control over it. My mom was dying of cancer, and my addiction was destroying my life. My mom died in the spring of 2009 at the age of 54. My mom was gone and my life was in shambles. I looked in the mirror and I saw a face staring back at me I didn't even recognize. I saw a face full of anguish and pain. What had I become? Who was this person?

A week after mom's death, my husband approached me about my addiction. I broke down and told him I needed help. I had tried many times to quit on my own. Every time I would try, the physical withdrawal would get so bad that I would start using again. We decided I needed to go to an inpatient treatment facility. We didn't know where to turn, so I went to a local outpatient treatment center and they sent me to an inpatient center. I was in there for five days and got through the worst of the physical withdrawal, but I wasn't prepared for the mental withdrawal.

After I was released, I went home and all I wanted to do was get back to work. Financially, we needed me working and I truly loved my job. Unfortunately, I went back to work in the same capacity way too soon and began using again. It didn't take long before I got caught. They wanted to do a random drug screen on me and I tried to fake it. Not a smart thing to do at all. After that, I lost my job. Another low.

Now, you would think that would be enough to get me to quit. But my body was still craving the drugs. The mental aspect of addiction is so powerful. So, I forged a prescription and got caught. That was one of the scariest days of my life, but it was also the day that changed my life forever. Not because I got called to the police station, but because through that encounter, I got introduced to another nurse who had gone through a narcotic addiction. Meeting her and seeing that I wasn't alone, I wasn't the only nurse with this disease. Before that, I had felt so alone and alienated. A nurse with an addiction is a very shameful place to be. I had finally found someone I could tell everything I had done to, and she would understand. I had been holding so much in and now I could let it out. That nurse is now my sponsor and my friend. That is the day my true recovery began.

Anyone who tells you recovery from any addiction is easy is lying. Or they aren't really in recovery. Recovery is a roller coaster. You may have your good days, but you have a lot of bad ones, especially in early recovery. A sponsor is a vital part in your recovery. You have to find someone who truly understands what you are going through and who also holds you accountable. I am also involved in my state's nurses assistance program, so I am required to have a sponsor, go to AA/NA meetings, see an addictionist, and so on. I am very grateful for this program and the guidance it gave me. It told me what I had to do, and these things are what I needed to do. I don't believe I would be where I am today if it wasn't for this program and my sponsor.

A nurse with an addiction needs specialized treatment because we are surrounded by these medications whenever we are at work. We have to have a strong recovery foundation to be able to go back into acute care nursing. Some nurses never can, and that's okay. There are other areas of nursing to pursue. That is why a state's nurses assistance program is so vital. It provides that guidance and support needed for a strong recovery foundation.

Many times, I would lie there at night and wonder why God spared me. With the amount of drugs I was ingesting, I should be dead. Why was I still alive? I believe I am here today to help others who are struggling with addiction. There are so many things I know now that I wish I had known when I first started to look for help for my addiction. To help others, I have developed a Web site with a wealth of information that includes links to helpful sites as well as personal experience. I want to share what worked and didn't work for me. Anyone with an addiction needs caring, compassionate treatment. Recovery is a lifelong process. There is help. There is hope. I am living proof of that.

6

Eating Disorders

INTRODUCTION

Previously considered to be particular to Western, industrialized societies, anorexia nervosa and bulimia nervosa are now found around the world with prevalence rates among adolescent and young adult woman ranging from 1 to 4% in the past two decades (Yager, Devlin, Halmi, Powers, & Zerbe, 2006). Anorexia, with its self-imposed symptoms of starvation, has been known for centuries, but the eating and purging patterns of bulimia were not recognized formally until relatively recently in the 1950s. Both disorders involve an obsession with weight and body image as well as strategies to lose weight that are excessive. Most common among young, White, middle-class, and college-bound women, anorexia can be life threatening and puts sufferers at great risk for many medical problems. Mortality for people with bulimia is a rare occurrence, as they are usually at or slightly above normal body weight, but serious health consequences of bulimia such as electrolyte imbalance and cardiac problems are possible. As women from other cultures immigrate to the West and adopt Western body ideals of thinness, eating disorders are becoming more common among these groups. Men make up only 5–10% of those with eating disorders.

Two other conditions that involve problems with eating (but are not covered here) are listed in the *DSM-IV-TR* under disorders usually first diagnosed in infancy, childhood, or adolescence. In *pica*, children (or adults) engage in persistent eating of substances that are nonnutritive (e.g., dirt or plaster). In *rumination disorder*, repeated regurgitation and rechewing of food is the key feature that can lead to failure to thrive in infants. The disorder can be fatal, with mortality rates up to 25% of those meeting criteria for the diagnosis.

Anorexia nervosa involves an obsession with or fear of becoming fat or gaining weight in the presence of being underweight. There is a misperception about weight and body image or denial about the reality of extremely low weight. Individuals with anorexia resist maintaining body weight that is considered normal for their height and age or fail to gain weight that would bring them up to an expected level. They remain below 85% of that expected weight. If a woman, she must have amenorrhea, the absence of three or more menstrual cycles. Anorexia may or may not include binge-eating and purging behaviors. *Bulimia nervosa* is characterized by repeated episodes of binge-eating and purging behaviors to prevent weight gain that are excessive such as vomiting, use of laxatives, diuretics, or enemas, fasting, or intense exercise. The bingeing and purging must occur on the average of at least two times a week for 3 months. The person with bulimia also experiences perceptual distortions of their body weight and shape.

This chapter consists of four narrative accounts contributed by people with eating disorders. Emily Troscianko's beautifully written but sad story refers to anorexia as "a quiet but dreadful illness" that "replaces character with ritual and life with survival." She talks about losing her identity to the illness and the accompanying depression and OCD that became part of it for her. While anorexia involves denial and control, she has been able to recover and holds out that hope for anyone with the disorder. In *Big Little*, Priscilla Becker describes the height of her anorexia as "eternal elitism" of "will" and "wit." Food had an extraordinary power in the household where she grew up, and the refusal of food became an act of power and control for her. She went to the depths of despair in her worst times with it. In response to the alarm of family and friends, she has improved her condition to the point of it being a "working anorexia." Next, a revealing account by an anonymous author describes her experiences of having the "addiction" of bulimia, the "irreconcilable urge to binge and purge." To control her weight, she became obsessed with weighing herself before bingeing and after purging. At one point when she started throwing up blood, she thought she was going to die of it—but now she is "bingeing and purging to survive." Finally, Laura Bette tells the compelling story of the obsessions and compulsions that were part of her anorexia. In acting on these, she exercised to an extreme and allowed herself only 400 calories of food a day. While pretending that everything was normal on the outside, she was filled with rage, depression, and self-hatred—and dying on the inside. Her recovery began when she started working with a therapist, and she now greets each day with a smile.

QUESTIONS FOR REFLECTION

In thinking about these four first person accounts (FPAs), what, if any, are the psychosocial factors that appear to precipitate the development of eating disorders? Are the experiences of people with anorexia different than those of people with bulimia? If so, why and in what ways? What are some other common themes that emerge from reading these various accounts?

REFERENCE

Yager, J., Devlin, M. J., Halmi, K. A., Halmi, K. A., Herzog, D., Mitchell, J. E., . . . & Zerbe, K. J. (2006). *Practice guidelines for the treatment of patients with eating disorders* (3rd ed.). Washington, DC: American Psychiatric Association.

Dying by Inches

EMILY TROSCIANKO

Anorexia nervosa doesn't necessarily begin with childhood trauma. Someone saying you're fat doesn't necessarily spark it off. It doesn't necessarily involve surviving on a slice of apple and a cup of black coffee a day, nor need it lead to heart failure or time on a hospital ward being drip-fed. My anorexia was much less dramatic than that, and became its own inevitable cause: Beyond a certain point, malnutrition itself created the mental rigidity that perpetuated the eating disorder.

It started like ordinary teenage dieting, and even at my skeletally lowest weight, I never ate less than 1,600 calories a day. But it consumed me and my whole life for more than a decade: it made me wraithlike, solitary, and scary. It gave me depression and obsessive-compulsive disorder. Here I want to tell the story of anorexia as a quiet but dreadful illness of starvation that replaces character with ritual, and life with survival. I also want to make it clear that such a story can have a happy ending, despite what many people say. It is possible to recover fully from anorexia, and, in the past two and a half years of my life, I have done so.

When asked where it all began, I usually fall back on the memory of a family ski holiday in France at age 16. I got quite drunk on the last evening and couldn't join the others for a last morning's skiing, instead sitting in the car with my hangover, and suffering all the way down the hairpins into the valley when it was time to leave. That evening, my queasiness remained, and I couldn't eat anything except a few salty crisps. I still remember the exact place where I was sitting cross-legged on the living-room floor of the house where we were staying the night, when I realized that—contrary to all my previous experience—it felt good to feel hungry. I felt lightened in body and mind, exhilarated because of, not in spite of, my hunger-induced weakness, and entirely indifferent to food. My diaries before then are scattered with remarks about thinking myself too fat and therefore unattractive to boys, but this was, I think, the first moment at which the possibility of eating less became something that appealed in itself, rather than as a means to the end of getting slimmer.

This isn't to say that I had no interest in being thin or losing weight while I was ill. In some ways this was the primary obsession, and by the latter years I was weighing myself every morning, fearing an "inexorable rise" and longing for a "magic drop," checking my tummy in the mirror dozens of times a day, inspecting upper arms, spine, sternum, ribs, and hip bones every time I undressed. It always made me feel good when the numbers on the scale were lower than ever before and when the bones and hollows of my body were more clearly visible.

Long before I became ill, I was writing in my diary about "the flat tummy I've always wanted," and that was also the center of my compulsive checking and mental measuring habits. I'd turn this way and that in front of the mirror, pressing my tummy in, breathing in, wishing it could always be as flat, or as concave, as it was when I breathed in, wishing nothing I'd ever eaten could be seen there, so that it could look perfect in the present.

At the same time, though, there was no practical point to those infinite "checks;" what numbers or what body shape I saw never caused me to alter anything of what I ate or when or how much, or how I exercised, because my rules about those things were, by about six years in, not debatable. Eating less was almost as inconceivable as eating more; the only possibility was perfect predictability. The point, then, was not to lose weight; it was to live life with the illusion of perfect control. This illusion could survive only if control was of a negative kind, of not allowing myself to eat more. The amount I ate changed through the years, as did the type and the timing of food, even though at any given time the current routine felt like the single possible type and time and tiny line between too little and too much. The equally urgent point of it all—the deferral, the restriction, the minute weighing of every gram—was to be able to get through the day without misery overcoming me. That was possible, I believed, only because I had the guiltless ecstasy of perfectly orchestrated food to look forward to at the end of it.

Paradoxically, then, the ultimate goal of the anorexia, in the later years, was to allow food to be the ultimate pleasure. I couldn't believe that any other pleasure people told me their lives contained could be comparable to the agonized anticipation, throughout the long hours of hunger and cold and tiredness, and finally the half-delirious consummation of the act that was eating my nightly 450 calories' worth of cheap milk chocolate (nearly a whole 100-g bar). That act made my muscles relax and my mind soften with the sheer delight of feeling the squares of dissolving, creamy sweetness in my mouth, with the sensual bliss of chewing them rapidly, in bed with eyes closed, the entire day having been a prelude to this moment, and nothing more to do now but turn off the light and sink down into the covers, warmed by the electric blanket I needed even in the summer, and fall asleep in the brief calm of the sugar high.

My aunt told me I should want to go to parties, go skiing, have boyfriends, have sex, but I found most people dull and I feared the cold more than anything. I needed privacy and predictability more than anything and I felt no physical desire for anything but food. No one else understood how complete the delight of guilt-free eating was for me; no one else who wasn't starving could possibly understand. I felt I'd found the key to the most sublime happiness possible on earth, and yet the tiniest thing could make me cry, and laughing was far too much effort.

All the arguments for change that were put to me by my family, by my few remaining friends, and, in my bleaker moments, by myself, were completely impotent because of my certainty of two things. First, that without this all-defining entity that was the anorexia, I would no longer know who I was or have any identity at all. Second, that life would be even more unbearable if I relinquished this way of giving every day structure, purpose, and certainty.

As to my identity, to me, "Emily" became nothing more or less than anorexic Emily. My blank, distraught, irritable, or fragile moods, my need for routine and privacy, my slight figure, my lack of friends and my worship of academic achievement, all seemed like innate parts of me. There seemed no reason to believe that eating breakfast or lunch would make a difference to any of them. The extent to which "I" was the product of years of malnutrition and the rigid, ritualized mental life and physical limitations that malnutrition itself created was not something I was capable of comprehending, since to do so I would have had to imagine my life as otherwise than it was. I had neither the ability nor the desire to do that. It was a perfect vicious circle: The anorexia had become so completely what I was that I couldn't see how completely it had taken over "Emily," nor could I therefore have any motivation to try to find her again.

In a much more pragmatic sense, anorexia gave structure to my day and to my life. The majority of my anorexic years were spent at the University of Oxford, first as an undergraduate, then as a master's student, and finally as a doctoral student. I lived on a traditional English narrow boat in the marina in Oxford, with a friend for a year, and then with my brother, Joly, for a year (while he too studied at the university), and after that, alone. The marina was pretty and quiet, and the boat a perfect size for one person—and living there in the latter years meant that there were no intrusions on a life that was as completely controlled as a life ever can be, once one has ceded all control to an illness that allows one to pretend that this is not the case. There was no longer the guilt and resentment of sitting wraithlike in my armchair wrapped in rugs while my brother lived a real life—a life in which he would have liked to invite people back to his home, but couldn't expose them to my cold stares and superior-seeming, life-draining presence.

Once he'd graduated and moved out, I got up when I wanted; went out on my bicycle straight after getting up; shopped for myself; "cooked" (i.e., boiled vegetables) for myself; counted the hours of solitary academic work, which were how I earned the right to eat; made my daily series of drinks at their proper (always a little later) times; kept the place cold so as to burn more calories keeping myself warm; and kept it dim (for I lived mostly at night) so as to save money and make it feel more romantic, or to give the world softer edges. How odd it feels to look back on all that and to wonder how I survived even a day like that, let alone so much of my 20s, whereas at the time I didn't believe I could survive if I did things any differently.

I simply couldn't imagine not riding my bike for an hour first thing, on one of two routes, one for weekdays, one for weekends. I couldn't imagine not going to a supermarket nearly every day for more lettuce or cabbage or apples, or cheap bread or chocolate, or low-fat margarine, or low-cal chocolate drink powder, or three different sorts of milk according to which meal it was for, or two unvarying types of cereal, or the particular brand of "yogurt break bar" that marked the daily transition from just drinking to starting to eat. I couldn't imagine not returning to a cold and silent boat to prepare my food—not to be eaten till many hours later—while listening to a favorite radio program, or not then sitting down with my laptop on my rug-covered knees to begin to read and type with hands encased in fingerless gloves, the first of two cups of tea (with milk) beside me to help the words and the thoughts flow.

I couldn't imagine not following those two teas (both made with the same teabag) with a cup of hot fruit squash (the amount carefully gauged by eye), or the squash with a cup of milky coffee, always aware of how long a two-pint bottle of semi-skimmed milk should last, and trying to reduce the quantities I used against an imagined norm so that there would be more left to add, indulgently, to the mixture of skimmed milk and water with which I ate my muesli, one day in three. I couldn't imagine not deferring the preparation of each of these drinks, because the longer I went without, the later it became, the stronger and more implacable I had been, and the more quickly I might then legitimately consume all the food that was to come, with a pleasure tinged with well-earned urgency.

I couldn't imagine not resolving, every day, to get to bed earlier, and failing every day to do so, because failing was also a sort of success in that my willpower was proven—even as it was disproven. I couldn't imagine not making the cup of Highlights (artificially sweetened chocolate drink) to have with the yogurt-coated GoAhead bar and finding something that needed to be done while the drink cooled to a drinkable temperature, and always taking a little too long with whatever it was I was doing so I ran the risk of letting it cool too much and it being ruined because it could then be drunk too quickly, imparting no warmth.

I couldn't imagine not longing for the moment at which I'd open the cereal-bar packet (having weighed all six in the box to make sure that throughout the week I ate the lightest first and had the heaviest left till last), turn the two pieces of yogurt-covered biscuit over so the biscuit was showing, find a magazine article of a perfect length to finish just before I finished eating, and eat while reading, using the trashiness of a short hotel or restaurant review or a recipe or a fashion article as a completely neutral foil to the sensation of, at long last, eating.

I couldn't imagine not crouching by my bed, "pre-reading" the hoarded magazines and newspaper supplements, which I would skim for matter light on food-related material to be suitable to accompany my nightly feast. Crouching in order to induce a bowel movement, in order that I might go out to the toilet block and empty myself as much as possible so that I should be as desirous and worthy a recipient as possible of the food that was now imminent.

I couldn't imagine not wearing myself out with pointless compulsions. On the way to and from the loo I would, in the last year or so of my illness, get caught up in nonsensical obsessive-compulsive habits that I found it impossible to refuse. I had to memorize all the writing on the hand-dryer and the toilet-roll dispenser before leaving. Then I had to memorize all the number-plates of the cars parked along the track to the boat, and pause or return (this all in the middle of the night) if I couldn't recite each one back to myself. Then I'd often start to worry whether the plants around the boat had been watered recently, and whether they needed slug pellets putting down, and then had to check that my bike was locked securely. All things I never gave a moment's thought until this time of night, just before it was time, at last, to eat.

I couldn't imagine not returning and finally allowing myself to turn on the electric heater, because although I found the cold relatively easy to bear before it was time to eat, I would somehow grow unbearably cold as soon as I began. I don't know how much because my body then needed its little available energy for digestion, and how much because I couldn't bear the loveliness of eating to be marred in any way by the cold that had plagued me since I'd woken.

I couldn't imagine not being reduced rapidly to cursing rage or tears if anything at all should interrupt this sequence of events, this ascending arc to brief happiness. I couldn't imagine life being bearable without such an internal structure, without each day rising to a peak, but instead just dull flatness with a little bump now and then where meals were. I couldn't imagine that anything but food might constitute a feature in one's mental landscape.

As for the food and the eating itself—it was, like so much in the existence that anorexia creates, a thing of paradoxes. Its perfection mattered more than anything else in life, but I threatened that perfection myself by the compulsion I felt to delay it, suffusing it ever more with guilt and with the sadness of knowing myself incompatible with the rest of the world. I threatened it, too, with my compulsion to record it. For many years I wrote in my diary once a day, at varying times, but toward the end I started to find it necessary to write down every aspect of the build-up to eating, and the act of doing so, pausing between bites to take up my pen and scrawl something predictable and nearly illegible. I don't know whether this was because the pleasure of eating grew greater the thinner and more chronically malnourished I became, or because this was just one of the obsessive-compulsive behaviors that took an ever stronger hold over me in the very last months of my illness, as my body and brain shriveled into the repetitive litanies of thought and action. Or, finally, whether this was my way of pretending to myself that there was any real pleasure there at all, rather than just a total emptiness that had to be clothed by words in some grander garb. Perhaps all of these.

The things eaten were a paradoxical mixture, too. On the one hand, they were the ultimate diet foods, the tired clichés of "moderate" anorexia: lettuce and boiled vegetables, the lowest-calorie margarine to be found, skimmed milk and soya milk, low-fat yogurt, All Bran (fewer calories per 100 g than any other breakfast cereal, as far as I knew, and I'd scoured many supermarket shelves checking). These foods made it possible to enjoy a great deal of eating—the sheer act of filling one's mouth with food, chewing, swallowing, feeling one's stomach fill—without sacrificing too many calories. On the other hand, some of the things I ate were the antithesis of diet foods: a substantial amount of bread (150 g), cheap and filling muesli (100 g), a selection of sickly sweet things making up 850 calories on the night when I didn't eat cereal, a token half an apple preceding instant custard or Angel Delight (a mousse-like sweet dessert, in chocolate, strawberry, butterscotch, and other flavors), cakes and biscuits and chocolate, and of course the 450 calories' worth of chocolate on the two cereal nights. These foods were what it was really worth stopping fasting for, because the rapture they imparted was unlike anything else on earth.

How did the 16-year-old who weighed 61 kg (135 pounds) and skipped breakfast turn into the 26-year-old who weighed 38 kg (83 pounds) and whose nocturnal life was nothing but longing for food? The transformation was a gradual, insidious one. I was a happy teenager, working too hard perhaps, but with enough friends and more than enough energy to go out drinking and dancing on weekends. No one noticed that I started to go to school without eating breakfast. My family didn't think it anything much out of the ordinary when I refused to go to the canteen at lunchtime, and instead took little bags of dried fruit and nuts to eat secretly in the library. For some time I at least ate dinner with the family in the evening; they assumed that must be enough to keep me going, and things couldn't be too bad.

But when I went traveling in Europe on my own, the summer after my first public exams, aged 16, there was nothing to keep me from eating as little as I liked, ostensibly to save money, and increasingly because I couldn't help it. Restricting what I ate had become an end in itself, and ignoring hunger had become the norm, although I saw how it separated me from the people I met. In my diary I wrote, "Everyone else is eating dinner—I'm a bit hungry but I shouldn't be—maybe I'll buy some more bread and fruit at the station (13.07.98)."

When I returned I'd lost a lot of weight (11 kilos, or 24 pounds, in six months), and my mother, Sue, realized something might be really wrong, as did I: "I've been looking at myself in the mirror and I've just realized, my body's disgusting. I'm too fucking bony. It's horrible (13.09.98)." Nothing about food was calm or easy anymore: When eating with the family, I'd constantly compare how much everyone ate, and ensure I ate more slowly than everyone else. I'd avoid eating with others at all, whenever I could. I vacillated all the time between hunger and nausea, between revulsion at my thinness and addiction to it and my hunger, between not caring about the way it was all going and acknowledging the danger. I felt crippled by the confusion of trying to reverse, or at least stop, the process of losing weight that the past six months had been consumed by, but still not quite daring to want to gain weight:

> Oh, I'm so confused. I don't know whether I want to put on weight or not. I know I don't want to lose any more, that's all I know. Which is a bit ironic because that's what I've been trying so hard for the last six months to do—all my willpower's been concentrated on not eating, on refusing desserts and beer, on finding bread and fruit instead of anything else. And now there are no rules that I have to stick to—my self-imposed restrictions are pointless now. So today I've again eaten more (Gayle, my friend, even bought me crisps today and I think she was amazed I allowed her to), and again I feel sick. My stomach feels bloated (if it's shrunk, I don't want to make it bigger), but I look in the mirror and I tell myself I ought to keep on eating. It's just I feel so much better if I don't. . . . Is this anorexia? I'm beginning to wonder (22.09.98).

My periods, which had only recently started, stopped. I had a stern talking-to from a pastoral tutor at school. I struggled to eat with the family, and my father, Tom, started to bring special meals to my bedroom—peeled apple with sugar, chocolate, and boiled eggs. I veered between gratitude and anger, between being a contrite and loving invalid and an angry victim. The crying, the shaking, the wanting to throw up made me hate him for bringing me the food and aware of how wrong everything had gone. I binged, for the one and only time, on chocolate. It never happened again. I despised the weakness of bulimics, who admitted by eating that they couldn't resist their appetites and fooled themselves that they purified themselves afterward by getting rid of it. Mine was the infinitely superior power, not to succumb in the first place.

My mother read up on anorexia; I felt my life drifting away from me, and the frightening attraction of quietly wasting away into oblivion. She asked me several times throughout my illness whether I wanted to die, and I always said no. In my diary I mentioned now and then the desire to die, but it was usually only a brief emotional response to the nausea that food induced: "Tom keeps forcing me to eat Milky Ways and he's about to bring me sausages. I can't bear it, I want to die. I don't want to think, talk, have any contact with food, ever again. That's why I'm killing myself, I suppose (17.01.99)."

When other people told me that they were scared I would die, it always moved me to improve things, however briefly and minimally. It was hardly bearable when, years later, Adam, my mother's partner, a grown man and not even related to me, e-mailed me in Germany to say: "Thank you for your lovely e-mail. I cried as I wrote the last one, for I am exceedingly fond of you and hate the thought of you dying. If I can help in any way, including getting on a plane, please let me know. Let's face it; if one of us is going to die, it should be me, since I have done everything useful that I am going to do, whereas you are just stepping off into what should be a fabulous life. May it be so! (01.03.03)." The guilt and sadness of having made kind and loving people feel like that is still hard to bear.

Over the years, the long weariness of starving sometimes made me feel I couldn't be bothered with anything anymore and wouldn't ever care about anything anymore. But my later routines of perfect food helped ward off that deep tiredness with life, because there was at least one pleasure left, one thing to care about. I had no idea what full or hungry meant any more. I drove away my boyfriend with my physical and emotional coldness. At age 17, I started seeing a child psychiatrist and made a recovery plan. I put on weight (reaching a high point of 50 kg, or 110 pounds, exactly), went clubbing every weekend, got together with my boyfriend again, began drinking instead of eating, was juggling exams and piano practice with drugs, was offered a place at Oxford, started losing weight again, and made plans to gain weight. Succeeding, I was delighting in the success that freed me from the grotesquery of anorexia as cliché:

A lazy day—the one burst of activity was cycling to the hospital for my appointment with Dr. Shoebridge, who seemed much reassured by my weight and reports of postdinner chocolate eating. We had the shortest session yet—less than half an hour—and we're to meet again in two months' time. It's reassuring to me, too, to go there and compare my state to how I was 18 months ago. I feel in control now and it's not an illusion anymore. What brought my relief home to me was the smallest thing—he opened the door to the "weighing room" without knocking and there was another teenage girl in there on the scales, her doctor peering anxiously over her shoulder. The utter ridiculousness of it all overwhelmed me; we all think we're so new and special and important, we stupid anorexics, but we're not, we're among millions of women equally self-centered and shortsighted, and it's not a clever thing to do. It doesn't make you special. It makes you a tormented bony creature perched on a weighing scale (21.06.00).

So I went up to Oxford having pleased the psychiatrist with my excellent recovery. At my all-female college I felt instantly out of place, superior intellectually and in life experience. I took pride in being abstemious where everyone else excitedly stayed out and got drunk with new freedom. I was *sensible* in a way more like my preteen self, but very lonely. In the second year I moved from longing for my boyfriend's visits to dreading them. I didn't eat breakfast; I ate lunch only when the friend I lived with on the boat was out. I ate less and less and worked more and more and discovered the joy of muesli and chocolate for dinner, "entirely alone. Nobody knows me. I don't know anything about myself or anyone else (18.08.02)."

I went to Germany for 9 months in the third year of my B.A., having split up with my boyfriend for the last time, and drowned my anguish in hunger. I terrified my parents and myself. I made, then, my most concerted effort ever to bring about a full recovery, but despite the weight I gained, I lost it again during a miserable summer in Switzerland. By my final year at Oxford everything was set in the pattern it would retain for the next 4 years. The rigidness of thought and habit and the mental and behavioral patterns that my starved state made so hard to tackle, were too much for me. Late attempts at compromise, like the plan of eating with my mother and her partner just on Sundays when at home, were abandoned when my fear of it all week, and my visible suffering throughout the day itself, made it more of a burden for them than a solace. I simply couldn't make it through the pain of a day without the comfort of knowing I had gone hungry and in the end could legitimately eat.

No step deeper into illness was noticeable, except with hindsight, and each was made inevitable by the greater mental rigidity born of malnutrition, which made food the center of all thoughts and behaviors. Thus, everything in the final iteration of my illness had its precursors in more benign variations. The ultimately unvarying alternation of three different "menus," for instance, was something that emerged out of a less deathly pattern. In the earlier years, one of my meals was proper pasta with a sauce of fried vegetables, crème fraîche, and pine kernels, but I gradually found reasons why it would be a nuisance to have to cook, especially when I still lived with my brother, and he might interrupt. Thus, cooking was gradually reduced to nothing more than boiling the cabbage or other vegetable to go with my bread and margarine. Except when I was at home with my mother and her partner; I'd cook elaborate and beautiful meals and watch them eat, delighting in all contact with food, and in the vicarious experience I had from watching them eat.

The "main course" of bread, etc., was also a bastardized version of something that had started off quite lovely and ordinary. I remember how back in my school and early university days I used to buy fresh rolls and spread them with butter, cream cheese, a few lettuce leaves, and a sprinkling of salt and pepper, and just eat. Then I started to weigh the bread to check I wasn't having too much, swapped rolls for cheap loaves, and swapped butter for margarine.

By the time I went to live in Germany, I needed the lowest-fat cream cheese and then watery fromage frais instead. A couple more years and the "cheese" had gone altogether, and the calories saved were then transferred to allow me to have 450 calories of chocolate rather than just 400. I could no longer just spread the margarine on a couple of pieces of bread, either. I had to cut four very thin bread fragments of graded sizes and leave them plain, to pile with vegetables, and have one very thick piece to eat last, which I smeared very thinly with the margarine except in one bottom corner, which I would pile high with most of the 25 grams of it (weighed with electronic scales, with spare batteries always on hand), so that my very last savory mouthful was an indulgent excess of starchy bread and slimy fat, and a great deal of salt.

I craved salt and still more salt on everything. I knew that this was typical of anorexics and that it was probably a symptom of all sorts of mineral deficits, but I didn't feel shame or anxiety at this, or think of doing anything to deal with the underlying cause. I just felt an undebatable need and ground more and more salt onto everything, and allowed myself two raw cloves of coarsely chopped garlic on muesli nights, just to make it all taste more. The whole "meal" makes me feel quite sick now even to think of it.

Similar implacable progressions toward the deviant and ultimately unalterable happened with all the other things I ate, too. The milk with my muesli shifted from semi-skimmed to skimmed, and was then stretched out with water and eaten with a tiny teaspoon so that it lasted as long as possible even though I ate (couldn't help eating) as fast as I could, burping in the brief intervals between mouthfuls. A reasonably sensible mixture of bread and savoury biscuits congealed into the collection of the sweetest chocolate-equivalents imaginable.

My meal times used to be distinct and reasonably normal, too. Breakfast was abandoned and reintroduced several times over the course of years getting worse and trying to get better again. However, lunch was for a long time a separate meal from dinner. Only when I spent 9 months in Germany as part of my Modern Languages degree, and taught in a school several mornings a week, and thus had a reason for lunch to be delayed, did it start to creep back and back until it became an integral part of the day's single meal; once all the work was done and I could sink into my mindless magazines and a brief relaxation of my willpower.

Naturally, these complex necessities made spontaneity impossible and any extended departure from the boat was fraught with difficulties and the paraphernalia of sickness. I couldn't go on holiday without weighing my frail frame down with an enormous rucksack full of kitchen scales, special milks, cereal bars, cereals, margarine, lots of books to read for work—because a holiday from work was unimaginable—a hot-water bottle, and warm clothes whatever the destination. There wasn't much point in relaxing holidays anyway since I would sleep all morning and then need to go for a long walk to tire myself and burn some calories, and after all that, even on the Greek Islands where we often went as a family, the sun would be too low in the sky for me to be warm enough sunbathing; I'd be ashamed of my body anyway (even while also secretly proud). Then the evening of the others drinking and eating would have to be endured before I could start on my sequence of drinks, sitting out in the mosquito-filled darkness with just a candle or two, and then finally eat again, as it got light. I love sunlight so much—and always have—it pains me to think of how many years I spent living mostly in darkness.

Relationships of any degree of intimacy were also made impossible by all of this. I had one long-term boyfriend, a lodger with my father, for about four years starting in the first year of my anorexia. However, once I left for university I became ever less able to take time off work for him to visit me, or to go out to eat with him, deferring the pleasure of his visits until a perfect time that never came, because once he was there all I could think of was the time being wasted that could have been used to work, and the food that

I couldn't delight in on my own because I had to eat with him. My desire for sex diminished until I found the very idea of it made me sick, and my temper shortened until almost everything he said and did made me snap at him with impatient disdain. Nonetheless, when he officially broke up with me just before I left for my year abroad, I was devastated and drowned myself in the emotions that welled up with photos of him and the music we'd listened to together, even while I starved myself more and more rigidly to stop myself from being able to feel anything at all except a constant low ache. Two other men, one in Germany and one back in Oxford during my master's year, were both driven away by my secrecy, my impatience, my sexual deadness and emotional flatness, and my all-encompassing obsession with work.

My anorexia brought me closer to my mother and alienated me from my father. They had separated when I was 11, but had become better friends over the following years, until their disagreements over how my illness should best be dealt with caused a deep rift again. My mother refused to throw me out of my teenage home, and my father believed she was colluding in my sickness and that I needed to be sent far away from home and from Oxford (Oxford never was "home" until I got better and finally grew up enough not to need my mother's home for holidays) in order to be forced to start a new and healthier life.

Ultimately, I don't think any such radical tactic would have made the slightest bit of difference. I would have continued to live in the only way I knew how, with all the more freedom to do so for being in Manchester or Moscow or wherever else. I would visit my father, who lived quite close by, when I was home for vacation, but neither of us understood the other and there was nothing we could share except tea or a little wine, and the deep sadness and perhaps residual anger that the prospect of my being like this forever brought him.

As a child, when his parents were splitting up, he had used not eating and not sleeping as a way of stopping their arguing, but once at boarding school, where no one really cared whether he ate or not, he had learned to eat normally again. I don't know whether he thought my anorexia was in any sense a belated reaction to his and my mother's separation; I'm not sure myself, but in any case, there was no such obvious cause. I think I longed to be left alone to do as I pleased rather than seeking to attract attention, and the effect on my parents and their relationship was only negative. I was similarly alienated from my brother, who lived a full and sociable life at university, bought himself a house and a car and started a PhD, and believed that he'd lost his sister forever. My mother's partner found things very difficult, too. Not just the incomprehension and anger, but also the day-to-day depressive effect of my sleeping most of the daylight hours and sitting at the dinner table unable—or unwilling—to partake. As my mother put it in a radio interview with me (BBC Radio, Scotland, 2010):

> He got exasperated and we tried to have a rule that she had to be up by lunchtime, even though we knew she wouldn't eat lunch with us, and even that she didn't seem able to manage. So imagine the depths of winter, in the city, we got up at seven, or whenever, and had been working, and had our lunch, and by half past three or four o'clock we've done most of our day's work. We're having a cup of tea and Emily finally wakes up. It's already getting gloomy, in December or January, and she goes out on her bike; she's terribly, terribly thin; puts on layers of clothes; and you *know* she's still going to be freezing cold and need me to rub her hands when she comes back. She goes out and bicycles for an hour, with no food in her, and then she's back at five o'clock or whatever it is, and her whole day is starting then, in the dark.

My mother was the one person I felt understood me and my inability to change how I was. This wasn't to say that I didn't feel her sadness or her fear or worry, but she was the only one with whom I could discuss all the dangerous paradoxes of anorexia, all my perceptive reflections on the reality of my situation, and the impossibility of translating that lucidity into any sort of remedial action. Perhaps those analytical yet emotional conversations, and her patience and ability to understand, helped turn the anorexia into a sort of intellectual curiosity, or sheltered me from the full impact of being isolated from the whole world by it, but I don't think so. She had her moments of rage, too, and the rest of the time it was simply a slight softness in a life of hard edges—pain, hunger, fear—to be able to talk to her. I even managed to laugh with her, occasionally, at the sheer ridiculousness of it all. I took her a tiny fruit cake for a birthday breakfast one year and made myself swallow a tiny crumb of brown cake, a white one of icing, and a yellow one of marzipan, and laughed at how grotesquely silly it was, to try to keep myself from thinking of how difficult it was. Since recovering, I've realized that many of the traits my mother has been defined by all her life—valuing her academic work and intellect above all else, suffering guilt at Western wastefulness and overprivilege, not tolerating stupidity or the waste of time—were also those that defined my anorexia, and that maybe this was why we were so close when I was ill.

I had only about three friends, one from school, one from university, and one a former teacher. In their various ways they managed to put up with my weirdness. Everyone else I drifted away from, and barely even felt any regret at doing so. Less and less mattered except the academic work I did and the food I deferred for so long and then ate so feverishly. Emotionally everything was almost entirely flattened by starvation-induced depression and by the starvation-induced irrelevance of anything that could not give me the pleasure food did. Anorexia was its own protection from the horror of realizing its full awfulness, and only some chance occurrence might now and then shock me into seeing what I was doing to myself with complete and devastating clarity.

One such moment was when I'd returned to a clothes shop to look again at a beautiful chocolate silk shoulderless evening dress, which I'd noticed there before, and decided to try it on. The sight of myself there in the harsh changing-room light, my deathlike torso sticking up out of the lovely soft-ness of the dress that I'd never be able to wear because it looked so horrific, because I'd be too cold in it, and because I never went out anyway, made me cry uncontrollably. Any accident or upset in my routine could reduce me to tears and deep despair in an instant:

> The day began badly because of the weight [being higher than expected]. And it hasn't improved much. When, this afternoon, I'd just made some tea and then Joly did the same, and I was sitting there listening to him slurp, and feeling quite ill, and unable to drink my own, I began to cry. The very fact of my cup of tea, so long longed-for, being spoiled, and the knowledge of the triviality of this momentous pain were unbearable. (21.05.04, 43 kg)

And although it never happened, I knew that any physical accident or illness could easily have killed me. When my mother fell off a horse in Corfu and broke her hip, she had a dreadful time in the hospital there, being operated on incorrectly and contracting MRSA. My love for her and pain at her suffering was all the sharper for my terror that she might die before I could eat with her again, and for my knowledge that in her situation I would probably die.

This brings me to the time at which the awareness of what my life had been reduced to started to have an effect. It did so for many reasons, none of which could have sufficed alone, but which taken together made seeking some sort of escape, or at least trying something different, with however little belief that it could help, a necessity. Many of the triggers to awareness came from other people. My mother and her partner were moving out of the house we'd lived in since I was 11, and they realized that they couldn't bear the thought of me—a collection of antisocial habits, food-related secrets, and deadening moods—coming to install myself in their new home.

The first I knew of this was during one of my usual Sunday evening phone calls with my mother, in which I was talking about how I'd have to find a doctor in the new place and whether I'd bring my bike down each vacation. The certainty suddenly crystallized for her that, "You are welcome at our new house, but your anorexia isn't." When she said this, it seemed to me like being rejected by my own mother, and I was devastated and furious that she could presume to draw a meaningless distinction between me and my anorexia, as though there were any way in which I could separate myself from it. In practical terms, her unplanned honesty had the effect of making me proudly pack up all my things and decamp completely to the boat in Oxford. Psychologically it contributed to a vague sense that there was no refuge for me as an anorexic, nowhere except the tiny boat where it was acceptable to live as I did. This didn't immediately make me wonder whether I could live differently—everything in me veered away from the mere hint of that.

But then two friends stepped in. Phoebe, more or less my only friend from my undergraduate days, had previously not noticed that I was really ill. I'd been good at concealing the extent of my thinness and at avoiding situations where eating was necessary, and she'd thought I was just naturally the way I was. But in the last year of my illness, my weight was for the first time consistently below 40 kg (88 pounds)—a boundary that my body had for a long time somehow refused to move below, which marked a rapid deterioration once crossed—and at last she couldn't help realizing. She spent days researching anorexia and treatment possibilities online and by phone and found an eating-disorder clinic in Oxford (The Centre for Research on Eating Disorders at Oxford, CREDO). She came with me to my doctor to get a referral for a first assessment there, and a prescription for Prozac, which quite quickly, in a small but crucial way, helped to loosen up how I thought and felt. Without her, I would never have known about the treatment-research program being conducted at CREDO, and would have missed their deadline for accepting new patients. Without the 9 months of cognitive–behavioral therapy that I received there, I would never have recovered with the completeness that I now have.

One of the many paradoxes of my anorexia was the condition upon which I entered treatment. The program was an outpatient program, and since they had no medical support team or medical training themselves, they couldn't accept patients with a Body Mass Index of less than 15 because of the significant risk of heart failure and other medical emergencies. When I went for a second assessment session, my BMI was 14.2, which meant that if I wanted to make it in to the program, I would have to gain 6 pounds (3 kg) in the next 7 weeks. My mother was with me and we were told that the maximum reasonable weight gain I could expect was a pound a week and that I would therefore have to start immediately, on my own, and be consistently successful—and both of us heard the skepticism in her voice that I would ever do it.

Partly I was proud, proud that while moving from academic success to academic success I had managed to reach a weight that made me too thin for the anorexia treatment program. Partly I was angry; this was supposed to be a treatment to make anorexics fatter and I was told I had to get fatter myself to qualify for it. Partly I was frightened at the alternative prospects; if I didn't do this now, and carried on getting ever so gradually thinner, in the future my only means of recovery would be the shame and complete loss of control that was inpatient treatment (I despised anorexics who were reduced to that even more than I resented the achievement it represented in them), that, or death, which I occasionally acknowledged to myself as never far off. Partly I was frightened at not knowing whether I could do this now, whether I dared, and what would happen if I did.

My other friend, Edmund, came up by train that evening, and we went out and drank wine and talked and talked about whether I could, should, and would really make this decision to change my absolutely unchanging daily diet and eat enough to put on those 3 enormous kilos. After some number of hours it was finally clear that there was no way, anymore, of avoiding the momentous necessity of trying something different at last. Edmund came with me then to the supermarket and wandered around with me suggesting things that might make up the 500 extra calories I'd been told were the right amount to add. I'm not sure why I knew that I wanted to start having breakfast again, and something in the afternoon, rather than just adding the calories to my evening feast, but I was somehow sure of that. Perhaps there was still something in me that not only longed for breakfast but could somehow already imagine the sheer delight there would be in breaking the rule, which for years had made it impossible to eat before dawn at the end of a day.

We decided on a pain au chocolat for breakfast and a custard tart for a teatime snack, and he bought me a 4-day supply because I couldn't bear to spend money on the food (and its effects) I was terrified of. Keeping a meticulous record of everything I spent, and working out monthly and annual totals, and working out what proportion had gone on food had been a habit since first going up to university, and I couldn't have coped, on top of everything else, with the compulsive calculations about how many loaves of bread, lettuces, or bars of chocolate I could have bought for the same amount that these relatively expensive pastries cost. In my diary that night, Friday, July 19, 2008, I wrote:

> 40.1 kg. 1:27 a.m.: All is changing. All has changed. Today is my last day of starvation—and I feel as though I'm losing, bidding goodbye to my most beloved companion. Yet already all *has* changed, today hasn't been starvation. I drank so much wine *so* quickly with Edmund, talking about the appointment, the need to reach 42 kg by September 4, the practicalities of how to do it, and now I still feel quite disconnected, weirdly blithe at all the mess here, and I've eaten so much today already—crisps at lunch time, a whole brownie with the coffee we had while waiting for the taxi that never turned up, bread when I got back from seeing Edmund, then the licked lid of the prawn cocktail, then a slice of brie, then a bit of Sue's muesli, then a handful of cooked rice, then finally just now the After Eight I'd taken from the hairdresser and, as ever, left to go squishy and sticky in the depths of my bag—I found it, unwrapped it, ate it, felt an undercurrent of fear—mustn't go down

the binge-eating/bulimic route—but mostly the indifference, the ease, the pleasure of eating it.

And so—I'm to have a breakfast of pain au chocolat (241 calories), and an afternoon tea of custard tart (235 calories). Edmund had to try to choose stuff for me, and then buy it for me; I couldn't. He's been unimaginably generous. [...] Sue got back home at 11-ish; we spoke and I told her tomorrow's provisions. I don't know how terrified I am. [...] 3:15 a.m.: I should try to record all this as best I can. [...] In a way, just in a tiny, scared, guilty, whispering way I'm really looking forward to it, the hot chocolate croissant before my bike ride. Is this really me? What am I turning into? For now, though, lovely low-cal soya milk to finish. Still as me.

In the following months Edmund was unstinting in giving his time, money, and emotional support. He would come by train from Bristol to Oxford with more supplies of food and encouragement and analytical or humorous discussion. I never believed that any of this would change anything, but perhaps he knew that it would.

Many other things in life conspired to make the decision to eat 500 calories more every day possible, and necessary. Obsessive-compulsive behaviors emerged and worsened with a speed that made me feel I was going mad. Waking up freezing cold to a wintry sunset for a night's work was only slightly more depressing than closing the curtains against a sunny summer morning for a day's sleep. There were episodes like that of the evening dress, in which I became sickeningly aware of the awfulness of my own body. There was a day down by the seaside, on which I sat for hours staring at sand and sea while my mother handed me grapes, and I experienced what it meant to live in the present moment, rather than be eternally deferring pleasure to heighten it—but thereby destroying life by living only in the future, in the brief ending of every day.

There was another story in the news about an anorexic academic dropping dead of heart failure while carrying heavy shopping bags up to her flat filled with the mess of hoarded objects. There was the sadness of not going skiing with the family, as I'd so loved to when I was younger, because it was too cold to be bearable, let alone fun, because I couldn't get to bed early enough to make a day's skiing possible, and because I was too weak to ski at all. There was, every single day, the dread, loneliness, and sadness of waking up in the afternoon and contemplating the joyless process of getting up out of the warmth of bed, cycling for an hour, getting trapped in a supermarket looking at labels, returning to make food and work and drink my drinks and work and finally eat my food. Occasionally there'd be a coffee with a friend, acquaintance, or colleague, or during the vacation there'd be dinner to shop for and cook, and a little wine to be drunk while the others ate. But I felt the total emptiness of my life every time I woke up to another day of it, and perhaps I knew that nothing could really be worse than this.

That first breakfast may have been the greatest pleasure I've ever experienced. It was a miracle to me. I woke at 2 p.m., got my bicycle ready to go out on, lit the oven, and warmed the pain au chocolat. Then I ate it. I ate outside for the first time in years, with fitful sunshine warming me as the dozen delighted mouthfuls of crispy pastry and hot molten chocolate entered my mouth, entered my stomach, and signaled the start of something. I took my plate in, set off on my bike, and the rest of the day was the same as usual, except for the custard tart with my first cup of tea, which I ate quickly and delightedly. The extra eating made remarkably little difference to the rest of my life, given the extreme effort of will and internal negotiation it had taken to make it happen, by breaking my so long-standing rules.

Throughout the following months, as I negotiated the "firsts" of recovery—first lunch with family, first birthday meal being able to eat, first steak in a restaurant with my father, first night without chocolate (last thing to send me to sleep), first day waking up early in the morning without an alarm—all these rites of passage were striking in their total *ordinariness*. There was still a place for me at the table, there was a new and beloved boyfriend to snuggle up to, and there was daylight to wake me. It was almost as though the 10 years of impossibility had never been, or as though all through those years something in me had never forgotten how it was to do these things, and had never stopped wanting to, despite the many congealed layers of fear and refusal that I had overlaid that normality with.

A strange little help in the first weeks was that I *lost* weight in the first few days, and then for three weeks or so my digestive system couldn't quite cope with the increase. This felt as though there was some magic that meant I could eat but not gain weight, that I could be brave and do the right thing, but not bear any of the "costs" of doing so. Perhaps, I thought, my body had become so used to the previous amount of food that it had no use for any more. By the time the weight was consistently above 40 kg again, I'd had time to adjust to the new normality and was able to bear its consequences. I was also deeply moved by the experience of the Western privilege of being able to reject food for all those years and of then finding it still there, ready for the taking, in any form and any quantity I wanted. Once I chose to eat again, this tempered my fear with deep gratitude.

That isn't to say that recovery wasn't terrifying, and difficult, at times. The hunger that was unleashed in me almost as soon as I began to eat more was the most frightening thing I've ever felt. Now that I was eating, and trying to gain weight, the hunger no longer felt like power, like something chosen; it felt inescapable, uncontrollable, illegitimate, and infinite. I managed to avoid slipping into binge eating or bulimia, but I'd never understood more clearly why that was where most anorexics end up. In my diary, I wrote:

> Once you've opened the floodgates, what is there to stop the great flow of appetite? Only it's not floodgates, it's a small hole that's been opened up in the great dam of self-restraint; and as Sue said in a text this evening, having sent a lovely one this morning, wishing me well in my new life, I should just use the hunger to eat the 500 extra calories, and then stop. And I think that's what I've done.

It took a year, and over 30 kilos (66 pounds) of weight gain, until at last I realized that I wasn't hungry all the time anymore, and that I was able to feel actually full, whereas until then I'd had to guess, and pretend, and wonder what it might feel like. In that time of recovery I couldn't stop thinking about food, because nothing was stable or self-evident anymore, and because the calmness that I'd created by living at the bare minimum of what would keep me going (physically and emotionally) and my brain working well enough to think and write was completely gone. There were many moments when delight at being "allowed" to eat more veered into deep nausea, deep internal resistance to anything that felt like being normal, being greedy, or being spontaneous, because all these could be the heralds of a spiral into obesity and a disordered life, and into the vacuum of no longer knowing who I was. There was the terror of feeling emotions again—of falling in love (with the man I now live with) and being initially rejected, and feeling the full depth of the dimensions of life I couldn't control.

There were moments of succumbing to the cripplingly low self-esteem, self-loathing even, that my decade of illness had brought about, and that made me question my right to recover. There were chance remarks from other people about it being "naughty" to eat pudding, or about some meal I'd also eaten having been too big, or about the changes in me and my eating, which threw me off balance and made me scared and miserable. There were times when I couldn't do what my therapist asked me to; couldn't eat within an hour of getting up, couldn't replace my breakfast porridge with something different, couldn't shift the chocolate drink and cereal bar from their position at the start of the evening's eating, even when they'd been made superfluous by all the rest of the things I now ate before them. But I did manage all these things, eventually.

There were other things that I've often heard reported as insurmountable obstacles to successful recovery from anorexia, and which for me simply weren't an issue. I had no trouble in incorporating long-untouched foods into my diet. Indeed, I loved the exploratory attitude of finding silly new toppings for my porridge, or weird cheap snack foods in the supermarkets. I'd been a vegetarian since age 11, but my cravings for meat were such that I soon loved it more than anything else (except chocolate). Partly this ease was due to the fact that my diet had always included very calorific things, so it wasn't a case of moving from one extreme to another. And then, I never planned to eat something and then failed to; I never sat down with food and failed to eat it, except on the occasions when, in company, I'd gone too long without eating and my hunger had flipped over into nausea, or when there was some emotional tension with others around me. The company of my new boyfriend, who moved in with me 6 months after I began to eat more, also helped me to exchange the monotony of a private routine for the dynamics of routines shared, and to learn how close a bond food shared can be.

In the early days, the new routine was no more questionable than the old one had been. There was no option but to follow it. All those years I'd intellectually understood the illusory nature of the control I was exerting by not eating when I recognized all the reasons to eat, and now, at long last, I was able to translate this knowledge into positive action. I was able to reverse the polarities of my willpower and use all that determination to heal myself instead of making myself ever sicker. The hours during which I made the decision were more difficult than anything in the months that followed. After that, after knowing that I really meant it, it was just a question of doing what I'd decided to, even though I never believed it would make any real difference.

I often ask myself what single crucial factor—or what combination of factors—made this possible for me, where for so many others it's so different. They decide, they try, they flounder, they fear, and they fail. I don't remember once asking myself whether I shouldn't put a stop to this, and go back to the old ways, perhaps because by the time the weight was going up consistently I'd already been granted a few glimpses of how life might be different; like eating a biscuit in company, eating a whole lunch at a conference, not putting people on edge with my inability to eat, tasting a bright new flavor, feeling a little spring in my step, looking forward to something other than food, giving pleasure and hope to those who loved me.

It's been a long path since then, a path toward where I am now, which is still working hard but knowing how to relax of an evening, a weekend, a holiday. Loving my boyfriend and living with him, being cooked delicious meals by him, laughing with him dozens of times a day, sharing food and drink and time with colleagues in an exciting research job, lifting weights in the gym and feeling my body still growing stronger and healthier and building up all its muscles and ligaments and cartilage, planning trips and gradually expanding my small circle of friends and interests, weighing myself once a month or so, and not particularly worrying about what the numbers will say, weighing 68 kg (150 pounds, BMI 24.7), and having never felt better.

I still see thin women in the streets and feel envious or insecure sometimes, but more and more often I feel pleased not to be thus, knowing what it would require for me to be as they are; and I feel proud to exemplify an aesthetic that judges women by criteria other than thinness. I am still reminded sometimes how easily my eating can be thrown off balance by an argument or upset. I still worry now and then about the shape of my tummy or about having eaten too much. But these are things that few women (or even men) could claim to be entirely immune to, and I feel bizarrely blessed, now, by my history of anorexia.

Yes, anorexia more or less ruined what could have been one of the best decades of my life—but it's also taught me all I need to know about food, starvation, my body, my mind, and society's sicknesses. I am completely sure that I will never go back to anorexia, because I did it so well, with such complete control, that I have no doubt that all its promises are dead ends, that to go back I would have to ruin my life again, and that to do it better

I would have to kill myself completely. There is no romantic seduction left in starving, no uncertainty as to its consequences, no little surreptitious internal voice to ask me whether this or that wouldn't be better if I weren't just a little slimmer. I have all the answers now. I know what it's like to die by just eating a little too little, every day, forever. I know what it's like to lose the will to live for anything but eating. I know what it's like for a concave tummy never to be concave enough and a hollow sternum never to be hollow enough. I know that this can all happen on 1,700 calories a day. I have all the answers now, and know that anorexia has none.

Reference

BBC Radio Scotland. (2010). *A life in limbo* (presented by Clare English), Series 2, Episode 1, first broadcast June 29.

Big Little

Priscilla Becker[1]

It began immediately after a comment made to me by a boy in the hall my freshman year of high school. The boy was Scott Calipari, my boyfriend. He was looking at my pelvis, squinting as though bringing something far-off into focus. He seemed to be registering an unbelievable truth: "Your thighs," he said, "they're kind of," and here he paused, "big."

I had eaten until then without concern. I was thin and active. I ran track and cross-country. I danced ballet. I was fourteen and probably on my way to developing the body I was supposed to have. Meaning, I have fat genes—Hungarian and German. Great-grandmothers, dead before my birth, are described by my father as "big *mahoskas*" (fat). I could feel my body lurching toward its true form, poised to realize its heredity. But what I was about to do would interfere with that, and prevent me from developing according to my natural physiology. Eating was never again to be a natural thing.

That night at dinner I didn't eat. The next morning I opened the cupboard door. It had dark oiled wood, the kind with black eyes and a hinge clasp that had to be depressed for it to open, which would occur with a distinctive

---

[1]Priscilla Becker, copyright 2008. Reprinted with permission of the author.

click. I learned to depress it very slowly so that the click was suppressed. I fit my hand silently into a bag of dry-roasted peanuts and split one open inside my cupped hands. The peanuts were reserved for my father; he ate them while watching sports late at night. There was food in the house designated for my mother and my father, but no special foods for my sister or me.

This was to become my morning routine. I would try to find a shell that contained just one peanut. Many, however, contained two. It is difficult to keep from lying about what I would do in the event of a two-peanut shell. The truth is, I don't know what I did with the extra peanut. I only know I didn't eat it. I probably wouldn't have thrown it out, either, because that would be wasteful, and waste offended either me or my parents, though at that point it wasn't clear which. We saved everything. Rather, I should say, there were two opposite and potentially canceling forces at work in the household: my mother accumulating and my father eliminating. In our case, the former has always won out.

I thought about composing a paragraph about my elaborate removal of the extra peanut, my systematic ritual. But that is because I know the stories, and I am assuming you do, too, the story of the cookie dissected into thirty-two equal segments, the story of the hour-long apple-eating excruciation; and I am competitive and don't want you to think I was a bad anorexic—sloppy, slack, fat. In any case, this was to be my breakfast throughout high school, which actually adds up to many, many peanuts, the exact number of which I am restraining myself from calculating, as it has been part of my recovery not to weigh and reckon. But I did wonder (and still do sometimes) about my father puzzling over the little pile of unshelled peanuts accumulating in his bag.

My sister's body, which I was jealous of, was shaped like a boy's, hipless and naturally strong. Mine is not. I curve at the hips, and extra, incomprehensible flesh accumulates there. Thankfully, I am small-breasted. Also, I am delicately framed, which makes thinness look thinner and weight more noticeable. While some girls eagerly checked mirrors for signs of development, looking toward the onset of puberty with excitement and curiosity, I was horrified and deeply embarrassed. My tiny breasts looked ridiculous to me, but I had not been warned of my first period, and when it came I thought I had injured myself by overmasturbating.

I prepared lunch at home and brought it with me to school: a bundle of carrots and celery sticks. If you were to make a circle with your index finger at the first knuckle of your thumb, that would be about the width of the bundle. The sticks were cut very thin and were three inches long. I carried them in a plastic sandwich bag. Dinner was a slice, a perfect square, of cheddar cheese. It had to be translucent; I would hold it up to the fluorescent kitchen light with one hand and, with the other, wave to myself from behind the flimsy screen of cheese. No, that's a lie. Actually, I had already lost, with alarming speed, my sense of humor. If I laughed, it would veer off into private uncontrollable laughter, the kind I've always thought to be the hallmark of insanity. It was better not to laugh, just as it was better not to eat; with both I feel that if I ever started, I wouldn't stop.

The family dinner was insisted upon, mostly by my mother, as some sort of symbol of normality. We rarely spoke. Currents of anger spiked around the table in complex cross-pollinations. Early in my refusals of food there were terrible fights. My mother thought my starvation was an exercise of my will, an arbitrary challenge, and that I could just as well have held my breath or repeated her phrases or stuck my fingers in my ears when she spoke. And so she attempted to force me to eat. I tried the usual tactics, lying that I'd already eaten, which further angered her, or I'd say that I felt sick, an indefensible position because we were Christian Scientists.

My father and sister were mostly silent, although their faces were disgusted. My sister stopped talking to me entirely in high school, and her lip curled as if she were tasting sour milk when I passed by. When she *had* to speak to me it seemed to physically pain her and she'd release a few syllables from between clenched teeth and stare at a fixed point in the distance, as people do when they are addressing large groups or no one in particular. Eventually, I removed myself from the fray by staying later and later at track practice or pretending to do homework or to practice the violin. Diligence, even the ruse of it, trumped the ruse of the family dinner.

I am writing in the early 1980s. I had never even heard the two words together: *eating disorder*. It was before such a condition was talked about, or at least no one I knew had ever had one. However, I knew very well the connection between what one ate and the size of one's body. My mother was completely taken over by physical concerns. She was generally on some sort of diet, although I hesitate to call her eating choices that, because they seemed to offer transformation beyond the body. Food had an extraordinary power in our household. As a child, I was generally recruited to follow these plans with her. There were weeks of fasting on hot lemonade and long stretches of extensive juicing during which my mother's skin turned orange. We exhausted many models of juicers and extractors, even the Champion, which was the most expensive and technically advanced, yielding the driest pulp, and to which a plastic bag had to be affixed like a diaper. We watched while orange and green waste coiled out the back like the bowel movements we hoped to enact.

We "sprouted" for a while, seeds insinuating their hairy tendrils from beneath moist towels, ate only raw food while horrible fermented almonds overtook the refrigerator, drank fizzy acidophilus from a champagne-shaped bottle (it tasted like sour socks), and lay on a "slant board" to restore our energies. Then the *Fit for Life* phase as well as monofasts of "perfect" foods—once bananas, then avocados, then pineapple. We activated our thyroids in shoulder stands before most Westerners had even heard of yoga, jumped rope in the garage, and rebounded—which is not exactly exercise, but a lymphatic-system stimulator. We drank fish oil from a spoon, hydrogen peroxide from the bottle, apple-cider vinegar containing the "mother" (the mucilaginous substance produced by mold fungus during fermentation) lurking at the bottom of the glass like a living ghost, liquid chlorophyll, spirulina, and barley grass. All the while, the water distiller, its presence on the counter, like a small silver nuclear reactor, sucked the minerals out of our water only so that we could replace them, including arsenic, in a liquid, extracted from a virgin sunken shale deposit below the sea in Tempe, Arizona.

Bran was to be found lacing every dish, powdered bone meal clogged our morning juice like paste, carob bean pretended to be chocolate, and hills of vitamins waited for us at every meal. We snacked on Scandinavian crisp bread, which boasted 85 percent bran. Buckwheat and beer pancakes were a favorite for a while. Anything ancient or tribal was taken to be superior, and so the Dead Sea was popular, as was the Essene Gospel of Peace. My mother was sometimes heard to exclaim, "Jesus cleaned himself out with a gourd!" Every ancient grain was experimented with for a time and left behind: teff, amaranth, kamut. We chanted at Hare Krishna meetings in the Village and attended powwows on the eastern tip of Long Island.

We *fletcherized,* as per Horace Fletcher, "the Great Masticator," a Victorian-era health advocate, by chewing each morsel thirty-two times before swallowing, this breaking down with our teeth the cell walls of all vegetables. We took pains to ingest liquids and solids separately, as combining them would weaken the digestive fire. But when we weren't eating, we flooded our systems with liquid in order to keep things moving along. We composted, ate the seeds and skins of all fruits and vegetables, as well as the white membrane surrounding citrus (vitamin P), and we ate unpasteurized cheese and milk before it became illegal in New York State (enzymes).

I always felt we were doing much more than eating certain things and not eating certain others.

Only one thing in our household was imbued with greater importance than ingestion, and that was elimination. It seemed that no sooner were we eating the foods than we were trying to get rid of it: aloe vera, pectin, wheat germ, senna, fenugreek, psyllium, cascara sagrada, flaxseed, Amrutadi, stewed prunes, beet juice, charcoal, licorice, enemas, high colonics. These were just a few of the household remedies. There was a shelf about three feet long at the bottom of the stairway down to the cellar filled with discarded powders with such names as Colon Blowout, Intesti-Cleanse, Bowel Broom, each one defective ("This one has added sugar, this one is rancid, this one contains aspartame, this one made me gag, this one constipated me, this one was infested with tiny grain bugs …") in some particular way, but all joined in one common offense: They did not work; they were no good.

I suspected that *no good* for my mother meant much more than that they had failed to produce a bowel movement. I think she meant something much more devastating and less physical, something about my father or God. I cannot remember a time when I wasn't constipated. I wondered what was happening to the food. I thought it must be poisoning my system, or worse, gathering as fat. Perhaps it was waiting deep inside some cavity and one day all the unexcreted peanuts and slivers of cheese would burst out on my thighs.

So I began taking laxatives, herbal ones such as Swiss Kriss or Tam. I took them every day. Because they did not contain harsh chemicals, I let myself believe they were not harmful to ingest. I had such morbid and special knowledge of nutrition that I was continually at cross-purposes with myself. I would apply a double standard to my behavior; adhere to that part of a rule that served my concerns. I looked ahead to a time (presumably now) when all the damage I was inflicting upon myself would be corrected, as though I'd be to one side of my life, the opposite one, standing in a frozen beam of health.

I remember the day I was caught short by this behavior. By this time I had been through four years of college, but had yet to earn my degree. My boyfriend and I were visiting New York and staying at a friend's apartment on King Street. The friend was very health conscious (years later, he would burn a hole in his stomach by eating raw jalapeños), as I claimed to be. By this time I had been swallowing laxatives every day for eight or nine years. There was a place mat on the kitchen table with a chart listing just about every possible physical and mental complaint and the vitamin deficiencies and bad nutritional practices that could cause them. As my eyes looked down the chart, I saw the word *laxative, laxative, laxative, laxative.*

In that moment I knew that I was really starving, that the few nutrients I was ingesting weren't in my system long enough to do me any good. Yet as quickly as the recognition had descended, it was gone. Of course I couldn't stop taking the laxatives, because by this time I had no peristalsis of my own. But in high school, when I was just embarking on my life of nutritional poverty, my body was still resilient. True, I was constipated, but this might have been normal enough, given my small allotment of food. I thought then it would all be temporary; I thought I was on a diet.

I would cut school by locking myself in my closet. I spent much of my time staring deeply into walls. I suppose it felt most like having been sucked away from everyone I loved, and from all desire, which is where I thought my trouble lay, with desire. I had never shared the sense of emptiness I often heard people describe, the hollow feeling, boredom. My trouble seemed the opposite: I felt too much. I was always bursting with some uncomfortable emotion or expression, feeling foolish and inappropriate.

So instead of figuring out how to get what I wanted, I slowly figured out how *not* to want. I was shocked to discover that desire is like most things, responsive to practice. I studied joylessness. I removed expression from my face and inflection from my voice. For the first 20 years of my condition, I was constantly hungry and wanted nothing more than to eat. But even hunger finally ceded. I overcame my sex drive (temporarily) in like manner; I felt peaceful, less human.

Every social situation was a test of endurance that I couldn't wait to end. I failed even to imagine enjoyment. I wanted only to be alone, hidden; once alone, I longed for love and people, for activity and interest. For each public thing I wanted to do, I had an accompanying proviso: I could do it, but just not now. I would stare at the hipless images in fashion magazines; these were the girls who desired nothing and so were desired. It never occurred to me that I might have a desire that could be met.

I had many male friends of the sort that wait around for you to love them. It was the only kind of friendship I could have, based, as it was, on their doomed admiration of me, and requiring almost nothing in return. They must have imagined a future payoff. But I slept with other men, just about anyone else, though it helped if they were ugly or abusive or actively hated. And I also pursued sex. It had no meaning for me, only purpose: to momentarily quell my nervousness and to feel me. I lived on it.

I kept extensive lists, documenting every calorie ingested in each twenty-four-hour period, and balancing this figure with the amount, duration, and intensity of exercise, and, because I was a runner, this meant mileage and pace I had exercised. On the reverse side of my calorie and exercise chart was my list of things to do for the day. Most of these tasks I would not complete, but I loved little more than crossing things out of my life.

As a child, I'd read biographies of the great composers again and again. I remember that more than stories, I had a deep affection for words. But in high school I lost the ability to finish reading a sentence without its trailing off into white gaze. I suspected I was stupid. I could read the words on the page but they didn't correspond to anything, just symbols without meaning. In tenth grade, as a book report, I made up a book, reported on it, complete with bibliography, and got a perfect score on the paper, which impressed my friends. One of them, unaware of how it makes me wince, still tells this story as proof, I think, to her, of my ingenuity. I would gaze at the books on the shelves in my house and my friends' houses, touch the covers and rub the pages between my fingers. I would smell the paper. But books may as well have been buried in the earth. I knew it was a world that could save me, but I did not know the way back.

So much of my condition, with the help of my silent complicity, seemed ready to be interpreted as will and wit; idiosyncrasy and special talent; superiority. And, in fact, this was the secret consolation: an internal elitism. My behavior seemed to prove a strange endurance because it did without a basic component of life: food. And, just as I think some non-anorexics fear, I *did* think everyone was fat and undisciplined. Anorexics generally don't like to admit this and I shouldn't speak for them, but denial, after all, is our medium.

While I felt a kind of dark pride when my body fit within my miserable limits, if anyone called attention to it, whether in alarm or praise, I would be filled with instant embarrassment. I dearly hated to be noticed. At the same time, I had intense yet stagnant ambitions for myself; talents that, although untried and undeveloped, I violently hoped would emerge one day, intact and whole, like an ejected egg, as though all that was required was the perfect form.

My hopes at that time were more like dreams, or really fantasies in which I was a famous musician. I had no plan to bring this about, although by high school I was a fairly accomplished violinist. That is to say, I went as far as talent could provide. I had weekly private lessons and was expected to practice every day. I was always first chair in orchestra and would score As in the yearly New York State competitions. I won a scholarship to study violin after high school at the Crane School of Music. The music school had a good reputation and the college itself, part of the SUNY system, was cheap. I chose it for this reason. I knew I was not setting off into promise. I couldn't tell my parents this, so I did the next best thing: I decided not to waste their money.

Musicianship was a requirement for membership in our family. Of the two musical choices presented for the girls (violin and piano), I preferred piano, but my sister, who was just enough older than I to choose first, had already claimed that. So I had the violin. But what I really wanted to play was electric guitar, though I had never even seen a girl holding one. Besides, guitar playing would have implied an interest in pop music, which was beneath contempt in our family, and which was also, as I left more and more behind, the only thing I was able to keep loving. I loved it in secret, keeping myself alive for it as others might go on for the sake of the children. *What if I died*, I wondered, *having not yet heard my favorite song?* Of course, by the time I was able to turn my attention to my real interests (which did not occur with any reliability until my early thirties), I found them decayed and immature. It was something like how I imagine the Sphinx must feel, arching up and gazing out of its stone form: I was an anachronism. This, at least, is one of the theories I sometimes use to explain to myself why I still look so young.

I hobbled through high school, by the tenth grade quitting most activities I once had loved or excelled in. I watched effetely from the sides of my life as my parents grew disappointed in me, then furious. I covered my tracks in a shroud of apathy equal to the intensity of my regrets. I quit track, unconscionable to my father, and would rejoin and quit several times during the rest of high school. I began to do badly in school, meaning I continued to get mostly As, but no longer because of my performance, rather because I was an excellent fake, a seasoned impersonator of myself, and because brilliance was what by this time everyone and all my teachers had come to expect and thought they were still seeing in me.

I could immediately sense the most minimal passing requirement and, at the last split second, would most often fulfill it. I would rather have continued in my former excellence and obedience; I would have given anything for it; I still would. The way I lived seemed so strange to me, far from anything that had been presented as acceptable life or even as life. I imagined myself telling someone, and the only reaction I could conjure was deep perplexity and revulsion. I threw a hardback book at Mr. Lamoureaux, my French teacher, who threw it back at me but had excuses: A former fat man on an extreme diet, he was going through a divorce (still an uncommon thing in that place and time). I got cited for insubordination in gym, now the most troubling subject of all because it involved exposing my body—something I could not do. And in my senior year I actually managed to fail gym; I hadn't shown up for even one class. Instead of going to class I would hide in the woods just off the premises, crouching in the bushes, waiting for time to pass. Failing gym threatened my graduation and, rather than submit to summer school, shorts, and public perspiration, I refused to acknowledge the grade. I simply did not allow them to fail me.

This sort of defensive offense was to become a characteristic of mine— that and the reliance on my former nature. Tactics worked for a long while. With the first, people simply did not know how to respond, and with the second, a lot could be squeezed from my past. Later, however, there would be nothing to fall back on, no remembered or defendable former life. I would rely on what had crept up in its stead: lying, secrecy, and omission.

I am assuming that I had begun much differently, but this is not necessarily true. One supposes all children are open, so I adopt this for myself as well. Actually I am mostly missing from my parent's specific memory. So, although I have asked what I was like, no real sense of me assembles. My father claimed I was putting him on the spot and so he failed to produce an anecdote. My mother has the two stories, set pieces, that to her illustrate my precociousness. In the first one, I am an infant, breast-feeding, constantly distracted by some bright object on the floor and yanking my mother's nipple along with me as I jerk my head to explore. In the second one, I am also an infant, singing to myself and walking hand over hand around the perimeter of my crib. As the story goes, my parents would find me this way in the morning, the tiny disembodied hands grabbing and releasing.

My sense of myself can best be explained by a phenomenon that I have come to call Big Little: a waking dream, not quite a feeling, but an intimation of one, a sensation. It is difficult to tell if it comes from inside or out. It slips over the body, yet has form, a column, that expands and contracts flickering as though trying to be brought into focus. When I would try to hold it though, as I often did (or else close my eyes and wait for it to pass), it would escape. Big Little *is* my body: *Is it big? Is it little? Does it have feeling? Will it stay?* It is as though I am approaching myself from a distance, almost touching down, before being quickly sucked away. I rarely experience Big Little now, although for years it was a very common feeling. I suppose it has been replaced by the sense of an actual body.

I had been sleeping dreams also—nightmares for me—one that I had eaten at McDonald's and another that I had moved into a fat person's body. I would awaken in terror, filled with an overpowering shame and dread. My waking thoughts were much the same: I wanted to become ever lighter, smaller, for my step to be soundless, my presence completely unknown. It occurs to me now that I have not been wholly unsuccessful. Many people I have lived with have been startled by my sudden presence, materializing without warning out of silence. Not one former roommate has ever neglected to mention how he didn't know I was home, didn't hear me come in, never heard a sound from my room, or would never have known I was there.

This is, as those obliged to share their living space well know, arguably the most valuable attribute and the highest praise for a roommate to possess and elicit. And once I lived five years in an apartment in which everyone who entered left saying the same thing: "There is no evidence you live here." I liked to say I had to be ready to go, to pack up and leave at a moment's notice, but I have never been particularly adventurous, romantic, or nomadic. Rather, I have always had the sense that someone or something is going to *make* me go and that I will not have the chance to collect my things, which brings to mind another of my nightmares: I return to my apartment to find my key no longer fits the lock.

The ability to leave, an antinesting instinct, is generally regarded as a male characteristic. It has been ascribed to me, bafflingly, when the truth is pretty much the opposite. I *stay* well beyond good sense, personal safety, propriety, and I have spent a good portion of my writing life identifying with statues, sculptures, blighted and frozen things. But I've noticed that most often people take *appearance* as reality and the subject of one's art as pretense.

To be fair, I probably confuse people by my other "male" characteristics. I wear no makeup and have been "cross-dressing" for most of my adult life; although this is less noticeable when one is female. I have managed, by practice of my condition, to completely suppress my reproductive system (I began, and stopped, menstruating at age fifteen and seemed not to go though puberty until I was thirty-six, having a similar reaction to the return of my period as the first time around—I thought I was dying). Until recently, I have had primarily male friends. As employment, I have mostly worked in privately owned record shops and, as anyone who has spent much time in them knows, they are almost exclusively the province of males.

I have felt separate from girls and women by nature, and I have also knowingly separated myself from them. It is at once painful and satisfying. I hated emotions and anything at all I came to associate with women: vulnerability, tenderness, manicures, compliance, shopping, Diet Coke, mollifying, heels, apologizing, deferment, flirting, dresses, asking permission, chit-chat, jealousy, nurturing, pleasing, breasts, neediness, laughter. I don't think I hated women so much as I hated the assumptions about them. But these I could not change, so I removed myself from women. It wasn't hard to do; they had never been kind to me.

I had always wanted to be a boy. Or perhaps I should say I have never wanted to be a girl. Boys seemed to have a natural resistance to doubt that I had detested and envied. Perhaps this is what their straight bodies suggested to me—arrows, direction. I felt gluttony or bulimia would have suited me better, that it was the very "choice" of my condition; always trying to be something I was not—and not the condition itself that suited my personality.

Recently, a male friend made a casual comment to me on the phone. "Well, that shouldn't be hard for you, you're practically a man anyway," he said. Many friends have said similar things, probably because of the masculine characteristics I've mentioned, especially the quintessential one: sleeping around. Their confusion reminds me of one relationship I once had with a boyfriend who I thought might be gay; he was boyish, social, and passive. It was a new model of maleness for me, one which, wanting to call it something, I sometimes settled for homosexuality. While no one has ever taken me for gay, I'm sure because of my appearance, I think what my friends might see in me is the female corollary to this: the absence of conventional womanliness combined with girlishness. It perplexes some, because the underfed form speaks, although softly, a confused and confusing opposition of signals: *I have no needs; take care of me.*

My immature figure is also why, I have come to think, a certain type of male finds me irresistible: generally in his late twenties to early thirties (although it has happened with much younger or much older than this), probably gay, and making a last desperate swipe at heterosexuality. For them I think I offer hope. I do not overpower with breasts and hips. I do not coax pronouncements of fidelity or commitment. I do not express an interest in marriage. I do not look like a promising candidate for childbirth. I appeal to the aesthetic sense of these men. I satisfy the condition, however slightly, of *femaleness.* And so their illustrations can be pursued with minimal discomfort. I have sensed their desperation, their disappointment that I wouldn't just love them and so save them from pain of their sexual futures. But I think, at least hope, that I have provided for them some other form of help, like a gender halfway house.

In college my tastes broadened: I began to substitute drinking for eating. A calorie was a calorie to me, and with drinking at least I had the hope of unconsciousness. And for a little while I could forget I was hungry. But I've never found drinking gratifying. It doesn't obliterate as promised. Neither do any of the drugs I have tried—I think a fair cross-section. There is always a reservation, however slight; a region unaffected by my considerable attempts, like a maddeningly alert night watchman.

I binged my first year in college and returned home looking like everybody else who had been freed from their parents and done more of what they'd wanted. Only I hadn't. My extra weight was a product of the same old rules except that I was losing my powers. That summer my father took me aside and informed me that if I didn't do something about my weight now, it might be a problem for me later in life. My mother was away that summer, and I can't remember if my sister was home, probably because she had long ago given up acknowledging me. I had a job that summer picking up trash on the beach; at night I would ride my bike three miles, run six miles, and walk one mile, returning home well after my father had eaten. He seemed content that I was tackling my problem. I returned to college having lost more weight than I had gained, refocused in my purpose. My father never mentioned it again.

But what had begun for me that day at the start of high school, with a comment that I am certain Scott Calipari never thought of again, was an approach to life that I am tempted to say I would never shake again. Twenty-two years have passed since that comment in the hall at school, and I still cannot imagine my life entirely free of rules about food. Not long ago, talking to a friend who has known me for fifteen of those twenty-two years, I remarked how far I had come, and she conceded my view—up to a point. After all, many things are different, better. Whereas once I wore baggy clothes from neck to toe never allowing an unnecessary inch of flesh to show and never ate in restaurants but would order various flavored waters while my friends dined self-consciously away, I now have come to some sort of resigned and inevitable terms with my body and generally wear clothes appropriate for my size. And I eat in restaurants almost every time I go to one.

Guilt does not describe my feelings about eating, although there is always a moment, a change, during a meal. Perhaps it happens when I have finished half my food, or depending on what it is and also how it appears on the plate: one-third, five bites, or two-thirds. Usually I cannot eat beyond two-thirds of the food on my plate; at that point I fear it might seem that I am eating too much, or that my interest in food might be apparent. Certainly it is not a sense of satisfaction that I am responding to. This is the point at which all enjoyment is over. Sometimes I will eat on, shamefully; sometimes I will stop, disgusted and sad. Not guilty, but ugly and conspicuous, as though I'm sitting under a hot white lamp.

What my friend had said, however, sounded about right, although I remember being startled by it at the time. I was on the way to proclaiming near recovery when she said casually, "It doesn't sound like you've been cured of anorexia, just that you've raised the bar a little." What she meant was that I now permit more calories and a broader range of foods, and I don't exactly count calories anymore, I don't have to, I calculate them instantly, reflexively, so quickly that the math is subsumed. I know the science behind all food, even in the case of foods I've never seen before. I can accurately hypothesize the ingredients, their proportions, and the caloric content. So now, when selecting what I am going to eat, I weigh my considerations in a flash and make my choice accordingly. You cannot see me do it, although I imagine that in that flash, my brow nettles and me eyes cloud. There are now also smaller considerations of desire, mood, and hunger, and a larger one of nutrition, because of the damage rendered to my body from decades of abuse. But there was a time, most of my life, in which only the math had authority.

So if I was premature in the assessment of my progress, perhaps it is closer to the truth to say that my behaviors are less extreme and my appearance less severe. I have settled into a kind of *working* anorexia: not careening toward death, but, in line with two words frequently used to describe me, disciplined and self-contained. It is, I suppose, anorexia's middle age, in which I give up my ideals and try to be more reasonable.

Binging and Purging to Stay Alive

ANONYMOUS[2]

I hear it so often, "I could never be bulimic. I hate throwing up." Yeah? Me too. I laugh every time because it implies I must have started purging because I have some weird fondness for throwing up. That's not true. I don't like it, but that is practically irrelevant at this point. Bulimia is my addiction. I binge and purge because I feel an irreconcilable urge to do so. I never planned on making this my life, it just kind of turned out that way.

I spent the first six years of my eating disorder trying to convince myself I hated food. I considered it a sign of weakness to admit I was hungry or that I had any desire to eat. During those six years I secretly longed for the ability to make myself throw up. It is a sick thing to wish for but not entirely crazy when I considered what I thought to be the only alternative, depriving myself of any food I deemed "bad." If only I could purge, I could eat all the things I so rarely was able to enjoy. To the casual outsider, that is what bulimia is, "eating whatever you want and then throwing up." It is only those who have experiences both its glory and its horror who know it is actually much more than that.

I quickly caught on to the mechanics of successful purging and in the beginning, it was great. I started trying things I was always too afraid to try before. Food was fun again. I still remember the first time I ate an entire box

[2]From "Binging and Purging to Stay Alive," Anonymous, in M. Stavrou (Ed.), *Bulimics on Bulimia,* 2009, London, England: Jessica Kingsley Publishers. Copyright 2009, by Jessica Kingsley Publishers. Reprinted with permission.

of chocolate chip cookies. I stared in amazement at the empty box for a good five minutes. I was both horrified and fascinated all at once. I had just done what I never would have done before. But it was okay because I could get rid of it. Erase the guilt and go on as if it never even happened. I was going to be okay. Or so I thought.

Bulimia quickly took control of my life. School, friends, and anything that once meant something to me were now secondary to this new activity. Life now revolved around food, reading about it, looking at it, finding it, buying it, and binging and purging on it. I started rearranging my life to accommodate my obsession. Classes were no longer a priority. I went when I could tolerate sitting still for more than an hour. Homework and papers were something I did while waiting for food to cook and in between binge and purge sessions. I was late for everything. I always thought I could fit in just one more binge and purge before I left. I learned to be fairly quick when I needed to be, but usually not quick enough. Three-hour night classes were a nightmare. I tried to binge and purge quickly on the ten-minute break they gave us but always lost track of time. I got tired of walking into class late so I just stopped going.

The library was no longer a place to study but a place to purge when I felt too ashamed to purge in the dorm bathrooms again. I made at least two trips a day to the grocery store to stock up on more food. I quickly learned to vary the places I went so as not to look too suspicious. At first I tried to hide it all from my roommates. I didn't want to binge in front of them so I was constantly stuffing my backpack full of food and carrying it around campus searching for new places to binge and purge in private. When people asked me why my bag was always so full, I told them it was full of books and I was on my way to the library. They believed it for a while.

Soon it became too much to hide and I decided I didn't care anymore who saw me binging. I openly binged in my room in front of my roommate. I stayed up all night on my computer, getting up sometimes eight or nine times to purge. She knew what I was doing but didn't know what to say. It was soon so common it was not awkward at all. We even joked about it. She saw me coming in with armloads of groceries and knew it was going to be a busy night.

I was constantly exhausted and tired but there was no time to sleep. I thought every binge and purge would be the last one of the night but it never was. I started to judge the quality of my purging by how dizzy and shaky I felt afterwards. If I felt fine I must not have purged everything. I would eat something to keep from fainting, but nine times out of ten this just led to another binge and purge session. The cycle repeated itself until I was literally too tired to stay awake. Sleep was the only welcome interruption.

I quickly started losing contact with friends. I made excuses as to why I couldn't go out when really I was just too afraid to be away from the one thing I had come to both crave and despise. When I did go out, I felt unbearably anxious and uncomfortable and couldn't wait to get back to the familiarity of binging and purging. At the end of my junior year my roommate and once best friend decided to stop talking to me. She told me she couldn't live with me anymore. The same girl who watched it all happen and laughed about it with me was now leaving. I hated her for it but at the same time understood and wondered why she didn't do it sooner.

The things that would have once repulsed me no longer did. I refused to start shoplifting food like so many other bulimics do, so I had to learn to be creative about finding cheap or free food. I never turned down food offers. I used to take advantage of campus events where I knew food would be provided. Food left lying around or even in the trash suddenly didn't look so bad.

I was always hungry because I didn't allow myself to keep much down without purging. Eating a normal meal was too complicated. Somehow, binging and purging all day became easier than eating breakfast, lunch, or dinner. Why drive myself insane trying to find something to eat that I won't feel guilty about when I could just eat whatever I wanted and then purge? I became obsessed with food. When I wasn't buying or binging on food, I was reading about it, looking at pictures of it, dreaming about it. My idea of normal was extremely skewed. I knew this and yet I couldn't seem to think any other way.

I longed for restriction. I missed the days when I could easily control what I ate. I missed being able to survive on minimal food. I still craved feeling completely empty, only now I could only achieve that through purging. Anorexia was definitely its own nightmare. I got to a dangerously low weight of 62 pounds while anorexic. I was constantly tired, weak, and hungry. I was left almost completely isolated from the outside world. Despite all of this, I still found bulimia more debilitating. Anorexia was clean, quiet, and simple.

Bulimia was messy, loud, and complicated. I used to be neat and organized in everything I did. I had the perfect bedroom, the perfect grades, and a seemingly perfect life. Bulimia left no room for organization. I dreaded the post binge and purge cleanup because I knew things would never stay clean for long. I filled up two large garbage bags every night. The carpet around and under my desk was ruined by food stains, and my computer had been spilled on so many times there were several keys missing. I had to be careful not to get puke on my shoes. "Aim straight to avoid splashback," I told myself.

Everything would be done "right after this purge." A lot of people describe experiencing a "high" right after purging. For me, the high was usually right after the binge and before the purge. I had this idea of the purge being the end of the madness and thus once it was over, all would be well. It was almost a manic feeling right after a particularly out-of-control binge. I felt larger than life, like I could accomplish anything just as soon as I purged. The purging would cleanse and empty me in such a way that I'd feel renewed and full of potential. I'd finally be able to write that paper, clean my room, whatever. I felt awful now, but all would be well just as soon as I purged. I continued to think this way even after learning otherwise. Everything would not get done "right after this purge" because "right after this purge" I usually felt even more miserable.

There is a common misconception that the act of purging is very straightforward. The movies make it look so simple. A girl eats an entire pizza, feels guilty, and then goes to the bathroom and gets sick. All this takes place in a matter of minutes. Sometimes it was that simple, but most of the time it was much more laborious. I quickly learned a simple heave or two wasn't going to cut it in terms of getting everything out. I was going to have to be more careful if I wanted to keep from gaining weight. I decided I needed to start weighing myself before binging and after purging in order to ensure I was emptying completely. I discovered the phenomenon of "rinsing," which is really just a term for drinking glasses of water and then purging over and over again until "rinsing clear." This is when I knew I was getting everything up, or as much as I possibly could. Sometimes, though, the scale would refuse to budge. When this happened, I would panic. How could there possibly still be stuff inside me when I just spent the past 45 minutes purging? I started feeling unaccomplished until I was throwing up blood on a regular basis.

Today, most of my friends are the people I met in hospitals or treatment centers. My best friend is also bulimic. I worry about her every day. It hurts me that she is in such pain. It's not fair. She deserves to be happy and healthy. I want her to like herself. I want her to see what everyone else sees when we look at her. I'm mad she has to go through it all and I'm upset I can't seem to do much to make it better. Her being self-destructive is not okay. I don't know why I hold myself to such a different standard.

If this life is making me so miserable, why do I continue to live this way? Most people don't understand that eating disorders are about a lot more than food or wanting to be thin. There are hundreds of reasons why people develop eating disorders or why they continue to deal with them for so long. It can take years of therapy to uncover all of the reasons. Often, eating disorder symptoms are used to cope with difficult events and situations. Binging and purging and self-harming have become my most frequently used "solutions" to problems. I turn to them when I'm stressed, angry, sad, or anxious. They are very flawed coping mechanisms in that their effects are usually very short lived. In treatment I have learned all about alternative coping skills, but somehow being self-destructive still seems like the most available option. I usually crave immediate as opposed to long-term gratification, making the symptoms seem worth all of their accompanying side effects.

There are also those times when I felt like I was passively trying to kill myself by staying in my disorder. There have been periods in my life when I felt so defeated and hopeless that I was pretty certain I wanted to die. I was using bulimia as a slow way to bring about my death. I no longer see my eating disorder in this way. Bulimia now feels like the only way I know how *not* to kill myself. Now I feel like I'm binging and purging to stay alive. Sometimes the urge is so strong I feel like I'll literally collapse and die if I don't act on it. It makes no sense, but this has never been and never will be a logical illness.

There is ambivalence in recovery from any eating disorder or addiction. It is not as simple as just wanting to get better. Getting better comes with a whole slew of responsibilities and unknowns that often seem more daunting than staying sick. I am stuck. I am stuck between wanting to get out of this terrible place and clinging on to something I'm not sure I know how to live without.

Life With an Eating Disorder

Laura Bette

When I was in my eating disorder, I was living in my own prison cell—the one that existed only within the confines of my own mind. Every day was a struggle, from the time I woke up to the time I went to bed at night. Normal life was not possible, as I was trapped within my own obsessions about food, weight, exercise—all intertwined with extreme rage, depression, and self-hatred. I hated life, yet I could never escape. Suicide was not an option—my religious beliefs and concern for those who loved me stayed me from that path. Because I wouldn't kill myself, yet had to find a way to release some of the pain, I turned to cutting. When I cut, I could express the pain I felt inside, yet was still able to cover it up and appear to be normal on the outside.

The eating disorder all began around age 14, when I was in the eighth grade. Naturally, there were social pressures to stay thin, which, as it turns out, came at a very inopportune time (as I was entering adolescence and my body was undergoing several awkward changes). At that time, I attempted to diet by eating less at dinner, cutting back on sweets and fattening foods, and starting to run. At that time, I was still fairly healthy, and led a generally satisfying life.

By the time I reached high school, however, my efforts to diet had spiraled out of control. During my freshman year, I joined the cheerleading squad, and encountered an even more overwhelming pressure to be thin than I had ever felt before. I also ran track and cross-country, so constantly being around all those extremely thin athletes exacerbated my drive to be thin and my rapidly declining self-esteem.

School was not the only place that held triggers for me. Life at home was probably not only the root of my anorexia but also one of the biggest driving forces. Although prior to my teenage years, my mother and I were very close, our relationship became very rocky during adolescence. We argued constantly, and neither of us could stand even being in the same vicinity as the other. This was rather unfortunate, as Mom assumed most of the parenting responsibilities; Dad mostly worked. My father was around a fair amount of time, but most of the parenting decisions and responsibilities were left in my mother's hands. Dad and I had a good relationship, but did not interact nearly as much as Mom and I did.

My mother and father were always dieting, and my mom appeared to sometimes diet to the point of starvation. She was always on those extreme diets; for example, on one diet, she was only allowed to eat 1,200 calories a day, had to measure everything she ate, and wrote down every single calorie she consumed. Another diet she tried only allotted her 800 calories a day and called for the consumption of pregnancy hormones to trick the body into burning fat instead of muscle (as the body typically breaks down muscle during times of starvation). Regardless, this kind of constant, extreme, yo-yo dieting really interfered with my concept of normal behaviors, health, and self-image.

My dad, who has always been thin, also exhibited unhealthy behaviors with regard to exercise; he expressed his constant drive to be thinner through excessive exercise regimens. He would walk between 4 and 8 miles a day, ride his bike about 10 miles a day (almost every day), and sometimes even used workout videos. Essentially, being exposed to the extreme diet and exercise behaviors of my parents on a routine basis demonstrated to me that these were normal and healthy behaviors.

I also had a pretty poor self-image and self-esteem, so I always strove to do the best in everything I could. Academics were my high point. I achieved straight As all the way up to high school, but there came a point when my parents got so used to me excelling in school that another semester of straight As became something that was to be expected, and nothing to get excited about. Looking back now, I'm sure they were very proud of me, but at the time, I was so starved for acceptance and love that everything short of heaven was a detrimental blow to my self-esteem.

As far as I know, eating disorders never ran in my family, but there was a history of depression on my mom's side. My mom also had a condition for which she experienced sudden, uncontrollable rage; she took some antipsychotic medication for it, and the condition seemed to dissipate over time. Other than that, I do not believe my family had any history of mental health problems (unless you count my uncle's alcoholism, which no one else in the family seemed to struggle with).

Looking back at the way my mind worked and the behaviors I would engage in makes me never want to go back to the time in my life when I had my eating disorder. I remember having so much rage, especially toward my mother. I also remember always putting on this ridiculous show of being happy all the time, and always being extremely energetic and fun. That was a crock; I felt like I was slowly dying on the inside. The anger and the depression were so great that it is a miracle that I didn't do anything worse than I did, such as getting into drugs or alcohol or getting in trouble with the law.

The things that are most vivid for me are the obsessions, that no matter how fast I ran, I could never seem to get away from. When I entered into high school, rather than being a healthy activity and outlet for myself, running became an obsession. At the peak of my eating disorder, I felt the need to run between 8 and 12 miles a day, whether it was 110 degrees outside or freezing cold, whether I was tired or having constant asthma attacks, I had to finish. And I had to run at least 6 days a week—Sunday was usually my day off. Not only did I run, but I had to do 800 crunches every day, in addition to sometimes walking, roller-blading, and any other form of exercise I could imagine. The obsessions and compulsions to exercise were so overwhelming that most of the time, all I could think about was how to burn more calories. Sometimes it even came down to twitching my leg in class or running around at lunchtime just to burn some extra calories. It is still very surprising to me that while all these obsessions and compulsions were dominating my mind, I was still able to do so well academically and socially.

The exercise was definitely excessive, but the obsessions with food were just as bad. I remember trying to find any kind of diet food I could get my hands on—I was always so hungry and dying to eat, but the obsession of being thin kept me from it. When I couldn't handle the hunger pains any longer, I would turn to strange combinations of low-calorie foods. For example, I would eat crushed ice with a cinnamon and sugar substitute, because I knew it had no calories in it. I would also eat lettuce and "I Can't Believe It's Not Butter," as I believed that the stuff actually contained zero calories like it advertised. Sometimes when I would get extremely hungry, I would suck on bouillon cubes just to make me feel nauseous and make me not want to eat. Most of the time, I would try to eat nothing until dinnertime, and then would restrict severely at dinner; I would say my average daily caloric intake was around 400 calories.

Even though my food intake was so severely restricted, I still counted every single calorie and obsessed over everything I ate and how I could burn it off. I remember eating half a gummy bear during class and feeling such guilt and shame for the rest of the day because I had eaten at a time I normally didn't allow myself to eat. I also remember being so jealous of my brother one day, because he had gone to a concert, and I found myself obsessing over how many calories he was burning and how I wasn't burning any. The obsessions became so overwhelming that I honestly felt like I was a prisoner trapped within my own mind—I just didn't know how to let myself out.

When I was about 15 years old, my mother grew very concerned over the amount of weight I had lost (I was down to about 87 pounds, at 5 foot 3 inches tall). She sent me to an individual therapist who specialized in eating disorders, who, although I resented at first, I found myself eventually being able to trust and surrender to her care. After about two years of individual therapy, I was able to venture back into the world on my own and face my life without an eating disorder. What an amazing experience it was to finally be able to live without being under the spell of obsessions, and to be able to live my life to the fullest, without having to succumb to any forces that I did not want to. Finally, I could smile; and that smile was really real.

7

Impulse Control Disorders

INTRODUCTION

Most of us at some point in our lives have experienced making a decision too quickly, making a snap judgment about someone or something, or engaging in a behavior impulsively. We do these things and then realize we did not give the necessary thought or consideration to our decision or action. Usually, little harm is done and we move on, having learned something from the experience. Impulse control disorders as defined by the *DSM-IV-TR* are quite another thing. These disorders involve the inability to resist an urge, impulse, or drive to engage in some action, behavior, or activity that the person knows will be harmful to him/herself or to others. People with impulse control disorders feel increasing arousal or tension before they commit the action or while they are trying to resist it. Engaging in the act or behavior brings them a sense of pleasure, gratification, or relief, and may or may not result in regret, remorse, or guilt.

Other *DSM-IV-TR* disorders sometimes include difficulties with impulse control. Problems with impulsivity can be part of the profile of people with attention-deficit/hyperactivity disorder (ADHD), conduct disorder, bulimia nervosa, bipolar disorder, substance-related disorders, borderline and antisocial personality disorders, or paraphilias. However, lack of impulse control is the *essential* feature of the five disorders listed in this section of the *DSM: intermittent explosive disorder, kleptomania, pyromania, pathological gambling*, and *trichotillomania*.

Three narratives written by people who have experienced serious problems with impulse control are presented in this chapter. Their stories recount both the obsessions to engage in particular harmful behaviors and the inability to resist the temptation to do so. Each author describes the impact that having an impulse control disorder has had on his or her life. Mia Zamora tells the reader in revealing detail about her experience with trichotillomania, which literally means "hair-pulling mania." Her narrative conveys both the struggle she has faced and the coping strategies she has used to deal with "her strange obsession" to pull out her hair as well as the "rigorous vow of silence" she kept until writing this account. In the next first person account (FPA), Sarah Wheaton talks about her fascination with fire since preschool age and the depth of her obsession with it. This account of her behavior and her feelings before, during, and after setting a fire describes the classic symptoms of pyromania. In "Dan's Story," the anonymous author writes about how gambling as a social family pastime became an addiction that cost him the love of his parents.

QUESTIONS FOR REFLECTION

How are the problems with impulse control described in these three FPAs similar to the addictions of the substance-related disorders? Are they similar to the obsessions and compulsions of obsessive-compulsive disorder (OCD)? How are they different?

The Numbers of My Obsession

MIA ZAMORA

Are not five sparrows sold for two pennies? And not one of them is forgotten before God. Why, even the hairs of your head are all numbered. Fear not; you are of more value than many sparrows (Luke 12: 6–8).

Trichotillomania (TTM) can be broken into three Greek words: *trich* (hair), *tillo* (pull), and *mania*. The definition of the word *mania* is up for discussion. It can mean craving, excessive activity, or craziness. When you put the three parts together, like some mental health *Sesame Street* game, you get an "impulse control disorder" that results in obsessive hair pulling.

There are some basic questions that arise whenever someone without TTM is told what this term means. Doesn't it hurt to pull out your own hair? No. In some cases, people describe going into a trancelike state, not even being aware of what their hands are doing. Others say that it's a "good hurt," or that it is a response to a sort of mental itch. Still others just say "No. It doesn't." Why would you do that to yourself? For me, it's an urge that I cannot resist, possibly akin to smoking, although having never smoked, I wouldn't know. It's an urge that becomes all consuming if ignored. I find it difficult to concentrate on anything else, I get jumpy and anxious, feelings that build until I pull. Where do you pull? I pull the hair from my head, and only from specific areas on my head. Other people pull generally from all over their head, many pull out their eyelashes and eyebrows. Some even pull out their pubic hair and body hair. One misconception is that people with TTM simply have no pain receptors in their hair follicles. However, people who pull the hair on their heads, for example, often can't fathom pulling out their arm or leg hair without pain.

Despite years of therapy, both behavioral and traditional, in which I was told over and over that it is not about being crazy, it's about having a chemical disorder that has not been entirely explained yet, there's still a large part of me that stares at my hair in the mirror and thinks, "Yep. I'm really crazy." Hair pulling has traditionally been considered the first sign of a psychological break, or a sign of extreme anguish. Everyone from Shakespeare to Homer has described characters rending their hair in a high emotional state. Hippocrates offered one of the earliest accounts of this phenomenon in his work, *Epidemics III,* "From the start she used to wrap herself up, always remaining silent while she groped about, scratching and plucking out hair, and alternately wept and laughed." I like this particular quote because I have spent so much of my time dealing with TTM by doing just that: weeping or laughing.

When you encounter someone who pulls out their hair on a regular basis, it certainly seems like a sign of more serious mental health problems. Perhaps it is the seemingly casual destructiveness that makes hair pulling so frightening to contemplate, or the strange immunity to a pain that most people would find hard to bear. There is a part of TTM that scares the people who have it—people who wonder why their hands seem to obey an order that they did not issue, and cannot override. Perhaps that is the reason no one talks about it.

The first thing that you hear from anyone who has this disorder is that they are so ashamed, so embarrassed. To a certain extent I don't even understand why it is so emotionally painful to go through this, even though I am terrified of revealing this secret. People who have TTM go to extraordinary lengths to hide their condition and maintain a rigorous vow of silence about it. I am one of those people. I had only told my closest friends and family about the disorder until now. But I insist upon writing these words, the words that I have fought against saying for so long: I have trichotillomania.

I have had trichotillomania since I was a baby. That's my theory, at least. My mother tells me that when I was a baby and I wanted to nurse, or I was tired, I would reach up and rub the back of my head. She said that I eventually developed a little bald spot, like a monk's tonsure. But at some point I stopped. I don't actually remember pulling my hair until I was 7 and moved to Phoenix from St. Louis. I remember sitting in my fourth-grade classroom and twisting the hair above my ear into a huge knot, at which point I had to borrow scissors from the teacher to cut it out. My best friend stared in astonishment but found it more funny than anything else. I guess I did, too. It didn't seem like a big deal at the time. I discovered later that this sudden reoccurrence is apparently common. According to the Trichotillomania Learning Center Web site, TTM most characteristically appears in late childhood or preadolescence, or is triggered by a life change that causes more stress than the brain can handle. It could be considered a strange kind of coping method.

Despite the sudden appearance of this strange compulsion, it wasn't a prominent feature in my life for several years. It existed, but I think that I was too miserable in school and life in general to really take notice of it. But as my life calmed down, and I settled into a less panicked existence, the TTM became the intense frustration that it is today.

In high school, I started cutting my hair shorter and shorter in an effort to make the thinning hair on my right side less noticeable. By the time I entered college my once waist-length hair only fell to my shoulders. However, I had never tried to get professional help. I discovered in high school my strange compulsion had a name, thanks to a Dear Abby column. My mother wrote away for an informational brochure, which I glanced at, but couldn't bring myself to investigate any further. I now knew that other people had this problem, and that it was probably more than just a bad habit. Sadly, that relief didn't extend to getting help or talking to people about it.

My parents tried to help by telling me when I would start to pull, since oftentimes I would start to do it unconsciously, when I was reading or watching TV, but that just made me resentful and embarrassed. I was seeing a therapist for clinical depression, and she knew about it, but I always made it clear that it was something that I did not want to tackle in our sessions together.

Later, I discovered on an informational Web site (http://home.intekom.com/jly2/indexp1.html# P1b1) that approximately 51% of TTM sufferers also have problems with clinical depression. The idea that these two things are connected is not too far off, both chemically and psychologically. There is evidence that both depression and TTM are the result of an imbalance of a person's serotonin levels. Serotonin is a neurotransmitter that controls mood, emotion, sleep, and appetite. Studies have found that people with depression are less likely to have correctly working serotonin systems and that the use of serotonin-boosting drugs often has a positive effect on patients' depressive symptoms. Many of the same drugs, called serotonin reuptake inhibitors, or SSRIs, have been used to lessen the urge to pull for people with TTM. Brain scans done of people who have TTM show a similarly inadequate production of serotonin. There are so many theories about what causes TTM, and because the problem is so rarely discussed, it is only just beginning to be studied.

The psychological side of it is far less complicated. One of the main problems doctors and patients have to deal with is the intense feelings of shame and embarrassment that come with this problem, and the depression is a natural reaction to years of negative internal dialogue. People with TTM will do anything they can to make their hair appear normal. Oftentimes the fear of discovery will cause people to avoid common activities like swimming, participating in sports, or even going outside on a windy day. People limit the number of friends they tell about the problem, and most people don't pull their hair unless they are alone, or with close family or friends. I am lucky. I do not have it severely enough to need a wig or curtail my normal activities. But the way my hair looks is a constant obsession. My roommates used to joke that they could always find me because I leave a trail of bobby pins wherever I go. I am constantly rearranging my hair to cover bald spots, or pinning back wisps of hair that are growing back in.

Two years ago I was finally reduced to cutting my hair extremely short because it was so thin on one side. Haircuts are a special form of torture for me. If you can imagine having to get undressed in front of a complete stranger and have them examine your body for deformities and flaws, that is what getting my hair cut is like. I have had two haircuts in my entire life, and both times it was a big production. My mother called the first hair-dresser before I came in, and explained to him my problem. The second time, my behavioral therapist called a hair stylist that he had found, and she arranged for me to come in on a Sunday when no one was around so she could cut my hair. Both of these times I have been blown away by the kindness of these people and their willingness to accommodate me. It is partially because of their sensitivity that I have conjured up the courage to write about this.

The shame that people with TTM feel makes it extremely difficult to conduct scientific studies on the disorder. It has been estimated that 1–2% of the population of the United States has TTM, but that is a number that is virtually impossible to verify because so few people come forward for treatment. Women are far more likely to seek help, probably because men are more able to pass off their bald spots as thinning hair, or have the option of simply shaving their heads. A result of the secrecy of TTM is a large Internet community of "trich-sters." By avoiding face-to-face contact, it has become easier to form a close-knit community of fellow sufferers while maintaining a crucial anonymity.

I have come across numerous Web sites with message boards, diet tips, suggestions for ways to hide bald spots, and stories from people who have recovered from TTM. There is no definite cure, so there is often a massive exchange of ideas for cures that begin to sound so random they could be a solution for almost any problem. There are testimonials from people who have cut yeast and sugar out of their diets, have gone on SSRI medications, or have turned to Jesus for help. But for every triumphant letter of success, there are 20 messages from people who are spending their nights sitting alone in a room, slowly pulling out all their hair, and can't stop. Knowing that there is a larger community out there does help, though. If nothing else it makes me feel like I'm not alone and I'm not crazy. I even found a TTM joke online:

Hello. Welcome to the Psychiatric Hotline. If you are obsessive-compulsive, please press 1 repeatedly. If you are co-dependent, please ask someone to press 2 for you. If you have multiple personalities, please press 3, 4, 5, and 6. If you are paranoid-delusional, we know who you are and what you want. Just stay on the line until we can trace the call. If you are schizophrenic, listen carefully and a little voice will tell you which number to press. If you are manic-depressive, it doesn't matter which number you press. No one will answer. If you have trichotillomania, please stop trying to pull the buttons off the phone!

After having this disorder for so many years, I have in fact developed a strange sense of humor toward it, as has my family. My mother called me once and, giggling madly the whole time, told me that she had just read about a study where they isolated the TTM gene in mice, and discovered that after the mouse had pulled all the fur out of its own body, it would start pulling the hair of other, nonsuffering mice. In a similar case, I saw a picture of a woman who attended a TTM conference (they have conferences!) who was holding a completely bald teddy bear. According to the caption under the picture, her mother had forced her to bring the bear that she had had since childhood. It was bald because as a baby she had pulled out all of its fur. My boyfriend calls the little balls of hair that litter my apartment, my clothes, his clothes, and my car "bunnies" and jokingly offers up his perpetual five o'clock shadow for my twitchy fingers, so he can skip shaving that day. After a while, there's really nothing you can do but laugh. Or cry. But right now I'm trying to choose laughter.

There are so many "cures" that people swear by. Some people swear by the John Kender Diet. John Kender is a professor who has TTM, and has constructed a diet around the chemical processes that he hypothesized as the cause of the problem. It mainly involves cutting out sugar, yeast, legumes, and caffeine. I am immensely skeptical of this approach, perhaps more because of convenience since breads, sugars, and caffeine make up the majority of my diet. There are behavioral techniques that work for some people, like relaxation exercises and object replacement. Some people claim that hypnotism works, and others say to go ahead and just shave your head. There are medications that have had varying degrees of success: Paxil, Prozac, Zoloft, Celexa, Elavil, Nardil. . . . The list is endlessly long because no one drug works for everyone, and most of the drugs work for at least one person. I have been on several of them, and none of them are perfect.

There is something interesting about the people who profess one treatment or another to the rest of us "trichsters:" Everyone allows room for disagreement. Unlike religious discussions or political discussions, or even forums for cancer treatment, people dealing with TTM all seem to understand that what may have worked for them won't necessarily work for someone else. The amount of compassion and tenderness that is exhibited in online forums is something that you would be hard-pressed to find anywhere else. People offer tips that did not work for them, in the hopes that they will work for others. People submit pictures of their hair, both to demonstrate solidarity and to provide proof that success is possible. There are discussions of the best ways to hide bald spots, and names and addresses of sympathetic hairstylists across the country. It is a grassroots effort that seems to have expanded beyond each individual's quest for a cure: it has turned into a community that won't rest until everyone has found peace.

Part of the shame stems from the fact that we recognize the ridiculousness of our actions. We are disgusted by the intensity of the obsession and our inability to quit. As you read accounts of people describing their pulling habits, so often they repeat the same phrases, "I can't believe how crazy that sounds" or "I know how grotesque that sounds, after rereading it." The sense of shame is what keeps me locked in my own head. It is only in the last couple of years that I told my closest friends, ones that I had known since elementary school. It took me at least 5 years of knowing what TTM was before I could seek help for it. And actually getting that help took even longer. I finally felt forced to get help when I had a roommate for the first time. My pulling got worse and worse during my freshman year of college, and it was getting hard to hide it from my roommate, someone who I didn't particularly want to talk to about it.

I finally went to Campus Health, which was excruciating. It turns out the mental health division is upstairs, and so I had to ask at the front desk, and was directed to the elevator. As I was waiting for the elevator, next to the big red sign that said "MENTAL HEALTH SERVICES," someone I knew from one of my classes came up to me. A particularly inept, rude person from my French class, not someone I would want to talk to on a good day, much less today. But, being the dense person he was, he came up to me and said in a piercing tone, "So! What do you need to go upstairs for?" This would be the part where I'm supposed to come up with some kind of witty reason for needing to go the second floor, or the ground is supposed to open up and let me fall mercifully into the bowels of hell, which would have been a paradise compared to standing in front of him. However, the only thing that happened was my mouth dropped open and my cheeks flamed into a brilliant shade of red. This is the same guy who walked into class one day and, seeing me sitting with my head down on the desk, said in that same earth-shattering voice, "Hey! A bald spot!" I don't know what happened to this guy after that day. I assume he vanished back into the ether, having accomplished his life goal of single-handedly orchestrating the two most embarrassing moments of my life.

But I digress. The result of this first reluctant step was me, sitting in an office with a triage nurse and a box of tissues. As I tearfully tried to explain the last 12 years of this strange habit, she asked to see any bald spots. In order to show her I had to kneel on the ground with my head bowed, as she parted my hair as delicately as she could. In terms of worst nightmare situations, this made the incident at the elevator seem like a walk in the park. I found myself crouched there as if in prayer, trying to keep the tears and snot from rolling down my face, offering my sins up to a higher authority. It was this moment of helplessness that made me give up some of my self-imposed prison of shame. I have never understood the need to prostrate oneself upon an altar, but that's what I was doing. I knelt there, feeling this woman's hands touching my hair, my defenses, and decided that I needed to fight. In a way, they were tears of relief, of surrender. Surrendering to the reality of this disease, and to the necessity of the fight that was coming.

I write this as if it were the finale, the triumphant climax. And in some ways, sort of, it was. I finally tried to find a doctor who could help me, and started taking medicine to alter the chemicals that seemed to be causing the problem. I tried actively confronting my actions using behavioral therapy. I slowly started telling my friends about my problem, and tried to accept the help that my family had always been tentatively offering me. But, like anything in life that isn't scripted, that moment wasn't even close to being the end of the story. The medicine I've been taking is working less and less effectively, and I keep cutting my hair shorter. I still flinch when anyone touches my head, and I carefully use bobby pins and elastics to conceal bald spots and asymmetries. I still look in the mirror and cry, and wonder if there will ever be a day when I will have long, beautiful hair. And a lot of the research I've done tells me that no, I won't.

Trichotillomania is often a lifelong condition, one that may get better as I get older, or remain the same. Despite the increasing scientific interest in the disorder, there is still no "cure." Nor is there any really solid evidence as to what causes it, or what will make it go away. But there are people who have beaten it. There are testimonials from people who have been "PPF," practically or perfectly pull free, for 20 years or more. There are also letters from people who insist that "beating" TTM really means accepting it as a part of your life. These are people who have quit wearing wigs, false eyelashes, and painted-on eyebrows, and simply accepted this disorder as their lot in life.

But I don't think I'm one of those people. I do not like being incapable of controlling something so basic as the movement of my fingers. Maybe it's because I thought for so long that it was just a "bad habit," so now the idea that I cannot train myself to change is abhorrent. It could also be the simple longing of a girl who once had beautiful long blond hair, and desperately wants to get that back, to get back the part of her that will make her whole and happy.

Endnote

In my experience, every time I get the courage to tell someone about this, they end up knowing someone who has it. Part of my reason for writing this essay was to broaden people's awareness of this disorder, in the hopes that if they know someone who has it, as most people probably do, they will have a better understanding of what they are going through. I'm still struggling to believe that this disorder should not carry with it the shame that it does, as are most people with TTM. If you do know someone with trichotillomania, or would like more information on it, I would recommend a Web site with an amazing repository of information on all aspects of TTM: http://home.intekom.com/jly2/index pi.html#P1b1 or the Trichotillomania Learning Center Web site: http://www.trich.org/home/default.asp?FC=740709.

Memoirs of a Compulsive Firesetter

SARAH WHEATON[1]

During the early summer of 1993, when I was finishing my freshman year in college, I was admitted involuntarily to a psychiatric hospital and stayed

[1]From "Memoirs of a Compulsive Firesetter," by Sarah Wheaton, 2001, *Psychiatric Services,* 52(8), 1035–1036. Copyright 2001 by American Psychiatric Association. Reprinted with permission from Psychiatric Services.

there two weeks. The following are edited excerpts from my discharge summary.

Reason for admission: *This 19-year-old single female was living in a dorm at the University of California at the time of admission. The patient had been involved in bizarre activity, including lighting five fires on campus that did not remain lit.*

History of present illness: *This young lady is a highly intelligent, highly active young woman who had been the president of her class in her high school for all four years. She had been going full-time to the university and working full-time at a pizzeria. She had called the police threatening suicide. When she was brought in, she was in absolute and complete denial. Patient claimed that everything was wonderful and she did not need to be here. She was admitted for 72-hour treatment and evaluation.*

Hospital course: *The hospital course initially was quite tempestuous. It was difficult to determine what the diagnosis was, as the patient was on the one hand very bright and very endearing to the staff and on the other hand was very unpredictable. She jumped over the wall on the patio (AWOL). The police were called and ultimately brought her back. She was subsequently certified to remain in custody for up to 14 days for intensive treatment because she attempted to cut herself with plastic and/or glass. She became more open after this, more tearful and at times more vulnerable. She tended to run from issues, to try to help everyone else, and not look at herself. Her father was seen in family therapy with her by a social worker. Mother is reported by father to be both an alcoholic and have a history of bipolar illness. The patient herself reported sexual abuse by an older stepbrother when she was about age nine to age 11.*

Initially I intended to use antimanic medication with her, either carbamazepine or lithium, but opted not to as she was adamantly against medication. The patient did seem to stabilize without medication. She showed dramatic improvement, although the staff and I still have concern. The stable environment she has been able to pull together may not exist after discharge. She is scheduled to go to Washington, D.C., on July 1 to work as an intern in the office of one of the congressional representatives. She had done this two years ago working as a page.

Aftercare instructions: *No follow-up appointment is scheduled because she is discharged today and will be leaving for Washington on the first.*

Fire became a part of my vocabulary in my preschool days. During the summer our home would be evacuated because the local mountains were ablaze. I would watch in awe. Below I have listed some of my thoughts and behaviors eight years after the onset of deviant behavior involving fire. I have also included suggestions for helping a firesetter.

Firesetting Behaviors on a Continuum

Each summer I look forward to the beginning of fire season as well as the fall—the dry and windy season. I set my fires alone. I am also very impulsive, which makes my behavior unpredictable. I exhibit paranoid characteristics when I am alone, always looking around me to see if someone is following me. I picture everything burnable around me on fire.

I watch the local news broadcasts for fires that have been set each day and read the local newspapers in search of articles dealing with suspicious fires. I read literature about fires, firesetters, pyromania, pyromaniacs, arson, and arsonists. I contact government agencies about fire information and keep up-to-date on the arson detection methods investigators use. I watch movies and listen to music about fires. My dreams are about fires that I have set, want to set, or wish I had set. I like to investigate fires that are not my own, and I may call to confess to fires that I did not set. I love to drive back and forth in front of fire stations, and I have the desire to pull every fire alarm I see. I am self-critical and defensive, I fear failure, and I sometimes behave suicidally.

Before a fire is set. I may feel abandoned, lonely, or bored, which triggers feelings of anxiety or emotional arousal before the fire. I sometimes experience severe headaches, a rapid heartbeat, uncontrollable motor movements in my hands, and tingling pain in my right arm. I never plan my fire, but typically drive back and forth or around the block or park and walk by the scene I am about to light on fire. I may do this to become familiar with the area and plan escape routes or to wait for the perfect moment to light the fire. This behavior may last anywhere from a few minutes to several hours.

At the time of lighting the fire. I never light a fire in the exact same place other fires have occurred. I set fires at random, using material I have just bought or asked for at a gas station—matches, cigarettes, or small amounts of gasoline. I do not leave any signatures to claim my fires. I set fires only in places that are secluded, such as roadsides, back canyons, cul-de-sacs, and parking lots. I usually set fires after nightfall because my chances of being caught are much lower then. I may set several small fires or one big fire, depending on my desires and needs at the time. It is at the time of lighting the fire that I experience an intense emotional response like tension release, excitement, or even panic.

Leaving the fire scene. I am well aware of the risks of being at the fire scene. When I leave a fire scene, I drive normally so that I do not look suspicious if another car or people are nearby. Often I pass in the opposite direction of the fire truck called to the fire.

During the fire. Watching the fire from a perfect vantage point is important to me. I want to see the chaos as well as the destruction that I, or others, have caused. Talking to authorities on the phone or in person while the action is going on is part of the thrill. I enjoy hearing about the fire on the radio or watching it on television, learning about all the possible motives and how the fire started.

After the fire is out. At this time I feel sadness and anguish and a desire to set another fire. Overall it seems that the fire has created a temporary solution to a permanent problem.

Within 24 hours after the fire. I revisit the scene of the fire. I may also experience feelings of remorse as well as anger and rage at myself. Fortunately, no one has ever been physically harmed by the fires I have set.

Several days after the fire. I revel in the notoriety of the unknown firesetter, even if I did not set the fire. I also return again to see the damage and note areas of destruction on an area map.

Fire anniversaries. I always revisit the scene on anniversary days of fires that I or others set in the area.

Fires not my own. A fire that is not my own offers excitement and some tension relief. However, any fire set by someone else is one I wish I had set. The knowledge that there is another firesetter in the area may spark feelings of competition or envy in me and increase my desire to set bigger and better fires. I am just as interested in knowing the other firesetters' interests or motives for lighting their fires.

Suggestions for helping a firesetter. The likelihood of recidivism is high for a firesetter. The firesetter should be able to count on someone always being there to talk to about wanting to set fires. Firesetting may be such a big part of the person's life that he or she cannot imagine giving it up. This habit in all aspects fosters many emotions that become normal for the firesetter, including love, happiness, excitement, fear, rage, boredom, sadness, and pain.

A firesetter should be taught appropriate problem-solving skills and breathing and relaxation techniques. Exposure to burn units and disastrous fire scenes may be therapeutic and may enable the firesetter to talk openly about physical and emotional reactions. Doing so will not only help the firesetter but also give mental health professionals a deeper understanding of the firesetter's obsession.

Prognosis given by psychiatrist: *Prognosis is very guarded given the severity of her condition.*

Mental status: *She firmly denies ... destructive ideation, including firesetting at this time.*

Discharge diagnosis *[33 hospitalizations after the initial hospitalization]: Axis I. Major depressive disorder, recurrent, with psychosis. Axis II. Obsessive-compulsive personality disorder; history of pyromania; borderline personality disorder. Axis III. Asthma. Axis V. GAF 45.*

Having been diagnosed as having borderline personality disorder with a history of firesetting led my therapists and me to use intense biofeedback therapy, social skills training, and an amazing psychotropic drug called clomipramine. As a result, I have been fire-thinking free for eight months. Have we found a cure?

Dan's Story

ANONYMOUS[2]

In the Beginning

I was a spoiled brat. My dad was a very successful businessman and well respected in the community. Despite his busy schedule, he always attended my school activities. He encouraged me to do the things that interested me. He tried to motivate me in anything he saw as a plus in my life, and he often praised me in front of others. I was an only child, and I truly felt he was proud of me. My mother wrote children's stories (one was made into a

---

[2]From "The Afflicted," Anonymous, in *Losing Your Shirt: Recovery for Compulsive Gamblers and Their Families,* by M. Heineman, 1992, Center City, MN: Hazelden. Copyright 1992 by Mary Heineman. Reprinted with permission.

movie). Since she wrote at home, she was always there for me. Sometimes I felt she was too focused on me and overprotective, but even at an early age, I knew that she always had my best interests at heart.

If compulsive gamblers need parents to blame for their addiction, I am out in the cold. I loved and respected my parents more than any kid I knew. They did everything they could possibly do to show me their love. Gambling was part of my family's lifestyle, and it was never a problem. Both my parents loved to visit the casinos a couple of times a year, and they'd have dinner at the racetrack every few months. It was one of their leisure activities, among many others: opera, theater, tennis, golf, traveling, and socializing at the country club.

My dad thought of gambling as a macho activity, so he didn't discourage me from an occasional wager on my favorite games, even at a young age. As a matter of fact, he often wagered with me. I enjoyed that because it gave us a common interest. I started to gamble without my parents' knowledge when I was in the ninth grade. I was fifteen years old and the smallest kid in class. Although I loved sports, I never tried out because of my size. I did the only thing I could think of to get involved with sports: I became the high school bookie. I ran the pools for the weekend games. While I was managing the money and keeping book, I started to wager heavily myself. I didn't wager because I needed the money (my parents were always generous with me). I wagered heavily to show off in front of my school friends. I wanted them to see me as a risk-taker, not a wimp. I felt that some of my classmates looked down on me because I was short and slight. They never really said anything derogatory, but they were somewhat sarcastic and I felt hurt. I needed their acceptance. I did not want to feel different.

At any rate, I found out very quickly that gambling was one way I could get what I needed. My reputation as a successful sports bettor spread fast and stuck with me throughout high school. Gambling afforded me something my parents could not buy: the acceptance and respect of my schoolmates. I loved it.

In the End

Gambling made me believe that all the things my parents said about me were true; that I was bright, creative, and intelligent. Before gambling, I never believed in myself because I never felt accepted by my classmates. I always felt like an outsider.

My first big win proved to me I could be popular. I fooled myself into thinking the kids liked me when I now know they liked my money and my generosity. Before I started winning, I was never invited to join the others at school activities. Because of my size, I couldn't get a date. I stopped asking girls to go out with me by the time I was a junior in high school. However, in my senior year, I had a number of girlfriends because I could afford to take them wherever they wanted to go. Gambling and winning allowed me to grow approximately six inches in the eyes of others. It made me feel six feet tall.

Today I know it is more important for me to remember what gambling did *to* me and not for me. By the time I graduated from college, I had few coping skills. I was irresponsible, very immature, and totally consumed by my gambling. The amounts I was betting and the frequency of my gambling caused many problems. The more problems I had, the more I gambled; and the more I gambled, the more problems I had. My parents bailed me out over and over again to the tune of over thirty thousand dollars. Each time they came to my rescue, I promised them, often with my tears, that if they helped me I would never gamble again. I would have promised them anything, as long it got me whatever I needed to remain in ACTION.

Gambling made me so incredibly selfish. I felt resentful on the night our American prisoners of war were returning from Vietnam because I had to miss the football games that the news coverage preempted. Gambling made me hate any family occasion when it was necessary to give a gift, because I wanted to spend my money on nothing but gambling. Gambling made me make a new friend only if I thought he would be good for a touch when I was in need of money. Gambling made it so that the only time I ever felt emotionally comfortable was when I was in ACTION. Gambling convinced me that my problem was money and that one more big win would solve everything.

What did gambling do *to* me? It removed all the positive characteristics my parents worked so hard to foster within me, and it destroyed them emotionally. I knew that when they first realized my gambling was a serious problem, they blamed themselves. I used my knowledge of their guilt to manipulate them. They raised me in hopes I would adopt their most precious values, but I ignored every one of them. I didn't care about their values; I didn't care about their feelings; I didn't care about anything but being in

ACTION. I cursed them, blamed them, stole from them, and, in the end, I attacked them physically—one day they refused to give me the money I needed to pay gambling debts in order to keep my credit with my loan shark and thus stay in ACTION.

What did gambling do *to* me? It resulted in losing the people most dear to me, my parents, the two people who would have died for me, the two people who gave me their hearts. I took those hearts and broke them.

8

Delirium, Dementia, and Amnestic and Other Cognitive Disorders

---

INTRODUCTION

The aging process involves changes in cognitive functioning that are natural, can be amusing or annoying, but do not lead to severe problems in the activities of daily living. Many of us experience these to one extent or another—the *DSM-IV-TR* calls this *age-related cognitive decline*. Some of the cognitive disorders, however, can be extremely disabling. The manual includes three types of cognitive disorders in this section delirium, dementia, and amnestic disorders. Currently, these disorders are assumed to be the direct result of a medical condition, the use of or exposure to a substance/toxin, or both. Older versions of the *DSM* referred to these as organic brain or mental disorders. Beginning with the *DSM-IV,* these terms were no longer used because they implied that nonorganic mental disorders (those not a direct result of a medical condition or substance) have no biological or physiological basis. More recent research has shown this not to be the case.

Delirium means "to rave" or "to be crazy" in Latin (*delirare*). It involves a clouding of consciousness and a shift in cognition that comes on rather quickly (hours to days) and results in a reduced state of awareness that fluctuates during the day and night. Disorientation and recent memory loss are hallmark signs of delirium. Someone in a state of delirium has trouble focusing, sustaining, or shifting attention, and experiences at least one cognitive deficit in memory, language, or orientation, or a problem in perception (e.g., illusions or visual hallucinations). There may be disturbances in the sleep–wake cycle. These changes are not caused by a prior or developing dementia. Most deliriums resolve themselves when the medical condition is treated or the exposure to the substance or toxin is eliminated. Children are susceptible to delirium because of their developmental stage, and older adults as well as those with medical illnesses and/or dementia are at greater risk for a less-than-full recovery.

A *dementia* is a "mental deterioration" that involves memory loss and other cognitive deficits such as language problems, inability to perform motor activities, inability to identify or recognize objects, and difficulties with executive functioning. The name comes from the Latin word *demens,* which means "out of one's mind." It is probably the most familiar cognitive disorder, it often has been referred to as *senility,* and the key features are memory loss and the decline of intellectual functioning. Personality changes, impaired judgment, and poor impulse control also are common signs of dementia. Dementias have a gradual or insidious onset and are classified by etiology (e.g., Alzheimer's type, vascular, HIV disease, head trauma, Parkinson's disease, Huntington's disease, Pick's disease). Mild cognitive impairment (MCI) is a neurological condition that is often a precursor to dementia. More than 60% of all dementias are of the Alzheimer's type, and it is the fourth-leading cause of death in this country. The current number of people over 65 with dementia (35 million) is expected to triple in the next twenty years. The already huge economic and social costs continue to grow as the population ages (Alzheimer's Association; Changing Aging in America, 2008; Maxmen, Ward, & Kilgus, 2009).

Amnesia means "forgetfulness" in Latin, and that is exactly the most notable feature of the amnestic disorders—problems in memory. This can involve both the inability to remember things from the past and the inability to learn and remember new information. The memory problems are serious and cause marked impairment in social and/or occupational functioning. If an individual also is exhibiting the cognitive deficits listed above for dementia, he/she is not diagnosed with an amnestic disorder. Onset can be acute or gradual, depending on the direct physiological effects of the medical condition or substance that is the cause. Amnestic disorders should be distinguished from dissociative amnesia and amnesia that may be part of the symptom profile for some people with other dissociative disorders. The inability to learn and recall new information is a sign of an amnestic disorder but not of dissociative states. We discuss this further in Chapter 10.

This chapter includes three first person accounts (FPAs) by people who are experiencing many of the signs and symptoms of the cognitive disorders described above. We think you will be impressed with the courage and strength these authors display in facing the challenges of their conditions. First, Jane McAllister writes her fascinating and in some ways frightening narrative about having Alzheimer's disease while she is experiencing the effects of it. She made a conscious decision to do this, and the reader is quickly drawn into her story. In *Poor Memory: A Case Report*, Malcolm Meltzer provides a detailed account of the memory loss he experiences as a result of having a cardiac arrest that put him into a coma. He describes its overwhelming impact on every area of his life, but he also tells of the coping strategies he has developed and shares some ideas for those who also have memory problems. The chapter concludes with Sydney Dorros's tale of the progression of Parkinson's disease that he experienced, how he could not accept the diagnosis at first, and how the more he ignored his increasing limitations, the more they became obstacles to living with the illness. In the end, the emotional support and love he received from others with the illness made all the difference.

QUESTIONS FOR REFLECTION

How has each of the authors of the FPAs in this chapter come to terms with his/her condition? What common strategies did they employ? What coping mechanisms were unique to each?

REFERENCES

Alzheimer's Association. Retrieved from: www.alz.org.
Changing aging in America. (2008). Retrieved from: www.almosthomedoc.org.
Maxmen, J. S., Ward, N. G., & Kilgus, M. (2009). *Essential psychopathology and its treatment* (3rd ed.). New York, NY: Norton.

Before It's Too Late

JANE McALLISTER[1]

The idea of writing a book has been with me for a long time. Like so many other things I think about but never get to do, I decided a book would never really materialize. But suddenly at age seventy-eight, time is growing short, and I feel it pressing against my procrastinating nature. In the last few months the idea has weighed more heavily on my mind. During hospitalization for surgery two years ago, I had some additional "thinking time." The title came to me as I contemplated a recent dire event in my life, an event which sharply confronted my tendency to delay.

Now, there are two purposes for writing. The first is to tell in a simple manner the story of my life. The second is to record, as well as I am able, what happens in my mind as a person with Alzheimer's disease.

Writing

I have to hurry ... write before the thought is gone. It does that in a second. I lose the thought. At this time in my life my mind is still full of feelings, yes, feelings unwritten, and soon to be forgotten.

There is no way for anyone to know so many things about me. It's all right. There's no need for most. But there are a few people I want to tell. There are lots of things about me you do not know ... things I care about ... things I think, want to do, have done.

So much has happened. I've become 78 for one thing. I am so much closer to insanity. Will I be able to continue to write? Not for my life!

How, all my life I wanted to journal—with my head always full of thoughts which were never to be heard by anyone, and now forgotten by me.

What is "book worthy" and what is not? In my head forever so long—to write on a page, especially in a mostly new, blank book—ahh. Not so now. It is mine to write in ... and the thoughts come to me ... only now I am aware of how quickly they are gone ... not remembered.

The unsentenced words reach out ... touch my heart ... not my mind. The page being read by another—the pain I must consume ... alone ... in the space where my brain fails and again the child returns.

My feelings flow ... I can feel them going from me to the page! Yes, I love to write. So I go on ... there is never a Jane's day in my mind—never. This is today though I never know the name of it! I need to write, forgive me if it seems strange to do so!

The change in my handwriting disturbs me somewhat when I come across notes written so long ago in some ring book—each letter clear, each word as if there had been lines on the page, holding the names I now cannot remember. I feel flushed and not relaxed as the letters grow crooked making misspelled words.

Alzheimer's

4/16/06: I love my life the way it is and being forgetful is an opportunity to be philosophical. When we talk about each period in our life, one of our great joys is to remember things we've done, places we've been, people we've known. I will eventually forget those things. They will be gone from my mind. That is frightening to me when I think about it, and I wish it would not happen. But as I thought about it now, I realized that I can have a philosophical attitude. We have experienced the world together, life together in the broadest sense. That's how I seek to look at it, how I plan to look at it.

You said something you had told me, and I said I don't remember. Then I thought—that's the way it will always be. You'll tell me what you said. Then my realizing will still be there, and what I always knew to be true will be there. This is a better thing. It will help me to think of that as I go along on the path of forgetting. This is a good thing to think about. I can do it. I didn't want to look ahead. I was frightened of it. This helps me not to feel that, gives me courage. I don't allow myself to be depressed, but sometimes it comes ... just like a wave. It has the control, the power. The reassurance you'll stick with me is important, but for a moment the wave is strong, too strong.

It's like being some place you've never been before. When I wake up after 12 hours of sleep I don't feel any better. What went wrong? What happens when someone doesn't understand any more? I guess they still feel lots of things.

Still so much to do—after years of wasting time, thinking incorrectly. The pain burns my heart. I want this monster disease to end—and let me rest in peace, or begin the price for all those years that were supposed to be happy, good, and clear and instead are an opening to this hell on earth and forever.

I'd be happy if I was crazy at night. Do what I have to do in the day and then happy hour at night. It takes a while to get revved up in the morning.

Remembering something that I loved and lived with ... there was always a picture in my mind ... I lived with pictures ... pictures that I could describe ... because I saw them from memory of them. Now it becomes a feeling. I think to acknowledge that will help. There are so many things I remember loving, but because I can't see them in my mind doesn't mean I don't remember them.

My notes have been strange I know. My mind is failing continually. I feel it in so many ways. Yes, I am sad because it is such a huge loss. Expecting it was of no help, nor is it a help to pretend it isn't happening when I feel it constantly.

Alzheimer's is like traveling a road that one has never traveled before ... without a map ... without directions. I know that others have traveled it, but I also know that no one ever comes back to tell about it. I wonder what it's like up ahead. It feels like I get off in different places. They seem real ... like I'm familiar with them. But then before I know it I'm back on the road which seems to move under me, rather than me moving ahead on it. I don't want to move ahead because I'm afraid of what's out there but the road keeps going by me anyway.

Finally, why me? Punishment that ends all potential? I never understood this "punishment disease," this that is happening and increasing all those years with my not knowing. Today it hurts my heart to know, my eyes to look at where I am ... my home ... all the other homes run through my head, each corner sometimes ... all the while not being able to recall which house sometimes.

I do believe this is a punishment ... this dread disease that destroys a bit of my brain every day. When did it start? How will it end? Will my breathing, seeing, speaking, living continue even after my brain is dead? I say all day, "I can't remember." Will I stop when there is no brain to know, to understand, to think? I know it is happening ... this daily changing ... the wafting between contentment and uncontrollable anger ... mostly that. I grasp at a thought and can't let go ... if it passes it's only for a little and it's back ... it returns. I do remember details of the hurting things ... the losses ... the mistakes. There is some part of my thinking that dreads, fears, mourns ... and of course the "why me?"

The day dawned and everything was painted the same inside my head, even though the blossoms and the leaves had grown and changed. I am not afraid. I accept the disease I have.

I clearly noted how differently I often feel between the morning and the evening. It feels like I'm running out of fuel later in the day ... particularly when the day has been full ... not full of our talking or our being together ... but full of … I don't know what … maybe the unfamiliar. Yes, it is the unfamiliar that seems to take more fuel … or whatever keeps me going.

It is so hard to lose control of one's life … as if we ever had control! I have been frightened all my life … of making mistakes, of people not liking me, of sudden changes, of all things unknown. So when I feel I have some control of a situation, it reduces my anxiety. With wanting to control such a high priority, I am devastated when I lose control of myself in some fit of rage. I am totally humiliated, scornful of myself, deeply embarrassed … coming away feeling that I should be punished.

I sometimes tell Rob that my head feels like crossed fingers, and I cross my fingers to show him how it is inside my head. The experts talk about "tangles" in the brain of Alzheimer's patients. I celebrate when my head is working … it feels so wonderful. But when it gets "crossed" and little things start to go wrong: I can't get the top off a bottle, I spill something, I can't find something … I see it all changing … going. And very quickly I discover myself sitting in a wheel chair, slumped over, unaware of my surroundings … or maybe acutely aware of my surroundings, but unable to communicate with those nearby. I'm old and wrinkled and ugly, and I don't want anyone to see me, and I don't want to see anyone.

It all goes through my head, and I don't want to be here. I plunge into the abyss … dark, frightening, cut off from the world … from life … living. All of this brings fear … no terror, anger … no rage, loneliness … no abandonment. It is a punishment from God for my life. I keep saying, "I'm a good person." But how can I be, and be under this curse.

It is almost like the pieces in my mind are not discrete thoughts but rather separate feelings that act like they are chained to one another and force me along into the words and actions that come out. It is terrifying to watch my feelings take over and put ideas in my head that I don't want to be there and cause me to say hurtful things that I don't want to say. When it's over (and I'm not really sure why it is over, how it is over, or when it is over) I am remorseful, apologetic, and embarrassed. Then with the return of clarity, I wonder how Rob can put up with all of this. But he does, and I know he always will because in the core of myself I know he loves me deeply and everlastingly.

Last evening I talked to Robbie about Alzheimer's. I sounded angry. I was angry. I want to know what is going to happen to me and I want to know when it is going to happen. I want someone to tell me, to explain it to me, to let me know. Sometimes I think I want it to go quickly so it will be over. And other times I don't dare hope that it might progress slowly. I had a hard time getting it out of my head last night. No wonder, my head is where it is.

This morning I woke up feeling depressed, tired, uninterested in anything. After breakfast I wanted to go back to bed. I didn't want to think any more today. I couldn't stop the constant negative thoughts and the noose of worry that strangles me. Now I am "injected" every waking morning with the word "Alzheimer's." It has been five years since I was first told. I criticize myself for slowing down or completely stopping doing so much that I loved all my life ... while at the same time I've given up trying in a deliberate manner ... and it doesn't hurt.

Poor Memory: A Case Report

MALCOLM L. MELTZER[2]

Past Memory

The loss of past memory was not as extreme as it is in amnesia. When I came out of the coma I had been in for 6 weeks I knew who I was and I knew that I was a husband, a father, and a psychologist. I knew my family, but I had difficulty recognizing some of my friends. In the beginning I thought I had two children, but I have but one. I thought my daughter was 13, but she was 15 at that point. I also thought I was 33, but I was 44.

During the drive home from the hospital (after 11 weeks), I saw that I did not recognize the route home, even though it was a route quite familiar to me. At that point, I realized that some of the geography of the city was lost to me. But I did recognize my home and the neighborhood when we arrived there. My house was familiar to me, but I didn't remember where some things were kept and how some things were used. I had to relearn how to play the stereo, set the alarm clock, use the calculator, change a razor blade, etc. All of these things were relearned but because of the short-term memory problem it often took several trials to relearn and keep these things in mind.

The feeling engendered by this inability to do things done in the past was that of incompetency. When should bills be paid? What is used to fix a

[2]From "Poor Memory: A Case Report," by Malcolm L. Meltzer, 1983, *Journal of Clinical Psychology, 39*(1), 3–10. Copyright 1983 by John Wiley & Sons. Reprinted with permission.

broken chair? When should the oil be changed in the car? Where is the best place to buy a new washing machine? What kind of machine would be best? How do you get from one place to another? When guests come, how do you prepare some drinks that might be requested? What must be done to ready the house for winter? Which are good places to go for a vacation? How do you get there? Where do you stay? What have you enjoyed and not enjoyed in previous vacations?

So many things I had learned and that had made me feel like a competent person seemed to have been lost, and I wondered if I could be an adequate husband, father, or worker again. Combined with this, I felt to some extent that I had lost my identity. This was not total or extreme, but there were some questions in my mind about beliefs, values, and purposes in life. In addition, I felt that I had lost some of my cultural background when I had difficulty remembering some of the customs, traditions, and beliefs of the groups to which I belonged. This produces a feeling of being somewhat alone.

Short-Term Memory

This information about short-term memory function was collected in a 2-week period in April 1975, 6 months after the cardiac arrest. I carried pencil and paper and wrote down each indication of memory difficulties. The information is organized into five categories: Cognition, recreation, living, interpersonal relationships, and personality.

A. Cognition

Organization of thinking was hampered. Problem solving often involves the organization and reorganization of data. The sequences or the relationships of the data must be coordinated, but I had trouble keeping the facts in mind which made it difficult to organize them. Sometimes I had decided beforehand that a particular fact or idea was important and must be included in making a decision, but then the idea was lost, or if written down, the importance of it was lost. Sometimes this resulted in the usual organic confusion.

To problem solve effectively, it is important that all the variables be included and the way things have worked in the past be considered. But the history of the variables may be lost and then some of the variables to be considered may not be remembered and included. Deficits in past and present memory combine to make it difficult to think in an orderly way. Too much is missing.

Then when you are on the track of something, any distraction can cause a loss of train of thought, and that means you need to start over again. Of course many distractions come from the outside, but many distractions can be inner. The difficulty in remembering and thinking is constantly in your field of awareness, and it often intrudes as you are thinking. Once again the train of thought is broken and you go back to the beginning.

Difficulty in conceptual thinking has been considered a hallmark of some types of organicity. Sometimes it was hard to think conceptually, and it was easier to deal with things at a concrete level. But it appears that memory is a crucial part of conceptual thinking. How is it possible to organize, to see similarities and differences, or to extract the essence from a variety of objects or events when you cannot keep the objects or events in mind? Comparing things along a number of variables is difficult to do when you cannot retain the variables or retain the comparison after you have made it.

Therefore, thinking becomes a real effort and sometimes there is no reinforcement if you lose the product of your labor by not remembering the conclusion or decision you have made. It is difficult to exclude negative thoughts when you are faced consistently with evidence that your memory is poor. These thoughts act as a distraction and they interfere with the train of thought. The slightest distraction may mean that you have to remind yourself of what you are thinking. Soon you become reluctant to reason something out. What's the use? You decide that you can't do it, so stop thinking and accept the simplest solution.

B. Recreation

The memory (or cognitive) problem interferes with the ability to understand and enjoy a variety of activities.

Movies and TV watching become work. If it is a story, the trouble is remembering the beginning of the story or who the characters are. If it is a complicated plot, it is hard to follow or understand. Even if it is a simple plot, you may be puzzled about the people together in the second act if you forget that they smiled knowingly at each other in the first act. And you can't enjoy the story by talking about it with friends because you don't remember enough about it to talk about it.

In terms of sports on TV there is trouble remembering which team is which, which team is ahead, which players did the scoring, and how it all relates to their past performance. The thrill of the moment is still there, but part of the excitement is relating it to past performances and to the situation as a whole. Some of those things are missing, and missing also is the pleasure of sharing these experiences with friends.

Reading becomes difficult (partly because of a perceptual problem) because the meaning of some words has been lost and rereading is necessary to remember what already has been read even in the same paragraph. Rereading is also necessary because the ideas that are being expressed may not be understood since the sequence of thoughts can't be kept in mind. Especially difficult were complex and scientific materials, often because the words or terms were understood but they could not be related to other things. The terms or words lacked the richness of meaning they once had.

Playing games, once a pleasure, also became work. The game enjoyed most in the past was a form of duplicate bridge. Memory and cognition are crucial in bridge and it became difficult to remember things like the bidding sequence, the meaning of some bids, what has already been played, what is still out, and the strategy decided upon to play the hand.

Sight-seeing also becomes a chore. I had trouble remembering where I just was and what I had just seen. Seeing the sights had less meaning because I had trouble relating them to the history of the place or to other places. There was some joy in rediscovering places I had previously visited, but with new places, and some of the old ones, the unfamiliar stimuli were confusing and the awareness of the memory problems intruded on the pleasure of being on a vacation.

C. Living

This section relates to a number of activities that have to do with daily living and that were hampered by the memory deficit.

Directions, geography, locations, and the way to get around were difficulties that recurred. Even inside a building, getting lost was commonplace, and sometimes it took days for me to figure out and remember how to get out of a building. In taking walks, even in a familiar neighborhood, I could get lost. In taking a bus, I occasionally would get on the wrong bus or get off at the wrong stop. Remembering the right bus number was difficult. I started driving again about a year after being discharged from the hospital, and at first I needed to get instructions and directions from others on how to get to places not far from where I live.

One role in being the 'man of the house' is being able to take care of some things that have to do with the operation of the house or the family. It was difficult to play that role. Taking care of financial matters was especially difficult. I couldn't keep in mind information about interest rates, types of accounts, types of stock, or bonds, and I kept forgetting what my family already had in terms of these things. Since my arithmetic and spelling skills were hampered, I was reluctant to take over responsibility for things like paying bills, filling out the income tax, or dealing in any way with finances.

I never had been especially competent at repairing or building things, and the memory problem made it even more difficult. There was trouble remembering where things were kept and how things were used. Simple things like how to tie a tie or change a razor blade had to be relearned. Things that were slightly more complicated were relearned, but there was difficulty retaining new learning. I had trouble remembering where things were kept or where I put them to use them later. Losing or misplacing things was a regular occurrence.

Sometimes I didn't remember if I had already done something, like on two occasions I wasn't sure if we had had dinner yet. Dates, phone numbers, license plate numbers, and addresses were hard to keep in mind. Sometimes I wasn't sure what day of the week it was.

D. Interpersonal Relations

Having conversations could become a trial. Often in talking with people I was acquainted with, I had trouble remembering their names or whether they were married or what our relationship had been in the past. I was worried about asking how someone's wife is and finding out that I had been at her funeral 2 years ago. So there was the worry of saying the wrong thing to people, and this made me cautious and reticent in my interactions with others.

But there were other reasons to be reticent. Often if I didn't have a chance to say immediately what came to mind, it would be forgotten and the conversation would move to another topic. Then there was little for me to talk about. I couldn't recall much about current events or things I read in the paper or saw on TV. Even juicy tidbits of gossip might be forgotten. So in order to have something to say, I'd tend to talk about myself and my 'condition.' My conversation became rather boring.

Interacting with others often made me anxious because I would worry about appearing too organic or might act inappropriate in some way. I was reluctant to make a suggestion for fear that it might be inappropriate. I was fearful of making a promise to do something because I was worried I might forget to do it. So being quiet and playing it safe became the watchwords.

E. Personality

The terms that best describe me during this period are passive, dependent, self-conscious, and withdrawn. But none of these was to an extreme degree. I was active in many ways and I stayed involved as much as I could stand it. But in comparison to the way I used to be, I became a narrow, passive, dependent person.

I was less confident that I could handle things so I resisted trying some things or getting involved in some things. I was more cautious than I had been, and I waited for other people to suggest things. There was more dependency on others and more expectation that others would take care of things. There was less willingness to take responsibility or to make decisions. Along with this was a tendency not to speak my mind, not to stand up for what I thought.

Also there was less involvement with friends and family. It was hard to follow up on things that had been planned, it was difficult to know what role I should play, and there was an unawareness of how to participate in things. In whatever I was doing, I was repeatedly reminded of how poor my memory was, and this led me to pay less attention to what was happening around me. Often I was locked in self-preoccupation, and too often this increased my degree of depression.

But on the positive side, I also became more sympathetic, more accepting of things, and more patient. This became more possible because at that point I wasn't supposed to be assertive or responsible or productive.

Recommendations for Patients and Therapists

Following are some of the things that I have learned that seem important in rehabilitation work with patients with memory problems. Of course, many of these may be important in rehabilitation for a number of different kinds of problems. First, some suggestions for the patient:

1. It is important to stay involved in things. It is easy to withdraw because of the difficulty and embarrassment of being involved with people. The embarrassment will come when you do not recognize or remember the name of someone you have known well. More embarrassment comes when you ask someone how his wife is, and it turns out that she has been dead for 3 years. Anxiety comes when

you are asked a question or to do something you have been able to answer or do before. Also, it is uncomfortable to be with a group of people and to have nothing to say. But you do need the stimulation, and you need to prevent yourself from withdrawing into a state of self-preoccupation. The stimulation helps bring back old memories. These old memories have not been erased, but the problem is how to retrieve them. Being involved helps.

2. Do try things even though you feel that you won't be able to do them. Of course, try things that are at a lower level than you were able to do before. Try again a few weeks later, and then try again. Realizing that you now are able to do something you couldn't do before is very encouraging.

3. Do try to find some things you can do fairly well. It is important to feel competent at some things, even though those things may not be related to your previous work.

4. Write everything down. If you do want to remember something, make a note of it as soon as possible.

5. Keep notes on your progress. It is important to keep progress notes because you will not remember what it was like a few months before. By keeping the notes on what you have and have not been able to do at a particular point and then at a later point, you will be able to see the progress. The steps in improvement are very small and slow, and you will not be able to recognize the improvement unless you have notes over time.

6. Do not try to conceal the memory problem. If you do try to conceal it, you will be even more anxious, and you may do some ridiculous things in trying to cover it up.

7. In conversations, you may feel that you don't remember something, but the first thing that pops into your mind is often the correct thing. Take a chance. Say it.

8. Do not keep thinking you will be returning to the same level at which you were previously. Set some smaller goals for yourself, and think about some things you might want to do and be able to do in the future. If it turns out you are able to do more, that would be a happy surprise. But if you set larger goals, you are likely to become depressed.

9. Read some success stories of people who have overcome intellectual difficulties (Moss, 1972), and read some books on training memory (Lorayne & Lucas, 1974).

10. Say 'be patient' to yourself every time you find you cannot do something. You must wait; things will be better.

11. Accept the difficulty of things and learn to live with the anxiety you feel when you try to do things. Tranquilizers may be helpful. Things will be easier, but this will change slowly, very slowly.

References

Lorayne, H., & Lucas, J. (1974). *The memory book*. New York, NY: Ballantine.

Moss, C. S. (1972). *Recovery with aphasia*. Urbana, IL: University of Illinois Press.

Parkinson's: A Patient's View

SIDNEY DORROS[3]

Parkinsonism does not suddenly attack its victim. It sneaks up on one—slowly, quietly, but inexorably. Its initial signs are so subtle that Margaret Bourke-White, famous *Life* photographer, in writing about her heroic battle with parkinsonism, referred to the first evidence of the condition as a "wisp of a symptom" (Bourke-White, 1963, p. 359). In her case it was a slight dull ache in her left leg which she noticed when she climbed stairs.

In my case it was a slight ache in my left shoulder and then a hint of a tremor in my left arm while raking leaves on a beautiful Indian summer day in October. I attributed the ache to fatigue; my wife thought I wanted to avoid an unappealing task—and we both thought little of it. But the ache in the shoulder did not leave with the leaves of autumn. So I consulted a physician, an internist. He diagnosed the condition as bursitis and suggested a shot of cortisone.

"It only hurts when I do something like rake leaves," I told him. "I'd rather quit raking leaves than risk the possible ill-effects of a drug as strong as cortisone." "Hmpf," he snorted, "I can't do anything else for you."

When I told my wife about it, she too said, "Hmpf!" But she did do something to help my shoulder. She raked leaves. That was the first of many burdens that she took on as the symptoms of parkinsonism gradually stooped and stiffened me.

When my fingers began to lose their nimble touch-typing pace, I thought it was due to typist's cramp. When my wife pointed out that my shoulders seemed to be more rounded than usual, I thought I was too tired to sit or stand up straight, or perhaps I wasn't getting enough exercise, or maybe I just had bad posture habits. I would often get impatient, nervous, restless, or irritable, which surprised my family and friends. This too was attributed to fatigue.

It was our family physician and friend, Bob Jones, who first recognized that I had symptoms of parkinsonism. Bob was an ideal general practitioner —broadly knowledgeable, considerate, and available. He lived in the community he served, and he even made house calls. He dealt with the patient and his or her idiosyncrasies, not just the ailment. He had a zest for life that was infectious.

During a routine physical checkup, I told Bob of the slight ache and tremor in my left shoulder and arm. He noticed that I didn't swing my arms freely when I walked, that my movements were a bit slow, and that my facial expression was somewhat frozen; but he didn't announce these observations at the time.

"You may have a neurological problem," he said. "I'd like a neurologist to check you out." ...

About a week after the initial examination, I got the diagnosis from Bob Jones. He took the time and exercised his skill to minimize the trauma when he broke the news that I had parkinsonian symptoms. He said that the ailment follows many different courses, and that some cases progress very slowly, or arrest themselves, or are limited in their symptoms. He told me that I didn't require any medication at the time but that there were medicines and exercises that could alleviate the symptoms considerably.... Superficially, I went along with my designation as a parkinsonian, but deep inside of me a voice said, "It can't be!" And for nearly a year, I really didn't accept the diagnosis....

As I returned home from Bob's office, I wondered why I still doubted the diagnosis of parkinsonism. I remembered that ever since early childhood, I had harbored a secret desire to accomplish something memorable in service to mankind. Suddenly I understood. I had been afraid that by accepting the diagnosis I would lose all hope of realizing this dream.

I've since come to believe that many other people, for reasons of their own, carry within them equally strong drives and aspirations. These strongly affect a person's reactions to a chronic ailment such as parkinsonism and need to be recognized, understood, and somehow accounted for by the patient and those who wish to help him. This is not easy when the motivations are well hidden....

I began to get symptoms that were noticeable to others. Slight tremor in my left hand was the first perceptible sign, but this could usually be temporarily alleviated or obscured by moving my hand and arm about or by resting my hand on some surface at the appropriate angle and level. My handwriting also became noticeably smaller and uneven. Sometimes I would have difficulty walking, especially after standing or sitting still for a while. At other times, I would be unable to lift either foot. I felt frozen to the spot. But I soon developed a strategy for breaking the ice. I would kneel down and pretend to tie one of my shoelaces. This movement usually loosened my muscles enough to enable me to step out when I stood up. After a while, though, friends began to wonder out loud why I had to tie my shoelaces so often.

Like many parkinsonians, I was reluctant to tell people that I had the ailment. However, when I thought that they were noticing and wondering about the symptoms I did try to tell them the cause as matter-of-factly as possible. I learned that people often misinterpret some of the symptoms if they don't know their origin. When I told them about my illness and its effects, it eased some of their concerns. For example, I remember one time while I was interviewing a candidate for a position in the Publications Division of NEA, I got the feeling she was becoming tense. I told her, "I have a chronic ailment of the nervous system called Parkinson's disease which affects my facial expression. So if I appear to be frowning at you or at your papers, please remember that I'm not really frowning. It's just tight muscles." ...

Despite the tribulations I endured during the ... years ... when parkinsonism first became a serious problem and ... when it became almost intolerable, I resisted accommodation to limitations imposed by the ailment. Instead, I tried desperately, in the words of Dr. Oliver Sacks, "... to transcend the possible, to deny its limits and to seek the impossible ..." (Sacks, 1974, p. 226). That is, I tried to conduct my life as if I were not ill. My efforts to transcend the impossible resulted in a vicious cycle. The more I ignored my limitations, the greater those limitations became. . . .

I hit new lows: physically, mentally, and in key human relationships that eventually forced me to accommodate to reality—to adjust the style of my life to the conditions of my life.

I was pushed deeper into the valley of despair by pressures at home and at work. At home my wife's buoyant spirit and emotional support weakened as she herself became overwhelmed with problems. About that time her period of menopause began, bringing with it physical discomfort, emotional upset, and depression. I have known women to have been pushed into depression by any one of the problems Debbie faced: adjusting to four independent-minded, adult and teenage children; living with a husband whose frustrating, mysterious illness often made him seem a frightening stranger; and experiencing the trauma of a difficult menopause. Yet most of the time Debbie was able to cope with all three situations at once. Friends and relatives, and even her own children, hardly ever saw her lose her cool. . . .

But while Debbie appeared to be laughing on the outside, she was sometimes bitterly crying on the inside. . . .

It was during this period that we changed from sleeping together in a double bed to sleeping in separate beds. Perhaps it doesn't seem so serious for husband and wife to sleep in separate beds. Many spouses do it all their lives. But Debbie and I were lonely, isolated, and frightened by the separation. After nearly twenty-five years of togetherness, each of us came to feel rejected by the other. How then did it happen, and why didn't we remedy the situation when we became aware of its implications? Partly because the situation grew slowly and unplanned and partly because it was accompanied by emotional crises that were too strong to overcome.

I previously described the problem of restless nights. At first I used to return to bed, but as the problem continued I found it increasingly difficult to get back to sleep. I was plagued with fears and restlessness, especially in the dark. Debbie was a light sleeper and my tossing and turning disturbed her. We both sought the security of sleeping in each other's arms, but my compulsion to move was too frequent for her to be comfortable. . . .

I had become so emotionally unstable that I would fly into rages upon slight provocation. Despite my wife's tremendous patience and support over a period of years, as my frustrations grew I would blame her for not being sensitive enough. . . .

I found it increasingly difficult to concentrate for long periods of time or to make decisions. It was difficult to tell whether my illness, the side effects of the medication, or emotional reactions to life's problems were responsible.

At work, I found dealing with personnel problems and changing organizational and operational conditions increasingly difficult. When asked to draw up a reorganization plan for the publishing function of the organization, I reorganized myself, with the approval of my supervisor, into a consultative position entailing hardly any administrative responsibility. . . .

The most difficult part was getting to and from the office. The twelve-mile drive became too much for me, or too scary for my car pool associates, and so when my turn came someone else drove. But then a new problem arose. I would often have difficulty walking out to the car or getting from the parking garage to my office. I could sometimes make it only by running. A friend would go ahead of me to clear the way, or follow carrying my briefcase. I was fortunate to have such good and patient friends. Some days they would wait for me because I could not make it to the auto and had to rest or wait for my medication to work. When I had such a bad day that I felt I had to see the doctor on an emergency basis, or just couldn't bear to be at the office any longer, they would take me home early. . . .

"If you get a lemon, make lemonade."

As we learned to adjust to retirement, we found some advantages in my relief from the pressures of time and responsibility. Retirement enabled us to enjoy our lives more, to cope more effectively with my ailment, to improve our relationships with our children, and to render increased service to others. Like many other couples, Debbie and I had feared that too much togetherness might break our already strained marital relationship. However, within a year after retirement our love and respect for each other began to increase. After more than twenty-five years of frustration over differing attitudes and habits on a few crucial matters, we began to accommodate to each other. My adjustment to retirement was aided also by the introduction of a new medication that increased my ability to function—not enough to resume remunerative work—but enough to improve my roles as husband and parent. . . . I tried to arise, eat, move my bowels, exercise, and go to bed at regular times.

I also tried to stick to my schedule for taking medication more rigidly than in the past. Instead of taking emergency doses of medication when I felt unable to move, I took emergency rests. . . .

Norman Cousins has publicized the idea that if negative emotions produce negative chemical changes in the body, positive emotions may produce positive chemical changes. . . .

He asks, "Is it possible that love, hope, faith, laughter; confidence, and the will to live have therapeutic values?" (Cousins, 1979, p. 35). I can attest that they have. I believe it's been love and the other positive emotions listed above that have sustained me as much as medicine since the loss of my wife. First, memories of our love and faithfulness to each other for thirty years helped counteract the grief I continued to feel and still feel over her death. Then, just as new medications have appeared to rescue me each time I have come near the bottom physically, new sources of emotional support came forth when my morale needed boosting.

In addition to the increased attention from my children and other relatives and friends, members of the Parkinsonian Society provided an important source of emotional support. When the leader of a well-financed but differently organized local Parkinson program in another state came to visit PSG\V; he observed: "You don't have as much money to work with as we do, but you have a much more important ingredient. You have love!" But all the emotional supports mentioned above did not keep me from experiencing many hours of loneliness and depression.

References

Bourke-White, M. (1963). *Portrait of myself.* New York, NY: Simon & Schuster.

Cousins, N. (1979). *Anatomy of an illness as perceived by the patient.* New York, NY: Norton.

Sacks, O. (1974). *Awakenings.* New York, NY: Doubleday.

9

Somatoform Disorders

INTRODUCTION

In somatoform disorders, patients or clients report symptoms of physical illness or medical conditions that cannot be explained completely by tests or on a physiological basis. The symptoms cause distress and/or dysfunction and do not occur voluntarily or intentionally. The symptoms are experienced as real by the person and are not a result of a substance or another mental disorder. Because of the nature of complaints about physical symptoms, people with these disorders are frequently seen in medical settings. People with somatoform disorders engage in hyperbole and high drama about their symptoms. Their medical history often is vague, and symptoms shift and change. Even after extensive diagnostic procedures have been performed showing no physiological basis for the symptoms, clients/patients still insist on physical causes of what they are experiencing (Maxmen, Ward, & Kilgus, 2009).

Somatization disorder involves a pattern of somatic complaints that begins before age 30 and occurs over several years, causes distress or dysfunction, or leads the person to seek treatment. This is a complicated disorder to diagnose. Each of the following must occur: pain symptoms related to four different body sites or functions, two gastrointestinal symptoms other than pain, one sexual symptom other than pain, one pseudoneurological symptom not limited to pain. Additionally, the symptoms cannot be explained by a medical condition or substance, or the complaints or dysfunction are more than would be expected from the medical condition. *Undifferentiated somatoform disorder* requires there to be unexplained physical complaints for at least 6 months that do not meet the criteria for somatization disorder. *Conversion disorder* is characterized by symptoms or deficits that are not explained by, but do suggest, a medical or neurological condition. These impact voluntary sensory or motor functioning and are judged to be related to psychological factors. Pain is the key feature of *pain disorder*, but its onset, maintenance, level of severity, and worsening are thought to be influenced by psychological factors. *Hypochondriasis* is the fear or obsession that one has or might have a serious disease that is founded on an incorrect judgment about somatic symptoms or bodily functions. And, finally, *body dysmorphic disorder* involves misperceptions about a deficit in one's physical appearance that reach the level of obsession and result in distress and/or dysfunction.

This chapter presents three first person accounts (FPAs) written by people experiencing the symptoms of somatoform disorders. Fredric Wertham composed his classic personal narrative in reflection on the borders that lie between the physical and the psychological. The anonymous author of the next first person account provides a look into the world of bodybuilding when it takes on pathological proportions. In his description of "bigorexia," the author details his struggle with muscle dysmorphia and the impact it has on his life. And, finally, Heather Menzies Jones paints a classic picture of hypochondriasis in her humorous narrative about the disorder.

QUESTIONS FOR REFLECTION

How do the personal accounts in this chapter touch on similar aspects of the human condition? How have the experiences of having these disorders affected the lives of those involved? Can you identify the strengths that each author possesses? In what way might society contribute to these disorders?

REFERENCE

Maxmen, J. S., Ward, N. G., & Kilgus, M. (2009). *Essential psychopathology and its treatment* (3rd ed.). New York, NY: Norton.

A Psychosomatic Study of Myself

FREDRIC WERTHAM[1]

The method of introspection has much against it. In the first place, the number of cases is restricted to one, if the observer is the same. In the second place, there are many sources of error. We all have a certain image of ourselves, and what does not fit into that picture we may overlook in any introspective efforts. For example, one may not want to admit that one is afraid and so may overlook the many disguises of fear. This source of error is even greater if one wishes to communicate the results of the introspection to others. There is also the complicated problem of amnesia: some things that seem to be genuinely forgotten may be recalled very clearly when—as the lawyers put it—one's memory is "refreshed." All these sources of error are particularly great when the borderline of the abnormal is reached. Yet no one can deny that certain psychological phenomena are open only to the introspective method.

While I was in the hospital with a severe physical illness, I began early to dictate my mental experiences and at the same time noted my interpretive comments. The background for my interest in this psychosomatic study is a great deal of work as psychiatric consultant in general hospitals. In such work I have found how important it is that certain psychopathologic syndromes in physical disease be diagnosed very early. It is sometimes difficult in severe cases or in postoperative cases to distinguish minor transitory mental symptoms from beginning stages of more serious syndromes, such as depression or delirium. But from the point of view of prompt and proper therapeutic steps, it is very important. I believe my own introspective experiences during the course of a severe physical disease are significant for the practicing physician and also have some importance for the theory of psychopathology.

Some of these experiences of mine, which I would classify as distinctly abnormal, have never been described from inside. The so-called phenomenological school of psychopathology promised us such studies, in general and theoretical articles, but has actually furnished little that is valid or

[1]From "A Psychosomatic Study of Myself," by Fredric Wertham, 1945, *Journal of Clinical Psychopathology and Psychotherapy.* Reprinted with permission of the Association for the Advancement of Psychotherapy.

practical. No psychiatrist has ever recorded his own abnormal mental experiences, with the exception of the cases of *cerebral vascular accident* described by Forel, *hallucinations* related by Kandinsky, and Cajal's discussion of his *arteriosclerosis*.

I developed a thrombophlebitis in the right leg without known cause during a period of excellent health and activity following a vacation. Under the treatment of a private physician, I followed a course of complete bed rest for about three weeks. Then, what was evidently a small pulmonary embolus was followed within a week by further pulmonary emboli. Altogether there were probably three or four. I developed a high temperature, took sulfa drugs, lost all appetite, and became very toxic. When taken to the hospital, I was in a very critical condition. Within a few hours after reaching the hospital, I had an emergency operation, a ligation of the right femoral vein. The same night a course of penicillin was begun. Owing to the fact that the thrombus extended very high and that there was an anomaly in the location for the blood vessels, which were deeper than usual and differently placed, the operation was more difficult and lasted longer than usual. It was carried out under local anesthesia, preceded by scopolamine, 1/150 grain, and morphine, 1/6 grain.

I deliberately refrain from giving complete surgical or medical details of my case history. They are not pertinent to the points I want to make here. The emphasis is more on the qualitative aspects than on the causative aspects of the mental state. It would be difficult to isolate the causes exactly. High fever, a general toxic condition, and possible scopolamine toxicity were present.

As far as emotional factors are concerned: before the operation, when one embolus followed the other, during the operation and immediately after it, I was in danger of death. As a physician, I should have known that merely from the objective medical symptoms, which I understood intellectually. It should have been even clearer to me when the director of the surgical service came from some distance to perform the operation at once as an emergency on a Sunday afternoon; and when the head of a medical service also came, on a Sunday afternoon, to see me at once. Moreover, I remember the serious faces of some of my medical friends who were there at the time. But I interpreted their concern as sympathy with the pain the emboli were causing, and at no time before, during, or within a few days after the first operation did the idea even remotely enter my consciousness that I was critically ill or in danger of dying, as I now know I definitely was. One might call this a protective mental amblyopia.

My experiences confirm the generally known psychological law that one is apt to forget unpleasant experiences and remember pleasant ones. Two factors have become clear to me with regard to this amnesia. In the first place, pleasant or indifferent experiences are forgotten, too, in such circumstances as severe physical disease. Secondly, there are two types of amnesia: forgotten experiences that cannot be recalled even when one's memory is refreshed, and others that are recalled easily. I have been told of some more or less indifferent things, which I said that I have completely forgotten. I have been told of others which I seem to have forgotten but which I immediately recalled.

For long periods of time during the first operation, I was in a state of sleep, or at any rate without full consciousness. At other times I was fully awake and clear. My main concern was with pain. It seems to me extraordinary how much I have forgotten about this pain (now, many weeks later). But I have not only a distinct memory of the pain; I have also the notes to go by which I dictated soon after I got a little better.

At times during the first operation I suffered great pain. When I had this pain during the operation, it filled my whole mind. There was literally no room for anything else. It is difficult to verbalize these pain experiences. For considerable periods when I was clear, there would be no pain at all. Then suddenly it would come. On account of the danger of further emboli, spinal anesthesia was contraindicated. As I understand it, the deeper structures are less accessible to local anesthetics, and certain types of pain, like that of actual ligation, are not susceptible to complete anesthesia at all. It is hard to describe one's emotional reaction to pain. It is partly a fear of more pain to come, of its continuing or getting worse; partly a hope that pain will cease—which, of course, it often did—or lessen, the *"speranza di minor pena"* that Dante wrote about.

During the first operation, I was emotionally reduced to a most primitive level of hope-fear. My attention was focused on concern with my body. Freud made a well-known statement about the distribution of "libidinal interest" in physical illness: "It is universally known and seems to us a matter of course, that a person suffering organic pain and discomfort relinquishes his interest in the things of the outside world, insofar as they do not concern his suffering. Closer observation teaches us that at the same time he withdraws libidinal interest from his love-objects: so long as he suffers, he ceases to love. The sick man withdraws his libido back upon his own ego, and sends it forth again when he recovers."

It is true, according to my recollection, that my libido certainly was withdrawn to my body and that my interest in the outside world was decidedly restricted to what had direct bearing on my immediate situation. But in the midst of the operation, during a period when I was either anticipating pain or enduring it, I asked one of the physicians standing near me to find my wife downstairs and tell her everything was going fine. This preoccupation must have been very strong, because after this physician had carried out my request and told me about it, I asked him the same thing again some time afterward. This would indicate, in the light of my experience, that Freud's formulation is an oversimplification of the very complicated levels and processes of emotional thinking. One functions on several levels at the same time.

During the periods when I was conscious and there was no pain, my intellectual capacities were greatly reduced. Some medical friends were standing near me during the operation. (I was separated by a screen from the operating surgeon.) On a number of occasions they talked to me in an effort to cheer and encourage me. Most of what they said was away over my head. I simply did not understand, though I heard the voices very clearly and was aware of their words, the finer modulations of their voices and their friendly intent.

The contrast between my keen awareness of the modulation of voices and my lack of intellectual understanding of what the voices said astonishes me now. At that time, however, the fact that I did not understand most of what was said to me caused me neither surprise nor anxiety. It seemed to me self-understood. For example, one doctor remarked to me—and I recognized the friendly, humorous tone—"just like a psychiatrist, you are constituted peculiarly." (He was referring to the anomaly in location of the blood vessels, which caused prolongation of the operation.) Ordinarily this is the type of joke I would enjoy, but I understood then neither the joke nor the meaning of the sentence. Yet I took it for granted that I could not understand and asked no questions. It was as if I were a child or an infant among grown-ups.

Mannheim, an author who made experiments with scopolamine upon himself, mentions among other things, "deterioration of comprehension and of intellectual performance." My experiences throw a clearer light on the nature of this disorder of comprehension. Toward the latter part of the operation the anesthetist removed the gauze that was over my face, because she felt I was getting too warm. As I looked sideways I saw a large clock on the wall. I remember distinctly what was in my mind. I thought the operation was lasting very long and I was fervently hoping it would be over soon. I thought I would read the time on the clock, figure out at what time I had gone up to the operating room, and then I could figure out about when the whole thing would be over.

When I looked at the clock, I saw numbers in a circle. I recall particularly the six and the seven. I said to myself that the position of the numbers on the clock—at the top, the bottom, or the side—had a meaning for telling time. But I could not figure out how. I remembered that each number meant something. But I was not sure how one picked a special number. I do not know whether or not I saw the clock's hands. At any rate, I did not comprehend that they pointed to the numbers. According to my recollection, I spent considerable time trying to comprehend this clock. What surprises me now is how indifferent I was at my inability to solve it. I have no recollection of any anxiety in connection with this lack of comprehension. My attitude was: This is the sort of thing well people know about, and it is quite natural that I don't.

Neither did it occur to me that the whole problem I was working on was meaningless, since I had no idea of what time it was when I had been taken to the operating room, and since I had no way of knowing, in any event, how long the operation would continue. Diagnostically, my inability to read the clock was a form of agnosia. Agnosia is a symptom that we know best from organic lesions in the occipital lobe, such as occur frequently, for instance, in carbon monoxide poisoning. I could recognize the object, know its name, differentiate its details; but could not apperceive it as a whole nor make use of its function. I conclude from this that definite disorders of the higher processes of perceptions, such as agnosia, may be a component of the disorder of comprehension in scopolamine intoxication.

I remember only two factors that alleviated my general feeling of insecurity while on the operating table. One was the voice of the operating surgeon and one was the reassurance derived from definite physical contact. The surgeon's voice was deep, calm, and authoritative. It was not raised at any time. One episode was characteristic of my mental state. I developed a very disagreeable pain in the right calf during the operative procedure. Somehow it seemed to me that this was due to my leg's "falling asleep," as if it were in an awkward, hanging position from the knee down (not true, of course).

I remember that several times I moved the leg, seeking to ease its position—not exactly an appropriate behavior in the situation. I recall very distinctly the surgeon's voice saying quietly but definitely: "Don't move your leg, Dr. Wertham." My emotional response to this remark is difficult to describe. From that moment on, it was unthinkable that I should move my leg, however it felt. The remark had such an authoritative effect on me that—pain or no pain, impulse or no impulse—the idea of moving my leg did not come up again. I would venture the speculation that the building up of the ideal ego in the very young child or infant comes about by a mechanism comparable to this response.

The second factor alleviating my insecurity was even more unexpected. Words spoken by medical friends present at the operation—even words that I understood—had relatively little helping effect. But physical contact did have. One woman physician who assisted at the operation had to lean over me in such a way that she touched my arm. I remember her asking me at one time whether I minded that she had to lean over my arm and my reaction of astonishment at the question. I tried to figure out how to tell her what great help it was to me. But in my overanxiousness to make it clear to her, I could find no words at all. Much later she asked a second time and then I asked her to stay as she was. (She was actually performing a difficult, prolonged task of retraction.)

Another woman doctor present at the operation touched my forehead once and said something, and I remember her touching me as a soothing event. Evidently friendly physical contact of this primitive type is not sufficiently recognized as a helpful procedure. I have since spoken to physicians who have undergone operations or performed them and they have confirmed my own experience in this respect.

My general mental condition during the operation and during the next two days and nights was much the same, with very little interest in the outside world. What preoccupied me most was what I would call pressures within the body. I had the typical postoperative difficulty in urination, a great difficulty of peristalsis, with gas formation, and some difficulty in breathing. All these pressures, as far as sensation goes, seemed to combine into one.

If I tried my best to answer a question about what my mood was during this period, I could not answer. One young doctor who gave me penicillin said, "In those days you were in the carrot stage." But the facial expression—mostly on account of pain—was apparently one easily confused with that of depression. As a matter of fact one young physician said when he saw me again a few weeks later, "Well now you're not gloomy anymore." This shows a type of misjudgment important for the psychiatrist who does consultations in a general hospital, and for the general practitioner. Actually, I was then in a stage far below that where there can be such clear-cut differentiated emotions as depression with a content of intellectual worry.

At no time during this period were there any delirious or delirioid features. But one evening I thought I was confused. When the nurse who had looked after me following the operation came on duty the next day, there seemed to me something strange about her. I was not sure whether she was the same person or not. She looked different, and I remember thinking that maybe I was mixing people up. I asked her. She laughed and said: "I just had a permanent wave." And so I was reassured. While such comparisons should not be carried too far, the whole condition I have been describing invites one to view it in analogy with the mental state of a very young child who lives in a world of adults who talk of things he does not understand, hears words not always comprehended, reacts quickly to modulations of voices and physical comforting.

While I was still in a very serious physical state and a very reduced mental state, I had a dream. Later I interpreted it very slowly by free association[1]. When I woke up from this dream, it seemed it had a great significance for my life. Only a fragment of this dream and its interpretation are of interest here:

> I was talking to President Roosevelt. There was a question of what kind of speech he should make. I advised him to make about the same speech he had made a year ago, but to leave out the introduction. He took my advice, but added that he'd have to make an introduction, which would take at least an hour. I advised him against this introduction. He offered me a cigarette. I told him I do not smoke.

Complete interpretation even of this fragment would be too long here. At first my free associations to Roosevelt seemed to lead me nowhere.

---

[1] Dr. Emil Gutheil aided me in the interpretation of the dream and my associations to it.

Suddenly I realized that the President in this dream symbolized a man who had lost the use of his legs but carried on successfully despite it. In the dream, my being with the President was a grandiose idea; no less a person would do. In addition, further to exalt my ego, the situation is one in which he seeks my advice and I tell him what he should do. Obviously there was a compensatory mechanism at work at a time when my ego was crushed. This mechanism meant a rallying of the ego. Such compensatory dreams in response to physical insult have been discussed by Ferdern.

The question of offering me a cigarette is a sign of cordiality; my saying that I do not smoke was tantamount to saying that I was a "good boy." Actually, I had stopped smoking over a year before. The doctors who examined me in the hospital and had great emotional interest for me had brought up the question of smoking. There is also the angle that in the dream I tell myself: Suppose I can't ever walk again; I can shift my abilities to the intellectual sphere to make up for what I will lose in the physical sphere.

From the many ramifications of this dream, one more part has to be mentioned. I had this "recovery dream" while I was still very ill. But if this interpretation so far is correct, there would seem to be an interesting error. With me only one leg was affected, whereas with the President there were two. As a matter of fact, on the basis of slight sensations there, a vague fear of phlebitis in the other leg had been in my subconscious mind. In other words, this compensatory dream came at a moment when I feared the worst. The dream said: "Even then, it won't be so bad."

Soon afterwards thrombophlebitis did become manifest in the left leg, and femoral ligation was carried out in that leg too. Before the operation I received scopolamine, grain 1/100 and morphine, grain ¼. The second operation also presented some complications and lasted longer than usual. My mental state during this operation was so abnormal that it deserves description. While my *feeling* was one of insecurity, apprehension, and at times great pain, I *expressed* a general euphoria.

I remember the very beginning of the operation and my general apprehension. But some time later I can still hear myself addressing the operating surgeon (whom I could not see): "I feel very frivolous, Dr. D." This was a most abnormal statement to make. In the first place, I had and have the greatest respect for this surgeon and would not address him like that—certainly not during an operation. In the second place, I would say that "frivolous" was about the last word that would describe my mental state at that time.

From then on throughout the operation I laughed, told all sorts of funny stories, and made puns. For example, I said, "I am against all -isms, especially embolism," and when during the operation I heard the pathologist ask for a specimen of my vein for biopsy, I asked the surgeon not to give out any "free samples!" A considerable number of my medical friends were present in the operating room. They laughed at my jokes and told funny stories of their own. It all sounded very gay. On many occasions during this operation, I suffered terrible pain. I tried not to show it but could not help contorting my face and exclaiming "Ouch!" on a number of occasions. Anybody who did not see my face would have thought I was having a good time. One nurse, on the other side of the screen during the operation, told me later: "You were so cheerful and took it all so easily. I have never seen anything like it."

This state of mind has to be differentiated from that of a manic or hypomanic condition. It is characteristic of a manic that he thinks things funny that are not funny at all. My jokes and puns were funny, and would have been appropriate had the situation been different. I also laughed heartily—and at the right moment—at the stories of others. There was no flight of ideas and no simple sound associations. An example of the puns I made: The pain after the first operation was relieved greatly by Demerol. So I said during the second operation: "I have a new slogan. Don't get demoralized; get Demerol-ized."

Towards the operation's end, I suffered particularly severe pain during the litigation of the larger vessels. As I recall it, I was really in agony. At that worst moment, the internist who had been most aware of my actual pain, and helpful about it, saw my contorted face and said, "Anybody can tell stories like you did. *Now* is the time to tell us a really good one, and from your life as a psychiatrist."

If I had been asked whether, according to my best psychiatric judgment and according to my best knowledge of myself, I would have been able to tell a funny story at that time or whether I could have forced myself to smile at anything then, I would have denied it without hesitation. Yet fully preoccupied as I was with pain, I immediately told a story with great gusto and with all embellishments. This was the story. As a young doctor at Johns Hopkins, I spent a vacation with a psychotic millionaire and his male nurse at a lodge in New Mexico. We had all our meals together in the general dining room. I observed that when the waitress served us, her hands trembled noticeably. After a few days of this, I asked her whether something was wrong. She said: "Well, it's like this. I know one of you is crazy, but I don't know which one it is!"

There is evidence here of clear dissociation between actual mood and behavior. On the whole, my insight into my general condition was very poor. I did not think of my behavior as being caused by a drug, although intellectually I might have guessed that. Yet I evidently had lucid moments with psychological insight. For instance, at one moment I said to the surgeon, as if to excuse my "frivolity:" "What I am really doing is whistling in the dark."

The term *euphoria* does not cover the whole of my behavior, because at times I spoke seriously of serious things. In response to remarks made by physicians near me, I made true but indiscreet comments on the treatment of mental patients in New York, and specified where I believed the responsibility lay.

There were a number of things that I thought I'd only had in mind but which I was later told I had said aloud. There was also an incident where I *did* something, which according to my memory I had only thought and talked about. When the operation was over, I thought of getting up from the operating table, walking across to the stretcher (which I thought was across the room), and getting up on it. This was a complete misunderstanding of the situation. I was in no condition to get up and the stretcher was right next to the operating table. I learned later that I actually attempted to sit up with this purpose in mind, and I lay still only when told to do so and actually held down by a physician. A few hours after the operation, I returned to my normal state of mind and realized how abnormal my behavior had been.

The mental condition during the operation was a form of scopolamine psychosis. It was characterized by euphoria, overtalkativeness, general lack of inhibition, euphoric misjudgment of the situation, side by side with more-or-less clear consciousness of apprehension and pain. There were no hallucinatory, delirious, or dream-like experiences. This particular form of scopolamine psychosis with such a dissociation within the mental life, I have not seen described before. It is probably only by self-observation that such a contradictory psychological syndrome can be delineated, but it can be diagnosed objectively.

Actually the euphorization of my behavior was a great help. What did it accomplish? It seems to me that it counteracted the anxiety that was undoubtedly present. While telling jokes or listening to them, I was distracted from anxiousness and the strain of experiencing pain. Such a contrast between euphoria and anxiety occurs in experimentally induced mescaline psychosis, as shown by the retrospective accounts of subjects.

With regard to the subject of pain and analgesics, some of my observations are significant. I believe that in studies of pain, the threshold of pain is too much emphasized. Actually, the *quality* of pain is very important. I could, after this operation, have enumerated six or eight different kinds of pain, each distinguishable from the other in quality. To express them in words would be impossible. Had I given each of these pains a number as they occurred, I believe an observer would have found that I could have identified, by its number, the special type of procedure by its accompanying kind of pain.

Some of the qualities of pain are:

1. *Localization.* Some of them I could not have localized at all; some I think I could have indicated exactly.
2. *Duration.*
3. *"After-image effect."* I use this for want of a better term, because some kinds of pain continued even after I knew they were over. This is comparable to the phenomenon of after-images and eidetic images in visual perception. Such phenomena are easier to investigate in the sphere of vision, but they also exist in other forms of sensation. It is possible that this type of pain refers to a more primitive, undifferentiated kind of sensation. Just as in the physiology of the special senses we know that there are phenomena between vision and visualization, so there is an analogous phenomenon in the sphere of pain-perception. I call this "eidetic pain" and believe it is of considerable significance in psychosomatic medicine.
4. *Special qualities of pain,* as when a nerve is touched.
5. *Association with fear.* Some types of pain seem to be more associated with fear than others.

If psychological factors play a great role in physical disease, as I believe they do, it may well be indicated to stimulate the productive activity of patients in the early stages of their physical disease. I believe that my interest in dictating these observations at the time—they were much more detailed than this paper would indicate and the paper itself was written during my hospital stay—helped me to rally the recuperative forces of my organism. As Heine said:

> It was disease—the truth to tell—
> Which gave impulse to my creation.
> Creating, I got better.
> Creating, I got well.

From a practical point of view, this study shows that there are definite and diversified psychiatric aspects of physical disease. Physicians are apt to neglect such experiences, but they are a grim reality. The psychopathological aspects of physical disease demand and deserve attention. They may make the difference between life and death.

Medical and surgical patients need psychological advice about how they should act, what their experiences mean. They need psychological preparation for what to expect. They need guidance so that they can make the best of the possibilities. As a physician, I was less handicapped than the general patient in coping with these experiences.

All these psychological and psychopathological features of physical disease are part of medical and nursing care. It is a problem that can be attached along three levels: The first is the part of the nurse. The second is that of the medical man and the surgeon. The third is the part of the psychiatrist, who should be available for the diagnostically doubtful, the more severe and prolonged abnormal manifestations. Here is one phase of psychosomatic medicine, which can be put into practice immediately without waiting for further investigation. Only in this way can psychiatry be really incorporated into a general hospital.

It is now five and a half years since my illness. During all this time I have never had any desire, speaking of operations, to tell anybody the story of mine. Apparently I got that all over with in writing the paper. But I have made use of my experiences in my psychiatric consultations in general hospitals. I have become more and more aware of how much can be done by psychotherapy for patients who have physical diseases. For one thing, the psychiatrist can help to prevent anti-psychotherapeutic actions in a hospital. It isn't so easy to know what a doctor should or should not say to a very sick patient, especially in the operating room. But it is a safe rule to assume that the patients are apt to take anything wrong. For instance, a postoperative patient recalls: "One doctor said to me, 'You don't have a thing to worry about.' I thought that was silly. I wouldn't have been there if I wasn't worried about it, if you get what I mean."

I did not include in my original paper some of the discouraging remarks made to me by friendly doctors visiting me during my illness. Dictating them soon afterward evidently helped me not to be upset by them. But it is what I call anti-psychotherapeutic for doctors to say, to a critically ill patient, things of this sort:

- "It's very common. It's nothing to worry about. I've seen hundreds of these cases at autopsy."
- "Sometimes there's no embolus at all. Sometimes there's only one. I had a patient with just one. It was in the arteria centralis." (Such an embolus causes blindness.)
- "Of course the edema often becomes chronic. But then it gets better with a spinal block. I had a case just like this where the edema lasted fifteen years."
- "Usually these cases get better. Of course there's always a percentage that become chronic."
- "In the beginning we doubted your ultimate recovery. But now we think you really have a chance to pull through."

None of these comments upset me, or had any bad effect on me so far as I recall. I evidently was not alert enough to take them in and was reminded of them later only when I was dictating my notes. One medical remark, however, did sink in and stayed with me for a long time. A physician explained to me that phlebitis in the legs is not so bad; but it can happen that the arms also are affected. As a result of this remark, I began to have—or thought I began to have—peculiar feelings in one arm and then the other. I remember that I was very anxiously concerned about this, watched whether the feelings got worse and thought at times that they did. Evidently the position in which one lies in bed for a long time has something to do with it. Here, evidently, a chance remark induced a hypochondriacal trend of thought that I would not have had spontaneously.

In psychiatric cases in general hospitals since then, I have often noticed that patients were more concerned with something they feared or fancied than with their real illness. It is probably not easy to prove that a good mental state aids recovery while a bad mental state impedes it. But I am sure that, especially in old people, both chronicity and fatal outcome may be conditioned by an adverse emotional attitude caused by the family or the hospital or both.

The concept of "eidetic pain," that is, the assumption of a more primitive type of pain not clearly circumscribed or localizable either in space or time, has proved useful to me. It is never superficial, never brief, and is apparently related not only to the deeper structures of the body but also to deeper psychological layers. It may be one of the avenues for understanding certain forms of so-called imaginary pain. Amplifying or enlarging the scheme of Guttman and Mayer-Gross (in their *Psychology of Pain*), this classification may be useful:

- overwhelming pain;
- severe pain;
- sharp, short pain;
- negligible pain;
- eidetic pain.

After speaking to many patients with physical illnesses, and comparing their reactions with mine, I am convinced that organic and neurotic symptoms may be subjectively experienced in the same way. Some men cannot urinate in a public place. Their experience is very much like the organic difficulty following operations. Such a physical difficulty may become easily neuroticized. Appropriate and simple psychological methods, which many good nurses know instinctively, can make an enormous difference in the course of a physical disease.

Strange though it may seem, we physicians are apt not to acknowledge the tragedy of pain. Even though I no longer remember clearly my pain experiences, I still have with me the realization that it is easier to be philosophical about death than about pain. Death is the transition from biochemistry to chemistry, but one can't make wisecracks about pain. As scientific physicians we want to find causes, trace processes, cure, and prevent. But every patient who comes to us has at the back of his mind a simple and what you might call primitive or infantile wish: He wants the doctor to alleviate his pain and banish his fear. That is where medicine and psychiatry meet.

Bigorexia: Bodybuilding and Muscle Dysmorphia

ANONYMOUS[2]

I guess I've always been fixated with my body shape. As a kid I was scrawny and I used to envy the popular athletic boys on the rugby team. I began lifting weights when I was about 14, using this tiny multi-gym in the school lunch hour. I discovered I was pretty strong for my size and quickly I began to see results. My mates and I used to mess about on the back seat of the school bus, flexing our biceps to try and impress the girls; pretty soon [*sic*] found I had the biggest arms, it made me feel good about myself.

When I arrived at university I got into boxing in a big way. My coach encouraged me to diet down from 70kg to 57kg in my first year so that I could fight as a featherweight. It was a ridiculous thing to be doing to my body but that was the only way he would let me compete. Basically, I had to live on a diet of Slim-Fast milkshakes, whilst still keeping up this six day-a-week training routine of running, sparring and weightlifting. I became fixated on food; after a hard training session I wanted to eat a big plate of pasta like other normal sportsmen, but I had to content myself with an apple and protein shake! I checked on the Internet and my new weight made me officially anorexic, which was something I was actually proud of at the time because it proved how hard I'd had to work.

Each session I concentrate on a different body part; for example in a given week I might work chest on Monday, back on Tuesday, legs on Wednesday, etc. Splitting the different muscle groups lets me really blast each one and allows me to train more regularly without getting fatigued. For each muscle group, I have a repertoire of exercises that I've picked up over the years, just from watching other bodybuilders and from reading magazines. I find which ones work for me and stick with them, but I'm always looking to incorporate new techniques so as to shock the muscles into growth. I have a little notebook in which I chart all the exercises I do and the weights I lift, so that when I analyse my workouts I can see if I'm getting stronger.

[2]From "Bigorexia: Bodybuilding and Muscle Dysmorphia," Anonymous, 2008, *European Eating Disorders Review, 17,* 191–198. Copyright 2008 by John Wiley & Sons, Inc. Reprinted with permission.

I definitely think about how the weights I'm lifting are going to affect my appearance. For example, I might choose to train legs twice per week if I feel my quads are lagging, or change the angle of a bench press so that it accentuates my upper chest. I'm very serious about my training; if I haven't pushed myself to the limit then I feel like I've wasted my time. If the gym is crowded and I can't complete all the exercises in my program then I get really irritable.

When I'm bulking I always try to keep my muscles supplied with protein and carbohydrates so they can grow. Each day I'm aiming to eat 3 grams of protein for every kilogram of my bodyweight, taking a meal every couple of hours to keep my muscles topped up, even if I'm not hungry. When I'm in a cutting phase I'll restrict my carbohydrate intake to almost nothing so as to lean up and make my muscles stand out. I read about this carb-cycling diet in Flex magazine, which some of the top pros use to help them shred body fat. It does involve controlling every gram of carbohydrate that you take in each day, which is frankly almost impossible, but I try to follow it as best I can. I do prepare all my food in advance so I can be sure I'm getting clean calories and I never have to fall back on junk food from the cafeteria. It is really hard to keep this kind of diet up and maintain any kind of normal life, but I persevere because that's what it takes to build the kind of body I want.

I've done three cycles of steroids in the past year. I don't see it as cheating, because everyone else in the gym is using them and besides, even on gear you still have to put all the hours in at the gym and stick to the same diet, they're not magic. I know steroids are bad for you in the long run but frankly I'm not that bothered about how healthy I am in twenty years; I want to feel good about myself now. And are steroids that much more unhealthy than living off junk food like most other men my age? Those people are messing up their bodies too.

The medical profession is always very quick to highlight the dangers of steroids, but I reckon that's motivated just as much by some puritanical desire to control what people put in their bodies than by hard fact. My doctor knows no more about anabolic steroids than the average man on the street whereas I've read up on all the different chemical structures of the various steroids, how they get metabolised in the body and all the side effects, so I've educated myself and I feel I've reduced the risk. Although when I came off my last cycle I got really depressed and even felt suicidal for a few weeks, which really worried me. But I don't want to stop juicing now because I've seen the results and I don't want to lose that edge.

Bodybuilding is my life, so I make sacrifices elsewhere. I'm always thinking about the nutritional content of food and how it would affect the way I look, so I can never eat out at restaurants or go to a friend's for dinner because it would mess up my diet. And I spend so much money on stuff like protein-powders and fat-burning pills that I have no money left to go out drinking; to be honest I don't have that many friends anyway. Not enough time for them. I often arrive to work late or leave early because I have to train, and even when I am there my mind is always on my next meal or gym session. I guess my ideal job would [*sic*] to be a personal trainer, and then I could just live in the gym.

Do I have a problem? I guess so. I sometimes wonder what the point of my life is. I work so hard at my body but underneath I still hate the way I look. In my mind I know I am bigger than most of the guys on the street but I still feel inadequate. I don't like undressing in front of my girlfriend and I don't enjoy sex because I'm too busy worrying about the way I look. Even just looking at my body in the mirror when I come out of the shower makes me feel horrible.

Hypochondria

HEATHER MENZIES JONES[3]

I wrote this piece in the late 1990s after living in the north of England for six months while my husband was on sabbatical. References to Mad Cow Disease and its human equivalent seemed to be everywhere at the time and provided me with a rich source of stomach-lurching terror. Heather Menzies Jones

I am a hypochondriac. I am not proud of this fact but I think it is part of my genetic make-up, for it is a trait I share with my father. I write for other hypochondriacs and the people who struggle valiantly to live with them.

If, dear reader, you are also a fellow sufferer, I know only too well what you have been obsessively worrying about for the last month and a half. You

---

[3]From "Hypochondria," by Heather Jones, *Confessions of an Upstate New York Mother,* 1996. Reprinted with permission.

have been turning the pages of your memory, back, back, back, and you have been trying to figure out just how much British beef you could have possibly consumed during the last decade. I know you have been doing this, because it is what I too have been doing. My worry has been fueled, no doubt, because my family and I did spend six months in England in 1989 and I have tried to piece together every meal I cooked in that six-month period. That bit of ground beef, it all seemed so innocuous at the time. While we were in England the only food items *they* were worried about were salmonella eggs and listeria-laden cheeses, not the beef. I think of those meat pasties and sausage rolls, so many consumed and all of dubious origin. Why, why, why?? Could we have eaten the flesh of a mad cow? Could our family be stricken sometime in the future with Creuzfeldt Jakob disease? Even now, when I forget a name or a telephone number, I feel that panicked realization that my brain is already sponging up and will soon have the consistency of a Nerf ball.

My hypochondria took a significant upward spiral three years ago when I actually did come up with something that could have been serious, and fatally so. If you are also a hypochondriac, you will know the answer to the following question immediately. If you are not a fellow sufferer, think carefully about your answer because it should be obvious. Just what one disease or condition would give the average, garden-variety hypochondriac the daily wobblies and nightly sweats? What one organ does everyone have miles and miles of? Skin of course. On that skin what does the average person have plenty of? Moles. These moles are at the crux; they are the matrix for much hypochondriacal musing. Has that one changed? Does this look irregular to you? Is that one darker?

My hypochondriac's nightmare assumed reality when a mole on my leg turned out to be melanoma. I couldn't believe it. Hypochondriacs worry so much and yet usually nothing ever turns out to be anything; I was dumbfounded. That wore off quickly enough, and I wish I could report to you that I reacted to my doctor's news with calm equanimity. I truly wish I had accepted his diagnosis with magnanimous grace and had not grabbed his white coat lapels and demanded that I be allowed to live to see my precious babies graduate from high school.

The dermatologist told me that I would have to have my entire birthmark removed and he looked at me kind of peculiarly when I asked if he would be doing that procedure himself in his office. After I had the surgery done at the hospital I know why he looked at me as though I were nuts. The surgeon must have used an ice-cream scoop to get at that birthmark. The stitches were these big, thick, black affairs and there were many of them. The bandage was huge and I realized a career as a leg model, while never in the cards before, was definitely out now. Some months later my trendy sister-in-law saw my leg and said, "cool scar." I shot her a withering glance and realized that I, as an uptight, prissy, PTA mother did not want a "cool" scar. What I wanted were long, lean, tan, suburban legs.

I spent the week after the surgery worrying about the biopsy report. To divert myself a bit, I decided to plan the readings for my funeral. My family and I attend a Unitarian Universalist church and if left up to someone there, I would be eulogized by having our parish minister read *Goodnight Moon* or something dreadful like that. I decided to write some extemporaneous words my husband could memorize beforehand and thereby rouse the congregation to weeping levels found in African American churches. I abandoned this effort when the thought of Bill saying things like, "she was the beacon of light shining in my life," or "I will never, ever, love another woman as I have loved Heather and will spend the rest of my days as a celibate father immersed in the raising of our three children" simply didn't ring true. I spent the rest of the week thinking about all the women who would make great future wives for Bill and wonderfully superb mothers to the kids. I know there are women in our acquaintance *now* who think Bill is poorly served by his present companion. To boost my flagging spirits, I decided to turn my trauma into art and wrote a short story about a woman who sees malignancy in everything around her: the brown spot on the apple, the eye on the potato, and the little red dot on the top of her electric curlers turning to black when heated. The biopsy report came back and it appears that I'll be able to see my children in cap and gown unless, in the poetic words of my dermatologist, I'm "hit by a bus first."

Americans adore the silver lining and there was one exquisite moment during this ordeal. It occurred when I called to tell my hypochondriac father that I had melanoma. I absolutely love it when people close to me behave in completely predictable ways. My father, true to form, spent perhaps thirty seconds making soothing parental noises about how everything would be okay and how much he and my step-mother would be thinking of me. I had my watch out and had to stifle a laugh because I had been eerily accurate about just how long it would take for him to begin to muse aloud about whether or not *he* should be checked out at the dermatologist's and about the mole *he* had been worried about recently. We ended the conversation by my giving him words of bucking up and encouragement. I happened to call him on a Friday at his place in the mountains in North Carolina, far, far away from his retinue of doctors in Charlotte and virtually not able to make any medical appointments until after the long weekend. It was immensely cheering to think of someone else whom I love writhing in obsessive panic about the possibility of having skin cancer. Hallmark should come up with a card for this.

Now that I have inched my way back a bit from the yawning abyss, I have a word of advice for those suffering from something serious. I had heard people can be unwittingly undiplomatic when responding to bad news from another, but like so much else, you don't believe essentially well-meaning people can say such numbingly stupid things until the horrible happens to you. Be judicious upon whom you spring crummy news. There were some people, who upon hearing about my melanoma, gave me detailed lists of people who had died from the same thing I had. I have one friend who grew up in Southern California and let me tell you, her list was prodigiously long! One friend grilled me about past sun exposure and whether or not I had ever used sun-block. My gynecologist, to cheer me up, said, "Well, Heather, statistically speaking, you're much more likely to die of breast cancer." Someone else breezily said, "They must have caught yours early because otherwise you'd be dead." No matter how tempting it is to fill someone in with grisly stories you've heard of their recently diagnosed illness, resist the temptation, literally hold your tongue if you have to, strangle out a "That's too bad," and leave it at that.

We hypochondriacs are a quirky group. I know I don't read many women's magazines and it's not because so many adopt such an irredeemably inconsequential tone about anything truly mattering in life. I don't read them because they all seem to feature an account written in breathless first person about a "disease of the month." These stories all employ the familiar trope of using hypernormal beginning gambits like: "It was just a regular, sunny day here in Pasadena when I heard the piercing shouts from the guests around our pool," "Nothing really was wrong, little Angelica just didn't seem to be herself, I thought she was only teething. Little did I know the diagnosis would be leukemia," etc. etc. I can't stand them; they are too similar to my own pulp fiction turn of mind.

Finally, I shall leave my fellow hypochondriacs with this: remember, if you are a woman, your primary care physician's level of respect for you will plummet dramatically if you ask him about the advisability of having a PSA test done because you are experiencing all the symptoms of an enlarged prostate. Sometimes it is helpful to learn from the mistakes of others.

10

Dissociative Disorders

INTRODUCTION

More than one piece of literature or film has portrayed characters with the symptoms of dissociative disorders as part of the story plot to create suspense or to illustrate the dramatic impact of early childhood trauma on the development of psychological problems. Many of us remember Gregory Peck in *Spellbound* (1945) as the lead character who has amnesia—and how the film's engaging plot was built around it, with Ingrid Bergman as the dedicated colleague and lover who insists on his illness and innocence. Those of us who have seen *Three Faces of Eve* (1957) will never forget Joanne Woodward's Oscar-winning portrayal of Eve, a woman who has a "split personality"—and Lee J. Cobb as the psychiatrist who helps her. Sally Field won an Emmy for her performance as a young woman with split or multiple personalities in *Sybil*, a made-for-TV movie based on a shocking but true story. Today, these problems would be classified under the *DSM-IV-TR* section on dissociative disorders, with little being said in the manual about the etiology or origins of them.

What are dissociative states? Are they always a sign of pathology? Most of us from time to time have had a few moments in which we blanked out or spaced out when someone was talking to us or we were listening to a lecture or a speech. This seems normal enough, and we might not remember what was said or done, but we are aware of this lapse in attention. The *DSM-IV-TR* defines dissociative disorders as disturbances in the normally integrative functions of consciousness, identity, memory, or perception that cause distress or impaired functioning (an exception is dissociative identity disorder). Dissociative states that are acceptable and common parts of cultural, spiritual, or religious activities, practices, or experiences are not viewed as pathological if valued and shared by the group involved. Examples of these such as a stupor, trance, or spirit possession are plentiful.

Dissociative amnesia is characterized by an inability to remember important personal information most often of a stressful or traumatic nature. The memory loss is beyond that of common forgetfulness, is not due to the direct effects of a medical condition or substance, and cannot occur only during the course of any of the following disorders: dissociative identity disorder, dissociative fugue, posttraumatic stress disorder (PTSD), acute stress disorder, or somatization disorder. The memory loss can be of a variety of subtypes (e.g., selective amnesia, in which the sufferer can recall only some of the events during a particular period of time). Finally, the symptoms must lead to distress and/or difficulties in functioning. *Dissociative fugue* is an interesting and unusual disorder that involves unexpected and sudden travel away from home or a work setting during which time the individual cannot remember his/her past. There is either confusion about one's identity or the assumption of a new identity. The symptoms cannot be the result of a medical condition or substance use/exposure, must cause distress or dysfunction, and are not happening at the same time the individual meets criteria for dissociative identity disorder. This describes precisely the character that Gregory Peck played in *Spellbound* in which he appeared as the new director of a psychiatric institute but had no memory of his past.

Dissociative identity disorder probably is the most well known of the dissociative disorders because it used to be called multiple personality disorder. Rather than an individual having two or more separate personalities, it actually involves identity fragmentation. Two or more distinct personality states or identities take over the control of behavior of the individual, who frequently cannot remember critical personal information from one identity to the other. The switch from one identity to another usually is triggered by stress and often happens quickly, within a matter of seconds. The symptoms cannot result from a medical condition or a substance. Both Eve and Sybil suffered from this curious, rare, and difficult-to-diagnose and -to-treat disorder.

Depersonalization or the experience of feeling detached, removed, or estranged from one's self is not an uncommon occurrence, but *depersonalization disorder* is. In this disorder, the individual has ongoing or recurrent episodes of depersonalization in which he/she feels like an outside observer of his/her mental processes or body including the feeling of lack of control over actions or speech. Derealization or the feeling that the external world is unreal or strange can be present. The size or shape of objects may appear altered, or people may seem unfamiliar or strange. For the diagnosis, the symptoms must cause marked distress and/or impaired functioning and not be caused by a medical condition or substance. Depersonalization is a symptom common to many other disorders, and the disorder is not diagnosed if it occurs solely during the course of another *DSM* disorder (e.g., schizophrenia, panic disorder, acute stress disorder, other dissociative disorders). But the disorder also can co-occur with other *DSM* disorders (e.g., depressive disorders, anxiety disorders, some personality disorders, hypochondriasis, substance-related disorders).

Amnestic disorders need to be differentiated from dissociative amnesia and amnesia that may be part of the symptom profile for some people with other dissociative disorders. Learning and remembering new information is not part of these memory problems. It is the inability to remember specific stressful or traumatic events that characterizes memory loss in dissociative disorders.

The authors of the three accounts in this chapter describe their experiences with the signs and symptoms of dissociative identity disorder (DID). It is not unusual that one of them mentions being diagnosed with other disorders because often DID co-occurs. Ruth Dee focuses her story on the coping mechanisms she has used at different times in her life. First and foremost was her ability to dissociate automatically during the trauma and abuse she experienced from age three. As an adult, she used a rigid set of coping strategies to keep up the pretenses of normality even though she knew something was drastically wrong. Eventually, she became depressed, and then had a breakdown. It was then that she got professional help that has given her the support she needed to recover. Having been diagnosed with PTSD and DID at age 49, Barbara Hope uncovers in therapy that she was sexually abused by her father. She discloses this to her four children and apologizes to them for leaving them with her alcoholic husband but learns that for the family to heal she must forgive herself. Robert Oxnam's personal narrative tells of the 11 separate identities within him that developed through dissociation during his experience of severe trauma in childhood. Through therapy and the process of integration, he now has only three. But he continues with the work of "putting Humpty Dumpty back together again."

QUESTIONS FOR REFLECTION

How does dissociation used as a coping mechanism by these authors differ from the coping strategies they have developed in their recoveries? How has this disorder impacted their families and their lives? How are the symptoms described in these accounts similar to those of anxiety, phobias, or obsessive-compulsive disorders?

Coping Strategies

RUTH DEE[1]

Coping strategies are essential to any persons survival in daily life. They are even more important to us in times of stress and mental illness.

I believe that the majority of us are born with coping strategies and then adjust and further develop them throughout our lives. For me, coping means being able to have as great a quality of life as is possible at the time, to maintain good relationships with my family and friends, to be integrated into my community and to feel life has a purpose. I also want to be as independent as possible, to feel I can do things with less and less support from family, friends and professionals.

I began to use the coping mechanisms that I believe we are all born with at the age of three to survive mentally and physically. I did this without even knowing I was doing it. It was an automatic response to danger. I began to dissociate on a regular basis. We all have the ability do this; for example, it happens when we become so absorbed in a film that we don't notice the passage of time. In a life-threatening situation, like a car crash, we feel as if

---

[1]From "Coping Strategies," by Ruth Dee, in *Voices of Experience,* by T. Basset and T. Stickley, 2010, Hoboken, NJ: John Wiley & Sons. Copyright 2010, by John Wiley & Sons. Reprinted with permission.

we are watching ourselves, temporarily relieving us from the trauma of the event. As children we use this skill often, but lose the ability as we get older as most of us don't need to use it in our daily lives.

I used the coping strategy of dissociating because of severe trauma and abuse on a sustained basis from the age of three. Dissociation allowed me to disconnect my mind from my body. During this dissociative process, thoughts, feelings, memories and perceptions of the traumatic experiences were separated off psychologically, allowing me to continue my daily life as if the trauma had not occurred. As the abuse and trauma were repeated regularly and over a sustained period of time my dissociation became an automatic coping strategy. As it was such an effective coping strategy I used it whenever I felt threatened or anxious.

Dissociation can be as simple as completely forgetting the event, or the personality can separate into different parts. These different parts then become the individual, additional personalities, or 'alters,' as they are often called. However, when the personality has split into different alters, each one can take control of the host. This is called dissociative identity disorder (DID). I developed DID.

The process of developing and living with alters and dissociation is a complicated one and inappropriate to this chapter. However my full story about developing and living with DID can be found in my book *Fractured* (2009).

During my adult working life I had already realised that I was mentally ill but didn't know what was wrong with me—nor did I understand the symptoms and behaviors of DID that I was experiencing; in fact, they frightened me. The coping strategies I had unerringly developed as a three year old had enabled me to successfully progress to adulthood, raise three children, have a good long relationship with my husband and a career as a senior manager in education.

In DID all the feelings, memories and thoughts about the experiences of abuse and trauma are stored in the alters and therefore hidden/shelved from the child's daily memory allowing the child (me) to continue to live as if the trauma had not occurred. My mind developed separate neural pathways to deal with different aspects of the traumatic experiences. Nowadays, brain scans can show this to be an observable reality.

With my DID the memories of my early abuse and trauma eventually started to come through. I began to lose a lot of time—I was unaware of the passage of time and what I had been doing during the hours I had missed—

even though I had apparently still been working. I started to talk out loud to myself, or rather to my alters. I was petrified of being 'found out.' I knew I was mentally ill, but couldn't make sense of my symptoms. I didn't approach my general practitioner for many years as I didn't know what to say. So I had to keep going on my own or completely give up.

At this point I think it may be helpful to describe some of the coping strategies I developed and used to cope with my mental illness at work and to enable me to be able to function generally. It shows that I was able to develop my own coping strategies even though they did eventually fail me. Surely this ability could be tapped into by professionals when I eventually went for help.

I developed a whole range of coping strategies:

- I was embarrassed by the fact that I was talking out loud and was concerned about how it would be viewed by my colleagues, so I always hummed a tune when walking from office to office. People interpreted this as my being happy; and I encouraged this. Humming also kept the internal chatter in my head quieter, allowing me to focus on a single issue.

- I would end up in unknown places when I dissociated when driving home or to a meeting. This really frightened me and I would panic, which in turn caused more dissociation. So I agreed with myself that I would always drive to the next roundabout or crossroads and take the road to a place I knew, even if it wasn't where I was actually going. This calmed me sufficiently to be able to think logically and I could then often read the road map before needing to travel too far out of my way.

- I began to dissociate through the entirety of meetings I was chairing and therefore had no memory of what was discussed. But it was obvious that no one realised that anything was amiss. I was in the fortunate position of having a personal assistant and I insisted that the writing up of meeting notes was a priority. A strong filing system was developed so I had ready access to information that I had missed. My recording system became famous and was often used by my colleagues because of its quality.

- I used memos with all staff at all times. I wrote memos as soon as I knew I needed to see someone or wanted some information.

(I carried them with me at all times at work.) Staff were then asked to bring the memo with them when they came to see me as I knew there was a good chance that a different alter would be in charge and not know what was going on. Because of my elaborate systems, I was considered efficient.

- I developed a relationship with my senior staff and secretaries that they considered eccentric. I had to be lively and outgoing at all times. I also said I had a poor memory and had too much to remember so they humoured me, apparently willingly. I was already humming, so it was easy to build on this. Being seen as an eccentric enabled me to cover up my unusual behaviours, such as talking out loud, forgetting my way round a very familiar building, completely and constantly forgetting the names of people I worked with every day and jumping at the slightest sudden noise.

- I would arrive at a meeting in a dissociative state and not know what the meeting I was obviously supposed to be chairing was about. Therefore, meetings invariably began with my asking people in turn what they wanted to achieve by the end of the meeting. This was usually enough for me to 'catch up.' People also felt they had a substantive say in the outcome of the meeting.

- As my talking out loud to my alters became more erratic and unexpected I had to attempt to cover this up. Initially, I tried to say that I wanted to say something, but this understandably annoyed people as I was interrupting them. So I covered it up by apologising and saying I had thought of something and needed to make a note of it. From then on I always had a notepad with me. I used this to just write down any words I said as I realised that if I did this, I was less likely to lose time/dissociate/switch. I couldn't doodle, as people would think I was uninterested in what they were saying. I therefore pretended to make my own notes.

- An advantage with DID is that the host is totally unaware of stress and tiredness. As a result, my capacity for work was enormous. The disadvantage is that my body became exhausted, but I was unaware of this until my breakdown.

The above coping strategies at work all seem to be very small things, but they allowed me to function as a senior manager in education without anyone becoming aware of my problems. I know I succeeded as, even on the day I left work to enter an acute psychiatric unit, no one even realised I was mentally ill (except the one person I had confided in). I had needed to keep working as it helped me focus, with the result that I didn't dissociate as much and I could keep the raging fear I felt for much of the time at bay. It also gave me a real sense of purpose.

During these years I developed a coping strategy for each little problem that arose. Life seemed to be all about having to get over one hurdle after another. It became harder and harder to cope with my alters and the memories and feelings of the abuse and trauma that had taken place over the first 16 years of my life. I became more and more depressed and dissociative and began to feel I couldn't cope. Finally, I had a breakdown and entered the secondary psychiatric services.

The coping strategies that I had unerringly developed as a child, and that had saved my life, had eventually become inadequate and inappropriate. I had tried adding to them on a daily basis as new problems arose, but I was fundamentally using the same ones. Now a whole new coping strategy was needed. This time I wasn't alone. I had my husband, who was now aware of my disorder and what it meant, and I had a care team who cared enough for me to help me develop new coping strategies. It has been their determination that I should have a good quality life and lead as independent a life as possible that has encouraged me and my husband to develop a whole new set of coping strategies. Unfortunately, it took a complete breakdown to reach that point.

It has not been easy to develop new skills and strategies and there have been many setbacks. In the seven years since the breakdown to the time of writing (August 2009), there have been several stages in developing coping strategies, each requiring a different level of input from professionals. What has been vital to my ongoing recovery is the way my care team have worked *with* me. They have supported me, encouraged me and, at each stage, made it clear they want me to recover and believe that I can. It is their 'we *can* do' approach that has helped me so much. They supported me when I felt I couldn't go on, when each new stage of my recovery was frightening, and they always helped me find a new way through.

I want to spend the rest of this chapter describing a few of the ways in which the professionals in the mental health services helped me develop new and appropriate coping strategies since my breakdown which have helped me progress so far.

The Mental Health Physiotherapist

I was referred to the physiotherapist (the physio) as soon as I entered the acute psychiatric day unit. At this point I was dissociating and switching into different alters constantly. One of the effects of this is to make me feel that I am floating and I can't feel any of my body. The physio initially worked on me so I could gain some level of feeling in my hands and feet. Once I began to gain some feeling when grounded, she worked with me to develop strategies I could use daily to ground myself. I learned to rub my hands together vigorously, to stamp my feet, to feel the arm of the chair that I was sitting in, to feel the heat from a warm drink. (I didn't know to feel these things before.) I would then practise these with the physio there to remind me to do it and then I would go through the activities when I was alone if I needed to 'ground' myself. They began to make a difference and often helped me to stop switching so often. Note that the physio used a graded strategy—first doing the work for me up to my being able to use the coping strategy on my own. I still use it today.

The Mental Health Occupational Therapist

I had once been a very independent woman, but during my breakdown I lost my independence. I wouldn't go out. I was referred to the occupational therapist (OT). I will use the example of catching a bus to my nearest city so I could go to a cafe or shop. Initially the OT visited me at home and we planned what I would like to achieve. On her next visit we went to bus stops, the route the bus would take and then the shops I wanted to visit. On the next visit we took the bus together to the city and stayed in the bus station for 15 or so minutes discussing where I would walk the next time. On the next visit we went on the bus together and then walked round the shops together. As can be seen, she was taking a staged approach of support with me. A few weeks later I caught the bus on my own, did some shopping and came home—I was delighted.

I added some strategies of my own to make me feel even safer—I bought a watch with the day and date on it so I could check this when I was getting anxious and repeat the day, date and time to myself. I would get anxious and would feel as if I was going to switch/dissociate as I was walking round the shops and on the bus. I also used the hand-clapping and foot-stamping strategy to keep me grounded. I made sure my husband's mobile phone number was the first on the speed dial. And I would write on my hands where I was going. In addition, I always take the same route round the city, the idea being that as all my alters use the same route even if I did switch we would all know the way home—it worked for me. Again, a staged approach had been used by the OT from full support in doing something I really wanted to do in order to improve the quality of my life to my being independent.

My Care Coordinator

My care coordinator has always made it clear that in graded steps I could develop new coping strategies. Even during my relapses he has said that I could get through the difficult times and then move forward again. This is an enormous support to me. He gave me hope even in very dark times. The immediate support may be going into a crisis day unit for a while or even onto a ward. This was to help me get through the immediate problems, but we still looked forward to when I could be discharged. He could tell me what progress I had made over the years and remind me what the next steps we had agreed were. I can't stress enough the power of having a professional who reminds me that he believes I can make progress, who tells me often of the progress I have already made, who wants me to be independent and who is there for me when I need support.

Together, we developed an advanced directive that I carried with me at all times as at this point I was often switching into a different alter and getting lost. The directive explained my condition, how to speak to me and whom to contact if I was found. It has worked with the police and the Accident and Emergency department after I had been found wandering. Having this gave me the confidence to try going out. As I am now at a different stage in my recovery we are just renewing the directive.

My care coordinator worked with me on developing a daily chart when I was very depressed. I made a time chart with targets such as: what time to get up and get dressed, when to have a meal, what activities I was going to undertake each day and for how long. It was very practical. I would tick off the things I had done and on his next visit we would look at it together. He was very careful to praise me for what I had achieved and then discussed with me how we could add more of the tasks I hadn't achieved. This step-by-step approach with a chart on my kitchen wall to tick was very motivating.

We have drawn up other working charts for different situations over the years. The charts themselves are a coping strategy.

He also developed a relapse signature with me. We spoke about early warning/sign scale identifiers; marked or daily signs; moderate signs and sources of help. We discussed these over a couple of sessions and then he had them typed up and they are hung on my kitchen wall. Because we worked on it together I feel it is a valuable document. I said what I thought and he raised points for me to consider and to agree to or not. As it holds both our opinions, I trust it.

Another little but significant strategy we have developed together to help me overcome the embarrassment of talking out loud to myself and having people stare at me was for me to wear earplugs. I can plug them into my ipod or pretend I am using my mobile. This really works for me and I feel more able to be in public without being embarrassed all the time.

Importantly, I feel we problem-solve together. He has said often that his role is to enable me to live successfully in the community as well as to coordinate my care. It is the working partnership that looks at problem-solving in a positive way that is so helpful and encourages me to take risks and to develop new coping skills.

The Psychotherapist

It is a little harder for me to describe the new coping strategies the psychotherapist and I have developed together as they are very personal and most are related to my DID. What I can say is that anyone who has DID has a good imagination. They have created a whole range of coping strategies and worlds in their head that has allowed them to survive horrendous abuse. My psychotherapist has used this ability to enable me to cope with the fears my alters held, to bring them into the present and to enable me to communicate effectively with them every day. For instance, when a child alter first expressed her fears out loud in therapy it was frightening for me and for the alter. We both needed a way to cope. Through discussion we agreed that I would create a bubble around the child alter that would inflate and shrink as she wanted. I put a rainbow between her, me, and the past to block it out. I tried to hold this image in my head every time we were scared. Over the next couple of weeks this worked. We were both calmer, and gradually I was able to talk to her and finally she integrated. This may be difficult to understand, but the key points are that my psychotherapist used a strategy that built on my known existing skills; she needed to make sure I could cope on my own and not just when I was with her; she needed to move my knowledge and understanding of my DID along at my pace and with some encouragement to take risks; she ensured that I was in control of the strategy and we worked out one together. After some initial difficulties it proved to be a strategy we have used again and again over the years, though obviously the imagery changes to meet different alters' needs.

She referred me to a sensory-motor psychotherapist to help me through the dreadful fear I felt constantly as we were working through the alters' feelings. This is a period people with DID need to go through. I was still seeing my psychotherapist as I trusted her absolutely and was very wary of the new one. However, by using a sensory-motor approach, which entailed knowing how my body was feeling, what I was thinking and then managing my fears, together we increased my ability to cope with my fears. After six months I was far better able to cope with my fears. She had used my knowledge of my body, added some theory and together we made huge progress. She always gave me the confidence that I could make progress. In this case it was explaining the biological theory behind fear and anxiety that helped to move me on. I then stopped seeing this psychotherapist and continued working with my long-standing one. An important factor here was my psychotherapist's ability to say she felt someone else could better work with me on a particular issue. I didn't lose confidence in her and she was able to make the suggestion in a professional manner.

Later in psychotherapy we began looking at how to manage my DID in the here and now. After much therapy and discussion I now have strategies that enable me to cope far better with my disorder on a daily basis. I can now talk to my alters to ensure each of them has their needs met, that we can live together in relative harmony and each is present at the appropriate times. All of these are essential new coping skills that enable me to live comfortably. They have taken years to develop. It has been the trusting relationship with my psychotherapist that has developed over the last five years that has been so crucial in this. She is there to support me and to challenge me to move forward. She has used the abilities I have and built new coping strategies with these as the foundation. She has ensured I develop coping strategies that allow me to survive in the community and that don't rely on her to work. She ensures I know she thinks I can make good progress, which is so encouraging to me. Above all, she has given me *hope*.

A controversial coping strategy I have is the possibility of suicide. To me it is a logical strategy. If I can't find a way of keeping going, of making progress, and lose that sense of hope, then I could always die. It isn't a dramatic gesture or thought; to me it is realistic. Having this escape route enables me to think about and develop new coping strategies. I can keep going as long as I have an escape route if my quality of life is too poor and I can't make progress. It gives me the strength to keep trying. I want to get well and work hard with my care team and my family to have a good quality of life; having an ultimate escape route—death—helps me. This is difficult for people to understand as suicide is often seen as cowardly, a cry for help, or a dramatic gesture. Nevertheless, it can be seen as something else: a coping strategy.

Conclusion

As a child my body and mind had found an extraordinary mechanism for allowing me to survive unbearable trauma and abuse. I was too young to do this knowingly; it happened automatically.

My breakdown was the start of learning a whole new range of coping strategies. This time I had professional support. I am lucky enough to have a care team who support me to be as independent as possible, slowly, step by step, and always looking to the future with me. At the same time I receive enough support and care when I am really struggling. I believe this model of patient and professional working together is one that may lead people to be able to find new coping strategies, at their own pace.

Whereas in childhood I was unaware that I had developed coping strategies I now *choose* to develop new ones. I use the word 'choose' because it is a choice. No professional can develop them for you; it has to be an active partnership and one where trust exists. It requires real caring and creativity on the part of the professionals to ensure the coping strategies developed together are appropriate to each individual's needs and build on skills they already have. The patient needs to trust the professional enough to take a huge risk and try something new they are at their most vulnerable.

As can be seen from what I have written, the smallest coping strategy has tremendous potential for helping someone in their daily life.

Family Talk

Barbara Hope[2]

In my family of origin, talk was buried under layers of fear and silence. It wasn't until I was 49 and diagnosed as having posttraumatic stress disorder and dissociative identity disorder that I broke through the wall of speechlessness. In the intervening years, mental illness had ripped me from my four young children. My fragmentation, although unconscious, could not bear the weight of child rearing. My mind was lost in visions of a special spiritual mission in the world. Although my children and I managed to maintain our disrupted relationships, I had no words to explain why I left them in our home with their father. Even in the therapy room, speech was beyond my reach. When I once broached the subject of changing the world, my therapist looked at me and said, somewhat sarcastically, "What could you do?" Neither he nor I were able to explore the troubled world that lay within me.

After a decade of community organizing, I returned to school for the study of social work. I learned about family dynamics and unresolved intergenerational pain. With a new therapist, words began to rise slowly in my mouth, words like abuse and violence. I was beginning to make sense of my history and recognized how critical it was to end silence in my family.

As I worked in therapy over a ten-year period, words became bridges that linked my history with the lives of my children. The first disclosures were in 1989. I needed them to know that I had been sexually abused by my father, that what happened to me impacted my mothering of them. I wanted them to know that I left them because my anger and anxiety frightened me. At an unconscious level, I left out of fear that I would hurt them.

We sat around the old family table. Their father was now dead and I could be in the house with ease. I spoke slowly, crafting words strong enough to stand on. My daughters, now 16 and 18, reached out for my hands, expressing sadness that such things had happened to me. My older son, age 24, looked quizzical and wondered what it had to do with him. I said that family secrets divide us, that if we can heal the wounds of one

[2]From "Family Talk," by Barbara Hope, 1999, *Psychiatric Services, 50*(12), 1541–1542. Copyright 1999 by American Psychiatric Association. Reprinted with permission.

generation, they will not burden the next. My younger son, who was 22, rose from the table and hugged me. "My friends tell me that I'm a good hugger; I learned it from you," he said, offering me comfort.

That moment in our lives was deeply painful. I knew that I was telling them that the grandfather they had never known had assaulted me, that his hands reached beyond me to shape their lives. I was also telling them something important about myself, something that they perhaps would have chosen not to know. Despite this pain, I felt convinced that these words needed to be said.

Three years later, my younger son shared with me some poems about his childhood. He wrote about his alcoholic father, the physical abuse he inflicted, and his own rage. I pictured the little boy hiding in the woods to avoid his father—with no one to protect or nurture him. I also remembered how in adolescence he closed himself in his room, unwilling to talk to me. His honest poems gave me the courage to tell more of my story. I disclosed the dissociation and told him about the multiple parts of myself. I wanted him to understand that it was not for a lack of love that I left him, but terrible inner confusions that overwhelmed me. "The family should know about this," he said.

It was difficult to talk about my fragmentation and about the fact that disconnected parts of me were involved in their young lives. I felt ashamed. I had come to understand that inconsistencies in my behavior, confusions in memory, and emotional instability were linked to dissociated alters. I wanted them to know these things. I hoped it would help them come to a deeper knowledge of themselves and an acceptance of me.

My older son was disbelieving, stating that memories could not be forgotten, then remembered. Multiple personality disorder was in the news, along with reports about false memories. The pain of his childhood made it impossible for him to hear my story. By the time I spoke with my older daughter, she had already distanced herself from me in protest against the harm I had done to her. Like her brother, she believed I was making up reasons to excuse the bad choices I had made in my life. Her understandable anger remains difficult to bear, but I have hope that we will someday talk with each other. My younger daughter asked serious questions. She wondered about a link between her depression and my mental illness. I let her know that her depression had a genetic component and that it wasn't her fault.

As the years went on, my multiplicity was never mentioned. At times, my behavior was erratic, but nothing was said. I came to sense that, for them, turning a light on the past was much too difficult to be endured. To speak directly of their mother's mental illness was too frightening. In my profession as a clinical social worker, I listened to clients talk about a parent's mental illness and their fear that they might be "crazy" too. I thought of my children and wondered if they had the same fear.

We have never talked about this matter. I apologized to my children repeatedly, seeking forgiveness for the hurt I had caused. My entreaties embarrassed them, I think. After a while I concluded that I had to forgive myself, a seemingly impossible task. How could I reconcile with the young mother who left her four small children in the care of a father who had a serious drinking problem? I prayed, exposed the problem to the light of therapy, and tried to mother well in the present.

Last year, after a lengthy therapeutic process, I accepted the additional diagnosis of a thought disorder underlying the dissociation. I reached a new level of clarity about my history and myself and saw the limitations that shaped earlier life decisions. I began to hold my parents in a different light, believing that they likely suffered from untreated mental illness.

Forgiveness toward myself, them, and others spread in me like a wild vine. I gradually accepted my own genetic vulnerability to mental illness and the possibility that this predisposition could emerge in family members. More than ever, I felt it was important to talk to my children. If it was difficult to reveal abuse and dissociation, it was even harder to disclose psychosis. The need to tell was heightened by my younger daughter, who showed symptoms similar to my own. I carefully planned the conversation. I talked to her about mixed-up thoughts about myself, others, and the world, as well as intense physiological experiences.

I was also able to tell her about the kind psychiatrist who had treated me and prescribed medication to stop my bizarre thinking. I wanted her to know that medication might hold out the possibility of a clear mind for her as well. My disclosures exhausted and distressed me. I left her apartment abruptly and refused to respond to her phone call. Revealing the secret had been a positive step, but one that I hadn't been ready to make. I fell into bed, shaken by what I had done.

The next day my daughter and I talked about what had happened. She heard me with compassion. As of yet I have not told my three other children about my thought disorder. I am waiting for the convergence of clarity, opportunity, and personal strength. I'm confident that the moment will come, that I will find the necessary words to expose the reality of serious mental illness in myself and in our family. Silence is no longer an option.

Fractured Mind, One Heart?

ROBERT B. OXNAM[3]

All my life, now more than sixty years, I've felt a kinship with Humpty-Dumpty, that hapless egg with human features who toppled from his perch. As a child, I often leafed through my English nursery rhyme book, staring at Humpty-Dumpty, proudly teetering on his wall, a fat little egg dressed as if going to some nineteenth-century London men's club, not a care in the world. There was only one illustration, a "before" portrait, leaving the reader to imagine Humpty-Dumpty's fate after he splatted on the busy roadway below. Perhaps the story was poking fun at pretentious English merchants. Maybe it was to remind us of the biblical verse "pride goeth before a fall."

What caught my attention was not the jolly "before" picture, but rather imagining the terrible aftermath of the fall, with a broken yolk, oozing whites, and eggshell fragments everywhere. It seemed impossible, but I wondered whether "all the King's horses and all the King's men" might find a way to put Humpty-Dumpty "back together again."

I'm quite serious. I thought long and hard about how it might be done. After all, I knew you didn't really need the yolk and the whites. I'd seen those "blown eggs" at Easter time. Wasn't there some way to glue the broken eggshell pieces together and bring Humpty back to life?

Today I understand why Humpty-Dumpty caught my attention so many years ago. Multiple personality disorder (MPD) might just be called the Humpty-Dumpty disease, but psychiatrists now call it dissociative identity disorder (DID). I didn't know that I had MPD until 1990, when a remarkable psychiatrist, Dr. Jeffery Smith, made the diagnosis. Since then, I have met with several other dissociation specialists, mainly as a talking

---

[3]From *A Fractured Mind: My Life With Multiple Personality Disorder*, by Robert B. Oxnam. Copyright 2005 by Robert B. Oxnam. Reprinted with permission of Hyperion. All rights reserved.

case study of an MPD patient. But I want to emphasize that I am neither a specialist in MPD nor a psychiatrist of any kind. What I have learned about the disorder comes from my own experience, from a few books I've sampled since being diagnosed, and from the insights of Dr. Smith.

My name is Robert. I'm one of eleven personalities whom you'll meet in this book. At one time or another, all eleven personalities revealed themselves as part of one human being, officially called "Robert Bromley Oxnam." On the outside, "Robert B. Oxnam" has done reasonably well for himself as a specialist on China and Asia, a published writer of both fiction and nonfiction about China, former president of the Asia Society, professor of Asian history and contemporary affairs.

But that's not the point. I want to be very clear that this is not an auto-biography of "Robert B. Oxnam." This book gives limited attention to what happened in the "outer world"—the world of professional life, family ties, of relationships, of successes and failures. We did not write it to reveal "who did what to whom." Instead, we wrote the book to convey our inner experiences with MPD—surprising discoveries, arduous therapy, and a lifetime of coping.

For those with MPD, these personal pronouns—*I* and *we*—get pretty confusing sometimes. Remember that I told you there were once eleven personalities. Now, I'm proud to say, we have whittled it down to three remaining personalities through a process of "integration." The three who remain—Robert, Bobby, and Wanda—made a joint decision to proceed with this book, and all three of us agreed to very clear rules about how it would be written.

Since I'm the most outspoken in the group, I get the job of "narrator," but don't think for a moment that either Bobby or Wanda is powerless. Quite the contrary, both are potent personalities, as you will discover. Indeed we agreed that, to portray accurately our inner divided reality, each of the eleven personalities would speak in his or her own voice.

So, in one sense, this book represents eleven autobiographies. But it also seeks to capture the constant inner monologues and dialogues that are common with multiple personality disorder. Life inside the world of MPD is filled with squabbles and power struggles, often over which individual personality will dominate on the outside. Since all of the personalities eventually communicated with Dr. Jeffery Smith, the book also reveals the enormous complexity of conducting therapy sessions with an MPD patient.

When Bobby and Wanda first pressured me to narrate this story, I was very reluctant. Imagine the daunting task of narrating the sixty-year history of eleven personalities to an outside world filled with people who have never experienced extreme dissociation. Wanda sought to persuade me with quietly passionate pleas: "None of the rest of us is a writer. It's a story that should be told. It's eleven personalities in search of one soul." But I think it was Bobby, our naughty imp, who sold me. "Robert, you're such a worrywart," Bobby said with a laugh. "It's not such a big deal. Think of it this way. You're the tour guide on the starship *Enterprise*—exploring the farthest reaches of *inner* space."

So, we—Bobby, Wanda, and Robert—all decided that this book would not focus primarily on the "outer world," which was really quite remote from many of us, but rather on our "inner world" of severe dissociation. We do not seek to destroy or protect reputations of anyone on the outside, living or dead, but rather to explore the inner MPD psyche that we have occupied.

But how can readers possibly believe this story? For a while, we all fretted about this issue. We vowed to tell the story as accurately as we could, letting each personality speak for himself or herself. We carefully corroborated our own recollections with the records and remembrances of Dr. Jeffery Smith in the long therapy process. We cross-checked our memories with several of those close enough to have witnessed our multiple personalities firsthand. Finally, we came to believe that we could do no more than that. The ultimate verdict on credibility will rest with you, the reader, after you have absorbed the story.

If this book raises more questions than it answers, then we will consider it a success, as long as the questions are more sophisticated by the end of the book than they were at the beginning. Indeed, it is our hope that you, the reader, will be asking questions throughout—not only about us and our story, but also about yourself and the society in which we all live.

Over the past seven years, I, Robert, have related shortened versions of this story, always on a confidential basis, to roughly a hundred people, either individually or in small groups. With few exceptions, the response has been riveted attention, people often nodding their heads affirmatively as I described various personalities or inner episodes.

When I have asked why they were reacting so strongly, the response was almost always the same. "I'm nodding because it's my story, too. Don't get me wrong. I don't have MPD. But I can really relate to different inner personae. Unlike people with MPD, I don't have memory blocks between those personae, but I act so differently with different people, in different places, at different times." One person elaborated: "When I have a difficult decision to make, I always convene an inner committee meeting. I allow all parts of me to air opinions; that way I know that all of me owns the decision."

I have come to think that a lot of people, possibly all people, have multiple personae. Everyone I know reports feeling differently and acting differently in different places and with different people. Many describe various "roles" or "masks," suggesting that my experience may be an extreme exaggeration of what is normal human behavior.

Probably the biggest difference between "normal multiplicity" and MPD is that most people recall what happens when they move through their array of personae. By contrast, MPD is characterized by rigid memory walls that prevent such recall until therapy begins to break down the barriers. While normal people have "multiple personae," they do not suffer from "multiple identities." In this sense, the new term, *dissociative identity disorder,* is more descriptive of what is commonly called "multiple personality disorder."

So, while acknowledging that my case is extremely rare, maybe the multiple framework is embedded in all human beings. If this unusual tale helps shed some light on what we often call "normal human behavior," then I (and we) will feel both gratified and, to be honest, somewhat vindicated.

For those who have experienced abuse and dissociation, I hope this story has some special resonance. For me, the hardest thing was not suffering severe trauma, but rather suffering a lifetime of consequences—finding out what actually happened, understanding the devastating impacts on my psyche, and, hardest of all, trying to rebuild my life based on hope, trust, and love. All of us inside reach out to all those on the outside who have confronted similar challenges in their own lives.

But we on the inside hardly have the last word on how those on the outside might find our MPD perspectives useful in their own lives. Unlike Dr. Smith, none of us is a professional psychiatrist, and all of us have been distracted from such outer issues. We have been much too busy trying to put Humpty-Dumpty back together again.

11

Sexual and Gender Identity Disorders

INTRODUCTION

Sexuality plays a critical role in human development and is considered an essential part of the human experience. Indeed, some theorists identify sexuality as a central source of one's personality (Russon, 2009). The field of psychology was largely built on notions about how sexual development related to one's psychological adjustment. Freud's psychoanalytic model of human development emphasized the role of psychosexual development and its impact on one's personality.

Today, we recognize that individuals vary greatly with regard to how they express their sexuality. Human sexual activity is complex with biological, physical, and emotional aspects related to its expression. It is recognized also that different cultures express sexuality in many different ways (Barlow & Duran, 2004). What constitutes "normal" sexual behavior? Society continues to struggle to answer this question because what is normal sexual behavior in one culture is not necessarily normal in another culture and because there is such a wide range of sexual practices. More than any other diagnostic category, sexual and gender identity disorders raise the question of when differences should be classified as "disorders." The common criterion for making such a distinction is whenever a sexual behavior leads to impairment in one's functioning.

This section introduces three types of sexual behavior disorders: *paraphilias, sexual pain disorders,* and *gender identity disorders.*

Paraphilias are sexual deviations and include any disorder where sexual arousal occurs in the context of inappropriate objects or individuals. Most people, when they become sexually aroused, are attracted to adult individuals, but some people find their arousal is activated by an object—for example, women's shoes or undergarments. The development of a fetish is an example whereby individuals are sexually attracted to such objects. Other examples of paraphilias include exhibitionism, frotteurism, pedophilia, sexual masochism and sadism, transvestic fetishism, and voyeurism. Paraphilias are not considered to be widely prevalent; however, transvestic fetishism is the most common paraphilia (Bancroft, 1989). The paraphilias are almost always associated with men; the one exception is women involved in sadomasochism.

Sexual dysfunctions are characterized by problems in sexual desire and in psychophysiological changes that cause distress and interpersonal difficulty. The three stages of sexuality—desire, arousal, and orgasm—each can be associated with specific sexual dysfunctions. Examples of sexual dysfunctions include hypoactive sexual desire, sexual arousal disorders such as erectile disorder, orgasmic disorders, and sexual pain disorders such as dyspareunia or vaginismus. One of the most common disorders in this category is hypoactive sexual desire (deficient desire for sexual activity). Some studies suggest that half of all patients seeking help from sexuality clinics complain of this issue, and it appears to be relatively common from community studies (See Barlow & Duran, 2004). Erectile dysfunction and premature ejaculation in males is a fairly common complaint, with estimates of about 4–10% for erectile dysfunction and 36–38% for premature ejaculation. Inhibited orgasm is a fairly common complaint for women, where 5–10% of females never or almost never reach orgasm (Barlow & Duran, 2004). Also, vaginismus, where the pelvic muscles in the outer third of the vagina undergo involuntary spasms when intercourse is attempted, is estimated to occur in 5–15% of women.

Finally, gender identity disorders occur when there is gender dysphoria (discontent with one's biological sex and/or the gender one was assigned at birth). This is not a sexual disorder *per se* but a disturbance in one's identity as a male or female. Individuals who have gender identity disorder often describe their experience as one of being trapped in a body of the wrong sex. Gender identity disorder is different than transvestic fetishism where individuals are aroused by wearing clothes of the opposite sex. With gender identity disorder, the goal is not sexual gratification but the desire to live one's life in a manner consistent with the opposite gender. It is also important to note that gender identity is independent of one's sexual arousal pattern. In other words, a male-to-female transsexual (a male with a female gender identity) may be sexually attracted to females, making the arousal homosexual. The most common treatment is surgery to change a person's anatomy to be consistent with their gender identity. Gender identity disorder is considered rare with a prevalence of 0.001–0.002%. In some studies it has been found as high as 1 per 12,000 individuals (Campo, Nijman, Merckelbach, & Evers, 2003).

Most transgendered individuals have advocated for the declassification of gender identity disorder as a mental disorder given research that has found brain structures and hormones as a key factor in its development. The *Psychiatric News* (2003) reported arguments by Darryl Hill, who contended that the distress associated with the disorder reflects parents' difficulty in relating to their child's gender variance. The issue remains controversial within the *DSM* community.

The first account in this chapter begins with a narrative about a serious paraphilia. The author wrote the story from prison, and he reveals the psychological and social factors that contributed to his masochistic tendencies and led to his criminal behavior. This is followed by an account of sexual dysfunction by a woman who suffers from vaginismus. Interestingly, she describes a new procedure that is being used to treat this disorder. As you read this account of her experience, the distress about having the disorder and her ultimate gratitude in finding a resolution to her problem are apparent. The final two first person accounts (FPAs) are stories about gender identity disorders. Both of these accounts describe the struggle and transformation that these authors have in common as they redefine who they are and establish new lives for themselves.

QUESTIONS FOR REFLECTION

How did these accounts of sexual disorders impact each person's view of him or herself? What theories or conceptual frameworks might be used to explain how people develop sexual disorders? How can variations across cultures and individuals be differentiated from disorders?

REFERENCES

Bancroft, J. (1989). *Human sexuality and its problems.* Edinburgh, Scotland: Churchill Liningston.

Barlow, D., & Durand, V. M. (2004). *Abnormal psychology: An integrated approach.* Pacific Grove, CA: Thompson.

Campo, J., Nijman, H., Merckelbach, H., & Evers, C. (2003). Psychiatric comorbidity of gender identity disorders: A survey among Dutch psychiatrists. *American Journal of Psychiatry, 160,* 1332–1336.

Psychiatric News. (2003). Controversy continues to grow over DSM's GID diagnosis, July 18, retrieved from: http://pn.psychiatryonline.org/content/38/14/25.full

Russon, J. (2009). *Bearing witness to epiphany: Persons, things, and the nature of erotic life.* Albany, NY: State University of New York Press.

SEXUAL PAIN DISORDERS

Vaginismus: The Blessing of Botox

Rachel[1]

I first discovered that I had vaginismus on my wedding night. What a horrible way to start a new life with your husband. My battle with vaginismus was very long and heartbreaking. In the following paragraphs of my testimonial, I will tell you about my journey to finding the "cure" for this horrible disorder.

When I was five years old, I was sexually molested by the husband of my babysitter. I can only remember bits and pieces of the heinous crime, but enough to know that it did a tune on my subconscious mind. Growing up, I never thought that anything was wrong with me because my brain was just blocking all of the painful memories. I never was able to use a tampon from puberty through my adult years; in fact, I still cannot use a tampon. I had always said that I was going to wait until marriage to have intercourse and any other types of insertion ... tampons included. I know it sounds silly, but I had always told myself that the first thing to enter my vagina was going to be my husband. So, I had no doubts that on my wedding night, I would be able to perform. Oh boy, was I wrong.

In January of 2004, I went in to see my doctor and be put on birth control. I was getting married in May and I wanted the pill to be 100% effective by the night of my wedding. I was told after I arrived at the office that a pelvic exam would have to be performed to check for certain things before they could give me a prescription. I was very nervous and upset, but I figured that this was something that I had to do. I had to be a woman. When the doctor attempted to insert the speculum, I freaked out. I began to shake and shiver and break out in hives. I began sweating profusely and crying uncontrollably. It was like I was having a seizure. No matter how much I tried to relax and calm down, my body would not respond. I had not told anyone about the abuse as a child, but it never crossed my mind that maybe this was the

---

[1]Reprinted from www.plasticsurgerypa.com. For additional information, see *When Sex Seems Impossible: Stories of Vaginismus and How You Can Achieve Intimacy*, by Peter Pacik.

reason that I was panicking. My doctor scheduled me for a hymenectomy, for concern that I was anxious over the pain of it tearing.

In March of 2004, I went in for my surgery to remove my hymen. It took about 6 weeks for the area to heal. I was told that once healed, I would have to use vaginal dilators to help loosen the PC muscles and prep my vagina for sex. When the time came for me to use the dilators, I tried once and it hurt so bad that I never did it again. Once again, I went into panic mode and could not even look at my vagina in the mirror without feeling queasy. I went back to my doctor for additional guidance. I was given Ativan (an anti-anxiety medication) and Prozac (an anti-depression medication). I was told to do breathing exercises and I should be fine by our wedding.

In May of 2004, I was wed to my husband. Halfway through our reception, I started to feel very nauseous. I brushed it off and tried not to think about it. That evening when my husband and I tried to make love for the first time (he was a virgin also), I began to react exactly like my pelvic exam attempt. This time, I began vomiting and urinating uncontrollably. My husband tried to get me to try different positions to help me relax a little, but each movement made me even more queasy. I immediately began to think that something was physically wrong with me and that I would never be able to have sex. My husband was so frustrated with me that he rolled over, made a nasty comment, and went to sleep. I cried myself to sleep on my wedding night. It will be a night that I will always remember, but not in a joyful way.

When we returned from our honeymoon, I was scheduled to speak with what I thought was a therapist. We met with her and she gave me the Kinsey 12-step program to read over and utilize. It talked a lot about getting to know your partner and various other things that I did not feel pertained to me since I had known my husband for 14 years. She told me that I could call her at any time with any questions and she would be happy to help me. When I did have a question, I picked up the phone to call her and she completely brushed me off. Needless to say, I did not go back to her again.

After the failed attempt with the first lady, I decided to see a sex therapist about 45 minutes from my home. I went to her twice a week for about a year. We focused on breathing exercises and relaxation techniques ... things that had not helped me previously.

After making zero progress and feeling very taken advantage of, I decided to terminate her help. I had heard about hypnosis for the possible treatment for vaginismus. I found a hypnotist in my town and called him up. The sessions were terribly expensive, and were not effective in the least bit. I would NOT recommend this to anyone. I felt completely uncomfortable the entire time, and the hypnotist seemed to be saying very inappropriate things to me. I went through three sessions (I paid for a package of three … non-refundable) and decided that it was a very bogus process.

Feeling extremely helpless and hopeless, I went about eight months without any therapy or medication or anything. My husband was beginning to become very distant with me. I knew that I had to do something soon or my marriage would be ending. I spoke to my family doctor and he suggested a woman who is a marriage counselor that specializes in sexual dysfunction. I called her up and made an appointment for the next week.

I met with my therapist weekly for the first few months and then bi-weekly after that for the next year. She was the very first person that I opened up to about the sexual abuse that I had endured. The majority of my sessions were working through the abuse and the feelings that were associated with that. I was put on several medications to the point where I would lose my memory for a few days. She helped me overcome the mental trauma, but I needed help with the physical side. She was a big help to me in overcoming my fear and anxieties about the sexual abuse, and I thank her for that. I had asked her about the use of botox to treat vaginismus, but she had little information about it. She recommended that I continue my Kegels, but I knew that I needed further help.

I began to research botox for the cure of vaginismus, but there was very little information. Then, I came across Dr. Pacik's Web site. I was so excited to see that there was a facility in the United States that was offering botox for the vaginal muscle spasms. I called the Plastic Surgery Center and spoke to Gloria. She was very helpful and friendly and answered all of my questions. I hung up the phone with a feeling of hope. I knew that the cost of the procedure and the drive from Indiana to New Hampshire would be well worth the outcome.

I scheduled my appointment for the botox injections for August 11, 2008. I arrived at the facility on Monday the 11th at 10:30 a.m. After being introduced to the staff, I was taken upstairs to fill out some paperwork. I was then taken to an exam room where Dr. Pacik spoke to me getting additional information. I was told that I would have an external examination only. He attempted to examine me externally, but I was so nervous and anxious, I made it a little difficult for him to do. After speaking with him for a few more minutes, I was taken downstairs to my bed in the recovery room to wait for my procedure. I was given two Valium pills to help me relax. I was originally going to have just light sedation, but once on the table, I was so jumpy, the decision to put me completely under was made. I cannot remember anything about the procedure.

I believe the procedure took roughly 20 minutes, but then I had recovery time due to the fact that I had general anesthetic. Dr. Pacik administered 40 injections of botox into my vaginal muscles. When I awoke from the anesthetic, I did not have any pain, just a mild discomfort similar to what you would feel after a long bike ride or a steady horse ride. I spoke with Dr. Pacik about follow-up care and then I was released. I believe it was about 1:45 when I left the office.

Dr. Pacik had told me that the botox takes 5 to 7 days to become fully effective. So, basically, the first week after you have the injections is time allowed for the drug to take effect. The second week is time spent practicing with your dilators, and the third week is time that you need to slowly practice with your partner in getting accustomed to how things are going to feel. Don't feel like you have to rush, or become discouraged. In my case, I had waited 27 years of life and 4 and a half years of marriage to have sex—what was 3 more weeks?

On the 10th day after my procedure, I decided it was time to start working with the dilators. I was unable to do a Kegel exercise, or voluntarily stop my stream of urine from flowing. I knew that the botox had taken effect. I wish that I could give everyone a small glimpse into my life so that they could see how badly I had vaginismus (in fact, when I called my therapist to tell her the good news, she said my case was the worst she had seen in her entire therapist career). Just the thought of something entering my vagina would make me queasy. I knew that I had to do this because I had just traveled 2,400 miles round trip to have this procedure done. I grabbed my smallest dilator that I had purchased from Vaginismus.com and drowned it with lube. On the third try, it slipped right in … all the way!! It was like I had been doing it for years! I was so happy that I called Dr. Pacik and interrupted a Sunday dinner with his wife's family (bless his heart for being so patient with me!) and told him the good news. My husband had been out running errands and I called him and he rushed right home … delighted.

Throughout the next couple of weeks I progressed through to the third dilator. It took me longer than what I had hoped only because my husband

and I welcomed three foster children into our family unexpectedly and my priorities were a little off there for a while. I never did use the fourth dilator.

On September 6, 2008, my husband and I made love for the first time. I cannot explain the emotions that overcame me. Please know, if I can do it, ANYONE can do it! Four and a half years of sexless marriage is enough to drive anyone batty. Not only is it trying on the woman, but it is excruciating for the man. I watched my husband grow farther and farther away from me over something that I was unable to control. He is the most patient man that has ever entered my life. The first time we made love, I was pretty motionless. He did the movements, and I just learned to welcome the sensations. Over the next few weeks we had intercourse almost every day. I wanted to make sure that my body would adjust quickly to the stretching of the PC muscles. I never had any spasms, and even now, it has been two months and I am just starting to get the slightest of movement back in those muscles ... not spasm ... just movement. Sex is enjoyable for me. I look forward to it, rather than dread the attempt of it.

I am so thankful to Dr. Pacik and his staff. I have told him that he is truly my angel. I would highly encourage any woman with vaginismus to seek his help. Botox is a blessing—it was for me. I cannot imagine not having it done. My only regret is that I did not have it done sooner.

PARAPHILIAS

The Armed Robbery Orgasm: A Lovemap Autobiography of Masochism

RONALD KEYS AND JOHN MONEY[2]

It was the foreboding night of my arrest. For the first time in my awareness or experience, my erotic thoughts and genital arousal were aborted. Throughout most of my forty years, it seemed, I had been possessed by erotic imagery and orgasms.

Caged in the Baltimore City Jail awaiting trial, I began the only criminal incarceration of my life. While watching a video movie at the jail, I questioned why I had arrived there. What made me commit multiple armed robberies with my young dominatrix as a prelude to our sexual activities?

The movie we were watching starred James Garner. In it, a man coerced his girlfriend into illegal actions with threats of punishment for failure. She failed to follow his instructions. Her cruel boyfriend scolded her, then removed his belt to strap her buttocks. Tugging her tight shorts down her shapely legs at his command, she lay down on the bed with her bare rump exposed. The whipping commenced and the video showed her grimacing face as he beat her squirming body with his leather belt.

A surge of erotic excitement suddenly permeated my body. Ambivalently, I experienced genital stimulation by that scene of a girl being lashed with a strap. That started my discovery of my perplexing sexuality.

The jail's psychologist eventually referred me to the Johns Hopkins Hospital. After several calls to secure an appointment at the hospital's Sexual Disorders Clinic, I asked my lawyer to arrange for my transportation from the City Jail. Someone there possessed some knowledge about what had happened to me, and I depended on this appointment for the answers.

Actually, without my mistress's sexualized influences, I would have starved to death before committing armed robbery. Yet, I followed my lustmate into twenty-four eroticized armed robberies. Now, I'd need to explain

---

[2]From *The Armed Robbery Orgasm: A Lovemap Autobiography of Masochism* (pp. 25–28), by Ronald W. Keyes and John Money, 1993. All rights reserved. Used with permission of the publisher, www.prometheusbooks.com.

to the specialist at Johns Hopkins what happened to me under her alluring influence.

On November 15, 1984, I was transported to the Johns Hopkins Sexual Disorders Clinic. Dr. Gregory Lehne greeted me and my escort. Initially, I spoke only with Dr. Lehne. He probed into my past with pertinent questions, and I replied candidly.

Contrary to my prosecutors, who miscast me, I didn't care about a pending prison sentence. However, I yearned to know why I behaved as I did, and why I needed spankings by my dominatrix. What arcane force made me, at forty years of age, jeopardize my future by following my young dominatrix into criminal activity that I would never have performed otherwise?

After listening to fragments of my sexually unprecedented history, and my criminal behavior with my young mistress, Dr. Lehne excused himself to phone John Money, PhD, professor of medical psychology, professor of pediatrics, and director of the hospital's Psychohormonal Research Unit. Dr. Money expressed interest in my case and asked to interview me.

Along with my escort but without handcuffs, I accompanied Dr. Lehne to the Meyer Building, Room 3–171 to visit Dr. Money. I pondered notions of escape, but I had no interest. My enemy resided within me—I couldn't escape it so easily.

My escort sat outside Dr. Money's office, and Dr. Lehne and I greeted the sexology expert. I shook hands with a truly interesting man in his most curious office. I was seated in a comfortable armchair, and graciously offered a cup of coffee, which I welcomed. Dr. Lehne seated himself to my left, while Dr. Money sat directly in front of me at his desk. He turned on a tape recorder, and Dr. Lehne commenced the interview by explaining briefly what had brought me there.

I sensed that Dr. Money possessed the answers to my sexually perplexing life, which consisted of inopportune penile erections, intrusively unacceptable erotic imagery, and finally criminalized activity with my lustmate, followed by incarceration.

Tangentially, we traversed my sexually unconventional life. During my discourse with the doctors, I wondered why I didn't meet with Dr. Money on my visit to the Henry Phipps Clinic at Johns Hopkins in 1972. Perhaps I wouldn't be here today—under arrest.

Unfortunately, I lacked a sufficient vocabulary to explain what took place in my mind and body for the prior forty years. However, I determined to seek and discover my sexual quandary. After all, I had nothing to lose. Not even my life seemed important. It had been systematically yet inadvertently vandalized, and by the very people and society who condemned me.

The diagnosis by Dr. Money, in addition to bipolar disorder, was a paraphilia of masochism. I knew little about either one of those uninvited conditions. However, I proposed to discover everything about these conditions that had brought havoc into my life.

Dr. Lehne inquired, "Have you read *Love and Lovesickness,* by Dr. Money?" I replied, "No." Obviously, I'd wasted my years of study in psychology attempting to discover my sexological problems. Thus, after my return to the Baltimore City Jail, I called my dear friend Nancy Jones and asked her to mail me a copy of *Love and Lovesickness* by John Money, PhD, and she agreed.

Inexplicably, I hadn't experienced any erotic fantasy or genital orgasm since the night of my arrest weeks earlier. That absence of familiar horniness perplexed me greatly.

When Dr. Money's book arrived, I read it avidly and repeatedly. There wasn't enough heat in the jail that winter. Yet, I allowed nothing to stop me from studying Dr. Money's book. Besides discovering about my sexual self, I realized that most inmates had paraphilias. However, they didn't understand their criminal acts to be related to their sexuality.

Had I not read his book, I might not be writing this book. It revealed to me who I really am, a question everyone inquires of themselves. During my punitive incarceration, I traced my masochism's onset to the significant incident that precipitated its deleterious effect on my life, academically, socially, economically, and erotically.

Criminally, my alluring dominatrix and I perpetrated twenty-four armed robberies, all for the sole purpose of facilitating our orgasms. We didn't do the robberies so much as have them happen to us.

During my pernicious and useless incarceration, I commenced an extensive study of my masturbatory fantasy and orgasms. After each of my approximately seven hundred orgasms per year, I recorded the accompanying erotic imagery along with the interconnections to my childhood. Faithfully, Dr. Money helped me to discover the significance of orgasmic fantasies, imagery, and ideation. Historically, my erotic fantasy research is one of a kind.

GENDER IDENTITY DISORDERS

A Rose in Bloom

April Rose Schneider[3]

April 12, 1951, dawned over the town of Dayton, Ohio, like any other spring day. A few wisps of clouds, a light breeze, and plenty of sun. Generally speaking it was a day without distinction—unless you happened to be Roland or Doris Schneider. For them this day was portentous. This was the day of the birth of their first child. Doris wanted a boy, Roland a girl. Everything seemed normal as they took their first tentative steps toward building their all-American postwar baby-boomer family. In 1951 life was good, and the future looked even better. The fifties were pregnant with possibilities, so Roland and Doris could afford to have high hopes for their firstborn. Boy or girl, the Schneiders didn't care that much, as long as it was a healthy, happy child. What they did produce would inevitably far exceed their parental expectations.

My name is Rosie Schneider, and the first five years of my life were the happiest I've ever known. I was too young to understand the contradiction that would eventually haunt me. Unaware of the shame that would eventually be heaped upon me, I lived a relatively normal childhood. Societal judgment had not yet been internalized. Happily ignorant of the struggles for life and sanity that lay ahead, I lived in prophetic dreams. It was in these dreams that I felt most comfortable, because in my special dreamtime I was a little girl.

In early Native American culture, the kind of dreams I began experiencing in early childhood would have been a sign from the Great Spirit that I was destined to be a "two-spirited person." Most indigenous Native American tribes believed that the Great Spirit chose certain special members of the tribe to be two-spirited. These people exhibited preferences for behavior outside the boundaries of the normally gendered early in life. The most convincing indicator of their special status was revealed to the young person in the form of dreams. These dreams set in motion a specialized regimen of training designed to guide the young person toward their future roles, which ranged from healer to mediator to substitute wife. Their legacy, now largely forgotten, was one of value and honor in their respective tribes. By comparison, my experience would be the very antithesis of theirs.

My dreams have always been a part of my consciousness. From an age before I could understand their significance or future importance, they were the mainstays of my nightly bedtime routine. For the years prior to entering elementary school, they were the means by which I achieved sleep. Each night I would put on my pajamas, clutch my stuffed dog to my chest, close my eyes, and become a little girl in a perfect world. In the bliss of my youthful innocence, there was no contradiction, no shame, no guilt. I dreamed I was a little girl, and I was happy. At first it never occurred to me to tell anyone because it was such a natural part of my consciousness. Just a few years later I realized that to reveal this component of my personality would lead to most tragic consequences. What if they tried to make me stop? What if they sent me away? The possibility was too much to bear. I kept the dream to myself.

Dancing With Madness

My adolescence was filled with swirling, powerful, wordless emotions, much like a tornado whose fury I first sought to suppress, then fled from in fear of disintegration. As my childhood progressed, so did my awareness of some apparent contradiction between the way I felt and the way I was perceived. Identifying as a little girl seemed quite natural until I gazed at my reflection in the mirror. As my self-awareness progressed I would spend much time crossdressing and posing in front of a mirror. And eventually all mirrors became my unforgiving captor. No matter how hard I tried, no matter what frilly thing I wore, the mirror was a constant reminder that regardless of what I felt in my heart, the reflection was that of a little boy. Here was the dark genesis of my dance with madness. Here was the first sign of stress fractures in my fragile eggshell personality. As I matured, the stress fractures eventually combined to create one huge schism that threatened psychic destruction.

On the first day of my first year in kindergarten, September 1956, I experienced the first assault on my innocence. I learned my first lesson in social intercourse when it became necessary for the class to be divided into boys and girls. It immediately became obvious to me that a really big mistake had been made when I was put into the little boys' group. I was mortified, and vowed to take action at the first opportunity. I saw my chance at naptime. Laying my head down on my desk, I dramatically beseeched God to change me into the proper feminine form by the time I woke up. Profoundly disappointed upon awakening, I saw that my wish had not been granted. At that moment a young atheist was born. I would gradually give up all hope that this god cared a pittance for the misery of a young transsexual.

By the age of ten, I had developed a growing fascination with girls and all things female. This fascination would create in me a keen observer of human behavior. I found myself studying the girls in my peer group with a passion. I felt inexplicably drawn to them. Way deep down in my young psyche I secretly shared their adolescent need to express themselves in the way that only girls were permitted: to skip rope, wear dresses, grow their hair, and attend pajama parties. This was my secret passion. This was the real desire that dare not speak its name.

An Epiphany

Then on one particularly poignant spring afternoon around 1962, I experienced a profound epiphany that seemed to certify my status as a pariah. I remember it as clearly as if it was yesterday. I had been experimenting with my mom's clothes and makeup for a couple of years. I used any and every opportunity to stay home alone and indulge myself in the contents of her closet. I never questioned my behavior, and my parents never suspected. I had begun crossdressing as a natural progression of the dreams.

On this particular day my mom was at her therapist and my father was at work. I was sitting on the floor of our living room in my favorite full-length crinoline petticoat—the kind often worn under a poodle skirt. The sun was shining, and a warm breeze blew in through the window, carrying the sound of boys playing. As I sat there and listened to those happy sounds, sadness overwhelmed me. I remember thinking, "That's what it must be like for normal kids." Slowly my gaze dropped to the petticoat, then returned to the scene outside. Sudden realization raised the veil of youthful innocence from my vision, and tears fell from my eyes. How melancholy I felt to be so different.

At that moment I felt the first inkling of the isolation that would eventually both protect me and drive me to the brink of suicide. I was struck by the gravity of my predicament. The sun was still bright overhead. Breezes still blew and birds still sang. But for me a subtle shift had occurred in my self-perception. I was a little boy whose idea of fulfillment was staying home alone and wearing my mother's clothes. And from that day forward, a part of me knew for certain that I was headed for stormy seas in a leaky dinghy.

Thus the strangeness of my neophyte transsexual life had begun in earnest. Without fanfare or ticker tape parade, with shaky faltering steps, I had embarked on my transsexual path toward an inevitability that I could not have imagined. And this benign ignorance was perhaps the kindest gift that cruel fate would ever bestow upon me. Painted on the canvas of my future was a portrait of despair, confusion, fear, and loneliness. Somewhere it is written that the easiest way to rob a person of their humanity is to place them in permanent isolation. Transsexualism is the epitome of isolation. It is the transsexual's body that betrays the spirit. It is the body that imprisons and isolates our true selves. It was my body that offered the pretense of masculinity, forcing me down a path I would gladly have forsaken.

As I look back to my earliest realizations, two things stood out. I knew there was something very different about the way I felt and that I was the only person in my little world who felt the way I did. I did not question for a minute the rightness or wrongness of my "unusual" impulses. I did what I did for the same reasons that fish swim—it felt right and natural to do so. But as I was also a product of my environment, wherever I encountered moral judgment and bigotry I internalized those feelings. Tragically then, at such a tender time in my life I was doomed by a paradox of staggering proportion. What I felt to be completely right and natural was perceived by my society to be immoral and perverted. Eventually an expression would be coined that put all of this misery into a neat little box. The name for my particular brand of madness is gender dysphoria. I still believe it to be a measure of my parent's infinite capacity for denial that they never once suspected or perceived anything untoward in my unusual behavior. I also believe that it was one of my innermost desires to be found out. As dangerous as it seemed at the time, discovery still seemed preferable to living in fear and isolation. As I entered my teens, I began nursing an invisible little emotional bruise.

But as with all wounds that do not get proper attention, what had begun as a tiny little innocuous hurt had begun to fester. The gnawing pain in my heart would eventually find expression in a litany of neurotic behaviors that ranged from alcoholism to near-fatal risk-taking behavior.

At the apex of adolescent need for attention I went into a department store, grabbed four or five baby-doll nighties and brazenly threw them over the door of a locked dressing room. I then asked an attendant to let me into the room, where I stuffed the nighties under my coat. If this was not a cry for attention, then I don't know what would qualify. Naturally I was apprehended as I exited the store. The security guard was a little confused, but he sent me home with a promise to notify me of a court date. Terrified as I drove home, I quickly came to the conclusion that the best course of action was to tell my parents so they would know why I would be summoned to court. Admittedly they did appear momentarily perplexed. They asked some superficial questions, such as, "Why women's lingerie?" But I mumbled a few "I don't knows," and the issue was quickly forgotten. Ironically, for whatever reason, I was never called upon by the justice system to explain my heinous behavior. The whole incident did teach me another valuable lesson—apparently my parents' capacity for denial far exceeded my need for parental attention.

Dante's Inferno

High school. Or Dante's Inferno, as I have come to think of it. While so many of my peers were apparently adapting to this final stage of their public education, I was becoming obsessed with my pubic frustration. The full onset of testosterone signaled the real beginning of my darkness. From a male-to-female transsexual's point of view, nothing epitomizes hopelessness like the burgeoning presence of virilizing hormones as they invade our bodies, creating all the wrong changes in all the wrong places. I had always been at odds with my male body. I appreciated it as a pretty decent male body, it was simply the wrong one for me. If I was condemned to live in this male body, so be it, but the chest hair would have to go. Thus began a thirty-year struggle to rid myself of body hair.

High school for me felt like being tortured on that famous device known as the rack. Drawn and quartered by forces I barely understood at the time, I often feared my own dissolution in the midst of a psychic tug of war. With no real self to operate from, I did the best I could to fake it. My grades were above average, my teachers liked me, and all together I'm quite sure they had no clue as to my inner turmoil. The only exception to the rule was a psychology teacher to whom I shall be forever grateful. It was the tenth grade. The stress I was feeling was so great that I can only assume that my subconscious was operating on its own when I wrote an "anonymous" note to this teacher. In my pain and confusion it never occurred to me that he could match my handwriting with other papers I had written. When he approached me about it the next day after class and asked me if I wanted to talk about it, I froze in terror. I was paralyzed by the desperation to speak my truth and by fear of the consequences of telling the wrong person. I quickly denied authorship. The subject, to my relief, was never brought up again.

As I eased, or uneased, into the eleventh grade, I felt hormone-driven changes happening all around me but not to me. For me, sexual development was an abstract concept. The big lesson I learned about sexuality was that it could not exist when the body and soul are at odds. My hormones only forced me deeper into despair. Hopelessness grew daily. I knew, based on observation, that certain behaviors would be expected of me. I knew that most of these behaviors were masculine in essence and that I had better start studying, and fast. The two male behaviors that I passionately abhorred were concerned with various aspects of male aggression: fisticuffs and sex.

The matter of physical confrontation was not as much of a concern as matters of the heart. I was not physically imposing in any sense of the word, nor was I inclined toward aggression. So keeping my head down and staying out of the line of fire would be fairly easy. The other problem, though, was going to be a bitch, plain and simple. Behaving like a male was the toughest role I would ever attempt. The consequences of being found out in the enemy camp were unpleasant to say the least. But like the dedicated actress that I was, I studied hard and succeeded. Some might even say that I overdid it, but I survived. Looking back now, I often joke that I was a double agent, an undercover transsexual agent stranded behind enemy lines. Deep cover, for I alone knew my real identity. There were no reinforcements, no manuals, no maps, and no survival kit that described the intricacies of being a male impostor. I studied hard and faked it.

For the next two years until my graduation in June 1969, I was the consummate actress. I played my part as if my life depended on it. I ingratiated myself into the company of men and listened to their boastful speech.

I tolerated their young sexism with tacit disdain, nodding and occasionally grunting for effect. But my sympathy inevitably lay with the recipients of their crude, unpolished advances. The young women who were the subject of so much salacious gossip could never have guessed that I listened for them and defended them when possible. To them I was just another high school boy trying to find his way through the morass of sexual vagaries that boggled the mind. I even went as far as to date a couple of girls who seemed to like me. I tried really hard to do the "right thing," but the truth is that I was lost at the moment when most men seemed unstoppable. I simply did not have what it took to do the manly thing, and I knew it. I just didn't have the words or the heart to tell them.

So to all the girls I've known before, I would like to take this opportunity to apologize. I knew from the look in your eyes, the smile on your lips, and the sensual toss of your hair that you were ready for me to do what came natural to a boy. How could you have known back then that I was dying to be one of you? How could you have seen that the only lust in my heart was to be one of you, and that everything that happened between us only reminded me of the hopelessness of my situation?

As my senior year came and went, I glided through the halls of college like a cipher, bereft of hope, friends, or plans for the future. There was a period of months during the latter half of the year when I thought I had a friend, knowing full well that friendship with a ghost like me was impossible. Still, for a short time friendship seemed possible, and then like everything else in my young life, it too faded away into the mist of disillusionment. As my peer group focused on their plans for the immediate future, graduation found me surrounded by family turmoil, seething neurosis, enough self-hate to float an armada, and a really bad case of hives. I wanted to die.

Sword of Damocles

Fortunately I remained alive long enough to learn another really important life lesson. In the absence of positive planning, fate can throw a monkey wrench or two into the proceedings. One of those wrenches turned out to be my personal Sword of Damocles. At first it appeared more like a panacea for every single thing that I thought was standing between success and me. Then it would become the noose with which I almost succeeded in committing suicide. Alcohol and I began our twenty-five-year affair in the summer of 1969, not coincidentally immediately following graduation from high school. We got close really fast. So fast in fact that I would become a burden to the few people who could tolerate me until they embarked on their own life. I took to drinking like a drag queen takes to high heels, and it did for me something that no one or nothing had been able to do up to that time: it erased my pain. Unfortunately, it also exacted a toll on my self-respect, integrity, honesty, physical coordination, and memory.

Alcohol was also the culprit responsible for a most egregious case of bad judgment on December 31, 1970. That's the day I got married. In a state of screaming denial, I married the first person to come along with a car and a job. All I wanted was to leave home, but it cost six years of my life to escape the marriage. I'll not waste precious words on the debacle, save to describe it as odious from beginning to end. Remarkable in one and only one respect—that a reasonably intelligent, responsible woman would voluntarily marry a neurotic, confused, unmotivated, unemployed, alcoholic, drug-abusive, self-loathing transsexual. Then incomprehensibly produce two children using my drunken sperm, divorce me, and then keep the children away from me. Nuf said!

It isn't always darkest just before the dawn, but it certainly seemed that way to me. As bad as my marriage had been, it had also functioned as a flotation device. But by 1976 huge gaping leaks had sent it plummeting to its briny demise. The next year found me adrift on the streets of my hometown. Everything seemed so unreal. I felt as if I was outside a bubble looking in, the warmth and spirit of life denied me. Again I was the specter on the outside, where cold wintry blasts rattled my bones, ever reminding me of my isolation and my frozen heart.

On the Road

Perhaps it was a death wish or the desperate need to flee from the forces of imminent psychological and spiritual collapse that propelled me on a three-year hitchhiking odyssey that would eventually cover approximately twenty-five thousand miles. Between 1977 and 1980, I ranged from Ohio to San Francisco, from Los Angeles to Fort Lauderdale, then back to Ohio. With my personal demons ever hot on my trail, I sought nothing more than surcease on the open road. For a few years the plan worked. I found necessary distraction in long-distance travel. My existence was simplified to primal elements. I slept outside in ditches, in fields, and on mountains. I ate out of cans, was chased by wild dogs, and passed out pleasantly drunk under a million stars. I got into a car with anyone who would take me anywhere. Looking back now on my abandon, I realize that I was lucky just to survive.

In 1979, at my wits end, I found myself standing on the Golden Gate Bridge. I truly had nothing but the clothes I wore. I gazed longingly at the water over four hundred feet down and tried to will myself to jump. But something stopped me, and I experienced a sudden epiphany. I had found something that I thought was lost forever. Hope. Nothing else had changed. There was no real reason to be hopeful, but I had found its essence within, and I would not question its arrival. Considering the state of my consciousness, just finding this little glimmer of hope was miraculous enough to keep me going.

So I went back to the only home I had. My family had all eventually moved to Florida, and the climate was perfect for the life of a beach bum. I hitched to Fort Lauderdale and lived for a year by selling my plasma, eating happy-hour cheese crackers, and sleeping on the beach or wherever I could. Ah, the good life! For a while it seemed as if the past would repeat itself. There were more itinerant jobs, more nights sleeping anywhere, and more drunkenness. In fact, I had unconsciously changed my self-image from tragically transsexual to sadly besotted. I was a reprobate who wanted nothing more than to drink my life away in my favorite bar. That's exactly what I was doing on a balmy night in April of 1980 when, ever so subtly, my whole life changed forever in the time it takes to open a door.

My new adopted home was an earthy sort of drinking establishment called the Draft House. Anyone who saw me sitting in that bar would have typecast me as just another beer-drinking, pool-playing, rock-and-roll biker type. My consummate disguise had become my reality. I had long hair, a beard, and bad teeth. I wore dirty jeans and a cutoff T-shirt, and I carried a knife purely for the sake of image. A twenty-nine-year-old drifter, I had no friends, no money, no job, and no prospects. I was interested only in replacing a lifetime of pain with alcohol. In the program of Alcoholics Anonymous this is referred to as the jumping-off place.

As I sat there with one eye on my beer and one eye on the entrance, I noticed a young wild child as she opened the door and glided in. I quietly watched her as she lit the place up with an inner fire I had not seen in quite a while. She left after a short while, but I was still in the same seat when she came back in two nights later. We struck up a conversation, and I finally got around to asking her for a ride to my apartment. She stayed for a drink, then she stayed the night. And the night turned into weeks, and the weeks turned to months. Miraculously, we recently celebrated twenty-two years of marriage.

The Power of Love

In a fairy tale, she would have kissed me early on and I would have turned into a princess, but the truth is far less dramatic. It took all of those twenty-two years to explain to her that I was really a girl in disguise. For her to have come so far philosophically, from a Pentecostal upbringing to living as an agnostic lesbian married to a transsexual, is a miraculous feat and a tribute to the enduring power of love. She now says that she always knew I was "special." She just didn't know how special! In 2001, she supported me while I worked and saved and flew to Bangkok, Thailand, for sex reassignment surgery (SRS). She is my one and only love, my soulmate.

Yet some dreams refuse to die. Previously in this text I alluded to the only person in high school with whom I felt any kinship at all. His name was Paul. He was 5′8″, fair skinned, slight build, and blond. Paul and I spent hours talking about everything. I felt a closeness with him, a trust that transcended words. With Paul I experienced a degree of emotional intimacy that I shared with no one else. I was fairly certain that I knew why. Paul was gay, or at least he was destined to be gay. It was a moot point in 1967. Don't ask, don't tell was the ethos. No one had to tell me. Paul was gay, and I was a closet transsexual happy to have found an unwitting ally. Then one day, inexplicably, Paul pulled away from me, and I lost the only friend I had in those troubled times. Later I would see him pal around with a female schoolmate who I assumed was a lesbian. I thought Paul was in youthful denial.

In May of 2002, five months after SRS, I was visiting a website that provides a cyberplace for alumni of high schools all over the country to find each other. When I saw the name that I had kept in my memory for thirty-five years, my heart leaped with happiness. Finally a small chance for even a tiny bit of redemption. Expectantly I sent him my e-mail address, using my high school name of course. Within days I received an enthusiastic return from Paul. My inhibitions were overwhelmed by my passionate need for resolution. My correspondence began, "Dear Paul, there's no easy way to say this, but I'm a transsexual."

Oh, to be a fly on the wall! When the poor man recovered from his seizure, we began a period of torrid correspondence that rekindled the flame of our youth and fanned it considerably. The story that emerged is a clear case of mistaken identity and unrequited love. In a convoluted plot befitting Agatha Christie, desire drew us in at intersecting tangents. As it turned out, Paul had a monumental crush on me back in high school. At first he thought I was straight, then he thought I was leading him on. I personally didn't have a clue. I just couldn't fathom the idea of having sex while stuck in the wrong body. Paul took it hard. He felt rejected. That's when he faded out of my life.

As we reconnected from adult perspectives, our realization of what had happened and not happened propelled us to a greater understanding of the sacrifices we made in the name of self-preservation. Somehow amid the social facades of our youth revisited, we emerged with a finer perception of the paths we had traveled together and apart. And while thirty-five years hadn't diminished our affection for each other, there was one little matter that still required closure. And this was the most delicate issue of all. Apparently neither time nor space nor gender had assuaged his ardor for the person he knew thirty-five years ago. I must admit that I was flattered, yet puzzled. I thought he was gay, but then he explained that he was bisexual. Oh! Even so, it seemed to me that he was taking a big chance. Though I had sent him a picture, I knew there was a recently emerged version of me that he was not at all acquainted with.

His next communication to me was the apex of resurgent passion. We finally spoke on the phone, and it must have been disconcerting for him to hear me as a girl. He said that he had a question to ask me via e-mail and that he hoped I wasn't shocked. Shocked indeed! Paul suggested that perhaps if our partners "loved us enough" they might understand our desire to consummate our long-lost lust. Mostly his lust. So I decided that the least I could do would be to ask my partner. When wisps of steam began to exit her ears, I adroitly retracted my question. Paul took it hard but made a speedy recovery, and has promised to visit soon.

The year 2002 is the year of my rebirth and a celebration of the first year of my new life. The ominously dark cloud of fear that once hounded me has broken apart, and now sun shines on my life every day. My self-image is radically improved. I am a spiritual warrior on my own path to a greater understanding of myself. By virtue of my life as a transsexual, I have learned many lessons about the world I live in. I am fiercely proud of what I am and what I have accomplished. I held fast to my dream, nurturing and protecting it from forces that threatened destruction. I never gave in to fear, even as I clung desperately to a tiny ray of hope. I survived drug and alcohol abuse, murderous sexism, religious intolerance, inept psychiatry, legalized bigotry, and socially reinforced oppression. And despite all these threats to my sanity, I have emerged victorious. With the reconciliation of mind, body, and spirit, my focus now rests heavily on the development of spiritual principles: integrity, humility, compassion, and gratitude. Especially gratitude. For today I am so very grateful to have something that I thought was lost forever. Today I have myself.

Time for a Good Transgender Story

KAM WAI KUI[4]

The philosopher Nietzsche argues that people will only become conscious of themselves when injuries are inflicted on them, because in being able to prove what's done to you, you have to give an account of yourself.

I cannot help but agree with these words, for I have been writing countless journals that reflect my struggles to come to terms with my inner turmoil. Long descriptions have been given to my first encounters with transsexuality and the endless negotiations that followed: the search for a way to make transsexuality an acceptable concept against my Chinese background, heated discussions with siblings about whether or not to come out yet, big questions about whether I can find someone who would care for me as I am, with all its complications. But there were also gaps, huge gaps between those journal entries. The gaps, or the unwritten, reflect the happy times, when things were normal or simply very pleasurable.

I wonder sometimes what would have become of my ability to reflect, articulate, educate, and explain if transsexuality hadn't come into my life and

[4]From "Time for a Good Transgender Story," by Kam Wai Kui, in *Finding the Real Me*, 2003, Hoboken, NJ: John Wiley & Sons. Copyright 2003 by John Wiley & Sons. Reprinted with permission.

asked me to live my life this way, to feel the pain, but also learn to forgive. What if, to paraphrase Nietzsche, I have no emotional injuries that need to be addressed? What would have influenced my consciousness of gender and my search for other possibilities to make my life enjoyable and acceptable? What would happen to my consciousness of the flaws within contemporary Chinese society toward people who are considered to be outsiders?

Nowadays I find myself in those days of unwritten gaps, but I'm still aware of all those negotiations with pain, and the anxieties I had felt before I came to terms with who I was and who I am now. To achieve anything in life, a quest needs to be endured first. The painful negotiations are still present, but they occupy a peaceful place in my life, like a book sitting on my shelf. I now focus on sharing our stories on screen with a wider audience through organizing transgender film festivals, so that people can contemplate the myths and meanings of trans narratives and understand our struggles better. My own life is a transgender story that came out of a classic transsexual narrative.

A long time ago when I was still very little, I was put in a position in which I needed to choose between being good and being special. Without hesitating, I chose the more difficult option.

The Conformist

Nothing could prevent me from being a good child, but in my young consciousness it was somehow clear that one thing was more important than my gender, which was to be a good Chinese person. I was born in Hong Kong in the late 1960s and moved to the Netherlands in the 1970s. So I spent my first eight years living in the city that has shaped many aspects of my life. I had a short but effective and tough education in Hong Kong. I can still remember the nuns who ran the school. They wore long black dresses that came down to the ground and seemed to glide through the alleys because no one could see their feet while they walked. These strict and supernatural creatures made a huge impression on me as figures of authority. Discipline was necessary according to the adults, for I had no sense of fear: I hung my head out of the window from the eleventh floor to imitate prison scenes that I had seen on TV; I crossed the streets without looking out for traffic; I let my classmates read my answers while doing an exam. It was a time when I had to learn to listen and obey.

Hassle about my gender started even before I was born. I grew up in a middle-class family with three kids. I am the youngest and originally wasn't part of the family planning. My grandparents from my father's side were very unhappy about my mother bearing another child. They would not approve unless it turned out to be a boy—as if my mum could have any active influence in this matter! However, my mother decided to keep me, even though the pressure on her was huge. To the dismay of my grandparents, I was born a girl. Still, I was greeted with joy by my two older siblings. I was a smiling baby.

My father was hardly around, as his job required him to travel nine months out of the year. It was the only way for him to support both his own family and his birth family. For the kids it was just fine. Somehow we found a harmony in the family, even though it was hard for my mother to bring up three kids on her own. We stayed in Hong Kong until the mid-1970s. Despite the rather complicated living situation, I had a good time in those days. I did have problems attending the elementary school in a girl's uniform: it was a great drama every day to get me dressed on time for school. When I was outside of school, my mother actually let me dress as a boy because I was very determined about it, and the family managed to deal with my particular behavior with humor. At that time, my behavior as a-girl-acting-like-a-boy did not cause too much shame. It was just another addition to the collection of fun family moments. Complications came much later on in life.

It's a virtue for a Chinese person to know how to behave according to their position. For some people, this knowledge serves them too well. I knew how men were supposed to behave, and I was certain that I could become the best model of such behavior. I was convinced that my grandfather's model sucked, and I hardly knew my father's. He was the man of exotic postcards and foreign currency. Most of all, my father was the man who was never at home. Instead of him, I would be the responsible, loving gentleman who would provide his mother with the happiness she had missed in her life. I would fill the gap. I took on this task as a secret mission. Was I trying to act like the man of the house because I missed my dad's presence? I guess I was. At least it distracted me from my own negotiations with my gender.

Perceptions of Gender

The first memory of my trans behavior was a story that my sister remembered very well, and my mother would always eagerly confirm it with a smile.

Apparently when I was four, I tried to pee while standing up, but all I could achieve was to dirty the toilet. When mum confronted me with my funny behavior, I told her that boys don't sit when they pee. Mum was quite embarrassed but at the same time very amused to have that discussion with her four-year-old but already quite stubborn kid. This is still a great family joke.

Not unlike the rest of the world, my early perception of gender was that there were only two. I was just unlucky enough to have been in the wrong category. As a kid, I thought that being a man meant to drive a car, to wear a three-piece suit, to have a secretary and lots of meetings. This strange perception of manhood was projected from Hong Kong's popular culture, which preached no other ideology except the dream to get rich. The major themes in television soap operas were all variations on this dream to climb up the social ladder. Being a real man meant looking sharp in a three-piece suit. That was also how you would get a girl too!

The other popular genre in Hong Kong during the 1970s that shaped my early perception of manhood was that of the martial arts stories adapted for television. In the world of martial arts, or *mo lum,* the hero is a man who can conquer all other fighters but remain untouched by the power struggles around him. My favorite characters were those who were powerful but chose to live outside the rules of power. Their character was pure. These heroes had their own codes of honor that remained outside of the complex hierarchies of Chinese society.

A hero is a man of virtue, a man of honor and honesty, a man of discipline and responsibility. However, a hero is not independent. To look for independence is a selfish act. This was my cultural baggage. Heroes sacrifice their lives as an act of honor, for they are good men; but the rules of society are golden, and mortals cannot overrule them. But what is the path of the contemporary man of virtue? What is the realistic substitute for the trope of honorable death? The portrayal of the guy in a three-piece suit with money and power was the only option represented. It may sound absurd now, but it did influence my determination to be a good student at school, to get a good job that pays well, and to gain respect. Born as a girl, I was supposed to find a good husband who could take care of me financially, but that option never occurred to me at all. No one takes care of me; it has to be me who takes care of others.

When we emigrated to the Netherlands to reunite with my father, we moved to a small town in the north of Holland. It was a weird experience for us because we were the only Chinese family in town. Yet moving to the Netherlands had also provided me with many positive changes: I was no longer obliged to wear girls' dresses to school, because the Dutch system didn't require uniforms. Unisex clothing was a big trend at the time, which made me suddenly less strange than other kids. Being a rebel and a dreamer in Hong Kong, I got lousy school grades, but once I had left the strictness of Hong Kong's system, I flourished in school and became one of the best pupils in my class. Even more important, I was able to create spaces where I could stay true to myself.

Although categorized as a girl, I was popular with boys as well because we shared many interests. I found out that I would be accepted as a boy if I did boyish things at their best: I learned to become cool and competitive and to stay well informed on the latest gadgets, games, and especially pop music. The head of the school once asked me whether I wanted to change my Chinese name into a Westernized name, but I refused. I enjoyed my un-gendered name, which initially caused confusion for my classmates because my appearance did not help them differentiate my gender either. That served me perfectly, as each time I met someone new, I could prolong the perception that I wasn't a girl.

In the relatively safe and closed space of the elementary school, I had learned how to flourish and to be popular. However, it was a different matter in college. Negotiations for gender-free spaces became a difficult business. The college world was incredibly competitive. Class, money, and good looks would provide you with status, but inventiveness and good grades would not. Dating became a hot issue. However hard I tried, it wasn't possible anymore to escape gender division at that age, and a relationship with a girl was not immediately within my reach. It thus became impossible for me to escape the stigma of being unloved.

Have the Chinese Never Learned to Enjoy?

Taking up responsibilities early in life is not uncommon for a Chinese child. There is a constant pressure on you not to fail your family. To change your gender more or less means carrying the burden of shame for your whole family. Even if you decide to go your own way, the family is still judged as a whole; the absence of a family member is seen as a crack in the mirror. Many young Chinese people that I encounter nowadays still live under such expectations. I was no exception, despite my optimism and will to change the situation.

Nonetheless, I kept on doing what I knew was right for me, despite the knowledge that pursuing boyhood was an unusual mission for a girl. I would dress as boyishly as possible, and I distanced myself from any sort of girlish habits or behavior. My mother was not unfamiliar with these gender expressions. Sometimes she let me have my own way. Other times, she would make me feel ashamed of my behavior. However, we never sat down to talk about it. We lived above the restaurant, which opened seven days a week. We spent most of the time together during business hours in the restaurant. Apart from that, there were always other people around, as there were often relatives and employees staying at our place. Due to this lack of time and privacy, my mother and I became very bad at communicating with each other. We never talked about our feelings. We just made sure that we moved on without apparent problems.

For many years, two boys were my best childhood friends. We often pretended that we were detectives from television soaps, or warriors from ancient China and masters in martial arts. We even shared our childish boy fantasies of making out with a girl. We spent hours and hours at night trying to reach the highest level of computer games on my Commodore. Those were great times. The boys' attitude toward me changed only when we got older, when our parents and siblings told them that it was uncool for a boy to hang around a girl. The fact that we had a genuine friendship seemed unimportant to our parents. These young men were shamed for their association with a girl as their playmate. What an effective social tool; it made us fragile, and our social status became dependent on the approval of this network of adults. The three of us shied away from each other in silence because of shame.

During my adolescent years, it became harder not to acknowledge that my gender identity had become a real issue. The incompatibility of my outer appearance and my inner gender expression was starting to cause serious problems. The growth of my female breasts especially was killing me, turning me into this monster with all the wrong body parts. The obvious solution to this problem also scared the hell out of me: the only option was for me to break away from this complex system of rules and obligations. Like many people who had to break hearts to break free, I discovered that my heart was that of a conformist. The conformist found himself on a lonely path toward his freedom and destiny, and somehow that pursuit of independence felt extremely lonely to him. It just didn't occur to me that the Chinese were not brought up to be independent and provocative. It didn't occur to me that we were simply taught to conform.

Active Negotiations

The concept of transsexuality took a long time to come into my life. I was fourteen when I first ran into a depressing autobiography of a transsexual woman. Reading that account really scared me off from thinking about the issue. Later, when I was seventeen, I saw a program on TV about the transitioning of two older transsexual women. There were still no representations of female-to-male transsexuals. Acknowledging that I was one of them did not fill me up with pride. The result was another two years being wasted on this refusal to accept my condition. I knew the concept of homosexuality by then, but unlike transsexuality, it didn't provide me with any identification at all. I struggled to understand how I could identify as a transsexual without making myself ridiculous. It was almost impossible to take a middle path because transsexuality would put me in the spotlight and give me a nasty reputation among my huge extended family.

Our family situation wasn't very helpful either; my father was not capable enough of succeeding in the businesses he started, and his incompetence eroded my mum's spirit. The tension in the family was high. The only way to support my parents was to behave well, knowing that at the same time we could never ask for any emotional support from them at all. We all turned to a hobby or something that we could control. My brother turned to upgrading his car with the latest gadgets; my sister devoted her time to setting trends at school. I tried to use my artistic expressions in drawings, but they got stuck in my anger. So instead, I approached my problems intellectually by turning to the arts and literature. It was a time of insomnia. Midnight radio shows kept me company in the hours when there was no pressure.

My years studying at the university finally offered a change in my environment. I left my parents' place to live nearer to the university, and without the immediate pressure of my parents' judgment on my behavior and clothing, I became more at ease with who I was. I even started hesitantly to identify more openly with transsexuality, but it wasn't until I discovered the difference between having crushes and falling in love that I made the final step to the gender clinic, because being in love created other urgencies. I believed that in the state that I was—a nonoperative transsexual—I could not have any relationships, so something needed to be done about it. But there were conflicts too. Even though I may have considered myself to be a true transsexual for a long time, somehow in the back of my mind, I never wanted to pursue the medical solution entirely. To be dependent on hormones for a lifetime was an unacceptable condition for me; I don't want my body to be chemicalized to that extent. To be a transgender person was an unknown option at that time: "in-betweenness" was and is still considered to be too frightening. You either choose to go all the way as a transsexual, or you stay in your "original" gender role: The gender clinic wasn't helpful for those who looked for other options.

Fortunately for me, around the same time, four FTMs founded Het Jongensuur (the Boys' Hour), a support group for FTMs and those who are questioning, with more emphasis on creating a space for the latter. I benefited a lot from these meetings. Meeting new people made me realize that I wasn't playing madman all by myself. We laughed a lot about our different approaches to dealing with transsexuality. All kinds of life stories and lifestyles appeared in front of me; I took them in thankfully as future possibilities. All of a sudden, it created so much mental space. Also, I was tired of being angry all the time, so instead I became more tolerant toward transsexuality and started to talk about it more in depth. All my friends were supportive, whether they understood the condition fully or not. Even my decision to wait to find out what sort of medical help I needed was greeted with understanding. For my part, I've taught my friends to talk about my transsexual condition without treating it like a disease.

I remember there was one time when I could bring a family member with me to a session with the psychologist at the gender clinic. My sister came with me because she was my closest ally. I was twenty-two by then. When my sister and I sat there in front of my psychologist, all we did was explain to her how we wanted to change Chinese thinking about outsiders and outlaws. Looking back at our attempt, we thought it was impossible for me to receive acceptance from our Chinese family, and their acceptance was needed first before I could continue with any treatment. We were in pure fear of unpleasant reactions from our family and relatives. We have a huge extended family, and my sister and I just couldn't foresee the consequences of dealing with them.

Living among foreign people brings your own cultural identity to the surface. Where are you from? Do you like it here? Negotiating and adjusting started early on. I was constantly in a process of comparing, analyzing, and negotiating these apparently separate worlds that I lived in. To add a third one—the world of an outlaw—was simply too much. To unite the apparently conflicting worlds of my parents' and mine was already a process that tore me apart too often. It turned my body muscles to stone.

Reconnecting Body and Spirit

By the time I was writing my master's degree thesis, I suffered from all kinds of complaints. I was eating badly and suffering from panic attacks and hyperventilation. My therapist told me many times that I treated my body only as the bearer of my mind. As long as my body was still bearing features of the female gender, it was simply untouchable, even after the woman I loved told me how much she appreciated me for how I was (read: not operated on). The decision was my way of remaining pure to my trans self. I had an infinite trust that my intellectual mind would help me resolve my problems, but without any physical intimacy, my body collapsed from exhaustion and neglect.

A friend decided to send me to a hapto therapist, a person who practices therapy through the sense of touch. It was the right thing at the right time. Experiencing my hidden and problematic feelings through simply feeling the touch on my skin was a powerful and at the same time scary revelation. Every word that I said, I realized now, was connected with parts of my body. Intellectual solutions were useless. I learned in this process that I had been looking for answers to deal with my problems all my life, and those endless negotiations without a break had worn me out completely. It had put too much responsibility on my head, which had begun to feel heavier than my whole body. So my body bent forward; my whole bearing was forced in the wrong position, and it became too painful. What I always regarded as an act of purity, sacrificing my own needs in favor of saving my parents' honor, was, in the end, pure destruction to my true self. I had to learn again to let go of my tears and to walk straight. When that moment finally came, I could hear my crying coming from deep inside, like a caged animal that was finally released after sitting there for ages.

The physical breakdown brought back what was most important—the care of the body. It took me another year to restore my sense of intimacy by letting go of all those obstacles that I had put down for myself a long time ago. I realized that it wasn't my transsexuality that prevented me from starting a relationship. Chances and opportunities were there, but I used to let them go; it was the intense feeling of shame that was projected on me by my overly modest mother, limited as her view was, like many of her generation.

Is There a Chinese Way?

Although I pretended I didn't need my parents to help me in my own process of coping with transsexuality, emotionally I was very angry with them for their lack of support. Deep down I was unforgiving. It was love from my side that kept them away from the negativity around my transsexual condition, but why couldn't I receive love from them in return? I could easily accept the argument that free Westernized society is better in its tolerance for outsiders, while Chinese society should be blamed for being backward in this matter. But why was such an argument unacceptable to me? Because despite everything, there is love from all parties. Certain forms of love just served my condition better than others.

Within Chinese culture, the self-sufficiency of its network has been able to work in such effective ways that it does not need new influences, so revising old habits is never an issue. My parents' behavior was correct according to the rules of that social structure, despite the fact that the rules were and are no longer adequate for the younger generation. My parents did what was required: they devoted all their time to providing financial security for the kids, but showing intimacy and support wasn't particularly important in their job description as parents. Most of the Chinese parents that I know are too modest to show pride in their kids or encourage their efforts. I would like to see that kind of communication more, so that a visible space can be created for intimacy among family members. Love is there, but it needs to be communicated to be understood.

I have devoted quite some time to figuring out how to change this common fear of new thoughts and lifestyles, but that aim was too far out of reach for me alone. Now I'm excited to find increasing numbers of young Chinese scholars emerging all over the world who explore contemporary Chinese society and search for new critical frameworks. I find the development hopeful and encouraging. Besides, why not let myself be part of something new?

A New Condition

To accept my body, my being, is an unbelievably powerful experience. It cured me of my adolescent melancholia about lost chances. I began to enjoy losing bad habits, outdated concepts, and idle expectations. I decided not to take male hormones, for I hate the idea of a lifelong dependence on the distribution of chemicals from outside my body. Despite the fact that taking hormones is almost considered to be a must in the whole process of being trans, I'm happy with my principal decision. Not taking male hormones means I need to keep my reproductive organs that produce my hormones and also my monthly periods. However, these monthly painless "interruptions" are too short to cause me any real identity crisis. So apart from the mastectomy that restored my male torso, I have no wish to pursue further medical intervention of my body. The classic transsexual narrative, once my framework, starts to lose significance for my current situation. I used to believe that complete transition would cure me from all my insecurities; it may make a man out of me in appearance, but it certainly won't make a man out of me in essence. Since I pass easily as a man, an entire transition was not urgent to me. The current possibilities of medical intervention are far reaching, but they cannot provide any FTMs with the ultimate masculine body, especially that important organ for men. I don't mind waiting for the next great invention, but as far as I am concerned, I won't wait any longer to live my life in my version of manhood.

I find the discussions that I have with my dear female friends on gender, femininity and masculinity, and especially on the fear of staying in between the two genders, tremendously helpful. Being transgendered actually creates opportunities for new forms of manhood and masculinity. I find it interesting and exciting to explore the possibilities to engage in a form of new masculinity without the actual biological male body. This could be called transgender masculinity.

When I applied for a mastectomy operation at the gender clinic, it was difficult to get treatment from them because of their fear of creating "monsters" or "in-betweens." I was warned that I would face great opposition from some doctors, but my wish was granted after all, due to the strong influence of my psychologist, who backed my decision, and a few doctors who were sympathetic. The provision of care for transgendered people is still an open secret in the gender clinic. In some cases requests for surgery are granted only after records are falsified to meet with the classic transsexual narrative. This attitude still worries me.

I didn't dream of becoming a transgendered FTM because it's a trendy thing to do. Being a transgendered person still requires a lot of courage and especially a healthy sense of yourself. You need to be able to sustain the constant questioning of people around you. But now, since my sense of my body has become strong and healthy, I have learned to read the auras of people around me and to distinguish the positive from the negative. It taught me a lot of boundaries and about kindness at the same time. Here, I would love to say something about kindness.

I have read and seen many classic transsexual narratives, and most of them are goal- and appearance-oriented in their search for happiness. I seldom read or see an approach of the issue where the trans person is kind to, and not so hard on, themselves in their journey to self-acceptance. However sympathetic these narratives are, they also feel too restricting for me now. Society tells us that in-between genders or gender confusion is something frightening, so in return, I want to create friendly spaces for all of us, so that it's OK to feel confusion. Nowadays I'm using the same kindness that I needed to accept myself to explain to people about my transgendered condition. I liberated myself from harshness and strictness with kindness, so why can't I give the same to people that I encounter?

Now

In the early 1990s I gave several interviews on transsexual issues, in which I confirmed the distress a person has to go through as a transsexual. I don't think I could have imagined then my openness now. Moreover, I never imagined that the good boy and student, the conformist and the loyal son, would rebel and even become politically active for transgendered people by organizing transgender film festivals. Yet sharing the goodies with others is so rewarding! Once upon a time, love and relationships were foreign to me. Now, love is a gratifying and sweet thing. I can listen to and watch my love, who enjoys life in so many different aspects. The fact that she is Chinese as well is very special to me—we have both fought for ways to deal with our alternative lifestyles (queer and trans), but now it's an enjoyment to find each other on the path that we walk together. Funny, once I was taught to hold back, and now I cannot be happier than being in this position—holding hands with my love—to give people a good transgender story.

12

Sleep Disorders

INTRODUCTION

The study of sleep disorders is a relatively recent field because the electro-encephalogram (EEG) was not developed until the late 1920s. It enabled the discovery of sleep stages and paved the way for the field of sleep medicine. The first hospital department for EEG services opened in 1937 at Massachusetts General Hospital. In 1951, the identification of rapid eye movement (REM) and non–rapid eye movement (NREM) led to significant progress in the understanding of sleep problems. Today, sleep clinics around the country engage in the diagnosis and treatment of sleep disorders. The International Classification of Sleep Disorders-2, 2005 (ICSC-2) lists eight categories of sleep disorders and these correspond with those in the International Classification of Diseases (ICD-10) and the *DSM-IV-TR*. Sleep patterns of Americans were surveyed in the National Sleep Foundation's 2008 Sleep in America Poll, and the results were alarming. Almost a third of the respondents claimed to get a good night's sleep only a few times each month, and over a third said they had nodded off while driving in the past year. Sleep problems are not simply personal problems of the individual sufferer but have a huge impact at the societal level in terms of safety issues in the home, on the road, and at the job, and lost productivity in the workplace (Maxmen, Ward, & Kilgus, 2009).

The *DSM-IV-TR* categorizes sleep disorders in four areas based on assumed etiology. Primary sleep disorders are those that involve problems in the sleep–wake regulators and are of two types. *Dyssomnias* include problems in the timing, quality, or quantity of sleep. *Parasomnias* involve behavioral or physiological difficulties related to sleep, specific stages of sleep, or the transitions from sleep to waking states. There are three additional categories that cover sleep disorders (1) related to another mental disorder that merits independent consideration, (2) due to a general medical condition, and (3) due to the use of or exposure to a substance/toxin.

The dyssomnia category includes *primary insomnia* that involves a problem falling asleep, staying asleep, or dissatisfaction with sleep (nonrestorative sleep for at least one month) such that it impacts daytime functioning and there is distress or impairment in functioning. This cannot occur only in the course of other sleep disorders: narcolepsy, sleep-related breathing disorders, parasomnia, or circadian rhythm disorders. It cannot happen only in the course of other mental disorders and is not the direct result of a general medical condition or substance. *Primary hypersomnia* involves excessive daytime sleepiness for at least a month with the same other criteria as for insomnia. *Narcolepsy* is characterized by being sleepy in the daytime but not at night. It involves falling into a refreshing sleep that cannot be resisted and must occur daily over the course of at least 3 months. The person must experience cataplexy and/or intrusions of REM sleep into the transition between sleep and wakefulness (hypnopompic or hypnogogic hallucinations) or sleep paralysis at beginning or end of sleep episodes. The symptoms are not due to a general medical condition or substance.

Sleep-related breathing disorders require there to be sleep disruption that results in sleepiness or insomnia due to a sleep-related breathing condition such as obstructive sleep apnea (OSA) or central sleep apnea. In *circadian rhythm disorders*, a person's sleep–wake cycle is out of phase with the actual time and leads to excessive sleepiness or insomnia. This can occur because of shift work, jet lag, or delayed sleep patterns and must cause distress and functional impairment.

The parasomnias involve the activation of physiological arousal mechanisms at the wrong times in the sleep cycle. Examples are *sleepwalking* and *sleep terror disorders* (normal in children 4–12, but not in adults), and *nightmare disorder*, which is a REM-associated parasomnia.

The two accounts in this chapter provide excellent, descriptive examples of what it is like to have a sleep disorder. *An Insomniac's Slant on Sleep* is Gayle Greene's fascinating and well-documented account of primary insomnia. For her, and for the many others who access Web sites to get and give support for this disturbance, it is "more than a 'sleep disorder'": it's "an all-day disorder" that is highly stigmatized. She goes on to explain the drastic effects of chronic sleep loss and how insomnia robs its sufferers of motivation and vital energy. It is the "loneliest of conditions" with serious consequences. She implores doctors and other professionals to listen to the stories of their patients/clients because insomnia puts people at risk of depression, alcoholism, and suicide. Patricia Higgins writes freely about her experiences with narcolepsy, which she describes as a neurological sleep disorder that, for her, also involves cataplexy (sudden loss of muscle tone usually accompanied by intense emotion). She explains that she has had vivid nightmares from childhood and remembers being clumsy and falling down a lot. By the age of 32, the falls started becoming worse, and she lost her driver's license and time at work. After innumerable incorrect diagnoses and years of torment, she finally ended up at Stanford's sleep disorders clinic and was diagnosed with narcolepsy. Now, she engages in advocacy work to inform the public about this disorder that almost ruined her life.

QUESTIONS FOR REFLECTION

In what ways are the experiences described by our authors in these two first person accounts (FPAs) different? In what ways are they the same? What role has social and mutual support played in the lives of these two people? What other strategies have they used to deal with their experiences?

REFERENCES

Maxmen, J. S., Ward, N. G., & Kilgus, M. (2009). *Essential psychopathology and its treatment* (3rd ed.). New York, NY: Norton.

National Sleep Foundation. 2008 sleep in America poll. Available at www.sleepfoundation.org

An Insomniac's Slant on Sleep

GAYLE GREENE

Most people know what it's like to lose a night's sleep and drag through the next day. Multiply that out over months, years, a lifetime, and that's what it's like to have chronic insomnia. Chronic insomnia is more than "a bad night." "Chronic"—as in lasting, constant, continuous—is many bad nights, and as many ruined days, since insomnia wrecks the next day. Insomnia is more than a "sleep disorder": it's an all-day disorder.

Talk to insomniacs, trawl through Web sites like Sleepnet and Talkaboutsleep and Sleepstarved, and you'll hear what it's like to have this problem: *It's like someone opened a tap at the bottom of your body and just tapped out all the blood. . . . It's like I'm wasting away, slipping away, losin' it. It's like I'm being sucked dry, eaten away, stolen away, swallowed up, coming unglued.* We use words like *zombie, zomboid, zombied out, comatose* to describe the effect of sleep loss. And no wonder: sleep is the fuel of life. It is so fundamental to our physiological and psychological well-being, to energy, consciousness, creativity, our better selves, that to be deprived of it is to be drained of a vital energy: *It's like some vital juice is drained away.* Sleep is as crucial to our survival as eating, drinking, reproduction, but of all the instincts, it's the strongest, since you can refrain from the others, but you cannot not sleep: sleep will overcome you.

I don't think anyone can understand what it's like, the bone-aching awfulness of it, night after night, when all you want is sleep, when all you need is sleep, so you can function the next day, but there you are killing time till you get sleepy or the night is over, whichever comes first. Insomnia is the loneliest of conditions: You're awake when the rest of the world's asleep, and then, when the world's awake, you're too wiped out to reach out and make contact. *I can't date, I can't connect with anyone anymore, I've lost all my friends, I feel so isolated and alone.* Friends, family, physicians, and psychotherapists have a hard time understanding how undermining it is when sleeplessness goes on *night after night* and we never get the restorative effects others get from sleep.

"Voltaire was right when he placed sleep on the same level as hope," wrote the celebrated Swedish physician Axel Munthe in his 1929 bestseller, *The Story of San Michele.* Munthe, who had success treating the sleep problems of others but could not cure his own, spoke from personal experience: "It kills his *joie de vivre*, it saps his strength, it sucks the blood from his brain and from his heart like a vampire. . . . I staggered on with my work as best I could, careless, indifferent what happened to myself and what happened to my patients. Beware of a doctor who suffers from insomnia! My patients began to complain that I was rough and impatient with them, many left me."

Studies show that motivation is the first thing to go: Even when the sleep-deprived are capable of performing tasks, they become, as Munthe says, "careless, indifferent." Often sleep loss renders us incapable of performing tasks, functionally disabled: *I can't work I had to drop out of school. I was a teacher once, there's no way I could face a classroom now. I used to be a lawyer, now I'm the walking dead. . . . It destroyed my ability to hold a full-time job.* The anecdotal information I pick up is confirmed by studies that show that insomniacs have a hard time getting jobs, keeping jobs, getting promotions. "There's a built-in glass ceiling for people with severe sleep disorders," a psychiatrist friend told me: "It's a career-killer."

I'd have been one of the causalities if I hadn't found my way to academia, where I can schedule classes late in the day and do writing and research on my own time. On days I haven't slept, I can barely string words together to make a sentence, and my mood hits the wall. "Sleep-deprived people," writes Paul Martin in *Counting Sheep*, "perform badly on all aspects of creative thinking, including originality, flexibility, generating unusual ideas, being able to change strategy, word fluency ... thinking becomes rigid. . . . They are more reliant on routine responses. . . . They also start using inappropriate, monotonous, or flattened intonation when reading out loud. Tired people are bad at finding the right words. Their language becomes less spontaneous and expressive, and they are less willing to volunteer information that others might need to know. All in all, they are worse at communicating their thoughts, feelings, decisions, and actions." People who are locked into 9 to 5 schedules, especially mothers who have to get up and get the kids off and then have to function at a job, take the hardest hit. I talked to women who didn't trust themselves to drive; I talked to a woman who went back to school to get a higher degree so she could get a better job and then stayed at the old job because she couldn't stand the stress; I talked to several who had to retire years before they wanted to.

"Nobody ever died of insomnia," we are told. But "people die of insomnia, all the time," says a character in Stephen King's novel *Insomnia*, "although the medical examiner usually ends up writing *suicide* on the 'cause-of-death' line, rather than *insomnia*." "Sleeplessness is the most common cause of suicide," writes Axel Munthe. Rumanian writer E. M. Cioran concurs, on the basis of his experience with insomnia: "In my opinion, almost all suicides, about 90%, say, are due to insomnia. I can't prove that, but I'm convinced." When suicide was mentioned on a panel at the 2005 NIH conference on insomnia, "Manifestation and Management of Chronic Insomnia in Adults," you could hear a pin drop during the intense conversation that followed: "How often do we hear, 'if you don't give me a pill I'm going to kill myself,'; "I, too, have heard such things. . . ." I got the impression that these doctors were speaking from personal experience of losing or nearly losing patients.

Heath Ledger's friends described him as going, night after night, on two hours of sleep. The drugs that were found in his bloodstream—three types of benzodiazepines, an antihistamine, two pain relievers—were pharmaceuticals taken for sleep. Michael Jackson, Judy Garland, Marilyn Monroe, Anna Nicole Smith, Elvis, were similarly hooked on sedatives. Maybe it wasn't reckless living and pleasure seeking that killed these stars, as we assume when a celebrity meets an early end: maybe they were just desperate for sleep. The insomnia Web pages were buzzing after Ledger's death, as they were with Jackson's. The situation is all too familiar; insomniacs well know how it might go: you need to function the next day, you take a pill. It doesn't work, you reach for another, then another of another kind. Still no effect. You add in a little more. *There are nights when I'll do anything for sleep,* an insomniac told me, and I knew what she meant: *You get to a point where you just don't care: At least if I died, I'd get some rest.*

Then, too, there's the death by a thousand cuts we suffer on account of chronic sleep loss. Depriving subjects of even a few hours' sleep over several nights, as Eve Van Cauter's work demonstrates, produces an insulin resistance like that in people with diabetes and the elderly. The sleep deprived have lower levels of growth hormone, a hormone essential to cell repair, and higher levels of stress hormones, which, when elevated over time, do damage to the brain and body. Since hormonal imbalances come about in the course of normal aging, chronic sleep loss makes us old before our time. It creates other sorts of hormonal havoc that leaves us longing for junk food and predisposes us to weight gain. It compromises immune function and leaves us more vulnerable to disease. No wonder that we have two to three times the rate of doctor consultations as people without sleep complaints, twice the number of hospitalizations, and more than twice the rate of auto accidents.

So we may not drop dead of insomnia the next day and we may not overdose accidentally or on purpose, but insomnia may be taking years off our lives. A 2003 study by Mary Amanda Dew et al. looked at healthy elders and followed them up at 4 and 19 years and found that those who reported sleep difficulties had mortality rates, within these years, almost double those who do not report such difficulties. Add to this the suffering: "People with chronic insomnia are distressed," summarized Myer Krieger at the 2005 NIH conference. Their quality of life is worse than "patients with congestive heart failure, in terms of pain, emotional effect, and mental health."

No surprise that studies find that insomnia is a risk factor for and predictor of depression, alcoholism, and suicide.

"Nothing wrong with you except you can't sleep," said a doctor, reading me the results of my physical. I tried to imagine a doctor saying, "Nothing wrong with you except you can't breathe." These are the kinds of things I hear when I go to a doctor: "You probably just need more exercise." Actually, I'm pretty good about exercise. "Don't worry about it. You're probably getting all the sleep you need." Actually, I'm very clear about how much sleep I need—7 hours, like most people. I'm not one of those people who can function on 3–5 hours, like Napoleon Bonaparte, Margaret Thatcher, or high-powered politicians and CEOs who boast about how little sleep they need—General Electric's Jeffrey Immelt brags he can run a dozen multi-billion-dollar divisions on five hours sleep a night. These are short sleepers, not insomniacs, and their ability to withstand sleep deprivation isn't about character or will power: it's a genetic endowment, as recent research has found.

"You worry too much," "you work too hard," "you're stressed out," says the doctor, moving on to that catch-all diagnosis, depression and anxiety. When I say I'm not particularly depressed or anxious, except about my sleep, and my lifestyle's less stressful than that of many people I know who sleep like babies, I get offered an antidepressant. When I protest that I'm nowhere near as crazy as my friend whose love life and work life tie her up in knots of rage, or the husband of a friend who drinks himself into nightly oblivion and beats his children, or the colleague who obsesses about things that happened 15 years ago and has anxiety attacks if she has to spend the night alone—they sleep like stones—I get told to keep a regular schedule, use the bed only for sleep or sex, "avoid caffeine and alcohol," "have a hot bath," "a glass of warm milk," have an antidepressant.

When 501 physicians were interviewed about how they treated insomnia, "they revealed that they asked an average of 2.5 questions and their questions were most likely to be about psychological problems." Fewer than a quarter "even asked about patients' evening coffee intake." "The patient with a chronic complaint of insomnia (even though it may have a purely physical etiology) will usually be referred to the psychiatrist," concluded Daniel Everitt et al. No wonder that many of us have given up on doctors, when insomnia is so likely to be trivialized, talked away, blamed on us, said to be something we're bringing on ourselves which we could change if we'd clean up our sleep act, and if we can't, we probably don't need all that much sleep anyway. Get over it, get a grip—this from doctors whose training was a hazing in sleep deprivation, who pride themselves on how little sleep they need. It may be that insomnia is not taken more seriously because sleep itself is not, in a 24/7 society where "sleep is for the weak," "you snooze, you lose."

Insomnia is a confusing condition. It is, as James Horne says, "one of the few disorders where the diagnosis lies with the patient and not the physician," since the physician only knows you have it by what you say. It doesn't show up in a blood test, a tissue sample, an x-ray, or even on an EEG. There is no biological marker for it, no indicator of it as a disease. It is not even defined as a disease, merely as a symptom of some other condition, usually psychological. When a problem is so invisible—when you can't see it, palpate it, measure it, test it—and when it's so little understood, there's a tendency to refer it to the psychopathology of the sufferer, a tendency especially pronounced when the problem affects more women than men, as insomnia does. Hence it is defined as a secondary, not a primary condition, secondary usually to depression, anxiety, or some sort of psychopathology. It is also defined as a "complaint," since it is dependent on patient report.

"Complaint" is an unfortunate term, since it turns insomniacs into "complainers." As if there weren't enough already going against us in our interactions with physicians: "The only thing I like to see come through my door less than a kid with ADD is an insomniac," said a sleep doctor I overheard at a sleep conference. "An insomniac comes in and we dread it; it opens a huge can of worms," says Dr. Jed Black, director of the Stanford Sleep Disorders Center, urging his audience *not* to take this attitude. "Physicians don't want to get into it because it seems to open a can of worms that might bring up psychological issues they don't want to go into." Doctors don't like problems they can't solve and we're a time sink, to boot.

And by the time we get ourselves to a doctor's office, we may not be in the best of shape. After a bout of insomnia, we are likely to be stressed out, anxious, depressed, and likely to fulfill the worst stereotypes about us: fixated on our sleep, anxious and upset, querulous, unpleasant, withdrawn, depressive. Terms I find for us in the insomnia literature are: "emotionally seclusive and socially withdrawn," "mentally and physically inactive, uncomfortable, sleepy, indifferent, not enjoying themselves, and depressed;" they are "a distressed, pessimistic, worried group who face the world with apprehension, anxiety, and self-deprecation," I read—and these unfortunate personality traits are what's keeping us awake. But if you were to take normal sleepers and deprive them of sleep, randomly and unpredictably deprive them, over long periods of time—an experiment that would not be approved by any "human subjects committee"—you could make them anxious about sleep, somatically preoccupied, socially withdrawn, mentally and physically inactive and unpleasant, and all the rest. Doctors and researchers (and psychotherapists and friends and family) are looking at the effects of the disorder and mistaking it for the cause. Sleep loss saps us of strength and motivation; we cut ourselves off from people and then get depressed about being cut off; we fall behind and get anxious about falling behind and fall behind more: And since we never do get that rejuvenation that comes with good sleep, and since sleep affects everything in our lives, everything gets sucked into the downward spiral: mood, motivation, energy, capabilities.

Some insomnia is caused by anxiety, depression, worry, or stress, no doubt. But the more that is learned about conditions, the less psychosomatic they seem. Many medical problems that were once pinned on the attitudes, habits, or psychopathology of the sufferers turned out to be, with further research, rooted in biology. People with ulcers were told to take a vacation or a tranquilizer, then somebody found a bacteria. Hot flashes, migraines, and multiple sclerosis were once thought to be psychosomatic but are now known to have organic bases. In recent years, several sleep disorders—narcolepsy, restless leg syndrome, REM behavior disorder—that were once blamed on psychopathology have been found to have neurobiological causes. People with narcolepsy, a disabling and often dangerous condition whose sufferers experience extreme daytime sleepiness, and, in some cases, collapse, were thought to be lazy or crazy and given all sorts of useless advice about diet and habits. Then in the late 1990s, in one of the most exciting breakthroughs of recent sleep research, postmortem examinations of the brains of narcoleptics turned up a defect in the receptors for hypocretin, a neurotransmitter that promotes wakefulness. A similar breakthrough was made with REM behavior disorder, where men (mainly men over 50) try to act out their dreams, leaping from bed in their efforts to slay dragons and wild beasts, kicking, punching, throttling their wives. The condition was attributed to psychopathology, but was discovered to be a glitch in the brainstem. Sufferers of restless leg syndrome, which drives the afflicted to spend night after night pacing the floors, were told they were crazy and offered all sorts of advice about their psychological problems; they are now known to be suffering a deficiency in a receptor for iron transport.

But there have been no such breakthroughs with insomnia. "We do not know ... the nature of the basic neural mechanisms underlying primary insomnia. Nor do we know the identity of specific neurotransmitters that might be involved, or even whether specific neurotransmitter systems are involved. The genetics of the disorder are also not known," say sleep researchers Gary Richardson and Thomas Roth of Henry Ford Hospital, Detroit. As long as so little is understood about insomnia, it is chalked up to psychopathology, and as long at it's assumed to be psychopathology, there's no point in directing scarce research funding to investigating it—and so it continues to be not well understood and ... chalked up to psychopathology.

Surveys suggest that 10–15% of the U.S. population suffers with chronic insomnia and about a third suffers with it enough to complain about it. Among the poor, female, and elderly, incidence is much higher. Women are half again as likely as men to suffer from it, and in people over 65, estimates are as high as 60%. Yet in spite of the millions who suffer with it and the enormous toll it takes, the National Institutes of Health, the source of most biomedical research in this country, spent, in 2005, less than $20 million on insomnia research, and most of that went to treatments, therapies, and "management" of insomnia. (Pharmaceutical giant Sanofi-Aventis spent *$123 million,* that same year, advertising Ambien.) Of the $20 million spent by NIH on insomnia, only about $3.8 million went to investigating the neurobiological mechanisms and pathophysiology of the problem, the kind of basic research that might lead to an understanding of underlying causes.

In 2005, the NIH had a conference on insomnia, "Manifestations and Management of Chronic Insomnia in Adults," the first insomnia conference to be held in 22 years. It was originally to be a "consensus" conference, but there turned out to be so little consensus that it was designated a "State of the Science" conference. At this meeting, researchers made a pitch to define insomnia as a primary condition that exists in its own right, rather than a symptom of some other cause—a major step forward—and issued a call for more and better research. More needs to be known about the neurobiology and neurochemistry and genetics of sleep before we can say what makes the difference between robust and fragile sleep. Sleep science has shown that there is enormous variability in the sleep system and that the variability is inborn and genetic: Long and short sleep, morningness or eveningness, the ability to withstand sleep deprivation, are inborn and genetically based, not matters of character, will, or even habit. Researchers suggest that insomnia may someday be on that list, along with narcolepsy, RLS, and RBD, of conditions once thought to be psychogenic that are now understood as organic.

I wanted to ask (but did not have the nerve to), "Why not bring insomniacs into the research process?" We live in our bodies, we often have hunches about where problems come from, a sense of what's gone wrong. People who live with conditions have inside information, information that's crucial with a condition that's entirely dependent on patient report. Yet there has been little interest in what we say, whether in the doctor's office or the laboratory or the literature: in all the insomnia literature I read, researching my book, I found insomniacs quoted maybe half a dozen times.

Insomniacs have always known what sleep does for us and what sleep loss does *to* us, an understanding that seems beyond many in this society, who so carelessly toss sleep away. We've long known that when we don't sleep, we have a longing for junk food, though this seems to have come as new news to researchers in the 1990s. We know firsthand that sleep loss lowers the pain threshold, that missing a night's sleep leaves us wracked by aches and pains—yet research has been slow to make this connection. Women have always known that insomnia is worse at certain times in the monthly and life cycle, though it took researchers till the late nineties to begin to look seriously at the role hormones play in sleep disturbances. If doctors and researchers had talked to us, kept an ear tuned to anecdote, found out what we know, they'd have come to these realizations much sooner, and to others besides (e.g., women have long suspected that birth control pills worsen sleep, and this too is being borne out by research).

It can be dangerous not to hear what patients have to say. We were not heard when we told doctors we were becoming addicted to the Valium and Ativan they so casually prescribed for sleep in the 1960s and 1970s. Physicians turned a deaf ear to our complaints, believing instead what the drug companies told them, that the benzodiazepines were not addictive. It was assumed—it still is assumed—that the pharmaceutical companies do adequate research. But most medications are tested only 6 weeks to 2 months; Lunesta was tested for 6 months, the longest of any sleep med—but 6 months is a trifle compared to the decades these drugs are taken by chronic insomniacs. Besides, the testing and research are usually done by the producers of the pharmaceuticals, who famously downplay their dangers and overemphasize their safety and efficacy. We the users, the consumers of these drugs, are how their long-term effects are known.

Talk to us, listen to us, take complete histories, try to troubleshoot our problems. Find out whether our insomnia is sleep onset or sleep maintenance, whether it's brought on by psychological upset or we've just had it always. Hear our hunches, find out where we think the problem comes from, hear us women when we talk about hormones, and keep an eye out for thyroid problems, which are way underdiagnosed and can wreak havoc on sleep. See if certain illnesses or conditions—thyroid, hormonal, auto immune, intestinal, cardiovascular—correlate with certain kinds of insomnia. Doctors and researchers acknowledge, theoretically, that insomnia is a multifactorial condition, that it may be caused by many things, but the treatments offered us are numbingly uniform: behavioral modification or medication, one size fits all.

Of course doctors will need more than the 7 minutes allotted them to see a patient, and the state of knowledge on insomnia will have to be a lot more advanced before therapies can be targeted to our individual sleep problems, whether it's hormonal, behavioral, genetic, or some defect of the sleep system or the arousal system. For this to happen, we need more and better research—and more imaginative kinds of research.

Advocacy groups have shown doctors and researchers that people who live with afflictions have something to teach, that nonscientists can play a role not only in fundraising and lobbying but in working with scientists to help direct research efforts. But there is no patient-organized advocacy group for insomniacs. There are groups for far rarer sleep disorders, narcolepsy, restless leg syndrome—and for just about everything from dog bite to bee sting—but none for insomniacs. How is it that a condition that makes so many people so miserable has no patient-supported advocacy group? There's a stigma attached to it that makes us reluctant to own up to it. (I can't tell you how often people have said to me, "I'm not an insomniac; I just can't sleep," and then gone on to describe a sleep pattern as broken as mine.) It seems we've been so talked out of our condition, so persuaded that it doesn't exist except insofar as we bring it on ourselves, that we haven't organized on our own behalf.

It is dismaying to see how thoroughly insomniacs have internalized the stigma. These are things I've heard:

> *I know I'm neurotic about this; I'm sure I think too much about my*
>   *sleep.*
> *I'm not as disciplined as I ought to be—I ought to be better about keep-*
>   *ing to a schedule. . . .*
> *If I was better about expressing my emotions. . . .*
> *I'm sure it's true what they say about secondary gains—I'm not sure*
>   *what they are in my case, but I know they are there—why else*
>   *would I be doing this to myself?*

"Quit apologizing," I want to say: "You can't sleep! It's a miserable way to be—don't make it worse by blaming yourself!" But when blame is encoded in our proverbial expressions—*There's no rest for the wicked; The best pillow is a clear conscience* (I found this proverb quoted in an article on insomnia)—it's impossible not to internalize it. When guilt is assigned by our medical lore and literary lore ("Macbeth doth murder sleep"), it's no surprise that we don't speak out for ourselves. A support group for insomniacs? "Chronic complainers," "all in their head," "bringing it on themselves," "why don't they just shut up and take a pill?" And in our heart of hearts, we probably agree, or part of us agrees—I know it's in me, this voice—if I were more sane or more normal, I'd sleep *the sleep of the just.*

We need to break the silence on insomnia, to come out of the closet and say, look, this is a serious problem that is making a lot of people miserable and is putting us at risk. It needs more than a hot bath or warm milk. It needs to be taken seriously by our doctors and psychotherapists, by friends, family, employers, researchers—and by us.

My Story of Narcolepsy

PATRICIA HIGGINS

Narcolepsy is a nervous system disorder, not a mental illness. Anxiety does not cause narcolepsy. What is a mental illness? If you do a Google search of mental illness, you will be directed to topics such as depression and schizophrenia. The National Alliance of Mental Illness states:

> Mental illnesses are medical conditions that disrupt a person's thinking, feeling, mood, ability to relate to others, and daily functioning. Just as diabetes is a disorder of the pancreas, mental illnesses are medical conditions that often result in a diminished capacity for coping with the ordinary demands of life.

The truth is that mental illness in our culture is a derogatory label that results in negative reactions and judgments. Chronically mentally ill patients are often most vulnerable, disenfranchised, underfunded, and often forgotten. Most health insurance limits the allowable limits for mental health care in ways they do not limit care for other diagnoses. If we were to label mental conditions *brain conditions,* what gain might there be? Could we mitigate the negative association with the "mental illness" label? Could there be more focus and support for brain research? Science is constantly evolving, and we understand very little about the brain. I wish narcolepsy could be labeled "brain illness," "brain disorder," or "brain condition." Labeling narcolepsy under mental illness keeps it in a classification system that is poorly understood and also poorly funded for research purposes.

The diagnosis of narcolepsy means something is wrong with the brain. Narcolepsy by definition is a neurological sleep disorder. It is organized in an informational system in the *DSM-IV* that allows clinicians to categorize it with a diagnosis code. These codes assist with direct funding and more importantly allow insurances to direct billing. Maybe it is time to change this classification as mental illness.

Allowing the vernacular brain illness, it allows mixed features to go to a generic catch-all diagnosis code where insurances allow potential reimbursement.

I am resentful of narcolepsy being classified as a mental illness, though I positively believe the mental component treatment is a huge part of successfully living well with narcolepsy. I truly believe that this classification as a mental illness negatively impacts funding, communication, and status. Mental health clinics open up in the poorest of neighborhoods and are not looked upon in a positive light. On the flip side, brain disorder clinics denote edgy, scientific evidence–based research, labels that are looked upon more favorably by the community. It is easy to see why people back away from the term *mental illness* and are reluctant to tell their stories.

After that introduction, and much angst and contemplation, I would like to tell my story.

Where do I begin? Attempting to write a history about my symptoms of narcolepsy does not come easily. For with this history a huge wave of emotions surfaces and makes me feel vulnerable and unsure all over again. Years of reflecting on unusual symptoms, falls to the ground, hallucinations, automatic behavior, and extreme sleepiness evolved into something called *narcolepsy*, a neurologic sleep disorder. These symptoms, unexplained for so long, now have a name and an accurate description. At age 39 I received the diagnosis of narcolepsy with cataplexy. Being unable to explain differences between my siblings and me has always bothered me, even after many years of living together under the same roof. I always felt different. I had some unusual symptoms as early as a toddler. Then I did not know how to explain myself. I will try to do so now as a middle-aged adult. My story begins.

For as long as I can remember I had very vivid dreams. Dreams for me were always nightmares. I never knew dreams could be positive or tender or even fun. They happened often, and my dad would be found many nights comforting me after screaming or thrashing in the night from a vivid nightmare. I also believe I was always clumsy. I tripped over things; I didn't notice the obvious. Things needed to be pointed out to me. But I could always sleep or nap at any moment. I loved car rides. I could fall asleep quickly, and long distance car rides were always pleasurable to me. I was considered quiet, maybe even shy. Interesting, though, I still managed to gain some key roles in events that would put me front and center on several occasions. I did not particularly like that. I am not comfortable with being the center of attention. I was pudgy as a child and that was different, because the rest of my 12 siblings were skinny and athletic. I always felt somewhat different. I even asked on many occasions if I was adopted. My parents assured me I wasn't, but I still continue to question how different I am from my siblings. I was always the sensitive one. I got the sensitive gene. To this day I am the most compassionate of my siblings. I am the thinker, the peacemaker, the most easygoing. I don't get too rattled, and I continue to hate confrontation.

We grew up playing kick the can and build up the army, and we played endlessly in the tree house. Sleeping in the tree house was forbidden until I stopped wetting the bed. So it seemed forever until I finally got my turn to sleep outside in the tree fort. Interesting to note, many people with narco-lepsy also have enuresis late in childhood.

Athletic endeavors were especially thrilling and played a significant role in my development as a person and team player. Everything for the good of the team, and I was skilled in athletics. I wasn't the fastest or the brightest; I was average, mediocre, and that was okay by me. Mom stated that when I was quite young I would hold my breath, turn blue, and fall to the ground. My parents were advised by the pediatrician that I had a temper and that if they just ignored it, it would go away. I do not have any memory of holding my breath, but I do remember falling and tripping lots. It wasn't until age 16 that the falling became a problem once again. Many times during wind sprints, successive runs of sprinting, short rests, sprinting, and short rests, the outcome was often the same. I would be on the ground looking up wondering what had happened to me. The general practitioner stated that I was hyperventilating, so a brown bag was placed over my mouth and nose on several occasions. It was then that I stopped trying to be the fastest, the best. I learned that pushing me beyond my limits often seemed to lead to another fall to the ground. Each fall would baffle me. I would always try to be in the middle of the pack, try to go unnoticed per se. All my life I must admit I felt tired. I believed that tired feeling was normal. I believed everyone felt this way. I had no reason to think any other way.

In college many unexplained falls on campus while dating made me the bizarre girl at times. I knew that drinking alcohol seemed to increase the frequency of these falls. I was mistaken for being drunk on several occasions. I decided early on that alcohol only complicated the situation so I stopped drinking all together. It is rare for me to ever have a drink of alcohol. Being referred to as a "drunk" was ingrained in my brain, and I never want that false accusation again. My life is complicated enough without alcohol so I avoid that altogether.

I used to try to spend all-nighters in college preparing for my nursing courses, and inevitably I would fall asleep before anyone else. I also was a B student. I tried the hardest and put more hours by far into studying than my contemporaries, yet they would get the As and I would not. I then noticed my note-taking lapses and unfinished sentences. I had no explanation for that. After each class I borrowed someone's notes and compared them to mine to find the missing comments. I don't remember falling asleep, but that must have been the explanation. I also worked several jobs while attending college, played two Division 1 sports, and was a resident director, so, yes, I was busy and trying to do studies just like everyone else.

Life continues to charge ahead full force with marriage, three children, husband going to school for postgraduate degrees while working full-time days. I worked off-shifts and weekends so that the children would be left with either my husband or me most of the time. We did what most couples did—we passed each other in the middle of the night doing shift work, to accommodate small children and provide as much consistency as possible.

At age 32 the falls started again and were more frequent than at any other time in my life. These falls to the ground were more alarming and disturbing and were happening in my workplace, the emergency department. Many were witnessed by medical staff, but continued to remain a mystery for several years. A medical workup stated stress, and I took off work a few days and totally wondered what was happening to me. Unfortunately, over the next few months the falling continued and the guessing game of diagnoses began. It was first diagnosed as stress, and the second diagnosis of seizures remained for the next 8 years. Trials of countless anticonvulsants yielded substantial side effects. My work hours significantly decreased, my driving license was revoked, and being confined to home sent me into a deep depression. Fortunately, my husband continued to have faith in me that whatever was happening would eventually figure itself out. Now I was not so certain—I was anything but certain. I researched the Internet, medical libraries, anything I could get my hands on. I was also seeing a psychiatrist for the first time ever and I was scared and withdrawn. I had never seen a psychiatrist, and now I was convinced I was mentally ill. Being placed on antidepressants during counseling began to slowly improve my outlook. I was still upset with the not knowing and positively sure that it was not a seizure even though the neurologist was trying to assure me that this was the best educated guess; the trials of medications continued. The falls did become less frequent. After trialing many different medications for seizures I had come to the end of my rope. I decided to go for a second opinion and agreed to long-term monitoring at a hospital in Boston. This required careful planning for the entire family. I was willing to do anything to find out what the falls were all about. Once in the hospital, I agreed to be the case in grand rounds and an entire arsenal of physicians and students entered my room to question and examine me. I wanted an answer and I knew I was not finding it on my own. I left the hospital after being spoken to by a psychiatrist and neurologist and left with the diagnosis of somatization disorder. He stated that the falls were due to something that was bothering me and until I discovered what that was, the falls would continue. I was sent to a psychiatrist and told him that diagnosis though tears and sobbing. He hesitated and then told me that clearly I was upset and needed to feel better and that what was what he intended to work on. I remember shouting to the psychiatrist that I just spent 8 days in a hospital in Boston and this is their conclusion and that he needed to believe it so that I could believe it, and only then would I begin to feel better and the falls would stop altogether. The psychiatrist allowed me to rant and cry and carry on until I had nothing left else to give. He made a profound statement to me on that day. He said, "I went to medical school, too. I have a medical degree and I am telling you that I do not believe that you have somatization disorder. I think we will eventually discover just what is causing these falls, so hang in there. I intend to continue to treat you and help you begin to feel better about you and what is going on."

It was then that the first life preserver was thrown. He repeated, "I do not think they know what you have." I have always wondered why the medical profession is so darn afraid of saying those words. It would have made the entire self-doubt and total loss of my self-esteem go by the wayside. On that day, my life took a significant change. It was on that day that I finally thought I just might make it in the world. I might not be so abnormal after all. The impact of those words carried me through the darkest days of my life.

I can honestly say that those words catapulted me through several great years now. My primary care physician had a pulmonary practice, but we met while in the emergency department years before. He took a trip to Stanford and met Dr. Mignot and saw the narcoleptic dogs. It was there that he figured out what might be going on with me. He returned from his trip, found me at work, and asked me to agree to do one more test. Eight years of not knowing, and I was adamant that I could not face one more negative test result. I told him that I did not have it in me any more to search for an answer. I could not go through any more tests. By this point I was exhausted, skeptical, and afraid to try anything more. I felt totally fragile, and that was not something I ever got used to. I used to be a doer. Now I was barely hanging on. It was because I had the kids to focus on, and the business of life allowed only that. I did nothing but get rides to and from work and take care of the family from home. I became reclusive and scared of everything. I no longer went out, ignored social gatherings, and hibernated. I stayed at home, because falling in my home remained undocumented. My husband and physician literally dragged me to my first sleep study, and I was anxious and upset, totally defenseless.

It was there that the clinician talked to me and asked me about my story. Well, the tears fell and the catharsis began. I had never had anyone inquire about my history and really care to listen to the bizarre claim. Well, it was in that sleep study and follow-up MSLT (multiple sleep latency test) that the unknown became front and center. The diagnosis of narcolepsy with cataplexy was given to me. Then and only then did the mystery unravel, and things began to make sense in my life. Falling, for me, had a name, and it is called *cataplexy*. Muscular weakness caused by strong emotion paralyzed my muscular system and I would collapse to the ground. Medications have been extremely helpful. With stimulants I notice things in my life that I had never noticed before. Things are much clearer than they have ever been.

I now work tirelessly for NN (Narcolepsy Network) as president to make people aware of this nonprofit organization. I want to get to people before they give up on themselves, due to the depression. It almost killed me. Without my husband allowing me to laugh, cry, and vent, and telling me to pull it together for the kids, I would not be where I am today. Once the children were in bed, it was my turn to collapse, laugh, cry, and vent in his arms. What an amazing individual my husband is. He is the center of my life. Today I am most grateful for all my experiences. It has made me who I am today. It has made me compassionate and driven to help those who cannot help themselves. This is the journey I was supposed to take.

13

Disorders Usually First Diagnosed in Infancy, Childhood, or Adolescence

INTRODUCTION

As the *DSM-IV-TR* acknowledges, there is not a clear distinction between "childhood" and "adult" disorders. The idea behind grouping together disorders first present in childhood is simply that most of these disorders emerge during childhood; however, this is not always the case. Sometimes these disorders are not diagnosed until the person reaches adulthood. Also, many "adult" disorders occur in childhood; for example, depression is not listed in this section, yet children can experience enough symptoms of depression to be diagnosed with this disorder (*DSM-IV-TR*, pp. 353–354, 356, 372). The *DSM-IV-TR* lists the following disorders that are usually first diagnosed in infancy, childhood, or adolescence: *mental retardation, learning disorders, motor skills disorder, communication disorders, pervasive developmental disorders, attention-deficit* and *disruptive behavior disorders, feeding* and *eating disorders, tic disorders, elimination disorders*, other disorders (separation anxiety disorder, selective mutism, reactive attachment disorder, stereotypic movement disorder).

According to the Methodology for Epidemiology of Mental Disorders in Children and Adolescents study (Surgeon General's Report, 1999), 21% of U.S. children ages 9 to 17 have a diagnosable mental or addictive disorder associated with at least minimum impairment. Some of the more common disorders break down as follows: anxiety disorders, 13%; mood disorders, 6.2%; disruptive behavior disorders, 10.3%; substance abuse disorders, 2%. With a prevalence rate estimated at 20%, there are almost 14 million children with significant impairment due to an emotional or behavioral problem. In real terms, that means "approximately two children in every classroom across America are suffering from a mental illness" (LeCroy, 2011, p. 3).

Children and adolescents who experience significant behavioral difficulties most often come to the attention of a professional through a referral initiated by someone else. Although it is unusual for children and adolescents to seek services themselves, this is sometimes the case. It is interesting to note that while the initial focus in working with children and adolescents experiencing symptoms of a mental disorder is whether the child has a clinically significant disorder, this may not be the focus of the person making the referral (Rutter & Taylor, 2002). Instead, frequently the main concern is what the family or school should do regarding a particular behavior that is distressing to individuals in the school or family environment. Administrative decisions often are the focus: Is the school environment a good fit? Should the child be removed from the home? Does the child need a residential treatment setting? More so than with adults, it is common to find differing viewpoints about the nature of the problem and solutions to it. Mothers and fathers frequently have different perspectives, as do school officials, the family doctor, and the mental health professional.

If it is determined that the child is experiencing symptoms that may meet criteria for a disorder, the focus becomes, "Which disorder?" For the childhood disorders, the *DSM-IV-TR* acknowledges that "good well-validated empirical evidence is lacking on how to decide on the precedence to be given among differing patterns of symptomatology" (Rutter & Taylor, 2002, p. 23). This suggests that when multiple symptoms are present, the mental health professional should examine all patterns that meet criteria for a diagnosis. As a result, there is a significant amount of comorbidity (the co-occurrence of two or more different disorders). It is not unusual to find children with four or more diagnoses, either because of comorbidity or because of disparate understandings of the underlying symptoms. As in other areas of classification, children and adolescent diagnoses have come under increased scrutiny about the "applicability of 'mental disorder' status to many conditions and situations" (LeCroy, 2011, p. 28) described in the *DSM*. For example, a recent book, *Toward a New Diagnostic System for Child Psychopathology: Moving Beyond the DSM* (Jensen, Knapp, & Mrazek, 2006), provides a stern critique of the *DSM* and its utility for use with children and adolescents.

Perhaps more significant in thinking about the nature of childhood mental disorders is that many of these disorders do go beyond a simple *DSM* diagnosis. Current research suggests that the clinical problems experienced by children are often the result of a mismatch between developmental needs and environmental resources, problems in successful adaptation to difficult environments, or the impact of adverse events (Jensen et al., 2006; Hibbs & Jensen, 2005). The *DSM* system of classification is grounded in adult disorders, and its use implies a static conceptualization of disorders rather than the more current dynamic and complex understanding of childhood disorders. Nonetheless, the *DSM* is the predominant method of researching and treating childhood mental disorders and remains an integral part of our system of mental health service delivery.

Perhaps more so than in any other section of the *DSM* and of this book, little is known about the subjective experiences of signs/symptoms of mental illness in childhood and adolescence. Not surprisingly, most children are not equipped cognitively to document their experiences. However, like the trend in adult memoirs and first person accounts, an increasing number of narrative accounts have been written and published by adolescents about their mental health problems. As Jared Douglas Kant (2008) notes in the introduction to his book,

> I was 12 years old when I came to terms with the idea that I would live my life with obsessive-compulsive disorder (OCD). I distinctly remember looking up at the sky and saying, "All right, fine, but something good better come out of this." Strangely enough, I remember thinking to myself at that time that, if I ever found my way out of the fog, I would like to write a book about my experiences. (p. xiii)

This chapter of our book begins with the FPA written by John Elder Robison, a well-known author who writes about autism. He talks about Asperger's syndrome and its impact on a person's communication abilities.

By focusing on communication, he sheds light on one of the most challenging difficulties for those who suffer from Asperger's syndrome. This account is followed by another story about Asperger's told from the point of view of a middle-aged woman, Stephanie Mayberry, who describes her daily reality in superb detail and reveals how she eventually makes sense of her life. Tony W. provides a fascinating account of infantile autism, reprinted as it was written, including misspellings and incomplete sentences. It is a rare look into what life is like for someone with this serious disorder. The next personal narrative discusses one of the most prevalent mental disorders in childhood and adolescence: attention-deficit/hyperactivity disorder (ADHD). Katy Rollins writes as an adult but starts by recounting her early childhood experiences in first grade. Her account is a good example of the mismatch between her symptoms and the demands of a school that failed to understand her unique challenges. The descriptions of how she experiences ADHD provide a glimpse into her day-to-day reality. Crystal Thomas, a teenager, shares a compelling story about her experiences with Tourette's syndrome. Like other children and adolescents with multiple difficulties, Crystal also suffers from ADHD and obsessive-compulsive disorder. Her account is an all too common description of what many children and families go through to find a medication that works to reduce the symptoms that are experienced. Finally, Rick Fowler's more classic case of Tourette's syndrome helps readers understand the mental torture experienced by those who contend with a disorder that exerts so much control over them.

QUESTIONS FOR REFLECTION

How are child mental disorders different from adult mental disorders? Is the application of the *DSM* appropriate for children and adolescents? Why or why not? What role does society play in helping families who have children suffering from a mental disorder? What are the biggest barriers in helping families cope with the mental disorders of their children?

REFERENCES

Hibbs, E. D., & Jensen, P. S. (2005). *Psychosocial treatments for child and adolescent disorders: Empirically based strategies for clinical practice.* Washington DC: American Psychological Association.

Jensen, P. S., Knapp, P., & Mrazek, D. A. (2006). *Toward a new diagnostic system for child psychopathology: Moving beyond the DSM.* New York: Guilford Press.

Kant, J. D., Franklin, M., & Andrews, L. W. (2008). *The thought that counts: A firsthand account of one teenager's experience with obsessive-compulsive disorder.* New York: Oxford University Press.

LeCroy, C. W. (2011). *Parenting mentally ill children: Faith, caring, support, and surviving the system.* Santa Barbara, CA: Praeger Press.

Report of the Surgeon General's Conference on Children's Mental Health: A National Action Agenda (Washington DC, 1999).

Rutter, M., & Taylor, E. (2002). Clinical assessment and diagnostic formulation. In M. Rutter & E. Taylor (Eds.). *Child and adolescent psychiatry* (4th ed.). Malden, MA: Blackwell Science.

PERVASIVE DEVELOPMENTAL DISORDERS

Communication Impairment

JOHN ELDER ROBISON[1]

Everyone with autism has some sort of communication impairment. The terms *autism, Asperger's syndrome,* and *PDD-NOS* describe some of its different flavors. The various conditions that make up what we call the autism spectrum differ greatly in their impact upon us, but the one diagnostic feature they all have in common is communication impairment.

All autistic communication problems stem from brain dysfunction. Autistic people can see and hear just like anyone else, but our brains may not make sense of those inputs in the conventional way. The same is true for speaking or moving our bodies to convey messages. The physical parts are all there and working normally, but we have trouble using them in the expected way due to our neurological differences.

The most obvious autistic impairment is the inability to understand or deliver speech. In our society, if you can't understand what others are saying, you are going to be disabled. If you can't speak for yourself—whether through speech or writing—you are going to be disabled. If you can't do either, you are doubly disabled. If you can't make sense of a phrase like "Bob will pick you up at five," how will you ever get home? The short answer is, you won't. An autistic person who cannot understand speech might be likened to someone who speaks English in a town filled with Chinese speakers, none of who speak a single word of English.

However, there is an important difference between a native English speaker in China and an autistic person. The English speaker has all the wiring in his brain to converse. In a matter of days, he will be working out the meaning of simple Chinese phrases. The autistic person does not have a system for learning language. So he can't adapt. For autistic people with

---

[1]From John Elder Robison blog (jerobison.blogspot.com/). Reprinted with permission. For further descriptions, see John Elder Robison, 2008, *Look Me in the Eye*, New York: Broadway Books.

language trouble, understanding speech can take years. For some, it never happens.

Speech and language impairments are what we might call left-brain afflictions of autism. What about the people with right-brain issues? Those folks may understand the logical meaning of words just fine, but they cannot grasp the emotional undertone. That's always been my problem. I have no problem with logical meanings, but the unspoken subtext—so vital in expressing emotions—goes right over my head.

For example, when I hear, "That's just great!" I cannot tell if I'm hearing praise or sarcastic criticism. With no clue how to answer, I respond incorrectly much of the time. That's the silent communication disability in autism. People who can't speak are obviously disabled, and cry out for compassion. People with good command of language, but no sense of the unspoken undercurrents, are often perceived as obnoxious, arrogant, or disrespectful. Those negative reactions lead to depression, anxiety, and in extreme cases, suicide or violence.

Some people on the spectrum have a hard time expressing themselves because they are, for lack of a better word, clumsy. That may sound strange, but issues with coordination and fine motor skills can make it hard to form facial expressions or make gestures to convey a message. If you are really ungainly, your meaning may be lost in a dance of strange-looking movements, or rendered invisible with no movement at all.

Where's Bob? He's over there. Most of us take for granted the ability to swivel and point so that you are sure to recognize Bob. A person who can't do that effectively is handicapped just as surely as someone who cannot utter the words. Unfortunately, many individuals who have problems controlling their bodies also have trouble forming the spoken responses, so they are doubly impaired. Physical responses are an expected part of ordinary interchange; people who cannot do that tend to be ostracized, ignored, or subjected to ridicule.

People with traditional autism—also called Kanner's autism—tend to have both verbal and physical challenges of varying severity. People with Asperger's syndrome (like me) are more likely to have impairment in reading or conveying unspoken communications. Some of us have challenges in both areas.

We now recognize that early and aggressive intervention results in far better adult language skills. That's why we feel it's so important to identify and address autistic communication problems as early as possible. Technology plays a key role in both the identification and resolution of childhood communication issues.

For most young people, autism therapy ends when they leave high school. One-on-one therapy is costly; few people can afford it on their own. Adult health insurance is often limited in coverage. That's why we look to technology to help adults with communication issues. I hope to see the development of devices that assist adults with communication issues at all levels, from helping severely impaired people with basic communication to helping less impaired people interpret the subtlety of facial expressions or nuances of spoken meaning.

One of the biggest problems of Asperger people in love is that we can't tell a false "salesman" smile from a genuine nurturing smile. One smile is delivered for the benefit of the smiler; it's essentially predatory and self-serving. The second is delivered for us, the smilee. It's true, open, and giving.

However, without the mechanism for instinctively evaluating other people's facial expressions, we may use the wrong evaluation criteria. You see, the salesman is often loud and expressive in her expressions, where the true friend is much quieter and more reserved. In the absence of working instinct, we may choose the salesman's louder signal as the better one simply because it gets through to us where the subtle signals (those that are really true) are totally missed. The result can be disastrous, when it comes to romance.

When we respond positively to the salesman, we are in essence accepting her pitch. In commerce, the message might be: *Look at me, I smile and make you feel good, so you will buy your next home from me and I will get a big commission.* In love, the message might be: *Look at me, I smile and make you feel good so you will fall in love with me and buy me things and give me the life I know I deserve.* There is nothing for the recipient of the smile in either of those messages. In contrast, a true message, delivered in the realm of love might be: *Look at me, I smile because I love you and I want to make you happy. When you look happy, I feel good inside.* That message implies a strongly positive and essentially equal exchange for both parties.

Laid out in that manner, no rational person would choose to be in the presence of a "salesman" smile when he could choose a true smile instead. Unfortunately, when people smile at us in real life, their expressions do not come with honest interpretive guidebooks. We have to judge with the tools at hand, in our heads, heads that are all too often inadequate for the task. How do you recognize the genuine smile? How do you tell the person who is true from the one who sees you as a resource to be used, enjoyed, and discarded?

The first tip is that real smiles are not this black and white. Everyone has a mix of salesman and true lover within him or her. Even the hardest-hearted salesman will give a true smile every now and then. And the truest and most nurturing person in the world will still succumb to moments of greed. So it's a balance; we want to find a person who is mostly true. So, what do we look for?

In some cases, we can look for sudden and dramatic changes in the other person's indicated mood. A true person, when feeling a strong emotion, will not be able to change their feelings, or their display of feeling, suddenly. A salesman or trained actor will display any emotion required, at the drop of a hat. That's a skill that comes from one of several sources: In the case of an actor, it results from years of careful practice. In the case of someone else it may indicate a narcissist, a sociopath, or someone who is simply totally superficial. Needless to say, none of those latter things are good attributes in a potential mate. Therefore, the "trueness" of a person whose signals change suddenly and dramatically is open to question. Tread carefully if you see this.

Another clue comes from the smiler's other behavior. A true person will display a consistent positive attitude toward you whatever you do, within reason. A salesman, in contrast, will only like you as long as you are doing what she wants. Ask yourself the question: Is she nice to me all the time, or only on her terms? If you suspect the latter, be wary. Finally, you can look at the requests that accompany the smile. Are they self-serving, or altruistic?

Think of Mom, who smiles and says, *Smile for Mommy. . . . I get so happy when I see you smile!* That's altruistic, and a fair exchange. Now think of the salesman who smiles and says: *Please, will you buy this refrigerator?* The smiler's sole purpose is to sell a refrigerator and earn a commission. To the smiler, the recipient is nothing more than a source of money and a strong back to carry home his purchase. Requests in love can be complex, but with careful observation, a pattern can often be seen.

Remember, there is always a balance. Some smiles will always be self-serving, even in the best of people. What we want to do is weed the totally or mostly self-serving people out of our lives while keeping those that are true close. Here are a few other thoughts:

True love, and the smile that goes with it, is not manipulative or controlling. True love is unconditional. True love does not appear overnight, or after two dates, or even after a month. True love builds over time. A true person may not smile much in the beginning but smile more as feelings develop. A salesman smiles more in the beginning, and less later as your feelings develop because her purpose has been achieved and the smile is no longer needed. True love, and the smile that goes with it, does not hurt. If a person smiles at you, and you wince inside, or wonder what's next, be very, very careful.

I wish I could say, read these rules and avoid the pain I've been through. Unfortunately, life doesn't work that way. As a realist, the best I can hope for is that you'll feel the same hurts I have known, and read this story, and have a flash of insight that perhaps keeps you from being hurt the next time. As my farmer friends say: "There are some men who read the manual. There are a few more who learn by watching. And then there are those who have to pee on the electric fence themselves." Which kind are you?

For many of us on the spectrum, a parent's stated quest to "cure" autism feels sort of like a divorced parent constantly criticizing her ex in front of us kids. As that kid, I know I am half Dad, and half Mom. So when Mom tells me, "Dad is no good," what is she saying about me? For those of you who think this is metaphor, let me assure you it's not.

If much of my life is defined by autism, and autism is a terrible thing, how do you think I will feel about myself? I ended up in special classes because I am autistic. I flunked out because I am autistic. I already know I am disadvantaged with respect to others who are not autistic. I don't need more stuff to feel bad about.

I want useful help. I want to learn how to hold a conversation, how to make a friend, how to get a job. Practical skills are what I need, not moral judgments. That's why it is vital to embrace neurological difference. It is not going to go away, whatever a parent may wish. Demonizing the way we are only makes us feel bad.

And that's not all. I am a logical fellow. When I consider the situation, it's obvious that autism is not evil. It's not good or bad. It just is. There is no morality hidden inside neurological difference. It's not logical. It's taken a lifetime to begin to understand the myriad ways that autism has shaped me. Indeed, as an adult, it's just one of the things that make me who or what I am. It's easy to dwell on what I can't do, and from there I can surely blame autism or anything else for my failure. But I know that's not a line of thinking that leads anywhere. So I try to focus on what I *can* do, and it makes me feel good to say, "See this great gift I have? It's because I'm autistic!"

Maybe you don't agree, and maybe it's not even a gift in your opinion, but why not let me have my joy over that bit of being? Life goes better for all of us if we change what we can, and accept what we can't, with some semblance of a smile. There is nothing wrong with wanting to take away a disability. That's a great goal, and one I fully support. What's wrong is making something out to be "bad" and then failing to take it away, leaving us stuck with the "bad" irremovably bonded to us. Moral judgment has no place in the world of remediating disability.

Alien: A Story of Asperger's Syndrome

STEPHANIE MAYBERRY

I used to beg my mother to "admit" to me that I was adopted. I just knew that had to be why I was so different. Later, about the time that UFOs became popular with *Close Encounters of the Third Kind,* I was convinced I was an alien—or at least an alien hybrid.

Then I grew up.

Thirty-four years later, at the ripe old age of 44, I sat across from a doctor who told me he was giving me a diagnosis of Asperger's syndrome.

And a lifetime of wondering suddenly had all the answers.

Asperger's syndrome is a neurobiological "disorder" that is classified under the autism umbrella (meaning it is an autism spectrum disorder—there is no actual umbrella). People with Asperger's syndrome (AS) may think and act in ways that neurotypical (NT), or "normal," people may consider odd, strange, or even offensive.

I know that there are times I say things that upset people. Over the course of my life, I have done things that caused people to think I was strange. Many even told me so. I never really understood it. Then again, I don't really understand people.

I can't speak for others with Asperger's; I can only talk about my own symptoms and struggles. We are all different, just like "normal" people. There is a saying, "If you have seen one person with Asperger's, you have seen one person with Asperger's." There are some common traits that we Aspies often share though.

I guess I should tell you, Aspie is a moniker that many people with Asperger's use to identify ourselves. It is "politically correct" and perfectly okay to use.

Communication and Social Interaction

I am not a very social person; many Aspies aren't. Some just don't really like people, but many don't know how to function effectively and appropriately in social situations. Sometimes I like to be around people—not too many. I think sometimes that it would be nice to have a friend, a real friend. But people exhaust me.

It is very stressful trying to communicate with people. The things that interest me don't interest them. I am fascinated by neuroscience. I also really like law. My job has to do with law. But when I talk to people about it they tell me that I am talking "over their heads." I am not, I am talking to them, but someone explained to me that that is an expression that means I am talking about things that they can't understand.

Oh, I am a very literal thinker. If you tell me that it is raining cats and dogs outside, the picture I get in my head is of cats and dogs falling from the sky. I know now what that means, but it is still confusing for just a second as I process it. This can make it difficult to talk to people sometimes. Neurotypicals (NTs), or "normal" people, use a lot of terms like this. It can make talking to them very confusing and frustrating for both of us. They say something, I take it literally, and they get frustrated with me because I don't understand. I have been through this a lot. It is not fun.

Many Aspies tend to be very honest. You might think that that is a really good thing, but it has gotten me into trouble more than once. It has also caused me to hurt people's feelings, which is something I never, ever want to do. But they ask me and I answer with the truth.

This is where a lot of Aspies get into trouble. Most of us don't know what to say and what not to say. We can't tell what is appropriate and what isn't. When it comes to our minds, we just say it. When I have tried to explain this to some NTs, they often respond, "Oh, I am like that, too."

The first time this happened, I said, "No, you aren't, not really." They got really offended. But I was just helping them understand. When I was first friends with the man who is now my husband, he spent a lot of time saying, "Wow! You are honest!" He was surprised a lot—he told me I surprised him. I didn't think it would be a surprise because I am the way I am and I don't change.

Most people with Asperger's don't have that intuition, that "knowing," that NTs have. They can "read" people, understanding what facial expressions and vocal tones mean. We can't much of the time. I can tell when a person's expression changes, but I have no idea why. I can't read expressions and it is really confusing because someone can be angry or sad and still smile. How am I supposed to understand that?

They use the same expressions, and sometimes vocal tones, for different emotions. A person can frown when they are angry or when they are concentrating on something or when they are trying to sort something out in their head. Apparently, there are subtle differences that most people would understand to know if the frown was angry or concentrating or whatever. I don't have that.

A lady at work tried to teach me how to "read" facial expressions. She went into this long explanation, telling me that I should pay attention to what emotions I am feeling and what I think that person is feeling or may feel at that time.

I was polite. I listened and said "okay" a bunch of times. But it made no sense. I am not an emotional person and I don't understand emotions in other people. People act on their emotions, and many times they become completely irrational. It just doesn't make sense to me. Plus, how can I know how someone else is feeling if I am not them? Her explanation did not work. But I still thanked her because that is the polite thing to do. It is a rule.

Rules and Routines

Aspies tend to be very rule focused, and I am no exception. I like rules. I like having rules to follow, knowing exactly what I am to do in given situations. I like having a set time to get to work and to go home. It is a little upsetting that they don't have rules at work for breaks and lunch. I am afraid to take breaks sometimes because I don't want it to be wrong and for someone to get upset. I made my own schedule, though, and it works for me. I made my own rules.

Routines are very good, too. I don't like change very much. I don't rearrange my furniture in my home. It changes the way the space feels and I don't feel like I am in my own space. It is upsetting and takes several days or even weeks for me to get used to it.

My morning routine is very precise. I wake at 4:00 a.m. My husband puts his arms around me and holds me for 7 to 10 minutes. I get up and take a shower while he makes coffee. We have our coffee, talk, and sometimes I write while he reads. At 5:00 a.m., we pray together. At 5:15 a.m. we finish praying and I get dressed for work. I leave at 5:27 a.m. The light at the end of the street turns at 5:32 a.m., so I make sure I get to my car out of the parking lot and to the light by then so I can catch a green light. I catch the 5:37 a.m. commuter bus. I always pull into the commuter lot at 5:35 a.m. When my husband drives, though, my schedule gets way off. It makes me feel like I can't breathe. I don't like it when my routine is messed up.

Sensory Defensiveness

I am sensory defensive. Many Aspies are to one degree or another. Sensory defensiveness is a hypersensitivity to one or more senses such as taste, smell, hearing, sight, or touch. Taste isn't bad, but smells and noise can make me very upset. Bright lights are bad, too. When I am in an area where there are bright lights, lots of noise, and activity, I get very agitated and anxious. I just want to run away.

I have worked in situations where people were cruel. Once, I worked for a government agency. I told my boss about my Asperger's and my sensory issues. She acted like she understood, and she did help me for a while. Then one day a coworker told her some lies about me and she got angry with me. She moved me to an area where there was a lot of noise and people moving about all the time. The lights were very bright. It was awful.

Another supervisor arranged for me to move into an office, but for the week I was in that other area, I got very little work completed. It was very stressful.

Noises that bother me the most are noisy food (celery, apples, carrots, chips) and beeping or humming at certain levels. It makes me feel like my ears are going to bleed or like my spine is getting shocked.

I am hypersensitive to touch, but I am not sensitive to pain. I don't really feel pain all that much. However, if I wear the wrong material it will feel as if I am wearing sandpaper. When I shop for clothes (I hate to shop but I have to feel the clothes to make sure I can wear them) I usually go to thrift stores because the clothes are soft and "broken in." As I shop, I look at skirt length first (I only wear skirts, long skirts), then I feel the fabric to make sure it is the right kind. Then I look at the waistband. I have to have an elastic waistband because anything else feels wrong.

When I get stressed, though, all of these things get way worse. Even my softest clothing feels scratchy. Noises seem even louder (I hear really, really well, things other people don't) and lights seem brighter. Smells are stronger.

Right now I am sitting in my living room in my apartment. I can hear the cars out on the street. Someone is setting off fireworks (very stressful—too intermittent and not rhythmic). I can hear my computer running, my refrigerator, my dog breathing, the light on the range buzzing, the crickets outside, my husband breathing in the other room, and the people upstairs walking around in their apartment. The thing is, my brain can't filter the unimportant sounds from the important ones, so it treats each of these sounds as if they are top priority. I am almost always in a state of hyperalertness. You might know it better as "fight or flight."

It is so hard to think with the fireworks going off outside. It is really bothering me. It is also against the rules because it is after 10:00 p.m. That is very rude and inconsiderate. But I wish they would stop because my anxiety is starting to bother me. The sound is too inconsistent and at a bad level.

The Loop

Sometimes a thought gets stuck in my head. I can't get it out. This is a common thing with Aspies. I get the thought or idea and I analyze it, question it, and discuss it. Sometimes it is a concern I have. Other times it is something that really bothers me or I don't understand it.

My husband has gotten very good at redirecting me. He will do something to get my attention on something else. Usually, it has to be something visual and he talks while he shows me. It can be a book or a photo or an electronic device (I like electronics—I am very good with them).

But when these thoughts get stuck in my head, I call it "the loop." My head feels tight and my brain feels like there are gears inside that are grinding, freezing up. I can't think or do anything but concentrate on that one thought. My anxiety gets really bad then.

One thing that gets me in the loop is my face-blindness. If a person isn't where they are supposed to be and I see them, I usually don't recognize them. For instance, one day I went into a convenience store and a lady walked up to me, called me by name, and started talking to me as if she knew me very well. I had no idea who she was. It was very upsetting because I knew that obviously I should know this woman, but I did not. I was looking at her and listening to her, trying to find some clues so I could determine her identity.

I walked out of the store and felt terrible. I was afraid she knew I did not know who she was. I was afraid that I hurt her feelings. It is a terrible, very sad feeling when this happens to you. I went into the loop and kept asking my husband if I had hurt her feelings. I even asked him if he would go back and see her to see if he knew her (I had gone inside by myself). But he said she was probably long gone. That Sunday at church a friend of mine mentioned seeing me at the store. I know this woman well, but I only see her at church. She was not where she "belonged" so I did not recognize her.

Lying will put me in the loop, too. I don't lie. I get very, very upset when someone lies to me or about me. When it happens I feel very violated and helpless. I get very anxious and want to right the wrong. I want to bring the truth to light. Sometimes people don't understand this. They say to just ignore the lie. But that breaks so many rules!

Patterns and Analysis

We Aspies are logical, analytical beings and we usually love patterns. I know that I am drawn to patterns and often find them where other people, NTs, don't see them. While I do tend to analyze things a lot, even overanalyze things, it is very useful.

I think that Asperger's left me with the inability to read people, but God gifted me with a gifted eye for patterns and a sharp mind for analysis. It makes up for what I lack. I like being intelligent.

I can also use these skills to do my own type of "reading" people. I had a supervisor who was very quiet. In the morning she seemed almost crabby. She would frown and sometimes raise her voice a little. Everyone was afraid of her.

I watched her, though, because it seemed that she changed slightly at about midmorning. She seemed to be a reserved and maybe even shy person, but she seemed different later in the day. So, I watched her patterns and analyzed the differences in her demeanor between the time she arrived at work and midmorning. I catalogued responses, the words she used to answer questions, the way her face looked, such as muscle tension around the eyes and mouth, and her speech (did she talk fast or slow, loud or soft, flowing or with spaces between her words?).

What I found was that in the morning she did have a lot of tension around her mouth and her eyes, like the muscles were clenched. Her eyes stayed downcast and her posture was slightly droopy. Her speech was at an odd pitch and her words were not spoken fluidly, but more broken with irregular spaces between.

By afternoon, her facial muscles looked relaxed, her eyes were looking about, above her shoulder level, and they were shiny. Her posture was straighter and stronger. Her speech was much more fluid and seemed to come easier.

I suspected that she was not a morning person (she probably stays up too late and does not get enough sleep). My coworkers were afraid to talk to her at all, but I started talking to her later in the day. She was very friendly.

Finally, I asked her if she was not a morning person. She admitted that she was not. My coworkers were very surprised that I had asked her that. They said they would never ask someone something like that. But she had not reacted badly or like she was offended. She seemed happy. It made our interactions much more pleasurable because I waited until around 10:00 a.m. to approach her on issues. Then she would be awake enough to effectively address them and would not get irritated.

The God I Know

The most important thing about me is that I am a Christian. God is the most important thing in the world to me. Without Him, I would not have the life that I do. And I have a pretty great life. He has guided me through some terrible times and protected me from some very dangerous situations. He has shaped me into someone I actually like.

Even though I grew up in the church, I was not "settled." It seemed that many of the churches I attended would take only parts of the Bible and toss out what they did not want to use. I think a lot of people do that: accept the parts of the Bible that they can live with and discard the things that would infringe upon their lifestyle or hinder their fun.

It doesn't work like that, though. The Bible is God's Word and we are to follow it. That is why I love the Bible. It has such straightforward rules. I can read the Bible and find the answers to just about any questions I have.

True, sometimes the terms are confusing. I am Apostolic now, and when I first started attending I heard the pastor talk about "fruit." There were "fruits of the spirit," people would "bear fruit," and people were told to be "fruitful." That really confused me. I asked my husband and he explained that a person is fruitful when they share the Word with others. They are fruitful when they do things and act in a way that shows people who Jesus is. He explained it better, but I do understand it now.

I haven't always acted in the way I am supposed to act, but God has forgiven me and now I live for Him. He works through me, reaching out to others. I began my blog TheChristianAspie.com because I felt pressed by God to write about what it is like to be a Christian with Asperger's.

I started writing and people started reading. I get letters and comments from people all over the world. Some have questions, some want to tell me that they have Asperger's or someone in their family has Asperger's, some want to ask me how they can best minister to this special group. This has become my ministry.

I never thought I would ever be good enough to minister to people in this way, but God is amazing and He works through me. I have even spoken on Asperger's and accepting people who are different or strange.

He has instilled in me a fierce drive to reach out to this population. There are many, many Christian Aspies out there who want to worship and attend services, but people don't know what to do with them or how to interact with them. The things I am writing are educating those people so that when an Aspie shows up at their church, they can effectively minister to them. And God has blessed me in ways that are just incredible.

My Job

I work a full-time job. It is estimated that approximately 86% of Aspies are not able to keep full-time, permanent employment. I know I have had a lot of different jobs. But I have been on this job for several years now.

It isn't easy. On jobs they expect you to be social. They expect you to attend office parties and go to lunch with people. I don't see work as a social situation. I am there to work, not go to parties. But I am polite so I go for just a minute, then I leave. I am not comfortable at those things anyway.

I have had jobs where I was treated very badly. I have had managers who were very mean to me. Most of it I did not realize, but people I worked with told me. The managers would use sarcasm, and I don't understand sarcasm most of the time. I did not realize they were being mean.

My husband says that it is a good thing that I don't "catch" a lot of that stuff because it did not affect me too much. But some things made me sad. They were really mean sometimes.

Marriage

God has also blessed me with a great marriage to a wonderful man. Many Aspies don't do well in relationships. I did not do well for a long time. I had several marriages and they were very abusive. I don't like to be hit. I don't think it is right, no matter how angry you get. These men hurt me. They hit me and yelled at me. They called me names and told me I was worthless and stupid.

My husband now does not do that. He is very kind and patient. He loves me, but he loves God more and that is the difference. He helps me navigate this world and helps me spiritually. I know that God sent him to me to help me.

The world is a scary, confusing place. Imagine that you are in a foreign land. You don't know the language and you don't understand the culture. Wouldn't you feel much better if you had someone with you who did speak the language and understood the culture? That is what my husband does for me. He is my best friend and I thank God every day for bringing him to me.

I do my very best to be the best wife I can be. The Bible gives us specific instructions on how husbands and wives should act, and we both try very hard to follow them. I am loyal and faithful and loving. I cook for him and keep our home. I am his friend and helpmate. He says I am his best friend.

What Asperger's Means to My Life

Well, I guess Asperger's impacts my life because it is a part of me. I can't imagine being any different. If I had the chance to get "cured," I don't think I would do it. I am afraid it would change too much of me and I wouldn't be me anymore. I like being intelligent and analytical. I like being logical and less emotional.

My husband loves me just as I am. Sometimes I say I wish I had friends or that I wish people would not ignore me. He says that if they took the time to get to know me, they all would love me. I don't know about that, but it sounds nice.

God is using me through the Asperger's. I know this. I see it at work. I can only see my Asperger's as a blessing. Sure, there are struggles sometimes, but in the end, it is well worth it all. I am so very blessed, and I must use that to show others, to give them hope. I can't hide my light by denying my Asperger's and pretending to be normal. That is not the plan, God's plan.

I'll never hide my light.

The Experience of Infantile Autism

Tony W.[2]

I was living in a world of daydreaming and Fear revolving aboud my self I had no care about Human feelings or other people. I was afraid of everything! I was terrified to go in the water swimming, (and of) loud noises; in the dark I had severe, repetitive Nightmares and occasionally hearing electronic noises with nightmares. I would wake up so terrified and disoriented I wasnt able to Find my way out of the room for a few miniuts. It felt like I was being draged to Hell. I was afraid of simple things such as going into the shower, getting my nails cliped, soap in my eyes, rides in the carnival—except the Spook house I love it, I allso like Hellish envirments such as spookhouses at the Carnival, Halloween, and movies—horror. I daydreamed a lot and tryed to actvly communicate and get into that world. I rember Yale Child Study Ctr. I ignored the doctors and did my own thing such as make something and played or idolize it not caring that anybody was in the room. I was also very hat(e)full and sneakey. I struggled and breathed hard because I wanted to kill the gunia pig; as soon as the examiner turned her back I killed it. I hated my mother becaus she try to stop me from being in my world and doing what I liked; so I stoped and as soon as she turn her back I went at it agen. I was very Rebellious and sneaky and distructive. I would plot to kill my mother and destroy the world. Evil thing astonished me such as an H.Bomb. I loved cartoons and their envirments. I also (had) a very warp sence of humor and learn(ed) perveted thing(s) verry quickly. I used to lash out of controll and repeat

[2]From "The Experience of Infantile Autism," by Tony W., *Journal of Autism and Developmental Disorders, 15*(1), 1985. Reprinted with permission of Springer Science + Business Media.

sick, perverted Phrases as well as telling people violent, wild, untrue things to impress them.

In school I learned somethings verry quickly but other were beyond learning comprehenshion. I used to disrupt the whole class and love to drive the teachers nuts. When I first started talking—5 years old—I started talking about an inccendent that happened a year before. I was obsessed with certain things and played in my own way. I make things with Garbage or Junk and Play with them. I like machanical Battery Power toys or electronic toys. Regular toys such as toy trucks, cars that wernt battery powered didnt turn me on at all. I was terrrified to learn to ride the bybycle. One thing I loved that not even the Fear could stop was Airplanes. I saw an air show the planes—f4s—were loud. I was allway(s) Impressed by Airplanes. I drew picutres and had severeal Airplane models. The Test came when we went to D.C. I was so Anxious and Hyper to go on the plane I drove my Parrents nut. The only peace they had is when I heard the turbines reving at the end of the runway. Then I knew we were taking off. Soon as the plane took off I was amazed. I started to yell y(a)h HO! I loved every minuit of it. I allways loved Hi tech thing(s)—Planes, Rockets. I watched a lot of coverage of the rocket launchings, moon landings, and splash downs; I love it. I like Plants too. I grew a lot of Plants too. And I liked Animals to, after the gunia pig killing. I hated sports and still do. (I was) horrified (the) first time I saw my own blood—cut I allso was very hard to assure or convince and allways need reassurrance and still do today. I dont or didnt trust anybody but my self—that still (is) a problem today. And (I) was and still (am) verry insucure! I was very cold Harted too. I(t) was impossible for me to Give or Receive love from anybody. I often Repulse it by turning people off. Thats is still a problem today and relating to other people. I liked things over people and dint care about People at all. I was Verry Fussy about everything and damanded comfort and pleasure and (was) Very Hyperactive and smelled thi(n)gs all the time. I spent hours Flicking books and was thirst(y) all the time and drank a lot—not booze. And was verry Fussy about eating, loved sweets and Junk Food. I was verry unthankfull and Greedy and hard to satisfy. And had and still have some mental blocks and great difficult paying attention and listining to people and was verry eas(i)ly distracted. I damanded to be amused by people and got board verry eas(i)ly and cant deal with stress. And had great difficulty fullfilling oblagations. I woudl hear electronic Noises and have quick siezious (seizures) in bed and many other ph(y)sical problems. Often I have to be Force to get things done and (was) verry uncordinated. And was verry Nervious about everything. And Feared People and Social Activity Greatly. Then I was sent to (another school). My behaivior hasnt change(d) at all or Problems listed before But more physcial problems started shortly before and after leaving (this school). I hated and rebelled. (This other school) was mostly cold harted disipline. There was verry little physical abuse by the staff. Finily My Shrink Pescrided (prescribed) Tillifon (Trilafon) to calm my behavior. The only phsical, medical attention I had was a quick 5 minute Phscial and shots and a blood test to make sure I wouldnt croke by eating 4 Trillifons a day. Those pills knock me out. I had to Fight to stay awake. I complained to the shrink and all he said was my body had to get use(d) to it. He was only 25% right. Once I got use to it I bearly mange(d) to stay awake. But I was mor a vegatable then I was before. I was drowzy all the Time. Shortly before leaving (this school) physcial problms were on the Climb—pounding heard Migranes, headachges, cronic peeing, seeing white bubles, heart pains, and Cronic Fear of Dying. After getting out I complained to my shrink about (it) and my dad—I lived w/my father after (this school)—my parrants divorced. I was deprived (of) physcial treatment becarse of my mental illness. My mother all(ways) wanted Medical testing done to see If There was a Medical problem causing This hellish disease. I(t) was never done and I was often told she was crazy hypocondriat (hypochondriac) and the physcial problem was allso caused by nerves and it was all in my heard. I belived it all for a long Time! And (I) was pescrided Vallium for a short while.

After I left (this school) The physcial problems continued and The list gets longer. I lived with my father and the(n) saw the so call(ed) normal, sick teenage world. I was 14. I set my will (to) be normal like everybody else. (I) look(ed) up to people in school and did what they did to be accepted and put (up) more of a show to hide the problems and be Normal. I forced(d) my self to Know all the top rock groups, smoke pot, and drink and (tried to) have a girl friend. This was the 9th grade and 10th. I constantly got in trouble in school and did som(e) real crazy things to be cool. Like everybody else I thought I was all normal. Most of it was a failure. More people hated me then ever. My interests were destroyed becouse I thought they wernt normal. Things were going bad at home. My Father and I were not getting along becouse of trouble in school. I wasn't getting along with No one. I got my (drivers) license and tryed to impress people at school and girls by driving like a nut. IN tenth grade I quit school and worked washing cars and work(ed) many other Jobs too. I was verry derpressed and Hyper at work. I got along with my boss at all my Jobs. I tend to get lazy and had trouble getting along with other people. So in (an) effort to keep my Jobs I avoided many people. I found It a lot easeyer to get along with older people and FEARED People my age because of school. I went into to the army and got in lots of Fights with people. So I got dicarged (discharged). I allso have great Troub(l)e getting thing(s) organized and missunderstand almost everything. I worked a few more Jobs and hung around w/some Crazy people I knew from school and got drunk a lot and did distructive things, Magnified Fears and Peronia on pot. I never got Fired from a job. My problems havn't changed at ALL from early childhood. I was Just able to Function. And it still (is) the same today—1983. Plus more physcial problems in 1982 knowing that NONE of these problems are gone but only sepressed (suppressed) by Physcatric (Psychiatric) treatment. Then (I) insisted on their was a medical problem but IT programed that Medical Help was a cop out and after (I) Find out more truth about lie and rebelling and hating its and doubting it. And then all the childhood problems and physcial problems starting eating me like a cancer. I then felt The medical help in one of the only hopes for my well being and (that of) Approx. 500,000+ Autistic kids.

ATTENTION-DEFICIT/HYPERACTIVITY
DISORDER (ADHD)

The Only Me That We Have Ever Known

KATY ROLLINS

It's challenging describing something that for your entire life has been your normal. That out-of-step feeling is the only thing I have ever known. You may mourn the out-of-step feeling, but still know it as normal. It means I am always either 20 steps ahead or 20 steps behind. Learning coping skills has allowed me to reconcile the distance between the two, but I still work hard to do so. Medication makes it easier, but the experience is not a perfect one. And it's hard not to criticize yourself for the inconsistency. The scenery never stops moving, but sometimes it's the scenery that's moving and I can't keep up, and other times I move so fast that I outpace it. Medication is what works the best in chronologically synching me with my scenery.

There is a lot more to me than ADHD. I am an intelligent person. I have a master's degree that I worked my ass off for. I work hard in my community because I'm very value driven, and many people in my community consider me successful and a unique, energetic thinker. But even so, I struggle with feeling out of step. I struggle with valuing my own intelligence.

I have never felt out of place in my own family. They say that ADHD is a genetic issue, and in that case my family displays all the signs you would expect. I am not unusual among them. They are vivid, energetic, entrepreneurial, and inventive; they are adaptive, creative people, and logical thinkers, if nonlinear in their approach to life. When I began school as a little girl, I learned what it meant to feel different.

I recall first grade vividly. I could read before I got to first grade, and was a bright child, so my parents were perplexed that my teacher was so critical. She told them I was stupid at math. She kept me indoors every day at recess because I was unable to finish my assignments. I watched the other kids out the window playing at recess instead of finishing the work I was there to complete. ADHD was not a commonly diagnosed phenomenon among little girls then, and I was not disruptive, I was simply elsewhere. I was watching everything.

Later teachers would find me perplexing. Bright, but unfocused. They would try to find educational opportunities that were appropriate. I was not challenged enough to need "special education" but I was unable to reach my "potential." How many ADHDers have spent decades tortured by that nasty concept? I know I'm not the only one. I was kicked out of an honors program for gifted students in the eighth grade. My parents, having their generally high opinion of my intelligence, were appalled. But I know why I failed. . . . I could not keep up. I did not know how to organize and pace my work, and at that age I did not know how to separate the lack of skill from a feeling that something was simply "wrong" with me because I could not succeed.

That same year I failed a reading class. That situation was a little different. Again, my parents' minds were blown, and rightfully so. When they asked me what happened, I said, "It was stupid, I can't believe I had to prove to them that I can read." Perfect ADHD logic. Perfect logic, really, but the school system isn't always based on logic, and I hadn't learned the fine art of just jumping through hoops. I still struggle mightily with the fine art of jumping through hoops and accepting things that don't make logical sense to me. By "struggle mightily" I mean rant and rave about it until those close to me can hardly stand to listen to it anymore.

The differences between how I was perceived at home and at school caused me great pain and depression as a child. I contemplated suicide before reaching middle school, because I did not understand why the rest of the world seemed to find me odd, but my parents found me normal. I assumed that my parents must be the wrong ones, and it broke my fragile heart that they couldn't see what was so wrong with me, even though I myself could not have told you what was "wrong" with me. I just knew something didn't line up.

When I was a child, schools were not prepared to meet the needs of a child who was gifted, but also gifted with ADHD. In high school, I delighted teachers with my intellect but continued to baffle them with my seeming inability to grasp deadlines, occupational focus, or prioritization of any kind. Not to mention that I was always losing things, locking myself out of the house, 20 minutes late for school every morning, and constantly in detention for either chatting or tardiness. When one teacher said, "You are the brightest student I've had in class in 25 years of teaching; I don't understand why you can't focus," I did not think to myself, "Maybe there's a reason." I simply thought, "I must be lazy, and I need to try harder." And I tried hard. I liked grown-ups. I was hungry for information and was a fiercely thorough thinker. But the details of everyday life often overwhelmed me.

One of those everyday details is that I often find human behavior perplexing. It's not because I don't pick up on social cues. It's more like I pick up on so many of them that I just come to different conclusions. I often find that, later, other people understand what I'm saying, if they don't understand it right away. I used to think that meant there was something wrong with me. Now I just understand that at times, my mind has raced ahead, made connections that have simply not been made by the rest of the room yet. Other times, in meetings or conversations, my mind has gone elsewhere and I've floated off because I'm busy thinking about something else and I can't stop. Medication helps me to feel calmer in these situations. Medication allows me to enjoy more of the moment instead of grabbing onto the wind's tail. Medication lets me eagerly engage in a conversation but remember to ask the other people questions, instead of feeling as if I might explode or that I cannot stop an intercontinental leap of thought.

I have always told people that if I seem like I am not listening, it's not because I'm not interested in what they are saying, it's generally because I am *so* interested that my mind riffs on the subject until the subject at hand is no longer recognizable. And I am embarrassed when I find myself so far detached from the conversation. I might be described as a bit hyperactive. But to me it makes more sense to say that my enthusiasm pours out of me in language. I don't jump off of cliffs or drive too fast, but my thinking and talking are hyperactive. This is another area of my life where medication seems to assist. I am more able to "do" and less driven to monologue. In my natural state, it's very hard for me to divert my mouth. I have tact, I have the ability to edit myself, but I just can't stop talking sometimes. People in my life have found it exhausting. Especially when I'm stuck on a particular topic.

And I sometimes don't understand why other people don't see the things that I am seeing. I'm not saying that I am always right, just that often it is much later that people understand what I am really saying. I work to mask impatience because it is not appropriate to display in public, but it takes work. I do the work because it is important to me. I'm not interested in dominating conversations or thinking. I am mostly interested in being heard, and it's hard to be heard when people don't understand what you are saying.

At parties, I cannot sit still in a conversation with people. There is an almost horrifying amount of activity and stimulation, and I can't shut out the distraction. So here's what I do: I'm a matchmaker. I look for people who I think would have fun talking to each other and I introduce them. Or I look to the edges of the room, for shy people who might not be comfortable going up and talking to other people. I go talk to them … and then I match them up with someone. It gives me something fun to do that isn't stressful. When I was younger, to cope with party stress, I would drink an obscene amount of alcohol. Matchmaking is the preferable coping behavior in my mind.

They say there are "types" of ADHD. I'm not sure what I think of that, or how useful it is to my daily life, or to understanding my life as a whole. At some times in my life, some attributes have been more prominent than others. But for many years, even before diagnosis, I told people that I suffered from inertia, inertia in the true physics definition sense of the word: Once I start I can't stop, and once I stop I can't start.

As a child, I was often not focused on what I was supposed to be focused on, but my mind was always busy in a very layered way. And I often found myself in the throes of what they call hyperfocus, to the point where I would literally pee my pants, or not go to the bathroom for hours and hours because I was busy. My mind was busy. I was reading books; I was listening to music. I was busy. And I could not stop. As I grew older I seemed to lose my ability to focus at all, I think because as you age, you interact more with the bigger world, and as you gain independence you have to start prioritizing things for yourself. That's hard.

A comorbid issue for me is anxiety. I seem to be affected by an ambient anxiety that lives in my body, but I also seem to experience anxiety generated by the interaction of my brain with the world. At times, small things are very stressful for me; for example, the sound of a power washer on a construction site across the street, the sound of a bathroom fan, the assault of fluorescent lighting, the intrusion of any overhead lighting for an extended period of time, or the ping-pong of multiple sources of sensory stimulation demanding my attention at once. When a fire truck drives by with its horn blaring I experience a panicked feeling so intense that it makes me want to start screaming and running in terror and I have to consciously stop myself. The sound of my family all talking at once at a holiday dinner (granted, they're objectively *very loud*!) at times sends me upstairs to the quietest room I can find.

My emotions have always been *large*, and one of the biggest ongoing challenges of my life had been learning to guide my emotions in socially appropriate and healthy ways. I had the advantage of a mother who was a social worker, who was able to help me gain awareness of my behavior and the limits a decent person should at least try to work toward. Because I started dealing with this at age 9, I've had a lot of time to really become quite adept and articulate about dealing with my feelings and reactions to things. It's so important for children to have access to these types of interventions. I was arrested once as an older teenager for one of my *big* reactions; and, truly, on the scale of "disorder" I'm probably on the mild end. Learning positive coping skills is absolutely critical.

So what's it like inside my head, inside my life? One of the defining features is a lack of certain types of consistency. My mood and reactions actually fluctuate quite a lot. I've just learned to temper them superficially. And when I can't, I know to give myself a new environment and choose a new path; this is a recent adaptation though. I can pass for "normal" if I have to. The important consideration is how much effort I had to spend to appear that way. As my therapist pointed out, it's simply not healthy to have to spend that much effort fitting yourself into a box. Much better to find a place where you naturally fit. I try to let this consideration guide my decisions now, and my life is starting to feel more comfortable.

What does treatment do? Even when someone tells you that life will be better if you try medication, you don't know what that means. Having my brain means thinking, "Isn't there an off switch for this brain?" on a regular basis. It is exhausting to harness a train every minute of the day, and medication allows me to harness it for at least a portion of my waking hours.

Treatment for ADHD is something that nobody can describe to you. They can tell you the basics but those don't articulate the experience. Medication does not fix you. It does not cure you. It does not make you whole, or make you normal, or make you better. It's sweet heaven to feel that first sense of "focus" from a stimulant medication, and then it's heartbreaking to realize that the unfocus will come back to you. Why would it not? It has always known you. It is also hard to learn the lesson that sometimes when you are taking medication you get so used to it working that you don't feel like it's working. Then you want to stop taking it. So you do. And the "way things used to be" comes back in a horrible way. I become more reactive, moody, stressed out, and anxious—it's awful. Back to the meds, please! Only had to learn that lesson a couple of times. As my prescriber says, I'm really very compliant. It was actually probably valuable for me to see that difference.

And my life *is* different now (I was diagnosed at age 33 when I was in grad school and I'm 35 now). My life has improved, but it is not perfect. I take stimulants and a low-dose antidepressant to ease anxiety. I go to therapy, too. In the mornings it still feels like I am being assaulted by the world from the second a single eye opens. Now, I can take stimulant medication, and after about 10–20 minutes I feel calmer, more able to just be and less apt to react to every small piece of my environment. My morning preparation to go out into the world is less frenzied, which makes it easier to leave the house in an orderly fashion (though I still struggle with timeliness).

Overall, though I still get frustrated sometimes, my life is much better. I used to be up every night until 3 a.m. because my thinking would not shut off. Now, even though I still don't get enough sleep, I can fall asleep by midnight. See what I'm saying? It's not perfect, but it's much better than it was. Medication reduces the amount of general frustration in my life, too. It reduces the number of things that are overwhelming to me. It helps me continue to make better choices. For example, I used to have a bunch of big boxes of stuff from years of my life that I moved around with me (and I moved a lot). In the past two years I have unpacked all of those boxes, and now if I move again I don't have to drag them with me. And I have made a habit of keeping my life a little more orderly and not just stuffing things into boxes. I remember the first time I opened them to unpack them and I turned to my boyfriend at the time and said, "Oh my God, a crazy person packed these boxes," and I laughed and cried because for the first time I was actually *seeing* what was in those boxes. Before, I had only truly been able to throw the things into the box. Medication made me able to *see* things in my surroundings that I never saw before.

One other thing that helps me be me in a more positive way: movement. Even just in a meeting, if I move some part of my body in a quiet way, it's like a switch that allows me to actually hear what people are saying. If I stop moving, my mind starts roving again. Sometimes, truly, I do it just because it's fun to shut the process in my mind on and off—refreshing to have a little control, I suppose. Dance is another love of mine. Flamenco and Latin are my favorite. And I do my best thinking while riding my bicycle, though I don't mind driving, either, because I come up with good ideas and connect things well there, too.

TIC DISORDERS

A Tourette Story

RICK FOWLER[3]

Everyone who has experienced Tourette syndrome (TS) has a different story to tell. Tics and obsessions vary tremendously. Individual reactions to them vary as well. Yet there are basic experiences that many of us with TS tend to have in common. All too often, these include an unfortunate series of misunderstandings and fiascoes in the early stages of diagnosis and treatment.

Over a period of twenty years, I was tested and treated for everything from eye problems to manic depression. The possibility of Tourette syndrome was never mentioned; the cause of my odd behavior remained a mystery. Perhaps by telling my story, I can help others avoid the frustration of a similar ordeal.

As a child, I had boundless energy. I loved to run, climb, and stay constantly busy. Although this is normal childhood behavior, I was more than just a busy kid. My activity level was excessive. I was constantly fidgeting, jerking, and squirming, especially when eating or trying to relax. My parents became concerned and had me examined by a number of physicians. The diagnosis was always the same: "He's just hyperactive. Eventually, he'll grow out of it."

As the years went by, it became apparent that this hyperactivity was something more than a temporary childhood ailment. It was a preface to a much more complex problem. By the time I was twelve, my nervous energy had started to evolve—it seemed to be taking on a life of its own. Rather than disappear, my movements became more exaggerated. My first real tics appeared in my early teens. I began to blink my eyes rapidly and repeatedly, and started jerking my arm up and down by my side. By the time I was a sophomore, these movements were occurring every day, and continued to increase in both frequency and complexity throughout my high school years.

[3]From *The Unwelcome Companion* (pp. 33–44), by Rick Fowler, Athens, GA: Silver Run Publications. Copyright 1996 by R. Fowler. Reprinted with permission.

As I developed so did the tics. The blinking and arm jerks would dominate for a while, and then a new set of gestures would take over, followed by another. I started jerking my head to the side, and at times would touch my nose repeatedly. Periodically, the old tics would return and combine with the new ones, creating a virtual repertoire of unusual movements. Over the years, I learned to disguise a few, but was never able to hide them all. I had no idea why I moved this way, only that I could not stop.

As a result of the tics, I began to develop problems in school, both socially and academically. Due to the twitching of my hands and arms, my handwriting was poor and erratic, often bringing complaints from teachers. I began to feel inferior, and grew somewhat shy and reclusive because of my strange fidgeting. The constant struggle to conceal my symptoms was becoming more difficult. It was embarrassing and frustrating to have so little control over my body.

Still, I was lucky compared to most children with TS, because my symptoms remained relatively minor until my late high school years. By this time, I had already established friendships, and most of my classmates seemed to accept my odd nervous habits. I was also fortunate with regard to vocal tics. The only ones I remember were an occasional clearing of the throat, snort, or grunt. I eventually learned to disguise most of them as allergy problems.

During this same period, obsessive-compulsive rituals also began to develop. I recall counting the cracks in the school lunchroom ceiling tiles. At first, this felt like nothing more than a harmless game to occupy the time, but over the course of a few months, it grew increasingly necessary to count those cracks. Obsessions of this nature became more intense around my senior year of high school. I was rapidly becoming a slave to meaningless mathematical rituals.

The symptoms grew worse as I entered my early twenties. I quickly became out of control. The struggle against tics and obsessive-compulsive rituals took every ounce of my time and energy. Fighting this battle became the sole purpose for my existence. At this point, I began an exhaustive search for answers. Through it all, my parents did everything they could to find the proper help for my condition, help that was then relatively unavailable. They were always supportive, and I often felt guilty for causing them to worry. I was totally baffled as to why I acted so strangely. I knew about hyperactivity, but had never heard that it could cause such bizarre symptoms. There had to be some other explanation.

By the time I had reached my mid-twenties, I had been examined by several doctors, and had been given a number of medications for a variety of possible disorders. I had been addicted to (and had withdrawn from) a couple of different tranquilizers, and had also been prescribed some powerful sedatives, as a restful night's sleep had become a rare luxury. Still, the tics continued, so my family doctor advised me to seek psychotherapy.

My first psychologist thought that he could cure me through hypnosis, but the therapy proved to be unsuccessful. I was never able to relax enough to allow myself to be hypnotized. We had several long sessions, and he concluded that my twitches, jerks, and grunts were a physical manifestation of a deep psychological problem. After a few months, he diagnosed my condition as manic–depressive illness, and he recommended several methods of treatment.

I followed the psychologist's instructions for improving my condition, but nothing seemed to work. At his recommendation, I remained on tranquilizers and learned some relaxation techniques. I also read the self-help books he suggested. Even with this combination of therapy and medication, I continued to fidget, jerk my arms and legs, and clear my throat continuously. Eventually, I began to doubt the psychologist's assumption that manic-depressive illness was the true source of my problems. I decided to go back to a general practitioner, searching elsewhere for the elusive cause of my strange behavior.

My next doctor insisted that I was hyperactive and should try a stimulant. He explained that stimulants had worked well in hyperactive children, and might be able to help a twenty-seven-year-old. Although he said that this was an experimental treatment for someone my age, I was ready to try anything. He instructed me to immediately stop taking my tranquilizer (I had been on the same one for a year and a half by now), and prescribed a drug called *Ritalin* instead.

For the next two weeks, I was in a daze. I could not eat or sleep, and went through a rough withdrawal from the tranquilizer, suffering from vomiting, headaches, confusion, and extreme depression. The jerking symptoms became unbearable. I finally had to stop the stimulant experiment, for fear that it was beginning to cause serious harm. I began to feel as if I had reached an all-time low. No one could figure what was wrong with me, and every treatment I tried seemed to make things worse. As I became more and more depressed, this doctor, having exhausted his repertoire of therapy options, recommended a psychiatrist. Once again, I had come full circle.

Although attempts at psychotherapy had failed in the past, I followed up on the suggestion and had several sessions with a psychiatrist, hoping that his extensive training could help find some answers. After questioning me, he concluded that I suffered from self-induced stress, which caused the tics and obsessions. He also thought that my excessive blinking resulted from eye problems, and he referred me to an ophthalmologist. The eye doctor prescribed some drops to help reduce dryness, but found no major problems. I tried the drops for months, but they proved to be of no avail.

During the months of therapy, the psychiatrist taught me a few techniques for breaking self-destructive mental habits. He continued to insist that excessive worry, overconcern, and a tendency to focus on the negative were the roots of my problem. His methods helped my attitude, but did nothing for my tics, so I moved on.

The guesswork continued for years. I was referred to specialist after specialist. The doctors checked for thyroid disorders, diabetes, and numerous other diseases. Perhaps the absence of profane outbursts prevented anyone from considering TS as my problem. After all, virtually every report published at that time focused on one Tourettic symptom, coprolalia. In retrospect, I can only speculate.

With each failed diagnostic attempt, I became more discouraged. It is ironic that during this long period of trial and error, I probably did develop a few psychological problems. The long and unsuccessful search for the elusive skeleton in my mind's closet may have actually created one. I knew that something was very wrong, and that its origin was likely to remain a mystery forever. This knowledge was an unyielding burden to my mind.

I was finally diagnosed with Tourette syndrome at age 32. Although I was not particularly pleased to have a strange neurological disorder, at least I came to know the identity of my enemy, and this was a great relief. Although it appeared that the battle was almost over, I soon realized that the struggle had just begun. It took years to discover the right combination of drugs for managing my tics and obsessions, and some of the prescribed medications created severe side effects, rendering me unable to function in everyday life.

Since that time, I have researched TS extensively in an effort to understand and cope with my condition. The sensations and emotions associated with it are interesting, varied, and complex. Words alone cannot adequately convey the mental activities endured with this disorder, for printed and spoken dialogue are limited forms of human communication.

Although Tourette syndrome originated in the human brain, it embodies, and more importantly, embraces that which is inhuman.

An Interruption of Regular Programming

A person with Tourette syndrome must live two lives, one dealing with the everyday stresses of health, career, relationships, and finances—the other, a life of struggle, an existence dedicated entirely to battling an invisible enemy. While one portion of the mind maintains contact with the outside world, another is engaged in intense combat with invading Tourettic forces, fighting for the control of conscious thought and actions.

Using an arsenal of ammunition, the foe attacks. One of its most effective weapons is the obsessive thought. An overwhelming notion is introduced, which interrupts concentration, breaks down the rational mind's defenses, and allows this intruder to quickly establish a state of mental mutiny. Its prey becomes oddly convinced that a ritualistic sequence of tics must be carried out immediately. Within a fraction of a second, the initial obsession is followed by the enemy's second line of attack, an intense physical urge to tic.

In order to understand this combination of sensations, imagine you have a horrible itch that is driving you crazy. You must scratch it immediately and repeatedly until it can no longer be felt. Until it is scratched sufficiently, you are overpowered by a feeling that disaster will surely come. The nature of the disaster is not always clear, but the feeling of impending doom is without question. When the consequences are known, they frequently involve your worst fears. The enemy may convince you that you will die, your house will burn, or a loved one's plane will crash if you fail to follow orders.

Whether vague or specific, the fear is just as real and overwhelming as anything in the universe, but it creates no actual terror or panic. These sensations are not perceived as immediate threats, but rather omens, urgent needs to take preventative measures. The rational, analytical mind is fully aware that there is no logical connection between moving a body part and preventing a disaster, yet it is convinced that there may be a connection, one which was somehow overlooked. It is therefore an absolute necessity to tic and continue ticking until the tension relaxes and the sense of premonition dissipates.

Searching for Answers

Crystal Thomas

My first day going into eighth grade, I felt like a psychological prisoner being forced into a physical prison cell. I'd spent the entire summer fighting an enemy that had no name, an enemy inside of me. That entire year, I was bombarded by accusations of every conceivable sort. In May, I'd spent days tormented by incessant worries that I had committed blasphemy, that I had done something terribly immoral, just by reading a book that expressed views that contradicted my deeply held religious beliefs. A debate continually raged inside my head: Were my beliefs true, or had I put so much hope into something that was nothing more than a fable? This thought, which might seem a normal, rational question of any faith, in my mind, burned with a deep, unfathomable pain of guilt. I couldn't think without pain, I couldn't breathe without pain. I was horrible, I was deviant, I was terrible.

This grief sat in my gut for months, chased out all contentment, all peace of mind. I could not eat, sleep, go to swim practice, without the barrage of guilty thoughts pounding me from the inside out. Sometime in June, when the pain had become unbearable, when I had failed to sleep more than a few hours a night for over a week, kept awake by the need to distract myself from the accursed thoughts, I did break down crying, confessing everything, to my mom.

I was terrified of what she'd say when she heard my secret. I feared she'd confirm my deviancy. Yet all she said was that she understood, and that it would be all right. At the moment she gave me her perspective, I loved her more than I ever had before. Eventually, she explained that she too had terrible worries that wouldn't go away, irrational worries that had made her life a hell.

She took me to my developmental pediatrician, Dr. Freeman, who had been following me since I was 10 for care of my then moderate Tourette's and ADHD. Dr. Freeman explained that I had obsessive-compulsive disorder. I didn't know anything about OCD, other than people with it were supposed to wash their hands hundreds of times for no reason. I didn't make the connection, at the time, that the drive behind the endless compulsions were irresistibly terrifying thoughts, nauseating perverse impulses, which sickened those subject to them, who felt no other escape other than to repeat their compulsion time and again. I didn't recognize that I, too, had compulsions, that my thinking certain thoughts a certain way a certain number of times, and praying a certain way a certain number of times, were compulsions.

After an entire summer of psychological torture, I was exhausted. I didn't want to go to school; I didn't want to do anything. I had been on an SSRI antidepressant for about 2 months, but my anxiety was still barely tolerable. This was compounded when, on the first day of school, I discovered that I had been placed in a different class than my friends. While most 13-year-old girls would have taken this with a moderate amount of anxiety, it only added to the near-crippling burden I held inside. On the second day of school, I didn't attend. The afternoon before, I had spent hours crying, overwhelmed, talking about the emptiness of life, the pointlessness I felt in living. I spent the second day of school at a psychologist's office—an emergency appointment. What we talked about I can barely remember. All I can recall is the overwhelming helplessness I felt, the despair that had eaten away everything I cared about.

The next day, I went back to school and settled into a routine, which I dreaded. I was in Algebra I, because I had chosen to retake Pre-Algebra my seventh grade year. Because of my math class switch, I was shuffled into a different class than I'd been in for the last 2 years, away from my few friends, and into a group of students who didn't take as well to my idiosyncrasies, my introversion, my strange twitches and grunts and nods and blinks and shrugs of my tic disorder. Every look someone sent my way I interpreted as a patronizing, falsely friendly laugh sent between two or three other students in the vicinity. I wasn't simply being paranoid; in elementary school, several children had discovered a weakness of mine: my tics. At the time, I had a frequent involuntary vocalization, a pronounced grunt.

Several students enjoyed devising creative ways to exploit my weakness, to point out my tics, to make me feel stupid and useless. So whenever someone in my eighth grade class laughed while looking in my direction, I felt a sting of embarrassment and helplessness; I thought I was being mocked yet again.

By December, my mom had talked the school principal into letting me go to different classes, so that I would be able to be with my accustomed classmates, who were more tolerant of my tics, and with whom I was able to interact without devastating self-consciousness.

It was around the third week of December that I began to feel a gnawing, yet indescribable feeling that something wasn't right. It was like an itch inside my brain that I couldn't scratch. I had noticed I was ticking more, my shrugs and back twists and knee pops becoming more frequent, more severe. One morning in math class, which was still with a different group of students, the teacher asked me to leave so she could explain to the other students why it wasn't acceptable for them to ask me to "shut up" when I kept grunting during a test.

One Sunday, when my family went out to eat, I had to leave the restaurant, as I couldn't take the volume of the noise inside. My cousin asked if I was all right, but I had no answer for him. I didn't know why I felt strange, nor could I imagine what this vague feeling would turn into. That night, I noticed my nodding tic was especially vicious; in my blog post that night, I described the headache the nodding seemed to have given me.

Then, on the following Tuesday, December 15, 2008, I was in band class when my arms started shaking. The movement was a flapping motion akin to what a child does during the "chicken dance." And it didn't stop. I couldn't make them stop; I couldn't hold a pencil to write, and had to ask to go home.

My mom made an emergency appointment with my developmental pediatrician, Dr. Freeman, who was stunned to see the persistent flapping, at first mistaking it to be me shaking water off my hands as I'd just walked out of the bathroom. When she took my vital signs, my pulse was fast, she couldn't get my blood pressure from all the movement, and I was covered in sweat and flushed from the exertion of the continual flapping. She said it must be a tic, and wrote a prescription for Lamictal, and told my mom to make an appointment with my neurologist immediately.

I soon discovered that deep-breathing exercises temporarily slowed the movements, but didn't have any effect after I stopped the special breathing pattern. I didn't go to school that week, nor would I for most of the next 2 years.

When my neurologist's appointment arrived, 2 days later, on December 17, my symptoms had expanded to include convulsive jerking of my body, barking, screeching, echo-like repetition of others' speech, repetition of my own speech, and random bursts of words that seemed to come from nowhere.

That morning, as I watched TV, I began saying "shark" over and over, and then it morphed into "shit-shark-shit."

By the time we arrived at my neurologist's office, an hour-long car ride away, I was coated in sweat and had peeled off my jacket, pushed up my sleeves, already exhausted by the near continuous convulsions and outbursts. In the waiting room, I sat, feeling as if every eye were on me, like a freak in a circus sideshow.

When the doctor entered the room, she checked my chart, and noting it was my birthday, said, "Happy birthday." Between barks and screeches, I replied, "Fix me."

That was her only interaction with me; she checked a couple reflexes, and then turned to my parents as I sat on the exam table, convulsing rapidly, my head lolling back so that it banged against the wall behind me. I kept repeating what the others in the room said, screeching, flapping, jerking. At the end of the appointment, she ordered a routine blood test and wrote a prescription for Risperdal to slow my tics.

After a few days on Risperdal, it became evident it wasn't helping. Whenever I took it, I would sleep for hours, and when a dose wore off, I would continue to tic violently. One night in Walmart, I began squatting every few steps. This became persistent, to the point I could barely get around my own house without being out of breath from the extraneous movements that walking triggered. Dr. Freeman was concerned that I might have an autoimmune reaction to strep, which could be worsening my tics, so she sent us to a walk-in clinic for a rapid strep test.

The doctor at the walk-in clinic was an older man, Dr. Creech, who looked at me for a moment, convulsing on the chair in the exam room, my elbows slamming into my ribs, producing all sorts of noises, and asked what had been going on with me. His tone was that of a concerned professional; he stated he was worried for my safety given the violence of the movements I was experiencing, that perhaps I needed to be in the hospital. When we declined the suggestion, he mentioned he had trained at a prestigious Maryland hospital, and that he might be able to get us an appointment there. I had the rapid strep test at the lab, and then we left.

Dr. Creech was true to his word; a few days after Christmas, my family packed into our truck and headed off to Maryland, a 5-hour ride. We rented a hotel with a medical floor that had a shuttle to the hospital, and went sightseeing as we waited for the appointment day. I was humiliated each time I went out into the streets; heads turned at me, the girl in the wheel-chair, who jerked, shrieked, barked, and shouted strange words.

At our visit, I was nearly petrified by the sheer size of the building, and in turns, startled by the stares of all the doctors who walked around. My mom joked doctors were worse when it came to staring than the general public.

The neurologist we saw examined me, taking various reflexes and testing sensation in my extremities, testing my coordination, and then talked to my mom. He said I had been on Risperdal, a drug in a level of treatment akin to a second line of defense, but it wasn't working properly for me. He recommended fluphenazine, an even stronger medication, with a somewhat higher likelihood of diminishing my tics. He ordered various blood tests and an EKG to make sure nothing else was wrong, that my tics were from my Tourette's, and sent us home with the prescription.

A few days after we got home, having taken a longer route to show my brother the battleship yard at Norfolk, Virginia, my parents had the fluphenazine filled.

We nervously anticipated the relief it could bring. Two days passed uneventfully after starting the medication, but on the third morning, I woke up feeling a nagging dread that intensified by breakfast, when my head abruptly angled to one side. Lying down and deep breathing didn't help, so I called for my mom. I was terrified; the rest of my body began to bend itself into odd angles, my back and legs bowing, my feet folding in. My mom called Dr. Freeman, who told her to give me some Benadryl and call poison control. I began vomiting, too, so the Benadryl didn't stay down. The ridiculous posture was extremely uncomfortable; my neck hurt, my back was so contorted I couldn't lie flat; I drooled because my spasming jaw and tongue made it difficult to swallow. At this point, my mom called my dad to come home, and when he arrived, he carried me to the truck and raced away to the hospital.

When we arrived, I was rushed straight through triage, taken to a bed, and nurses established an IV, stripped off my clothes, and put me in a gown. They asked me questions to check my mental status, but I could barely speak; my mouth was locked in a position that I couldn't move from.

I was given an anticholinergic, Cogentin, and Benadryl in my IV, and within 15 minutes, my head had begun to go back to its normal position. After another 10 minutes and a second injection into the IV, my back straightened, and the rest of my body slowly relaxed from the contortions. I was able to speak again, and with that, came the ability to tic. When the nurse came in to do an EKG, I was already back to my moderate vocal and movement tics. Later, my mom told me what was going on: I'd had an acute dystonic reaction to the fluphenazine. I had no choice but to discontinue the fluphenazine to keep the reaction from continuing.

A few days later, Dr. Foreman called in a second prescription, Haldol, another potent antipsychotic, which was also highly effective at reducing tics, but less likely than fluphenazine to cause such a reaction. As a precaution, I took Cogentin with each dose of Haldol to prevent another reaction. Two weeks passed uneventfully, save for the continual cycles of tics. I was at an appointment with an immunologist, to check for further possibilities of immune disorder, when the lip-smacking began. It continued through the hour-long appointment, at which point I told my mom guardedly, "This doesn't feel like a tic." She nodded, and called Dr. Foreman, who said we should see her immediately. At her office, she said it looked like dyskinesia, a repetitive spasmodic puckering of the mouth, and that this, too, was likely due to my medication. By then, I'd done enough reading about antipsychotics and the side effects they cause to know that dyskinesias and dystonias caused by them can become permanent with continued use. This unsettling knowledge lent the situation yet more urgency. My mom gave me another dose of Cogentin. In about 15 minutes, the puckering had stopped while we were in a Staples. I wandered around the office supply store in my wheelchair, lamenting the fact that yet another treatment had failed.

Crisis

Over the next few weeks, into February, my tics continued to mushroom. I was by now punching and slapping myself in the face, head, and chest, slamming my feet against each other, squatting and hopping every few steps when I walked, swearing and saying racial slurs, spitting and striking at walls and objects. During this time, I tried a few more medications: Lamictal for my mood, Xanax as a sedative to give me a little relief from the tics.

However, none of these seemed to help. One afternoon, on the way home from town with my dad, I kicked the car windshield. A large spiderweb crack spread under the toe of my shoe. As soon as I saw the crack, my heart sank. But my dad was incredibly patient; he swore and told me it was okay. At that moment, I knew my disorder was truly out of control. When I got inside the house, the same urge in my foot came up; I was walking to my room as fast as I could, but something inside me pulled me toward the dining room wall. My foot kicked out, and smashed a hole 3 inches wide into the wall.

That night, I was ticking continually, crying because I couldn't make my body stop despite the exhaustion I felt. My parents took me to the ER of a university hospital an hour and a half away, hoping to get a line through to their anxiety clinic. At the ER, my mom had to help calm me down before the staff could get an IV in to give me a sedative.

All I can remember after the injection of the sedative, Ativan, is how my vision went fuzzy and I felt drunk. I have no memory of the rest of the following night.

For the next couple days, I drifted in and out of a stupor, caused by oral Ativan tablets the ER doctors had prescribed. Yet, somewhere in the trance, my personality changed. Whenever I was aroused, I became hostile, ripping at my own clothes and body. I knocked a hole through my bedroom window by slapping it. I still recall vividly the awful sinking in my stomach as the glass tinkled down to the floor, and my recoil, filled with dread and a surreal horror. More continual tics followed, and by mid-evening I was so agitated, my parents took me to the ER of University Hospital II. On the way, I'd first bitten and scratched myself, then the car door, then chewed the sleeve off my own shirt. I must have looked like a madwoman upon arrival. When we went into triage, I poked the nurse on the shoulder, and he called security. A scuffle ensued; my dad says I drew blood on the guards. All I can really recall is being pinned on the floor under other peoples' hands, jerking, screaming, and being placed in restraints, a mask over my face. I continued to tic, but the restraints held my body down despite the violent spasms, sending shock-waves of pain up and down my limbs. Someone gave me more Ativan, but it didn't help. My mom says I was screaming, first that it hurt that I couldn't tic, and then that people were going to eat me. I was terrified, in pain from my tics and the restraints pinning me down, my thoughts distorted by medication to the point I believed my own doctors were plotting to kill and eat me. The doctor eventually gave me a second injection, and I passed out.

I woke up in a tiny room with rubber furniture, where my parents were sitting, by some miracle allowed to stay with me through the night. We spent 30 hours in that tiny, miserable ward, until a neurologist visited and convinced the attending doctor that I was safe to go home. Later, I'd find out that Ativan, a sedative, can cause unusual paradoxical reactions in some individuals—for me in the form of paranoia and agitation. The medication built up in my system over the few days I was on it to the point that whatever reaction I'd begun to have culminated in the terrifying episode of psychosis.

Shortly after that incident, I tried another medication, Abilify. It's commonly used as an antidepressant, but it acts to reduce dopamine, so it is, theoretically, beneficial for tics. I took the medication at night. The next evening, I was out shopping with my aunt, when I began to feel nauseous. I grabbed a fast-food bag just in time before I began vomiting. I continued to spew stomach contents for an hour, until I got home and my mom gave me an antiemetic the ER doctors had given us in case of another dystonic reaction with vomiting. Two days later, I took the medication again, on my doctor's advice, and the next evening, the same continual vomiting ensued.

It was easy for Dr. Freeman to see that I couldn't take Abilify.

In March, we got a call from the anxiety center, that they had a spot open for us to make an appointment. On the day of the appointment, my parents wheeled me into the waiting room where I proceeded to throw magazines and toys from a toy chest and scream, jerking on the floor. At the time, my mind was lost in the awful behaviors, and the shame of being so out of control.

Dr. Danning came out of the hallway and showed us the way back to her office. It was a small room, with a couch and office furniture, and a window that showed a large apartment building and parking deck on the other side of the block.

Over the coming sessions, I'd sit staring at the buildings out the window, trying to listen to what Danning was saying. But I was barely able to think—disjointed, strange things, of misery, of pain—of my disorder. I was prescribed Topamax by the neurologist I saw at Danning's request, which he said would be extremely efficient at slowing my tics, and the only side effect to look out for was difficulty thinking. But what I experienced wasn't just cognitive dulling. My personality was radically changed; I couldn't muster a smile, at times my words came out slurred, I slept most of the day and ate little, and could barely get up off the couch for fatigue to go to the bathroom. And every waking moment, I punched myself in the head, slapped my own face, slammed myself against the walls of my house until the Sheetrock crumbled into gray dust with chips of paint cascading to the ground. Soon our house had more holes than walls.

Meanwhile, Dr. Danning tried to educate me about my disorder; she said my real issue was compulsions in my OCD. When my mom mentioned the mounting destruction of the holes, Danning asked me if the holes had to be symmetrical, if that was why I kept making them. I vaguely wondered if she'd heard me say I didn't have any reason at all to destroy my parents' home. The holes were simply there because I involuntarily, repeatedly, slammed myself into the wall—a tic. I didn't want the holes…[I wanted her to understand] what I was trying to tell her.

One afternoon, I asked my dad to kill me. I had been thinking and talking about dying, about the relief it would be, for weeks. A few days later, over the weekend, the last shreds of control I had over myself vanished. I spent hours lying on the floor, screaming, jerking, banging my head into the laminate flooring. I kicked a hole through a wooden closet door. I broke all the way through the second pane in my window. I talked about killing myself and my parents. Late that night, my mom called 911. For some reason, police came instead of an ambulance. By then, one of the episodes had waned, lessened, and I was lying relatively quietly on the floor of the dining room, after nearly an hour of jerking, screaming, banging. The officers who came didn't try to hold me down—we just talked. One of them had a medical condition, too, which had landed him in the ICU in the hospital on his 19th birthday. He seemed to understand what it was to have lost control of one's body.

After a while, the police called for an ambulance and left. It came, and I was taken to the local hospital's ER, where I was given a small dose of Ativan. By midnight, my parents were asleep in the bedside chairs, but I chattered endlessly, watching the news about the swine flu epidemic. Around four in the morning, a nurse realized I hadn't slept, and gave me an injection of Geodon. It took effect quickly; I slept through the morning, as my parents took me to my appointment with my oblivious Dr. Danning.

Panicked after hearing the events of the preceding weekend, Dr. Danning called an ambulance, which took me to another ER, this time at university hospital. By evening, the nurses had become tired of my tics and gave me an injection of Ativan. Mistake. I became wild, pacing aggravatedly, only complying with orders to lie back down when the nurses threatened to restrain me. At the end of their patience, several nurses took me in my bed to the crisis unit and injected me with Geodon in the thigh as I struggled under them. My bed was wheeled into a dingy, padded cell where I quickly passed out.

Sometime in late morning the next day, I was allowed back into the regular ER where my parents were. Dad supplied pizza for a late lunch; afternoon hit with a new wave of tics that again angered my nurses and earned me another spot in the dirty, padded cell, this time on a plastic bench built into the off-white vinyl walls.

In late afternoon, an episode of shaking wracked my body, forcing me to lie on the floor, where my head and body jerked until I felt nauseous, calling out for help until an irate nurse peeked in. But by the time they came back with medication, the episode had ended, the tics calmed to my continual barks and swears and twitches.

In the evening, a stretcher was wheeled into my padded cell, and someone told me to get on it. In the back of the ambulance where I was taken on the stretcher, I was told I was being taken to a psychiatric hospital. I kept thinking: I'd rather be dead now. This can't be happening. Within a few minutes, the EMTs on the ambulance had noticed my tics. I kept hitting myself, then tapping on the cabinets in the ambulance. One of them told me to stop. But I couldn't. So they got the straps out. The ride to the mental hospital was 2 hours—2 hours in which I continually fought the straps, screaming, spitting, jerking, biting the straps the EMTs tied perpetually tighter around my arms. It hurt horribly; my body kept trying to tic only to contract uncontrollably, wrenching my joints in the restraints, as my urges to tic built up.

Eventually, I was wheeled through the hospital to the psych floor, where personnel surrounded my stretcher, explaining to my parents dumbfounding news: I wasn't going to be accepted there. Their facility wouldn't admit me because they hadn't been informed of the violent nature of my condition.

The psych ward personnel sent my parents, the EMTs, and me downstairs to the ER, but the ER personnel soon tired of my outbursts and sent us back upstairs to the psychiatric ward. Over a period of a few hours that we sat in the psychiatric ward entrance, my parents explained to the EMTs what was going on. I also had time to calm; eventually, I had to relieve myself, and they took off the restraints so I could use the bathroom. Not long after my release from the restraints, someone told my parents I could go home. My dad had doubts, but my mom convinced him to let me go home.

On advice from Dr. Freeman, who answered their desperate phone call the night the psych ward refused me, I withdrew from the Topamax, and within a few days, I was no longer suicidal. I now had a new symptom, however—anxieties about security and emergency personnel, psychiatric wards; one afternoon I saw a nurse's uniform in a drugstore and began to hyperventilate and cry. I had nightmares about psychiatric wards, restraints, and injections that caused dystonic reactions.

A new counselor I began seeing diagnosed me with posttraumatic stress disorder.

Despite all this, I attended Camp Twitch and Shout a month after being "kicked out" of the psychiatric ward. Camp Twitch and Shout is a weeklong summer camp for teens and kids with Tourette's. At camp, I was normal; I had friends who understood my tics. I didn't want to leave when my parents came to pick me up.

Over the summer, two more medication trials ensued. Moban, another antipsychotic, gave me severe restlessness and mild dystonic reactions. Namenda caused the worst dystonic reaction I ever had; its pain and spasms surpassed those of fluphenazine.

In the fall of 2009, I participated in a research study on a noninvasive brain stimulation technique for Tourette's. It didn't improve my tics, but the doctor conducting the study began seeing me as a patient, and has had excellent recommendations for novel treatments, which other doctors hadn't conceived of.

In the coming winter, I began having muscle spasms similar to those of dystonic reactions, continually, but I wasn't on any medication that could cause a dystonic reaction. From December through March, I had muscle spasms of every part of my body, which made walking impossible and contorted every part of my body: face, hands, arms, legs, toes—everything. No doctor my parents could find seemed to know what it was. Dr. Freeman had never seen the likes of it before. One neurologist was vague and said it would probably go away soon; another accused me of faking, which made me wheel my chair out of his office in tears.

In March, I saw yet another specialist, Dr. Bringer, who carefully explained to me that my dystonia was real, but its cause, so far as she could tell, was psychogenic. The afternoon of my appointment with her, I walked around the front yard of my house; the spasms vanished from my body. It seemed that the insight of my brain's trickery was enough to lift the symptoms.

On the researcher's advice, I returned to regular school. It took months of meetings with the school administration to prepare, but in the spring of 2010, I went to ninth grade English class for the first time. I had just gotten used to walking again, my feet still aching, weak from months of disuse.

The year 2010 was the beginning of a new life for me. My tics continue to be debilitating; I have an aide at school who follows me with a wheelchair wherever I go because I need it often due to large jerking movements and squatting tics, but I've realized I can still do things. I completed Driver's Ed this spring. I passed tenth grade with As and Bs. I have several friends at school, and trained to be a counselor at Camp Twitch and Shout this summer.

Dr. Freeman continues to see me, a guardian angel of sorts, helping my parents to find local doctors to carry out the novel approaches to treatment the researcher from the trial I was in recommends.

Now, I am 16, and an online activist of sorts for Tourette's syndrome and other movement disorders. I continue to search for a treatment that will relieve me of the debilitating symptoms I experience, but already have one valuable weapon: *meaning*. Through my disorder, I have discovered a passion for neurology and psychology. I plan to go to medical school after college and become double-certified in neurology and psychiatry. I wish to research Tourette's and related neurologic disorders, perhaps to contribute to a hope of a future cure.

Index

A

ACT (Assertive Community Treatment) Teams, 13
ADHD (attention-deficit/hyperactivity disorder),
    444–449
Adolescence, disorders usually diagnosed in, *see*
    Childhood disorders
Age-related cognitive decline, 303
Agnosia, 329
Ahern, L., 30
Alaoglu, Ann, 16–17
Alcoholics Anonymous, 222, 225
Alcoholism, 217–227
    and drug addiction, 232
    and insomnia, 407
Alcohol use:
    with ADHD, 447
    with anorexia, 274
    and mental disorders, 216
    and narcolepsy, 416
    and polysubstance abuse, 229–230, 232
    with social anxiety disorder, 124
    and transsexualism, 383–385
"Alien: A Story of Asperger's Syndrome" (Stephanie
    Mayberry), 431–440
Aloneness:
    with anorexia, 268
    feelings of, 22, 83
    as theme of first person accounts, *xxi*
Alternative health therapies, for schizophrenia,
    17, 18
Alzheimer's disease, 304, 306–310
Amenorrhea, 238
Amnesia, 304–305
    dissociative, 305, 346
    with severe physical illness, 325, 327
Amnestic disorders, 303
    characteristics of, 304–305

dissociative disorders vs., 305, 347
Amsel, Peter, 76–91
Analgesics, 335
Andrews, Linda Wasmer, 153
Anger:
    with Alzheimer's disease, 309
    and anorexia, 282–283
    and depression, 66
Angst:
    with bipolar disorder, 81
    with panic disorder, 109
Anorexia nervosa, 237, 239–276, 281–284
    and abandonment of talents and interests,
        270–271
    with BPD, 210–211
    with bulimia, 278
    characteristics of, 238
    early symptoms of, 239–241
    and family eating/health practices, 265–267,
        282
    and the feeling of hunger, 240, 260
    and identity, 242, 272–273
    internal elitism with, 269
    as means of control, 241–243, 269
    and natural body type, 263, 264
    obsessions and compulsions with, 281–284
    OCD with, 240–245, 258
    and weight for sports, 339
Antidepressants:
    for ADHD, 449
    for bipolar disorders, 77, 92, 102
    and tics, 462
Antipsychotic medications, 22–23
    cost of peer support vs., 34
    individual effects of, 32
    for Tourette's syndrome, 459, 460
Antisocial personality disorder, 198

Anxiety. *See also specific disorders*
    accepting, 119
    counteracted with euphoria, 334–335
    food, 135–136
    insidious nature of, 112
    inviting, 113–115
Anxiety and Stress Disorders Institute of
    Maryland, 118
Anxiety disorders, 105–195
    in children, 422
    demographics of, 105–106
    lifetime prevalence rate for, 50, 106
    obsessive-compulsive disorder, 142–174
    panic disorder, 108–121
    phobias, 122–141
    posttraumatic stress disorder, 175–195
    professionals' unfamiliarity with, 111
    symptoms of, 106
Anxiety Disorders Association of America, 120
Apprehension, in anxiety disorders, 106
Armah, Justin, 63–65
*The Armed Robbery Orgasm: A Lovemap
    Autobiography of Masochism* (Ronald Keys
    and John Money), 374–376
Armour, Mary Anne, 182–186, 188
Armstrong, Lance, 32
Asking for help, with schizophrenia, 16
Asperger's syndrome, 431–440
    and communication, 426–433
    and employment, 438–439, 443
    likely impairments with, 427
    "loop" thoughts with, 435–436
    marriage and, 439
    patterns and analysis with, 436–437
    and religious beliefs, 437–438, 440
    rules and routines with, 433–434
    sensory defensiveness with, 434–435
"Aspie," 432
Assertive Community Treatment (ACT)
    Teams, 13
Asylum, *xvi*, 24
Attention-deficit disorder, 421
Attention-deficit/hyperactivity disorder (ADHD),
    444–449
Autism:
    Asperger's syndrome, 426–440
    brain dysfunction with, 426
    as communication impairment, 426
    infantile autism, 440–443
    Kanner's, 427
Autism spectrum, 426
Automatic thoughts, *see* Self-talk
Avoidance:
    with anorexia, 272–273
    with panic disorder, 110, 114, 117
Avoidant personality disorder, 198

B

Banyard, V. L., *xvii–xviii*
Barlow, David, 109
A Beautiful Mind (motion picture), *xvi*
Becker, Priscilla, 263–276
Before It's Too Late (Jane McAllister), 306–310
Behavioral therapy, for panic disorders, 120
"Being Bipolar: Living on Both Sides of the Coin"
    (Susan Michele Vale), 101–104
Beliefs:
    and Asperger's syndrome, 437–438, 440
    in coping with bipolar, type II, 186
    in coping with PTSD, 186
    as disease triggers, 152
    and Tourette's syndrome, 455
Belittlement, 45
"The Best Medicine" (Susan A. Salsman), 6–9
Bette, Laura, 281–284
Betty Ford Center, 219, 221–226
Bibliotherapy, for PTSD, 184–187
"Big Little" (Priscilla Becker), 263–276
"Bigorexia: Bodybuilding and Muscle
    Dysmorphia," 339–341
Binge eating, 274. *See also* Bulimia nervosa
"Binging and Purging to Stay Alive," 276–280
The Biology of Belief (Bruce Lipton), 152–153
Bipolar, type I, 80
Bipolar, type II, 76–91
Bipolar disorders, 76–104
    with BPD, 210–211
    and creativity, 76–79
    cyclical patterns in, 81–82, 97–101
    depression with, 78–80, 82, 92
    distinctions among, 80
    personality changes with, 98
    psychiatric professional's experience with,
        101–104
    rapid cycling bipolar disorder, 91–96
    self-management of bipolar II, 76–91
Black, Jed, 408
Black, R., 29
Bodybuilding, 339–341
Body dysmorphic disorder, 324
Bola, J. R., 32
Borderline personality disorder (BPD), 198–213
    behaviors and symptoms associated with, 198
    comorbidity with, 210–211
    criteria for, 212–213
    emotional assaults with, 204–205
    how mental health professionals can help with,
        205–207
    identity with, 200, 202, 208–210
    misconceptions about, 203–204
    mood swings with, 211
    self-injury with, 200–201
    suicide attempts with, 203–204, 206

Botox, for vaginismus, 371–372
Bourke-White, Margaret, 317
BPD. *See* Borderline personality disorder
Breaking the Silence (Steven Hinshaw), *xvi, xx*
Brief psychotic disorder, 2
Brown, Les, 57
Bulimia nervosa, 237, 276–280
    with BPD, 210–211
    characteristics of, 238

C

Campbell, J., 39
Camp Twitch and Shout, 465, 466
Carbonell, Dave, 111
Cardiac arrest, memory loss due to, 310–317
Career shaping, as theme of first person accounts,
    xxii
Carlin, George, 153
Cataplexy, with narcolepsy, 402, 403, 415
Catatonic behavior, with psychotic disorders, 2
CATIE (Clinical Antipsychotic Trials Of
    Intervention Effectiveness), 33
Centers for Medicare and Medicaid Services
    (CMS), 29
Central sleep apnea, 402
The Centre for Research on Eating Disorders at
    Oxford (CREDO), 256
Chaos stories, *xvii*
Children, sleep terror disorders in, 403
Childhood disorders, 421–466
    attention-deficit/hyperactivity disorder,
        444–449
    diagnosing, 422–423
    pervasive developmental disorders, 426–443
    tic disorders, 450–466
Chinese culture, transsexualism and, 388–397
Chipmunka, *xvi*
Choices:
    in developing DID coping strategies, 357
    in schizophrenia treatment, 29–30
TheChristianAspie.com, 438
Chronic ailments:
    insomnia, 404, 410
    resistant reactions to diagnoses of, 318–319
Cioran, E. M., 406
Circadian rhythm disorders, 402
"A 'Classic' Case of Borderline Personality
    Disorder" (Lynn Williams), 203–207
Cleaning:
    and mysophobia, 137–138
    and obsessive-compulsive disorder,
        151–153
Clifford, J. S., *xvi*
Clinical Antipsychotic Trials Of Intervention
    Effectiveness (CATIE), 33
The Cloister Walk (Kathleen Norris), 183

Clumsiness:
    with autism spectrum disorders, 427
    with narcolepsy, 416–419
CMS (Centers for Medicare and Medicaid
    Services), 29
Cognitive-behavior therapy, for anorexia, 256
Cognitive disorders, 303–322
    Alzheimer's disease, 306–310
    amnesia, 304–305
    delirium, 303–304
    dementia, 304
    due to cardiac arrest and coma, 310–317
    Parkinson's disease, 317–322
Cognitive therapy, for panic disorders, 120
Coma, memory loss due to, 310–317
Communication:
    and ADHD, 446–447
    and Asperger's syndrome, 426–431
    and the autism spectrum, 426
    from peer supporters vs. traditional
        providers, 28–29
    of sleep-deprived people, 405
Communication disorders, 421
"Communication Impairment" (John Elder
    Robison), 426–431
Comorbidity:
    of ADHD and anxiety, 447
    with BPD, 210–211
    with childhood disorders, 422
    of depersonalization, 347
    with OCD, 156, 159–160
Compulsory admission/treatment, for
    schizophrenia, 19
Conceptual thinking, memory loss and, 312
Confusion:
    with schizophrenia, 20
    as theme of first person accounts,
        xx–xxi
Control:
    and Alzheimer's disease, 309
    and anorexia, 241–243, 269
Conversation, after memory loss, 314
Conversion disorder, 324
Coping skills:
    for ADHD, 448
    for panic disorders, 118–119
"Coping Strategies" (Ruth Dee), 348–357
Counting Sheep (Paul Martin), 405
Courage, as theme of first person accounts, *xxii*
Cousins, Norman, 322
Creativity:
    and alcoholism, 222–223
    and bipolar disorders, 76–79
CREDO (The Centre for Research on Eating
    Disorders at Oxford), 256
Creuzfeldt Jakob disease, 342

D

Daniell, Rosemary, 187
Danquah, Meri Nana-Ama, 61–66
"Dan's Story," 298–301
Darkness Invisible, xvi
Davidson, L., 29
Davidson, Neil, 217–227
DBT (Dialectical Behavioral Therapy), for BPD,
    211–212
Dee, Ruth, 348–357
Deegan, Patricia, 26, 29, 30, 34
DeFulgentis, Frank R., 142–153
Delirium, 303–304
Delusional disorder, 2
Delusions, 2
    with bipolar disorders, 93–95
    dismissing thought-voices as, 23
    with psychotic disorders, 2
    with schizophrenia, 10, 19
Demeaning experiences, 45
Dementia, 303
    Alzheimer's disease, 306–310
    characteristics of, 304
Democratic psychiatry, 24
"The Demons of War Are Persistent: A Personal
    Story of Prolonged PTSD" (Art W.
    Schade), 189–195
Demoralization, with panic disorder, 117
Denial:
    as defense, 8–9
    with transsexualism, 381
Dependent personality disorder, 198
Depersonalization, 347
Depersonalization disorder, 347
Depression:
    with Alzheimer's disease, 310
    as anger turned inward, 66
    and anorexia, 240, 283
    with bipolar disorder, 78–80, 82, 92
    with BPD, 211
    in childhood, 421
    and insomnia, 407
    as a mood disorder, 53–57, 61–66
    with OCD, 156
    postpartum, 66–75
    with postpartum depression, 74
    with schizoaffective disorders, 38
    with schizophrenia, 11
    and serotonin levels, 289
    with social anxiety disorder, 125, 131–132
    and trichotillomania, 289
"Depression: Disease, Loneliness, Social Isolation,
    Suicide, Negative Thoughts..." (Bec
    Morrison), 53–57
Depressive disorders, 53–75
    depression, 53–57, 61–66
    and meaning in life, 57–61

postpartum depression, 66–75
Depressive episodes, 50
Derealization, 347
Desire to get well, need for, 8
Dew, Mary Amanda, 407
Diabetes, comparing a mental illness to, 43–47
Diagnosis of mental illness, peer support and, 27
*Diagnostic and Statistical Manual of Mental
    Disorders (DSM):*
    age-related cognitive decline in, 303
    anxiety disorders in, 105–106
    mood disorders in, 49–51
*Diagnostic and Statistical Manual of Mental
    Disorders,* 3rd edition *(DSM-III),* 2
*Diagnostic and Statistical Manual of Mental
    Disorders,* 4th edition, Text Revision
    (DSM-IV-TR), xxiii
    and childhood disorders, 421–423
    cognitive disorders in, 303
    dissociative disorders in, 345, 346
    eating disorders in, 238
    impulse control disorders in, 285
    McNally's critique of, *xxiv*
    narcolepsy in, 414
    personality disorder in, 197–198
    psychotic disorders in, 1
    PTSD in, 106
    sleep disorders in, 401, 402
    substance-related disorders in, 216
Dialectical Behavioral Therapy (DBT), for BPD,
    211–212
DID. *See* Dissociative identity disorder
Different People, Different Voices, xvi
Disclosure, lack of:
    due to fear of professionals, 21
    in general, *see* Hiding symptoms
Discrimination:
    in hiring, 12
    against transsexuals, 380
Disease course, for mental vs. physical illnesses, 46
Disorganized behavior/speech/thought, with
    psychotic disorders, 2
Disorientation, with depression, 61
Disruptive behavior disorders, 421, 422
Dissociative amnesia, 305, 346
Dissociative disorders, 345–364
    amnestic disorders vs., 305, 347
    depersonalization disorder, 347
    dissociative amnesia, 346
    dissociative fugue, 346
    dissociative identity disorder, 346–364
Dissociative fugue, 346
Dissociative identity disorder (DID), 347–364
    characteristics of, 346–347
    coping mechanisms for, 348–357
    multiple identities with, 361–364
    and self-forgiveness, 358–361

Dissociative states, 345–346
Distraction, to cope with anxiety, 112
Doctor-patient partnerships, 88–89
Don't Panic (R. Reid Wilson), 113
Dopamine supersensitivity, 33
Dorros, Sidney, 317–322
Down with the Rain, xvi
Dreams:
    and gender identity disorder, 377, 378
    and narcolepsy, 415
Drinking: A Love Story, *xvi*
Drug use. *See also* Substance-related disorders
    with anorexia, 274
    and insomnia, 406, 412
    and mental disorders, 216
    with OCD, 156
DSM. See Diagnostic and Statistical Manual of
    Mental Disorders
DSM-III (Diagnostic and Statistical Manual of
    Mental Disorders, 3rd edition), 2
DSM-IV-TR. See Diagnostic and Statistical Manual
    of Mental Disorders, 4th edition, Text
    Revision
"Dying by Inches" (Emily Troscianko), 239–263
Dyskinesia, with antipsychotics, 460
Dyspareunia, 366
Dyssomnias:
    characteristics of, 402
    primary insomnia, 402, 404–413
Dystonias:
    with antipsychotics, 460
    with Tourette's treatment, 465

E
Eating disorders, 237–284, 421
    anorexia, 239–276, 281–284
    bulimia, 276–280
    reasons for developing, 280
ECT. *See* Electroconvulsive therapy
Eidetic pain, 338
Eiken, S., 39
Electroconvulsive therapy (ECT):
    for depression, 54, 56
    for postpartum depression, 71
Elimination disorders, 421
Embarrassment, with trichotillomania, 288, 289
EMDR (Eye Movement Desensitization and
    Reprocessing):
    for PTSD, 188
    for schizoaffective disorder, 38
Emerson, Ralph Waldo, 19
Emotional assaults:
    with BPD, 204–205, 211
    with gender identity disorder, 378
    with Tourette's syndrome, 455, 456
"Emotional Triangle" (Blazie Holling), 175–181
Employment. *See also* Reentering the work force

with Asperger's syndrome, 434, 438–439, 443
coping with DID in, 350–352
and insomnia, 405
and Parkinson's disease, 321
and social anxiety disorder, 127, 131–133
Empowerment:
    in learning about your illness, 85–86
    in recovery from schizophrenia, 17
    through choice of medications, 31–32
Epidemics III (Hippocrates), 287
Erectile disorder, 366
Everitt, Daniel, 408
Everyday lives and experiences, as theme of first
    person accounts, *xxii*
Evidence-based practice:
    patient access to information on, 30
    peer support as, 28–30
Exhibitionism, 366
"The Experience of Infantile Autism" (Tony W.),
    440–443
Experience Project, *xvi*
Exposure plus response prevention (EX/RP), for
    OCD, 155–156
Exposure therapy, for panic disorder, 119
Eye Movement Desensitization and Reprocessing
    (EMDR):
    for PTSD, 188
    for schizoaffective disorder, 38

F
Face-blindness, with Asperger's syndrome, 435–436
Facial expressions, autism spectrum disorders and,
    427–430, 433
Falls, narcolepsy and, 416–419
False beliefs, with psychotic disorders, 2
False memories, 359
Family:
    anorexia and eating/health practices of,
        265–267, 282
    effect of gambling addiction on, 300–301
    feelings of, with mental vs. physical illnesses, 45
    and mysophobia, 138–139
    SAD and social functions with, 126
Family support:
    with anorexia, 246–248, 252–254
    with Asperger's, 439
    with BPD, 201
    in dealing with mental health problems, 21
    with depression, 56–57, 64–66
    with DID, 358–359
    with mysophobia, 138–141
    with narcolepsy, 419
    with panic disorder, 121
    with Parkinson's disease, 320, 321
    and polysubstance abuse, 230
    in schizophrenia recovery, 11, 17, 18
    with Tourette's, 455, 461, 463–464

Family support (*continued*)
    and transsexualism, 390–391, 395, 397
"Family Talk" (Barbara Hope), 358–361
Fatigue:
    with bipolar disorder, 94
    with depression, 61
Fear. *See also* specific disorders
    and anxiety, 112
    of contracting a parent's mental illness, 360
    of meeting with mental health professionals, 21
    and pain, 337–338
    and substance addiction, 228, 229
Feeding disorders, 421
Fetishes, 366
Filson, Beth, 30
First break (schizophrenia), 1
First person accounts (FPAs), *xv–xvii*
    as challenge to service delivery systems, *xx*
    emerging themes in, *xix–xxiii*
    motives and purposes of, *xvii–xix*
Fisher, D. B., 30
Flashbacks, with PTSD, 179–181, 185, 186
"Flux" (Frank R. DeFulgentis), 142–153
Food anxiety, with mysophobia, 135–136
Ford, Betty, 221
Forgiveness, DID and, 360–361
Fowler, Kristen B., 38–43
Fowler, Rick, 450–454
FPAs. *See* First person accounts
Fractured (Ruth Dee), 349
"Fractured Mind, One Heart?" (Robert B.
    Oxnam), 361–364
Frank, Arthur, *xvii*
Frankl, V. E., 90
Franklin, Martin, 153
Fraser, Kennedy, 187
Freeman, Dr., 455, 457–459, 462, 465, 466
French, Aaron J., 228–232
Freud, Sigmund, 327–328
Friends' feelings:
    with bipolar disorders, 96
    with depression, 63
    with mental vs. physical illnesses, 45–46
    and transsexualism, 386–388
Frotteurism, 366

G

Gambling addiction, 298–301
Garland, Judy, 406
Gender identity disorders, 365, 377–399
    characteristics of, 366–367
    female-to-male transsexualism, 388–399
    male-to-female transsexualism, 377–388
Gene activation, 152
Generalized anxiety disorder, 106
Giffords, Gabrielle, *xviii*
Girl Interrupted (motion picture), *xvi*

Going Hungry, xvi
"Goodbye, Johnnie Walker" (Neil Davidson),
    217–227
Goodwin, F. K., 76
Gray, Benjamin, *xvi–xvii*, 19–25
Grazia, Daniela, 122–133
Green, Melanie, 199–203
Greenblat, Cathy S., 17
Greenblat, Leslie, 14–19
Greene, Gayle, 404–413
Grief, with depression, 61
Grounding strategies, for DID, 353
Guilt:
    with anorexia, 275
    with mysophobia, 139–140

H

Hallucinations:
    with polysubstance abuse, 230
    with postpartum depression, 74
    with psychotic disorders, 2
Hand-washing, with OCD, 142–145, 168–169
Hapto therapy, for transsexualism, 396
Health, as ongoing process of self-reflection and
    action, 18
Health services, overmedication in, 22
Health Talk, *xvi*
Hearing voices, *see* Thought-voices
Hearing Voices: The Personal Stories of Voice Hearers
    (Intervoice and Benjamin Gray), 24
Hearing voices movement, 24
Hearing Voices Network, *xvi*, 24
Helplessness, feelings of:
    with BPD, 206
    with schizophrenia, 20
Het Jongensuur, 395
Hiding symptoms:
    of bipolar disorders, 103
    of bipolar II, 76, 86
    of postpartum depression, 67–69, 74
    of schizophrenia, 21
    of social anxiety disorder, 125, 130
    with Tourette's syndrome, 451
    of trichotillomania, 288
Higgins, Patricia, 414–419
Hill, Darryl, 367
Hinshaw, Steven, *xx*
Hippocrates, 287
Hoarding, with OCD, 157–159
Holling, Blazie, 175–181
Holocaust, 90
Homosexuality, transsexuality and, 386, 394, 399
Honesty, with Asperger's, 432–433, 436
Hope, Barbara, 358–361
Hope, losing, 85
Hope and Help for Your Nerves (Claire Weekes), 118

Hormonal imbalance, insomnia and, 406, 411
Horne, James, 408
Hornstein, Gail, *xvi*
Hospital experience:
　with BPD, 204–206
　with mental vs. physical illnesses, 44–45
　with postpartum depression, 69–71
　with pyromania, 295
　revolving door syndrome, 15
　with schizophrenia, 10, 14, 21–22
　violence in, 22, 45
Human, being treated as, 17, 24
Hyperactivity:
　attention-deficit/hyperactivity disorder,
　　444–449
　with Tourette's syndrome, 450–452
Hyperfocus, 447
Hypnosis, for vaginismus, 370–371
Hypoactive sexual desire, 366
"Hypochondria" (Heather Menzies Jones), 341–344
Hypochondriasis, 324, 341–344
Hypomanic episodes, 50
　with bipolar disorders, 80
　mania vs., 80–81
　and rapid cycling, 82

I

ICD-10 (International Classification of Diseases), 401
ICSC-2 (International Classification of Sleep
　　Disorders-2), 401
Identity:
　and anorexia, 242, 272–273
　in bipolar disorders, 100
　with BPD, 200, 202, 208–210
　gender, *see* Gender identity disorders
　and memory loss, 311
　multiple, *see* Dissociative identity disorder
　　(DID)
Identity shaping, as theme of first person accounts,
　　xxii
Immelt, Jeffrey, 407
Impulse control disorders, 285–301
　gambling addiction, 298–301
　pyromania, 294–298
　trichotillomania, 286–294
Impulsivity, 285–286
Infancy, disorders usually first diagnosed in. *See*
　　Childhood disorders
Inhibited orgasm, 366
The Inner World of Mental Illness (Bert Kaplan), *xv*
Insomnia:
　with bipolar disorder, 85
　chronic, 404, 410
　with Parkinson's disease, 320
　physicians' approaches/attitudes toward,
　　407–409, 412

　with postpartum depression, 69, 73
　primary, 404–413
　research on, 410–412
Insomnia (Stephen King), 405–405
"An Insomniac's Slant on Sleep" (Gayle Greene),
　　404–413
Integration, of multiple personalities, 362
Intermittent explosive disorder, 286
International Classification of Diseases
　　(ICD-10), 401
International Classification of Sleep Disorders-2
　　(ICSC-2), 401
Intervoice, *xvi,* 24
Invisibility, feelings of, 22
In vivo therapy, for panic disorder, 119
Isolation:
　with panic disorder, 111, 117, 120
　with Parkinson's disease, 320
　with schizophrenia, 20
　with social anxiety disorder, 130–131
　as theme of first person accounts, *xxi*
　with transsexualism, 380
"It'll Be Okay. How I Kept Obsessive-compulsive
　　Disorder (OCD) From Ruining My Life"
　　(Shannon Shy), 160–174
"I Wish I Had Gotten Help Sooner: My Struggle
　　With Postpartum Depression" (Marcie
　　Ramirez), 66–72

J

Jackson, Michael, 406
Jamison, K. R., 76
Jensen, P. S., 423
John Kender Diet, 291
Johns Hopkins Sexual Disorders Clinic, 374–375
Jones, Bob, 318
Jones, Heather Menzies, 341–344
Jungian psychology, 197

K

Kam Wai Jui, 388–399
Kanner's autism, 427
Kant, Jared Douglas, 153–160, 423
Kaplan, Bert, *xv*
Kender, John, 291
Keys, Ronald, 374–376
King, Stephen, 405–405
Kleptomania, 286
Knapp, P., 423
Krieger, Myer, 407

L

Learning:
　after memory loss, 314
　of language, autism and, 426–427

Learning About Mental Health Practice
    (P. Amsel), 76–77
Learning disorders, 421
LeCroy, Craig, *xvii, xxvii,* 422, 423, 425
Ledger, Heath, 406
Lehne, Gregory, 375
"Life With an Eating Disorder" (Laura Bette),
    281–284
Linehan, Marsha, 212
Lipton, Bruce, 152
Living life, re-learning the activities of, 11–14
"Living with the Dragon: The Long Road to Self-
    Management of Bipolar II" (Peter Amsel),
    76–91
Loneliness:
    with insomnia, 404
    with panic disorder, 117
    with Parkinson's disease, 320
Loss, feelings of, 20
Loud in the House of Myself (Stacy Pershall),
    207–213
Love and Lovesickness (John Money), 376
Luchins, D. J., 34
Ludeman, Susan, 115–121

M

McAllister, Jane, 306–310
McCall, Catherine, 181–188
Major depressive disorder:
    bipolar disorder vs., 78–79
    lifetime prevalence rate of, 49
Major depressive episodes, 50
Mania, defined, 287
Manic depression, 79
Manic Depression (F. K. Goodwin and K. R.
    Jamison), 76
Manic episodes, 50, 80
    with BPD, 212, 213
    hypomania vs., 80–81
Mantle, Mickey, 221
Martin, Paul, 405
Masochism, 366, 374–376
Mayberry, Stephanie, 431–440
MCI (mild cognitive impairment), 304
McNally, Richard, *xxiii–xxiv*
Meaning in life:
    and bipolar II, 79
    and depressive disorders, 57–61
    and schizophrenia, 13
Medicaid coverage, of peer support, 29–30
Medical conditions:
    mood disorders due to, 50
    psychotic disorders due to, 2
Medications:
    addiction to, 233, 235
    for ADHD, 444, 446, 448–449

analgesics, 335
for Asperger's, 442
for bipolar disorders, 77, 83–84, 92,
    102, 103
for BPD, 200
for depression, 53–56
for DID, 360
and insomnia, 406, 412
and narcolepsy, 417–418
overreliance on, 22, 23
for panic disorder, 111, 113, 116–117
for Parkinson's disease, 321
patient choices in, 31–33
personal medicine vs., 26–27
for postpartum depression, 75
for schizoaffective disorders, 38
for schizophrenia, 8, 9, 15, 32–34
self-determination of, 25
side effects of, 22, 33, 103, 460
for tics, 452
for Tourette's syndrome, 457–463, 465
for trichotillomania, 289, 291
violence in administering, 21
Meltzer, Malcolm L., 310–317
Memoirs, *xvi,* 187–188
"Memoirs of a Compulsive Firesetter" (Sarah
    Wheaton), 294–298
Memory loss. *See also* Cognitive disorders
    with dissociative amnesia, 346
    due to cardiac arrest and coma, 310–317
    from ECT, 54
    suggestions for dealing with, 315–317
Mental Health Act of the United Kingdom, 19
Mental Health America of the Heartland,
    27, 29
Mental health professionals:
    for alcoholism, 221–226
    for BPD, 204–207
    for DID, 352–357
    fear of meeting with, 21
    impression of lack of interest by, 78
    for narcolepsy, 418–419
    for panic disorders, 118
    peer support specialists vs., 28–29
    for postpartum depression, 67–68
    and self-knowledge, 16
    and social anxiety disorder, 130, 132
    support of patients' proactivity by, 88–89
    and Tourette's syndrome, 452, 453
    understanding of mental illness by, 6–7
    unhelpful, 10, 16, 17, 130
    for vaginismus, 370, 371
Mental health system, needed transformation of,
    25–26
Mental illness/mental disorders:
    in children, 422, 423
    defined, 414

defining, *xxiii–xxiv*
distribution in general population, 49
power of learning about, 85–86
stigmatizing attitudes toward, *xviii*
substance abuse with, 216
Mental retardation, 421
Mental rituals, with OCD, 147–149
"Metaphor and the Role of Genes and
    Development" (H. F. Nijhout), 152
Methodology for Epidemiology of Mental Disorders
    in Children and Adolescents, 422
Mild cognitive impairment (MCI), 304
MindFreedom, *xvi*, 24
Mind Matters Monthly, 27
Mixed episodes, 50
Money, John, 374–376
Monroe, Marilyn, 406
Montgomery Community College, 17
Mood disorders, 49–104
    bipolar disorders, 76–104
    and BPD, 211
    in children, 422
    depressive disorders, 53–75
    distribution in general population, 49–50
    DSM criteria for, 50–51
    lifetime prevalence rate for, 49–50
    mood episodes in, 50
    signs and symptoms of, 50
Mood disorders due to medical conditions, 50
Mood episodes, 50
Morris, M., 24
Morrison, Bec, 53–57
Mosher, L. R., 32
Motivation, insomnia and, 405
Motor skills disorders, 421
Mrazek, D. A., 423
Multiple personality disorder (MPD), 346, 361,
    364. *See also* Dissociative identity disorder
    (DID)
Munthe, Axel, 404–406
Murder, witnessing, 179–181
Muscle dysmorphia, 339–341
My Confession: My Life Had Come to a Sudden Stop
    (Leo Tolstoi), 57–61
"My Journey Through Postpartum Depressions"
    (Jessica Rodorigo-Dunican), 72–75
"My Path to Recovery" (Melanie Green), 199–203
Mysophobia, 133–141
    and cleaning habits, 137–138
    emotions associated with, 139–140
    fear of germs, 133–138
    food anxiety with, 135–136
    how others can help with, 140–141
    others' perceptions of, 138–139
"Mysophobia" (Catherine Taylor), 133–141
"My Story of Narcolepsy" (Patricia Higgins),
    414–419

N

Napiorkowski, Michael, 97–101
Narcissistic personality disorder, 198
Narcolepsy, 414–419
    characteristics of, 402
    early symptoms of, 415–416
    as nervous system disorder vs. mental illness,
        414–415
    neurobiological causes of, 409–410
Narcolepsy Network, 419
Narcotics addiction, 232–235
Narratives:
    transformative, *xx, xxii*
    types of, *xvii*
National Alliance of Mental Illness, 414
National Comorbidity Survey Replication
    (NCS-R), 50, 106
National Epidemiological Survey on Alcoholism
    and Related Conditions, 49, 216
National Institutes of Health, 410, 411
National Sleep Foundation, 401
Native American culture, 377–378
NCS-R (National Comorbidity Survey
    Replication), 50, 106
Nettelbladt, P., 44
Neurosis, 1
Neurotic disorders, 1–2
*Never Tell: The True Story of Overcoming a Traumatic
    Childhood* (Catherine McCall), 187
Nietzsche, Friedrich, 388
Nightmare disorder, 403
Nijhout, H. F., 152
Nonverbal communication, autism spectrum
    disorders and, 427–430
Norcross, J., *xvi*
Norris, Kathleen, 183
"The Numbers of My Obsession" (Mia Zamora),
    286–294
Nunes, J., *xix*
"A Nurse's Journey Through Loss, Addiction, and
    Recovery" (Michelle Walter), 232–235

O

Obsessive-compulsive disorder (OCD), 142–174
    with anorexia, 240–245, 258
    cleaning habits with, 151–153
    comorbidity with, 156, 159–160
    EX/RP for, 155–156
    fear of germs with, 151–153, 157, 168–169
    hand-washing dilemma with, 142–145
    hoarding with, 157–159
    imagined violence with, 153–156
    mental rituals with, 147–149
    with postpartum depression, 70, 71, 74
    and practicing imperfection, 145–147
    and satisfaction of derivative desires, 150–151

Obsessive-compulsive disorder (OCD) *(continued)*
symptoms of, 160–171
and Tourette's, 455
Obsessive-compulsive personality disorder, 198
Obsessive-compulsive rituals:
with anorexia nervosa, 281–284
with Tourette's syndrome, 451
Obstructive sleep apnea (OSA), 402
OCD. *See* Obsessive-compulsive disorder
Öjehagen, A., 44
"The Only Me That We Have Ever Known" (Katy Rollins), 444–449
"On Madness: A Personal Account of Rapid Cycling Bipolar Disorder," 91–96
"On the Outside Looking In" (Daniela Grazia), 122–133
Orbison, Kelly, 108–115
Organic brain/mental disorders, 303
Orgasmic disorders, 366
OSA (obstructive sleep apnea), 402
Osmond, H., *xvi*
Ostracism, feelings of, 22
Outpatient programs, for depression, 56
Oxnam, Robert B., 361–364

P

Pacik, Dr., 371, 372
Pain:
with bipolar disorder, 94
with BPD, 205
eidetic, 338
emotional reactions to, 327–330, 332–334, 337–338
ending, 87
and insomnia, 411
qualities of, 335
with schizophrenia, 20
as theme of first person accounts, *xxi*
Pain disorder, 324
"Panic, Anxiety, PTSD, and My Experiences of Healing Through Multiple Avenues of Psychotherapy" (Catherine McCall), 181–188
Panic attacks:
feelings accompanying, 109
with OCD, 156
with polysubstance abuse, 229
with postpartum depression, 73–74
with PTSD, 177–178, 181
with social anxiety disorder, 128
Panic disorder, 106, 108–121
early symptoms of, 108–109, 115–116
self-management of, 111–115
stories with, 109–110
symptoms of, 116
Paranoia, with polysubstance abuse, 229

Paranoid personality disorder, 198
Paraphilias:
characteristics of, 366
of masochism, 374–376
Paraphrasing, in treating schizophrenia, 17
Parasomnias, 402–403
Parenting Mentally Ill Children: Faith, Hope, Support, and Survival (Craig LeCroy), 422, 423, 425
Parkinsonian Society, 322
Parkinson's: A Patient's View (Sidney Dorros), 317–322
Parkinson's disease, 317–322
Partnership-based care, 88–89, 355
Pathological gambling, 286, 298–301
Paulson, R., 28
PDD-NOS, 426
Pedophilia, 366
Peer support (for panic disorder), 111
Peer support (for schizophrenia), 25–31, 32–35
in challenging assumptions, 34
as evidence-based practice, 28–30
and medications, 32–35
services of, 28–29
to show choices, 30–32
Perception problems, with psychotic disorders, 2
Perfectionism, social anxiety disorder and, 123
Pershall, Stacy, 207–213
Persona, 197
Personality, 197
after memory loss, 215
with bipolar disorders, 92, 98
with schizoaffective disorder, 41
Personality disorders, 197–213
borderline personality disorder, 198–213
names of, 198
Personal medicine, 26–27
Person-centered psychiatry, 24
PERT (psychological emergency response teams), 69
Pervasive developmental disorders, 421, 426–443
Asperger's syndrome, 426–440
autism, 426–443
infantile autism, 440–443
Peterson, D., *xvi*
Phenomenological school of psychopathology, 325–326
Phobias, 122–141
mysophobia, 133–141
social anxiety disorder, 122–133
Physical contact, during surgical procedures, 330
Physical disease:
and insomnia, 409
psychopathological aspects of, 325–338
Pica, 238
Poe, Edgar Allan, 225
Polysubstance addiction, 228–235

"Poor Memory: A Case Report" (Malcolm L. Meltzer), 310–317
Postpartum depression (PPD), 66–75
OCD with, 70, 71, 74
panic attacks with, 73–74
screening for, 66–67, 72
Posttraumatic stress disorder (PTSD), 106, 175–195
early symptoms of, 175–176, 181–182
flashbacks with, 179–181, 185, 186
panic attacks with, 177–178, 181
psychotherapy experience with, 183–188
"Powerful Choices: Peer Support and Individualized Medication Self-Determination" (Corinna West), 25–37
PPD. *See* Postpartum depression
Practice:
for overcoming panic disorder, 119
Premature ejaculation, 366
Presley, Elvis, 406
Primary hypersomnia, 402
Primary insomnia, 402, 404–413
Primary sleep disorders, 402
Prison, feeling of being in, 45, 284
Privacy:
with mental vs. physical illnesses, 47
and schizophrenia though-voices, 15–16
Prozac Nation, xvi
PSR (Psychiatric/Psychosocial Rehabilitation):
Certificate Program for, 13
Core Principles 7 and 8, 10
PSR/Readaption Psychosociale Canada Ontario Chapter, 13
Psychiatric News, 367
Psychiatric/Psychosocial Rehabilitation (PSR):
Certificate Program for, 13
Core Principles 7 and 8, 10
Psychiatric Rehabilitation programs, 84–85
"Psychiatry and Oppression: A Personal Account of Compulsory Admission and Medical Treatment" (Benjamin Gray), 19–25
Psychopathological aspects of physical disease, 325–338
Psychopathology, 2
Psychosis, 1
"A Psychosomatic Study of Myself" (Fredric Wertham), 325–338
Psychotic disorders, 1–47
criteria for, 3
schizoaffective disorders, 38–47
schizophrenia, 6–37
symptoms of, 2–3
Psychotic disorder due to general medical condition, 2
PTSD. *See* Posttraumatic stress disorder
Purpose in life, rediscovering, 13
Pyromania, 286, 294–298

Q

Quest stories, *xvii*
Quitting the Nairobi Trio, xvi

R

Rage, with BPD, 204
Ramirez, Marcie, 66–72
"Random Scribblings on Bipolar Disorder" (Michael Napiorkowski), 97–101
Rape, as PTSD trigger, 185, 186
Rapid cycling bipolar disorder, 82, 91–96
Reactive attachment disorder, 421
Reading, memory loss and, 313
Reality, break with, 1–2
Recovery. *See also specific conditions*
ambivalence in, 280
choice-making for, 30
desire for, 90
due to hard work, 16–17
as getting life back, 203
goal of, 13–14
as learning to live life again, 11–14
patient's role in, 8–9, 18, 90
personal medicine for, 26
"Recovery as Discovery" (Paolo Scotti), 9–14
Recreation, memory loss and, 312–313
Reentering the work force:
after depression treatment, 56
after schizophrenia treatment, 12–13, 17, 33–34
through peer specialist training, 34
REM behavior disorder, 409, 410
Rescue, longing for, 204, 205
Restitution stories, *xvii*
Restless leg syndrome, 409, 410
Returning to school:
after schizophrenia treatment, 12, 18
with social anxiety disorder, 131
Richardson, Gary, 410
Ridgway, P., *xix–xx*
"Rituals, Routines, and Recovery: Living with OCD" (Jared Douglas Kant), 153–160
Robison, John Elder, 426–431
Rodorigo-Duncan, Jessica, 72–75
Role modeling, by peer specialists, 30
Rollins, Katy, 444–449
Romme, M., 24
Rooney, Andy, 225
"A Rose in Bloom" (April Rose Schneider), 377–388
Ross, Jerilyn, 111
Roth, Thomas, 410
Routines, Asperger's syndrome and, 433–434
Rowe, M., 29
Rules, Asperger's syndrome and, 433, 437
Rumination disorder, 238

S

Sacks, Oliver, 319
SAD. *See* Social anxiety disorder
Sadism, 366
Sadness, with depression, 61
Salsman, Susan A., 6–9
San Diego police, 68–69
Sanofi-Aventis, 410
Schade, Art W., 189–195
Schizoaffective disorders, 38–47
    compared to physical illnesses, 43–47
    first symptoms of, 38–43
    gender incidence of, 3
    psychotic symptoms in, 2
Schizophrenia, 6–37
    first break in, 1
    as fundamentally flawed label, 25
    medications for, 8, 9, 15, 32–35
    onset of, 3
    others' understanding of, 7–8
    peer support specialists for, 25–31, 32–35
    positive and negative symptoms of, 3
    psychotic symptoms in, 2–3
    reentering the work force/school with,
        12–13, 17
    self-blame for symptoms of, 10–11
    self-directed recovery from, 8–9
    thought-voices with, 10, 14–25
Schizophrenia Bulletin, 3
Schizophreniform disorder, 2
Schizotypal personality disorder, 2
Schneider, April Rose, 377–388
Schneider, Doris, 377
Schneider, Kurt, 2
Schneider, Roland, 377
School:
    for children with ADHD, 444–446
    for children with Tourette's, 456–457
    returning to, *see* Returning to school
Science-to-service gaps, in schizophrenia treatment,
    26, 32–33
Scotti, Paolo, 9–14
"Searching for Answers" (Crystal Thomas),
    455–466
Selective mutism, 421
Self-blame, for schizophrenia symptoms, 10–11
Self-determination, of medication choices, 32–35
Self-directed recovery, from schizophrenia, 8–9
Self-forgiveness, DID and, 358–361
Self-image, 325
    and autism, 430–431
    and transsexualism, 387–388
Self-injury:
    with BPD, 200–201
    and eating disorders, 281
    with schizoaffective disorders, 40–43
Self-management:

    of bipolar II, 76–91
    of panic disorder, 111–115
Self-obsession, with depression, 64
Self-pity, with schizophrenia, 20
Self-stigma, *xxi*
Self-talk, with social anxiety disorder, 124, 125,
    132
Self-worth:
    and anorexia, 282
    and BPD, 202
Sells, D., 29
Senility, 304
Sensory defensiveness, with Asperger's syndrome,
    434–435
Sensory-motor psychotherapy, for DID, 356
Sensory overload, with depression, 62
Separation anxiety disorder, 421
Serin, U., 44
Serotonin, 289
Sex reassignment surgery (SRS), 386
Sexual abuse:
    and DID, 347–349, 352
    as PTSD trigger, 185, 186
    and pyromania, 295
    and vaginismus, 369, 371
Sexual arousal disorders, 366
Sexual behavior disorders, 365–399
    gender identity disorders, 377–399
    paraphilias, 374–376
    sexual dysfunctions, 366
    sexual pain disorders, 369–373
Sexuality, 365–367, 382
Sexual masochism and sadism, 366
Sexual pain disorders, 366, 369–373
Shame:
    with DID, 359
    and transsexualism, 393
    with trichotillomania, 288–290, 293
Shaping identity and career, as theme of first person
    accounts, *xxii*
Shared psychotic disorder, 2
Sharing, to cope with schizophrenia, 16
Shy, Shannon, 160–174
Simmir, S., *xix*
Sleep disorders, 401–419
    circadian rhythm disorders, 402
    dyssomnias, 402
    narcolepsy, 402, 414–419
    parasomnias, 402–403
    primary hypersomnia, 402
    primary insomnia, 402, 404–413
    primary sleep disorders, 402
    sleep-related breathing disorders, 402
Sleep in America Poll, 401
Sleep medicine, 401
Sleepnet, 404
Sleep paralysis, with narcolepsy, 402

Sleep-related breathing disorders, 402
Sleepstarved, 404
Sleep terror disorders, 403
Sleepwalking, 402
Smith, Anna Nicole, 406
Smith, Jeffrey, 361, 363
"Snapshots: The First Symptoms of Psychosis" (Kristen B. Fowler), 38–43
Social anxiety disorder (SAD), 106, 122–133
    depression with, 125, 128, 131–132
    employment with, 127, 131–133
    panic attacks with, 128
    and perfectionism, 123
    support networks with, 128–129
Social stigma, *xxi*
Somatization disorder, 323–324
Somatoform disorders, 323–344
    hypochondria, 341–344
    muscle dysmorphia, 339–341
    and psychopathological aspects of physical disease, 325–338
    somatization disorder, 323–324
Sommer, R., *xvi*
Sorrow, with schizophrenia, 20
Speech:
    with autism, 426–427, 433
    with psychotic disorders, 2
Spoken word poetry, 28
SRS (sex reassignment surgery), 386
Stereotypic movement disorder, 421
Steroids, 340–341
Stigma:
    with insomnia, 413
    with schizophrenia, 25
    as theme of first person accounts, *xxii–xxiii*
Stigmatizing attitudes, *xviii*
Stimulants:
    for ADHD, 449
    for Tourette's, 452
The Story of San Michele (Axel Muntye), 404–405
Storyteller as hero, *xvii*
Storytelling, *xvii, xx*
Strength, as theme of first person accounts, *xxii*
Substance abuse, 216
Substance abuse disorders, in children, 422
Substance dependence, 216
Substance-induced mood disorders, 50
Substance-induced psychotic disorder, 2
Substance intoxication, 216
Substance-related disorders, 215–235
    alcoholism, 217–227
    narcotics addiction, 232–235
    polysubstance addiction, 228–232
    prevalence of, 215–216
    substance intoxication, 216
    substance withdrawal, 216
Substance withdrawal, 216

Suicidal thoughts (suicidal ideation):
    with ADHD, 445
    with anorexia, 247–248
    with bipolar disorders, 86, 91, 95
    and bulimia, 280
    as coping strategy for DID, 357
    with depression, 54, 56, 58, 61
    hiding, 86
    with mood disorders, 50
    with postpartum depression, 69–70
    with social anxiety disorder, 125
    with Tourette's syndrome, 463
Suicide:
    and insomnia, 406, 407
    as a "selfish" act, 87–88
Suicide attempts:
    with bipolar disorder, 101–102
    with BPD, 203–204, 206
    with depression, 55
Support networks. *See also* Family support; Peer support
    for alcoholism, 225
    for anorexia, 255–258
    for bipolar disorder, 84–85, 103
    for DID, 352–357
    for insomnia, 412–413
    for panic disorder, 121
    for Parkinson's disease, 321, 322
    for postpartum depression, 71–72
    for schizophrenia, 18
    for social anxiety disorder, 128–129
    for transsexualism, 395
    for trichotillomania, 290–292
"Susan's Story" (Susan Ludeman), 115–121
Svensson, C., 44
Szasz, T., 20

T

Talkaboutsleep, 404
Taylor, Catherine, 133–141
The Call to Social Work (Craig LeCroy), *xvii, xxvii*
Themes of first-person accounts, *xix–xxiii*
Thinking. *See also* Cognitive disorders; Thought-voices
    with ADHD, 448, 449
    with Asperger's syndrome, 432–433, 435–436
    disorganized, with psychotic disorders, 2
    and memory loss, 312
    suicidal, *see* Suicidal thoughts (suicidal ideation)
    and Tourette's syndrome, 454, 455
Thomas, Crystal, 455–466
Thought-voices:
    with bipolar disorders, 94–95
    with polysubstance abuse, 230, 231
    with schizoaffective disorders, 41
    with schizophrenia, 10, 14–25

Tics, with OCD, 156
Tic disorders, 421, 450–466. *See also* Tourette's
　　syndrome
"Time for a Good Transgender Story" (Kam Wai
　　Kui), 388–399
TMS (Trans Magnetic Stimulation), for
　　depression, 55
Tolstoi, Leo, *xv,* 57–61
Tourette's syndrome (TS), 450–466
　　diagnosing, 450, 452–453
　　double life with, 454
　　early symptoms of, 450–451, 455–456
　　hyperactivity with, 450–452
　　medications for, 457–463, 465
　　obsessive-compulsive rituals with, 451
"A Tourette Story" (Rick Fowler), 450–454
*Toward a New Diagnostic System for Child
　　Psychopathology* (Jensen, Knapp, &
　　Mrazek), 423
"Transformative" narrative story telling,
　　xx, xxii
Trans Magnetic Stimulation (TMS), for
　　depression, 55
Transsexualism:
　　female-to-male, 388–399
　　male-to-female, 377–388
Transvestic fethishism, 366–367
Treatment inadequacies, as theme of first person
　　accounts, *xx, xxii–xxiii*
Trichotillomania (TTM), 286–294
Troscianko, Emily, 239–263
TS, *see* Tourette's syndrome
TTM (trichotillomania), 286–294

U

"Understanding Health as a Continuum" (Leslie
　　Greenblat), 14–19
Understanding of mental illness, 6–9
Undifferentiated somatoform disorder, 324
Unholy Ghost, xvi
An Unquiet Mind, xvi

V

Vaginismus, 366, 369–373
"Vaginismus: The Blessing of Botox" (Rachel),
　　369–373
Vale, Susan Michele, 101–104
Van Cauter, Eve, 406
Vietnam War, 191–194

Violence:
　　in hospital treatments of mental illnesses, 45
　　in hospital treatments of schizophrenia, 22
　　images of, with bipolar disorder, 95
　　images of, with OCD, 153–156
　　or war, as PTSD trigger, 189–195
　　with polysubstance abuse, 231
　　rape, as PTSD trigger, 185, 186
　　witnessing, as PTSD trigger, 179–181
Voices, hearing, *see* Thought-voices
Voices of Experience, xvi
Voyeurism, 366
Vulnerability, as theme of first person accounts,
　　xxi–xxii

W

Wakefield, J. C., *xxiii*
Walter, Michelle, 232–235
War, as PTSD trigger, 189–195
Warmlines, 27
Wasted, xvi
Weekes, Claire, 111, 118
Weingarten, Kaethe, 188
Wertham, Fredric, 325–338
West, Corinna, 25–37
What Is Mental Illness? (Richard McNally), *xxiii–xxiv*
Wheaton, Sarah, 294–298
*When the Piano Stops: A Memoir of Healing From
　　Sexual Abuse* (Catherine McCall), 187
"Why Having a Mental Illness Is Not Like Having
　　Diabetes," 43–47
Williams, Lynn, 203–207
*Willow Weep for Me—A Black Woman's Journey
　　Through Depression* (Meri Nana-Ama
　　Danquah), 61–66
Wilson, R. Reid, 111, 113
Winston, Sally, 118–121
Work, see Employment
Work on Track program, 12
Wounded Healers, xvi
Wounded storyteller, *xvii*

Y

Yale Child Study Center, 440
"*You* Have Anxiety?" (Kelly Orbison), 108–115

Z

Zamora, Mia, 286–294